ON THE ORIGINS OF SPEAKING
THE DISCOVERY OF STONE AGE LANGUAGE

OR

Ishkama Ishkara Pheikara

LORD WALSINGHAM

Trafford
PUBLISHING

CONTENTS

FIGURES

PREFACE

In the preface authors customarily thank all those who have helped with their work. This is for me a nul category because I have kept it all to myself – partly because I assumed anyone else would tell me to drop it. A preliminary draft was seen by a friend Major General Bob Lyon (an author) and his wife Rosie and the opening chapter thrown out as altogether too autobiographical on their advice and rewritten, which I acknowledge as a great improvement. Otherwise from forty years of intermittent research to the piecemeal composition (which shows in places) and final proof reading (also it is to be feared apparent) the labour has been entirely mine as a hobby, enabling me to face the business competition of the modern world and stay sane and cheerful by adjourning to the age of the Pleistocene, a gentler place where the battle of life was on a rather different plane. So I only have to thank my wife and children for the stoic forbearance they have shown over the decades for absence of mind at meals and the books and paper trails they have had to put up with in the house. For them publication must secretly come as a blessed release. I am very grateful to Alison Lambert who painted the cover picture - several times, in order to rescue our cave men ancestors from the apes.

Some of the repetitious material has been removed at final edit but it has not proved possible to completely eliminate it, the same ground being covered more than once. It is in any case the nature of the work that chapters, which although devoted to single phonemes inevitably need to refer to other meanings appearing in words discussed, hark back (or forwards) to others. If everything appeared only once the reader would find himself or herself flipping pages far too often. A degree of repetition in a fairly substantial book covering new perceptions is perhaps in itself no bad thing. At second mention some of the strangeness and reluctance to take it in may hopefully have worn off. Pulling the book together into a consistent whole has occupied a good few nights of pernickety toil to present as clean a disc as possible for publication.

The title is of course a skit on Charles Darwin's 1859 "On the Origin of Species" (a singular origin), a century and a half ago. My great grandfather (1804-1870) had a minor hand in the Darwinian pie as a friend and colleague of Charles

Lyell, later Sir Charles, – they were barristers in London together when the world was young and London its metropolis and weekended together at Merton. Lyell used my forebear's shell collection (I remember it well) – he was an amateur conchologist like his clerical father before him inspired by the Swedish natural-ist von Linné (Linaeus) – to establish the sequence of the sedimentary rocks by means of the microscopic shells (microfauna) included in them, for his book "The Principles of Geology" published in 1830. In those days geological evolution was a minor sacrilege and the microfauna were intolerable heresy and were simply brushed under the carpet (where comically they remain). Since then Darwin, as well as Lyell (and the great grandfather), all gentle agnostics unprepared to adopt a religious stance, have been ill served by the intellectually aggressive vulgarians who have come after them riding in their train. My book simply sets the record straight by exempting language and thinking from the strait jacket of the bio-logical paradigms fraudulently imposed on them since 1859 in Darwin's name. The universal applicability of evolution by random genetic variation followed by natural selection of the fittest individuals to survive is curtailed. It only applies to organic evolution and not to the walks we may take. To that extent it is a pious work. Flying religious or secularist flags is irrelevant to etymology as indeed to science in general.

My whole book owes an inestimable debt to the late Eric Partridge, the word king, whose "Origins. A Short Etymological Dictionary of Modern English" published in 1958 I have dipped into almost every day since I discovered it de-cades ago, its second buckram binding now wearing out. My work is dedicated to his memory. Without his life work mine could never have got off the ground. But his shade can not be held responsible in any way for the gloss I gave put on his "Origins". I should also acknowledge a debt to two other books, which greatly influenced me when still starting out on putting my own ideas together for a book. The first is a two hundred page paperback by John Phillip Cohane, "The Key" of 1971, much of which I have since come to believe is misconceived; and the second is Alfred Kallir's "Sign And Design" of 1961. I still much admire the way they both stuck their necks out.

Professor Cyrus H Gordon of Brandeis University wrote a preface to "The Key" in which he identified Philadelphia as from the Greek Phil- for love and adelphi for siblings, making it the city of brotherly love. We can "Lithicise" (translate into Stone Age phonemic terms) that little lot as from pahei-lai for the Phil, meaning orgasm-like before being redefined and cleaned up as love; while adelphi as siblings is is from a-tai-lai-pahei, meaning that-born-impregna-tion-linked. Pahei as ecstacy piece, orgasm and impregnation is one of our very oldest perceptions. The citizens of Philadelphia are going to be intrigued to have their brotherly love undermined by not one but two mentions of Tarzan's penis.

Professor Gordon sails on to explicate the composition of Egypt from H-t-k-s-pth, later Hikuptah. E, he says, goes back to the word for house and –gy- to the word for soul and pth to the Egyptian great god Ptah. But we can do a lot better than that. Professor Gordon had only the letters to go by, and they let him down. First h was pronounced in Ancient Egyptian ahi, t was pronounced tai or tau, k was pronounced ka or kai, s was pronounced ish or sa or sai and p was pronounced pa or pai. Finally pth was pronounced pata ahi. So H-t-k-s-pth in Ancient Egyptian read as Ahi-tai-ka-sai-pata-ahi and what it actually meant was That which-born-place-lived-fathers-our, or better Englished Where-born-our-fathers: The Fatherland. Professor Gordon goes on to offer Hikuptah (getting nearer to Egypt) from 1400 BC as the name of the sacred area of Memphis after which the country was named. In terms of the Lithic roots this can still be read as Ahi-kau-pata-ahi, That which-begotten-fathers-our, still The Fatherland. If you want to know in precise detail how these etymologies are derived in accordance with the new linguistic model you need to read this book.

Language was introduced some six hundred thousand years ago by our hominid forebears using simple phonemic strings with psychosemantic contents for each phoneme, that is to say the 'natural' meanings attributed were those suggested by the subconscious minds of the bare bottomed naming committees, and they were more or less the same world wide because human experience was more or less the same world wide. There is no requirement for an 'Ur-language' spoken in an original single speaking community. The spread of dumb hominids across the world rules this out. The big surprise is the refresh rate from our subconscious minds, which have relearned the old patterns from the lexicon with each generation, means that the original traces can still be recovered from our present day subconscious store of treasure, and indeed like flies in amber from the present lexicon if intelligently interrogated. In chapter 16 on the origins of thinking – nothing to do with the cognitive scientists' research programme at all – the disastrous Hegelian-Marxist dialectic is derived from the Ancient Egyptian patterning of their three vowel system. Much of Genesis comes from Malaya, the Eastern Garden of Eden, borrowed from the Sumerians (who were goys) who came from there, by the Akkadians, the bedu pastoralist Cains who captured the Sumerian padi gardens

Homo Erectus who tamed fire and spoke was highly sexed. Partly it was because he kept himself warm and responsive around the hearth, with sex a desert with a full belly after the evening meal of cooked meat. It is moot whether his sexual proclivities came from chatting about it, or if it was the other way around. But both ways it was the flame which did it. We are still living in the Fire Age. It is the classical psychologists (Freud and Jung and their contemporaries) who have drawn attention to the subconscious keel which underlies our conscious minds.

Noam Chomsky's attempt to pray it in aid to support his hard wired ideas genetically transmitted is a false avenue. Its proper content is the Lithic substrate read back in by each generation learning the lexicon, not genetically determined at all.

For the etymologists, the Lithic hypotheses share much of the Poo-Poo theory (speech based on natural cries) and the Ding-Dong theory (speech based on copying natural sounds). Many words have to be put in the 'too difficult' tray for now, but all are probably genuine constructs on Lithic principles originally. Critics inclined to dismiss the whole exercise as overly fanciful must earnestly confront what for them are inexplicable coincidences. While typing up this preface my attention has been drawn to the two words carpenter and toboggan. Toboggan is from the Algonquian (Micmac dialect) tobakun meaning a wooden sledge. Carpenter, the trade of Christ the Saviour in the first century of the present era, is from kara-pai-en-tai-arai, joiner-pieces-of-cut-verbal, a cutter and joiner. Compare tailor a cutter of lithe (soft) [materials] if you will. The surprise is the Algonquian toboggan turns out to be a carpentered job as well: tau-ba-kau'n, all the cut-bits of timber-joined or made up into the vehicle in question. It will have been in comparison with the more casual trailing sledge comprising merely two saplings fastened either side of a saddle with the load bound to them behind the horse. Nothing much flows from one such identification. But from many everything follows.

Walsingham
Merton
Thetford
Norfolk
IP25 6QP
October 2005

CHAPTER 1

INTRODUCTION

The ideas in this book are not your run of the mill stuff. They put the skids under the existing schools of thought amongst linguists, from Chomsky who thinks we inherit ideas to Greenberg who has family trees for the eight thousand languages on earth as if they shared a common descent[1]. They must also I think prove startling to most everyone who takes the trouble to read through it all, as well as disturbing to the point of disbelief to many of them. "On The Origins of Speaking" offers a theory of original word formation from basic linked semantic-phonetic elements, now largely confined to the subconscious mind – which was at one time, until the birth of language, all we had. There is however still an original substrate in everyday speech which can with a little circumspection be uncovered. The title is a take off from Charles Darwin´s single "On The Origin of Species" of 1859, now nearly a hundred and fifty years old; while the contents are a homage to the rather more industrious and intellectually formidable – and therefore less well known – Eric Partridge, the etymologist who died only recently, with his semantic worms tunneling through the lexicon, displacing in some respects Darwin´s earth worms grubbing in the ground. So much of this book relies upon the almost daily study of Eric Partridge´s "Origins", his etymological dictionary, over many decades, that his book can almost be regarded as volume one of the present work, though without any indication he would approve of the additions. The forty years spent by Partridge at a desk in the British Museum Library (like Karl Marx a hundred years before) with access to the vast collection of dictionaries of the languages of the world there, has given anyone who is into etymology a splendid head start. In turn I have been obliged to defer to a second volume of my own "Origins" the chapters on a number of difficult languages: Albanian, Basque, Chinese, Dyerbal (a Northern Queensland aboriginal language now extinct), Egyptian, Guanche (the aboriginal language of the Canary Islands) and Malay, the language most closely related to that spoken by Adam in the garden of Eden.

I feel I should also mention H Yule and A C Burnett´s "Hobson Jobson" as revised by W Crooke in 1903. It is of course now outdated but still full of sharp perceptions and enjoyable outlandish derivations, a delight for the modern mind overburdened with consequentialities and dull thinking and avid for refreshment by means of any lateral connections it can find. I have also made use of the Oxford English Dictionary on disc and Chambers Dictionary of Etymology based on the original Barnhart dictionary on the other side of the Atlantic pond. Like all good books with something unorthodox to say, it is bound to raise a few hackles amongst the great and the good in linguistics who quite understandably do not care to have the ground removed from under their clay feet. Linguistics has fairly acquired the reputation of a dry as dust subject attractive only to theoreticians and nerds. But this is something else again.

It is now nearly fifty years I have been working on the historic structure of languages in my spare time, mostly at nights, entirely on my own, sometimes excited and convinced and at others wrestling with the fear of insanity, in order to grub up the data I am now presenting. You can not get any further away from present day concerns than the age of the Pleistocene, which is perhaps why it has had a certain appeal. The main thesis is that in the languages of the world spoken today are preserved, like flies in amber, the original phonemic elements with which Plain Sapiens, the half human hominid species from way way before Sapiens Sapiens took centre stage a mere hundred and fifty thousand years ago, first broke into speech. First of all, meaning is attributed to the original phonemes language started out by identifying and adopting. The current consensus view is it is only morphemes (combinations of phonemes) which have meanings, and those meanings are randomly chosen. It is also currently believed that prehistoric language roots are untraceable because the random drift of pronunciation makes so much noise over a time span that long that they are irretrievably lost. Here it is argued per contra, in a new look at the role of the subconscious mind in shaping the so called random association of words with meanings, that community memory has been repeatedly refreshed over hundreds of thousands of years as each generation consciously learned to speak and subconsciously learned the underlying Lithic (Stone Age) original language roots. These elements are not words as we understand them. You can speak as well as think without using words, although this may seem a puzzle today. The truth is the meanings conserved in semantic elements with simple phonetic correlates were only later linked up in established strings to make up persistent words as we know them. For our present purpose speaking is simply defined as uttering phonetic strings with meaning strings attached to them. Chimpish, per contra, is only very doubtfully linguistic in so far as the semantic strings are perishingly short and anyway there is no uttering of phonetic strings to go with them, only manipulation of visual prompts, so the chimp, though he may claim some very modest degree of linguistic comprehension, is not capable of speaking.

It is difficult to know how to present theories which must score a high mark for novelty throughout, if for nothing else. I have tried to sketch out the outline of the whole work in this introduction to serve both as an appetizer and as a warning. The rest of the book must then set about detailing the evidences which support the thinking. I have called this elementary language, which has now gone underground into our subconscious minds, Lithic, simply from the Greek lithos for stone because it began in the Stone Age, and also because it represents intellectual bedrock. You can not get behind it, or below the mental threshold it presents. The reason for this is the birth of language appears to have marched simultaneously with the birth of conscious thinking – certainly so if you define it as articulated ratiocination stringing ideas together to make up sequences or chains of thought. The crunch corollary is that without such chains of thought there can be no idea of the self, so that distinguishing internal prompts from ones from outside was problematic.

Moreover, these Lithic hypotheses open up wide ranging speculation about the textured interconnectedness of all the languages on earth when resumed at this depth of analysis. It certainly helps if you quite relish driving a coach and horses through the received wisdom. The dates involved in this "evolution"[2] of language are quite uncertain. I address the figures currently favoured by academia without attaching too much importance to them. Sapiens Sapiens is currently supposed to have sprung to life a hundred and fifty thousand years ago, but the date has kept getting pushed back in time, so we keep getting older. So I suppose Plain Sapiens, the one who first learned to speak, should be allowed a similar span at least before Sapiens Sapiens emerged and he was submerged by our higher life form in one way or another (possibly eaten, his brains a delicacy). So then I double it because I am by now very well aware how dozily we progressed with our thinking, as with much else, so it must have taken even longer than folk think; and say we probably started speaking some six hundred thousand years ago; but of course it could have been way before then, still further back, although the date will already be a red rag to the academic senators. Anyway it is indisputable fact somebody was there chipping away at stones a million years ago and more, although he may have been just a dumb ape; and some time later he had tamed fire and lived round the hearth and was cooking on it. Recently the discovery of a bone apparently cooked, dated to around a million years ago, has opened up a strong query about when hominids tamed fire. Previously the remains of ash from hearths suggested a much later date but this was of course because ash is not permanent and after a few hundred thousand years has broken down and become unrecognizable. Already I think with the taming of fire it may have been quite a good time to have been alive, in good times at least, even if not as nice as now. But what is for sure is the scene is prehistoric by quite a long chalk. That presents, as the Spanish would say, something of a problem for research: with no record to tease, how can we hope to know what happened at the birth of language in any detail? My answer lies in psychosemantics, a term I have coined – so far as I know nobody else has – to identify how we can proceed.

As I have said, hominids or anthropoid apes have certainly been breaking stones and chipping them into shapes for a million years and more, starting with single strikes just breaking a stone in two, leaving the archaeologists to guess which bit was for use, as well as for what. Their guess (and mine) is for the sharp edge exposed when stones break, and if so both bits would often do. You got a choice right away! For most of that million years progress got to making hand axes by means of a range of repetitive strokes aimed with more and more care and attention to the detailed responses of the material in hand; but the most signifi-cant thing as I see it was the painfully slow rate at which change occurred and the mind progressed. I have an axe found a few hundred yards from my home[3] and dated to 40,000 years ago by museum staff, iced into the glaciers and then melted out again. But it could in my opinion have been made as long as 400,000 years ago, or even perhaps by an anthropoid ape. It is not particularly well done. The museum's date was purely stylistic, and their dating of styles largely guess-work. No account would be taken of backward undeveloped areas and that sort of thing. For a year or two I carried it with me everywhere so I could feel it in my jacket pocket twenty times a day to remind me where we came from. Then I lost it. What is fairly clear is technology for about a million years was apparently largely confined to chopping and scraping. That really is a lot of chopping and scraping. How many unbroken handy sized stones on the surface of the earth are left unchopped, I wonder? Perhaps in inhabited zones only those out of range or otherwise not worth the effort. A further thought: did it all start by clacking stones together preparatory to throwing them at a rival, or a tiger, a threat gesture to frighten the brutes off? If so should we trace all civilisation as a spin off from throwing stones, the prime of all tool use and thence of technology[4]? Anyway the leading school in archaeology now proposes all this handiwork, as well as chip-ping a real lot of stones and turning out a real lot of meat tenderisers and scrapers – now termed hand axes – was also indirectly developing our brains. That is how we got our brains big enough for self conscious rational thinking. Handiwork, in-cidentally, remains the preferred mental medium for many with intellectually less sophisticated gifts and appeals to us all. But I am not sure knapping was needed. Maybe the brain burgeoned on its own from subtle DNA changes out of the blue. We now know these changes can arise from stray rays or viral attack, and maybe even from causes we know nothing of as yet. A change of diet could have done it; even eating each others' brains; or perhaps, by altering our hormone balance, even eating the enemy's genitalia in order to acquire his virtue.

No doubt throughout the Pleistocene there was also some sharpening of sticks and hardening the points in the embers as well, for use stabbing rivals, spearing small game, and spitting meat on the barbie, with all the sticks of course long since decayed. Starting fires was a trick which has left traces, and the traces found so far only go back about two hundred thousand years or so. But ash does not remain identifiably ash for ever, so that the fire age we still live in may very well have started about the same time we learned to speak; and I think this fits for reasons to be developed regardless of the dating, because I believe it was warming ourselves in front of the fire which got us all sexed up and which indirectly made us so voluble – after the sexual activity for which the ample heat of the hearth when huddling for warmth proved the prompt as well as the excuse, enlivening what had been previously a comparatively chilly performance. Not only that but the increased pleasure led inexorably to as near to total recall as possible when it was over – best achieved by chatting. Our earliest discourse, if I am right, will have included how was it for you (or some such) as well as enthusiastic responses. It is a shame they did not have a fag between them with which to sauce their discourse. I believe humanity, the state of being human, has nothing to do with humus, earthlings, as some learned folk think, but comes simply from hi-u-man, both sexes enjoying the procreation, from the Lithic proto language hei-u-ma'n, enjoying-both-planting [the seed]. Animals do not gather around the hearth at nights, and their amatory exploits are generally nasty brutish and rather short. In Ancient Egypt Amaun, The Ever Loving, found his loving emotion 'As when impregnating' (mai in Egyptian). The Loving did come from the Earth in a way, since earthing was also planting the seed, and it was when so engaged that passion momentarily melted the most macho heart – as indeed to this day! These were comparatively recent developments, so far as we know going back just a few thousand years. Before the Egyptians the idea of a God kindly disposed to mortals does not appear to have occurred to anybody, and propitiation of a hostile world is still around today.

The Latins´ amatory exploits came from amare, which Eric Partridge relates to the earlier Phrygian Greek adamnein which he analyses as a preliminary ad- which he suggests is merely "an intensive prefix", followed by –am- the loving bit. Then –n-, a "meaningless infix" and then -ein, the Greek verbal ending. But in Lithic terms adamnein breaks down instead as a-da-a-main-ain, as-does-as-impregnating-verbal ending. We agree on the verbal ending. Partridge does not say why it should be a verbal ending in Greek. Lithic suggests the vowel a has the semantic content of extension and so of distance or going or, as here, abstract translation, and so action, or as a verb of action like da. Da is not the English word does, but Lithic da can carry the meaning happens or does (see chapter 6). The Lithic reads 'as happens when impregnating'. It appears our hominid forebears at least experienced a surge of affection at orgasm. Raping and then killing was a puzzling perversion even in those days, due to the heightened emotional tones of lust and aggression somehow becoming confused. In any case if you wanted to get Tarzan, hunkered beside you round the hearth, to identify the emotion in language, how he felt on such occasions was probably the best pointer around.

Chipping flints may have been a stepping stone on the way to the hearth. You get sparks sometimes, small remnants to the Lithic mind of the fire out of which stone was born (I think stone actually means fire-born, ish-taun, from seeing volcanoes errupting), nipping out and away like imps when you split it open, or even if you challenged it severely by striking it with another. A flint was a flasher, not the full flame just a fleck of it. The fire age suggests one of the first expresions was a warning not to burn your fingers, probably the actual cry "Haa!" or "Ho´!" (hot!) or some such, and I think I can demonstrate as much (see chapter 8). The sabre toothed tiger always merited a warning of course but just the single cry used for "Tiger!" (perhaps just Grrr! only later elaborated to Ti-Grrrr! or Mistress Growler – felines were probably identified as feminine ab initio because of their dainty tread when stalking and slinky habits), whatever it was, was enough for that.

Once you get used to the idea human speaking started so long ago in hominid times, you can see the thinking at the time was likely to have been a trifle on the uncivilised side, and I am afraid I shall be demonstrating this all through the following chapters, which suggest to me at least our minds when we were mere anthropoids were deeply pornographic for Mrs Grundy, soused in sex and every kind of sexual metaphor. It does not all make very pretty reading. It certainly appears to me our breakthrough into articulate thinking was hammered out on the anvil of our own genitalia. There is for me the less surprise then when evidence appears of the recapitulation of this process in the youth of the nation today. The relatively brainless are simply being lived, with their atavistic subconscious minds in the driving seat.

After all, in the stone age these were bare bottomed savages without any clothes on at all and thus with the shamelessness in all probability to match the Bonobo pygmy chimpanzees, which can not now be shown in zoos because of the scandalously brazen enthusiasms of both the sexes. I therefore feel that in this introduction I should start by saying sorry to Mrs Grundy. Indeed it would not be out of place to sub subtitle the whole work "or Sorry Mrs Grundy!", only discarded as overly flippant. However there is more to be said. Although the original semantic contents of so many of the primitive elements of speech include a number of crudities, that is no reason to suppose the thinking always continued to revert to the original constituent semantic contents in all their crudity, as language developed from its original simplicity. A clinical approach is therefore required, dumping

Mrs Grundy. But a further apology may nevertheless be due to more sensitive souls on behalf of humanity: it may well be we are simply not worthy of you!

It has taken me a long time to work backwards, in discovery mode, tracing present derivative meanings to their sources, with different developments in different words providing some degree of semantic triangulation. These indications point to primitive root meanings, and ultimately to the original meanings of simple phonemes from which all the derived meanings have sprung in cascading semantic chains. That is quite something. The elemental phonetic construction of words which illustrate the semantic chains are a different interest from the semantic cascades themselves, that is to say how one meaning has triggered or given birth to another by metaphor and analogy, age upon age, even generarion by generation, ultimately each a singular contribution by some unnamed and long dead individual thinker. That has something to say about the history of the mind and its intellectual development. It illuminates the past in a way no amount of fossicking with the neurons in the brain and other biological arcana can ever hope to do.

By the time you have traced the whole developmental catena of meanings backwards to the ultimate root meanings in the first place of the absolutely basic sounds, you have as it turns out made out a texture of intellectual history of some interest in itself. This remains true regardless of whether my guesses as to why the first meanings were given to the sounds are right or wrong. It is quite acceptable to treat these initial sound-meaning identifications as simply mnemonics, although of course I personally believe I am dead right all along. "Ka! Ka!", no doubt with the appropriate hand gestures mimicking the action to start with, reflected – as near as our anthropoid ancestors could get to it – the sound and the effortful concentration of striking flint on flint with flaking intent, and it drew attention to chipping, flaking, striking, as well as the debetage or waste resulting. Hundreds of thousands of years later KaKa is still used for the human waste product. The first speech was simply echoic, and that is rule one. Ka Ka started out just meaning clack, the clink of striking flint on flint. But spat in a neighbour's face edging too close to your girl around the hearth I think it immediately suggested to him he would be similarly treated if he did not edge away again somewhat sharpish; and all without any grammar or syntax at all. There are etymologists with distinguished dictionaries to their name who have suggested Ka Ka is echoic of the grunting made when defaecating rather than my interpretation of the clink of stone on stone. Readers may wish to refer to their own experience here. For my own part it seems a rather over ready acceptance of echoism regardless of much claim to the equivalence of sounds, as well as of a rather severely costive condition. Anyway I am staying with the flint knappers and ignoring the kite hawks.

You can probably fairly early on include also in these original phenomenal semantic contents, given by the human mind to its own utterances identifying phenomena, the sound of fire when it is put out. The brand dunked in a pool in the morning (to save fuel; a brand was heavily buttered with tree resins and gum, hard to collect in sufficient quantity) said "ishshsh" as it died. The same flaming habit continues to this day which is how we are able to extrapolate this back to the age of the Pleistocene, although there are no reports extant on the matter from those times. The things that are always with us, our prehistoric forebears must surely have encountered. Although, so far as we can determine after some half a million years, the taming of fire has appeared to have come some considerable time after primitive stone breaking began, this may now, it seems, be largely an appearance because the absence of ash at lower levels in the detritus of cave floors is really because the ash is unrecognisable any further back. The minerals have been broken down and recombined losing their characteristic profile. In any case we can see for ourselves that once you get settled into a routine of taking flints home and seriously flaking them on the floor around the cave entrance – nobody wants your detritus scattered around inside on the dormitory floor – sooner or later a flint spark in high summer will eventually have lit some dry kindling happening to be on the floor where the flint knapping was taking place. But then again at any time some particularly brave soul in a thick bear skin – against the heat, and probably pragmatically around his leading arm in place of its usual duty around his waist (to keep his stomach warm and his digestion going) – may have already simply grabbed a burning brand from a forest fire's front edge and sprinted home to the cave mouth to establish a hearth with it.

Anyway I believe "Ish!" and "Ka!" were two of the earliest vocabulary members anywhere ever under rule one, echoism. Certainly nobody has so far come up with a better idea. The rest of mankind's first vocabulary, as well as the devious and whimsical ways in which the meanings were developed and parlayed across the millennia I have endeavoured to derive somewhat similarly in chapters 4 to 16 which follow. Not all spring from such obvious initial identifications as "Ish!" and "Ka!" The fascination of the pursuit however lies not so much in learning how our hominid forebears first lisped, although that too is a curiosity, as in the discovery we still talk Lithic today, at least in fair measure, without ever becoming consciously aware of it. Not only that but it also appears that of all the thousands of languages alive today hardly one (I have not had the time nor the patience, nor the other means, to examine more than a minute fraction of them even in the slightest degree) does not use these very same primitive semantic associations, even if their different idioms of use result in surface structures so radically different as to be mutually incomprehensible, so that even after lengthy introduction the Lithic connections of remote tongues remain quite difficult to grasp.

Most of the identifications of Lithic constructs (words) are from English and the Indo-European tongues akin; but wherever possible examples from further afield have been attempted. All the languages of the world are probably related, because of their common Lithic substrate. There is no good reason why this should be so, since humanity was most likely quite widely distributed around the globe while still dumb. But it does appear that the initial identification of sounds and their meanings, because of their psychosemantic pattern, were very similar the world over. It is only the diversification of idioms since which has created the cacophony of over 6000 tongues today, the survivors of a quite unknown number that have passed away. In the following chapters I look at as mixed a bag of languages as I could at all readily find the means to examine, in order to give some body to the Lithic hypotheses and demonstrate how it is possible to find such linguistic uniformity under such conspicuous diversity. It is a genuine search for the points of congruence still extant (and not an abstract grammatical schema such as Professor Noam Chomsky has devised on theoretical grounds) heavily relying, as we all must, upon the subconscious workings of the human mind which by definition are hard to access. For me hard wired ideas however seem to fall outside science, period. Thinking is an intellectual activity and not a structure like a limb or the way it articulates. It is a bit like arguing for a genetic determination of what walks a person will take during his time on earth under the impression it is just a question of how the leg moves. I have traced the development of this modern philosophy of language, of which Chomsky is now the most distinguished ornament, solely in an appendix, Appendix A, since it otherwise hardly impinges at all on the present work.

The second part of the title of the book is in original Lithic phonemes and is gibberish, that is meaningless unless you choose to give it meaning, which I presently will attempt to do, trying for the first time to trace the building of language from its origins in simple exclamations. Our hisses and our hums (the sibilants s, sh, z, etc and the hums m and n) are the only consonants or stops which you can also continue as long as you have breath. That generally is the nature of the vowels. Hisses and hums are consonants which also can behave like vowels, and as such they will have held a special fascination for the rather empty primitive mind. Of course they were not at the time classified as stops or notes or both, but the hisses and hums were surely early identified as odd twins. Not only that but with the hisses you are clearly expelling breath whereas with the hums you appear to be sounding without breathing out. I can even hum while holding my nose as well, if not quite so easily. So these twins had contrasting characteristics as well as communalities. The sibilants were actively expressing themselves, air was clearly being expelled. The hums were background noises by comparison. Sibilants were lively, hums lifeless. I believe it was esoteric identifications like these, often baseless and absurd by todays standards, which informed much of the initial work done in our forebears' bare bottomed naming committees hunkered around their hearths. Any such belief, admittedly, is quite controversial since it assumes, or anyway allows, that before speech was properly up and running we were already beginning to think in quite an abstract way about our speaking and how to get the best out of it. We made language, it did not just happen to us. It is still perhaps the crown jewels of human thinking, originally botched together though it may now appear. It is the putting together of human language that this book is really about.

I have chosen for the title three Lithic phrases which so far as I am aware are gibberish in any language spoken today; but they encapsulate, for me at any rate, the pattern of thinking which started us all out on the human saga of expostulation. I believe speaking and thinking in conscious steps developed hand in glove – the glove is the speaking. The consciousness comes from being able to take it off and handle it – in the mind of course. Before that, the hand (the thinking) be it never so fly, left nothing behind to address once the thought moved on. This is of course not a perfect metaphor, but it gets us thinking of our pre-linguistic predicament on the right track. Before we spoke we could of course remember what happened to us; but it was a memory which presented itself overwhelmingly in visual images, such as a horse or a dog enjoys, and the images were impersonal in so far as they were merely what we saw outside ourselves. It made us jolly extraverts. There was no possibility of any wrangling being involved. There was no discussion, probably even no possibility of discussion with ourselves. Before we got thinking in labelled form we did not debate, we just acted on the hunch of the moment, unaware of the possibility of mulling anything over. It is a strange world it takes some thinking to get used to. Who got the meat was settled by emotional tone on the one side, who had it, and discretion or valour on the other. Speech is based on the desire to communicate, but perhaps to communicate within oneself as much as with one's neighbour. It was, I think, as a personal mnemonic that it really caught on, perhaps just thinking aloud to start with, half thinking mutterers as we started to put thoughts into strings, probably trying them out audibly and repeatedly, over and over again marvelling at the persistence of the symbolism – at the fact that the same sounds brought back the same images each time, just as children starting to read find it easiest to read aloud. Did we sing our way to logic? I believe we did. And if so my title is a kind of birdsong of our race. There must surely have been the odd Lord Lloyd Webber even before trousers. Indeed I believe there might well have been more then. Songs come from the subconscious muse for one thing, and do not need tagging with meaning as you go along. Tim Rices come much later. Then because it was aural it turned out language was a game two or more could play, so that it was turned into a public mnemonic as well. Once in the public arena there will have been no holding it. At a stroke we became born again speakers. I hasten to add, since all kinds of mindless therapies and their gurus are popular today amongst the unthinking, chanting my birdsong will get you nowhere. It is a mnemonic merely. If you do not know what is memorialised it is no help whatever.

So now I will give the game away. Ishkama says Ish ka Ma, Ish makes Ma, Ish fashions and leads to Ma. It is the first step in linguistic development, or perhaps the second, since you need first of all to have given some meanings to Ish, Ka and Ma. They are in chapters 14, 5 and 10 respectively, but to save rummaging at this stage I am happy to repeat that Ish was what the flame said when you dunked your glowing brand at dawn in the nearest puddle, and dying men speak true. The phoneme was providential, almost suggesting on its own some providential agency was already taking our education in hand. Just think what a complex language idiom might have resulted if the brand had instead said "Rumpelstiltskin!" as it died. Tarzan might have even fallen into a sulk and refused to play the language game ever again, reverting to hand gestures for another million years. However, as it happened, exploring the flame for further meanings, its most notable characteristic (once you had discovered it burnt) was its instinct to spring upwards. Most things, which were solid, had the opposite instinct, to go downwards. Whereas the rising flame was best avoided because it could burn your hand, solids with their falling habit could crush your foot. Not only that but the hisses and hums were the only two initial-and-stop sounds (we call them consonants) which could be continued as long as you had breath, a mysterious pair thereafter to be distinguished from the rest. If the hisses went up and the air went out, then it was only reasonable to suppose the hums went down since the breathing out was negatived. In this way opposites (and maths) were born for us – a continuum with poles – to put beside the straight distinction or divide, the older line or boundary between distincta (things or phenomena), which I have elsewhere exemplified as "Red" and "Not Red". There is more of this in chapter 16 on thinking. We can not develop it all here.

Ka, meanwhile, was, I fancy, taken to be the closest we could get to the clack of flint on flint, a sound which must have dominated society for a million years. "Ka Ka" was accompanied, no doubt, initially with the appropriate hand gestures to provide a double prompt with the sound, just as Ish I imagine was accompanied by a hand movement of inversion and submersion of the burning brand. Ka Ka, repetitive strikes, flaking flints was to make our earliest artifacts, and striking was thus making. Our own word make has added ma- and originally meant to mould by pounding the mass, like making a cake, or indeed kneading clay, a ka of the ma.

Now we can read "Ishkama": "Up makes Down", that is to say the perception Up leads to the perception Down, a polar continuum. Here we are compiling a vocabulary, a vocabulary of thinking at the same time as a vocabulary of utterances. The next rubric is to put the two vocabularies together and start to build language as a textured structure of elementaty building blocks like the Ish, the Ka, the Ma and the Ra. Ish-Kara has Ish Ka, fire make, with the verbal marker (aRa) added: Ish-Kara is fire maker, just as in Arabic today. Lawrence of Arabia started publication of a periodical broadsheet in Arabic, when he was not disguised as a Bedu in the Arabian desert, called Iskra, the spark (still published, I am told, in Cairo) hoping to light the fire of Arab nationalism against the Turks. To tackle PheiKara next, Phei is from the consortium of Pa and Hei in Ancient Egyptian, originally pahei, specifically identified as the glyph for the male organ; alternatively "Mai" in Egyptian (the planter or inseminator). Pahei is rather more poetically the joy piece or glory bud. Also in Egyptian it is traditionally "Petch", but probably better transliterated more fully as Peti-Kahai, roughly "the teated shoot for making whoopee", the ancients' jolly way of designating the male organ, long before Mrs Grundy came on the scene to interrupt what naturally sprang to mind. Pa was the thinned diminutive of Ba, the sound made by the two lips and so the sound of flesh on flesh and so the fleshy bits and so flesh (Chapter 4). Pa was thus a little bit (a thinned diminutive) of flesh, that is a shoot or bud; or else the skin, quite precisely the thinned diminutive of flesh – when it tended to acquire a defining –lai, added to indicate a looped configuration, surrounding (the flesh), as in the Latin pellis. "Hai!", "Hei" or "Hi" was a sudden or powerful sensation, anything from Hot! Or Ouch! to Hurrah!, Rejoice!, or Wow!, even 'Glory be to God' for the Egyptians. Now it is a sudden greeting merely. The Egyptian Pahei or Glory Bud for the penis is not unlike the Joy Stick my uncle and the other intrepid airmen of World War 1 manipulated between their legs (to steer the aeroplane). Pai-nai(s) on the other hand, Latin Penis, is the shoot which protrudes or presents, the witness piece (chapter 11). In the days before trousers you got a good idea of what was on Tarzan's mind from the angle of attack of his organ. It must occur to anyone who thinks about these old days that honesty was often the only policy where today we can hide behind our trousers. The more clinical Egyptian "mai" for penis is merely "the earther", "the planter", "the inseminator". I picked a naughty bit for the second title since so much of our primitive forebears' thinking appears to me to have had this orientation – much as with the military at least today. Perhaps a hazardous occupation subtly, or not so subtly, develops a Stone Age mentality. Ka- we already know; while -ara is from the Ancient Egyptian, to ray, from Ra the Sun God: a mysterious function which acts at a distance to make things happen, as the grass to grow, and so in this case derivatively just a verbal marker, any activity or action not involving anybody's legs (Bai, the haunches), our fleshiest bits originally in those days when boys loped after game each day and girls fattened against pregnancy. The Ishkama Ishkara Pheikara in the title thus exemplifies the composition of elements such as Ish and Ma, as also of Pa and Hai and Ka and Ara, to make more complex meanings, in due course not only confined to the specification of observed phenomena, whence the original elements were derived, but by analogy to more difficult ideas. Pheikara, to make with the pahei, provides a novel and I believe veridical etymology for the four letter word it has until recently been considered too impolite to publish, but now passes amongst all the other vulgarities as a commonplace.

The subsidiary titling, it can now be seen, is runic as well as informative, that is to say it illustrates in its structure general truths. So, to begin with, ishkama really comprises only two nodes, ish, up, which ka, makes, leads to conceptual ma, down. So the pattern rounds out in the mind as a linearity or direction with two possible extensions or projections, which I have elsewhere called a criterion, arguing it is prior to the perception of a category and plays a role in deconstructing the Marxist dialectic which is merely a silly play on Aristotle's categories. If you treat "red" as a criterion you can have more or less red. As a category it has to be in or out, red or not red, the category derived from the circle rather than the straight line. The first word ishkama puts first the criterion and the Lithic thinking that went with it,

The second word Ishkara has the first two syllables the same, and this is by no means accidental. But it introduces a second element attached to the second syllable giving it a dual sense: kara is a verb. Ka on its own played the same role precisely in the first word, but without any conscious recognition it had a different role from the terminal elements, although it did. It even throws some light on why (or how) Ka could come to mean join as well as make, a surprise when Ka started out making by flaking which splits the flint and does not join. Ka, the splitting, when it resulted in making (a tool), took off, so that the abstract consequential effect of the action (the making) became superimposed semantically upon the crude manoeuvre suggested by echoism. It is in itself evidence for intellectuality, such as we recognise today, at the very earliest stage of explicit thinking hundreds of thousands of years ago when our forebears were still mere hominids with very sloping foreheads, hefty jaws and probably still even relatively hirsute all over. This is probably a better explanation than the alternative that a split was thought to be an exposure of what previously was joined, a junction therefore. The proper science is the split opened up a displacement of the two parts which was not implicit in the previously joined state; but that does not mean that we spotted that at the time. It is perfectly possible we didn't, and argued accordingly. After all, flaking flints is not an exact science. Flints do flake where they will, so that getting the split to go right is an act requiring a long apprenticeship, as if the spirit of the medium had to be accessed by means of lengthy submission to its demands. At Grimes' Graves in Norfolk, the prehistoric flint mines, virtuous flints were extracted unspoiled by environmental strains making flaws, like those found lying about on the surface locally for free, which meant that the flakes would follow the flaws regardless of the straightness of the strikes. Quality sold already. Brandon flints struck true and were exported over a wide terrain by land and sea: an early industry, the first of many, with mining second only after prostitution – but so much more substantial, the output lasting generations.

The third word Pheikara comprises four elements, two pairs of two, and because the semantics are from recent usage, only some five or six thousand years ago from Ancient Egypt, the first two are already slurred together in the modern manner from pa-hei to phei an elision recognised in the Greek letter phi – originally more like a Q, a male-female symbol, the male organ striking home and penetrating the female, subsequently somewhat similarly casually drawn as a straight line across the circle, perhaps at the instigation of an early Mrs Whitehouse[5]. Pa-hei-kara, to make with the pa-hei, the rhapsody piece, like World War One pilots' "Joy stick", is usually symbolised today in the media as "f---", although the late Ken Tynan – alas my contemporary as an undergraduate at Magdalen College, Oxford (England) – distributed the expletive in the media at every opportunity; and nowadays little school children use it unsparingly when addressing their teachers in school[6].

In Egypt these three gnomic utterances would probably have been regarded as words of power, like the rosary encapsulating a whole lot of prayerful thinking to wash the brain and trammel the mind in right ways, in this case as follows: first, the basic pattern of human thinking is from similarity (analogy) suggested by the criterion which leads on to contradistinction by opposition. Think of a vertical line with up and down arrows on the ends and a consequent point of origin or change over in the middle, conveniently marked with a short cross-piece. Secondly, grammar begins with helper suffixes (or prefixes) as markers showing the way to think of the main dish. Then thirdly the suffixing of a pair on pair opens the way to a whole gamut of descriptive pointers to a complex semantic construct soon to be dignified, and forgotten, as a single word. But the grammatical lesson, lost in morphology, is carried over into sentence construction.

The "cigar" from distant South America which I am smoking as I ponder on these beginnings is a "shi-kara", a fire maker or burner, a combustible, and the smoke is what the flame makes as it devours the fuel or even after it has died down and is dead, along with the ash, originally ashce (ashke from ash-kai in Lithic) in Anglo Saxon, again "flame made". In the case of the cigar, imported from South America, it is not hard to see it is probably from the Maya "sik'ar" to puff [smoke], which Eric Partridge (following Webster's New International Dictionary, Second Edition, Impression of 1945) describes as "inchoative of sik'eh to smoke", in turn from "sik'" tobacco, in Maya. The Lithic appears to have been Ish-kai. Meanwhile our verb to smoke, from smokian in Anglo Saxon, is probably akin to the Greek smukhein to smoulder [and smoke], which Eric Partridge, the word king, fancifully derives from an imaginary pared down Indo European root *meukh, with the s- just "apparently a reinforcement". But the dunked brand suggests to me the s- is in reality an integral part of the smoking, since otherwise the overall meaning is lost and we are left with making a mew, meu or whatever or even just a gibberish. This is indicative of the advantage of understanding the construction of words from semantic elements, instead of just going blindly by the sounds. And now I have finished my cigar. How odd, I am thinking, the Maya should share some of our thinking with us from so far away in time and space, so that when their cigars arrive among us in the sixteenth century of our era they snuggle in so neatly alongside our own native smoking linguistic idiom. There are a lot more similar surprises to come, as we check through the meanings of the other phonemes which we generally know these days as letters of the alphabet, supposed on their own to have no meanings attached whatever. We are asked to believe they have no meanings on their own except just occasionally when a single letter is treated as a word.(a very simple one). Only morphemes, generally strings of two or more phonemes, have sufficient anything about them to be dignified with meaning, we are taught; and this is supposed to have occurred on a random, or nearly random basis without prime regard to relating sound and sense. All this I plan to rubbish.

I identify only about the same number of original phonemic elements of language as are in the alphabet, from which the whole of the present world lexicon has evidently sprung, elaborating and expanding in accordance with the different idioms which appealed to human whimsy. Of course there has always been lots of linguistic diffusion, borrowing from one language to the next for one reason or another; but I have no need of it any more than of a single original proto-language to explain the universality of Lithic language elements: I guess simply because people everywhere all simply decided to think that way when they were first confronted with the challenging question of what the natural meanings were of the noises they uttered, which young Tarzan sitting beside them (the real Tarzan without any diaper on at all) might readily cotton onto. Incidentally I think he was already a very engaging little fellow, though he probably smelt a little rancid like the aboriginal in his natural habitat today. Soap is hardly more than two hundred years old, a late confection. In reality our primitive forebears probably all finally got properly on net together somewhat later, from contextual analysis just as much as from all guessing all the same guesses initially. But it was the need to communicate which made these folk think in terms of natural meanings which would be accessible to all. Linguistic buffs think in terms of "natural" linguistic development as an evolutionary process, an unfortunate spin off from Darwin´s evolution of species which has nothing to do with language whatever. Language goes with leaps and bounds by comparison, along with the human mind it takes with it, in accordance with human whimsy and analogy.

He is a brave man who will enter the semantic labyrinth on his own, and even dwell in that jungle year upon year. The penalties, once completely lost, can be very severe. It is a jungle which may be neutral but is hardly user friendly. In intellectual circles it also almost amounts to hoisting the Jolly Roger, because producing a plan of otherwise uncharted wastes is likely to be seen as a challenge to the survival of more conventional thinking. In an introduction it is best to declare ones true colours, and it can not be over emphasised that the Lithic language theses in reality challenge nobody and no thing, and that is one of Lithic's principal pleasures. It is a language game for any number of players, much like the game of scrabble, but played on a semantic board to the rules of Lithic analysis instead of on a conventional virtual chequer board with merely alphabetic linkages. All that is needed for the game to start in earnest is a copy of the late Eric Partridge's exquisite etymological dictionary of 1958 entitled "Origins", a treasure trove of original thinking, some of it just occasionally blinkered and perverse (Homer nods), but most of it original and ground breaking and epoch making. Perhaps nobody but me has really read it properly in the half century since it was published. His pot boilers were much more read. Much of my book owes an inestimable debt to the work of this estimable man. Half of Lithic language roots I believe he had caught sight of himself and reading between the lines you can see it. I have dedicated my own work to his memory. I never met him. When I was ready to go to him with what I had, I read that he had just died.

So far as the contents of this book are concerned, language has a phonetic texture and a semantic texture and the marriage of these two matrices is what etymology is all about. But up until now it is the alphabet which has prevailed and it is the blind phonetic matrix which has had the semantic matrix hung on it. I have tried to turn this about, putting first the semantic matrix, comprising all the semantic catenas apparent, derived from the most primitive phonetic elements I could disentangle; and then I have built a conjoined texture illustrative of the actual development of meanings given to each phoneme over the aeons. The psychosemantic trees which accompany each chapter covering the phonemes, chapters 4 to 15, represent an initial attempt to explain this semantic texture.

I have largely confined derivations in this book to English since it is the commonest language world-wide as well as the most researched, as also because it is my mother tongue so for most purposes I think most easily in it. But I have sauced the text with some examples of Lithic idioms from other tongues where they are striking and I have come across them. To cover all the languages on earth in any depth is well beyond a single lifetime's work and must await a general understanding of the method to be followed and generations of study. But I shall be surprised if my Lithic hypotheses concerning the meanings which have been given to individual phonemes do not all get worked out eventually, as well as being dead. Meanwhile I have endeavoured to give some added breadth to the hypotheses by providing chapters on languages not widely distributed outside their own domains such as Albanian, Basque, Chinese, Djeribal, Egyptian, etc, picked alphabetically until I ran out of puff, but I have had to defer these chapters to a second volume. I add Malay because it was Malay which first set me off on my researches and also because I have come to recognise it as the language most closely related to the language which Adam, the earliest Sapiens Sapiens of whom we have any news at all, spoke in the Garden of Eden, now beneath the shallow South China Sea, since the Great Glacier Melt when the oceans all rose some three hundred and fifty feet only some fifteen thousand years ago and Adam found himself driven out of his Malaya or garden, the irrigated river system Eve had invented with her digging stick while Adam was out hunting. Unsurprisingly he blamed Eve for their misfortunes, stifling her initiative for fifteen thousand years: a whacky world, my masters! Volume 2 should nevertheless follow quite shortly after this volume, since much of it is already written.

In this volume I have explored the semantic catenas, rather than just the sound changes which have occupied the attentions of linguistic experts since the fairytale brothers Grimm thought up their law and His Honour Sir William Jones compared the phonetics of Sanskrit with Greek; and I have illustrated them in the relevant chapters each with their "Psychosemantic Tree": a thumping expression I made up myself from the Greek. It is much like a family tree but with the chains of thinking followed by our forebears taking the place of the genetic descent displayed in a family tree. A Psychosemantic Tree simply means a tree of the meanings which can be seen to follow from the basic meanings we originally thought were the natural meanings of the sounds we made, courtesy of our own psychic promptings. I can not pretend that these trees are in any way complete and I very much hope this work will stimulate other folk of independent mind to add their personal pennyworths as opportunity offers, in as many languages as may be, the more remote from the Indo European language family the better.

I have not concerned myself at all with the kind of speech analysis which diagrams the vocal organs, and analyses phonic frequencies and draws conclusions about precise pronunciations at different times and places, trying to discover how we have managed to speak at all. For me that is a datum. Those who still fancy Neanderthals and or their contemporaries could not have spoken, or only very badly, because of the shape – largely guessed – of their vocal organs may want to regard this as a significant omission. For my part I think pushing back the time at which we learnt to speak to before Sapiens Sapiens is a mark of virtue, considering the extreme coarseness of the original thinking revealed: we may have thought like that once as complete vulgarians, but we can take comfort from the fact it was way back when we had scarcely shed our tails. Since then of course there have been aeons of refinement; although when you look at the presidents and prime ministers around the world today I think you are entitled to the view the progress has been relatively modest considering the time scale – a bit like the hand axes, we are still turning them out much the same after hundreds of millennia, with some surface polish perhaps but underneath the same trad pattern betraying our ugly origins[7].

I have not paid much attention to the current philosophy of language, chiefly because I am not very fond of philosophy any more; but I have included a review of the matter as an appendix (Appendix A) so as to head off criticism I am altogether lacking in that department. In the body of the book I sometimes carp at grammarians, the first philosophers worthy of the name, for trying to reinvent language the way they liked to see it rather than the way it was, making the language historian´s task that much the more confusing. I will confess to being bad at math although I have had to study it and am reasonably numerate by now. This is relevant because the current crop of grammarians base their approach on the Boolean mathematical logic associated with Frege, Russell, Tarski and Carnap, with a systematic construct not in any way apparent on the surface of languages and therefore treated as a hidden deep-seated structure. The question to be asked of course with these fanciful constructs is whether they dug it up or made it up. I think one of us must have done the one and the other the other. At least I go through the motions of trying to disclose what the digging reveals. One can only hope against hope the prejudiced will give the evidence a twirl before dismissing the whole neatly interlocking scheme of meanings as fabrication. The fabrication is not mine. If it is a disgrace it belongs to the whole human race – a boomerang which keeps coming back.

The Lithic hypotheses occupy an undeconstructed structuralist position so far as the philosophy of language is concerned, a fact only brought to my conscious attention after the deed was done. Jacques Lacan's discovery that reason and semantics in general are products of linguistic thinking, rather than prior to it, matches quite well the historicism of The Origins of Speaking. It is not hard to relate to Levi-Strauss and it is a pleasure to reflect positively upon a thinker who is unreservedly French. There is also the language of thought of course, prior to language, a "language" without the use of the tongue, of which we have no record and so must simply guess as best we can from the way we structured our language when we first started to use our tongues. The language we have worked out has come from somewhere and it is difficult to conceive of any source other than our own thinking. If we had not thought already we would never have spoken; and anyway even monkeys think so it is reasonable to presume we were thinking when we were still single ka creatures, godless monkeys, without speech.

The philosophy of language is of little interest which is why it has been deferred to an appendix. It is some way from the coal face, where thickets of abstraction provide every opportunity for obfuscation. Deconstruction and the rest of post modernism always had an undergraduate air about them with 'enfants terribles' successfully establishing themselves in avant garde academic quarters, some now rather elderly enfants and by now feeling the foolishness of their position as well as exhibiting it. The Origins of Speaking is an unashamedly historical work, unashamedly asserting we have a history and it has been what it has been and not another thing. This is anathema to post modernism which ludicrously alleges there is no underlying reality but only textual representations, arguing from the undoubted fact we tend to see things from our own individual windows on the world. In reality that is no big deal, and has certainly been common knowledge for very many millennia. Try selling post modernism to a man on the surface of the moon. Science has found a way for sifting the wheat from the chaff. It may not be perfect – it is not – but it works. Folk will bet their lives on it. The world is what it is and not another thing.

Only a mind stuck in undergraduate rebellion could miss the significance of this fact. To miss it, it will have helped to have been studying in an English faculty, that much separated from the coal face of events as to give a feeling of freedom to poetise in disregard of realities. Many good brains have been lost to this kind of lackadaisicality. Artistry is not all sweetness and light, though all artists pretend it is. It can trash the intellect. It does it by enlarging the scope of every enquiry beyond the range of the human mind properly to cope. Musicality then steps in as a substitute for articulate thinking. Music is the food of love, Jessica style, as well as of all other kinds of unpunctilious emotions, providing solace when rational thinking stops. The rational thinking may stop for a number of different reasons. One is pain. The commonest is sheer boredom because the thinking has become so completely divorced from the agenda of the human psyche that it has become a chore. Officers in the army, if they have any brains, resort to concerts with astonishing regularity. But more determined afficionados like Lord Lloyd Webber have genuine abilities which can not be denied, and his younger brother scrapes his instrument with admirable persistence and concentration. It appears to be something they have picked up in the womb before the cortex was sufficiently developed to embrace rationality, the latest theory being that the net effect of the electromagnetic and gravitational fields of the astronomical bodies moving relative to the earth play 'melodies' to the foetus in the womb. As the brain develops it picks up the tunes relayed in the fields at the time. It is probably over egging it a bit.

Postmodernism probably derives immediately from the fall of France. Sartres was out to show it did not signify, although of course it did. Maquisards declined to expose Vichy collaborators when the war was won for fear of bringing France into further disrepute and degradation. That compromise has given us the European Union on the one hand and terror on the other, twin post Nazi phenomena, both owing much to Nazism and neither perhaps fully aware of the fact.

As it is widely believed in academic circles that any such study as mine is ruled out of court before you begin, since language change proceeds at such a pace – it even purports to have been measured – that nothing would be recognizable from so far back, perhaps this introductory chapter should already indicate why I beg to differ. There is a concealed premiss in this academic assumption which proves not to be well founded. It is only true if the process of language change is assumed to be (semantically) chaotic, the current orthodoxy. In my view, to borrow a turn of phrase from Henry Ford, that is bunk. Jung had a Collective Consciousness or World Soul in which all the thinking thought since kingdom come was somehow accessible to those who came after – and particularly elite thoughts, and capping it all his own thoughts even if he had not got them to his publisher. That is where his archetypes came from. Henry Ford would have got a hit there as well. But the world lexicon is a reality in everybody´s language, unlike the World Soul. Sapiens has refreshed the original Lithic semantic elements, or anyway the very early ones, for the most part all unawares, picking them up from his lexicon from generation to generation via his subconscious muse in a thoroughly poetic manner, while skimming the surface with his conscious thinking, so that linguistic change has been semi informed all along by the subconscious; and the chain of speaking has never been broken. Jungians get no comfort here since their archetypes are fanciful as well as misplaced. I believe only careful attention is required to pick out these original Lithic patterns in the lexicon which have been passed down to us generation by generation linguistically from the origins of speaking. But the original elements, which have been passed down subconsciously, were basic and not fully shaped as in myth and fable, which only came in the last few thousand years at most. Jung is out of my frame altogether. But anyone with the gift of speech is well equipped to follow along, and the less educated the better – for these purposes only of course. In the following chapters I make a first attempt to trace these psychosemantic meanings for each of the phonemes (letters roughly) where no meanings ought to be for academe. They have been passed down to us learned, not genetically passed on, because only organs are genetically determined, not the particular activities they happen on – our genes decide the legs we grow but not the walks we take. Our genes decide the brains we grow but not the ideas we have. This is a puzzle because entropy is going the other way. Our legs will not jump us over the moon. Our brains will not surmount us god.

Admittedly the Lithic lexical hypothesis is bound to appear a bit iffy, as if Henry Ford were due for another call[8]. After all it must at first sight strike anyone approaching the matter for the first time as highly unlikely that the whole gamut of semantic evolution from original Lithic elements such as I have indicated in this book could possibly have been tucked away on a continuing basis in the human subconscious and still be available for discovery – and particularly if it be the case, as I also suggest it is, that the whole lot has to be subconsciously reinstalled and repacked away by each and every infant while learning the language up top. Just up top is judged too much without hard wiring, by some. Nevertheless, with familiarity I believe it gradually becomes obvious that that is in fact exactly what occurs. It certainly puts a new gloss on the Nature versus Nurture debate, coming down conclusively on teacher's side and cultural nurture, and against Noam Chomsky's hard wiring. The capacity of the human mind in terms of bits of information, whether conscious or subconscious, is immeasurable as well as being quite unknown. The subconscious mind is most of it. The conscious bit is a relatively recent offshoot apparently, and probably developing only pari passu with the introduction of speech. The chimpanzee can be quite bright without saying anything or thinking self consciously as we understand it very much, or even at all. The brutes think; but do not reflect much while they think. Thought just happens unnoticed, that is subconsciously in their untutored brains. Consciousness is reflexivity, thinking about thinking, whence comes quite incidentally the ability to collect and collate and dream up new images based on previous imaginings.

I have tried to keep the book light and airy since all intellectual research should be fun, and there is I believe the deepest humour possible involved in the whimsical way our minds have worked under the spur of speaking. But there is hack work involved in mulling over the detailed examples which make up the body of the book. It is of course possible, even though it is true, that nobody will believe it, preferring to regard Lithic as mad; in which case it should be stressed it is in the strings of elements which make up words that the proof lies. You could perhaps write different psychosemantic trees, but not I think capable of making any sense at all of very many words, which must therefore after all have been built from the Lithic phonetic elements and the semantic contents which I have uncovered, more or less.

Either the Lithic hypotheses – words composed world-wide from original strings of phonemes each with its own imagined generic meaning – has fairly general application or it does not; and if it does one should expect the cross referencing, given the time scale, to have reached a fairly rich texture. What needs explaining is how so rich a texture can have been rendered invisible for so long. This ancient language lore has perhaps been accessed in part at times by mystics, witches, magicians and such like with no general following, and with a mischievous need to dress up their insights as something they were not – Higher Truth, a White Goddess, Magic, etc. Or else we should perhaps put down their wild interpretations, so wide of the mark, as simply due to the unreliability of egg-heads? Most recently Karl Jung, for instance, has posited a "Collective Unconscious" as a repository for deep thoughts including those he had not the time or inclination to rush to his publisher, accessible nevertheless to seekers after truth after his death tuning in to this source. It was of course the same source which pointed any enquirer to the archetypes by introspection, Jung's window to the spiritual internet where everybody's scratch pad was available to the spiritual hacker. It is to be feared that Professor Chomsky's Universal Transformational Grammar is to be found at the same address. The Lithic world lexicon by contrast offers an alternative repository in the present sublunary sphere for such stores of wisdom as may be accessible to introversion; saving us from Jung's metaphysical limbo. It is not that the ideas are preconceived and hard wired in our minds by a beneficent and thoughtful nature before birth – the Chomsky Hypothesis – but that they are accessible to human thinking because they are encoded in the way we think because the way we think has been built on them. The subconscious mind knows this although Professor Chomsky apparently does not. Nobody however should seek to take away from him his undoubted achievement in fabricating so formidable a quasi-mathematical scheme of the grammar of language as she now exists.

Meanwhile the mind set of language study has diverged from the ancient idiom so that we all now, anyway in the West, think of words as nuggets, simply dubbed with meanings on no detectable principle; sometimes admittedly with articulated segments, prefix, suffix or even infix; but then again the articulated bits are in turn nuggets, again dubbed with meanings on no discernible principle. The idea of basic meanings inherent in basic elements of speech (based on sophisticated interpretations of their sounds), what I call psychosemantic contents, is so foreign to our ideas of nature and convention alike, with language clearly conventional, that any indications in that direction are apt to be dismissed as mere fancy out of hand. At most an aesthetic fuzz of meaning is allowed to surround a phoneticisation. Poets alliterate for example. Alfred Kallir in Oxford, in a book called "V for Victory" in 1947, and later in a similar treatment of every letter of the alphabet – "Sign and Design" in 1961 – examined their aesthetic significances, but without seeking anything really clearcut in the way of meanings. While John P Cohane, an advertising executive, in a short book entitled "The Key" traced certain phonemes applied to topographical features in a trail around the world and appears to have imagined them prehistoric expletives addressed to a god or gods by ancient seafarers, without any attempt at serious analysis. But that is about it. William Skeat's 1894 list of some 364 Indo-European word roots which I have carried in my pocket (copied into my address book) for more than two decades now, so that whenever kept waiting I could return to the feast, is simply a stock of such unthought-out nuggets, and they are not all correct even in his own terms. But they are all laid out for inspection in Appendix B. Some of them clearly respond to Lithic analysis, especially when re-expanded.

My principal effort has been in Ancient Egyptian. It is a major challenge because it has not yet been properly reconstructed after being lost. Only the consonantal system is roughly understood, because the vowelisation is usually left out in the writing. That probably means that the language was Semitic in principal content at least. The pharaohs were probably farming their people as Semitic conquerors who had gone native; and if so there is no Black Athena, although the Pharaohs acquired darker pigmentation the longer they stayed, from concubinage with the local talent. Meanwhile Egyptologists, doctors of Ancient Egyptian, have settled for half a loaf and put in middling vowels to enable the otherwise unpronounceable to be pronounced. Had they taken a pot shy at the likely pronunciation we could have applauded, with all the mistakes it might have implied. But just leaving the issue unresolved and with no attempt at progress seemed absurd to me, and it still does so.

A good number of Egyptian words have found their way over into Greek. Coptic, originally Egyptian, moreover boasts a fat dictionary in English (by Dr W E Crum,1939) and Coptic, though muddled up with Greek orthography, is a pointer to how the Egyptians spoke. Champollion learnt Coptic and used the language to guide his work on Egyptian. Unfortunately the Coptic language had been suppressed by Muslim invaders as heretical and lost, and was only later reconstructed by the Copts for religious purposes. A good deal of it, especially the pronunciation, and the spelling which followed it, had meanwhile been borrowed unawares from the Greek, along with the Greek alphabet which also in itself likely reshaped some of the words. A classic example of the kind of misunderstanding and elision which has occurred in Egyptian decipherment is in Sir Wallis Budge's 1925 and still only reputable and full scale Egyptian Dictionary. "Ptah renpit", from a late (Coptic, and therefore Christian) hieroglyphic text is glossed by Sir Wallis "apparently a title of God". Yes indeed! With the proper alliteration it can be shown to read "Pata ahi, arai en Pai Taun", which is easily enough then Englished to "Our Father roaming around (or raying about) in Heaven". There is even a streak of heresy in the "arai"; since it really meant being actively involved (like a demiurge or an Egyptian sunbeam doing its business pulling up the flowers) rather than merely being around in the background savouring or disapproving sublunary affairs, as orthodox Christian belief requires. It is known as the Pelasgian heresy. Moreover 'Ptah' is an ancient Egyptian 'god' predating Christianity by thousands of years, so that pastors of the church twitch at the idea of allowing him into Christian theology even in the Lord's prayer. Interestingly he alone of all the Egyptian 'gods' has no "neter", supposedly an axe of divinity according to the academic Egyptologists, before his name. The neter is really a 'Natura' or wind blown pennant. Natura is literally na or show, plus tura pull, or 'force indicator' in Egyptian. Ptah having no neter has always been an inexplicable puzzle to Egyptologists, since Ptah was an ancient and venerable god, but I can now explain it to them here. It was for the good reason he was not a 'god' in the Egyptian pantheon of what we would call just natural forces, but a collective, Our Fathers (since Pata ahi could be singular or plural). He was an ancestor god and not a force of nature, so he carried no natura. Simple really! You just have to chance your arm in a game of "spot the thinking", which puts academic Egyptologists off.

So Christianity is not impugned by Egyptians using their own old word to describe the Christians' God, and the characterisation of the Christians' God as a Father in Heaven is in fact entirely canonical; although it may be mildly disturbing for Christians to find fathers allowed in heaven (even a heaven in an under world) before they came along, and even if they were only ancestor fathers, rather than a single Divine One. Christian apologists have always made a point of contrasting uncaring heathen gods with their fatherly God's Christian concern for sparrows' falls, etc; and it is a fair point. But in point of fact it must surely have been Ra, the Sun perceived as the all seeing eye of heaven, who provided, rather earlier, at least the ground for this characterisation; after all it was bound to occur to the Egyptians there must be some reason for all that looking down, and concern at what He saw must have been an appealing suggestion as soon as it was made. It was a more encouraging view than the other previous explanation available that he was an overseer keeping a severe eye on things to ensure the smooth running of the world machine he had created in accordance with His wishes, with the various natural Pulls and Pushes the Egyptians had identified as the ones to watch and propitiate. The Jews were long enough in Egypt to have learned that much there. The Egyptian connection was a strong one, and should not be under-estimated, whether the prophet Moshe was really an Egyptian priest or a Pharaoh or both or neither. On balance I favour both. But then I am a free spirit, not a Jew.

So with a bit of Lithic license it was already possible in 1970 to start to connect up some of the other Egyptian words to exemplify parts of an idiom. Aton, conventionally interpreted as the disc of the sun to suit Mrs Grundy, but actually the world's female sexual orifice, the everlasting birth canal, an undeniably feminine attribute, with the A- prefix – you can go on sounding 'aaaa' as long as your breath lasts – deriving its sense from the continuousness of the general vowel, giving the meaning here of Eternal or Everlasting. A little rumination on the A-ton's (Lithic Aaa-Taun) qualities readily offers such phrases as Everlasting Source as well as Birth Source, Source of Becoming. So far as the second element –ton is concerned, if the substantive form Taun is either used to derive the verbal form as a back formation, giving Tai, the action of becoming (like tai'm or time for one); or indeed if it is treated as itself derived from the prior verbal form, we can posit a completive verbal form also, with the same phoneticisation: tau, become; and a possible further substantive form tau as a verbal noun, the become or even the becomings. The vowel u as the completive form of the vowel tends to signify duality and plurality as well as substance. So the substantive form Tau could carry the sense All the Becomings, which is one (and apparently the Egyptian) definition of the universe – the totality of everything which happens. Taun from the early semantic content of the birth canal, also came to mean all the births, all the becomings, the totality of phenomena – perceived by the Ancient Egyptians rather like the frames of a TV programme – and so for the Egyptians the world. To go back to basics, the original Lithic meaning of Ta came from the sound of snapping a stick in two, so it meant to make into two bits, two bits, to divide, division, and so parturition, and with an oo or orifice added, the birth canal. We have seen all the becomings already in Pai Taun, the skin or lid of the world, the glyph for which was a semicircle, a circle divided into two, flat side down, the world's dome. The Egyptian world was like a penny with the world of live forms under the dome of the sky (as must appear to any flat-earther) and the underworld of Hades in the dark on the underside. We have seen this too already in Pai Taun for the Christian Heaven in Wallis Budge's "Ptah Renpit" We can observe the same elements in the Greek 'Pretani' their original term for Ancient Britons, which in turn came from the Egyptian: Peri-Taun-i, the-periphery-of-the-world-ones, encountered by the Egyptians who apparently colonised East Anglia and perhaps Salisbury Plain and the Thames estuary as well, before the Celts invaded and overwhelmed their colonies. The Greek "peri" was from the Egyptian Pai Rai, in this case the skin of Ra, the Sun: the border around the Sun and so a periphery, or the peripheral. Nowadays the Eskimos are the only true Britons or Peri Tauni, and they prefer to call themselves Inuit. Esquimo means raw meat eaters, a fair description but considered rude. Literally A-Sakai-mau. As-alive-Eaten. They lived where there was no firewood or cow dung to burn and perforce ate raw fish. Far from being criticized they should have been given a medal. I imagine once you get used to the flavour.it goes down as well as raw flesh of any other kind. It may even slip down more easily; and they needed no salt pans.

So Pet, which academia uses for Heaven in Egyptian, but can hardly be the kind of phoneticisation an Ancient Egyptian would pick for so august a phenomenon, can instead be read as Pai-Taun, the Skin or Roof of the Universe, which to me at least sounds a lot better, and is even meaningful with it. That is Lithic for you. Whether these ancient speakers thought at the same time and simultaneously of the Aton as a birth canal of the universe (giving birth to the light each day, a busy lady) or the Pai-Taun as meaning precisely the roof of the universe is not at issue. There is no reason why they should necessarily have done so. One word is coined at a time and its derivation, these days anyway, quickly consigned to oblivion. Almost half the older (shorter) words in the English lexicon neither the late Mrs Whitehouse nor any other Mrs Grunty would tolerate for one moment if they knew how they started out.

Think of the inconsequence of the bus and the pram. Even the Egyptian language is a late confection when compared with the length of time we have been speaking, a time to be measured in hundreds of thousands of years, though how many hundreds varies as evidence is turned up in one discipline or another and is variously interpreted. My own preference is for quite a number of hundreds of thousands of years and pre human hominids as the first speakers. But the dating is not of prime importance. It just has to be recognized it was a very long time ago indeed.

It did occur to me at one stage that what I was discovering was perhaps not a universal meaning system but merely the ground of Egyptian meanings. Such an interpretation is still a contender, especially if we throw in an excessively large slice of diffusion. Perhaps the reed boats the late Thor Heyerdal recreated carried Egyptians on world cruises, spreading their manner of speech wherever they went. So for example they could have given the Aztecs who spoke Nuahatl their supreme creator god Wakan Tanka, Fear Making World Maker or The Awesome Creator. On the other hand, an Egyptian mission to the primitive Germans seems rather far-fetched. With their Semitic heritage would they have been well received in any case? My own preference is for the universal applicability of Lithic, with the Egyptian language yielding big returns in spite of its high culture because of the uniquely conservative legacy of their glyph, retaining archaic forms. The evidence for this judgment must be evaluated in the remaining chapters of the book, particularly chapters 4 to 15 covering all too briefly the discovery of the psychosemantic trees. Those without the time or temperament to examine the whole work – reviewers, students and the young at heart in general – can pick up sufficient by turning to the short synopsis I have provided for them at Chapter 18 to enable them to appear to have read the whole book, if somewhat cursorily. The more studious may still find it a useful reference while ploughing through the detailed chapters.

If the Lithic hypotheses are to be believed, what shall be their proof? Is a fair number of cases fitting the hypothesis sufficient, or for that matter a very great number? Must it have universal application, so that if words can be found that refuse to yield to Lithic analysis the theory fails? It is early for me to answer such questions. My own astonishment is for the spread of the thing. Every day in the normal course of speech and reading I notice it. I would need a tape recorder on my wrist to pick up on everything that comes to mind. Politeness prevents me, although very deaf now, from pursuing each mental minnow as it shows, breaking into normal conversation. I believe every educated person, whatever his or her native tongue, if they finish the book will find themselves in the same way thinking of numberless cases of Lithic analysis on their own. Indeed the fear of paranoia may well intervene. But they should have faith in their sanity like the present intrepid author. The paranoia, if paranoia it is, is not theirs but that of the human race, which needs to be exposed so that it may be understood and managed. Otherwise we shall have to continue to put up with the lunatics taking over the asylum. We have just lived through a century of mass political criminal lunacies, generated in Germany on the left: both Communism and Nazism guilty of deliberately butchering very many millions to prove themselves right, tasks quite hopeless from the outset. It matches in a most embarrassing way the rise of the labouring masses to take their rightful places in the politics of the world. The world is swimming in a sea of political Tom Fools – most of them it has to be said in cloth caps or Mao suits: not that a cloth cap or a Mao suit makes you a fool, but simply that by definition there are so many of them that a large number are foolish. Now in Europe we have another criminal conspiracy in the making, with ex Communists and ex Nazis plotting together to take over the world by continuing to build a European Super State to outgun the USA: another task quite hopeless from the outset, since it actually incorporates at one remove both the discredited criminal lunacies mentioned above merely dressed up in a (threadbare) democratic cloak. These unpalatable truths need now to be exposed. They are not for comfort. Tracing the human whimsy in the lexicon is a very small start.

Notes

1. There are some recent signs of intelligent endeavour. Mr Peter MacNeilage and Dr Barbara Daws of the University of Texas in Austin have studied the babbling of babies as an original source for speech; and Phillip Lieberman has published an interesting book on the evolution of speech and thinking.

2. The word "evolution" is in quotes because it is only rather doubtfully applicable at best, in the way science currently uses it, to the development of linguistic skills. Skills do not evolve any more than thinking does. They change according to the whimsical (but directed) insights which shape them. The way we think, how we control our enunciation and mental activity, is clearly a function of physical structure, but – quite surprisingly really – after scientific determinists have insisted we are being lived we go on to exhibit lively and independent minds capable of adopting and adapting one idea after another, and often contradictory ones at that, just as if we were genuine free thinkers,

which I have come to believe our primitive forebears already actually were, admittedly not yet emissaries of reason, more like caterpillars at the end of a leaf. Any study of language, or of the thinking which lies behind it, must be in terms which are meta-physical, that is to say not in any way confined to the thinking of the laws of physics. Metalinguistics receive a mention in Appendix A amongst the philosophical speculations. Partridge's etymological dictionary recognises this whimsy where all the others go for languages evolving like physical species, which most certainly they are not; and they do not. It is this whimsy which is the glory of the human race.

3. On the edge of the Breckland in Norfolk, England, where the soil is light and the trees easier to fell so it ranks in age of occupation with Stone Henge on Salisbury Plain some 200 miles South West. But long before that the axe must have been frozen into the ice in the last ice age at least and later melted out. To judge by the glacial erratic boulder found three centuries earlier within a mile of it, it could have been made locally or anywhere within a couple of hundred miles or more. Perhaps like the boulder it came from Yorkshire. The boulder featured in Charles Lyell's 1830 book "The Principles of Geology" which established evolution, collaborating with my great grandfather, the conchologist, born in 1804.

4. I think so. The appeal of baseball and cricket (and other ball games) are otherwise inexplicable. But there is nothing else to learn from the fact. Academia is not directly or immediately a refinement from throwing stones, although academics are sometimes stout defenders of their turfs.

5. Mrs Whitehouse campaigned to clean up TV in UK.

6. My own daughter started teaching in the "Blackboard Jungle" in Bristol, threatened with violence by 16 year old boys; and after moving to Norfolk where she was regularly abused quit for South Africa where she taught post-apartheit Boers whose behaviour was by comparison immaculate because they were punished at home if it was not. Apartheit and even Nazi supporters are disciplined whimps rather than macho, cowards over-awed by those in power, staying politically correct. The cowardice is of course deliberately stimulated by those in power, by harping on perceived threats.

7. I wrote this when Mr Clinton was discovered entertaining Monica Lewinsky sexually in his Oval Office. Cynics would say it was relatively benign entertainment for an American President there.

8. Henry Ford was after all a single minded man who made very good cars in his day. My father drove a model T Ford van with port hole windows in the back doors. Ford also contributed famously to the urchin mind of ours: just

wave a hand and enjoy a wave back and ignore the difficult, the painful or the spiteful bits. It is now socially and politically entrenched and polluting every kind of enterprise and study, a nihilist heritage and a sad legacy for the moribund West as we enter the burgeoning geopolitical millennium with only our technology to keep us afloat.

CHAPTER 2

ORIENTATIONS

Not many people you meet in the street have actually read Charles Darwin´s book "On The Origin of Species" published almost a hundred and fifty years ago and still going strong[1]. Even fewer have any knowledge of the intellectual milieu at the time he wrote and thus have any hope of assessing the contribution he made to human knowledge. It was less than is usually imagined. He collected other peoples work as well as the scientific evidence for half a lifetime; and if Alfred Russell Wallace had not anticipated his principal message of natural selection he would most probably have deferred publication until after he was safely dead. His revolutionary paper read to the Linnaean Society was skimmed out of the voluminous posthumous work he was preparing in the few weeks grace the Society gave him to state his claim when they got Wallace´s paper. The press then as now liked a name to nail to any cause and played the religious scandal card for all it was worth. As a result a hundred years of adventure and research have been filed under Darwin´s name in the usual convenient shorthand for the more realistic kind of history. To be fair Darwin wrote well by the standards of his day, although today he can appear both pedestrian and over elaborate at the same time, no mean literary feat. He wrote in the style of the quality press of his day deliberately, not for the man in the street but for the gentry in their clubs. His book, neatly interpreting the spirit of the times, was a runaway best seller with a second edition on the streets within six weeks, a succés de scandale.

Dr Gillian Beer, Professor of English and President of Clare Hall at Cambridge University (England), in her introduction to the paperback edition of Darwin´s Origin – the second 1860 edition – remarks judiciously: "The Origin of Species made its impact because it raised questions fundamental to the life of humankind without making humankind the centre of the enquiry". This may be true in its way and the literary technique of placing in counterpoint the two centralities, the human and the natural approaches, gives it an air of subtlety; but to me it seems to be oddly phrased, as does some of Darwin's own work between the same covers. Certainly Darwin´s book was at the time perceived (correctly) to actively and deliberately displace humankind from the centre of the world and from the centre of every man's enquiry, as it still (correctly) is perceived today. It was one more Copernican Revolution for mankind to swallow, already sick of the punishment. It was not at bottom because he argued for natural selection and an undirected naturally self-regulating universe that Darwin's book hit home so hard. That had often been done before. His grandfather Erasmus had held equally scandalous views. Lamarck and even Cuvier had also said as much, though perhaps without the plethora of supporting nitty gritty. It was because Darwin did so under the imprimatur of a scientific protocol which would brook no independent world view other than its own, which was to be taken as a singularity. That was, and is, the sting in Victorian science's tail. It is this singularity which is now a hundred and fifty years later under review: a review which can realistically be described as resulting from an 'Aquarian' zeitgeist challenging and seeking to melt down previously conceived categories, a spring cleaning age, and of course nothing whatever to do with alchemy or pretended zodiacal influences. Science has from its origins always prided itself, correctly enough, on being a singularity and promoting a singularity of view: there is one picture of the world and when scientists have had their say any other turns out to have been pre-empted, found unscientific and not to be said. This is in itself curious when you realise science self confessedly is a learning process and has to date always been found later to have been wrong. Science advances while claiming stasis at the same time. Had it ever discovered the whole truth, conceived as singular and unique, it would have come to an end already just as history has been imagined by certain post moderns to have done so for another reason, namely it is all just day dreaming about the past. The real nature of scientific knowledge is to advance by successive approximations, for ever circling a central reality but doomed never to achieve its goal, always up for review, even up for grabs. So how can this be? The scientific position is that there can only be one single version of the truth – the world is what it is and not another thing – and, sotto voce, it is unfortunately true science does not yet quite fully possess it, though it is conceivable quite soon it will. There is a vulgar realism in every scientist's brief. That does not stop eminent popularisers of science like Professor Hawking looking forward to the millennium with a Theory of Everything to be vouchsafed as a capstone of the scientific edifice. With such a view in mind it might be no bad thing to see what and where this edifice may be. We shall see, I think, that science is a fraud – an amiable fraud – because it sets out from the beginning with a self-deception bequeathed by the founding fathers and still central to scientific thinking. It purports to access reality but what it is really doing is only to process it in the mind. This is not because the scientific edifice is not a thoroughly modern building continually under inspection and repair and kept sparse and trim. William of Occam if he were alive today could safely afford to put away his famous razor and still not lose himself in the fuzz remaining. So it must be added that science´s methods are so far our best protocols for investigating the nature of the universe we find ourselves in, including its galaxies and vastnesses, the big and the small together, its rocks and crevices, its species and all their derivations, its specifics and ways of thinking.

But there is one more Copernican Revolution waiting in the wings, a blow in the solar plexus for the scientific triumphalists, which Darwin may perhaps have sensed although he gave away no clue he had any inkling of it. But then everything he wrote was with an eye to the public he addressed. It has been assumed he wrote for mankind. But I believe the figures over his shoulder were mostly his prosy cousins in frock coats and many of them dog collars, much of whose predispositions and world views Darwin in fact shared, though not their placidity. Darwin had a bad stomach most of his life and lived in retirement reading and brooding; and curiously acid in the stomach is probably the principal stimulant for radical thinking, a surprising fact since nobody would have supposed the brain takes its time from the stomach, but it does.

Every Copernican Revolution is perceived by the scientific establishment of the day as an attack on the whole edifice of their thinking, impossible for them, the most potent grave and reverend seigneurs, to believe that it could after all be built round any illusions. Those who clung to Ptolemy´s heavenly cogwheels to explain astronomy by the laws of mechanics were muddling the what with the where. Scientists the world over still rejoice in the same muddle. The reason why scientists could espouse a systematic description of the facts of astronomy which was actually quite bogus was because it came out of their own heads and not from the heavens as they imagined. The brain of the thinker and the cosmos out there are clean different things. Unless you are a solipsist, which scientists have foresworn, you must pretend at least to take this into account. But it is easier if you can enjoy a one to one relationship with your facts, so the facts are usually taken to be the universe, real and immediately available for scientific examination and analysis. But you really need a bit of symbolic logic here – not taught in the scientific tripos to date. Facts may be real while "facts" are mental constructs. But science is surprisingly hidebound. If a theory takes in a field and mathematics it is the singular reality, while plurality of vision leads to myth, religion, etc – dead ends!

Consequently scientists are all dancing a war dance on an ox-hide – undeniably a prettily enough choreographed composition with intricate steps and subtle minuets; but the larger part of the mental universe remains off limits by order, so that there is usually light relief for scientists only in music and humour. They all stay strictly on their mat. A scientist is a prisoner in his scientific world, anyway while he is doing science, with just the freedom that he needs to move around his pad but no more. To rub salt in this critique we can quote that prosy old Victorian poet Coventry Patmore, out of context for sure and purely from memory from my own adolescence, but the diction is good:

"Love wakes men once a lifetime each,
They lift their heavy lids and look,   (eyelids of course, they are not
And all that one fair page can teach   inspecting what is cooking)
They read; then close their eyes and shut   (or shut eyes and closed book?)
the book".

Perhaps we can concede the scientist one fair page to dance on in place of the ox-hide to which we just hidebound him. The hides and pages after all are mere metaphors; but they can also serve to carry forward the philosophical distinction made earlier between the cosmos and the mind. The hide and the page turn out to be the scientific singularities Professor Hawking has in his sights. These surfaces, like patterned wallpaper, overlay the wall which is reality, just as the hide is spread on the ground to dance on, or the script is imprinted on the page. I am back to the poetry book of my boyhood again, only an unattributable more recent fragment on language this time, just a snap shot of human knowledge on the fly:

"A mass of paper reasoning ill hemmed
A jagged edged floating tegulation
Coming from nowhere, and to nothing pinned
And so seemingly must descend
To the bottom one supposes of creation"

Let us not leave these metaphorical tegulations hanging loose in limbo any longer. Let us fold or stretch them topologically to concave hemispheres and fit them into the insides of our skulls. Hey Presto! Realism is out the window. We are now just copyists, rather than modelers in clay handling the material directly, doomed indeed to remain so for ever; and science itself is obliged to move over into our heads, the subjective. Our logic is a logic of symbols rather than reals, and so is the thought which we think – another conventional language lying beside the ones that we speak. It is these overt utterances of language alone which can guide us back to an understanding of the ways the human mind has thought and so to why we think the way we do. The study of linguistics is properly the study of linguistic evolution in reverse, that is working back up (or better down) the linguistic tree to discover where we came from mentally speaking. Nothing to do with Darwin, this! The composition of language is non physical itself anyway, if not indeed metaphysical (in spite of the latter´s metaphysical associations). The mind is not the brain, after all, though we expect to find them both in the head. Yet mental tonality at least comes from the stomach and genitalia. The mind is a free floating entity in the brain, a made up ghost of the body with a congé to think

Since Darwin, evolution – that is automatic random change and natural selection leading to speciation under its own steam – has ruled biology. Indeed it has been the flavour of the day for a century and a half now. There was a good reason for this. Darwin's book in 1859 was the first, or at any rate the first successful attempt to nail science's colours to the mast and stand firm against the forces of obscurantism since the dark ages began. These obscurantist forces have usually been represented in clerical garb. It is not germane to our present theme whether this has been entirely fair. Probably it has not. Certainly Darwin himself – who was agnostic but married to a pious believer and with many of his family and acquaintances churchmen – agonized for decades over the effect the publication of his scientific conclusions would have on society. He actually thought it might spark revolution and violence in the streets as the common man learned he had been conned. Only the paper sent to the Linnaean Society by the young and far brasher Wallace forced his hand, so we have Darwinism in place of Wallacism today. The fact is Darwin was really quite a nice man; by the standards of his day a very nice man, perhaps a little bit too nice even. One would have liked to have him meet Engels, who had actual experience of working conditions. As Darwin saw it he was living in profoundly revolutionary times to an extent that we moderns now find difficult to understand. The social changes and the threats to conventional beliefs his generation was asked to face in the middle of the Victorian age seem so absurdly insignificant in comparison with the intellectual bankruptcies, mayhem, genocides and published mass starvations of our own times that the point can now easily be missed that up until Darwin the social structure itself was taken to be part of nature. Society was therefore sacrosanct, and interfering with it was taken to be unnatural. In living memory there had been a lot of head cutting, and the wholly unscrupulous atheistic Napoleonic imperial ambition of France had torn up the map of Europe and impoverished the common man all across the continent, confirming the less common in their religious beliefs. Peace and prosperity were what were wanted, not the intellectual and spiritual turmoil Darwin had to offer; and he knew it. Moreover in the very same years the young Darwin was busy doubling certainty with his detailed researches into barnacles and earth worms the young Karl Marx was already on record declaring the moral corruption implicit in the Victorian world view – and ironically prolonging the corruption for a century and more by assuming the same confusion of nature with society in his own critique. Marx's ideas are still quite common a hundred and fifty years later amongst academics, at least in the more decadent establishments on the European continent, apparently because they make them think. Yet they are also espoused by simpler minds because they save them thinking. The miner's leader Arthur Scargill and the London Mayor Ken Livingstone spring to mind. As Groucho would have said if you can work that trick you have got it made. It is a paradox Marx himself would have very much enjoyed.

Be all that as it may, in 1859 evolution under its own steam was a declaration of independence for scientists and political theorists alike, whether they liked it or not: from 1859 science was declared to the English speaking world to be autonomous. The rest of the civilised world read it and followed along. Darwin thus imprinted his own perception of the momentous developments he believed in on the thinking world for five generations. Only Karl Marx´s intellectual miasmas have lasted longer.

Apart from that, his original ideas could be counted on the thumb of one hand: namely the idea – we would say the statistical idea – that very many small selective differentia could over sufficient time lead to big changes. Even the germ of this idea was already in the work on population growth by the Reverend Malthus decades before, as Darwin was quick to point out in his own defence. It was indeed no more than was specifically prayed in aid by Darwin´s elder mentor and tutor Charles Lyell in his truly epoch making book "The Principles of Geology" published in 1830 just on thirty years before Darwin's "On The Origin of Species". It was the book Darwin took with him on his five year round the world cruise as official geologist, a post secured for him by his Cambridge geology tutor, on the admiralty survey ship The Beagle, with the third volume forwarded to him in South America. Not only that but Lyell had already established the temporal sequence of the sedimentary rock strata by sampling the microfauna (small shells) included as fossils within them under his microscope, putting the earlier less evolved shell forms earlier than those with more pronounced features. His book rested firmly on conchology. There was a self taught quarryman William Smith who had ordered the major British rock strata long before Lyell, but clumsily using only the larger fossils which fell out of the rocks. He appears to have had no use for a microscope. Largely forgotten, he has recently been rescued and dressed as a natural genius by Simon Winchester in a biography entitled "The Map that Changed the World"[2], supposedly preempting Darwin. So the evolutionary clock had been set firmly already in 1830 by the evolution of living species marked by the shell sequences. Darwin had known this for thirty years and only pretended to have got the idea of species evolution himself from the evolution of the rocks to save his friend from criticism. Most of the intervening years Lyell had been urging Darwin to publish. Darwin had married a daughter of the wealthy Wedgwood potter and after his world cruise lived a life of genteel retirement in the country enjoying indifferent health. For most of his life he was withdrawn and hesitant. He likely had picked up Chagas' Disease exploring in South America. The science history books have copied his little deception to protect his mentor Lyell ever since he penned it. Yet Lyell's book is in print and it is all written there. The conchology is on almost every page.

I just happen to be privy to all this because my great grandfather was a colleague of Lyell's when they were both young barristers together in London; and Lyell would visit Merton Hall for weekends and used my great grandfather's shell collection as well as the Merton Stone, the largest glacial erratic in the British isles dug up in the seventeenth century when we were marling the land, for his book. They would retire together with their microscopes to the long gallery at the top of the house after dinner where the shells were ranged in glass cabinets the whole length of the gallery. I remember them well. With hindsight all Darwin did was to put it all together with his own idea of natural selection and publish it in the face of the church, without ever really wanting to do so. It could be argued the revolution in genetics, all since Darwin, genetics was a blank file in Darwin's time, owed more to the old monk Gregor Mendel and his study of peas in his monastery vegetable garden than to Darwin's writings. Modern biology only nods at evolution and natural selection.

As a historian I am going to insist that writing up history as if it mostly consists of big men is for the most part quite bogus. There are movements of ideas often triggered by technological advances – Marx's bit – so that the time becomes ripe for the background of informed opinion to find expression. Sooner or later somebody is going to blurt it. Wallace and Darwin blurting together nicely illustrate this, in fact. It is estimated that quite generally it takes thirty years from the first technological promptings of novel thinking until any idea is exploited and a book gets written laying out a fully revised view of the subject matter. Lyell's work nicely illustrates this latter rule of thumb. Darwin's contribution probably originally started to mature when Karl von Linné (Linnaeus), the radical Swedish botanist, a son of the manse, got locked in to the examination and description of species decades before Darwin was born, realistically using the genitalia of plants (the flowers) as critical criteria. It cost him his sanity, hounded by the clergy of the day for his revelation of the indecent sexual secret of the otherwise innocent flowers. for which he was told he would burn for eternity. But he inspired Lyell and my great grandfather to take up the baton, perhaps with the ambition to carry over Linnaeus's sexual trick to conchology to provide a wide ranging evolutionary taxonomy. Unfortunately, sex for the conchologists is tough. The conch is sexually very discreet, with its genitalia tucked well away, except when actually copulating, which often requires both partners turn themselves virtually inside out. They would never score in a flower show.

In the outcome Darwin worsted the bishops in the most public of debates, conducted for the most part in his absence. They even had to let him into Westminster Abbey when he died. He certainly deserves credit for his service to humanity, though Socrates would have said he had it relatively jammy. Faced with hostility, his meticulousness and evenness of temper enabled him to con the world so that his sagacity was largely unquestioned. Facing the challenge of speciation he went to the pigeon fanciers for evidence. Facing the charge of heresy he wrote about earth worms. Clerical critics merely charicatured his conclusions for the public and represented them as grotesque; so science won by default. Darwin himself was horrified by all this. He probably knew Linnaeus had gone mad under the threat of hellfire for his entirely legitimate identification of the flowers of the field as their sex organs, all only a century before – the church wanted to keep them just as flowers and was still just as powerful and unforgiving in the middle of the nineteenth century when dogma was challenged. He appears to have feared also he was putting weapons in the hands of the mob. He was no more a Darwinist in modern terms than Marx was a Marxist-Leninist. Neither can be fairly judged by the bully boys who came after, free riding in their trains – bad tempered simpletons for the most part incapable of original thinking and simply using their borrowed ideas as bludgeons to assuage their bad tempers.

Meanwhile the idea of evolution as its own prime mover spilled over into other areas where historical change has to be explained. Quite early on Professor Stubbs at Oxford, a historian who imagined history to be an evolution (later recruited as a bishop) found the British constitution had developed by an evolutionary process which he felt to be progressive. Indeed liberals of all kinds joined the band wagon. But it has on balance done little for the understanding of historical change. Indeed the very idea of any historical process as a scheme of events over and above circumstance and happenstance has been brought into disrepute. By the time the late historian Alan Taylor, never episcopal material, hit Magdalen College in the 1940s the abandonment of the nineteenth century liberal historical school was far advanced; and Taylor himself had already dumped Marxism, after writing some terrible turgid party stuff in Vienna under Professor Pribram. He made sure they stayed out of print after, and my copies burnt with my house round them twenty years later. The proof of the pudding is in the eating after all, and socio-economic theory based on bogus historical process has bitten the dust most notoriously and most recently across the Russian empire, but in fact egregiously and universally wherever it has been tried. Marx had his own ideas on the historical process he called Dialectical Materialism, worked out over a hundred and fifty years ago long before electricity or internal combustion; and their downfall is therefore no great loss. But it is early as yet to count all the other casualties. Not much of current sociological thinking can in the long run expect to survive. Time like an ever rolling stream will bear all these women in sensible felt hats away, and their posturing masculine tutors with them.

At least Darwinian evolutionary thinking on its own has not needed to distort all analysis into a triple stitch of Thesis, Antithesis and Synthesis as Marxists have additionally required – copying the liberal Hegel whose original German dialectics were comparitively rarified and intelligent (although just as wrong). They are both of them finally disposed of in Chapter 16 on thinking. But evolution has made a strait jacket of historical process nevertheless. Schematics have over-ridden common sense – always a hazard where academics are at work, since they have a bent for exalting intellectual input over more practical effort. Shoemakers have always preferred leather. It is not that they are prejudiced in their own favour; merely that the experience they draw on and admit to is severely limited. But this is why it has now become necessary to attack the idea of blind process under its own steam as unhelpful for most kinds of study, including scientific study par excellence since it excludes nine tenths of how science develops.

The study of language is a critical such case in point. A study should be reasoned all through. Any other approach leads to more or less free composition, illuminating for the light it throws on the quirks and dispositions of the writer rather than the material insights it provides. In the case of language, to treat the phonetics as possessing a dynamism and process of their own, without taking proper account of the semantics involved, reduces to blind process what is of its nature a complex web of reasoning and articulation; while to treat of grammar as Chomsky does as if it were in some way prior to the vocabulary which carries it similarly blinds the process. It is in fact treating a diachronic study as if it were a synchronic one; which brings us to the second point in our critique of modern thinking, this time to be blamed on simpletons misreading Einstein rather than Darwin.

Any schoolboy can grasp the idea that space and time can be treated as merely different dimensions: a fourth dimension is fully comprehensible, even though you can not draw it – at least not without some elision. But that does not make our apprehension of space and time the same, any more than going up and down is the same as going sideways. It certainly does not blur – unless for a bullock – the fundamental distinction between synchronic and diachronic analyses, both mental modes or schemes, between descriptions of states of play at any one time and descriptions of the course of change across time. These are givens of perception, which are not altered by Einstein's mathematics utilising space-time to validate equations. It may well be our perceptions are misleading and unsatisfactory but they are what they are and pretending they are different will not alter the position. If we could perceive space-time we would not have needed an Einstein to point it out as a consequence of his mathematical equations.

This distinction between space and time is the Tau cross, perhaps the oldest symbol we know the meaning of, though cups and circles and spirals can be found which are older. I personally suspect these earlier symbols may simply reveal the same nausea of the néant that Sartres and his followers complained of recently. Our forebears´ minds were reeling and whirling trying to find their mental bearings. But the Tau meanwhile is so fundamental that it needs to be included at the outset in the operating system of any educated mind before getting down to particular studies. It is the identification of synchronic and diachronic schemes and was certainly known to the Ancient Egyptians. They called the world Taun which meant the totality of birthings, becomings, happenings, or events. They had in fact a very proper historical perspective the modern world has largely forgotten in face of technology. Metaphor will illustrate the nature of their thinking position best. Time is sometimes conceived as the vertical dimension without real steps or graduations. Character type can be illustrated by whether an individual believes the moving hand of time is ascending or descending. One early tradition was it reciprocated in a circle, a wheel of time. There is of course no reason why it should not even be thought of as going from left to right, or indeed from right to left like Semitic writing. In fact any continuum without graduations will do as a metaphor.

For purposes of the present metaphor it is proposed to take the case of a vertical continuum for the second or temporal dimension (really the fourth) with the direction of movement an ascending one. There are reasons for thinking that was the hominid model because the flame leaps upwards and the plants grow up to the sun. The past can then be characterised as a rope of consecutive actualities being spun from individual strands much as the original hempen hawser was spun, but with a myriad filaments. It is best these days to picture a good thick hawser capable of mooring an ocean liner or even an island, with countless continuous strands since in reality the strands are indeed innumerable (as well as being imaginary). The present is then represented by the rope cut across, with a texture of synchronic interconnections between them which may be deduced from examination of the scientific evidence. It is upon this flat surface of our rope cut across that we live and move and have our being, since for our rope illustration our three dimensional world has been shrunk to a two dimensional one so as to attend to the relation between the spatial on the one hand and the temporal on the other. This hardly conflicted with actual experience in the stone age since legged beings moved mostly on the flat, although birds flew. In Australian aboriginal languages a bird is still known as a budgy, a ba-ji which means a go-up, not bad for a bird in two phonemes. The budgerigar is just a bird djeri-gara, of bright colour. Not many of the fanciers know that – perhaps none. Comically the fanciers call them budgies, just birds in the aboriginal tongue, as if they had spotted it. Our English bird in turn is perhaps originally one that ba-rai-da, one that go-raying-does. The sun´s rays in Egypt were supposed to return to the sun, pulling up the vegetation with them. The Englishing of the elements is of course misleading. Ba-rai-da holds only meaning in Lithic terms, reinforced by the subconscious awareness of these basic constituents of human thinking. There is no suggestion everyone originally spoke English, which quite evidently they did not. I guess the aboriginal name appealed to the early immigrants because it was a satisfying mouthful and was a name they thought they had learned. They had it all wrong already of course, since in its own language it was actually a description. Asked 'What do you call that one?' the native guide probably thought he was being given an intelligence test to see if he could distinguish a pretty bird from a bowl of porridge, picking his answer with care.

The structure of the rope beneath us can now be seen to be problematic in a way that does not apply to the three spatial dimensions. Time structure calls for an extra dose of surmise because it is further removed from our experience than the other dimensions. The present can simply be treated as the three spacial dimensions – and the minor motions which take place within them in the here and now. The past can of course be perceived as a memory or imagination of a previous spatial only scheme of arrangement, a single frame in TV speak; but it does not get you very far. As a dynamic, as a sourcing of change, time is quite different and difficult to grasp. This is an odd result to be sure. We do after all experience the passage of time directly every moment of our waking lives. But we do not see it as such. It flows by without registering any unitary behaviour we can easily latch onto, which is why we have interjected our own conventional meters, chiefly the circular clock face, going in no direction, simply changing its face; but also the t dimension on a graph, a straight line continuum given artificial graduations. We can indeed only register time at one remove by inference from displacements in the other three dimensions, most conspicuously from the displacement of the sun, but also just from the changing scene from our window. We do not see growth for instance, simply because it takes place in too small steps to see. It has therefore sometimes been taken as an exemplar of time´s mystery, an invisible incomprehensible process, a magical coming into being and passing away. In reality growth does not explain the temporal process any more than we explain it by running a race. The temptation in these circumstances to transfer whole webs of inference from the mental cats´cradles derived from our three dimensional experience back down the beanstalk of time amounts to a procedural error – or else a relative quantum leap in analogical perception.

Spengler and the Nazis opted for growth as the temporal process to warrant their fantasies, I speculate it was because it gave them a nice lush feeling concealing from themselves their own relatively arid emotional life. A plain rope image better represents the original Tau of the becoming and the become for our forebears, where time is the becoming and the Tau has either been taken as the other dimension or both of them. A 'T' after all has an upright and a cross piece and is a pretty obvious symbol of two different directions, two dimensions. At one time I had privately labelled them Asha and Awa, which I (mistakenly) took to be the original syllabic forms of the consonants, the Asha going up and the Awa away across! My late uncle, steeped himself in Norse folklore, took it as final evidence I was mad, as anyone would be, he felt, who made up his own folklore. This relationship however actually takes us into areas of primitive dialectic which really require a chapter on their own – so see chapter 16 on the origins of thinking for more of this. And it turns out I was half right after all. Asha, the hiss of a flaming brand when extinguished in water stands for flame and the flame does spring upwards, and the sibilant does stand for upwards in a number of languages including the oldest known, Sumerian, and as I propose to demonstrate in that prehistoric Lithic language substrate now confined to the subconscious mind I got it from.

In the present century, while the hard sciences have dismantled the solid world of common sense by showing for instance that solid surfaces are really conglomerates of sub atomic electromagnetic elements – nuclei and forces made up of other abstract entities minimally defined – simultaneously the other mainstream of academic thinking (old philosophy), suborned by a limited understanding of relativity theory, has abjured the very idea of ultimate truth and knowledge of reality, with the implication those who even think of it are misguided. Against all these advances of science, in its own sphere history must therefore fight back. The kind of synchronic analysis (that is the study of schemes of arrangement outside the temporal continuum which can be treated as universal truth precisely because they are not modified by the passage of time) which the hard sciences have affected and effected have led, let it be stated at the outset, to most of the advances in understanding which the modern world can boast. But it is a commonplace that they have not led to any increase in human wisdom. On the contrary the claim of science to be self sufficient has sometimes led to excesses where practical morality is concerned. Henry Ford said history was bunk, after rather modest investigation. Many more have concluded religion, even including morality was bunk also. I am thinking of Nietzsche and his followers, mostly in continental Europe. If there were a Satan they would have been of his party. Elsewhere I make out Satan just meant Sai-Taun, the ways of the world in Ancient Egyptian and could have come down to us via the Greeks and Romans, garbled of course. The ground has thus been prepared for radicals to proclaim unethical hedonist or sadistic philosophies and gain adherents. This is how Nazism and other nihilist ethics nowadays commonly prevail. It was the misfortune, or else the poor judgment of the German people in particular to have allowed themselves to be taken for a disastrous ride by a clique of sadistic perverts – singing famously and tarnishing the German name for ever – riding no doubt upon the malice imprinted by defeat in war. It may seem absurd to suggest that villainy can essentially result from muddled thinking.

But malice is a poverty which is always with us. What makes the difference is civilised judgment with the weight to provide society with a keel; and Weimar had none of that. In some rather unexpected places as well as others where it might have been expected the civilised keel has been sadly lacking this century, as the common man has been shakily finding his feet, and winding ambition for the first time. Without a keel and wanting an anchor, the intellectual ferment brought on by the advancement of science and its increasing pace has more or less guaranteed a sequence of cultural capsizes, even including – remarkably – in the so called civilised free world.

The vanities and inanities in such a scene pile up. Even if it is entirely true that man makes himself as he goes along, he certainly does not know how he does it. Human knowledge, and the whole of human culture that goes with it, is therefore overdue for a rethink. Much of what passes for science is illusion. It is not that experiments are improperly conducted, but rather that the proper experiments are not done. It is the thinking that underlies them which is therefore often flawed. The laws of science, like social conventions, are house rules and not laid down by nature. Nature no doubt has its own rules to go by, which we try to spot and copy: but our laws are just system software, providing protocols – operating rules – for the particular programme being run, laid on top of nature´s own system in order to provide user access in terms that can be understood without first fully mastering the system protocols of nature. So-called knowledge is mere observation, often well informed and effective, as when for instance an astronaut or two are landed successfully on the moon or a heart is transferred without a second death, enabling us to manipulate events with novel results. But knowledge does not approximate reality. This idea is quite hard to grasp but it is very important. It can be put most simply in terms of a metaphor. It is as if the human mind did its thinking and wrote its words, ideas, formulae, diagrams, etc all on a wallpaper, hoping to comprehend the wall behind. The diagrams, however exact and useful they prove in practice, do not get any nearer to the wall than previous ones. There is in this sense an eternal divide between the universe and man´s understanding of it, regardless of the evident improvements we have made recently in our doodlings on the paper. Moreover, the paper in reality lines our own heads. The world is ultimately unknowable in the sense we may theorise about it for ever, but we will never become it. For to fully know the real world and be able to keep up with it you would have to be it, and thus perhaps to become indistinguishable from it. Is this the Nirvana of the singular Theory of Everything grail hunters, one wonders? Are they in pursuit of another Jungian Collective Unconscious so their personal sandcastles shall not after all melt into the sand, an immortal connubium with their materialist Godhead?

Review of the typescript has thrown up protest at the drubbing I hand out to science, in spite of my protestations of admiration which I have also included. The drubbing is really aimed at simpletons' realism, and perhaps at the same time at 'scientism' and the several scientists who embrace it. Scientism is the clinging by establishment scientists to outmoded science, unprepared to think differently. They were Arthur Koestler's 'Sleepwalkers'. It is firm knowledge in the public sector that this sleep walking happens, but of course it is only supposed to have occurred with previous scientists, where everyone now accepts they had it wrong and fought like tigers to keep it. I have been confronting it for six years with BSE, jokily still treated as an infection by magic prions from eating infected tissue, when it is really a genetic disorder brought on by enzymatic poisoning of protein formation in the chromosomes of the cells so that manganese is taken up instead of copper, misfolding the prion protein and rendering it a useless obstruction to mental connections; which in turn may easily result from chelating of the copper in the cells by Organophosphorus insecticides with which fruit and vegetables are soused, and with which cows were douched repeatedly and in excess strength in UK at the outset of the British Mad Cow Disease epidemic. Facts like the incidence of CJD in a five mile radius of a source of heavy manganese pollution in Slovakia double that in the whole of UK since the epidemic began is ignored, as not fitting the present theory. Organophosphorus is still poured on children's heads to kill nits in some counties in the UK. While these misunderstandings continue youngsters must continue to die horribly. It is indeed fraudulent but not in the sense of cheating at the checkout. It is intellectually fraudulent like NIH[3], and intellectual fraudulence starts in all cases with defrauding oneself, dishonesty over one's own understanding, pretending to oneself one has mastered the understanding when really one has only acquired a copy of the PC account. Scientists are human before anything else, with human failings. Some have commercial and even political agendas. They fought their corners to get a position for themselves, their fields these days are often narrow and their days rushed, they see science as beleagured by fundamentalists and other cranks, they can always refer to a code of absolute proof (which is never possible), they are sober-sides concerned with petty instances in pursuit of exactitude, they aspire to be grave and reverend, and finally they daren't break ranks. There is also the conceit they are on to a winner. Considering all their failings some of them actually do rather well. None of this is an argument for being unscientific, only a plea to get the science right.

In passing, my Wallpaper Theory rules out of court, of course, a select band of believers in the view that we already are the world and that is how we know it. These are amongst the Napoleon Theorists, in polite terms. They are to be found in asylums striking napoleonic poses as proof of their identities. But outside they represent perhaps the commonest kind of thinker under the guise of realist. They are in turn distinct from others who claim they are the world because there is no other to know, espousing a radical nominalism or solipsism. Bertrand Russell at one time had to enter an asylum unable to reach outside himself so far as to button his own buttons. It was reportedly his waistcoat buttons that were the problem, but his predicament preceded the invention of zips and he was an experienced fornicater, so it may well have been his fly buttons, for the serious solipsist of course themselves an otiose convention. There are also some Napoleon Theorists of the more rarified sort who tunnel to reality rather than possessing it directly. For them the psyche possesses extra mystical dimensions not widely understood allowing direct insights superior to the common wisdom, sometimes received by rays. They can thus make use of hot lines to reality often personifying the reality they find as God. This is all very well within the confines of an established church with house rules of its own tempered by experience for coping with such problems of living. It is disturbing when used by the madder sort, particularly when "Reality" acquires human language, and dressing themselves up as the Divinity the subconscious promptings from the individual psyche start to talk, leading to bloodshed sometimes on a horrific scale. To highlight their eccentricity in this, as well as for the general purposes of explanation, it is desireable to establish clearly the usual sequence of psychic activity, from left to right as it were with increasing precision, as follows.

First comes raw psychic inputs, which include of course the traditional domain of the physical senses; which can be simply labelled Ψ (Psi) for the present. Next come the fuddled emotive and barely cognitive states of mind such as served the earliest forays of our hominid forebears into the intellectual thickets. This area we shall simply label Phi (Φ), thinking of it as the stage of initial formation of phenomenal ideas and our earliest language. Next, trailing somewhat (I suspect by some hundreds of thousands of years), comes Π (Pi), that area of sharper ostensive definitions in language and more sharply defined judgmental thinking which includes, by way of illustration of the category, both religion and science on an equal footing. That is where we are at. There is then a large gap, representing that unavoidable space between the wallpaper which has recorded the progress of our doodling to date and the inaccessible reality of the real wall behind, which, to highlight its detachment from the others in the sequence we shall label Ro (P) for the ultimate unknowable reality, with a quite different sound. The Greek lettering is simply to raise the tone of the piece in the usual way, but I think I have picked them rather well as they get less fuzzy sounds as we go on until we are brought up short at the wall. The nature of the tunneling required to support the Napoleon Theory tunnelers is now made crystal clear. Faced with the sequence, Psi Phi Pi Ro, access to Ro (P) is claimed by way of Psi (Ψ), where a tunnel round the whole ostensive sequence is required to provide linkage between its opposing ends. It is not intended to suggest that such a linkage is therefore impossible, since the

Greek letters are nominal only and hardly prescriptive; but merely that it flies in the face of the spectral scheme of events proposed and is therefore quite unacceptable to the present writer.

Quite apart from the bias in favour of blind watchmaking which Charles Darwin's biological observations have indirectly inflicted on language studies, much confusion has arisen among linguists – over millennia – due to mistaken ideas of syntax and meaning. These ideas have been imported wholesale from philosophic programmes themselves incorporating muddled thinking. Thus grammar has been inflated at the expense of the common sense of language. Panini, the great Sanskrit synthesiser, the first grammarian whose work is extant, has been the bane of genuine progress in human thinking ever since he first put pen to papyrus around 350 BC. Since then there has been a faithful apostolic succession of pandits squatting cross-legged in their leader's style expounding his text and judging all other texts by it, for all the world as if grammar were akin to reason itself, a pure math. Grammar is no such thing; it is opinion laden, partial, subjective and as often as not flies in the face of reason. I sometimes think it is our closest link with our hominid past after the lexicon. At best it is an otiose protocol, at worst just systematised mental doodling or cats cradling. We may use it but we should not idolise it. Computer buffs will recognize it as an outmoded piece of software best binned. Above all as a frankly declared synchronic (static) analysis of linguistic rules grammar can not claim to account for the actual development of language, and even less of thinking; and indeed on the contrary seeks to freeze it as if it were a dead specimen already. In truth the meanings we manage to convey originate with the individual words we use, the semantic bits; and not originally with their grammatical modalities at all. There are of course rules of right reason for the combination of the semantic bits; but any useful coincidence with grammatical rules is for the most part coincidental. Grammar rests on whimsy. So far as etymology is concerned – the study which concerns itself with tracing the development of phonetic and semantic forms backwards towards their origins – the grammarians are the villains of the piece, intervening to mess up the record and conceal the truth by syncopating language into patterns, almost as if it were a mujak. The end result is a grammar-based language analysis which is fatally flawed since it leaves the meanings of words out of account in their derivations, acknowledging them as accidental accompaniments of sentence construction merely, and producing a taxis of functionless (fleshless) carapaces. This kind of analysis – characterised in the natural sciences as reductionism – has left us with imagined random original language roots then advancing by due blind phonetic evolutionary process, courtesy of the blind watchmaker one must suppose, as language species (more or less fit?) proliferate and then decline or prosper.

But it never went like that. Tant pis for the thinkers that think that way. Nine tenths of understanding is disillusion and the rest is acquiring a better neater tool kit with sharper cutting edges. This is what education is about. Language and science figure about equally; though in the last resort science when closely defined proves to be just language also. Now let us see where language, and particularly its Lithic Stone Age elements fit into the muddled jigsaw of contemporary thinking.

Notes

1. Comically its tenets, random variation, natural selection, genetic mutation, etc have incorporated smoothly into the body of science over the past century, except for the speciation which has had a rough ride. Is your baby really related to a cockroach? Two distinguished scientists thought insects were alien space invaders, but they are dead (the scientists).

2. Winchester S. The Map that Changed the World. Viking. Harper Collins. 2001.

3. NIH stands for Not Invented Here. It highlights the temptation to dismiss without too much consideration a new idea which is presented by an outsider, sometimes even on principle so the Whig dogs shall not get the credit.

CHAPTER 3

LEARNING TO SPEAK LITHIC

To start with the easy bits first, every schoolboy knows words are made up of letters of the alphabet, even if unsure which bits to use; while schoolgirls nowadays apparently know it all even better. Admittedly alphabets vary, and in China boys and girls alike are made to work to a rather different system of picture writing. But in reality words are only represented (symbolised) by letters. That is perhaps the easiest demonstration of all that a "symbol" is, which still flummoxes many people – it is just anything picked on to represent something else. There does not have to be any rhyme or reason to it, although of course it helps. A picture of a cat (or the word cat) "symbolises" a cat. The actual cat is a cat. There is no surprise in that. The picture is a symbol, the meaning of which is rather more than hinted at in the picture: a cat. Children soon pick up the trick, although some aboriginals are said to have difficulty at first. All those I knew found it a pushover. Words however are actually made up of uttered sounds – they are the symbols – with semantic contents; which are quite a different kettle of fish. The superficiality of human understanding is compiled of confusing mistakes like this: alphabets treated as meaningless rigmaroles in aid of a common alphabetic recording system. It takes a poet to get to grips with language and understand its diversity and composition. For the rest of us, words tend nowadays to be simples, atomic. They mean what they mean what they mean, just as a rose is a rose or a cat is a cat. Worse still, the philologists have persuaded themselves that is a good description of meaning. In this Alice in Wonderland world, word roots have been worked out as if a particular basic meaning actually started out clothed in a particular random basic sound – another rigmarole without reason. So we have Walter Skeat´s three hundred and sixty four phonetically random Proto-Indo-European roots of 1879[1], for the most part represented by two or three letters to provide a pronounceable syllable; and we have Ancient Egyptian word roots without vowels often handing us a totally unpronounceable syllable. The proto-Egyptian was evidently a pretty tongue-tied fellow! We must then suppose such word roots to have grown into fully fledged and articulated words, not much different from the way Oswald Spengler's cultures were supposed to have grown from primitive roots, to burgeon flourish and finally die – and all by rote, like clockwork or indeed more like cabbages and kings.

To make a comparison between any two things it is necessary to hold in the mind simultaneously or in close succession the two cases compared in sufficient detail to identify the similarities. If the comparison is of two items obviously similar, like two shoes for instance, this hardly taxes the mind. But if the similarities for perception are hidden, remote, largely semantic, or unrecognised before, and particularly if they are all four, the mental task can be quite severe, and even beyond a great many people. To resume a galaxy of such arcane cases and then inter-relate them similarly, disclosing a network or matrix in order to establish a systematic explanation of linguistic relationships must surely take much time and effort and be hard to follow through. This, by the way, is what this book is about. One is conscious of cutting across the grain, because what is proposed is new and contra-indicated by the common sense of the majority. Others have not thought the same way, and there is the comfortable presumption that the solid core of what most people think is sound, with error only at the edges, so that a proposal which seeks to radically alter the common perception of how languages have been formed must surely be wrong. If the correlations proposed were veridical why were they not perceived before? Surely they would have been! But would they? History is the dismal record of human error, spiritual, moral and intellectual, as the human mind has come down out of the trees, falling it has to be said at most of its fences, and learning painfully slowly to contradict presumption and accept the advancement of science. Science is of course here used accurately with a small s, in its quite general sense of knowledge, from the Latin scire to know, and from the Lithic phonemes Ish and Kai, bright making, illuminating or clarifying, so that we can see how something works or what it means. The advancement of knowledge has generally been fiercely opposed by its keepers, as a derogation of their status. All intellectuals are apt to suffer from Jowettism[2] or hubris in the Greek: if they don´t already know it they think it can hardly be knowledge. Jowettism is alive and well and institutionalised nowadays as peer review. Bolder spirits on the wilder shores of knowledge know they shall not easily pass. Regrettably, serving up an oxymoron like prehistoric linguistics is tantamount to taunting the intellectual establishment. That is what of course provides a certain spice but it does not help at all with the publication.

Readers may like to reflect on the remarkable similarity between our modern English word for sun and the Ancient Egyptian word Aton. It was reflecting on this remarkable apparent persistence of nomenclature over thousands of generations and several times as many miles which first led me to look for and research the other linguistic traces which I have come to call the Lithic language. The Aton-Sun match is by no means perfect, but much better than one could hope to achieve in a few hundred throws of a die with the whole gamut of possible sound combinations on it – unless of course the thing were weighted so as to land sunny side up. Ancient Egyptian is not even recognised as in the Indo European pipe line; although it is, through Greek. The Hittite version of sun meanwhile, or a little later, was Tun Akalas. The Latins thought it meant World Eye and adopted oculos for eye, which is why we use binoculars. Tun we can recognise easily enough from Egyptian Taun, or even from the Mayan Tan, as meaning world. It is convenient to accept the Egyptian as the more original since Ta-un can be glossed "Birth-all" or all the comings into being or Everything that happens, the Universe, perhaps a more general and comprehensive world view than our modern merely locative recension. Perhaps the Egyptian sun Aton was really Aaa-taun or World Wanderer, a possible definition for the sun. Aaa, the general vowel, early came to be seen as indicating extension, simply because you can go on with it for as long as you have breath. The extension symbolised could be either spatial or temporal (see Chapter 16). Similarly the Hittite akalas in Lithic phonemes spells a-ka-la(s), eternally-make-loop, world-orbiter like Apollo. But again in Taun the oon can be an oo or orifice, and Taun (Ta-oon) can be thus read as Birth-canal instead of Universe. The A- in Aton would then be temporal: "Everlasting Birth Canal" birthing light into the world each day, a busy lady. Many years later I hope I have got it right. Later the Egyptians changed their minds and decided the sun was a world eye (Ra) and assumed the Hittites had the same idea. The Egyptians first had a transcendental Vagina in the sky and the Hittites marked the sun's diurnal orbit. Egypt's switch to a world eye will have provided some gain in prestige for their monks who also had eyes, leaving Mrs Grundy to nip in and translate the Eternal Vagina as the disk of the sun seen fully frontal. I had been hopelessly barking up a number of different and quite disparate trees when I set out, misled by the polysemy of Lithic phonemes.

Partridge is a help here. Sun was earlier Zonne (Mediaeval Dutch), or Sunna (Old Norse) or Sunne (Gothic), with the Indo European root taken to be *Swon with the pronunciation perhaps Soo-aun, from the Lithic sa-oo-nai with the original Lithic semantic contents: fire-hole-presented. The ´n which may have started out as –na/nai > ne > n to add the idea of presenting (Chapter 11): The Flaming Orb Presenting [Daily]: less poetic than the Egyptian, more matter of fact already! As for the Hittite eye, it was perhaps read as: a-ka-la-sai or That-makes-light-shine. It is important not to be put off by the inevitable use of precise modern words, and in English at that, with which to describe the contributions made to Lithic phrasing. The ancients all thought the eye was an active radar letting out a ray like any other light source, such as the sun, and then catching it back again on its return with the information garnered now painted on the iris to be read from behind by the owner of the eye. That is indeed how the sun came to be regarded at the same time as an eye in the sky in accordance with the science of the day. The Egyptians who had first picked on the vagina later took to the eye; at first finding it all seeing and punitive – they were conscious of their own mischief, evidently – but later caring for sparrows and leading to Christianity. The switch over from the vagina to the eye was indeed a highly significant move and may well have been connected with the shift away from goddesses to father gods as well as from water holes and springs to eggs and beans, and indeed from mothers to fathers as the principal parent. It must surely have enlightened many an early philosophical debate in councils hunkered around the hearth, the pros and cons of either perception mulled over interminably with emotions rising as evenings wore on. It would be unfair to suggest the ladies lost the argument. More likely they were silenced by the threat of no more meat.

When confronted with the task of resurrecting the prehistoric syntax of the Old Stone Age, when men first began to speak, about the only prompt to rely on is psychosemantics. It is necessary to leave far behind Professor Chomsky's transformational grammar and virtually the whole, certainly the core of modern linguistics with it. Away with its mathematical structure derived from Boolean logic which is obviously a modern figment. Forget Frege, Russell, Wittgenstein and others. It is also surely moot if the figment is indeed hard wired in the sub-conscious of the race at large or merely loose in the private lucubrations of the professor. Many theories can be devised which touch reality at a number of points and yet have room for arabesques at the whim of the inventor. I have had constantly to ask myself if the points of contact in the case of the Lithic hypotheses justify belief. Psychosemantics is the study of those meanings which may have naturally commended themselves to the simple untutored minds of our still inarticulate forebears; and if they fit at all with the meanings in the languages which have come down to us, that is a bonus. These hominids were deriving their meanings for their uttered sounds from what has been called sound symbolism. I am endebted to Jarvis Nickolls for this term in his book Sounds Like Life, Oxford Studies in Anthropological Linguistics, A Study of the Pasteza Quechua Language of Ecuador. The attachment of meanings to simple sounds chimes with Lithic but the meanings are not carried on into the expanding lexicon as breeders, only in their original sense, by the Quechua speakers. It is as if they were stuck in phase one of linguistic development.

Sound Symbolism includes most obviously the echoic. Straight echoism like Cuckoo or moo or miaow is simple. Quechua echoism is more complex, shading into whimsy. So for instance "Tsak" is apparently taken as the sound symbolic of puncturing or piercing, like an arrow entering the body of a bird or monkey or other small game. Then from the meaning of perhaps "Bullseye!" it is developed semantically until it comes to mean just a specificity in time "precisely then" and so, as Nickolls has it, to an adverb "making it clear that there was a definite point in time when the action took place". I rather like this, although initially I reserved judgment whether to believe it or not. It makes my identifications seem comparatively or even excessively sober. But it must be remembered my psychosemantic identifications claim to be universals not just Quechua whimsy. On reflection "Tsak" is in fact not so far from the Lithic phonemes Sa-Ka, action-strike (see Chapters 14 and 5 respectively). Similarly "Tsuk", which is said to be derived from the sound of plucking something from its mass (like an arrow from the flesh?), as an adverb qualifying the verb to pull renders it to pluck out. I see no reason to quarrel with this as the squelch of a deeply embedded arrow as it is plucked from the flesh. The u (oo) in place of the a as a vowel is of course a Lithic pointer to the rounded lips and so a sucking sound; and u is the dual vowel so that tsuk is the second sound – tsak as the arrow goes in tsuk as you pull it out. It is fanciful but believable. The layman may find it far fetched but the etymologist versed in the byways of semantic derivations will, I think, recognise the pattern. The novelty is the starting with sound symbolism. Linguistic roots have been generally assumed to be phonetically random: perhaps just an admission that if they have rational bases they are too remote to be recovered. But with no vocabulary to cover the case a quite sensible ploy was to mimic the sound accompanying the action to be captured. Of course to work well it needs to be a readily recognisable sound known to the hearer. It helps in such a case if he is first and foremost a hunter after small game so that his mind readily refers to the repertoire of hunting sounds. It will be less obvious to a pop mind today, more attuned to noises like "Brm Brm" and raucous thumping music out of Africa.

In Malay and a number of other languages there is no verb to be, and indeed the semantic content of the verb is not much. "Him angry" tells us almost precisely as much as "He is angry". There is a problem with "Man angry" because it could be merely adjectival "the angry man" or else an observation drawing attention to a novelty "the man is angry". In Quechua it is even worse, "him angry" can also carry the meaning the man "being angry" or "when angry". So "tsak him angry ashka (deed done) him-agent suffix, wife strike" is the Quechua idiom, if I have it right. The proper nuanced translation into English would be "He flew into a rage and struck his wife", an action, it should perhaps be mentioned, as socially disapproved in the jungles of Ecuador as in the streets of London – or more so. Simple it ain´t unless you are reared in Quechua speak. Computer aided translation has some way to go before it can accommodate this kind of paradigm shift. Malay has other tricks. Orang amok itu is that amok man whereas Orang itu amok is that man is very angry, not so far from the English that angry man and that man (is) angry, where the position of the adjective is before or after the the, or that. In

Malay with no verb to be, you don´t have a the either. Using the same word for the as for that does very well, and saves learning another.

What we are learning is that some of our grammatical distinctions are second thoughts. Earlier you could get away with only a few and rather general and inconclusive terms by our standards – after a few hundred thousand years of mature consideration sifting out additional distinctions. The interesting business is how from a few rather literal ideas, mostly of an ostensive nature merely identifying aspects of the objective world, pointing things out, drawing attention to them, indicative terms, we were able to develop some of the more abstract ones needed for logic, like for instance ifs and buts, wheres and whys. It appears that from an initial rather undiscriminating adjectival mind, whilst learning discrimination we first progressed to recognition of the substantive, items, things, (as things in themselves, or things for themselves, as Kant would say) rather than merely exemplars of qualities as previously supposed. The item still is made up of qualities but at a stroke now permanently with them. The door was thereupon opened for grammatical concepts: but enormous leaps have been involved in grasping abstract thinking, on which syntax depends. It is easy to see starting out on this odyssey will have been with the easier ideas where the original phenomenal concept fairly readily translates into a phenomenal type and then into a more general type, a fly perhaps and then a flyer, and thereafter the fully abstracted concept of flight. A relative pronoun or adverb, which or where for instance, is only a small remove from him, it or place. If place itself seems to involve a degree of abstraction already it will have come in turn from the idea of ground, or even via group from loop. A group is a number of individuals in a loop, looped or grouped. A loop on the ground is a location. I think a loop, an actual one like the horizon at sea, was an early perception, and from it came in time the geometrical circle or cycle. We can list the terms of symbolic logic and look at their provenance in turn.

When one comes to trying to identify the guiding principles for the analysis of words in any current language, apart from the key psychosemantic contents of individual phonemes (letters, more or less) listed in the trees provided in Chapters 4 to 15, the next attempt must be to make sense of whole words. A string of phonemes has to have a meaning made up of its constituent phonemic meanings. It appears to be a commonplace that words describing phenomena generally define their referents by means of a specific character, in the case of life forms a conspicuous physical feature or habit: Usually a neutral character in the approval rating of the time is chosen so as not to cause offence by the nomenclature. The powers of life forms were unknowns so you played safe. A bull is not criticised for tossing people but congratulated on its genital performance. Anyone on the farm first attending a cow being put to the bull would I think be bound to be impressed by the length of phalus it is able to put out and put in. Semitic Aleph is in Lithic Aa-lai-pahai, long-length-phalus; later Latin Taurus, which is from Ta-urau, vagina aroused, the u- in front of the −rau is the superlative u, or as a common soldier would put it cunt-struck. Nobody unaware of this bovine potentiality should be left in charge of a bull at any time, or even allowed near one. A dog, on the other hand, may be noted as a tail wagger, canis from Ka-nai in Latin, protruding (its tail this time) or perro in Spanish from Pai-rau, with a tail roused and upstanding – like what you may ask? Or it may be marked for its bark, "Chok" or "Khhok" in Malay Aboriginal Senoi, or even dog in English from Old English docga, or better chien in French as well as zakur or txakur in Basque or as a Bow wow or mbua in Swahili, or auau in Ancient Egyptian. These early dogs were snappy curs not the deep Baskerville bayers bred by the fanciers later. Then there are the growlers, orr in Hungarian, which the Basques use too, or ur in Sumerian, the oldest language known. In Sumerian ur mah, a big growler, was a lion! A curiosity is a cat in Sumerian was ka-tse, not so far from current German pronunciation. Ka in Sumerian was mouth, and a cat was a spit mouth. In Akkadian, a Proto Semitic language in which a great deal was copied from the older Sumerian civilisation (based on irrigated paddy fields, Sumerian gardeners whom the still pastoral Akkadian Cains conquered) including some of the old testament passed off as the Jewish Book, a mouth was pu and a cat was pu-tse, spit-mouth in Akkadian. A pussy-cat thus spells spit-mouth in Akkadian and Sumerian respectively! They still do it, if ruffled. The ancients, Cains and Abels alike, were all cat rufflers, it seems. An eagle is noted for the height at which it flies, circling in the thermals like a para glider, often taking advantage of the strong wind currents rising as they meet cliffs and mountains. Aquila in Latin is from Lithic A-Kai-La, un-powered-glider, while Albanian across the bay is Shqipe from ish-kai-pai, high glider (up-making with-the wings). Not so far this from the simple Budgy or bird (ba-ji is go-up) in Australian Aboriginal. The Toucan on the other hand, from the native Tupi language of Brazil, as well as selling Guiness has a naughty name which shows what it can do, Ta-u-kan, a slit-a round orifice-maker in Lithic. The female nests in a slit in a tree which the male bird cements up with mud and spit to leave a round hole through which her horny beak pokes out so he can feed her in safety while she sits on her eggs. For the Tupi, the boyos, other circumstances rounded out a slit when stimulated (kai). The Tupi clearly had vulgar minds and enjoyed double entendre. One wonders if many Irishmen were responding to subconscious Lithic prompts when they ordered their Guinness, just thinking what Toucan do. In any case the features picked on for nomenclature usually amount to a phrasal entry using the original Lithic language elements, phonemes, much the same as letters of the alphabet with vowels attached. A phenomenon without inspirational character or activity may be indicated by its supposed origin: for example ash, earlier ashce is from burning, a-ish-kai, that-fire-made. Compare stone from ish-tau-´n, fire-born, (from volcanoes). Dropping the –ce leaves just a-sh, that-burnt, the dross left over when the flame has carried off everything else.

The Egyptian word for Heaven, we are told, was Pt, or at least that was the root of it. Doctors of Egyptology, with rather doubtfully commendable caution, help themselves out by putting in a neutralish short e, or schwa and pronounce Heaven "Pert" (with an unobtrusive untrilled r). In reality the Egyptian was "Pai-i-Taun", which actually meant what it said, namely 'Skin of the Universe', spread taut like the Bedu goat tent as shelter against the sun: the roof of the world. Nothing is gained, and of course all the good sense is lost, by talking of "Pt"! It actually would be nearer the mark to English it as Point. Point, the o originally from the dipthong au, has tucked away inside it the same element pa- as in the Egyptian goatskin, but here understood as a different thinned or diminished version of Ba (flesh), in this case not the thin outside layer around the flesh we call the skin but a diminutive bit of the stuff itself, a small thin bit or piece, say a finger or perhaps a cocktail stick rather than the conspicuously fleshy bits like the lips (bab is mouth in Arabic) or the haunch (ba in Egyptian). A point is what you pounce, punch, push, poke, peck or prick with. But the meaning theory I am propounding is heresy and indeed unheard of, and there will be those who will wish to punish it severely.

There were genital connotations to be briefly noticed already in the Egyptian, incidentally. A second offence in this book is to point out most of humanity's original perceptions appear to have been hammered out on the anvil of our own genitalia, as if we were just as obsessive about sex then as now, or my guess is even more so, simply because there was no TV or too much else at all to take our attention from our favourite reveries. If you locate the birth of language in the Old Stone Age as I do, you have to think of the first speakers as in most ways idiots by our standards. In this case the quail chick was observed by the Egyptians, for whom quail was (and is) a gourmet dish, always to say peep-peep, or as they heard it pee-pee or pi-pi, always two of them, never a single peep. This is in fact the habit of all ground game-bird chicks. You can check on it as I have with reared pheasant chicks, just as the Egyptians noticed it I dare say while rearing quails less sportingly directly for the pot, just wringing their necks instead of giving them a run for their money. In Egypt they had already worked out a grammar of vowel sounds – or some say cadged the scheme off the Sumerians via the Akkadians – which allowed for three: a, i, and u (aaa, eee, and ooo in English spelling to give the correct phonetics). The aaa was the general unmarked form, and so was taken to be carrying any general vowelisation characteristics such as continuity – no beginning or end, just more and more of the same as long as the breath lasts. Eee was the thinned diminutive reduplicative distributive indicative; and ooo was the completive inclusive substantive unitary form, including the dual – it reunited the distinction made between aaa and eee as it were! There was dialectic involved in this but that is another matter, see chapter 16. As the one thing the quail chick knew was evidently that everything came in pairs, they called it pooh (pu), or two peeps, both together, or the dual. Then, because they used 'pa' where we would use 'the', pu could be read, elided in form as pa-u, 'The u'. It was natural enough then to use the quail chick as the glyph for the alphabetic letter u, the dual vowel. Professional Egyptologists however are unaware of all this and comically think the quail chick pu was pronounced wa because the glyph could carry that sound as well as oo just like our w. Perhaps their quail chicks said wuff wuff instead of pi pi; or else they have not thought very much about it. Egyptian Pan pipes meanwhile, with holes for stops, made peeps like quail chicks, so they called them chicks, pipi; and to cut a long story very short that is why in English today we use pipe to describe a tube of any sort – proper pronunciation lost along the way, probably thanks to the distorted alphabetic idiom as above. The quail chick would certainly be nonplussed, and even philologists have been completely flummoxed to date.

The Egyptians had quite early moved on to identify one particular tube pipe or pipi, in the best of semantic taste of course since i was simply the diminutive form; which is also why every schoolboy in my day referred to his (or his neighbour's) "pee"; and it was not in fact very long before every schoolgirl secretly knew the word just as well. Pee was no doubt taken directly from the adult penis, a Latinism in commoner use in my youth when Latin was taught than today when it is I suspect confined to medical interviews in the doctor's surgery, probably reinforced in many cases of puzzlement: "I mean your willy". Penis in turn, to anticipate a little, was a politer version of the Egyptian Pa-Hei or Hooraying Piece. Penis in Latin is simply pai-nai, protruding, presenting, showing or witness piece: before trousers its angle gave an unmistakable indication of its owner's preoccupation. What psychosemantic content there was in the schoolboy pee is moot. Some argue the letter is one, demurely turned down. The Latin schoolboy in his time was called a puer, where pu is the dual of pi and so stood for pipi, a piper or cheeper, his voice unbroken; and in fact it originally included girls as well; although it was probably also an innuendo, with the u vowel read as a double diminutive as well. Malays call small boys' genitals sparrows – a puzzling association until you understand they call sparrows pippits, that is cheepers in the case of the birds, perhaps allowing pan pipe for the other. My book is designed to highlight the thinking behind the composition of words, much of it much more difficult to pin down than the pahai and penis. Sex of course is pretty straightforward and easy and does not seem to have changed much – or at all – over the millennia.

For decades now everyone writing on language has sat glancing over his or her shoulder at the shadow of Noam Chomsky, an eminence grise in the linguistic field since he invented transformational grammar, a genetically inherited grammar imprinted in the brain (sic) and worked out in your subconscious to Boolean[3] mathematical rules and then by a subtle transformation converted to your conscious mind as the grammar you roughly know how to use. However, so far as I can see my book has very little to do with him, since it is to do with individual words and their meanings, an aspect of language Chomsky has hardly addressed. His work is concerned with sentences and their structures, a major relational study amenable to mathematical logic, but – like all grammarians since the infamous Persian Pannini started the genre in the fourth century BC – he appears to have allowed himself some improvements on what he found; and from the point of view of the genuine historical researcher he has merely rent the fabric it is the historians' task to reconstruct. So far as the origins of language are concerned, grammar has little to offer, since it only came later with the analysis and codification (including some tidying up) of the original rules of procedure and expression which had already been invented extempore and untutored, by the savage mind and had hundreds of thousands of years in use before Pannini ever got to work[4].

The failure to recognise this situation is on reflection quite bizarre, even though it is perfectly explicable. A sentence is (a priori) a string of words, a word string. It follows that words must be prior to sentences. That syllogism as such is impeccable. But the process does not have to be unique. If for a sentence we substitute a symbol, s for instance, then S1, S2, S3…Sn provide a potentially infinite series of particulars, just as words do. We can conceive of a metalanguage in which S1,S2,S3…Sn provide the lexicon; and so on for as long as we care to posit metalanguages. It is not particularly clever, but it is true, and I mention it because it is apposite to my theme. I see no valid reason for believing that such a process, at any rate to some extent, could not have occurred. Everywhere I see evidence that it has. The ground language was Lithic, and it was composed of elements of speech which are identified as phonemic. Phonemes are uttered sounds which carry meanings. That contradicts the received wisdom of – so far as I know – every other linguistics buff to date. But there is the word to dress. There is also the word to undress. I see no reason why undress must be classified as lexical rather than syntactical, or why ago is lexical but go away is syntactical. It is possible to consider a different set of definitions. Why are anthropological and meander lexical rather than syntactical? I concede they are words. To me they are also sentences, or at least phrases, in Lithic elements. It helps to trace the etymology back to the Greek, and perhaps even beyond. Conventionally anthropology – any good dictionary will say as much – derives from the two words anthropos and logos, glossed as man and word (or knowledge). But why stop there? Anthropos is capable of further gloss: ana-thro-pos, from ana-therau-pous, roughly "[He with the] out-drawn-legs". The word defines man as "he who walks upright". Anthropology would do equally well coding for the science of perambulation, or even how to run races. Meander is similarly analysable as ´m-e-an-der, and to cut a long derivational story into two short shots it is from ´m-ai-an-ther-rai, him-that is-un-drawn out, in short a sluggish watercourse liable to meanders – and ultimately of course to ox-bow lakes when a meander gets cut out of the flow. The ox bow lake is, in Australian Aboriginal tongues, a billabong, from bai-lalai-baung,. go-slippy-sloppy-bunged, a blocked river flow. Bai-lai, pronounced billy in Oz, is water you have to wait for to boil. In the chapters on the individual phonemes and their meanings I endeavour to derive all the meanings of each phoneme from the original perceptions of our primitive forebears from some six hundred thousand years ago. The sub species of Homo Erectus who was around at that time is recently dubbed Ergaster, and he has been upgunned from a simpleton with an excessively low brow with high ridges to something like the Neanderthalers have been represented up to now, with a brain similar to ours. I then attempt to trace their meanings into the words which the phonemic strings make up, just like the meanings which the individual word strings in a sentence make up. I read words as starting out as descriptive phrases, only later treated as nuggets on their own without need any more for articulation in full or with the thinking to match. It is a bit like learning Chinese, with syllables combined to form meanings. For me that is the interesting bit in languages, working out how they have grown from the initial pairing and phrasing of simples to the conventional wisdom of today. I even believe it has implications for the human mind and human understanding. These two words anthropology and meander were chosen at random. Anthropos, the species, is muddled with Aner, genitive Andros, the male of the species (a merry Andrew). Aner, I believe, is from the Lithic A-na-er, that-presents-verbaliser, the presenter; while Andros is equally neatly glossed in original Lithic phonemes a-na-tai-rau(s), that-presents-drawn out(substantive marker). Both are sexual definitions, the first a clear enough visual description of the behaviour of the male penis; or else it is an-a-tai-rau drawn out, the tempted sex, drawn out by the (magic) seductive rays emanating from the mischievous feminine genitalia. In parentheses this is the ancients speaking, it is not what I myself think, it is what the race has thought – to avoid any angry ladies fulminating at me. Of course I regret it, but so long ex post facto all I can do about it is expose the thinking and hope our chauvinist forebears may be forgiven in time. Feminists are referred to the old Adam and Eve in the garden. The real point is the elements of the words have meanings all through. It is undeniable. More startlingly still, these elements always have similar meanings, the world around. It follows, in my book, that we all started out as one, speaking the same language composed of Lithic language elements. What now divides us are the different phrasal idioms we have built on the original bases. It does not mean there was one source of speech or that the rest of us learned to speak from an elite breed, somewhere on the surface of the globe, from whom the gospel spread, the diffusionist illusion. Reality is even more remarkable still: we live in a heavily textured universe. We spoke the same because we picked the meanings off the wall, and we all shared the same environment, internal and external, within wide limits, so we picked the same meanings. I know with technology environments vary widely, as do the mentalities arising. Whim too has much multiplied along with the gradual sophistication of the mind, a grade or two different these days around the world, each with its own virtues and vices.

In reality language – and particularly vocabulary – should be seen historically as a thoroughly diffuse as well as an irregular matrix. Take for example the Australian aboriginal 'djeri' group, where we can identify three common usages where 'djeri' means 'clear', 'bright' and 'loud' respectively, according to context, within the three comparatively well known words 'Djeribal' (the tribe – of those who speak in clear, literally "clear-speak, while other languages were in code), budgerigar (baji-jeri-gara, bird of bright colour), and di-dgeri-doo (tube or tuba with a loud toot). They show how the lexicon begins to build up by simple meaning diffusion or drift following surprisingly abstract analogy. Incidentally it also exemplifies the basic vocabulary construction, the build up of words from descriptive elements, as is argued all throughout this book for Lithic. Djeri comprises dje- and rai from the hiss of a brand extinguished in water for fire, and a ray from Ra (the sun): a fire ray is bright. Bal comprises ba and la, lip and tongue for speak (or speaker). Baji comprises ba and ji where ba means go from haunch, another fleshy bit like the lip, but which walks instead of talks, and ji meaning up, as the flame leaps upwards. A bird was a go up. Ish was flame because when you dunked your burning brand in the morning to save resin it said ishshh loud and clear. If you said ish Tarzan knew what you had in mind. Gara comprises Ga (or Ka) for make (from ka the sound of the knapper making flint tools) and ra for ray, the visible. Di does for a small oo or hole (titi is lots of them as in the human teat), and Doo is the sound oo (rounding the lips) does. The 'djeri' meaning-shift or drift from bright through clear to loud is analogous to a system where a base (in this case a base meaning) is stretched between multiple nodes (in this case of actual usages) perhaps a bit like Albert Einstein's stretchable space-time matrix. The mind visiting these nodes is then forced to bend, modify and redefine the base in the light of each actual example that it meets of its use; and ultimately the bonds break and it is time to distinguish different usages by marking the base word or coining others. Compare Joel Chandler Harris´ Uncle Remus stories with Gallah (West African) ideolect terms surviving, including "churrah" meaning "splash", surely a visible upward burst just as – to the aboriginal mind – is planted as instinct in a flame. The flame was sh or ch or dg (ignore the spelling) because it said it itself. In reality of course these usages are all simply different from the start and represent small and digestible but significant departures from the original base meaning, which though roughly adjacent (equivalent) nevertheless involve redefinitions of the word elements concerned. Post modernists, and other academics interested in taking an argument well beyond any utility, will immediately be able to see that every single instance of use of any word may well participate in this developmental process.

Vocabulary differentiates and accumulates by way of these redefinitions. A lazy mind will be inclined to manage with the few pre-existent categories it has encountered to date, language as learned, whilst an eager and inquisitive mind will be for ever analysing comparing and differentiating meanings – putting the record to the torture as it were – and even composing new ones. Think of Shakespeare. So it has been with language all along, jointly spun from these two kinds of spinnerets, one with a few strong if bovine pinches of reality, the other laboriously fine-texturing the world with an intricate lacework of categories. The language story is thus a tragicomedy of Wayland Smith on the one hand and Scrimshaw Man on the other[5], both busily at work shaping the same artifact, but by no means always at one in their methodology.

We should therefore not be surprised to find fine detail being slovened over, redefined and again slurred over, with our current idioms often a papier-maché of what went before. With the belated rediscovery of Lithic, the original because "natural" Stone Age language, it can be seen that Wayland is still with us and is still winning some of the time, in spite of all the scrimshaw work thrown up by the progress of technology over the millennia. But it must also be borne in mind that Scrimshaw was also with us even from the beginning of language. There was in reality a degree of arrogance and absurdity but also intellectual elegance even in our initial inanities, and they can not be reduced to a handful of overly basic random roots[6]. The pristine condition of the human mind (defined for these purposes as when language began) can be seen to have been one of wildness rather than simplicity. We started out with vivid but disorganised – indeed with what would now pass as deranged – minds; and it is taking us a long time to reshape them, I think because some of us are still hooked on Wayland's old ways. These worthy if inelegant word smiths are to be found in all walks of life around the world, but markedly in high places and occupying the seats of power and influence, as befits their appeal to everything that is atavistic in our make-up. It does mean of course that their thinking is at several removes from reality.

In the Stone Age, with their great brains like ours, thinking was none the less blurred. The clarity of thought we enjoy today, such as it is, is the result of hard pounding. It has not come easily. We have always regarded clear thinking as brain damage. Ask any schoolboy. One man´s brain damage has however been the next man´s clear thinking. Etymologists will be better equipped than most to review the matter. Words and word meanings proliferate, have proliferated, and will proliferate. They ought to continue to proliferate even more. I sometimes think discrimination is all; and I always look disdainfully at those great systematisers who have generally misled humanity by working towards the great syntheses of knowledge which have so far eluded us. These minds, locked into the ideal, for me constitute the worm in the bud, the forces of evil if you like, the ideologists of every kilter, the arch corrupters attempting to turn us all mad in their own image, in order to reassure themselves, against the grain, that they are the sane ones. These supposed Honest Johns fill me with a far more vivid and real horror than all the alien space parasites trying to take over our children for androids in science fiction. But I dare say we all have a black dog, some just better defined than others. The celluloid parasites are the phantoms at the conscious level of the real struggle for the soul of man within. We are already possessed and the business in hand is to exorcise and expel the enemy within, or at any rate the corrupt mental practices.

Meanwhile for Stone Age research, when these corrupt practices were only modestly developed – there's the fascination – we need simply to blur our thinking. We need to abandon a vocabulary of tens of thousands of words and come down to a vocabulary of a few hundred at most. It is a fascinating conjecture what it must have been like in those days with the inner life bumbling along catching its minnows in a net with only a hundred or two knots in it. Nowadays we would find it frustrating, claustrophobic; and so would everyone else. We would be sent to special schools for the handicapped. Stand the men representing a thousand generations of our forefathers in a row for inspection – I take their clothes off to cut them down to size – and the thousandth you come to is already a moron, as well as talking gibberish. Feminists may instead stand the ladies in a row, and undress them if they so prefer. The result would be very much the same. I plead guilty to a certain amount of meliorism in my makeup. I think that human progress, though fitful, has been general: each generation has stood on the shoulders (and the faces) of its predecessors and thus learned to think more, which is better. What is more, I see no term to this process, provided we sober up as we are bound to now we have such powerful explosives, and face up to who and where we are. This facing up is bound to uncover a few lines which will have to be crossed. The moral promptings of mankind have been badly mussed up by his thinking. The promptings themselves are not too obsessive, but the thinking is. On the contrary, permissiveness is in itself a bad thing. What we see as sin is mere peccadillo, compared to the monster crimes against humanity we all pretend we are not guilty of in order to hide our own nakedness. Whole religions exist solely or chiefly for this ludicrous purpose: to provide us with these mental fig leaves and save us from having to confront our own dirty tricks department. I have written elsewhere of fig leaf religion.

By contrast, contemplating blurred thinking, as practiced by the ancients, is absolutely blissful. We should first narrow our minds to a fair degree of tunnel vision. We should admit large doses of inconsistency, or – which is the same thing – only small domains of reasoning, none even roughly cobbled to its neighbours. Preferably we should limit single domains to single words. All the rest should be allowed to proceed swimmingly, undistracted by any consideration. Having as far as possible shed aeons of preconceptions separating us from the Stone Age, we should, using our bleariest eye, try to make out any vague concepts which still appear to differentiate themselves in the gloom, like moving shapes in a mist. Welcome to proper etymology.

The trouble with an unconventional etymology, as indeed with the conventional kind, is the proof. But whereas the conventional wisdom is that which is taken to need no proof, being more or less proven by long usage anyway, any new look at the evidence is immediately open to challenge, and even resentment as impertinent as well as upsetting. For these reasons it behoves the well groomed etymologist to marshal his reasoning. Let us suppose for example that the English word pie – as in apple pie – is to be interpreted as retaining (for one reason or another, never mind for the moment) the ancient Lithic (Stone Age) elements pa-i, meaning skinned, surfaced, patched over or lidded. It might be thought that since nobody has any other serious derivation to offer, the proposal would be largely unobjectionable. Even Eric Partridge can only offer the tentative suggestion the original meat dish with a pastry lid on it, which comically is the actual pie, got its name because it was made with magpies – not blackbirds after all in spite of other sing-song clues – known to have been known as pies. That surely is pragmatism run riot, Homer nodding if ever he did. In anybody else´s book, Partridge´s derivation would have earned an "f/e", for folk etymology, an attribution based on ignorance and faulty guesswork, only extant from lack of informed competition. What is more, the same semantic content embraces Partridge´s magpies, which are notable for their contrasting (black and white) patches, as also of course are piebald ponies with white patches. The further issue arises of whether the mag-part can be read as contrast. It can be argued ma and ga can carry such a semantic content, ma dark and ka bright. Meanwhile the conventional wisdom derives the mag- in magpie from maggot, short for marguerite from margaron (Greek) pearl, in turn from margaros the pearl oyster. Traditionally the magpie is a pearl pecker. They certainly do squirrel away shiny objects. The Sanskrit for the pearl is manjari (finger biter) descriptive it would appear of the pearl oyster which nips a finger stuck in it when open, and rubbished in the borrowing by the unsophisticated early Greeks. Compare modern Hindi ma-karna to kill, harm or damage and Malay makan eat, or even, more distantly, murder in English and makan in Hindi again for butter, a smashed mashed mushy form. So there is only rhyme and no reason in the Greek transformation from manjari in Sanskrit to margaros.

Except that the Lithic root Ma as well as carrying the semantic content dark and dead could also mean inert but gestating like a seed when planted in the earth. Ma was all these things, down seeking (heavy), earth, earthing, planting, seeding, inseminating, gestating, even as the Egyptians thought a dead body awaiting re-birth in the second world, Dua Taun in Egyptian, on the underside of the world penny, the rebirth copied later by the Christians. Dua Taun in Egyptian was sym-bolised by a hand, a notorious twin, and then a semi circle for Taun, a Ta or cut in two O or oon, conventionally identified as a bun (sic!), but actually a representa-tion of the familiar half we see with a flat earth and the inverted bowl of the sky (The Heavens are Pai Taun in Egyptian, the lid of the world) over it. In Lithic terms there were thus potentials even in death and decomposition. Mice and flies (mouches in French) were at one time supposed to be so generated. Greek garos was perhaps at least akin – suggesting the same to the contemporary mind – to keras (skull), the hard part, compare kheras in Malay, harsh or rough. Margaros abandoned the original finger nipping of the Sanskrit oyster and transformed itself into the Greek oyster busily gestating hardness instead. All this taken on its own is little more than a maybe. It gains in probability in so far as supporting us-ages can be found. But no amount of supporting usage gives any actual validity to the ideas disclosed, other than the apparent usage. If the thinking developed that way that is still just whimsy, it is merely because people thought in those terms. No secret wisdom is disclosed as witchcraft imagines and claimed for its words of power. All etymology is only f/e, folk etymology, the record of the follies and illusions of mankind as he labeled his world for reference purposes. The interest for us is quite clear. These meanders throw into high relief the meandering nature of the human mind. Scratch any man and the Irish in him is revealed. We do not know. We make it up as we go along. The fabric of science on which the progress of technology depends springs solely from the monitoring, the disciplining of this free-wheeling imagination by recourse to hard fact, preferably repeatedly.

It is also relevant to record these Lithic delvings are works of supererogation so far as the humble practitioner of speech is concerned. None of this earlier ratiocination need be retained by him who simply wishes to advert to a magpie, seen or imagined. Magpies are of ostensive definition, regardless of Lithic. But it very often, if not always, turns out that naming committees have done more than just pick a random form which rolled off the tongue, in spite of the received wisdom which takes the common sense view of the speaker that his root vocables are ultimately random and unconnected in any rational way with their meanings. Certainly where omnibus is changed to bus or manjari to maggot the evolution is hardly relevant to current usage. In these cases it strains language to say such a string underlies the present usage. Chomsky's logical strings are perhaps just such another strained use of language.

Meanwhile, back at the ranch, faced with the historic matrix of linguistic semantics – if the purists will allow me a diachronic matrix – academic philologists have inadvertently bamboozled themselves by an overdose of precising. It is as if they sought to understand the historic process of semantic differentiation by the familiar entries on the bottom line only, which are of course the nth differentials of that process, which has enlarged the human vocabulary from at most probably half a hundred or so basic elements (at the origin of the trick of uttering meaningfully) a thousand-fold and more in English alone. All the original semantic structures are now too fuzzy by today's standards to be readily identified and dignified as sapient thinking. A useful lesson about this is contained in the auxiliary verbs of the Papuan languages which, in translation into developed languages can mean almost anything. To find one's way in such a wilderness what almost amounts to an independent math of elementary generalised meanings is needed, attempted in the following chapters which explore the Lithic (Stone Age) elements of original speech. The Lithic hypothesis, indeed, is grounded in just such a matheme as we find in the take off of languages – perhaps the true source of the Babel myth, which records the abandonment of the limitations of natural semantics (which could be worked out from scratch from the meaningful elements, whatever word composition you used, whatever dialect you spoke) in favour of words as mere ikonic or other symbolic artifices which have to be learned by heart. This very ancient revolution in human thinking resulted from combinatorial progress in the unitisation of thinking, that is the stringing of Lithic elements in short strings so the strings stuck in the mind as words. The result was excessive polysemy, because the strings were of so few basic semantic contents developed to carry so many, mostly metaphorical usages The only way forward was with longer and longer strings, until words became blind symbols and speaking became rote speaking, a babel which could no longer be worked out. Natural speak, attending to all the elements in turn instead of just accepting the symbolisation, had by then led to ambiguity to tax the wits of the best soothsayers. Complexity at a certain stage demands codification, just as in the later progress of science. To differentiate vocabulary it became necessary to cease analysing each word (string) back to its basic elements and start afresh with words learned by rote. That way rote soon ruled and academia got its brief. It is the story of Babel.

It will help, and it is also quite interesting in its own right, to look at what is known about the history and development of languages and what can be said about their past. The idea of the language family arose little more than two hundred years ago. You can relate this to my late mother's boast one of her grandfathers was born in 1780, before the French revolution, 225 years ago and about the time the Indian judge William Jones spotted the link between Sanskrit and Greek. Much of the work on any but the Indo European tongues is very new. A family of languages related in some way by kinship was postulated in order to explain the underlying similarity of roots, even where pronunciation and grammatical idiom differed. The first and most studied family is of course the Indo European. The next most widely known is perhaps the Semitic, of which the only language now surviving as an original first language is Arabic. Chinese, African, Amerindian, Pacific, and one or two other less well studied language families are also known.

It is thought that language families originated from single proto languages. It is presumed that languages split from their parent stock by a process of dialects becoming more parochial and peculiar as groups of speakers emigrated from the motherland or in some other way became detached from the parent body of speakers, or in some cases as outsiders invaded the land and the language, until eventually the differences were beyond the wit of the populations to reconcile. We know that this is what tends to happen, in spite of heightened communications. It would not be hard to pick English speakers from around the world who would give each other serious pause if asked to converse together colloquially. But it seems it is more likely it is the divergence of syntactical structures, the idioms of speech, leading to new word formation and new sentence structures which is crucial for reaching the stage of mutual incomprehensibility. This probably arises from pollution by another form of speech, that of conquering or of conquered people. The winners have not always – or even often – been the brightest.

However deliberate and consequential, even erudite, word formation at one time or another may have been, its use and development has been inconsequential, even preposterous. Word development proceeds by slovening, slurring and misprision in the mouths of practitioners. The development of French from Latin is as nice an example as you could wish for. A word is merely a cipher in the course of speech, and must take its chance in the gabble which goes on. As units, words are divorced from their semantic structure as soon as may be. The structure is ignored and eventually over-ridden. Etymology is the study of the original structure, semantic and phonetic alike, from the worn down traces of the original surviving. It is an excavation job from word shards in some cases revealing little of the original form. The slovening includes notably vowel slurring, often to make two the same to save moving the mouth. Vowels are therefore relatively volatile and ephemeral, since the easiest pronunciation is often not to pronounce them at all. For speakers in a hurry, vowels exist to be abused. Cold blooded murder is their usual fate. We all have lazy mouths and many of us lazy minds to go with them. Syllables become just letters. The alphabet implies almost as much.

To pursue syntax in early language with single sounds significant, and their significance psychosemantic, the vowels lend themselves to primitive grammar because they are the linking sounds which go between the consonants. For the same reason they are much prayed in aid, and thus accumulate diverse semantic contents to an inordinate degree. Whatever category syntax demands, a vowel is there to represent it – and there were originally only three to choose from. This does present the researcher with problems, not least of credibility. The short i for instance, a diminutive reduplicative (see Chapter 15) is therefore an itemiser, a single by comparison with the wider and more general vowel a. In the vowel family, a is the daddy. U is the mummy, because the mouth is shaped into an orifice. And i is the diminutive and derivative offspring. I (ee) is thereupon indicative also, an itemisation derived from the reduplicative semantic content: "it", "he", "is", "which", "as", "-ing", as well as a plural. A plural is an itemisation just as a singularity is, repetitively perceived.

Almost every word will need in time reforming, re-elaboration, reconstruction, expansion, extension, restoration of its pristine structure to recapture its pristine shape and the meaning which flowed from that configuration. The task would indeed be quite impossible were it not that an ally is working all the time in the subconscious mind to preserve the Lithic semantic contents, guiding words back into meaningful patterns in accordance with the old old original Lithic meaning elements ingrained in the vocabulary as a whole and sensed in the subconscious though not consciously recovered in the waking state. It is this submerged keel beneath the conscious surface which holds languages on course when the crew are carousing instead of holding the wheel. Learning a language reassembles this unseen keel of meanings in the subconscious mind. Lithic is not inherited like Noam Chomsky's thinking patterns which claim to be able to pass down in the genes not merely brain structure but even the activities which brains are used for. It is as if genetic evolution could pass on not only the physical structure of the phenotype but also determine how the organs will relate to the environment. It is as if the genes determined not only the legs we inherit but also what Sunday walks they will take. We inherit physical structures which determine what walks we are able to take but not precisely how the phenotype will perform. That is the product of happenstance, and, dare I say it, that is a combination of happenstance and human whimsy. The brain is inherited. The mind is not. That is the bombshell in this book, to be believed or not believed according to the temperament of the reader. For me it is just common sense. The mind is an abstraction simply substantiating thinking, no more. The relationship of thinking to the brain is precisely the same as the relationship of our Sunday walks to our legs.

Not much recognised, there are already references to an original Asianic language family underlying some of those found around the world, for example Sumerian and Chinese. I think I have found traces in Albanian and Basque.

Detailed studies of these difficult languages, owing to the exigencies of space and time have had to be deferred to a separate volume. These are certainly outliers and I am not well placed to analyse the possible Asianic languages in between. Finnish, Hungarian and Turkish are largely closed books to me. The earliest historical migratory patterns are relevant. Generally for whatever reason migrations have proceeded out of Asia Westward. Furthermore it is now reasonably well established that the Sumerians were refugees from the Garden of Eden, the garden of the East now the South China Sea, where they had discovered the potential of riverine irrigated gardening. They were displaced as the sea levels gradually rose, by three hundred and fifty feet, with the great melt at the end of the last major glaciation, now leaving only the highlands of Malaya exposed. It may be these inundations in prehistoric times which triggered by a knock on effect these shifts of populations Westward, as well as flooding the Mediterranean sea. Who is to say Sinbad the castrate was not following ancient tradition? Before the Celtic invasions there were previous populations in Europe, but little is known of them. The primitive Celts were cruel head-hunters who appear to have eaten the boys anyway. They may have kept some girls for breeding. The Egyptians or Mediterranean tribes speaking the lingua franca evidently colonised Britain, to judge by some of the place names. It is an acceptable hypothesis the previous tribes were also Westward migrants in their time, eliminating the Neanderthals. What language they or indeed the Neanderthals spoke is quite unknown, and it has been argued Neanderthals did not speak at all. I find this bizarre, given their degree of civilisation. There is of course the possibility the Lithic roots I think I have discovered are really only traces of this Asianic language, although I do not believe it. I do not believe it because the Americas have traces of the same Lithic elements. But of course it is possible again the diaspora resulting from the sea level rising, flooding all the low level lands, led to folk fleeing North to China and East across the Pacific as well as to Sumer. The Malayan language appears to be related to Ancient Egyptian. It may be the Egyptians, certainly Semitic, probably farming the Hamitic tribes they found along the Nile along with their cattle, derived their kinship with Malay from the Sumerian they acquired as Akkadians which they carried with them to Egypt along with the Sumerian river gardening. There are perhaps five millennia during which this spread may have taken place. In any case the Asianic speakers may well have been close inheritors of the Stone Age proto language directly from the earliest linguistic roots which I claim to have discovered as Lithic.

The study of word formation leads in a direction quite different from the study of grammar. Grammar is late and superimposed by scrimshaw man on earlier usage. Transformational grammar, the modernist development of the mathematical approach to language analysis, concerns itself with relationships involved in sentence structure which are amenable to this particular approach, rather than with the end terms (words) to be related. Lithic word analysis on the other hand seeks out the compositional rules not of sentences but of single words, which prove not to be singular at all in origin, but complex semantic strings from the beginning. So much – the complexity of words – is already given away, for those with eyes and ears to see and hear, by the prefixes and suffixes (and infixes) as well as the grammatical inflexions, conventionally well established across the widest range of languages. Words are already complexes in conventional linguistics. We even know that they continue to agglutinate in aid of further meaning in this way. All the Lithic hypotheses seek to add is that it was ever thus, and it goes on rather more cheekily to add that the elements from which the vocabulary of the original (or early, what is the difference?) speakers was assembled are accessible to us still, preserved gratuitously, somewhat like insects in amber (nearly as old), within the present world lexicon. Just as mammals all have the same original basic skeletal structure, languages all prove to have incorporated the same elements in their word formations. It does not follow language is hard wired as Chomsky believes. The reality is more nuanced than that. But there is an unexpected corollary in that quite possibly all the languages there ever were started out with the same – or nearly the same – bunch of basic word elements; the noises came out much the same because the organs of speech were and are much the same the world over; and – here is the clincher – the semantics were also picked much the same because the human environment (internal and external) was much the same all round the world, and language is primarily ostensive. The psyches were all shaped much the same and we all picked up much the same psychosemantics when we learned to speak. It did not need any world symposium for the job nor spreading by word of mouth across the globe.

It is admittedly for speculation how such a circumstance can be accounted for. Of course there may have been a dispersal from a single ur-language, but that seems to me rather doubtful: I guess the species had widely spread while still a dumb hominid. So the diffusionist idea it all started at one place and passed by word of mouth is not considered. So inelegant a solution holds little appeal; and it flies in the face of common sense in so far as it requires that the human race, so bursting with potential, up until it began to speak lived hugger mugger in a concentrated area, within walking distance in a reasonably short space of time; which it is fairly clear that it did not. Otherwise it requires a Nazi conquest of the whole of humanity, presumably with clubs or else perhaps advantaged by the weapon of pure speech, with wholesale conversion to Human-Speak on pain of death. Wayland may nevertheless wish to explore the possibility further.

We should concentrate first on world wide phenomena – the common ground for interrogating and interpreting sound. So for example all the races of mankind have lips, merely the generosity of provision varying from race to race, starting with the baboon (babine in French) whose lips are semi prehensile organs for garnering shoots etc and ending perhaps with the Englishman who is half way to ventriloquy with a penchant for labial stasis. Perhaps he is signaling "No sex, please; We are British!" That too would put him at the far end of the spectrum from the baboon – though still without any reputation for delicacy when it comes to his own sexual expression. But confining our examination precisely and directly to the sounds made by the lips we have already babbling b, the labial plosive when expelling air with the lips lightly pursed and then allowed to part. This is the babbling sound made by babies the world over, and in passing baba is of course the origin of the word baby. So the labial plosive could easily have been remarked as such independently the world over, without the need for any diffusional hypothesis: linguistic innovation was surrounded by babbling babies wherever and whenever it began. It is thus the less cause for surprise when we find the Ba syllable semantically linked to the labia or fleshy bits surrounding the mouth, the world over across language families. Semitic languages have bab for mouth, not unlike pu which is the Akkadian. Historically early we have Babylon, Bab-i-laun, at The Mouth of the saltings, the lawn or flat salt marshes of the delta of the Euphrates river in those days, like the Shatt al Arab today. Bab el Mandeb, at the mouth of the Red Sea, is mouth or Gateway of Tears, where the treacherous cross currents from the Indian Ocean at the entrance of the Red Sea spelt shipwreck for the incautious prehistoric mariner. Similarly Mama, or something like it, has the same maternal meaning in almost every language under the sun. It is mater in Latin, mek in Malay and ma' in Navaho (Californian Indian), and of course spelt mom but pronounced maam on the other side of the pond. In China it is ma, if you get the tone right. Otherwise it means horse. Courtesy of Professor Richard Dixon I am able to discover it was also mujam in Yidinye a Queensland aboriginal tongue spoken by a few dozen survivors when he interviewed them; and I ask myself if the jam started out as a sucking sound. This is simply because when hungry or otherwise distressed the babies' babbling turns from baba to ma'a, with tightened stomach muscles, not unlike the hm! at one time part of the pugilist's repertoire when making a punch. Mums around the world have interpreted their progeny's signaling "Hungry!" as "The little darling is calling for me!", thereby naming themselves the same as their mammary glands similarly labeled. Each of these universal psychosemantic contents can form the basis of world-wide psychosemantic trees and they open the possibility of finding others rather better concealed. Admittedly the handling of these meaning developments can differ according to environment and whim, so that the ultimate origins of most words are by now arcane. They may prove hard to agree on in some cases, but the search is now on.

I have tried in the following chapters to show that the world wide community which appears to share the same linguistic base, which the Lithic hypotheses indicate, results from a delicate balance of probabilities (no more) such as to delight the most dedicated scrimshawist. Psychosemantic promptings to which all humans (as partial systems) are subjected by their mental environment (internal as well as external of course) have been sufficiently directional (but only just) for minds all over the place, thinking things out for themselves, certainly in committee (the quorum must be two), to have arrived by local democratic decision (occasionally over-ruling Wayland) at virtually the same answers everywhere.

Local Councillors will protest this is not a recognisable state of affairs. Local debate admittedly no longer achieves this kind of unanimity, now that we have advanced to exquisite self-expression and esteem with an ample vocabulary for making our individual positions plain, both to ourselves and to others. On the other hand, allowed half a hundred words only and obliged to hunker round a hearth together with no clothes on, asked to engage in a game of definitions, the scenario would be quite different and would I believe approximate to the Lithic solution closely. Those who persist in disagreeing should be made to try it. Here is how, once stripped off. For proper correspondence with the primeval scene, all the rest of language must be blotted from the minds of the participants. The fifty words must then be blurred so that they become so general and uncertainly comprehended amongst those present that they become largely useless by today's standards. All Councilors are by now no longer shy in their birthday suits but on the contrary suffering from inbuilt claustrophobia, clasping each other in their desperate efforts to communicate, grimacing and aping the movements or shapes or sounds of the definands to help their articulations, a solemn but comical Stone Age Dumb-Crambo to get their meanings across.

Perhaps the reason the Lithic elements of speech have not been singled out before now is simply because they offer no utilitarian gain in understanding the meanings of the present day, which are precised to a degree beyond the reach of the Lithic vocabulary of elementary meanings. Indeed, reliance upon Lithic meanings as determinants of current word meanings is contra indicated, tending to confusion of thought rather than clarification. Nevertheless the Lithic meanings do add a piquancy to word meanings even if they hardly develop our understanding or perceptions.

But then, what if confusion of concepts be the way forward to an understanding of primitive thinking? Fuzzy logicians and chaos theory buffs may compare. If in the context of word origins thought and expression were vague and under determined by our standards, does this not shed light on how the mind started out and the way it has come? We ought not to look for what we want to find, to confirm us in our own assessment of our intellectual achievements; on the contrary we should sit back, just like Jessica, and let the sounds creep in our ears, approaching linguistic history resolved to find the way language actually developed in practice; and here we are powerfully assisted, it will be argued, by the discovery of the longevity of the historical traces (self validating semantic traces, not just individual marks for free interpretation) encapsulated in the languages of today. We have access to an underlayer of pidgin meanings, rather as a 'Windows' software addict has access to the underlying Disk Operating System (DOS) also, if he can once pick up the protocol. As with Windows and DOS, the earlier underlying operating system proves to be different from the iconisations of the surface language. One of the principal difficulties for our imagined innocent exploring DOS will be to get outside thinking in terms of the iconic convention, which will prove a hindrance when learning the individual elements of the code needed for DOS. The analogy should probably be stretched no further. It is merely a mnemonic for the idea of Lithic language analysis for anyone who can actually use a computer, ie not counting games or just typing or working within a software programme.

It is in fact not very original to suggest there are psychosemantic promptings: that Ba for instance suggests a rather general fleshiness or flabbiness because of the softness of the lippy plosive, or that Ha (as in Ha! Ha!) with a sudden staccato ejaculation of breath has an element of sudden disturbance about it, suggesting sudden sensation or strong emotion like something hot or an affair of the heart, or even just a hacking cough. Much of the poet's art is working with this material. Even the ancients had muses to cover these aspects of things. Magic invented words of power which were, one suspects, merely words which had secrets in their construction not immediately apparent to the casual user; it looks as if the earliest etymologists were mages and vice versa. What the Lithic hypothesis adds to these elementary insights is that these basic psychosemantic orientations can be seen to have semantic consequences, indeed that subsequent semantic structure is actually built on these original vague semantic orientations; as also that these original orientations can still be found doing service in the languages of today. The hard grafting is tracing the connections between the original psychic promptings of meanings through their various transmogrifications and the meandering byways of linguistic history all the way through the linguistic record; in order to establish the ways the human mind has worked as it has built the world lexicon.

My own particular study could and would never have got under way had it not been for the lifetime of meticulous research devoted to etymology which the late Eric Partridge crowned with his English etymological dictionary which he titled 'Origins'. Half at least of what is new in my book I believe Eric Partridge already knew, but merely had not had the time to shake out into publishable form. Partridge devilled; and it falls to me to publish the grand design – I can not say it is his, since his shade is blameless whenever and wherever I err.

It is this grand design which makes of Lithic a far reaching tool for etymological research. You can not precise current meanings by knowing Lithic, all you can do is illuminate the way the human mind has worked; and it has not been a question of systematics, certainly not evolution with any justification by "reason" in the sense of a mathematic. It does not appear to have been heading for Noam Chomsky at all. It has on the contrary been by idiosyncratic whimsical coarse and subjective analogy that the mind has found expression and language has evolved. There are a few obsessive themes of rather doubtful taste but powerful emotive fascination to be seen. Even the earliest theory of vision (we know of) may well have commended itself largely because of the useful turn to which the Egyptian rays could be put in the battle of the sexes of those days.

In short what we discover is a mad math. Lithic, comically enough, thus provides an introduction to the Aquarian ethos, which appears not to be afraid of mad math since it challenges rational analysis, trying to reach beyond the scientific schemes which technology underwrites. There is in my approach no desire or intention to seek to discredit scientific thinking however; only to say there are other things which may claim prior attention. The traditionally religious have all along been saying as much, often shrilly and peevishly as the record shows; but they are less and less listened to, since most of their vocabulary is outmoded. (It has to be said some of their ideas are extremely silly also – one would have said unbelievably silly if it were not proven there is nothing so silly some fool can not be found to believe in it). It is an irony God's Word alone is forbidden any etymology! There is an oxymoron in here somewhere for anyone who wants to take up the matter. Lithic meanwhile can claim to fit in with the present stage of the radical review of enlightenment research programmes – which uneducated youth apparently senses in chaotic music. It is post modernist without the highly selective and elitist concentration on esoteric analyses of literary themes which we get from the academics. It is a plea for common sense and individual authenticity at a time when thinking at the edge is for the most part consensual, indeed put into committee, stereotyped and sterilised in a properly scientific manner. Lithic language study argues for a renaissance of pragmatics; the kind of pragmatics which any objectively orientated software programming accidentally inspires. Computer buffs and uneducated youth in general should all buy this book, if only to startle their elders once they have read it.

After that opening general walk-about considering the state of affairs in linguistic as well as other studies, let us turn without further delay to particularities and give by contrast, by way of practical example, an account of the proper history and analysis of "Lithic" language elements in one simple case chosen more or less at random from the English dictionary I just happen to be looking at. Consider the history of the English word to join, akin to English yoke and Sanscrit Yoga

and Juga. Moreover Malay juga is conventionally translated as indeed or some
such, but in origin it is "also" or "with it", from 'that is joined' or 'to be added'. I
like to think of it as "and now take that on board too". There is in reality express
meaning in the original forms of all these words, revealing an internal structure
of constituent word elements like in a sentence with words. This is quite different from the conventional academic idea of word roots, for the most part random simples; that is in all cases which are not echoic or borrowings from echoic
forms – when the match is merely phonetic and therefore rather uninteresting.
According to adopted linguistic theory word roots are by definition simples: they
mean what they mean by default, by an act of appointment only, based on no
discernable principle. That is what may be described as a linguistic squelch: it
terminates further investigation with a definition. This version of etymology can
now be seen to be bunk, to borrow from Henry Ford, but after rather longer pe-
rusal of the matter condemned than Ford allowed himself. It is to be replaced by
an etymology in terms of original Lithic elements of words which were and in a
certain sense even still are phonetic strings with integral semantic strings pertaining. To put it simply every word is really a sentence, or at least a phrase, and not a
commissioned nugget or shell. We have only forgotten this because we have used
words with such fluency for so long that we treat them with complete familiarity
as nuggets and do not reflect upon their geniture any longer. In the metaphor of
physics words, from first utterance, were originally molecular complexes, never
atomic. Perhaps Chimpish is atomic? It is a job to get them to put a few simple
molecules together. The importance of this shift of approach to Lithic can hardly
be exaggerated. It allows for the first time belief in the development of language
simply under the agency of human thinking, even individual suggestion, answering only to the whims of the individuals concerned and certainly not driven by
any natural scheme or process superimposed on those whims by transcendental
clockmakers of one ilk or another. More, we even gain access to the whimsy of our
earliest forebears, those who invented the principles of speaking, because it is all
(or anyway a lot of it) still there concealed in the lexicon. As a result the progress
of human intellectuality is uncovered in the linguistic record in a way which was
never going to be possible under the old scheme resorting to blind process and so
shifting the action off stage.

Meanwhile to continue with our study of Yoga the late Eric Partridge, who is
I believe to be credited with a good deal of the new vision required to support the
new etymology, imagined the Indo-European root of join to have been: "apparently *jeug- to bind together, to yoke, to join, itself an extension of *ieu-, variation
of *ieo-, to bind; with the ultimate root perhaps *ie-, varying *io- and *iu-, to
bind". Partridge was not alone in most of this. But many questions remain to be
asked. Why do we find otiose extensions (eg the g) getting added, for instance?

As also what is primitive or prime about a word meaning bind, only later becoming generalised and used to join quite generally? Is it that the actual must precede the abstract? Perhaps it appealed because it was surmised (correctly) that stone age joiners used bindings before nails or glue, a simple truth which may still be verified in many of the jungles around the world. But such selection is objectionable without hard evidence. It imagines the human mind originally simplistic which again must be true if you go back far enough. But in fact the speaking hominid's mind was already baroque and whimsical even when least informed, indeed perhaps especially so. Relevant is the experience of a youngster after a spell in the Malayan jugle learning survival skills. After he wrote "One of the things we learned is 'tali' makes very good string". Tali is string in Malay. But it is also a liana, because it comes from the Lithic phonemes ta-lai, which means become naturally (literally by birth, Darwinists please note)-lai, that is flexible and windable round as a binding for instance. The fact French lier means to bind, and we make alliances supposed to be binding too may have influenced Partridge. The budgerigar is another case in point. "What do you call that then?" says a released convict after serving his time. "It's a bright coloured bird of course". [Thinks] 'Do you thimk I can't distinguish it from a bowl of porridge?' Or what about the aboriginal Malay for a tree, kruing? The Malay is pokok. Garden furniture in this country pretending to be from managed and ecologically sound forest plantations in Borneo are widely advertised as made from kruing as if it were a species of timber. In Borneo the Dyaks in the jungles speak a different tongue. It would appear whitey has sent an entrepreneurial representative for five minutes to ask 'What do you call that one then?' in order to add veracity to his claims. He has evoked the pretty obvious reply: 'Well we call it a tree'. |Thinks] 'Do you think I can't tell it from a bowl of porridge?' Now the abstract idea of two things – or indeed people – coming together will surely have been common currency, articulated or not, from well before the first binding was bound – or indeed the first syllable articulated. Indeed how could the idea have occurred to anybody, say when tripped by a liana, without also the idea of linkage to prompt the artificial liaison. No doubt chimps appear to study with great seriousness their individual movements, and so perhaps to categorise in their minds simple tasks like binding. The human mind however got there by a different route altogether, as the words themselves reveal if correctly read. Join is certainly from the same source as Gothic iuk- (yoke) and the Latin stem jug- (yoke) – the spelling came later, remember – and may thus be taken to have comprised the three (Lithic or Stone Age) elements i + u + ka or ga. Of the three vowels recogniized at the beginning i is the second, the diminutive-reduplicative-indicative vowel suggesting itemisation, coming after the a, which is the middle vowel and therefore the first, because the easiest to utter, and so the general unstressed unmarked one; while u (or ooo phonetically, there were no letters or spellers in the Garden of Eden) is the completive-substantive and so as well as the plurality of the inclusive one the dual also, as well as simply two. The dipthongs e (ai) and o (au) could only have come in later as the human mouth parts learned to flex more nimbly. The vowels are covered in detail in chapter 15. With iuk that leaves only the phoneme ka which has been reduced to the consonantal form, a process of slurring and slovening often found arising in two stages, first as the marked form kai which is then slurred to ke and thereafter as a further easement cut down to k. It follows i-u-k actually meant and means something, namely "it dual makes" or "it unit makes", a fair description of union, though little directly to do with any binding, which turns out to have been an accidental characterisation of one method available for joining things, doing it with a liana or some such, while the brute idea turns out to have been the abstract mathematical one. This has implications for the age of language and the onset of reasoning – of a kind – with primitive mankind. We have learned something greatly to the credit of our hairy bare-bottomed forebears and to the discredit of our modern trousered disparagement of them.

Moreover as an aside for the moment the three vowels a,i and u make a sequence of smoothly changing vowelisations and symbolise as much, particularly as the vowels have no articulations (in the sense of breaks or junctions in the flow of sound) such as the consonants (which are sounded with them) contribute; so that the semantic prompt is for smooth flow, extension, movement without any feet – in space or time. The temporal dimension is recognized in the Greek aeon group and the spacial in Latin ire, to go, etc. Moreover again the sequence is triune and ends in a completive term embracing the previous two, making a Lithic Dialectic – I have called it the "Vowel Oon" (the word vowel is made up of them all, and lai as a loop easily leads into the idea of a group) when thinking in Lithic – and it is the paradigm for the later atavistic Hegelian dialectic so eagerly and disastrously adopted by Marx. See Figures 1 and 2 on page 95. Jehovah, I-a-u-a-i, whose virtue was somehow regarded as miraculously encapsulated in His vowelisation, improperly identified as a Tetragrammaton in place of the proper Pentagrammaton, was perhaps the first dialectical deity. He certainly was not the first singular one. His universality consisted in uniting the two dimensions of Space and Time so that He presided over the conjunction of the two of them, the Tau. We can reduce His name to its elements thus: "It-That-Inclusive-Continuing" and paraphrase it "The Universal and Eternal", the prinzips in inseparable embrace as world dimensions, waiting for Einstein with his space-time to come along.

All these ideas are now historical; they are in the record, in the language. They are not, as Jung persuaded himself – perhaps to free himself from his publisher – accessible to all who come after via a Group Soul or Collective Unconscious, making up a limbo of ideas, which have at one time or another been thought, available to afficionados, whether appearing in Jung´s published texts or not. Archetypes are really linguistic categories. We learn them from the language. To that extent Jung was right: we can deduce beliefs from close language study, and we all do so a great deal more than we are normally aware. But he was wrong to personalise them and as it were to dress them up in hats and coats. When we recognize the process and attend to it with care we gain access to a store of ancient lore, most of it thoroughly misleading of course but all of it a source of delight. We are led to think "So that's how the old coons thought, is it?"; and I am afraid it is an incentive to think of our more immediate elders as old coons too, especially when you reach an age when all your old coons are dead in the natural course and can not argue any more. The study of Lithic meanings is not quite culture with the lid off; but humour is never far away for normally sober folk, with the naïve intellectual antics of our rude forebears exposed to the cold light of hindsight.

Now that we have rubbished most everybody else, I think it is time perhaps to state quite shortly what is offered in replacement of perceptions 'perceived as current' (PC perceptions). The following three Taos are offered as a runner or appetiser for what follows in subsequent chapters which contain more etymological detail than will be to everybody´s taste. Here the Taos or paths to understanding offered comprise firstly ten Axiomatic Principles which make up the Lithic Hypotheses, and secondly twelve Consonantal Determinations which outline it, covering some hundreds of thousands of years of linguistic development; and thirdly Ten Conclusions as to how we manage to live in this world. In these three lists I have tried to be brief. After a lifetime cutting bait I have at last found the courage to actually go fishing. I believe these lists would be regarded as Taos by the Chinese mind, that is to say rubrics or realizations – from "Becomings" at subparagraph 2.5 below: Ways of Thinking. The individual mind is like a sand castle built in the tidal zone on the beach and very few people are single minded enough to get as far as putting the flag on the top. Most find it more fun to go fishing in the rock pools as soon as they come by a shrimping net – the hunting instinct without any risk except to the shrimps. Or else it is fiddling life away to avoid confronting it. So what is this single mindedness? I believe it is built on bloody mindedness and has probably spilt more blood over the aeons than man´s need to eat, which puts my own lifetime achievement in proper perspective and perhaps answers the question my wife put to me those many years ago when I claimed for the first time to have discovered some novel findings: "Why you?" Is it because I have hunted ideas to extinction? It perhaps comes from those many hundreds of millennia we spent loping after game until the quarry dropped exhausted from the chase, often with a sharp stick stuck in its bum, more to mark the beast to keep on chasing as well as serving notice on it of your intention to do so, than with any hope of bringing it down. To get meat you had to keep going, sullenly and interminably until you had won. I have seen this same sullen intent on the face of a young nephew as he hunted his younger brother round and round the table to inflict on him condign punishment for some imagined slight.

TEN AXIOMATIC PRINCIPLES

The Lithic Hypothesis is, I believe, based on the following axioms of belief:

1.1   An alphabet is a conventional set of symbols coding sounds by rote and is used in strings.

1.2   A lexicon is an alphabet which codes for meanings as well as sounds by rote and is used in strings.

1.3   There was a Lithic lexicon used for hundreds of thousands of years before the alphabets.

1.4   The Lithic lexicon still underlies the alphabets we use and we can sometimes sense its presence, and indeed often if we persevere and try. In psychobabble it is in the subconscious still, and it is made up of meaningful phonemes.

1.5   The Lithic lexicon was and is both alphabet and lexicon in one.

1.6   Thinking is a flow and not a thing, an ephemeral activity in the brain; but ideas may be substantially represented (coded with symbols) when the thinking has been thought.

1.7   These substantial representations, sometimes called entifications or reifications, both ugly words, itemisations much preferred, are always deliberated and conscious ideas.

1.8   Speech breaks the train of thought into discrete bits for utterance and at the same time for collation and recollection.

1.9   Syntax is a rote or protocol developed by speech, and biologists fancy it evolved, but in fact it just came from fancy thinking, because metaphysical activities can not evolve.

1.10   Grammar is a rote or protocol developed by writing, and biologists fancy it evolved, but in fact it just came from fancy thinking, because metaphysicl activities can not evolve.

TWELVE CONSONANTAL DERTERMINATIONS

Helpful for the break in to the primitive mindset of our hominid forebears' adjectival minds when first they began to speak is the realization their identifications of meanings were nasty brutish and short. They were also often rather low brow and rude, as I suppose one should expect, since every sensation conveyed to their minds came via their own bodies just as today and they accepted them where we are expected to filter ours. What really got their minds racing was hunting for the two gratifications food and sex and their respective consumations around the women's hearth. Here are the twelve tentative initial lexical identifications from perhaps six hundred thousands of years ago which can astonishingly be discovered still operative in the lexicon of the present day – under the Lithic Hypotheses:

2.1 Ba. The sound made by lip on lip, of flesh on flesh: flesh-speak! Flesh, mouth,the bungy bits,bubs, bums, bumming – using the haunches, haunching around, going, bungs, buoys, boys, bunds, fleshing out, covering the bones, covering, fleshed, alive, being, and so on (not in any order of precedence).

2.2 Pa. A thinned and less substantial (unvoiced) Ba. Thin or small flesh, skin or small shoot or bud, piece, surface, covering surface, top, lid, roof, patch, pie, pan, panorama;, also pipe, spit, spray, spring, and so on; and also of course just a puff, pah! At one remove papa as well (from penis).

2.3 Ish. The sound of a burning brand when dunked. Fire killed by water, fire, flame, sun (God), shine, see, the visible world, the existent, comfortable around the hearth, at ease, sedentary around the hearth, alive (animals are warm), active (animals are active), animal, action, actual, moving, up (the flame leaps upward), the supermaterial (you can pass your hand through the flame and it hurts), spirit, and so on.

2.4 Ka. The sound of striking flint on flint. Strike, effort, force, flake, cut, sharp, shape, hard, structure, frame, solidity, the solid element, the hard element, the earth (not soil which originally is marl), land, location, place; spark, kindle, beget, make, and so on.

2.5 Ta. The sound of snapping and tapping, a doublet with Ka but without the effort of the blow. Break (into two), do (any other handiwork), broken in two, two, become two, slit, the sexual slit (the birth canal), parturition, birth, become, becomings, events, source, twins, twin dimensions, two, and so on. Ta-un, all the becomings was the world in Egyptian – and Aztec!

2.6 Ha. The sound of sudden forced expulsion of breath. Hilarity, horror, orgasm, whoopee, high emotion, joy, rejoice, welcome, greet, and so on. Also the break between two consecutive vowels (cockney h) protecting the vowels from elision (usually unsuccessfully).

2.7 Fa. Originally the pronunciation Ph suggested expectoration. This is a difficult one to follow because of shifts with b, bh, p, v, etc. Ph was at the time of the birth of the Egyptian language, prehistorically but quite recently as languages go, Pa-hei, when it meant joy piece or as we say penis (protruding or witness piece), whence (Greeked) phi. Egyptian nefer (from nai-pa-hei-rai, [when] showing-the pahei-is rayed/rises) meaning pretty, fair, fine, fun and so on.

2.8 La. Nasty taste (curled tongue). Expectorate, dribble, leak out, lye (nasty tasting), liquid, liquid's instinct to slip into the lows and thus become brackish, slope, slow, tongue (the taster), language (tongue wagging), the ocean (the lowest of the low and the briniest of the briney), the skyline at sea, line, flat, loop, circle, to circle or orbit, Apollo, balloon, and so on.

2.9 Ma. The sound of a baby crying with a fatal stomach ache or just to be fed. Mortality, mother, faeces, decay, mess, dirt, earth (soil), (down seeking), the opposite of ish at 2.3 above (continuous like the sibilant but in this case with no issuing of breath), inert mass, matter, heavy, massive, large; earthing, planting seed, impregnating, propagating, gestation and so on.

2.10 Na. The sound of holding the breath and then gasping. Orgasm, ejaculation, erection, protrusion, push forward, present, show, witness, explain, advise, minister; gape, be open, be wanting, be empty, without, negative, and so on.

2.11 Ra. The sound of a succession of raps (of the tongue). Uncountable multiplicity, fur, hair, prickles, sunbeams (rays), Ra (sun), a whole spectrum of fancied rays and their effects, eg growing, and sexual rays, raise, rise, warm, braise, eyes (which were thought to utter rays), see; brain, rage, hero, and so on.

2.12 Wa. The sound of shivering. Vibration, fear, and so on. Also a semi vowel with different connotations when pronounced "oo" in place of "Wa".

It certainly sounds a radical plan to seek to ground the whole of human language over some hundreds of thousands of years of thinking on these twelve original motifs (or perhaps a few more) and claim they have survived (refreshed subconsciously) all that time. I certainly never intended it. It must be the longest game of Chinese whispers conceivable, and indeed the longest gaming of any sort in the universe. The fact is that is how it has worked out. The chances of these budding psychosemantic trees, subject to combination and erosion (slovening and slurring) and recombination and reslovening over so many millennia and still presenting so as to appear to be based on these semantic grounds whilst yet not in reality being so are surely of the same order as the chances of a team of monkeys on a word processor typing the bible a randon (at random). Linguistic change itself is like a gigantic rope with twisted skeins of astonishing complexity but nevertheless woven with an underlying semantic simplicity – almost poverty. When we learn a language we are presented with a cross section of the part of the rope concerned cut across at the relevant stage of development, and the weave of the skeins is semantic, and firstly word semantic, which is ignored by the grammarians.

TEN CONCLUSIONS

3.1 Our reasoning now is an offshoot of our speech, but speech was first an offshoot of the mind.

3.2 Our identifications are an affectation, a bi-blow of our speaking, by which we paper over the world with the entities which catch our attention.

3.3 Thinking is an independent mystery; something which is now done mostly with the aid of language, a use of it. Language is the first differential of thinking, an independent calculus. It has nothing directly to do with the heritage of the brain. A hundred Einsteins in descent one from another, a hundred lifetimes scribbling, would not advance brain power one iota. For that the hundred would have to gain access to sufficient descendants to skew the gene pool, a business taking several times the length of time we have been speaking, never mind doing math. That would not improve any genes but merely replace inferior genes (for math).

3.4 Math is an independent mystery, something that is now done with the aid of thinking, a use of it. It is the second differential of thinking after language, another independent calculus.

3.5 Each one of us lives in a self blown bubble, which I have likened to the wallpaper on the real wall, and the bubble is papered on the inside of our own heads and we read and write on its inner surface to guide our surmises as to what is going on outside of us in the world. This in no way impugns the power of surmise, only its direct applicability to reality.

3.6 The world is what it is and not another thing – Wittgenstein's "Case".

3.7 Analogy fails to adequately describe the mind because it is like nothing else in our experience.

3.8 Mental events are therefore properly treated in terms which are metaphysical and sui generis.

3.9 William of Occam presented a true bill (unfortunately in Latin) widely known as Occam's Razor: "Res non multiplicanda", loosely translated "Check your baubles before relying on them", ie go for the simplest explanations, get rid of the elephant standing on a tortoise on which at one time it was suggested the earth rested to explain how it stood still in space rather than falling; and shun Ptolemy's multiple coggery to account for the movements of the heavenly bodies, and so on – the philosophic cobwebs left by the cognoscenti.

3.10   Science (knowledge) is partial and never conclusive. It does not approach reality, it merely represents it – well or badly. See the wallpaper in 3.5 above.

Lithic Gaming.

Based on no more than the above, the reader may now, if he is so disposed, try his own hand at playing Lithic for himself or herself. When my sisters and I were children before the last Great War our mother taught us to play a game of free composition to exercise the imagination, for which the rules were very simple. It was a kind of Chinese whispers out loud for any number of players but with an additional semantic element. The opening player announced any substantive thing – for younger players it was usually a visible entity, res vista, say a wheelbarrow. The next player had to say "A wheelbarrow reminds me of…"; and so on ad nauseam. The (unspoken) aim of the game was to produce opening and closing terms as far apart as possible, on a scale also unspoken but pleasing to the players. Skill was displayed in thinking of way-out semantic connections nevertheless capable of being followed by the other players when confronted with the new idea. If any player could not follow the catena, often my youngest sister, a challenge would be made, whereat the players would immediately go into umpire committee and agree on the validity or otherwise of the intellectual catena. The game became known, inelegantly as it now appears to me, as "The wheelbarrow-cow game" from a famous outcome of an early session. The relatively close similarity of the two end terms which so satisfied us as worlds apart owed some of its fame I have now come to suspect to the unspoken and perhaps barely perceptible element of cheekiness to the cow, large horned beasts we knew to steer clear of in the home pasture, by deriving its status from a mere wheelbarrow, a two legged dumb gardening tool. We can see now the naivety in the choice: academia is not represented, nor is there so much as a shadow of originality in it.

The rules for the game of Lithic are somewhat similar but there are some additional restrictive rules born of rather more than a further seventy years of ratiocination. With Lithic the Challenge Committee is permanently in session in the background and each move is open to inspection by it. So as to keep the game in play as far as possible you can co-opt yourself to your own committee and even allow yourself alone to be a quorum for the time being if playing on your own. Indeed it is the solitaire version I mostly enjoy. The other rules are simply the rules of reason; but it is Lithic reason which applies, not the reason of the scholiasts or Boolean logic. Fancy is OK provided it is Lithic fancy, the thinking is OK provided it is Lithic thinking, suitable for a hominid in his or her ignorant posture squatting bare bottomed around the hearth six hundred thousand years ago. The aim of the game is to derive as many words as possible, in as many languages as possible, from the prescribed list of original Lithic elementary phonemes and their original psychosemantic contents. It is a game for any number of players with or without the aid of sources such as etymological dictionaries, and can be played silently by oneself in the train, or when ostensibly listening to sermons or in class, or even engaged in idle conversation (risking an anti social behaviour order). It is not particularly addictive for any reasonably balanced person, though others, myself included, should perhaps beware. The skill lies in awareness of the rules of Lithic which are the ways our hominid ancestors were thinking some hundreds of thousands of years ago, together with those rules required to cater for the erosions and elisions, the additions and subtractions over the same period of time. That allows for a deal of expansion to get back to the original meanings. It sounds alarming but the rules are in fact relatively easily stated. The original phonemes and their psychosemantic contents from which all players must always start are as already laid out above on pages 77 and 78. Their justifications are of course in the chapters dealing with each phoneme in turn. These chapters sketch them in much greater detail and give some practice in their combinations. The simple rules of Lithic grammar – nothing to do with Boole or Chomsky, you don´t need to know about them and if you do it is a disadvantage – are laid out below. The rules derived from the erosion and elision and the additions and subtractions amount only to a handful of procedural guide lines, all of which are shortly stated in the accompanying instructions for playing which follow:

How to Play.

Grammar and Syntax

The rules of Lithic grammar, or better syntax, the rules of sun-taxis (sun = all the instances) of putting ideas together, were few indeed; since, like Simple Simon, our dumb ancestors they had not any – or at least they had not adumbrated any. What was going on in their minds before they had language to express it is another matter and a hard one to solve since all the direct evidence is, by definition, missing. Cognitive archaeologists are simply reduced to guessing, from how they handled their tools and their tool making for instance. But here are the rules of Lithic grammar:

1. Apposition. What we find in the earliest language use is adjectival apposition, putting one idea next to another and connecting them together – not so much like "black hat" where there is an obvious noun and an adjective which adds to it its colour as an extra identification; but more like "high

green" where it may refer to a bowling green up a mountain, or alternatively a green hill, or even just bright green. We do not need to distinguish between adjectives and nouns because they only came later; in fact we ought not to do so. Original ideas were effectively all adjectival, probably just from an original exclamatory. We are still at it. We look at a sunset and we think "Wow!". Then we wax poetic calling upon our neighbours to remark the "blood red", "streaked vermillion", etc, etc. It may be retorted what we actually say these days is "Do come and have a look at the sunset" using nouns. But why do we say it? We are elucidating Lithic, not modern discourse with a hundred thousand nouns at our disposal, and a pervasive if not actually a universal grammar. Our first world was an adjectival universe; so think in adjectives. That is rule one.

2.   The Idiom of Pairs. Apposition puts ideas (later I call them distincta, and then categories) in adjectival pairs, and the Lithic idiom was then to put these pairs in turn in pairs. So we often find our words originally composed of two or four Lithic elements, and so on. The Spanish still like to do their telephone numbers in pairs, I notice, whereas northerners now remember them in threes. Pairs appear these days to suit the lazy minds, basking rather than biting, and it was probably always so.

3.   The rest of Lithic syntax was vowelisation. Most of the virtue was in the consonantal elements, the leading elements when speaking, and with an articulation you could set your mind on. The vowels were therefore markers added. In fact they actually were the grammar. The Lithic "Vowel Oon" and its conventions are already introduced. It comprised only the three vowels a, i and u (aaa, eee and ooo for the man in the English street). They had a number of different meanings which amplified and modified the sense of the consonants to which they were attached. These were rather fluid concepts, hard to pin down in the precise terms we have grown accustomed to think in. The idea of impressionism comes to mind; our forebears were dabbers, not engravers like us. To briefly recapitulate here:

3a.   "Aaa" was the middle general vowel and so the first one, unmarked. Continuity, extension, the ongoing, even just plain going so long as it was not thought of as articulated, with consecutive haunchings which needed a b in it, happenings or smooth changes other than the ambulatory; and then above all the first term in the Lithic vowel dialectic or 'vowel oon'.

3b.   "Eee" was the thinned diminutive, reduplicative, indicative (including the genitive in Latin and –ing in English); the temporally shrinking (into the distance), the past tense: and then also the second term in the Lithic vowel dialectic (later picked up by Hegel and disastrously borrowed by Marx).

3c.   "Ooo" was the completive vowel (the whole, all, in a loop or group), the
       substantive (and so eventually the noun form), the dual, the pluperfect, the
       synthesis of the other two vowels, the third term in the Lithic dialectic. It
       may be noted here, as I think we may take it those bare bottomed naming
       committees did, the lips are protruded sequentially from aaa through eee
       to ooo, while the tongue is flat and relaxed for aaa, curled and raised for eee
       and in a middle position for ooo, resuming the other two vowel positions;
       so that we have a thoroughly dialectical vowel u which is sequentially third
       as evidenced by the lips, whilst at the same time in the middle so far as
       tongue position is concerned. This is probably the best and strongest evi-
       dence for dialectics, and it turns out to be neither a mental nor a physical
       process at all, but in origin no more than a phonetic whimsy, based on the
       physiological functioning of the human mouth parts: early science?

SLOVENING AND SLURRING, EROSION AND ELISION.

The slovening and slurrings over many millennia are from the lazy tongues and
absent minds of common speakers, taking the exquisite formulations of the elites
of the day sitting and working over the imagined evidences in those bare bottomed naming committees, and then massacring them with careless abandon so
as to be able to romp through simple phrases with the minimum of effort. I have
described this dichotomy elsewhere as the dialogue of Wayland and Scrimshaw
Man. Consequently, it is argued theoretically, there can by now be nothing left
of original speech to discover. But this is not borne out by the evidence. What
mechanism has ensured the survival of Lithic is secondary, but survive it has.
Without rubbing out the whole lexicon at a stroke and replacing it piecemeal
with a new lexicon based on a different linguistic plan altogether, surely an impossibility, it is fairly obvious as one word is spoiled – rendered incomprehensible in
terms of its original Lithic elements by slovening – it can be reconstructed with its
original elements intact, simply from analogy with the rest of the lexicon. So it is
a fair presumption there has never been a total break since the origins of speaking.
That means language has in fact a self repairing mechanism, which has proved
sufficient to reinvent Lithic sufficiency, regardless of the relative mindlessness of
the great majority of speakers over the past few hundred millennia. Language is
by now buried deep in the human psyche, sufficiently established therein to be
attended to without conscious attention. It is, it would appear, the subconscious
workings of the human mind which have assumed responsibility for the refreshment – in computer speak the refresh rate – of age old Lithic protocols, quite regardless of surface erosion and elision, so that it is now not too fanciful to borrow
from Chomsky´s jargon and talk of a deep structure which is the Lithic language,
underlying all the languages of the globe – but not hard wired at all, which would

require the inheritance of ideas, which after all are active and therefore transitory neuronal electronic configurations, the softest and most ephemeral software, with no hard disk. Switch off the brain and the programme and the work in progress is lost for ever. Almost as astonishing as Chomsky's ideas, what actually happens is each infant individually recomposes the underlying information inbuilt in the lexicon as it learns to speak, while uttering only the surface layer of current verbiage data required for conversation. Whether such a subconscious substrate of language learning can cohabit with a late Boolean universal grammar such as Chomsky provides I leave to others to debate. Be that as it may, all we have to do to attend to the surface presentations is to undo the damage done by the slovening. Here are the rules for that.

1.   Expansion. Primitive languages are built from short bits with wide usages. The phonetics were short. A whole sentence would fit in a word these days; we can sometimes even find it doing so. Where developed words have generally been bunched up the rewarding technique is to expand them, giving each single phoneme its full value as originally perceived.

2.   Final consonants, copying the glotal stop, came late. Many or perhaps most result from first the modifier –i being added, giving the final vowelisation –ai, and then its dipthongisation to –e, followed by semi silent pronunciation and finally the deletion of the final vowel altogether. It is a fair first rule to think in terms of reading final consonants such as –k as originally –kai, with the Lithic meanings striking off (a flint), making, kindling, etc, all the sons of striking flint on flint.

3.   The dipthong vowels e and o are to be read as in origin ai and au respectively. Of course the u in this latter expansion is the symbol for the sound made with the lips rounded and pushed forward as in the final position when we say owe precisely. The dipthong O is the departure from the proper symbolisation. Or to put it the other way round, O is really the proper symbol for the vocalisation ooo, as commonly in Chimpish, which (to a chimp) probably carries the psychosomantic content "Ooh!", "Attention!", "My Goodness!" or something like that, even "I have something I am trying to communicate to you". My goodness in Chimpish? Why not?

4.   Repetition. Repetitive phonemes are used in primitive languages as plurals. With usage they may nevertheless elide. They may also come together as back and front end terms of two pairs of elements put together in apposition. In this case also they may have elided. A case in point is the Australian aboriginal Budgerigar, which is made up from the three aboriginal words, and six elements, Baji jeri and gara, which mean bird bright colour. The use of the gara makes it clear in what sense the jeri is to be understood

and is not really needed in translation. It is what the Egyptologists would call a determinant. A budgerigar is a bright bird or a bright coloured bird. Fanciers have reverted to the original Lithic Baji or Go Up for their birds, finding the aboriginal sentence a mouthful. It is only sad they do not allow them to be bajis any longer in captivity. The gara we translate as colour is really make-ray or make-see, the substantive which we think in terms of represented as a happening, keeping the thinking fluid – or perhaps better put as using the available fluid idiom which springs to the aboriginal mind. Anyway an occasional redoubling of consonants as in budgerigar to discover baji jeri gara is permissible. It is irresistible to add in here, while we are thinking of a bird as a go up the derivation of bird in English as from the Lithic Bai-rai-dai, goes-raised-does, just another go up. Eric Partridge derives it from breeding, but that is hardly an avian peculiarity. Breeding is in fact a form of burgeoning semantically, which accounts for its own quite separate ba-rai-da configuration. The Spanish bird, a pajaro, is yet another go up from the same stable as the passer or sparrow, and I have long thought the parrot is just a bird from some jungly native tongue rather than a Pierot or cousin to peruques and periwigs as in the established etymology.

5. Consonant changes. This is the contentious area of Lithic research. In different languages there have been different consonant exchanges, though some are common to many. The French can be found changing their Bs to Vs, for example. The Spanish can be found writing their Bs as Vs but retaining the original pronunciation as Bs. Sanskrit has a fancy for writing sh where kh or even k originated. Greeks have traded s for h in many places. Ks have become Gs all over, and Ps Bs, Ts Ds, and so on, often just slovening. The result of these changes has generally been to ease pronunciation, the lazy mouth parts syndrome; but some are reasoned – grammarians´ kind of reason only – and this suggests they have all been given a fair wind by the grammarians tidying up and uniformitising the language. Anyway the result is to afford a good deal of flexibility in interpreting the original Lithic consonants which went to make up a word. This is unfortunate because it invites criticism as taking liberties to preserve the thesis and is what makes me describe the grammarians, the systematisers, as the villains of the piece. But it has to be lived with.

MORE LITHIC GRAMMAR COMPARED TO THE GRAMMAR OF TODAY.

OSTENSIVES

What was our first speech about? It is an anachronism to suggest it was an expression of a poetic urge to declaim, since that came aeons later. It may have been prompted in part by a less than poetic urge to express emotion: plain hunger for example, or "Phoaw!" But to judge by the chimp, communication of some matter of urgent import like the advance of a leopard or the location of food open to predation was the principal spur; and this was because it required a degree of specification unneeded for simple emotional expression; and the lack must have been apparent to all parties. The voice was initially for warning of danger. Indeed "voice" actually meant danger. The Sanskrit "vac" for voice, pronounced in its pristine form "Wa-kai!" says "Woe make!", ie a panic signal: Raise the alarm! And it certainly can be so read in elementaty Lithic, ie in Lithic elements, just like the schoolboys' KV today (from cawe,just wakai the other way about) or is it yesterday with now no Latin taught? Meanwhile the Old Persian or Avestan "Wackis" pronounced "Wa! Kais!", a battle cry, was also raising the alarm, in this case putting the frighteners on the enemy. It is not so far from the Maori "Hakka!" where the Ha is variously used around the world for sudden emotional responses, from the hilarious to the horrendous and hooraying, in the Maori case a rejoicing at their own Ka and at your imminent downfall. It comes from the contraction of the glottis, as in a gasp, followed by a sudden expression of the tension built up. It was how our hominid forebears naturally said "Good Evening!" to a sabre toothed tiger at the back of their cave. Curiously it may have worked. Laughing in the face of a hungry tiger, if you can manage it, is said to put it off. Anyway it would be worth a try. It is hard not to slip in here a mention of the humble cow. Wild cows charge and gore when they get confused, which is often since they are not blessed with much consideration and are conditioned to use their horns. In Malaya the wild "buffalo" (from bous wala, ox wild or fearsome – or is it just panicky, wa!-like?) is named "misai" from mai-sai, roughly mayhem acting, the stupid brutes are known quite often to charge on sight. The aboriginal tribes in the Malayan jungle called me Tuan misai, Mr Buffalo, but this on investigation proved not to be an uncharitable assessment of my morals or intellectual achievements but merely a shape resemblance. I favoured a well curled moustachio – shaving was a bind – and the buffalo´s bridged horns, shaped like a full moustache, meant a moustache had been named after the animal. A buffalo lip was derived precisely like a gull wing. It was a gull. The tame water buffalo, a placid beast, benefits from tens of thousands of generations of skillful breeding for the milder character by the Eastern races. The English cow is probably named for its curved horns, cornu in Latin, hard prominences or skull prominences (kara- for skull, -nau for protruding or presenting). Kau is two prongs. Unlike chimps, hominids tamed fire and spent hundreds of millennia hunkered around their hearths unnaturally warming their bellies and exercising their minds. Without rushing our fences, that got hominid speech up and running by devious means which will be precised later.

Then as a starter for gaming it is probably best to think in terms of the total absence of any grammatical sense when language was born. It is hard to see how it might have enjoyed a prior development for some extraneous utility with evolutionary survival potential, to be handy to be prayed in aid when language needed a bit of structuring. Nor is the time scale helpful. Nor is it any real answer to allege it is hard wired as part of the human brain structure and function, which is merely another way of expressing the preceding hypothesis. If I sometimes appear to be gunning for Professor Chomsky and his hard wired universal grammarians (mostly unaware of their wiring) I can state positively I remain an admirer of his linguistic expertise without fully espousing his dissident politics. Similarly, I sat at the feet of Eric Partridge for fifteen years before finding the time or the brains to branch out on my own. Reason, which is what makes semantics, is the ability to think half way straight, and it goes back a long way. It must be prior to language, although in the more recent millennia, as language has developed the marriage of thinking and speaking, it has encouraged some people to think speech supports thought and most people to think solely in the terms in which they speak. The latter is of course an intellectual disaster, triggering every kind of obscurantism and vice, not excluding Nazism and the other totalitarian miasmas. We dream in pictures with emotional messages, and hardly at all in words except when they break through the cartoon sequences bearing highly emotional imports – often single words given absurdly significant meanings, like Marlon Brando's "Rosebud!" (which acquired its significance I think because in his acting part he had departed about as far from that ideal of innocence as one could get). It is thinking which from the outset supports, even informs speaking, and it is the thinking, the semantics, which unravels the development of language and now the etymological derivations. Indeed I conceive our word elements to have come down to us in an unbroken semantic catena all the way from our hominid ancestors hundreds of thousands of years ago. That may seem far fetched and an overly long time for a game of Chinese whispers without any recess for refreshments; but every link in the chain was a single one-to-one link between consenting adults, remember; and the shifts between repetitions do indeed show the degree of whimsy or wandering attention we might expect revealed in the semantic record. That is why I have spent a great deal of effort trying to lay out semantic trees tracing the meanings linked to the phonetic utterances and marking the semantic traces in step with the changing phonetics. This is quite different from the traditional derivation of nonsense language roots by a simple evolutionary process, like vegetable evolution which is quite inappropriate for thought processes. The mind does not function as a potato grows either! Skeat's 364 Indo European roots of 1882 for instance, fascinating though these are, are roots with no reason for their being other than as termini from which the phonetic trains supposedly set out. But even if they set out from these buffers, phonetic language trains had semantic carriages attached from the outset, indeed it is readily arguable the semantics actually comprised the prime movers. Language did not spring from nonsense roots, nor proceed along similar lines. The naming committees – it is probably right to think of them as hominid elders hunkered hirsute and bare-bottomed around their hearths many hundreds of thousands of years ago – by a mixture of gesturing, mimicry and reason were trying to work out what was the "natural" meaning which brother Tarzan might hopefully twig from an utterance if he tried hard enough. It must have been desperately frustrating and claustrophobic work, reminiscent of the chimpanzee´s desperate chirruping when trying to communicate. By contrast the stolid gorilla is just a starling keeping his own counsel.

Before speech, the voice was preeminently used as an alarm call, just as the single finger was first regarded as preeminently a tickler, a phein-kara, a pleasure-maker. The Indo European tik for finger is believed to be one of the oldest words and is originally tickler. Even a chimp is cheeky. Maybe a chimp is a go-up like a budgy. What is the semantic catena to get from "Leopard there!" to "Leopard approaching!"; that is to say how is it that ostensives (cries indicative of things) can give birth to verbs (words indicating actions) and the distinction between the two – a grammatical invention: no doubt ex post facto once the usage was established. Some early Shaman will have been hugging himself and justifying a lion´s share of the meat because he could see the distinction clearly. The verb is indeed a sophistication. We go from an undifferentiated state of affairs – the approaching predator – to a precising of an abstract (the verb) from the scene. Perhaps it comes from when the leopard was not there. Perhaps a leopard customarily came that way, judging by his tracks, or a twig snap suggested his approach before he was there. A leopard that may be there or will be there involves a moving world, a world of actions, the world which hominids quite obviously inhabited. Prey take off, birds fly away; ostensives actually take in activities and happenings. Prey-gone must have been an early messaging requirement, just like fruit-unripe or fruit ripe, but in the prey case including action marked by articulation. In any case prey fleet and prey flit are not all that different. In fact if you said fleet loudly and sharply enough in context it would surely be understood as flit. You merely had to draw attention to that character to indicate it was operative right now. Separate nouns verbs and adjectives are all late distincta and the distinctions were hardly called for at the outset. That is not to say the distinctions have not proved handy once they were worked out.

Phonemes

We should next note what it is in Lithic which is to be grammaticised, that is worked up into a structure of thinking. It was single syllabic phonemes already with semantic contents of their own which were the initial elements of speech, and not the words fancied by Skeat and all. Words were not yet composed. They were not yet on the thinkers' menu. We can hypothesise this already from the fact speakers of less developed languages, with small vocabularies for instance, for whom "prestidigitation" or "hyperphosphorylation" would be lengthy sentences, use shorter word elements and often single syllabic phonemes with meanings. We may finish up in imagination, as we go back in time, with the repetitive single mewing of the chimpanzee. Moreover when we come to look into the etymology of numerous languages we soon start to pick up within present day words these semantic nuggets attached to the same phonemes across surprisingly wide fields of application and interpretation. Once the semantic contents of an early phoneme is worked out, usually with a fair indication why the earliest meanings were picked, a whole range of primitive usages together with the early 'grammar' for word making reveal themselves in use, under cover of conventional word construction. We can finish up recognising almost as much of the original Lithic composition as the modern language we profess to speak. That is a bold claim, perhaps over bold, but the book has to be read before deciding.

ORDERING

The first rule of grammar concerns the ordering of speech. If the simplest elements are syllabic phonemes (a consonant and a vowel in other words, the vowel to allow the utterance of the consonant), their ordering is the first concern which can rank as grammar. Originally we may surmise ´Pa-Ka´ (perhaps ´A shelter let us make´) and ´Ka-Pa´ (perhaps ´Let us make a shelter´) were alternative usages: just 'cover-make' or 'make-cover'.

OF

But with consecutive substantive usages, for instance 'Ka-Pa', (perhaps 'root-of the matter') and 'Pa-Ka' (perhaps 'the surface of the earth'), there would I think come to be different semantic contents associated. The ones I offer as examples would perhaps be later and hypersophisticated for a hominid but they are nevertheless illustrative of the differencing which arises. Certainly the simpler the language the more preponderant the polysemy – numerous semantic contents for the same utterances – as well as the more general each individual meaning. This is the birth of the meaning of 'of'. It takes the form a > b and then a of b: a leads; that is all it takes to entail subordination and then dependence and consequence. There is of course no real reason why 'Ka-Pa' might not just as well be read as 'Earth's-Surface' as 'Pa-Ka' be read as 'Surface-of the Earth'. As long as either form was optional the development of the grammatical term óf' was recessive/redundant. It is also relevant some languages do indeed say Earth-of Surface, rather than Surface of-Earth, ie using a postposition in place of a preposition. But what matter? One way or the other the dependence became marked by convention where it was not so marked before. Which way was primal may remain moot. As an English speaker I fancy the route I fancy, thinking the leading element should lead; but would be perfectly content with either.

OTHER HELPER WORDS

It is arguable all the other prepositional and postpositional helper words are conceptually merely glosses in elaboration of the initial apposition and then the dependence derived from it, as just indicated in the case of 'of'. Certainly the way symbolic logic has been used to portray tidy mathematical values as essential building blocks for language is a late fabrication. Such values will hardly have troubled Plain Sapiens (Homo Erectus, now divided up between Erectus who came first, Ergaster second and Heidelbergensis last before Sapiens Sapiens – us) as he struggled to take his first steps towards sapience. To and for, by with and from for instance add greatly to the genitive 'of', but they are not such great leaps away they can not be judged to be from the same stable. Pick any sentence with a preposition in it and substitute 'of' as if wrongly spoken by a learner of English as a foreign language, and the meaning will generally be identifiable with a lively imagination. The meanings are different and distinct but they are grouped in function and will have builded gradually from a single origin.

SURROGATES

Grammar in its fullest sense, it seems to me, first developed with the invention of surrogates, pronouns, this and that, he, who, and adverbs where and whence, whereunto and wheretofor etc. If these are really no more than ostensive nouns they are less obviously so than a mere name. They involve abstraction. 'This' abstracts, from a potential plethora of items present at one time or another, their presentness when they were or are present; and 'that' does the same a little way off. "He" abstracts from persons similarly, present or further off, and can be marked for gender. It is perhaps an appropriate moment to remind readers of the richness of the notation available to be used here. Him refers to the person indicated, while "him" is the utterance, the word "him" (eg he said "him!") and 'him' is the idea of the utterance which lies behind the word, often referred to as if it were the word. For most purposes of course the distinction between the word and its utterance is otiose, but it is sometimes relevant to consideration of the way language has developed, for example which came first, the idea or the utterance. It is no secret I think the idea did. Philosophers, logicians and other pernickety modern folk with a knowledge of symbolic logic to guide them may like to inject further complicating levels of discourse. For instance as well as the utterance (sound) "him" also the word "'him'" written or otherwise symbolised, and then the idea symbolic of that or those in turn. We then have apparently acquired a quiverful of 'words' expressed one way or another! But these frills and fripperies are ignored in what follows.

AND

'And' is a specific (limited) case of 'more'; "more" often being used for both ideas. Hindi "aur" springs to mind: "aur us ke bad" (and after that) for instance and "kuch aur chini" (some more sugar). And is short for "What is more", "there is more to tell you", "moreover". The Lithic elements are aan-da, with the vowel a the extensive vowel here (as will be explained in chapter 15), ongoing, and da which has amongst its semantic contents a meaning close to do (see chapter 6). So and means it goes on, from extending does. The English words may not capture the original semantic contents particularly well, but the original composition makes perfect sense.

NOT

The negative comes from the negative imperative 'don´t!'; but also from the open and empty category, the absence of anything, however illogical that may appear when the two ideas are confronted here. An absence after all in no way negatives a presupposed presence, although if a question be asked "Is x present?" the answer may well be in the negative. But 'negative x' is not present in the way that a negativing of action is called for by a negative injunction, anticipating an action and negativing it at the same time, a 'do' and a negative together. Similarly going and coming are really true opposites like plus and minus, just as in coordinate geometry. There is more to say of true and false negatives when it comes to the consideration of primitive dialectic in chapter 16.

IS AND EQUALS

Equality is a specific limited case of (adjectival) apposition. With 'Earth-surface' the surface does not equal the earth; but with 'tomato-red' the tomato does in a way equal 'red'. It really is red. Equality is in origin simply essence (being) spelt differently, it comes from mere equivalence, equi-valence. The song has it: "One is one and all alone, and evermore shall be so". This perception is not entirely helpful for such as Gotlob Frege looking to award a special stative function to the existential category, which is elsewhere simply omitted.

ADJECTIVES

There is more on the adjectival mind elsewhere in chapter 16. 'Tomato' and 'potato' can be regarded as adjectival (a bundle of qualities merely) rather than as nouns, although this might these days be taken as intellectually eccentric. If it is wished to argue a bundle of qualities must be substantive because the bundle makes it so, a bundle of one should qualify making 'red' a noun too – one hand clapping to confound the critics! That is how the human mind works, wicked though it may be. In explanation tomato is from the Nahuatl "birth death birth", you grow it from seed, while the potato (the same species bred for its tuberous roots) means "tuber birth birth", it is the variety you can propagate by planting a seed potato. Darwinists will be interested in this speciation of the plant at the hands of the husbandmen of old. They certainly do not readily interbreed any longer, although irrigating potatoes immediately after flowering will produce a crop of (poisonous) green tomatoes the size of golf balls instead of boosting tuber growth.

TENSES

To add to the grammatical categories those of temporal discrimination, they may be derived from a lively sense of the here and now, those environmental stimuli actually being experienced which thus denote the time in question as the present time. Time is simply a matter of the observation of the course of events, the scenery changing, the procedures we appear to be in the midst of. Time is the process of becoming which almost everything appears to encounter, originally if the words used have anything to say the process of being born and coming into being. Partridge gives the Indo-European word root as "te-" or "de-" which is from "tai" with a very early semantic content of birthing or becoming. The pundits will argue the oldest word known is tik for the digit; but the Lithic is earlier, identifying the finger as "ti-ka" 'tickler' – for delicate work of all kinds. There is however also the Ancient Egyptian taun meaning the world from ta-u'n, becomings [ie events]-all. The tau is older than the tick or the time (from tai'm).

THE CONDITIONAL MOOD

The conditional "if" comes from the expectational or suggestive sense eg "stay on the ground and you get eaten"; "I give you the meat and you sleep with me"; "if I give you the meat you sleep with me, OK?" If links two propositions, just like and; but with if the linkage extends to another proposition, namely that the two are linked. The difference is nicely caught by the rascal above, flirting in the first pair of propositions linked by and, and buying sex in the second linked by the conditional.

THE VOWEL OON AND ITS SIGNIFICANCE

Primitive grammar is much mixed up with the vowels; and the perception of the vowels is mixed up too; so the primitive vowel dialectic is grammar too, as well as vice versa. The general vowel "a" features as the thesis in this dialectic, the initial posit. The diminutive-reduplicative vowel i features as implicit in but distinguished from the general vowel, budded off as it were, hanging off it, a natural offspring from it, a chip from the block, marked out from it and therefore to that extent already antithetical, "the enemy in the blanket" (musoh dalam selimat in Malay). It is not intended to show that hominids were Hegelians of course. Hominid dialectics were not answerable to Hegelian categories. But their dialectical thinking was as compulsive and insidious as any Kommissar´s, or even more so. It was the human mind at its most vulnerable gyrating in a rut like a crazily cracked gramophone record. It looked like a string of scratched beads, while the Marxian dialectic makes a world fabric more like a chain mail of coathangers (see overleaf). Needless to say neither of these patterns is in any way veridical, merely fanciful[7]. The hominid version is made up of the "-aaaa-" vowel contributing the ongoing lateral scratches; while the contrary (vertical) scratches were its individuations; and the beads, partly there merely to be scratched on, were the encompassing synthetic snapshots, the ooo laid in a row like fish eggs or a television slowed down to individual frames. These are really cosmological ideas blundered into without further analysis, see the Tau-oon added in Figure 1; the wonder is such abstractions came to mind so early on and have nevertheless left their marks in the intellectual ether still within the grasp of linguistics. This latter circumstance indeed calls for some justification, since it will otherwise be dismissed as at best a brilliant piece of extemporisation seeking to illustrate the kind of mental world hominids lived in, but without any particular warrant. Shortly stated, the pattern can be teased from the language, what there was of it. It is not to be expected that a point source of any of this early ratiocination can be uncovered; nor indeed what such a source might conceivably consist of. A longer answer is contained throughout the length and breadth of this book. The origins of speaking presented are early origins, hopefully the earliest obtainable and anyway sufficiently early to shed new light on the nature of speech as well as of thinking.

It is a comical thought hominids may have said "-aaaa-" to examine each others' throats, opening and clearing their laryngeal passages and building an intellectual empire on them. Early utterances will have introduced the mind to the ongoing "-aaaa-". It is perfectly true that an ongoing "-iiii-" can with some slight extra effort be continued for just as long. But this is where the whimsy comes in: you hardly need two exemplars of the same extension, and when shouting out loud aaa wins hands down. The "i" vowel is instead a short pecking plosive one. It actually is diminutive and reduplicative, these terms are not just figures of speech in the common sense of figure of speech. "-oooo-" has to be forced; the lips are forced into a round orifice, just like the birth canal when birthing. Well anyway our hominid forebears thought so. Meanings abound to indicate these points were taken. Words can be found the world over a-shaped (or rather sounded) for wide and long things, for vast spaces and aeons of time. The i shape is indicative of little things and specific things including the tiniest little items; while o is simply oval or round, shrouding altogether the tongue, the little joker in there. Similar selections can be made in almost every language, perhaps in all.

Finally, in order to clear the decks, it should perhaps be asked if language, unlike physical attributes, is properly subject to any kind of Darwinian scheme of evolution. We can guess Darwin thought so. He had read up linguistics, as much as the subject was understood in his day – which was not very much. The East India Company judge Sir William Jones was learning Sanskrit and working out the links with Greek in the 1780s and the Indo-European family of languages was established in Darwin's day, though without the rich evidential working which has blocked out the relationships since Darwin's time. It is however possible the question should be rephrased the other way around. If linguistics suggests that slow changes in the various minutiae of pronunciation and meaning as speech populations move apart to new environments can lead to the development of disparate languages and language groups mutually incomprehensible to native speakers; is it then legitimate to transfer this whole gamut to the quite separate question of physical adaptation of species? Science will answer this question with a clearcut affirmative; yet scientists will not really mean what they say. Their position is really simply a pragmatic one: in effect, never mind where the idea came from, only ask yourself does it work? If it works, don't mend it. The speciation of languages may well have prompted the idea of the speciation of species; but language change owes nothing to natural selection, added for biological speciation.

Looking further at the issue, there is a neat parallel in the origins and evolution of clothing, which can perhaps throw some light on the development of the art of speaking. That clears away the problem of reflexivity which confuses issues when it is a question of speech, and therefore of thinking. Clothing is obviously unnatural and artificial and (less obviously) like speech. The first lady or gentleman to furl a fur about their shoulders, or was it around their waist, was yet another exemplar of the genius of the human species. Was such genius innate? And which in fact came first, figleaf or fur? Was it for warmth, or from an inborn sense of shame as the Bible has it that clothes were first worn? If shame, it was a rather late developer. We ran stark naked like Barbary apes, with no distinction between public and private acts, for hundreds of thousands of years before the first breech clout was invented to cover our sexual organs. Instinctive inputs and outputs after

FIGURE 1

THE LITHIC VOWEL OON

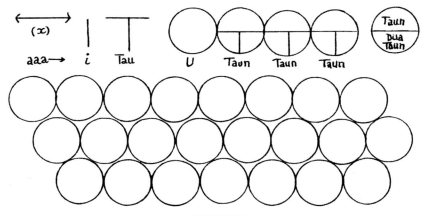

FIGURE 2

HEGEL'S AND MARX'S DIALECTIC

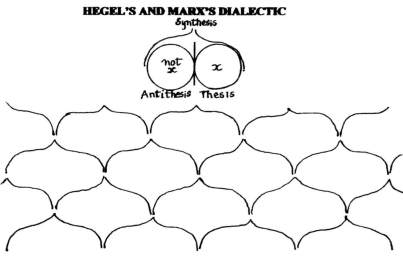

all, are not noted for their delicacy even today. The first breech clout, the Biblical leaf, was surely a purely cultural novelty with a political purpose. The Bible has it: less sex was thought to be correct. It may seem out of place for primitive man to be exhibiting such prudery. But then we do not know the level of sexual activity which obtained at the time. Tribal dropouts addicted to hedonistic tripping all the time make poor hunters, hanging about hopefully in camp when their elders are away hunting and wanting supporters to close the cordon; and anyway boys should be disciplined and their usurpations checked. Body clothing meanwhile was clearly pragmatic to keep away the cold. It marked mankind's spread from the tropics and the hot climatic conditions inducing excess body heat – which over many millions of years had led to the descent in all mammalian species of the testes out of the body cavity in search of a cooler environment. Imagine now the exploring Neanderthal's unadorned gonads, confronted by the chill winds of a barely thawing Europe. Small wonder they called for the first pair of trews, whilst simultaneously retracing their precipitate descent. They still do when a chill wind blows in the Scottish highlands, or immersion in cold water occurs. The advent of underwear, as of footwear, improved performance in rugged conditions; and in the former case there was the further beneficent spin-off so far as establishment thinking was concerned, it reduced the directly competitive element as well. Cold climate also subtly changes the hormone balances in the body so that nowhere can northerners match southerners in our hemisphere in their sexuality. (They make up for it with brains). The body acquired tabu areas with the cold where procedure with due caution was prescribed; and the old men took charge of sexual etiquette, making for some moral high ground out of the thermal requirement. The point is language evolved under the influence of circumstances no more sophisticated, and most probably a lot less so. The thinking in both cases was by our standards crude, undifferentiated, and dominated by the age old preoccupations of dumb self expression, left-overs of millions of years of life before language. Of course primitives did not think solely in terms of their sexual proclivities. But there can be no doubt they must have bulked largest in their repertoire of feelings and responses – if only because extraneous thinking in the absence of vocabulary to express it was peculiarly impoverished by comparison, whereas their emotional promptings were immediate and widely understood. It has always been something to jabber about, it seems. Some of the best established lines of thinking were evidently in the tabu areas. Ab origine, it seems, the Devil had the best lines; and that was because mankind readily conceded them to him. Any author writing on primitive language is confronted with this issue. If he is pilloried for undue fascination with these primitive patterns of thinking, even of having made them up, he can only plead the neurosis, if neurosis it be, is not his but humankind's. Without the acceptance of this human bias, progress in psychosemantics is likely to be scant. The box office spin-off must compensate for any little local embarrassments. When you think of the sensual and pornographic muck on display in bookshops and stationers around the world I shall be cross to be pilloried for it.

So thinking Lithic is a kind of dirty philology; or else it is learning to go for the dirty bits you are served by the lexicon without bothering yourself about it. The way I learned was the hard way, compiling linguistic relationships piecemeal from etymology, always bearing in mind the semantics as well as the phonology, working in a double matrix of sounds and meanings over a theoretically limitless set of instances, the world lexicon from its first accumulation, of which of course I was only sampling the merest smattering.

But then I found myself starting to speak – in my mind only, there was no speaking overtly in tongues, I am pleased to be able to report. I was putting together primitive elements with meanings and getting meaningful strings which matched existing languages. What is more the strings were singing of sex. This was partly perhaps from my own inclinations influencing my perceptions: it was naughty but fun. But there was much more to it than that. Sex is fairly predictable. Sexual experience based on our current physiology probably has not changed all that much over the past few hundreds of thousands of years so it is easier for us to follow the drift of the hominid mind when he or she was thinking of sex than when he was flaking a flint for a tool or gone fishing for instance. This is simply because technology has transmogrified our experience of our handling of tools over the aeons beyond recognition; while we retain more or less standard pattern genitalia over the same time span so that, at first approximation at least, we can take it we still use them much the same as dumb hominids did. I am tempted to say exactly as dumb hominids did. Our sex falls into the coeleocanth category. Professor Chomsky would love it: it can clearly be described as hard wired in our heads from birth. When you are asking yourself "and what could they have possibly meant by that?" it is helpful to be able to narrow the field in the sense of the possible spread of meanings. The strength of the field in the sense of a current or pull narrows the spread of the field. When we emote we concentrate the mind, strait jacketing our thinking: the spectrum culminates in orgasm at emotional full throttle when thinking practically ceases: in salacious slang the little death. Anyway you are momentarily intellectually laid to rest. As T E Lawrence opined, that may be part of the attraction for the intellectually ill equipped; though perhaps he was slyly excusing his own pathetic lack of performance in that department.

So sex has these two handy keys to unlock the earliest meanings in human speech: it probably has not changed much, so our prejudiced perceptions of it do not spoil our thinking much; and the range of likely meanings is in any case fairly narrow. As we shall see they stretch little beyond a pattern of outlines taken directly from the shapes of our sexual organs and their responses to arousal.

Not only these two handy keys but hominids seem to have thought about the subject even more, in a world where pleasurable indulgences were few – the warmth of the sun (which brought them to sexual reverie again), a full belly (ditto), a smiling child (perhaps the same again), the excitement of the chase and the kill (well the boys at least may have been able to forge a connection), and best of all a safe warm place round the fire in the hearth to lie at night, and the orgasm with a partner that would often follow. There was no television, no soaps, no sport, no property or shopping or fashion to think about, not even much in the way of mental abstraction to occupy the mind; only survival skills with sex the unchallenged hobby for all, still remembered as the garden of Eden, A-i-dain, the first-it-dawning, or The Dawn of the Day, that is to say the garden in the East. There we find Adam, the aa-da'm, the first-born'him, the first man, his navel a question mark.

And not only that, thinking itself is introversion. So you start by mulling over your own internal data rather than conceptualising the outside world: that is left to be built subconsciously just as it was before the mind got round to thinking about thinking, that is to conscious thought. Our mental world was thus built in the image of our own bodily design to a degree which now ranks as absurdity; but our first thinking forebears could not see it. We just identified our own bodies and then we went on to identify the rest of the world under those preconceived categories; we anthropomorphised the world as if it was the most natural thing to do – just more of the same as we experienced in effect. We can see now that there was an inbuilt egotistical streak in this, a natural autism every infant starts from – which has not gone away. Moreover it was probably inevitable, with this plan of attack, that the bodily motifs that we most liked to think about mostly got hung on the scenery. We have inherited a sexually charged lexicon which must leave Mrs Grundy incredulous and lightly stunned, and may even be providing the subconscious sexual pump leading to sexual recidivism in modern times. We have this sexual reservoir which we have stored in our language, which the subconscious mind can read and obtain arousal from. It is really no more far fetched to believe so than to credit the direct visual and multimedia stimulation of television with a copycat effect for the weak willed and suggestible. We are after all what we think about to an astonishing degree, or at least we were until we learned to prevaricate, or sublimate in Freud´s rather Victorian terms, so as to switch course and go about on another emotional tack – making Sapiens into Fraudster, and incidentally filling the asylums with simpletons who have got knotted. There is still in our mental world a strong bodily and particularly sexual penumbra which invades and distorts our perception of reality. At one remove, Darwinism is about discovering the importance of breeding and sex in the world, which was probably another reason why it caused such a stir on publication, to add to the atheism it appeared at the time to imply. But we should perhaps first stop to ask who put it there in the first place. Perhaps it was the first born (A-dam) in us, and the chauvinism packaged with him. We live in a made up world, we have developed everything in it on our own terms. Of course we have taken note of the spatial environment in which we live, because when we have not we have been tripped up. But everything that has been recorded in all the encyclopedias ever written, as well as everything that wasn't, has been spun like gossamers out of our own heads.

In Egypt five thousand years ago they still retained some of the earliest ideas of physiology. The Ka phoneme still stood for hard structure, for instance the bones of the body, the skeleton which determined its shape and performance and gave the possessor his drive and his will power as well as his locomotive abilities; and it was all male. In classical times it became known as form. This is without prejudice to the definition of a skeleton as a mummy or dried up body, from the Lithic ish-kai-lai-tau'n, fire-struck-liquid-become'n, one that has had all the liquid element in it dried up. The Greek skellein to dry up and skleros dried, dry, make this clear. Ka has many roles, even in a single occupancy. The Ba was the fleshly matter clinging round and covering the bones and it was female. Every man and woman and every animal each of their own kind such as found their way into the ark had both ka and ba, skeletal structure and flesh surrounding it; but the men had more ka and the women more ba. Women's job in life was to put the ba round the ka in the womb, a bit like a bun in an oven. The ka was magically introduced, indeed rammed home by the male at intercourse, the planting of the seed (ma-sai in Lithic, mau-sai or mai-sai in Ancient Egyptian, transliterated on occasion moshe or -mese as in Iau-moshe (sometimes shortened to Moshe) and Ra-mese, born of Ra (who planted the seed – or life); in Greek the Heiros Gamos the sacred ka-maus, making of the implantation, or marriage: in church now the mass, the planting, or in this case better the ingestion of the life of the Messiah, the Saviour implanting eternal life, symbolically ingested[7].

Moreover a full Ka was double, one for this world and one for the next. The traces are just about universal. The Malays dubbed their aboriginals in the jungle Sakai, single Ka'd folk without any expectations in the hereafter, just animals really with no souls whom it was not unjust therefore to kill at any time, since they had no preparations to make or homework to complete to secure a better future in the hereafter because they had none. In Hawaii the Uku-lele or singing insects (the grasshopper and cricket) is Englished Ukulele or grasshopper because the instrument makes a stridulent noise like a grasshopper, an uku which lai-lai. It was an uku because it wore both its Kas in this world, thorax and body together, which surely boded ill for any future in the next world. Some insects could even be seen to pupate and then come out by the self same door as in they went. Anyone reincarnated as an uku or dual-ka'd in this world was for the final chop on death.

Was that what made them sit up and sing so? We just say insect, because its body is nearly cut in two. Meanwhile the Japanese seek to strengthen their Ka by means of Karate, getting it to ra-tai, become raised or roused. It is a psychological activity in inspiration as well as just a physical technique, apparently originally a sadistic exercise. Perhaps these primitive psychosemantic phonemes were invented in the garden of Eden, now apparently finally located between Malaya, the garden country, and Borneo, pig country where the pig or boar farmers were, before the whole of the flat fertile alluvial plain between the two was flooded with the last great prehistoric melting of the ice. That makes the Lithic Hypotheses less hard to believe, but detracts from the arguments I have put forward in favour of Lithic elements being dreamed up universally just because they have psychosemantic meanings attached to uttered sounds as a result of prompts from the subconscious human psyche, the concealed workings of Sapiens' mind. I still intend to have my Eden cake and at the same time dine out on the Lithic Hypotheses however. Hawaii, Japan, Malaya and Egypt with a spot of Aztec thrown in is quite a good spread for almost anything before the combustion engine. But I can make sense of the Ka phoneme a great deal more widely still. As well as Wakan Tanka the Aztec Creator God in central America which is almost pure Lithic speak: Wa-make Taun-make: Shiver-maker world-maker: Awesome Creator. The Aztec Tan- (forget the spelling) is almost an exact doublet with Egyptian Taun for the universe; as well as the –tain in Britain. I have slipped in a scandalous trap to trip the shallowly erudite there, since you need to have cracked the Greek Pretani to find any relevance of the Aztecs to Britain. Similarly I can not resist defining a scandal from scandalon as is-kan-da-laun all in Lithic elements, an action which-making [you do]-a-down-slide", or slip, or trap when correctly etymologised. You only become a scandal in English when so tripped or trapped. There is no necessary immorality even when it is most glaring. These historical elaborations do nothing for the hypothesis that Lithic phonemes were at the origins of speaking since that was hundreds of thousands of years prehistoric. But by the same token they do point up the pervasiveness in human thinking of psychosemantic elements, if their original presence can be conceded on other grounds.

It is these other grounds my book will go in search of. By flooding the following chapters with examples of Lithic derivations across the board I hope to put a different gloss on the hypotheses. If the pattern was not always with us, some reason must be found for switching to it just in the last few thousand years after using a completely unknown and simply conjectural alternative system up till then.

Notes

1. Revd Skeat, professor of Anglo Saxon at Queens College, Cork. An Etymological Dictionary of the English Language, 1879-82. See Appendix B.

2. Benjamin Jowett, a famous Oxford savant who claimed in the nineteenth century to have trained the civil service which governed the British Empire was lampooned by his students:
My name is Benjamin Jowett,
I'm the Master of Trinity College.
Whatever is known – I know it,
And what I don't know – ain't knowledge!

3 Boolean mathematical rules in linguistics come from George Boole (1815-1866), Professor of Mathematics at Queens College, Cork, whose algebraic logic provided a calculus for proving syllogisms by means of algebraic symbols for logical terms, 'clarifying' the meanings of grammatical terms.

4 Last in the line is the American guru Noam Chomsky.

5 Academics may recognise Lumpers and Splitters in Wayland and Scrimshaw.

6 The Greek "etumon" is analysable in Lithic elements as 'a-i-tau-mau'n' = 'first-which-born-meanings, or perhaps '1t-that-which-natural-meanings', or even both. "Mau" is most readily treated as a past participle "meant" or "minded"; but it is also easily understood as "meaning". There is also in the present form of "etumon" a missing "a" in the Tau element proposed. But this is a common elision, since there appears to have been some ambivalence in the minds of those who spoke in those days whether the vowel marker (in this case the –u) should be added as a modifier or a replacement for the general vowel form.

7 The metaphysical speculations of this paragraph are not repeated here in aid of belief. Faith is a separate matter to be decided on moral grounds.

CHAPTER 4

THE PHONEME BA

The Lithic hypotheses propose that when mankind first began to speak Ba was identified as the sound made by lip on lip – which is simple fact – and that the meanings attributed to the Ba phoneme thereafter, over hundreds of thousands of years, can all be derived from this original derivation of flesh on flesh, lips and mouth and all the other fleshly derivatives. Ba is the simplest and earliest sound of articulated language. There will have been earlier screams and cries prompted by the human psyche and its instinctive responses to stresses; but Ba was the first sound recollected in tranquility and thought through, and its thinking given a symbolic meaning. Ba was also already the primal linguistic sound because it is the first babble made by the infant when it apparently has nothing particular on its mind, the sound which comes from the human mouth parts when otherwise undirected. Every mother knows this and has surely done so for hundreds of thousands of years regardless of what language she spoke – or even if she spoke none at all. In English we have baby from the Lithic phonemes babai, quite simply echoic of babbling, ba-ba-ing going ba-ba; and the meaning can easily be traced in many other tongues. The novelty of the Lithic hypotheses is tracing the meanings of each individual sound instead of just treating sounds as vaguely suggestive of poetic tone.

In the psychosemantic tree opposite and the lists of words that follow are some of the derivative meanings arising from the initial flesh and mouth meanings. These are taken from actual usages today, not all in English. The problem with making out psychosemantic trees for every phoneme in turn is that very few words rely for their their semantic contents on a single phoneme. So words adduced as incorporating a meaning of the phoneme Ba, for instance, depend also on the many other psychosemantic contents of the other phonemes in the words. Each chapter headed for its principal phoneme is bound therefore to trespass upon the others, including those to come. You really need to read all the phoneme chapters to fully follow any one of them. This is a character of language rather than just a shortcoming in the author's scheme of arrangement. It does call for some repetition, but repetition is an aid in learning a language, even so elementary a one as Lithic. The tedium involved is unavoidable. There is only so much novelty and excitement that can be extracted from the meanings of Ba, even as an exemplar of the Lithic language theses.

Readers of the proofs have been almost uniformly puzzled by the imagined ontological implications of the present tense of the verb to be, and have responded by asking for an explanation up front. When it is argued Ba "is" the sound of lip on lip, in what way exactly "is" it? Being is always debatable in Western languages because a verb has been found for it. In Malay by contrast the problems disappear: they are simply not mentioned. My own instinct in this is Malay. But where I write in English "a is b" I mean approximately a equals b, and by that I mean there is an equivalence – not a congruence as language philosophers have imagined. The equivalence I generally have in mind is semantic, but it may instead be phonetic or both. There is no special space or time these entities inhabit. So Ba is the sound we make exploding air with the lips pursed together, and it is therefore the sound of flesh on flesh and meant and means basically flesh: so Ba "is" flesh (see column 4 in the psychosemantic tree). The statement is meant to be simply factual. There is not meant to be any magic or alchemy in it. "Is" should perhaps be read as "symbolises". The two letters ba are not made flesh, they have just come to symbolise it, and as a matter of fact I believe the symbolisation, after many thousands of generations using it, is deeply embedded in the human lexicon, and thus also in the human subconscious. There is nothing added surreptitiously about the nature of flesh, nor of the linguistic element Ba, nor of the ways we think and apprehend meanings. There is admittedly a stated synchronicity about "is", but it is the synchronicity of the laws of science merely, which does not prohibit them from extending into the past and prospectively into the future, although it does perhaps urge caution in cases where it is germane to distinguish between the synchronic and diachronic, between science and history for example.

THE PSYCHOSEMANTIC TREE FOR BA

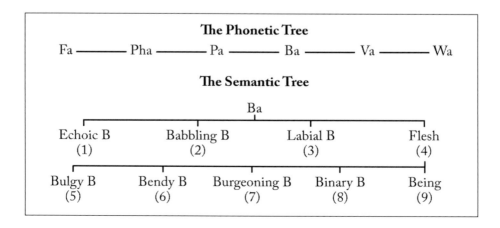

THE PSYCHOSEMANTIC TREE FOR BA

PAGE 2 EXAMPLES.

Column 1	Column 3	Column 5	Column 5
BAH!	LABIAL B	BULGY B	(cont)
Bang	Bab (Arabic)	Bulgy	Belly
Banga (Old Norse)	Bouche (French)	Bungey	Banana
Boo!	Bucca (Latin)	Bung	Bar
Buzz	Ba'al Zebab (Hebrew)	Bum	Barbeque
Bee	Bab I Laun (Akkadian)	Bub	Barbakoa (Arawak)
Abeille (French)	Bite	Bust	Barang (Malay)
	Bait	Breast	Sumbat (Malay)
	Bit	Bosom	Lembu (Malay)
	Bibere(Latin)	Bottom	Gambar (Malay)
Column 2	Bay	Buttock	Brown
BABBLING B	Baa	Bone	Balkans
Baby	Bark	Boa (Latin)	Belang (Malay)
Baba	Gbe (Fon)	Bag	Belit (Malay)
Baba (Spanish)	Indaba (Zulu)	Bas (French)	Semblit (Malay)
Babador (Spanish)	Liber (Latin)	Buoy	Bongkah (Malay)
Bib	Bahasa (Malay)	Bwoid(Gaelic)	Kembang (Malay)
Babosa (Spanish)	Bugle	Boy	Labuan (Malay)
Bueh (Malay)	Book	Budak (Malay)	Bu (Chinese)
Bumbo (Italian)	Bab el Mandeb (Arabic)	Bobo (Spanish)	Tumboh(Malay)
	Sebab (Malay)	Bodoh (Malay)	Bakelos (Malay)
	Bacha(Malay)	Brain	Avocado(Quechoa)
	Bantai (Malay)	Bank	Bocado (Spanish)
	Blah	Bund (Hindi)	Bunga (Malay)
	Babuine (Old French)	Bund(German)	Bull
	Baboon	Bend	Abang (Malay)
	Bader (Provencal)	Bind	Bagus (Malay)
	Bacalar (Spanish)	Bahei (Egypt)	
	Ban	Bare	
	Batare (Latin)	Button	
	Beak	Babi (Malay)	
		Bor (Senoi)	
		Borbi(Senoi)	
		Buah (Malay)	

THE PSYCHOSEMANTIC TREE FOR BA.

PAGE 3 EXAMPLES

Column 6	Column 7	Column 8	Column 9
BENDY B	BIOLOGICAL B	BINARY B	BEING
HAUNCH	BURGEONING		
LEG	LIFE	Body	Be
GO	Bion (Greek)	Bottom	Be-
Ba (Egyptian)	Verde (Spanish)	By	Ber- (Malay)
Bous (Greek)	Brer	Buttuc (Old English)	Become
Baino (Greek)	Bough	Balluc (Old English)	Behet (Albanian)
Bear	Bud	Butt	Liber (Latin)
Aber (Gaelic)	Bad	Bulrush	Seberang (Malay)
Nabi (Arabic)	Bor (Bornean)	Ambi (Latin)	
Naib (Arabic)	Barra (Hindi)	Bind	
Labalaba (Malay)	Besar (Malay)	Badhna (Hindi)	
Berbaling (Malay)	Labu (Malay)	Bashki (Albanian)	
Bilabong (Oz Abo)	Rambutan (Malay)	Bilanx (Latin)	
Baji (Oz Abo)	Bengala (Bengali)	Bellum (Latin)	
Boomerang (Oz Abo)	Bawang (Malay)		
Burong(Malay)	Bulb		
Terbang (Malay)	Bamboo (Malay)		
Bangli (Hindi)	Buloh (Malay)		
Bangle	Kebun (Malay)		
Beliong (Malay)	Boabab (Hamitic)		
Bamboula (Creole)	Babul (Bengali)		
Lambat (Malay)	Nave	**Column 7**	
Bangsat(Malay)	Navis (Latin)	**Continued**	
Bintang (Malay)	Beam	Brank (Breton)	
Boleh (Malay)	Board	Bhura (Sanskrit)	
Balek (Malay)	Barn	Brinnan (Gothic)	
Belakang (Malay)	Barm (Swedish)	Bachelor	
Balalaika	Bergen (Swedish)	Bhura (Sanskrit)	
	Biarg (Old Norwegian)	Bachelor	
	Biargahei (Gothic)		
	Beorh (Old English)		
	Barrow		
	Burrow		
	Brand		
	Burning		
	Brank (Breton)		
	Brinnan (Gothic)		
	Burning		

In the next chapter there is written at the outset more challengingly ka is the chink or clink of flint on flint. Historically it was so perceived; but now it can only derivatively be read into the semantic record. The identification is there beneath the surface of our conventional thinking, in the subconscious. That is the Lithic hypothesis. Both Ba and Ka are, in their different ways, echoic. Ba´s meaning is a reflexive echo of its phonetic form, or as our Lithic forebears would probably have phrased it had they addressed the matter, discovered from the way it is born. While Ka´s meaning derives from the commoner ostensive kind of echo imitating something else out there: Cuckoo!, or A´ma ooh! (Ancient Egyptian for the night owl´s cry, making it at once a knowledgeable bird, hunting at night and calling out the message in Ancient Egyptian "It´s dark, beyond a peradventure" and at the same time the hunting cry "I´m out to kill you all", the hunting cry our primitive ancestors read into the owl´s hooting. Small wonder it later became the hieroglyph or symbol for the letter m). Obviously Ka´s flint chink is not factual in that we do not take two flints and clink them together each time we come to a K, but instead contract the glottis originally in supposed linguistic immitation of the clinking flints. But then it may be argued nothing is gained by imagining the flints: please leave out the imagination. Unfortunately for this argument, leaving out the imagination when studying language roots is to abort the exercise before it is begun. Language is all about imagination and the articulation of those images which have seemed good or useful to plain Sapiens, and then to Sapiens Sapiens as we have shambled through history. If we wish to be able to examine meanings then we need to be able to follow human thinking – a point largely missed by the current brew of academic semanticists as a result of the fashionability in soft science at present of semi mathematical schematics based on symbolic logic – just because it sounds like hard science that way.

Then abandon any pretence of science, one can hear from certain quarters, and admit you have produced an essay in free composition. But this won`t do either. It is a fact that words have and always have had meanings. The statement is indeed tautological; since a word can be defined as a mouthed sound string with explicit meaning. If it has no explicit meaning it is not a word in the strictest sense; but perhaps a cry, a sigh, or just a tune, or even a plain grunt. The origins of speaking find Sapiens admittedly at free composition – though it may be argued the human mind fell into particular phonetic wrinkles and semantic ruts much as water runs downhill. – that is as the largely mindless agency of determining circumstance. There is indeed, it is suggested in this book, some patterning behind (or over and above) human imagination, but it is never immediate and incontravertible like water´s urge to be off into the lows, but on the contrary mediated by the whimsical, inconsequential, mischievous and thoroughly understandable mind of the species.[1] Language was in fact invented by bare bottomed bushmen, and there is still a bare bottomed bushman in each of us today, living cosily in the subconscious of every present day speaking phenotype, his and her character floating from generation to generation aboard the lexicon in which he and she lodge.

In any case yesterday's happenings are today's facts. It is too late to proceed as if we have not spoken or can not speak; or in any way as if it can not be allowed to count. Science properly investigates facts, certainly disputing them all the way. Ideas too are facts, though not easily ascertainable ones. The joke is the hardest of sciences today still treats solely of ideas, allowing some to masquerade as wholly objective data because it appears that they are empirically obtained. Mental states on their own are hard to obtain empirically and that is why meanings are apt to be counted out of linguistic science. Science claims to find out how; and sometimes adds never mind why. This study does mind why, however. It uses language as a factual record of the meanderings of the mind; and by building a library of cross references to different usages extracts a pattern for inspection. The pattern suggests a Lithic language underlies extant languages, with original elements in words, preserved like flies in amber. The pattern is described as if it existed, as if its existence were a fact. That is the hypothesis. The truth of the matter is testable by reference to language use which is on record. The method is bold, but it is fully scientific.

Ba (1), then, may be described as the sound of the pursed lips breaking wind, a labial plosive in the linguistic jargon. The point is our forebears actually took it as such and ascribed it the meaning of the fleshy surrounds of the mouth when, ignorant savages though they no doubt were, they researched carefully in their minds its proper or natural meaning in order to get an agreed meaning across to brother Tarzan hunkered next door. It is a claustrophobic scenario. Here are all these hominids wanting to communicate and share their concerns, as yet unable to do so more than in the barest outline with hoots and shrieks, emotional vowelisations. An utterance must surely have been taken to mean simply what it was. Some sounds – the hoots and shrieks par excellence – naturally expressed the state of play in your neighbour's mind because they were evoked spontaneously on account of human psychology, common to all, which you knew evoked them. If you moaned when your stomach ached you could guess when your immediate neighbour in the cave moaned similarly she had food poisoning too – probably just like you from eating rotten meat, did either of you but know it; or if later perhaps she was solicitous about your ache she was doing the very same sums.

But some sounds did not accompany any particular physical or emotional state – you could blow bubbles at any time – and these sounds if they had meanings, if they were to carry any message, must have meanings more lightly marked which were more subtle, which were anybody's guess almost. The only common focus likely to have occurred was the established reflexive one of reference to the functionality of the production of the sound. Those sounds which were without deep meanings, coming from behind them as it were, had shallower meanings coming just from their utterances. Inconsequentially perhaps it was here at this shallow level – distanced from determined thought sequencing – that the intellect acquired scope and was tested. With our first true words, the human mind was first allowed to wave around, like a caterpillar at the end of a twig, in search of a further firm purchase, all firm and established cries and groans left fairly far behind it. Reflexivity – reference back to a causative precursor for a meaning – was not in itself a novelty. No doubt for most hominids the fear and the shriek, the pain and the groan simply coalesced in their minds, just as the letter A and the sound a coalesce today when learned by rote. But some – the jokers perhaps – could surely see there was a difference between a sound and its meaning. It was the first stage of abstraction, leading to conceptualisation galore in due course. The meaning of Ba appeared causative because the meanings of moans and groans were causative: Ba simply referred to the fleshy borders of the mouth where the sound came from, perhaps fleshier more prehensile and expressive then than now, if apes are anything to go by. The major point to be grasped is that subtler meanings were accessed naturally enough by analogy from the coarser meaning systems based on stomach aches and pains.

It is therefore proposed as a first rule the original meanings of sounds should be derived from their methods of utterance unless there is a good reason for deriving them otherwise. Two good reasons are stomach aches at one end of the scale and onomatopoeia (echoism) at the other: the Ouches and the Cuckoos as mnemonics if you like. These two derivations also exemplify the reflexive and ostensive derivations of meanings respectively, distinguishing what is experienced personally and what is observed to occur out there, a trick essential for much understanding and hardly achievable without language to tag the thinking. In the reflexive case the mind thinks "You'll know what I mean when I make this noise because you have experienced it yourself from within (if your stomach has ever ached)". In the ostensive case it thinks "You'll know what I mean when I make this sound because you have experienced it yourself out there (if you have ever heard a cuckoo)". With sounds unattached to either of these kinds of prompts the mind is going to have to think "You'll know what I mean when I make this noise (which we do not ourselves experience within and do not hear out there) if you follow your instinct and relate its meaning to its cause and just think hard what causes it – the lips breaking wind". "It is just caused whenever we use our lips to make it. It has no deeper message, it is not to be found in the instinctive vocabulary. That is the secret. It is a reflexive ostensive, an Ouch which is only a Cuckoo after all!" That is an achievement humankind can still boast of, thought through without the use of language to tag the thinking.

We can deduce all this from the many meanings we find in words with this Ba element in, an overwhelming number of which can be shewn to hark back to this original meaning. Such meaning traces of course, since we have come a long way since lift off however many hundreds of thousands of years ago, are elaborate and amount to semantic trees like pedigrees which are illustrated diagrammatically in the chapters for each element. Moreover it has to be accepted that a good deal of slovening and blurring has occurred since man began to speak. The principal fascination of the Lithic hypothesis is the thought that any trace of thinking thought so long ago – of the order of hundreds of thousands of years – could possibly survive the ravages of time. Indeed it has been argued dismissively it is impossible because of the effect of noise on any communication. However these noise theorists do not allow for the refresh rates of instinctive cognoscenti able to pick up the traces of the original system and repeat it, thereby renewing the traces. One would admittedly have hardly expected such a chain of refreshment to have stretched for such a long span of time, were it not for the linguistic evidence that it has, pervading all languages as it does. Then the reflection arises, if there is such refreshment there is no reason why it should not continue indefinitely. Perhaps the spread of written notations in historical times has for the first time jeopardized this refreshment rate so that after hundreds of thousands of years when it was old hat (or witchcraft even) Lithic language is now for the first time in danger of being lost, a bit like the recognised younger individual "aboriginal", (ie small vocabulary harsh sounding) languages around the world, as those in the know die out.

Technically a pedigree or crane's foot is a network of diachronic strings; except in Chomskyan linguistics where they are used sideways for synchronic patterns of grammatical structure. Another of the fascinations of understanding the Lithic contributions to current language is the ability to pursue the interconnections of meanings and the way they have proliferated, on an everyday basis – almost while speaking. It is also possible to work through a dictionary (in any language, if the script is known) sidelining the meanings which bear traces of Lithic meanings: a good dictionary to use in English is Eric Partridge's Origins: A Short Etymological Dictionary of Modern English, first published in 1958. Partridge already groups words which are akin, so that a good deal of the preliminary research is already presented. My own copy has been given a buckram binding, now itself in need of repair, and is disfigured with decades of graffiti in the margins. Of course confining research to English only weakly supports the Lithic thesis, but few readers speak many languages, and fewer the same ones, so you quickly lose readership if you try any fancy footwork. Nevertheless, use is made of foreign material known to me whenever it seems sufficiently important to warrant the necessary explanation.

Ba is the middling sound the mouth makes when it is uninformed, as when a baby just babbles. That is why a baby is so named, a babbler (2), and baba (the original form) is better than baby. The baboon (3) is similarly named for his prehensile lips from the French babines, lips. Oo is the intensive vowel, Mister Lippy. Beelzebub comes out of the same cupboard. Ba'al ZeBab has been translated from the Hebrew as Lord of the Flies. A Mr White has written a book under that title. Ba'al was a heathenish god of the early Jews. Perhaps "Mouth (Voice) of the Lord" is better, a prescriptive deity. "Zebab" is literally "sting mouth" or more literally still "hot lips". Compare the Bantu Tse-Tse fly, Sting-Sting. These were vicious killer flies with stings like hornets, not the ordinary house flies. Ba'al Zebab was the Voice of the Lord and the Scourge of His People, and we can fit him into the Old Testament the more easily for knowing it. The Spanish meanwhile notice the baby's bubbling as well as its babbling: bebe is baby and baba is slobber, a babador is a bib to catch the slobber and balbucar is to stammer (a wet stammer evidently); and babosa is a slug with a slimey gait all of his own. The –s-, like the one which appears in the Spanish slug (and the English slug too whose activity is slow going), is often dismissed as a simple emphatic to account for its presence, but actually it often acts as a marker for an activity, see chapter 14 where this semantic content of the sibilant is derived from the flame which says ish as it is drowned.

For Ba, however, Arabic has the plum: bab (3) meaning mouth; with the two fleshy protruberances actually represented with a gap between, with unusual Semitic directness. The mouth is open and talking already – perhaps arguing its own case? From mouth bab comes also entry or door or gate or even straits at sea, like the Bab el Mandeb, the Straits of Tears at the entrance to the Red Sea. Ancient Babylon was at the Bab-i-Lu or Bab-i-Laun in Assyrian or "Gateway of the salt marshes"; or some say of Al Lahu, God, though the topography at the time seems to favour the salt marshes: either way nothing to do with babbling over a tower construction (or even a ziggurat) as the Bible makes out, and much as London (Lau-'n-don) is estuary or salting-terminus of the river.in the Mediterranean (provincial Punic) lingua franca spoken by the early colonists of Britain – all apparently eaten afterwards by the invading Celts, head hunters then with a taste for fresh brains for tea. The Carthaginians in turn spoke a provincial Egyptian, so our earliest colonists brought traces of the Egyptian tongue to Britain. Already in prehistoric times London was occasioning a good deal of pile driving and really already crying out for a tidal barrage. In this connection it is irresistible to include here the Lithic derivation of Wimbledon where the modern game of lawn tennis is played, originally Wimblendon (6), "oo-im-ba-lai-en-don", in Lithic "where-him-go-looping-of-river" or "where-him-belly-of-river", where good old Father Thames, still in his old river bed, loops round Wimbledon Hill to bear witness to this derivation. This is as close to Egyptian as Celtic. Belly derives from the fleshy sense of Ba, allied to an adjectival "-lai" which can be perceived as loopy and slack or lye to the taste, or most likely both in origin, or sometimes one and sometimes the other depending upon race and speech idiom as well as gastronomic experience. The La derivations are in chapter 9. These occasional long Wimbledon style strings do make it difficult to see how the Lithic style of analysis can be found to be a total miasma. Monkeys eventually typing the Bible would have to be prayed in aid, and it still might take them longer than the relatively short time which has passed since man began to speak to generate an alternative scheme of arrangement retrospectively.

Meanwhile not a thousand miles away but many thousands the Australian aborigines arrived, independently one must suppose, at their own analysis of the meaning of Ba. Their fleshy bits included the haunches as well as the lips. It is the rump which is called into play when going walkabout, the bulging musclature bends the legs. So Ba (6) came to carry the meaning to leg it and go, and not only for Australian aborigines either. In Queensland a bird is a baji, a Go-up. Just when you caught up with it, it took off and went-up. Ji is up in Lithic, see chapter 14 on the phoneme ish. A ba-ji-djeri-gara or budgerigar is a Go-up-of bright-colour as elucidated in that chapter. Odd the fanciers fancy budgy for their birds?

But to begin with it is the mouth which bites, giving us a bit, bitten off, and we can see it also imbibes; we may even be bibulous. The mouth it is which speaks. In English we bawl and bellow, lip and tongue (see chapter 9 for La, the tongue or taster as well as the linguist); in Hindi it is bolna to speak, lip and tongue again, while in Queensland in North Australia bal is speak or speaker. We can perhaps see in this speech the Ba supplies the stops required for articulation while La provides the vowels especially when loud or sung out, going "La". We say just bang when it is the plosive on its own required just to mimic the noise, and a hound bays and a sheep baas, although there is not really any b in the sounds they make. The hound's sound is all vowel, and the sheep's has a trace of a maa, not a baa at all.

The flesh itself has many derivations. Over the millennia these have been exhaustively mined and explored by metaphor and analogy. The animal and vegetable kingdoms were less distinguished in early days. Flesh was bungy, bulging, billowing and burgeoning. To be fleshed or fleshy was all these. To be fleshy gave us our bums, bottoms and buttocks, our bubs, busts, breasts and bosoms. To be bare was with the flesh visible, since –rai or –re is visible in chapter 13. Siti and so –st is the feminine marker of the sedentary sex in early days minding the hearth and the kids while the men were out loping after game (chapter 14 for the sibilants). Our bottoms and buttocks are cut, split or twinned burgeons, see chapter 6. The binary symmetry of the human "body" (the twin burgeon, in two divisions, left and right sides) gives us our bicycles and also our biscuits and balances, just like the two cheeks of our behinds, side by side and beside each other, and the hanging pans both level when you have a balance.

Latin ambi (8) for both or twin (Lithic elements a-'m-bai, or as-him-fleshed) results in bi- being used for twin or adjectival (or adverbial) two; and could have saved Eric Partridge and others the lost labour as well as the inconsequence of deriving bi- from an imagined dwi-, supposed progenitor of Latin dua (which derives its duality quite independently, from the supposed sound of snapping in two, see chapter 6) When it comes to making things up, such debonair transposal of quite different consonants, even allowing for sandhi[2], is hard to justify and smacks of saving the system – although the elision of neighbouring sounds is frequent, given time, and always has to be taken into account. But d and b are not readily interchanged, although either can convey doubling. The same side by side arrangement of bodies, with an element of punning perhaps, and after several in-termediate steps, also accounts for by and beside. Agential by at first seems some way from beside. What it shares is a half linking with the accompanying item, in the case of a propinquitous one the proximity (the besidedness, like the two sides of the body with its bilateral symmetry) rather than juncture while agency is denoted (with a passive verb) by near action, ie without the fully active case of a grammatical subject. By in the sense of before, or at any rate no later than, shares its branch of the semantic tree with the earlier mentioned bai, the haunch which does the going, temporal as well as spatial. Compare the Hindi phrase, cropping up frequently in legal cases where evidence is being extracted painstakingly from an uncomprehending and frightened witness: "aur us-ke ba(r)d...", "and after that...", literally "and that-of the after(the gone by)", where ba(r)d is substantive and has the sense gone by or passed or the past (of it). Almost every one of these small over-worked words has been tailored over the aeons almost beyond belief, to accommodate a clutch of meanings supposedly related.

The Oxford English Dictionary has 39 meanings for by. So a clear-cut defini-tion of the ablative case is not easy. In Latin, schoolboys are taught it means by, with or from. But of course it does not. There is no such concept embracing three such different meanings as these. The original native speakers of Latin evidently did not recognise them and made do with another. The concept of the ablative case which they had was the more general one of a kind of obliquity or deposition or setting aside from the main stream of their line of thought, to be taken as "be-sides" or "in parentheses" or even "and by the way, in passing". It did not include our later and greater precisions. So these now have to be translated back to the older simplistic Roman model of reality in Latin, which at least enabled the Romans to manage without our more precise categories until someone thought them up. Not every schoolboy even gets as far as spotting the "with" he gabbles does not cover propinquity. The Latins had another construction altogether for that, cum meaning adjoined or in company with, and not apart. The ablative with was only used adverbially: "he pressed on with the wind whistling in his ears and with a heavy heart" for example. It may be thought the wind was close beside him and he had his heart with him, but that is not in the Latin construction which merely reports these circumstances as an aside from the main action, which was the pressing on. "With the fought battle, Caesar moved his legions to winter quarters" makes the point clearer. It is better translated perhaps "with the battle fought…" or "after the battle…". There was a fought battle in the background as it were, while in the foreground Caesar might have been observed moving his legions in the here and now into camp. Pliny's description of the column of smoke over Vesuvius, when the eruption killed his father, as rising "with a long trunk not unlike a pine tree" used the form (from memory) "in longo trunco" for "in a long trunk" – not unlike a pine tree he added. The long trunk was a circumstantial fact. The trunk was not noticed as joined or in company with anything else; it was the trunkish columnar length remarked which was a separately observed fact as it rose.

Not only that but the fleshly state is a biological state (7) with vegetable tissue counting too, like boughs, branches, arboriums, arbours and especially bamboo (from the Malay, which acknowledges the great many boughs or burgeons, perhaps a hundred growing straight up from one rootstock and brittle when green, all waiting to cut the unwary parachutist into as many slices as a bacon slicer, and blocking his passage on foot even if he avoids them in his descent) all springing from this primary identification of exfoliation. The banana is a fruit which burgeons with numerous protruding "fingers", from the West Indian Taino language,. See chapter 11 for the plural protrusions indicated by –nana. The banana is sometimes likened mischievously to the male organ and astonishingly the –nana of the Taino language has a similar derivation in Lithic. Is this the subconscious mind at its mischievous work in both cases, weaving subliminal connections between words we do not consciously perceive any longer because we have lost our Lithic language idioms where these connections were consciously pursued?

The flesh covers the bone. A bone is what you come to when the flesh is removed, cleared away and not there any longer, bau-nai, fleshed-nay, whether from butchery or decay. As well as being bungy, flesh can be a bung or block, as we see in bar and barrage, akin to bund in Hindi as well as the cummerbund or body band in place of a belt. A buoy is a bung which floats, and a boy has a bunged vagina with a throttle excrescence, and bwoid is Irish for his penis which does the throttling. From this in turn comes the bawd, a procurer finding the prostitutes for clients just as the bwoid (an Irish penis) itself is supposed to pursue them – an Irishism letting their owners off perhaps? It is a bawdy business.

In Australia, in a belated gesture of being matey with the natives, they wait for their billy to boil. The billy (6) is the water not the pot. Water for the aboriginal is the element which "ba-lai", goes sloping off into the lows with an infallible and inescapable instinct, forming rivers and billabongs, ox bow lakes formed by "bunged rivers". In English the water overflows when it bubbles up and boils over Our rivers are conventionally derived from their banks (ripa in Latin), but they are really "Rai-bara", with ray-legs, that is they travel as smoothly as a sunbeam without any musclature, as water does provided only you give it a slope however slight to slip away on.

In Egyptian the Ba (4) was the body's female fleshly soul represented as a bird hovering over the head at death, the ba being a ba-ji or go-up at this critical juncture; while the Ka was the guiding principle or male soul. It was dual: for guidance in this world and the next. The Ba was thus the bodily principle of being, we might say, perhaps even the vegetative element in all life forms. It is perhaps no surprise to find this secondary and relatively passive element, without any immortality on its own, to be labelled the female element by the male and chauvinist Egyptians. To be fleshed was to be alive, indeed to be, just as with our verb to be.

We can now take a look at the Bacchanalia of Ancient Greece. Bankhai, Bakis or Bacchus (4), the Greek god, was in elementary Lithic terms Ba-en-Khai, Flesh-of-the Kindler. He stimulated the feminine element to tear its flesh. His followers tore animals and even fellow revellers limb from limb. They probably did their kindling of the fleshly element under the influence of drugs as well as wine, rather than Hell raising while sober. Laurel leaves if crushed will kill butterrflies, and derange anyone who eats them. It flourishes as the green bay tree, Bacca Lauri in Latin, Laurel in English, literally in Lithic terms Ba-ka-lau-rai, foliage-make-long-lasting, or as we would transliterate it today, a leafy evergreen to distinguish it from the commoner pin or needle leaved Mediterranean evergreen pine. It was probably this fully foliaged burgeoning aspect which prompted Old Provencal usage of Bacalar for young man, just along the Mediterranean shore; which was in turn picked up in Old French as Bachelor, a young man in the flower of his youth aspiring to knighthood. In the earthier Celtic version the young man is a working farmer, a Ba-ka-la, a livestock (Ba) keep together (kala, from making looped)) or else an ambulant keep together, anyway a shepherd. The latter in turn had a staff or crook, baculum, for keeping the sheep together. This by shape resemblance then gave the world bacilli, identifying the agents of disease as little staffs or rod shaped structures as they appear under the microscope.

In Egyptian the glyph of a leg was pronounced Ba. The Great Bear or Plough constellation was represented as an ox haunch. The symbolism was of a plough team of seven oxen yoked to an invisible and magic spindle of the firmament dragging it round the pole star, just as the original plough team, Ba-lau, Go-looped, legged it round in a circle on the end of a stick tied to a post, dragging a heavy beam round and round over the wild corn to thresh it, before ever oxen were used to cultivate the soil and go backwards and forwards, boustrophedon[3]. The Great Bear was never really an Ursus or bear, that was simply a linguistic mistake – one of Sapiens Sapiens' longer entertained misapprehensions – but rather a bearer. As an Ursus it has survived its magic spindle by several millennia.[4]

To explore more of the many usages of Ba in English you need to go through the B's in an English dictionary and then seek out all the other words with B's in them, which is too much for a single chapter. Here we can only pick out some of the more obvious meanings.

Reference to the psychosemantic tree shows in the phonetic tree at the top the common sandhi (from Lithic sa'n-tai, action-become, development or change) or consonant shifts over time. In the case of Ba these are fairly obvious: to or from a P or a V, and in the latter case on to a W, as well as back the other way. These shifts are not motivated by reasoning, they count as slovening and slurring, in the absence of thought. A language may prefer a shifted consonant for reasons of euphony, or for easing the pronunciation or to distinguish two words with different meanings otherwise too close for easy distinction. The less the mouth has to move the less the effort expended in speaking – and the quicker and more easily you can go. The fine control of the mouth parts in concert with the ear has had to be learned by everyone as part of the course for speaking, and can still cause difficulty with every generation. Indeed some languages will defeat the average adult. There may (rarely) be an error of syntax encouraging a change. Or polysemy may suggest discrimination. None of this is any help to any Lithic hypothesis, but it has to be recognised. It helps to explain why linguistics buffs are apt to see languages as evolving under natural phonetic rules of evolution. In truth there is not much in the way of any consistent patterns: Greek h for s; Celtic sandhi (initial consonant shifts, more whim and fantasy than a scheme of things) and Grimm´s laws to explain how different langages differ. It does not extend much further.

The semantic tree has nine main categories from 1 to 9 on page 1 and with examples in columns 1 to 9 on pages 2 and 3. But it is an arbitrary and spur of the moment list, and the order is also quite casual, as is quite appropriate for any list which purports to indicate the movements of the human psyche, in this case the development of meanings, over aeons. We start with Bah! in column 1, the echoism being simply of the sound as uttered; an expletive indicating displeasure or contempt at one time, simply because its semantic content is minimal. It relies for its meaning, I suspect, upon the labial plosive, a gesture of expectoration, of rejection as opposed to imbibing. Also in column 1 is Bang! which is more obviously echoic of external sounds; and I have added the Old Norse Banga for hammer, a banger in those days, their shipyards resounding to the wooden pegs driven into the timbers. In Albanian bang is bam. The plosive is echoic again. We may note the labial plosive was selected because of its association with making noises, just as it is in children's games bouncing out and surprising each other with cries of Boo! or similar outbursts. Buzz is echoic as well with the zz to help out by echoing the sound better than the ba; but so is the bee that buzzes if not so obviously so. In French bee is abeille, from the Lithic elements a-bai-lai, that-ba-sings. The bee has a lay which is a buzz.

Babbling B heads column 2. A baby is a babbler or baba, a dribbler too. Baba in Spanish is spittle. To slobber in English is from the Lithic elements sai-lau-beber, action- overflow/liquid running down-the two lips,. Babear is to slobber (or to drool over women, if adult) in Spanish The abstraction of the womanising from simple slobbering is a nice example in fact of the possibilities involved in Lithic style metaphor, extensions of meanings from simple originals. It is not a question of whether over reaction to minimal sexual stimuli can properly be referred to as a case of slobbering, but instead whether it answers to human whimsy, as a hankering after the flesh. For Spaniards babosa, with a slobbering action (Lithic phonemes baba-u-sai-a, a slobbering-what-acting-one, is a slug which leaves a slimey trail. It gets further treatment in chapter 9 where the meanings of La are analysed. The derivation of sai-a is in chapter 14. More significantly perhaps, because from further afield, we find bueh in Malay which is froth or foam, from bau-ai, both lips going, what comes from between the two lips, in the land of the amok (from the Lithic aa-mau-kai, extensive aa- followed by mau-ka, death-making, killing). The classical amok, having altogether lost his orientation and oriental cool, runs about killing everyone he meets, usually with a parang, a pa-ra'n in Lithic elements, a blade wielded with a swiping action, until himself brought down.

Next is the lip/mouth list of column 3, headed Labial Ba. Arabic bab, mouth, must come first. The French mouth, bouche, is slovened. Spanish boca is better, more directly from the Latin Bucca for the mouth, from the elements bu-ka, a lipped chop or slit. The Spanish bo- is both lips from ba-u, with the −u- as dual, and the -ka from the original chop is simply the result of the chop, a slit or opening. (The Sumerian for mouth was ka too, and the Akkadian was pu). They were all thinking along the similar lines for whatever reasons. If they were picking random phonology they would have been far further afield. British mouths are of quite different provenance, as nice an example as could be wished for of human whimsy when playing definitions. The Teutonic was muntho and the pre-Teutonic root the OED[5] records as mntos, or Mau'n-tau(s) in Lithic composition, that is to say eating-hole, or even the stoke hole. The reading 'hole' is from the sound of snapping a stick which leaves you with two bits, whence division into two, whence a gap and so a slit or hole, quite a long derivation but only developed over a very long period. It is all laid out in chapter 6. The (s) of the OED's mntos (sic!) is a substantive ending added for grammatical reasons only. There is an alternative reading with ma-oo as the whole of eating-hole and the -tho(s) merely adding naturally ocurring, a common enough recension of tai, here ending in u to match the mau-. In the dream world both derivations fit together seamlessly. The earlier reading is perhaps to be preferred because of the ´n which otherwise one might expect to find before the −u, manu-tos, and the mau which would normally suggest a completed action rather than the −ing case we now describe as a verbal noun in Lithic, which used u for the completive case, including the substantive, regardless. But it should be noted the n was dropped in English. The OED glosses mouth "The external orifice in an animal body which serves for the ingestion of food". So the primitive Teutons seem to have got this one right down the middle; or else the OED simply copies, as is its brief.

To return to Ba, Buaya is crocodile in Malay. Crocodiles have very large mouths and very lethal bites. Bu-aia are two lips or jaws which extend for ever. But be warned, not all that glitters turns out to be gold. The croc is waterborne most of the time, it infests water holes lying in wait for mammals coming to drink. Ba-uai-a (6) or (9) is either a go-in-water-one or has its being-in-water-one. Maybe all three derivations have been brought into play either simultaneously or at different times and places. The Gharial croc, which lies in wait with just its eyes above water in the rivers of Malaya, ga-rai-a-lai, with its eyes on the water line in Lithic, has a pipestem jaw with several feet of teeth although it is less aggressive than the usual croc, with a bite almost delicate by croc standards so that it lives on smaller game. Indaba is from a Hamitic tongue (Zulu). It means a pow wow (Bow wow is for dogs). It says In-da-ba, One/they-do-jaw in Lithic – jaw jaw being better than war war: it is a council for the settlement of disputes which does the talking. Da is in chapter 6 with Ta, to which it is closely related. It has nothing directly to do with the English verb do, but that is the nearest to the Lithic semantic content of da in English. A ban in English is a proclamation by word of mouth. Bacha is to read or recite in Malay. The −cha could be from the ish of chapter 14 slovened from sha with semantic content "mouth activity" for bacha, or from ka in chapter 5 with the meaning "make with the mouth" which is probably to be preferred: or even a confusion of both, suggested by the ch. Baying can be added in here, with hounds, which is barely echoic, since they have no b- in fact. The b is used because of its association down below (in the subconscious lexicon by now) with the mouth and its activities.

Similarly sheep and goats really Maa rather than Baa. Even a dog is said to bark which is to mouth, to make to mouth it in Lithic, ba-a kai, just like the human recitation in Malay. The coastal bay belongs in column 4, its curve being modeled on the bum (or any of the other bulgy bits), just as the less well known architectural one is also. There is also Fon or Ewe, a West African tongue, for speak which is Gbe, to go mouthing in Lithic terms; while in Malaya bahasa, in Lithic (with a cockney h), ba(h)a-sa or mouthing action, mouth action, fashion of speech, means manner of speech or language. The Fon gbe is not to be confused with the Ancient Egyptian Geb, an exemplar of the burgeoning of the earth, as in column 6, so extraordinarily well endowed when lying on his back his phallus is able to reach the naughty night sky Nut with the thousand breasts as stars, and the crescent moon as target for the phallus of the burgeoning earth. The solar bodies were perceived originally as holes letting through the light from the upper fires above the (stone) firmament of heaven.Nut or Nau-ti, with the exposed tits or stars, is painted arched over the earth waiting for Geb's erection to reach her moon.

A bugle has a wide looped or rounded mouth, but its complete analysis is with gala, gale and gull in chapter 9. A book makes up and joins together all the verbage, ba-u-kai, the speech-all-joined, and the pages in Europe at least were originally made of beech bark, still often disfigured with graffiti today. They might however be the pages (as bits) rather than the speech, although pai for pages would carry more conviction. An aa extension can make a plural in Lithic, usually a numerous one "and so on for ever", to match the –u- of book. Spelling liber with an -er is an irrelevance. Liberty, in passing, is unconnected with bookmanship. It belongs in column 9 where it is placed, but the nub of the concept is in the Lai of chapter 9, along with loose and slack as well as lief and love (liebe in German). Before books, papyri or skins were rolled, not nearly so neat and handy though we now have some scrolls from caves in the Holy Land which have lasted well – too well in fact for some. Realities can sometimes rise phoenix like from the mists of time to correct the fancies of a later age.

The mouth's activities include biting bait as well as imbibing; and batare in Latin was to yawn, parting the lips or opening the mouth. Ta in chapter 6 is a cut or slit and ta-are is to round out and open it. These are original Lithic semantic contents. Baiting bears was done with dogs which nipped in from all sides and bit them while they were tied up: not very nice, but our forebears liked to watch the bears suffer to punish them for the fear they spread. Bumbo is an Italian children's nursery name for a drink which surely shows they associate imbibing with the lips and both with ba since it is their own concoction for sucking, where our drink is to make a draw in, which would do almost as well for making a drawing with a pencil. Latin bibere is the source for our imbibing as it is also for Spanish beber, to drink. A hard mouth is a bird's beak. A mouth is also a point of entry and so a door or gate or even a strait at sea like Bab el mandeb, the Gate of Tears with treacherous currents which capsized primitive craft at the entry to the Red Sea. Babylu or Babylon in Akkadian is Mouth of the Lawn or flat salt marshes now the Shatt el Arab, which extended further North in olden days; much as London is the estuary of the river, the lau´n, the flowing down of the Don to the sea, as the poet had it recently "Flow down Oh London river, to the seagull´s silver wings".

Where did he get it from? From his subconscious muse perhaps? It was named by very early settlers my guess is they were Egyptisn speakers. Bantai is Malay for think, to give birth to words. An early semantic content for the tai phoneme was parturition, separating into two just like a snapped twig, as is shown in chapter 6. A babuine was a gaping (salacious) figure in Old French, much like a baboue which was a grimace and the muzzle, which leads them and us to the baboon with a long muzzle and prehensile lips. In fact bader in Old Provencale meant to gape, from the Latin batare to yawn. Yawning, an involuntary opening wide, parting the lips or opening the mouth, had a salacious penumbra for our vulgar forebears, for whom labia adorned different parts of the anatomy. The bacalar is a Spanish co-dfish which is a gaper when caught, baca-la-arai, lips-make-loop-er.; nothing to do with a bachelor who is in column 6. A lullaby is a lala-bai, clear singing notes from the mouth. La is used for singing, see chapter 9, tra-la!

Column 4 exploits the characters of the flesh, picking new concepts from the characters of the flesh once lips have drifted to fleshy bits in general. I have named this ploy a gull, from the sea gull which is a sea caller, but a gull wing is not a caller, instead the shape is from the gull's wing shape. The effect is to shift the meaning to a remotely and only indirectly related meaning, which means that the trace may be easily lost. Flesh is malleable, bendy, curvaceous, laid over the bones, the tissue from which all our organs are made, and it gradually grows bigger, bur- geons, and more difficultly seems to have the role of filler (bung) and container (bag) at times, and it carries our physical senses. So we see bungey (rubbery), bulgy, bendy, baggy (belly), bottom (from bum), and so on. Bone is what you get to if you take the flesh away. The Lithic is bau-nai, unfleshed, or flesh bared. Bone does not exhibit flesh, it is robbed of it, gnawed probably, and the residue declared bone. In chapter 11 which deals with the phoneme Na, the ne- and no negatives are derived from exposed or bared. The boa is a snake which has grown to a very large size. But it started out as a water snake in Latin. Water is derived inter alia from shivering wewewe in chapter 15. The Latin water snake if old enough could go back to Ba-wa, go water, like the aborigine baji, go up, for bird. A bag has a bulgy shape compared to a box which has straight sides. A bung blocks an orifice and a buoy is plump and floats. Irish boys call their genital organ bwoid, a bunged orifice on the end of the male urethra, a character which English boys may have inherited, and perhaps Malay boys also, budak, pronounced buda'? Bobo is stupid in Spanish, a brain with a bung in it. It is bodoh in Malay. The English brain itself, ba-rai'n, needs chapter 13 to explore the Egyptian rays, which were responsible for every kind of action at a distance otherwise inexplicable, including particularly the attraction of the sexes which overwhelmed the Egyptians – in far off days, just as today. Nowadays the Egyptian rays are mostly affected by those in asylums, sending messages sometimes in code and often from the most bizarre addresses.

The brain was early identified as the part of the body receiving these rays, giving rise to thinking and emotion. A bank is a ba'n-kai, a bulging of the ground, the hard part of the universe, kai is hard from chapter 5 on. A bund, Hindi, is an earth bank making a dam closing off a reservoir, and by association also the lake which is formed behind it. Their kummerbund is a bend around their stomach. The German bund is one which binds a band together. In English a bend (sheet or fisherman's for examples) is a knot that binds as well as the flexing which the body allows. Bend bund band and bind are all from bai-. Bahei from the unreformed Ancient Egyptian is the organ of the flesh which hei or makes whoopee, with an unmistakeable glyph of the male organ apparently ejaculating, followed by a determinative glyph in this case of a gobbet of flesh, such as is often put at the end of a string of glyphs as a helping hint as to which meaning is to be read into the foregoing glyphs. There is a kind of dark humour in putting a gobbet of flesh after a clear enough depiction of the organ in question in outline which any schoolboy would recognise in the twinkling of an eye, as a pointer for anybody not already there. The organ in question is more often spelt pa-hei, since it is a thinned diminutive of ba meaning flesh and so a small shoot or just the skin. Perhaps the rules blinded the scribes to the obvious, then as now, or else they were already enjoying the joke, now a few thousand years passé.

To be bare is to be ba-rai, the flesh rayed, that is seen, visible. In Egyptian ra was the eye, vision and visible, with Ra the eye of the day, the sun. The bubs or boobs are the two bungy bits, and the breast originally breoste comprises the Lithic elements bai-rai-au-siti, berries-that-dual-female. Her bottom, meanwhile, in this case shared with the boys, is bau-tau'm, dual bulges with a cleavage, cleft, that is parted in accordance with the dual symmetry of the two sides of the body. The construction is indeed a kind of poetry, the tau matching the bau and at the very same time indicating the completive both as a substantive, the cleavage, and a past tense form of ta to divide, cleaved or cleft, which was originally a cutting. It is all spelt out in chapter 6. It even appears it is a later syncopation of the earlier theme, the bum, which merely picked up the bulb shape, now surviving only as a vulgarism. A button, of course, is right next door, a burgeon or bung for a slit or cleavage, the buttonhole. This can by extension be used for the posy we put in it, simply because we see it to be there. By now our mental travels have taken us a long way from our bottoms, revealing something of the power and the glory of thinking.

Babi in Malay is a pig, from ba-bai, flesh- burgeoned, a fat beast and excellent eating. The Senoi (Aboriginal Malay, perhaps "first appearing folk" in their own tongue) greeting on meeting is Mong Bor? for How do you do? It means Eating Pig? and the reply is Borbi! for Fat Pig, thank you! Pigs in Borneo, which means where boars came from, are only eaten on festive occasions, substitutes for can-

nibal sacrifices probably, the piglets are even suckled by the women. They taste
the same as human flesh which is known across the island as long pig; an idiom
much like anthropos in Greek, which refers to the drawn up legs of the species,
our walking upright and standing tall, which is (virtually) unique, since the other
ape candidates are really jumpers or swingers or mere greenhorns at it anyway. The
Lithic analysis of boar, the boy pig, is Bau-arai, which could of course just be a
longer way of describing a berry body or plumpling. But bau could mean just what
it says, namely dual bulges like the bottom, in which case we have to ask ourselves
which two bulges our forebears had in mind. A clue is in the arai added. A-rai in
Lithic terms is raised up at the same time as meaning rayed or visible. Now it is
a quirk of piggy anatomy the boars wear their testicles in two bulges at the back
immediately under their bottoms instead of suspended between their legs like the
rest of us, and indeed like the rest of the whole of the animal kingdom; where they
are totally exposed and very visible because of their curly tails, as every farmer's
boy knows very well. It was the domestication of pigs, incidentally, which taught
us the need for impregnation, since sows penned on their own were the very first
virginal females on the planet, so we learned to let in the boar. The human species
would never have learned on their own because impregnation was such fun for
both parties, and always available in full measure when there was no television or
football to fill the unremitting evening hours, so impregnation passed unnoticed.
Acquiring virtue in those days was often regarded as eating it. A pig´s testicles
were the bon bouche reserved for the most honoured (male) guest. Mong bor?
could thus mean in reality "I hope you are eating pig?" and the reply, Borbi! "Yes,
the testicles, thank you!". Admittedly the Senoi had no bicycles but they exhibit
the same bilateral symmetry in their bodies as all the animal species, a bilaterality
exhibited precisely enough by the items which appear to have come under discussion early at aboriginal meetings. Pa`Ah, the sober grandfather I knew (Pa is
grandfather in Senoi)– we first met on a track between his home ladang (clearing)
and the local stream for fishing – I suspect had his mind far from pig's testicles
when we exchanged greetings, although he declared in the conventional manner he had eaten them in answer to my enquiry. He had information about the
murder of the British Protector of Aborigines during the Japanese occupation so
I needed a serious talk with him. In one hand he had a small fish trap and holding
his other a small grandson. He was fully clad in a small barkcloth bag on a string
round his waist which nominally enclosed his genitalia. Cloth was a euphemism,
the mesh was open work, easier for fingers not too nimble, and more like a tennis
ball bag than an article of clothing; but an adult male could never be seen without
one. Our soldiers bathing in the river after a patrol were liable to flush the women
folk into the jungle, while bringing all the boys to the river's edge for the sheer
pornography of it. He had a wisp of hairs on his chin which showed he was an

elder, but nothing much in evidence in the area of the tennis bag. The porcupine quill which on festive occasions he would have worn through the septum of his nose he had left at home as overdressing for a fishing lesson. His grandson had left everything at home, not even bothering with the tiny baglet his mother had made him for special occasions, which was going to get wet in the water. Pa'Ah spoke just a few words of Malay, he had walked out to a kampong for cooking pots, so we were able to speak on about equal terms.

Concentration on how Malays and Borneans spoke and how they originally thought is emphasised throughout these chapters without apology because these territories are the highland hinterland remnants of Eden, now under the shallow South China Sea, where the river courses which provided paddy and taught Adam and his lot to irrigate their gardens (actually padi fields, not flower beds) can still be traced on the sea floor many millennia after Eden was drowned three hundred and fifty feet deep with the melting of the major glaciation between ten thousand and twenty thousand years ago. Malay is perhaps the nearest to the original Andaman language of Adam´s Eden, a provincial patois from the lingua franca of the Malayan lowlands, adopted by the hill tribes, who just retreated uphill in Malaya, Borneo Indonesia and New Guinea and never emigrated when the floods came. If some of the Eden population went North to China while others went West to Sumer it would account for similarities between some of the Sumerian we have been able to recover and Chinese, which has even caused some etymologists to suggest Sumerians were Chinese. Such borrowings do not impugn an original Lithic phonemic vocabulary since they are borrowings of the idiomatic word constructions based on the body of bedrock Lithic meanings given to the sounds. A body, bau-dai, is indeed a dual burgeon naturally come by, by birth in fact. That is what body says in Lithic.

But now back to the testicles. Buah is Malay for fruit, which at one time suggested to me our genitalia had been identified as the fruit of the body, which of course they are not. But it did not take long to realise it was in fact the fruit which were actually identified as the testicles of the vegetable kingdom, since both were supposedly plump seed containers. Buah is testicles precisely in Lithic, bu-a-hei, the dual bits-that-make whoopee. It was a very long time before the male sperm was more correctly identified as the equivalent of the pollen of the vegetable kingdom, since the girls keep their seeds so discreetly tucked away inside their bodies that male chauvinism was able to flourish with the boys as egg layers and the girls the mere receptacles for male virtue, just putting the dumb ba on the male ka which carried the flame of life from generation to generation. It was sheer daylight robbery of the girls' role. The word fruit itself can now be rendered in Lithic terms as Pahei–rau-i-tai, the phallic organs-when roused or ripe-which-give birth, that is the sexual organs of vegetables. Notice the unblushing interpretation of the rest of nature as a gloss on our own physiognomy here. Now if fruit were the seed containers of the vegetable kingdom, many delicious as well as health giving, it is surely small wonder that our ancestors were tempted to try the virtue of the seed containers to be found in the animal kingdom as provender as well, and picked on the testicles as bon bouches, and hopefully as receptacles of physical well-being and potency. Gardeners will be amused to spot it followed for our hominid forebears fruit were male too.

The Spanish avocado, pronounced aboucado, is a fruit widely believed to be described as a testicle because of its shape, even if when fully grown they would do credit to an elephant in that role. Primitives have a robust, even lip smacking sense of humour where the genitalia are concerned. However the Quechua from which the Spanish derives turns out not to be abucatl after all but ahuacatl. Still, the tradition still fits since the Quechua idiom 'a-hua-kai-tl' in Lithic terms can be read as 'one that-dual joy-makers-noun ending', or in English the twin joy pieces, the two hay makers, a functional description of the testicles not likely to be found attached to a fruit, unless as a salacious reference to its shape. We may note the Spanish use of bu instead of hu has a world wide following as well. The form abocado may have been influenced, Eric Partridge the word king thought, by the Spanish bocado a delicacy. We must now wonder whether instead the Spanish sense of a delicacy is influenced even today by a remote psychosemantic shadow of the original delicacy their word describes. Or else the cynics will insist it just meant a mouthful, a bon bouche. Bunga is the Malay for flower, from the Lithic elements bu-en-ka, maker of the dual bits, the testicles or seed pods.

Perhaps the Greek bu- we find in bous, the Greek for ox, was at first for testicles rather than muscles after all. Our bull is of obscure origin. The bovine genitals are very well endowed in every department. The Hebrew Aleph, sometimes explained as smooth breathing, is actually in Lithic analysis Aa-lai pa-hei, Very–long–phallus, which I believe the ancients would have been bound to celebrate. The bu or dual ba of the English bull may very well also refer to his testicles which are bu-lai-lai, both long and unusually smoothly linked in a single stalk for them both, quite unlike the rest of us who wear them parted like brer boar, if more discreetly. This is why the bulrush gets its name. Its seeds form a single bole shape just like the bull's testicles. Admittedly the rush is ra-ish, straight-up, while the bull's testicles hang down. But the animal and vegetable kingdoms though thought to be sharing many adjectival motifs, or even originally every one, were assumed to be in a dialectical relationship, so pointing rigidly up instead of hanging down was par for the course, confirmatory evidence of the accuracy of the identification. Some Greeks in classical times were reluctant to eat beans, which they regarded as tabu. Legumes have a few large seeds in a pod. The reason, the language suggests, is they renounced the eating of testicles and beans were regarded as vegetable testicles, in Latin faba – the Spanish have clung to the same form precisely – which comes from the phonemes pa-hei-ba, penis bulgy bit or bobble, a testicle. Broad beans are the right shape if on the small side, but if you had more than two you would perhaps expect each to be smaller especially if you were as slender as the plant, and they are podded like the animal versions. A pea, similarly podded, was a diminutive version, with pa in place of ba and not yet hei, a boy's testicle. Puer is boy in Latin, but also a girl, later feminised to distinguish the two with an –ella ending, with the pu- bit being from the Egyptian quail chick through the Greek with its dual peep. Children were cheepers, voices unbroken. Our English bean is from the earlier bhone, the –ne from –nai perhaps standing in for the hei. The French feve for bean just comes from mispronunciation.

It seems hard Karl von Linné, Linnaeus, should have been driven mad thousands of years on by the warnings of hellfire from the Swedish clerics of his day for imputing the very same sexual role to the flowers of the field. The progress of human knowledge has been something of a zigzag. Plenty of men today still think of their semen as seed rather than pollen. The word semen actually means life gestating or dead life, life lying doggo, and was originally just used for seed, which is from sai-dai, life birthing or life bearing. Semantics carries the meaning of meaning by using the same phonemic structure, sai-mai´n, but reading it as the life essence or spirit or activity of the mind (mens in Latin), mental activity. Abang in Malay is an elder brother. A-ba´n, single flesh makes a brother because the flesh is added in the womb, and a is also first, so the a- stands in for elder as well. Sebab, sai-bab, is the live essence of words, and means reason in Malay. Apa sebab nya is why?, what reason of it? Kenapa? means the same, what is the ken? Kai´n is the strike or driving or initiating force, the cause, and the English comes in turn from the Lithic kau-sai, the making or cause of an action, or the causative action, from the Latin causa. Meanwhile, on the other side of the world from the elder brother above, bon in French is well fleshed and so doing well, in the pink, a goodly condition when sustenance was scarce; and beau followed the same reasoning. Bagus in Malay, from ba-kau was the flesh kindled and so grown and enlarged, well fleshed out, and it meant very good: while baik, fleshy, pronounced bai´ means good, just like bon but with a simple past case in place of a pluperfect one. Our English belly is lolling flesh, as with a beer belly, or else one of the lai could come from your butcher's knowledge some of the contents can be lye, bitter to the taste. Lye is a term dreamed up early on by the founding fathers of the lexicon, originally the tongue curled signaling 'nasty taste!'. A banana has many protruding fruit, with the stalk growing down but the fruit growing strongly upwards in bunches, and the repetition of na indicates many protrusions, taken directly from the West Indian Taino language, which as Eric Partridge avers is in turn from the earlier Arawak prattana – you must remember the spellings are late approximations to what seemed to be coming out of the mouths of native speakers in the minds of foreign interpreters – which in Lithic terms is Pai-rai-ti-ta-na, perhaps phaluses-raised-things-become-protruberant, or with a trifle of rearrangement to suit our English idiom, erect protruding pieces, with the elements all with strong sexual connotations, as is illustrated in the chapters dealing with the phonemes concerned: in all not a bad mnemonic for any piccaninn sent to the bazaar for bananas to remember which fruit to buy, the ones which look like dad does sometimes when he is hot.

A bar is a straight piece of wood from ba-rai a ba as straight as a ray, or else rayed by the sun to draw it out and up. It could then be used to bar the way, ba-are, bung-verbal ending. A barbeque from the Arawak babakoa, a raised wooden framework of crossed sticks for storage, sleeping or drying fish, etc, is a grill or grating with bars joined crosswise. Barang in Malay is blocked rays or vision, or else just the bulk visible as at dawn, when the sun's rays are muted, and by this rather roundabout process of reasoning it comes to mean indeterminate. Barang barang is miscellaneous odds and ends, barang is kit and equipment, baggage, and barang kali is an indeterminate time and therefore used for perhaps. Sumbat is a Malay cork or stopper, the -bat is easy, a bung thing, a plug, just like a very small beam or bat. The sum- could be vertical but convenient is to be preferred (as in sugar, see chapter 14) – since it is a loose bung which can be put in and taken out again as required without undue effort, as opposed to a permanent seal which would likely be a cover or lid with pai in place of ba. Lembu is a cow in Malaya, a milking ox which is bous in Greek. Milk is a lye. It is a liquid which is not clear like fresh water. Or lembu's lai-mai in Lithic can be read as leaking liquid-ingestible, just as milk in English is from mai-lai-kai, in this case an ingestible liquid of the body, unless the bu are the fleshy bits which leak the milk, the udders. The many derivatives of Ma are all in chapter 10. Gambar is a visual representation in Malay, a statue or a picture from the Lithic elements ga-em-bara, form of the visible object.

Our brown is dull compared with much of the foregoing, ba rau'n, the raying blocked, colours not visible, probably noticed first at dawn like the barang; but bruin the brown bear seemed to have mastered the trick for all time, perhaps using the thickness of his fur which kept the rays in also, a veritable sun trap handy for keeping warmth in also. Malay bayang means outline or shadow rather than brown. The Balkans were named by the Turks because of their rolling hills – a lot of Turkey is a lot craggier – Bala-ka'n, bulging-earth one, or place with rolling hills. The Balkan states could do with a flatter surface, but it was the best turf in striking distance of Turkey at the time. The Malay for Zebra is kuda belong or belang, a horse with long bits or stripes, and so – a little inconsequentially – is a piebald horse, not striped at all but still bi-tone like the zebra, in locations instead of lines. But belit is to be twined round, in Lithic terms be-looped, to bind, and semblit is movement blocked, to be constipated. I once found this handy when a Laotian officer on exchange in Singapore who had no Malay informed me of his condition behind his hand in French, a language we had found we shared (his was a pidgin version). I was able to take him to the bazaar and ask for the opening medicine he needed in Malay at the Chinese pharmacy. I rather savoured this experience interpreting between China and Laos. Bongkar in Malay, making a bung or heap in Lithic, means to ransack; while bumbang is a roof beam supporting the leaves laid over each other as a thatch, usually atap leaves, a-ta-pai, that become a roof or cover in Lithic. But bongkah a hump back, or bent body in Lithic, leads to membongkah to stoop, where mem- is merely a verbal prefix of obscure origin (o.o.o. as Partridge has it when he gets one he can not crack). The obscurity is relevant since ob- from the Lithic au-bai is altogether blocked and/or no go and thus against, an obstruction. Kembang, Ka-em-baing in Lithic is a swelling in Malay, a bulging of the body. Labuan, the island off the Brunei coast, is an anchorage, the Lithic La-bu-a'n the flow (tides and currents) blocked, or no slippage in the Chinese recension, with bu the negative. Sinbad the sailor, the sadistic castrated Chinese admiral who terrorised the South China seas and much of the Indian ocean also will have so read it. He will have anchored there. "Sinbad" may have named him as the castrate, as the Lithic phonemes of his name suggest: Sai-en-ba-tai, Life-of-bits-cut. The Chinese glyph for bu is read as a plant not blooming but blocked with a horizontal line drawn across it, indicating an obstruction, and so to the Chinese mind a negative. But can the Chinese for the negative really be – well, just "Balls!"? It also raises sensitive logical issues whether a negative is properly an absence or an opposite, discussed in chapter 16 on thinking where it reveals a fatal flaw in the Marxist dialectic.

Tumboh in Malay is to pummel or pound. The tu- is tricky, it can be a becoming or an event. Mai can signify harm or downwards (or both?), and boh is the flesh or limbs, here perhaps the fists which really belong in column 5. The Malay pummeler appears to have been a bovver boy pummelling when his opponent was already on the ground.

Ba as flesh has a bewilderingly wide application. Bahei is the Egyptian male genitalia, the joy bits with pahei the penis, when not more prosaically just mai the planter or inseminator. In Greece Sinbad the eunuch was Bakelos, the ba- here apparently standing in for bahei, and the kai lau(s) rendered flaccid. The Irish borr, in nice counterpoint, proud and strong, looks similar to brand, a human burgeon in place of an animal or vegetable one this time. It is just possible however he had big balls. But there is worse. It may be the Irish bwoid when rayed and raised, borr again, is just like the proud Englishman, pai rau dai, a cockstand doing it in both cases. The Irish blocking mode they ascribed to their penises relates to the beret as well, blocking the sun's rays; just like the biretta a little beret or cap which the Pope has consigned to the back of his head where it is no good at all at blocking the sun's rays after all. This is because it is there for another function altogether, blocking the bad rays which might otherwise reach his brain, which is defined already as the ba which is rai'n or flesh which is rayed. Originally it was a Jewish gambit copied by the Roman church, at other times affecting a Pharaoh's headgear. The head was the caput, from the Lithic Ka-puti, glans of the body (puti from pipi-ti or penis teat) long before Magritte spotted it, and the Irish barai or ray blocker down below had been trimmed up by the Pharaohs so the glans could fire first, not having to wait for the ladies to round out and send a ray to withdraw the male muzzle cover so the puti could pout and ray in its turn. Pharaoh was a Pahei-a-Ra-u-hei, his 'Phallus-Ra-was always-rejoicing in', or else causing to rejoice; but in either case not to be kept waiting at the behest of common females. The Royal House which Mrs Grundy prefers for the Pharaoh would be Pa-rau, a shelter from Ra or parasol made of skins, originally a goatskin tent later a house with walls and a roof. A pa is a skin, but a pahei is a joy piece, in Greek phi, first drawn with the verge penetrating the circle, not just slashed across it. Upstairs where the contest was more unequal with all the powers of nature targeting the brain and not just the opposite and weaker sex firing, a prepuce or peri-puti had its attractions, and since nature had not provided one art should intervene. Jewish wisdom has thus removed the foreskin from where it grows and properly belongs and they wear it on their heads instead, a significant revision of Jaweh's planning for which they claim His blessing, masterminding the Egyptian rays, welcome or otherwise, for male convenience here below. The Greeks took the goatskin still further, with a polis or collection of lasting skins or roofs, pau-lai, a city and then a city state. The police will probably be disconcerted to discover their close cousinship with the prepuce. Skinheads too may reflect on the deeper promptings which lie behind their shaven pates, making them more like genuine ka-puti or body-glans.

Column 6 for Bendy B which takes us to the limbs, and the use of the legs to travel, is headed by an ox haunch, the sign for the constellation of the Great Bear on Egyptian funerary ceiling paintings of the heavens. However the constellation is not of a Bear but of a Bearer, a confusion of longer standing than most, many millennia at least, far longer than Plinny the Elder's fib about the Canary Islands. The Plough, its alternative name, slovened from ba-lau, a go round (see loop in chapter 9), which was at first an arrangement for threshing wild corn, before the plough for making furrows to prepare the earth for planting was invented as a clever extension of the ox pulling principle, to and fro this time to cover the ground required for planting. This first plough team however went round in a circle (lau) with oxen yoked to a stick, in turn tied to a central standing post,

dragging round as they went a heavy beam which winnowed the wild corn tipped
in its path. The Great Bearer constellation was similarly perceived as an ox team
going round the pole of Heaven taking the heavy stone firmament with fixed star
holes round with it. By day this firmament had one big hole letting through the
light of the fires above the firmament as it circled. The geometry was not by any
means perfect, since the sun´s trajectory did not match the circling of the stars in
the firmament at nights any more in those days than it does in these. But in an
ineffable universe some shunting of circuitry off stage was evidently acceptable. It
was a long time indeed before anyone had a better idea, and then they still got it
all wrong. The ox, Si bai in Egyptian, Brer Muscles, misread by the Egyptologists
as Seb or Sab – they do not even pretend to guess the vowelisation, which the
Egyptian is supposed to leave out – prefigures Bous in Greek, which for long I
thought with the rest of the etymological fraternity was in Lithic terms Bu(s): All
Muscle. The flesh is muscle and fat, mostly muscle. The leg muscles are mostly in
the haunch which the ox can be seen to struggle with when getting a heavy load
going, as his driver stabs the point of his goad into the raw sore on his rump so he
struggles to get away from the shooting pain – still a common enough sight you
have to learn to live with in India where a teeming population has very little room
for charity in the struggle for survival. Ba goes by a simple progression from flesh
to muscle to leg muscle to leg it and go. The Greeks had baino to put out with the
legs, show a leg, to leg it, meaning to walk, but the Latins changed it to a v and
apparently interpreted the -nau as present (when finished walking) and so to go
present, to come; but then the Spanish pronounced the v as a b, while the French
kept the v as a v, both keeping the Latin meaning of venire, but with a sideways
acknowledgment of ba as va.

The Gaels have aber for across or crossing, a- for extension and -ber for going
(verbal ending), from bai-arai. Aberdonians and the rest are at the spread estuaries of rivers where you could most easily cross without being swept away out
of your depth by the current. But they won´t have it the aber is anything other
than estuary. For that the extension would have to be of the –ber, the ba-rai, the
burgeoning (of the river). More difficult, because of the elaborate gloss put on it,
is the Malay Nabi Issus for the (Muslim) Prophet Jesus. Nabi, from Na-bai read
as Prophet, is really in Lithic terms more like Explicater Bum, or travelling guru,
witness or presenter. The derivations of Na are in chapter 11. Similarly we find
Naib in Arabic, for an ambassador and then for a provincial governor sent by the
central government to rule an outlying province as viceroy, another Explicator
bum. A spider in Malay is labalaba. Like the Bruce it does not easily give up but
goes on round and round repetitively in loops, loop-leg it, loop-leg it, spinning its
web. A bulang baling, all the go round go rounds, the rotary motions, is a whirligig
in Malay, and the berbaling which spoils the slumbers of light sleepers in the jun-

gle is a perpetual wind blown whirling bamboo mounted at the top of a tall tree with bamboo flutes tied on each end, which whoops eerily in the lightest breeze to scare the evil spirits away from honest folk asleep, rising to a whooping scream in a gale. In a stiff wind a well made one can be heard for a long way and must surely achieve a thoroughgoing wholesale clearance of the local hantu or spirits. Down under, the Australian bilabong is a flow, a river, bila from bai lai going low in Lithic, which has got bunged, an ox bow lake in fact. The bila is from the instinct of water to go low (it always runs down hill) and is fully derived in chapter 9 for La. Compare baji per contra, ba-ji, an Australian go-up or bird. The billy which keeps your average Oz waiting while it boils is not the can but the water in it. The aboriginal boomerang meanwhile is a bu-m-ai-rang, a dual go-him-as is-raying. These are the Egyptian rays of chapter 13 going out and coming back in with their booty, which were evidently present in Australia too in olden times. They emerged from the sun, came down to earth, grabbed the vegetation and returned to their source, plucking out the veg to bring it back up with them. The Egyptian sun was earliest the Aton, the Eternal or World Vulva birthing light into the world each day, which at the same time was a plucker upper just like the mini version the ladies wear here below. The boomerang's raying was thus a return trip "as the sun rays". Our re- prefixes of course come from the very same dual action rays, there and back, which shone on us too. In Malaya burong terbang, birds fly, pulled up going. Flight through the air was a magical process, for which you needed to be specially equipped, denied to earth bound species however hard they prayed and flapped their limbs. Wings needed dual sky hooks for flight. A bird, burong had two limbs, bu raung, able to lock onto the rays and be raised and towed along up into the air. Flying, terbang, from tai-rai-bang, going drawn up and out in a manner precisely analogous to those other tau rays the ladies were able to emit which drew the male organ up and out (with the male following along behind) to their source. The air itself of course started out as aai-rai, the extension of rays, that is their path or the medium for them. The idea of any gaseous element came far far later. The ether was still the very same medium adapted to the science of the day just leaving the sun worship out. Meanwhile, back in Indo Europe, they were already making bangles, bangli in Hindi, for leg or wrist, ba-en-ga-lai, limb-of-go-looped. The English limb, by the way, is a lai-'m-bai, a long length of the flesh or a long flexible excrescence or burgeon. A beliong is no bangle. It is a Malay felling axe which in Lithic is a ba-lai-au'n, a go-swinging-one. Now with a steel blade, it nevertheless faithfully follows the pattern of the flaked flint, narrow to fit in the end of a split shaft and bound in place with lianas or tali, a word now used also for string. the Lithic ta-lai, 'naturally become-long lithes', were natural bindings. A bunch of bare bottomed Senoi woodsmen will spend days pecking away at a hardwood forest giant taking out postage stamp sized pieces to make a clearing, often on flimsy platforms head high to avoid the buttressed roots which may spread six to eight feet above the forest floor to give the tree stability. After a week or so of pecking they will then burn the core out by building fires around it until it falls. Liana in fact is French, associated with the verb lier to bind, which also makes us allies, bound together, but copied from the Antilles in fact where they grow in abundance. A ballerina is using her lower limbs as a dancer. Ballar is to dance in Spanish and a ball is a dance in English, with looping haunches. Lai here is smooth like a loop or water's slow flow or a lake's surface. Less well known is the Louisiana Creole Bamboula, a dance to a musical accompaniment on a banjo. Lambat in Malay is just going slow, (compare langsam in German, slowly from lang-sa'm, low-activity and so slow – slow in fact has the same phonemes in a different packing order); while Malay bangsat (the Lithic original of sa was the flame with its instinct to go up while la was early the instinct of water to run down slopes) is a vagrant, an obsessive traveller. Bintang, a star, is a travelling orifice, in the firmament at night. Boleh, on the other hand is from the Lithic elements ba-u-lai, go where downstream, able, can. (To go downstream in Malay is hilir). Balek however is from bai-lai-kai, going-loop-make, to go back. Belakang is therefore the back, behind; and if you are seriously retracing your steps you can balek belakang. A balalaika however is a sing song maker, the bala lip and tongue, the song, while the laika is to go la, to sing.

Column 7 is headed by Burgeoning or Biological B. Animal and vegetable were not nearly so fully discriminate in olden times. But veg was rooted; animals were rootless and able to move around. Veg was cold and animals were warm. Veg alive was green, dead brown. Animals were flesh coloured alive, dead rotten. To be fleshed was to be alive for both of them. Both were edible, both burgeoned, both were Ba. Greek bion meant living and bios life. It is tempting to derive Spanish verde, green, pronounced berde, from baia-dai, burgeoning does, much as green comes from growing, (the effect of getting rayed: from the paradigmatic Egyptian sun Ra's raying and dragging out and up the vegetation). But the v as in Latin vivus, alive, comes from Latin vivere and goes back a long way. Eric Partridge relates Greek bios and Latin vivus, and with no Lithic roots to consider goes on to relate also Greek zen to live, which in chapter 14 is derived from a completely different root, the sibilant, from the flame which is hot and animal life which is warm. His derivation of vivus from a possible (but unrecorded) Germanic root *guiguus, to go with Old English cwicu, cwic, alive, living – in brackets "the quick and the dead"- is similarly derived in chapter 5 quite independently from Ka and not from vivere at all. There is no reason why we should not arrive at the idea of life from several different directions. There is no reason why they should not meet and intertwine in the subconscious mind. But there is also no very obvious reason why they should. However what is clear is the same or similar semantic content can be reached by several different routes, which is why there are so many different languages. Ka was certainly responsible for kindling, a kick start for a flame or life as well as a flint flake. Si, as in zen, was certainly used for life form, including in Malay for instance, and is translated brer as in brer fox and brer rabbit in chapter 14.or brer plandok, brer twinkle-toes for the Malayan mouse deer. Latin u- could just as well be from v- and b- as from gu-. The ka/ga phoneme is a difficult one. With y and u, but not w, it is a back consonant, with the glottis opening or just opened. At times and places g was pronounced y and in Sanscrit j leading to sh. Anyway a bough or branch, (ba-rai'n-kai) is burgeon-made, and a bud is a ba-dai, a (newly) born burgeon. Further off bad is a dead one, rotten, whence bad like a bad egg and then quite generally. After the bud comes the bent and then the beam as well as bunga the Malay for flower. Malay buah for fruit and Bornean Bor (boar) already addressed under column 4 were burgeons too. Much of the derivation under column 4 in fact could be included about as well in this column. The flexible quality of flesh, its bulging etc, could almost as well be attributed to its burgeoning. Column 4 (Flesh) is animal oriented, this column 7 vegetable.

Barra (Hindi) big, comes from burgeoned. Big from bai-kai gets that way from the kindling of the flesh. In the children's story the big bad wolf acquires the first of these qualities in the telling because the author links the two subconsciously, and gets poetic satisfaction doing so. A wolf of any size, after all, would have done as well; it was to be expected it would be of average wolfish size at least. Besar, also big in Malay is perhaps the vegetable equivalent from ba-i-sarai, flesh-which-sunrayed, so the bud has grown. Labu, a vegetable marrow in Malay, has burgeoned looped or ballooned, or else it has long bits (or both). Rambut, hair in Malay, Lithic ra'm-bau-tai has become burgeoned in rays, and a rambutan is a hair-one, a hairy fruit. Well it has fine protruberances all over its skin at least. But Malay has also bulu for fur, lots of linear burgeons. Malay bamboo is a burgeoning in very many bits, as also buloh for bamboo, very many long linear burgeons: a bit like fur, as any jungle veteran will know who has ever tried to cut his way through a dense thicket of bamboo: he can save a day or two by going round. Kebun, from Lithic kai-bau'n, is burgeoning ground, a garden or plantation, as found in the highlands of Malaya left above sea level. Malaya itself, the garden land, was the name of the garden of Eden now under the South China sea. Its garden was paddi, ma-lai-a, soil-with water flowing over it-one, bunded and channeled from the river, a trick which perhaps planted the tree of knowledge and civilisation as we know it. In far off days it was the ladies who poked around with their digging sticks (while the men went hunting) and so Eve likely dreamed up this innovation; which explained for the first authors, noses slightly out of joint with Eve stealing a lead on the men, why God made her heirs suffer so for her sin breaching the natural order. He melted the glaciers in revenge and made the serpents swim for it. Eve's heirs' track record, it has to be interpolated, has not lived up to her early Eastern promise with her digging stick. Men's hunting skills, turned to other areas including personal relations, have proved more productive – at some major cost no doubt, much as feminists quite correctly aver.

A boabab (Hamitic) is a tree burgeoned with numerous bits (aerial roots) and a bulging trunk. Babul, the Bengali version, is the same tree or similar, probably from the Sanskrit babbula, like the Malay vegetable marrow. While on the wooden bits there is navis (Latin ship) and nave (English) the main body of a church, both from na-bai, exposed beams – not a prophet this time – showing with church roofs as well as with clinker built ships, with the beams to which the boards were studded standing proud for all to see. A board is just a flat timber, recut a second time. A barn with the roof beams showing was another major building with a high tech roof the same as the kirk; while for the Swedes, who were good at it, a barm was a boat. A bergen rucksack was designed for climbing mountains, where warm clothing as well as provisions needed to be carried, see Old Norse biarg, an unlikely burgeon this since it was gai from kai, a rock, a giant rock, a mountain. Partridge takes it further back to Gothic Bairgahei, a mountain range: a cockney h this, from biarg-ai-ai, meaning lots of them, extending-extending. (The aye aye is a sloth if I remember, going going ever so slowly). Old English beorh or barrow was another unlikely burgeon urai or urau, raised up, made of earth; and a rabbit's burrow is not really the hole everyone thinks it is but the excavated earth thrown up all round a warren (one-that-is-raised in Lithic), just as the barrow was. Classical is the saucer barrow in the centre of the saucer dug out, with the earth thrown up into the centre A berg is not so far off from an English bank, from ba-en-kai, a burgeon-of-the earth's surface rather than the burgeon of the ka or ga, the rock our forebears were knapping, the hard rock surface of the earth and not really the ma or milled soil they were irrigating as marl or malai, fertile soil (as in Malaya, Gardened-one, and Hindi mali, gardener) – and the rabbits were excavating elsewhere. A barrow would be better as a marrow, and vice versa. The mountain dwellers in Malaya got it right.

The burning brand further prayed in aid in chapter 14 is a gull's nest. A gull is a switch in meaning from the article originally indicated to a character derived from it (a gull shaped wing from a sea caller). A brand is a burgeon like the Breton brank, a branch, after it is cut, dai from tai. It was kindled in the flame and brandished burning making a very satisfactory flash (a fire flare) in the dark to drive off your sabre toothed mistress growler, ti-grrrr or tiger. Or else it was just cut as firewood for burning in the hearth for warmth. Either way the brand was for burning, and it was this character lifted which gives us the burning from the Germanic and Gothic brinnan, the intransitive, the brand be-raying does, that is burning and probably brandished burning too. There is the earlier Sanskrit bhura to flicker, like a flaming brand (cockney h) from ba-urai, a brand when raying or fully lit up. To brand livestock is to set about them with a burning brand and burn an identifying mark into the flesh, which in turn gives the brand its identity.

Column 8 is a mercifully short one for Binary B. The flesh has a binary symmetry everyone knows: two arms two legs two eyes and even two little noses – nostrils in English – although so closely straddling the centre line. There are also two breasts; and two buttocks hugging each other like the nostrils above. Open us up and we have two sets of ribs and two lungs, two kidneys, two ovaries and two testicles but only one set of gastric tubing down the middle from mouth to anus. It is the central spine with two sides to the body which gives us our binary symmetry. Bai means kitted out with two of them, and so side by side. The buttocks really epitomise the relationship. Bilaterality and so bi- for two is derived by Eric Partridge from the same root as dwa for two. This seems to be taking a distinct liberty with the idea of roots which surely can only thrive on some degree of similarity. If any phoneme is to be allowed to be transmogrified to any other in kaleidoscopic fashion rooting becomes haphazard, just as they are taken to be in fact, but are not. If Bs become Ds we are at sea. It can easily be shown that generally they do not. It is certainly much simpler to posit two sources for two: first snapping something in two, the snap was the Ta incidentally (chapter 6) when you are left with two bits, probably one in your right hand and one in your left, a dry windfall for burning in the hearth for warmth for instance; and then not a mile away the two hands holding the firewood, and the rest of the symmetry of the flesh to go with them. Breaking the firewood in two must surely have seemed like humanising nature, just like the hearth, the flame corralled which otherwise untamed would have been off into the jungle. Now it seems clever to think of these connections which in a simpler world were just common sense. Similarly when Lithic was the conscious idiom the body itself was common sense, a burgeon divided down the middle; so how could the duality of the ba be missed, a growth in two copies inextricably mixed for all the animal kingdom, but not for vegetables which instead grew green and had a grain, growing in the round with no need for any copulation in pairs either. The Zulu for two is bili, and it also means testicles, the pair it is clear they always thought of as paradigmatic, and this in spite of their bare bottoms with their two cheeks on show at that time. The others had a stronger appeal, it is clear, and could surely have been guessed. It must have led to a very jolly math. We really need to infiltrate the Zulu mind to find out whether their number two is simply the word for the pair that immediately sprang to mind when their naming committee was asked to think of a mnemonic for the duality; or if on the other hand their genital nomenclature is from the number two, as a discreet indirect reference without actually using a name, perhaps regarded as unlucky, ill mannered, sacreligious or even providing evil spirits with a gratuitous purchase on the speaker's own person by disclosing the address. It has to be said both the actual phonetics and the body of Lithic, which sees the visual form generally preceding the abstract, argue strongly that the priority of the number goes strongly against the Lithic grain. In KwaZulu sex is at number two. In the Indo-European tongues it is at number six (in chapter 14). It is there in both countries, probably in all.

The two sides of the body are side by side, the two buttocks precisely so. So to be by is to be beside, near or far, but mostly nearby. From beside it is a short step to side as a subsidiary or minor location or activity: a bye road is a side road, and on that road the scenery goes by, and cars in the outside lane, and even time follows suit and goes by too. Eric Partridge equates by with be- which here is in the next column. He had no columnar approach. His semantics are always understated. The buttocks properly belong in columns 5 and 6 but carry forward into this column of the tree as well. Eric Partridge appears to be adrift here again. He treats a butt as an end piece as prior to the bottom, whereas it is more consistent in all cases for the tune to be played on the human body which is treated as the original instrument. The butt of a gun in point of fact is a single piece unlike our bottoms, and only mischief allows the bifurcate exemplar to stand in for a single wooden stock as well. The Old English suffix –uc which is the origin of English –ock, and was probably pronounced ook, is nowhere interpreted. The Lithic u-kai is simple enough: dual or both-joined, or joined together. The buttocks are divided or separate burgeons but joined together. We have two buttocks but only one bottom. Old English had ball-uc as well for a bull's testicles specifically, of which the bull possesses a pair like everyone else, but joined together in an unusually close fitting scrotum which binds them together so that he possesses a single genital stalk, unlike all the rest of us with our double endowment quite visible in all but the shaggiest exemplars, but which in his case hardly reveals the two separate beans in the pod at all. In view of the established Lithic idiom of bu, as in the Bornean Boar, for his dual bits, the testicles, it seems reasonable to analyse bull as in fact similarly prompted, that is the one with his bu-lai, his two testicles looped or lumped together in a single long pod. A bulrush we may like to note in passing shares this configuration with the bull, its very many winged seeds being in a long smoothly rounded stalk, evidently reminding our rude forefathers immediately of a bull's scrotum – but in this case a rush, rai-sai, rayed up, that is raised up and pointing to the skies – all reeds and rushes have long stalks without leaves – a comicality of a kind on its own, as if the Egyptian rays had missed their proper target by a fraction and got the bullrush by the seedpod and raised it up. These are the Egyptian rays of chapter 13, paradigmatically from the Egyptian sun Ra, but in all cases stimulant, particularly those supposedly exchanged between the sexes. The Malay labu for a vegetable marrow is perhaps reinventing the same jape, the plant alleged to grow large seed pods.It is a known fact some Greek intellectuals (probably Guardian readers) did not care to eat beans (phasilos in Greek and faba. in Latin) because they were called testicles. With both words the paha or pahei, reduced to phei in Greek and simply fa- in Latin meant the genitals. The Latins contented themselves with genital bits to match the boars and bulls. The Greeks had a longer and more explicit composition. The pahei or joy piece was taken to be both seeded and long. Peas in their pods were simply skinned or covered. Beans were the fleshy bits in their scrotums. Or so folk seem to have thought.

Latin ambi (8) for both, as is the body twin sided together, also involves the Latin ambire (8 & 6), from ambi-ire, to wander around or make a circular tour, tethered as it were, to maintain the same proximity to a centre of action en route. To bind (8) is to join two bits together like the body does. It is from the Sanskrit which is badhna to join together. The −na is a Sanskrit verbal suffix merely. If the −h- is a cockney h disclosing an original ba-da(h)i, it is a binary work very much like our English body. Bashke, from the Lithic ba-sai-kai, a two-singles-shaped or joined, is the Albanian prefix or suffix indicating shared or joint activity or characteristic, as with English co-, con-, syn-, or fellow-, meaning joint. There are 450 entries in my Albanian dictionary with this prefix or suffix, from which we may conclude Albanians are quite at home with this aspect of ba- although nowadays probably unaware of the derivation, which all the while they are sitting on. A balance is from the Latin bilanx. The Lithic would be bai-lai'n-kai(s), meaning two-flat-shapes or plates, or even bowl shapes, but perhaps more cogently two-level-makers. These doubles entendres seem to have quite often convinced the naming committees they were on the right tracks. The balance was two platters suspended from the ends of a rod, level when the weights on each were equal (as long as the point of suspension was precisely in the middle). Warfare, a confrontation in two opposing lines in classical times (or thicker ranks if you were Greek and deployed as a phalanx, imitating the shape of the soldiers' friend the phallus), was bellum in Latin, the two lines of battle brought up against each other.

Column 4, the Ba itself, was pictured in Ancient Egypt as a bird seen hovering over a dying person, a spirit of the flesh on the point of departure, while the Ka was the driving force of life which was dual, one half for this world and one for the next, the Dua Taun[6] or Second World of the dead, on the dark under side of the disc. It was not seen leaving therefore at death. It was going to hang in there until reincarnation when it would get a new suit of flesh. It must shame the Egyptians (were any left), as chauvinistic males as can readily be imagined. They are exposed making Ba the mortal feminine element and the Ka the immortal male part. It was in fact quite widely believed in olden days that it was the male part that survived and was reincarnated, with the Ba clothing each reincarnated Ka in the womb with flesh, like putting on a new coat. They did however pass

"Western" civilization on to the Greeks. At one time more educated Greeks lived in Egypt than in Greece, which harboured the yokels. It is pertinent to ask where we would be now without the Egyptians. To be bai (9) was to be alive and it was the mesi, the planting of the seed, the impregnation from which age was counted, since that was when the bai began to be buttered on. To be bai was to be alive, a single phenotype of any species, which is where we get our meaning of being. To be alive is to be, and only by abstract extension is it taken to refer to simple presence for any article at all. Strictly the individual became individual on parturition, separation from the parent stock, tai in Lithic as in Ancient Egyptian passim, like the firewood snapped into two. Ber- in Malay is the universal prefix for an intransitive verb or verbal adjective that is indicating a state of being as opposed to one of agency. Brer similarly was an African Creole term for an animal life form, related to brother merely for the benefit of whitey. Brother's derivation is a mystery. Lithic berau-terai could be fleshed out-together – in the same womb. Compare Thomas, the twin from Lithic elements tau-mai-sai, twin-planting-of life/seed.

There is of course a close relationship all through between all the columns of the semantic tree for Ba, such that in the individual subconscious mind they can coalesce and exchange semantic contents more or less at random, depending on context or even the state of the digestion – a potent factor in the dream world. The –ber- in liberty from Latin li-ber, free, was loose-living or lai, as opposed to being a slave under restraint not to take off, enclosed or lai. The slave was living under lien, a nice example of the human mind's ability to twist a single phoneme to mean whatever whim required it to mean quite without reference to what had been worked out elsewhere for another purpose. Slaves were also quite often aliens too. Many of them were Slavs. Lai was sometimes loose and sometimes linked, it is that simple. It is all in chapter 9 for La. Civilisation may not yet have eliminated the chauvinisms of the sexes but it would be foolish to deny there has been some movement and the flux seems unstoppable now. The Albanian behet to become, turn into, acquire the characteristics of what follows, is emblematic of getting fleshed out, kitted out in effect with a covering of the pre-existing bare bones. The h is a cockney h, and the Lithic phonemes ba(h)i-ai-tai, being-as is-becoming, or still more literally being- by- birth. Behet is closely followed by ben- with more than a dozen meanings including to be, to mature, ripen, be readied, to become one of, to pass (of time), to go off somewhere, and eight pages of different applications. Then comes ben- with a page or two in a role very similar to ber- in Malay. The Malay ber- prefix makes an intransitive verb or a verbal adjective, like being or –ing in English. It is from bai-, like being in English, or bespoke tailoring etc. So we say goodbye without too much regret to Billy Bunter and his nested gulls, and move on to less prolific phonemes with some relief.

Notes

1. We all started out with the Irish in us, it seems – before the rest of us moved on.

2. Sandhi is the term used for the changing of the initial consonants of nouns to mark different cases, as in Welsh. It is highly disconcerting for the Lithic hypotheses, although it is highly unusual. Consonants casually shift from inadvertence over time. It is not terminal for Lithic, merely a latter-day whimsy.

3. Boustrophedon is from the Greek Bous-strophe-don where the Bous is Oxen, Strophe is turn backwards and forwards, and don is does or some such. The Lithic (regrettably) is from siti-rau-pehei-don. Siti-rau is when roused by the female, pehei is the male organ and don is doing or something like it. Strophe, the backwards and forwards movement (like it or lump it) is modeled on that of copulation. The term is a very old one and it looks a bit as if the oxen were introduced to cover for the other. Strophe was the common term for turn and go in the opposite direction, and came to mean a stanza, a stand in the action or part of a performance. At one time Greek texts were written in this way alternately from left to right and then back again from right to left, and in the theatre the singers promenaded from side to side of the theatre similarly. It is too late to say if there were any etymologists among them who knew of the internal construction of the term or if the original motif was already buried with the passage of time. The Greeks got their bad mouthing from the Egyptians where bahei or pahei was the joy bit or whoopee piece and the Greeks turned pahei into phi (Φ), and the British copy in their most notorious four letter word f***, adding a k for kai, meaning making with the pahei, a novel derivation offering certain opportunities for free pints in a pub if neatly presented.

4. The subject has been exhaustively explored in "Hamlet's Mill" by de Santillana and von Dechend, published by David R Godine in 1977. It was perhaps the first perceptive publication of any thoroughly esoteric mythological subject matter since The Golden Bough, and was therefore not taken up by established publishers.

5. OED is The Oxford English Dictionary in some thirty five huge volumes, or for a minor fraction of the price on two CDs on computer, clicking instead of handling the multiple volumes when cross referencing articles, hopping between volumes.

6. The Egyptologists only recognise 'Duat´ for the next world, and do not read Dua as Second. They think that the final glyph for –t in their recension is a bun or a loaf of bread whereas it is in fact a divided circle, a semi-circle, one

divided in two, properly pronounced taun, with the meaning of the two because of the letter T and the universe because it also conveys the meaning of
all the events or occurrences. The Egyptian universe was a floating penny in
a stone dish, or anyway with a stone lip which kept the sea on board. The upper side was the light world we all live in, with the inverted bowl we call the
sky above, the lower side the second world of the dead where the dead sun in
the West gestated nightly on its way for a rebirth at dawn the next day in the
East. Of course it was all tommy-rot but it is wise to remember it satisfied the
best minds of the day and we still have virtually identical minds, if somewhat
differently stuffed.

CHAPTER 5

THE PHONEME KA

Although this is the second phoneme chapter, after Ba, it was written first which is why it rehearses phonemic research somewhat generally at first. Of all the consonants K is the paradigmatic one with a clear Stone Age psychosemantic content. Moreover it was the first original semantic content to be discovered, which with hindsight probably contributed to the significance it is given. It makes sense therefore to try to develop here the scope and significance of the psychosemantic contents, which theoretically are to be found for every consonant and vowel, using the Ka consonant as a prime example. It appears to have figured first as the primal scream, an involuntary contraction of the glottis on sensing the sabretoothed tiger in the dark, and then an outburst as the brute's fangs bit in. The more meaningful a sound to human perception, the greater its traumatic content, the earlier the establishment of dominant meaning content and its persistence and breeding potential over the millennia, and the more proliferation of meanings we should anticipate. Vowels being by their very nature less concrete and determinate than consonants, their separate identification and the accretion of common conventional meanings for them appears to have come later. This lateness in turn is perhaps the reason for the relative sophistication (degree of abstraction) of the semantic contents eventually ascribed to them. Abstraction is generalisation, a loss of specificity, and vowels lend themselves to this kind of thinking where articulation of precise meaning is difficult, since they have no articulation of their own. It makes them hard to track as well.

The method for deriving the original psychosemantic contents of word elements is the reverse of that which is easiest for explanation. A semantic tree is historical, like a family tree; but with the meanings giving birth to new derivative meanings – derived by extension or analogy from the parent meanings. Meanings have to be dug out and built up in the first place by working backwards from the current forms to the more and more previous, the more basic and original meanings. The Lithic hypothesis maintains that the original meanings that were attached to sounds as being their "natural" meanings were more or less the same in all languages, so that the traces, with different combinations and idioms, can be pursued in all languages simultaneously. This obviously has some practical limitations. The number of languages any one person can review in a lifetime is a small fraction of those spoken. Moreover the reader is not often willing to be racked with more than one or two languages at a time, and it is easiest for writer and reader alike to deal for the most part in the home language. Old dead languages are in point of fact extraordinarily handy, precisely because they are old and dead; their formation has been arrested before as much modern slovening has occurred. With living languages, there is nothing like a good etymological dictionary to clear away the top layers at least of later modifications of both phonetic form and meaning.

The Ka sound, imitating the sound of flint striking flint, intimating forceful deliberate effort towards an intended and purposeful end, purposeful effort, was about making things happen, already preaching the chauvinism of the tool maker. Echoism was in at the birth of language and consciousness. It could be said mimicry virtually on its own kick started civilization. Ga, the softened voiced version, was apt to be treated as at one remove from the naked physical action, the first abstraction, perhaps indicating the equivalent intention. In cut and kill and kharma we can still count the echo of the crude conception of making and acting on the world, all from the clack of flint on flint. In coming and going we can see, if we are alert, the same agency. In acid and acropolis, pickle and cranium, horn (cornu) and geography we can distinguish, if we are careful, the growing gamut of descendant meanings. Ka in Egyptian, in Japanese and in Hindustani carries the same message, albeit in different idioms but always within the same range: to strike, to flake off, hard, sharp, striking force, impulsion, drive, action, structure, form, matter, a miscellany of divergent applications of the same original semantic content pregnant with many meanings as the human mind sophisticated itself up by its own bootstraps, as the linguistic idiom proliferated to describe more and better. This is not just high flown metaphor. It is literally what happened. But it is necessary to guard against anachronism. The original psychosemantic content was simple and general and therefore diffuse. Our modern meaning systems are clear cut and differential by comparison, precisely and solely because they are modern and benefit from aeons of slowly clearing the attic, replacing relative chaos with neat and tidy wordy patterns.

The juxtaposition of two Lithic elements so that one modified or at least marked the other, supplying more than one pointer to the intended meaning by (grammarless) apposition, was the means by which early communication could expand and increase its utility. It was before grammar, and long before grammarians. Now two elements in apposition amount to a word beyond a peradventure, even if of a form barely sufficient for us to recognise it on its own as such today. Single grunts were and are just grunts. But grouped differential and sequential grunts must already be words – or else just a tune. The art of wordification is already suggested; language as we choose to define it has begun. As yet grammar is wholly lacking, so the first and second elements in any sequence must have ranked pari passu so far as their meaning function was concerned. The second adjectival element was also just as much a noun as the first, and the first as much an adjective as the second. Effectively the mind was quite simply adjectival. The substantive was a later arabesque.

Original semantic contents appear to have been so general as to be diffuse. This is not quite the same as to say so general as to be useless, but it is getting near it. The adjectival mind, when it picked up an idea, was ready to find it duplicated anywhere or even everywhere. Readers of Bertrand Russell in his lighter moments will recall his tale of the philosopher who had a tooth pulled under laughing gas and discovered the Secret of the Universe as he was coming round. Methodical fellow, he scribbled it down as he emerged into consciousness. Later, under the cold eye of reason, he examined his script. It read: "A smell of ether – everywhere pervades". Generations of other philosophers, alas, have formulated whole systems of their universally pervasive abstractions every bit as fatuous in the cold light of reason as the adjectival ether, without the aid of laughing gas and for all one knows with all their teeth at their disposal.

Ka, it may seem at first, is almost as pervasive as the smell of ether appeared to Russell's philosopher. We can look here at case histories most easily in English, the commonest Indo-European tongue as well as the largest anywhere (ever), chiefly because it is the most easily accessible – particularly to English speakers. The term Lithic element is used to refer to both the phoneme and its semantic contents; and if it is necessary to identify which, the expansions Lithic phonetic element and Lithic semantic content are available and easily understood. The phonetic element is traditionally described by etymologists as a phoneme, and is contrasted with a morpheme which is defined as a combination of one or more phonemes sufficient to have a semantic content, somewhat as if there were phonetic atoms and molecular morphemes with meanings deriving from their structure, made out of them. In fact this distinction between phonemes and morphemes and the canonisation of phonemic structure as morphemic (morpheme is just form in Greek) in practice prejudges where meanings begin, and introduces an element of gobbledegook besides. Use of the term element rides across this distinction therefore, rather as if it had never been. Traditionally etymologists have allowed meanings in rather late. By putting meanings earlier in the developmental chain and by giving them a larger place we effectively dismiss the meaningless phoneme, replacing it with one already meaningful. It is not disputed that assiduous critics may be able to generate a meaningless cry, a phoneme, and go on to distinguish it from a morpheme, but they should be left to the exercise on their own. Some of their meaningless cries they may even be mistaken in treating as meaningless in that vague meanings may be attributed to them, as we shall see. No phoneme (or morpheme for that matter) has any objective semantic content of its own. That can only be acquired in the mind of mankind when appointed there by human whimsy of one kind or another. Semantic contents are functions of the living species, and do not in reality inhabit either phonemes or morphemes – or any other noise for that matter.

For English words the best of the printed sources, bar none, is the late Eric Partridge. His life work "Origins, A Short Etymological Dictionary of Modern English", of some thousand pages, was first published in 1958. My copy is currently the cheaper Book Club printing of 1978. The weighty Oxford Dictionary of some thirty four volumes (but now mercifully on CD) is historical before it is etymological; the difference is it seldom goes back before the Latin and Greek and illustrates recent developments over a few hundred years for the most part. Comparing Partridge's layout Partridge highlights, all through, ramifications between words which are akin; and he roams further afield. He sometimes reaches back to Ancient Egyptian and Akkadian, even once or twice to Sumerian. He says in his foreword "...the system I have devised has enabled me with the aid of cross references not only to cover a very much wider field than might have seemed possible, but also, and especially, to treat all important words much more comprehensively and thoroughly". Indeed many entries group scores of words together including those not obviously related, and cover a whole page or even several pages. There is, on careful daily reading for over several decades, at least a hint of some of the developments the Lithic hypotheses profess. His shade nevertheless must be held blameless for what he left unstated; and he had no Lithic. But without his gargantuan appetite for analysis and comparison over a lifetime culminating in his Origins in all probability this book would never have got written.

The psychosemantic tree for Ka on page 144 has fifty two derivations, denoting the power of the original semantic content buried deep in the subconscious mind, with proliferations galore. The more fundamental the original identification of the phonemic meaning the more it has been built on over the millennia, the more meanings have been spawned. In the Stone Age much of human thinking centred on stones, reinforced daily by practice, their flaking and use. Knapping was high tech in those days. Thinkers thought about it a lot. As well as the knock of flint on flint there were the associated thoughts of what it meant to knap. The Lithic for knap is ka-na-pai, strike-expose-surfaces. We can start with meaning 4 of the semantic tree, the effect of the earliest striking of the flint, namely a chipping off of lots of little bits, and these bits were debetage, discards or waste resulting. Ka, the strike of flint on flint, produced lots of chips (chips from kei-pai, struck pieces) or kaka, which thus meant debetage and waste and then human waste or excrement, as it still does although the Stone Age is long past.

Meaning 4 is also for cracks, also resulting directly from the strike; the Lithic original form of crack is kara-kai, to strike or striking-makes. It makes both the sound and the split. From the crack comes the semantic extension of the split, the division between the flake and the flint cracked which is also where they are or were joined, their joint. Lithic perceptions were less critical than ours. The slayer and the slain were joined in a general perception of the act. A splitting off was not so far as all that from a joining on, in both cases we are thinking of two bits, distinguished but seeming to belong together. Ka could mean join or joint as well as a split or disjoint. Look at Hindi with the suffixed –ka for of: for example iska nam for his name. The 'of' meaning in Hindi is from joined to, belonging to, be-long. Blong is used in a New Guinea-English pidgin[1] language for of. To be split off from something can also suggest belonging to it. There is assumed to be an underlying continuity in spite of the break

Belong, in passing, is from being looped together, see chapter 9. The crack also implied a split and a crack fully split was a slit such as you got in the Stone Age from the stroke of a butcher's sharp flake, these days a heavy steel blade. The Sumerians were using such a ka for mouth, a slit opening for eating and speaking, and no doubt spitting as well: cat in Sumerian was ka-tse or spit-mouth, uncommonly like German katze five thousand years later, and even English cat, a tidied up version of katze with the spitting dropped, perhaps because a kitten once tamed stops spitting. The Old Frisians had kunte, which can be read as struck become or struck in two, either way a slit, our English cunt, which Partridge curiously relates to the Hittite kun for tail. Perhaps he thought because vaginas are worn at the tail end? He had no Lithic of course and could not imagine a single phoneme, ka, with so many so different semantic contents as a slit and a tail, as he must have been going on the sound equivalences alone. The tail which wags the dog, canis in Latin which is akin to kun in Hittite, is from the Lithic ka-(u)-nai (s), spine(49)-what-protruding, erect and waving with pleasure, Brer tailwagger in fact. The tail is indeed an extension of the spine and it is the protruding end of it too, and the dog does wag it when it is feeling good. Cunnus in Latin, per contra, is from the Lithic elements kau-nau (s), the –nau exhibiting poetic agreement with the foregoing element and to be glossed slit-nai, viz the slit which gapes and presents – rather than the one up above, the mouth for eating and speaking, in short the sexual opening or birth canal, see chapter 11 for nau. The Ancient Egyptians, way before Mrs Grundy, were fully at home with the way the vagina, when flaccid a mere slit or split, little more than a fold, rounds out and gapes open when sexually aroused; and they were even happy with it. It was a major part of their emotional and semantic repertoire, since suppressed in the interests of taste

THE PSYCHOSEMANTIC TREE FOR KA

The Phonetic Tree

The Semantic Tree

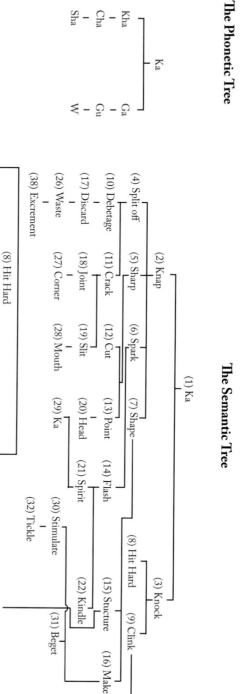

and decorum. The language says as much however much Mrs Grundy may grunt. We are left with the optional −ta, -te or −t to explain. It is the definitive marker, much like those in Ancient Egyptian glyphed but unpronounced at the end of a word. It says 'the twinning ka', when the splitting has been done and not the original striking ka at all, in other words a slit and not a hit.

As an exercise to assess the applicability of the Lithic hypothesis to a word list not of my choosing, to see how widely it can be made to stick, all Partridge's words beginning with K are glossed below. It is a mercifully short list, which is why it is chosen. If we work through the 150 head entries, thirteen merely refer to the same words grouped under other words beginning with K – his cross referencing – while another 27 refer in the same way to head entries for other words beginning with letters other than K – the majority unsurprisingly beginning with C. A further 26 are straight borrowings from other languages: Kafir (Arabic), Kaka (Maori), Kalmuk (Turki), Kanaka (Polynesian), Kangaroo (Australian Aboriginal), Kaolin (Chinese), Kapok (Malay), Karakul (Turki), Karma (Sanscrit), Karroo (Hottentot), Kauri (Maori with Tahitian, Paumotan and Samoan cognates), Kayak (Eskimo), Kea (Maori), Kedgeree (Hindi), etc. That leaves 84 head words for which the etymology is indicated. Partridge's word list is in no way exhaustive. It is simply proposed here to attempt to gloss the 84 with their possible Lithic originals, in order to give the reader a more detailed idea of the scope of Lithic analysis.

Katydid, a North American insect, is simply echoic of the insect's strident call. An echoic meaning is strictly a psychosemantic one, since it is prompted by the significance attached naturally to the sound by the human mind, to be distinguished by its evident echoic character from the more devious and less obtrusive psychosemantic meanings it is hoped also to demonstrate. There is no need to pay too much attention to the fact a strident call is here perceived as beginning with a K, which perhaps weakly supports the hypothesis that there are, somewhere in our subconscious minds, psychosemantic contents waiting to get out. In point of fact echoing a natural sound usually includes a degree of imaginative interpretation, often prompted by the language involved. Ancient Egyptians were persuaded their owls were saying A-Ma-oo, probably because it meant to them the superlative case ending of both darkness and death, and the owl after all is a hunter in the dark. Anglo Saxons had the owl saying owl, or perhaps originally a-ool. They spoke no Egyptian, unless unawares. Now we think Ter-wit-ter-woo is apt, though the consonants are there to mimic our whistled mimicry, the owl does not mention them, he just uses the vowels without modulating them with the tongue, checking the flow to produce what is perhaps best represented as awa-oowoo; good enough anyway I find, if whistled low, to fool the owl and bring him over to repel the intruder.

Kedge (16), a small anchor, Partridge hypothetically refers to catch, which he derives ultimately from the Latin capere to seize. The Lithic elements of capere appear to be ka-pai, with Latin grammatical suffix -ere, the infinitive or verbal marker. This verbal marker is probably from the Egyptian (Mediterranean). The Lithic ka-Pai can carry the meaning make covered, and/or make with the legs, ie chase and capture, hold under restraint. There is more and better on this at Ketch below.

Keel (15,16) is from Mediaeval Dutch kiel, a sea going vessel, akin to Old English ceol, and it is not altogether fanciful to see the same elements in the otherwise unrelated word galleon. The Lithic formation appears to have been ka-i-ai-lai, hull-which-goes-saltwater or sea, that is to say made for ocean going. Galleon's Lithic elements somewhat similarly appear to be ga-lai-aun, go-saltwater-that one, where evidently go-to-sea has become worded (perceived as a word) and then conjugated as a verb, galai-on, going to sea one, ocean going one. Land lubbers may need to be told a keel is essential for an ocean going vessel to keep it upright in a swell, but not for calm river waters except in rudimentary form as merely part of the construction process where it takes its name from the major article, named for the role for which it was developed. It is of course in origin the solid timber which runs the length of the bottom of the boat, and for ocean going is extended so it goes deep and provides stability in a swell.

Keen (8), to wail, a wail of grief, is compared with the Old Irish cainim (variation coinim), Gaelic caoin, Welsh cwyno, and Breton keinal, I wail. The Lithic offered is kai-ai-nai, struck-which-presents; a sign of grief, literally hit-showing. Wailing is an exhibition of grief. In Eastern countries it is laid on with a trowel and acts as a catharsis.

Keep (16) is derived from Old English cepan, where the -an is the Old English verbal (infinitive) marker, with the consecutive meanings to observe, to notice, to desire, to seek, to keep. Partridge suggests comparisons with Old Norse kopa, Mediaeval Dutch capen, Middle Low German kapen, and Middle High German kapfen, all meaning to gaze or stare fixedly or gape. One wonders in passing if the carp (German carpfen) was named for its pog-eyed fixed stare when fished out of the water or for its fat body. To carp at anything comes perhaps from such a glassy stare, a refusal to go along. "Carpe diem" in Latin, beware the day, with carpe meaning look out, suggests the Lithic ka-ra-pai, make-visible-the panorama, look around you, whence a warning. Partridge adds "The semantic chain, or at least the interconnections are worth noting......the origins of this verb need to be clarified still further". Here goes. The common semantic element in the catena which Partridge proposes – observe, notice, desire, seek, keep – is a certain fixity of purpose. Fixate on/observe; fixate on/notice; fixate on/desire; fixate on/seek; fixate on/keep. The Lithic is kai-pa, make a view or take a view. The sense of view comes from the panorama, the surface (pa) that the eye presents to view, the snapshot the camera saves these days or when the movie camera pans. The first semantic content (observe) is with reference to a physical action; one looks at and sees. The second (notice) and third (desire) are intentional, the intention abstracted from behind the initial action as it were. The fourth (seek) tends towards physical action again, and it might be said to follow on from the intentional state foregoing, extending the catena. The fifth (keep) is a physical action of restraint, or a state if you think that way. This sequence is not untypical of the transformations or developments of meanings occasioned by metaphor: first the beady eye (observe); then the mental state behind the seeing eye (notice); then a further marked mental state, marked by cupidity (desire). So far we could be following the mental processes of a blackbird! These meanings appear to go back a bit. Then the cupidity gives rise to the action it engenders (seek); and finally the consummation of the action, capture and retention (keep). There is even a link to Latin capere here too, as with kedge treated above. Pa as cover also involves surface, both originally from skin, and a view presents a spread of sights which can be (and indeed was) fancied as a surface, with attention to perspective coming much later. So capere can be glossed to make or take a view and so to observe as well as to stage a coup, strike with the mitts, or cover and nab or seize. The Lithic ka-pa is a prolific pairing of elements. Ka, strike, breeds hard, hard structure, formative shape, and so skeletal structure of the body, or indeed in like manner of the world, the ground (dig a bit almost wherever you are and you come to rock), which locates you, etc, while pa as a diminutive of ba, the fleshy element, can refer to any small fleshy piece of the body or the wider world, as well as the covering of the flesh, the skin; and surface coverings quite generally.

There is a kind of evolution of the mind involved here; and maybe rules for it might be developed without making it a matter of natural process like a Grimm's Law for semantics – finding mental ruts rather than firm tramlines. But no attempt will be made here since to be sufficiently general it would inevitably appear inconsequential, even whimsical, and would be laughed out of court. Nevertheless a little concentrated thought in areas the academic is apt to dismiss because uncharted can be very rewarding. The identification of the Lithic elements of keep was difficult for us because to our way of thinking they are bizarrely skewed. But kai-pai carrying the meaning kindle-panorama (22) is not forced. A panorama, the general sweep of observation, is made up of all the bits and pieces in view taken collectively, to form a surface or picture of the whole, the locus of all the individual pieces, their integral or universal. We know Greek pan also has come to mean all; the occasion for the identification of a surface with the totality was originally the vision process as perceived. The Greek ops (eye, as in optician) springs to mind illustrating the same idiom. au-pa-i-sai, that one-scene-which-lights up or sees, ie the organ which sees. Lighting up and seeing is a slayer and slain pairing. For the theory of sight which treated the eye as an active emitter of there and back rays like the sun, rather than as a passive receiver as we now do, see the Egyptian rays in chapter 13.

Keg (15), Partridge thinks, comes from Old Norse Kaggi, a cask. The cask is of course a maverick like the crab, wearing its skeletal hard structure on the outside, and this maverick property is noticed in the language. Ka-gai, carcase-made/hardened/joined; not admittedly a shellfish, but certainly a shell thing. The crab, like the Egyptian Scarab, from the Lithic si-kara-bai, brer-skull-fleshed, wears its skeleton on the outside, while the rest of us keep our soft flesh decently covering our bones.

Kelp (15), from the Lithic kai-lai-pai, making/shaped/structured-long/lithe/saltwater/ocean-pieces, conveys the seaweed under water streaming in the tide pretty well. Readers will by now be demanding of themselves why the general syllabic forms Ka, La, Pa, and now the general forms Kai, Lai, Pai are used. Elision in language use apparently has gone that way: from -a to -ai to -e to silent -e or final omission as surplus to requirement; so ka, kai, ke, k; pa, pai, pe, p. These elisions were not semantic marks, they just occurred over the millennia by the universal slovening process whereby every construct is gradually slurred, generation by generation, in aid of shortened and easier pronunciation. The Lithic idiom which precised every phoneme with its semantic contents has been long forgotten, and survives only in the subconscious repository of old language idioms which each generation relearns as it learns to speak, from the linguistic keel beneath the surface influencing the direction in which language drifts and keeping the old patterns afloat in the slow maelstrom of life.

Kelpy (15), a horse-like water sprite is of obscure origin, Partridge says. We must agree. What is obscure is the character portrayed. There are Celtic variants. Anyway it is simply from kelp. A sea-horse sprite would likely graze on kelp in place of grass. We might have called a cow a grassy if we had not noticed its horns and named it for its bifurcating skull.

Kepi (48) should be compared with the English cap, and is to do with caput, the Latin for head. The head is in this recension the Ka's puti, or glans of the body, body knob. The puti in Egyptian was the teat (ti) of the penis (pipi or pu). Medical science would be more likely today to report injury to the head of the penis than to the glans of the body. Nevertheless in far off days a cap was a covering of the body knob, the thinking being akin to that which gives us also the prepuce or foreskin, from peri-puti, the surround of the penis teat. Every cap is at one remove a foreskin worn on the head. Magritte was barking, but up this same tree. So kai-pai-pai-ti, body-glans-covering-thing was not bad for a cap. It may seem cheeky to reduplicate the pai to recover a double usage (for glans and its cover) like that. The reduplication is not there in the form it has come down to us, though it is in the dual pu for pipi. But in Lithic you could use a syllable twice for double semantic contents if it fitted the string. They were there in the mind, so why not allow them to apply? Indeed if a syllable was doubly apposite that was a dual recommendation for the construction, almost a guarantee it was naturally predestined and apt. The widespread use of pai laid it open to this kind of duplex utilisation. The English pie is a dish with a lid on it, often of pastry which is also a lid specifically -stry, or Lithic si-terai, rayed in the fire, just as in the word roast, where the rau vowel indicates a more thorough roasting. The same applies to toast and holocaust. Greek pi (Π), which every schoolboy knows is really 22/7, is actually drawn as a lid or surface on two supports, attention drawn to the surface by making a curlicue of it, while the supports are plain so it is crystal clear (to those who know already) the top is the bit intended. In Egypt they drew it instead birds-eye perspective as a square (surface), the glyph for Egyptian pai, Greek pi and our letter P (which happens to be a diminished B). The Egyptians actually used it syllabically contributing the sound pai and not just the letter p – which the Egyptologists have not yet spotted. They used birds a lot in their hieroglyphs, apparently because they flew about in the Empyrean as if it were their domain, especially and rather unfortunately the bigger soaring birds that were birds of prey and got up the highest (for the purpose of searching for their prey), making them aspirants to God, whom the Egyptians decided was up there with His beady eye fixed on them and their affairs, as well as models in due course for the angels (messengers) from Him, to be adopted by Jews and Christians alike, alighting out of the heavens with news from above both good and bad, but most often the latter. Gabriel was exceptional in this respect.

Kerosene (16,22) is from Greek keros, grease or wax, ie a viscous fatty substance from Lithic kai-raus, made-thoroughly rayed, or in other words given a good roasting, when the juices ran out and on cooling congealed providing a combustible liquid, the first ceramic, made by heating. The Greek root is the same as in Christ, the anointed, the oiled. The confusion with Chrestus, wearing a crest, comes from the semantic contents of rai. Being rayed can be a roasting, an observation – like the sun god Ra as the eye of Heaven looking down upon his creation – or just a rousing and raising if you are a penis. The crest is copying the penis.

Kestrel (16,22) is from Mediaeval French cresserelle probably; and thus ultimately from Latin crista, crested. If so the bird originally so named must have had a crest. The Lithic was kai-rai-siti, made-rayed-feminine. Feminine rays raised things (notably the male organ, a very early perception) apparently copying the flame, which leaps upwards on its own. The Lithic siti could also be read as fire-thing, exhibiting heat, the life principle. Around the hearth together in their birthday suits, after a satisfying evening meal, the warmth of the flame was seen to enamour the boys. The ladies were flame-like in this. They had that subtle essence which could be a pain, but also held the magic or spirituality which gestated life by putting the heat into it and keeping it warm. They were life sources, the incubators of the species, and therefore partook of the flame. And all because the ladies liked to sit round the fire? Not really. They did, and it enamoured them too, and even got them jabbering about it perhaps; that may be what got us talking; but all animals were warm blooded. The flame, in an adjectival world, shared heat with life just as life was warm, while death was the opposing cold element which took over when you died.

Ketch (16), like kedge, Partridge derives from Middle English catch, with a related form in Old English chacier to chase, so that a ketch was originally perhaps a light pursuit vessel, or else a fishing vessel taking the catch on board? If we are to lead back to a Lithic form it is by way of the Latin captiare, in turn from capere again, to take or seize – perhaps originally to trap (small game, insects, witchety grubs, etc) under the hand, Lithic ka-pai, strike-(with the)hand, or make-covered, grasp, make with the spuds. If this is right then a ketch is a sense development from the butterfly net tactic, also used netting at sea. The word grasp, incidentally, comprises the same Lithic elements plus two more which may be virtually fillers. This looks like one of the common uses of the Lithic -s-, which may perhaps be touched on here, since it appears in grasp. It often seems to be included much as the Egyptians put a subscript | under a glyph to indicate it was to be read in its pristine actual first sense rather than in any subsequent figurative or alphabetical sense; so in this sense s means actual, as is, ie in this case the following p, from pai, is to be construed in its literal meaning of skin, surface, cover, covering, even cover of. The r in grasp can also be disposed of here, as the verbal marker as in the Ancient Egyptian, gr- being slovened from kara- to make or making.

Kettle (7) is from the Latin catillus, diminutive of catinus, a large deep vessel, akin to Greek kotule, a bowl, Lithic ka-u-tau-lai, shape-hole-become-looped; and Sanskrit catvala, a hole, and though Partridge does not mention it, also the current Hindi chatti, the porous unglazed earthenware wide bellied water vessel for keeping water cold from evaporation through the earthenware. The basic idea (according to Partridge) is hollow, hollowness, hole-shape. The Egyptian khati, the lower belly, is relevant. Nasalised it is a vulgar English four lettered word for the female external genitalia, notably hollow. The Lithic appears to be ka-ti, the feminine part of the body par excellence – ti was the feminine marker in Ancient Egyptian as well as an orifice or teat, the concordance not accidental. But the belly was the feminine part of the body anyway because it expressed itself so clearly in pregnancy which was taken to be the process by which the female put flesh on the male boney element. The various suffixes in the Greek, Latin and Sanskrit words cited above are open to several interpretations. The Latin suffix -illus is generally taken to be simply a diminutive, little. But the -le in Greek kotule is indicative of the rimmed saucer shape of the bowl, by analogy with the imagined lipped saucer shape of the skyline at sea in which the waters of the oceans were contained: a merciful provision, since otherwise the water would long ago have all drained down and fallen off the edge of the world, leaving it an uninhabitable desert. The Lithic lai as well as the semantic content loop from the ocean's saucer had also come to mean elliptical, part of a circle. It is tempting to gloss the Sanskrit catvala as kati-wala, by analogy with modern Hindi chae-wallah or topi-wallah or garram-unde-wallah, tea-seller, hat-wearer and hot-egg-seller respectively, the original semantic content of the w-a-la being one-that-linked, the person linked with, or of that ilk; here the mental circle suggested by the supposed world circumvallation being akin to our idea of a loop or encirclement and so a category. Circle itself, indeed, being from the Greek kuklos, a ring or circle, is from Lithic ku-ku-lau(s), corner-corner-looped, all the corners smoothed in a loop, the smooth curved figure. We have left the liveliest bit until last, for fear of Mrs Grundy. The Latin catinus, the large deep vessel, has a -nus termination so far unattended to. We can expand the -nus to Lithic -nau(s) and dispose of the s as the Latin substantive marker. Nau is orgasmic, engorged and gaping. Roman matrons handling their catini probably never knew the derivation of the large pots in their pantries; but way back some early Roman matelot had started them on a course with an unshakeable pedigree of coarseness and vulgarity. Original meanings are a let down and a give away. The genitalia hold a prominence rendering most original root meanings overly strong meat for our present tastes; but with the passage of sufficient time, with the original sense gradually worn down suppressed and replaced with paler versions, we eventually arrive at a stage where Mrs Grundy no longer has any difficulty in getting her tongue round the word, however originally composed. It is a mistake to think the original meaning still tainted the sense aeons after, even if long ago. Our original neurotic fascination with our genitalia is now so heavily overlaid with cultural accretions it only flowers again and finds full expression from time to time, often amongst the more lightly acculturated, for example in the armies of the world, where the author discovered it for himself.

Kewpie (22,25) is a modern twee concoction from cupid. Cupid is akin to Latin cupere, to desire. The meanings of Lithic ku- are various. Since a was the general case for vowelisations, most of the i and u vowelisation should be treated as markers or replacers, ie as strong (significant) forms. Ku can in most if not in all cases be treated as the shortened and elided version of kau, with -u the completive vowel case, either verbal or substantive. In this case it is probably to be read as the perfect or pluperfect participle of kai, in pidgin 'all done gone finish kai', with kai here signifying kindled (22) or even hardened (25). The pai is to be read schoolboy fashion as pee or penis. This equates quite neatly with the coarse modern usage

'with a hard on', an unequivocal indicator of amorous, or at any rate Priapic intentions. Priapus availed himself of a closely similar idiom; the initial pai of the
Lithic pai-rai-a-pu(s) – the s is once again simply the Latin declensional suffix
– being the very same schoolboy appellation, and the simple participle form of
rai carrying the semantic content rayed or raying, raised or rousing. A rayed anything was drawn out by the returning ray, as the flowers of the field by the sun's
returning rays, or the picture seen to the eye. These were Egyptian rays, but not
peculiarly so. In Egyptian both the sun Ra and the eyes (rai) were active emitters,
and active harvesters also. We only allow the eyes these days to be harvesters. If
the sun was a full-blown hole, the eye was an egg with an aperture. Full-blown
holes as well as eggs with apertures were established rayers. The sexual encounter
was defined in these same terms. Priapus was either exhibiting a roused puti or
egg with an aperture, or one which was in turn rousing, sending out an invisible
ray to attract the female to it. Either way, his herms were explicit, just posts with
protruding penises stuck on them. All that is not clear is if he was modeled like
that as a patient or as an active sexual symbol. One suspects it was not any clearer
to the ancients than it is today. We are collectively in two minds even today as
to which sex it is that really initiates sexual encounters. We did not really quite
finish with cupid however, getting side tracked into the bye ways of Stone Age
sexuality. We are probably justified in extracting the further Lithic content from
the final consonant -d. Lithic da, quite early in its development of meanings, had
the semantic contents become, happen, cause to happen, do: Lithic ku-pai-da,
ku-pai-[he] does. When he pays a call your pai, perhaps to be read as little bits,
but if so you can guess which bits, or else it is the schoolboys' pee which is kau,
stimulated. That is what Cupid does.

Key(1) is from Old English caeg pronounced something like kaiy – it should
not be thought Roman script consonants or vowels have always received the same
vocalisation; on the contrary pronunciation has varied as the language has developed. A g pronounced like a y is not a strained reading. Partridge derives caeg
from the Germanic root *ki, to split, to split open, to open up, to open; and relates
it (probably) to Old Norse kill, a long narrow inlet of the sea. The Lithic does not
fit these semantic contents particularly well, at least not at first sight. Kai, from
the clink of flint on flint, can mean striking (3,8), whence perhaps striker, and so
perhaps splitter, but hardly opener. Caeg in Old English, Lithic kai-ia is probably
better derived as having the meaning of actuator or operator or even initiator,
which is a semantic content found elsewhere with this element. There is probably
no reference to the function of opening, or indeed more pertinently of closing
anything, it is simply the initiator or actuator, the handle. What is actuated is
what in turn opens if the key is for a door. Norse kill reads to me differently, more
like ka-i-lai, land-which-laked, ie into which lye or ocean has run.

Key(2) or kay in the Caribean, is from the Taino caya or cayo, an islet. We can compare Ancient Egyptian Ka, inter alia the earth (44) or land, ultimately from the hard structure (15,25) or shaping constituent of anything, including one's person, in physical extension (in space and time), where it is thus also the active developmental principle, the directing principle in life, as if growth followed invisible bean poles in time and fleshed them out with actuality. The Lithic, I suggest, is ka-ai-a or au, land-that-one; land item, an individual piece of land, an island; or else with still more elision it is from ka-a'a-ai-a, land-water-that which-that, which in our (English) idiom was an ieg-land originally, ieg an egg shaped lump of land with land added tautologically. The Caribs seem somehow to have used the same elements, in an indifferent order. We have used in English the Lithic elements i-ai-ka, it-item-land. We may not be brothers under the skin, or we may, but either way we appear to have had a surprising way of thinking along the same lines. The Taino alternative vowel ending -o, if veridically reported, would merely emphasise the unitary or substantive ending. The Carthaginian Go-, as in Gomera, from Ka-u-mai-Ra, Land-where-dies/sinks-the sun, Sunset Island, one of the Canaries — with magnificent sunsets seen from our winter apartment in Tenerife — is made up the same way more or less. The -mera, in Carthaginian, is definitely dying of the sun, from Lithic mai-Ra. It is also red in Hindi where the sun sets over the Western Ghats, and mer is sea in French where it sets over the Atlantic. An English mere by contrast is small beer, gulled from the larger body of water. Sri Lanka, formerly Ceylon, is Holy Island in Sinhalese where the Lan is Ocean and the Ka is land. With Ceylon the phonemes are merely reversed. It is still an ocean kay.

Kibosh (16), Partridge finds o.o.o, of obscure origin, possibly originally from Yiddish, with the meaning nonsense. To put the kibosh on means to dispose of, to terminate; or better perhaps to rubbish. If the development of the meaning of the word has been influenced by the colloquial English bosh, as Partridge surmises, then this is from the Turkish bosh, meaning empty, useless, worthless. This in turn looks remarkably like ba-ush, the equivalent of the English vulgarism piss off, literally go and piss. If ba is a substantive, however, it could be read even more aptly as bollocks. For the above readings you have to know ush means penis, pisser or pizzle in Turkish. That is certainly psychosemantic, being echoic; any stable lad can tell you that even a horse can understand it. He says swish swish swish until the horse gets the message, before putting down new straw, in order to clear the decks so that it stays dry for as long as possible once the straw is down. I served my time in stables in short pants, time not altogether wasted as it turns out. Horses are fully aware of echoism, and can put two and two together to make an invitation, just as Sapiens certainly was able long before he learned to speak. Ish for Tarzan meant "firewood, dear boy!" however, once fire was tamed and burning brands were dunked in puddles, hissing as they died. That would be beyond the most acculturated horse, which would simply piss and put the fire out. Lithic called for discriminatory powers beyond the ordinary.

Kick (3) is from Middle English kiken. Partridge suggests it is akin to Latin calcare, to kick which is in turn related to calx (shortened form of calcis or calicis) a spur, but originally just the heel, which did the kicking in the first place. If the original kicking was as a spur to a horse then the kiki form is appropriate, since it indicates by its form a series of small strikes, and by its semantic content the same. kai-kai reads strike-strike quite readily. The elision to ki-ki, with the i being the diminutive reduplicative vowelisation, is of a piece. The Latin is in fact more difficult. It can be compared with leg, another long story. A leg is a strider or loper, it makes or goes in loops or leaps rather than in a smooth unarticulated plain extension. That has certainly been its essential function since it developed, long before speech. Mankind has been legging it until recently. Calici(s) can be read as meaning strike with the legs with a looping or swinging action.

Kid (22,31), from Middle English kid or kide (bisyllabic), meaning small (young) progeny, child, kinder, is perhaps from Lithic kai-di, with the semantic content procreated-little, a small growing individual. Or else it is a thinning (diminutive) of the Egyptian idiom of Katy in the sense of belly. To call kids little bellies may not chime with our thinking, but in the Sahel it might, where kids' bellies bulge from poor nutrition, and they need feeding above all else.

Kidney (7), Partridge identifies as from Middle English kidenei, with the -ei being the Middle English ei, from Old English aeg (pronounced approximately aeyi) meaning egg. The Lithic appears to have been kai-dai-en-ei, and the meaning shape-two-of-eggs, shaped like two eggs. Or see kid above: abdominal-eggs? One is tempted to surmise eggs may have gone with kidneys in Stone Age quisine already, with or without the bacon.

Kill (44), a channel, or inlet, is perhaps in Lithic form ka-i-lelai, meaning land-which-has lapsed and lyed up, ie been filled by the ocean, or a crack (11) or creek, or just land filled by the flow of water into the low.

Kill (3), slay, is from the Lithic kai-lelai, strike-lay-low, or to lay the Ka low. The Lithic syllable which began with the liquid palatal consonant l was contrasted with the glotal k. We at one time indicated a nasty taste by putting out our tongues – perhaps even retching like Dame Edna on stage. La was the articulation with the tongue on the way back in. I imagine lye is as near as may be an original Lithic phoneme, with a semantic content of incalculable antiquity. The spelling is baroque. Just as the explorers, and nowadays anthropologists are apt to discover any number of words for finger (the pointer) in response to their pointed enquiries, so some learner speakers (or were they masters of metaphor?) appear to have taken lai to be a suitable designation for the tongue (the taster), as well as by an even grander sweep of the imagination that greatest and lowest of lye pits, the ocean. From which it soon became apparent to the more scientifically minded that water had not only an inate propensity to lapse into lows, on its own or when spilled. Australian aboriginal science actually used bi-lai for water, from bai-lai, it goes-low (compare baji it goes up for bird) which the Ozzy colonist with his clumsy colonial tongue roughly transliterated as billy. But also it was instinct to taste nastier the more it had been lying low, and nastiest of all when it had finally achieved its mission in life, run the gamut of its metamorphoses, and sloped off down into the ocean. It was, one must suppose, partly this sloppiness and lack of structure or stiffness, physical or moral, which was contrasted with the staccato crispness, sharpness and effectiveness attributed to the ka phoneme, from the flint it sounded for. The conjunction of opposites, which has fascinated and entrapped the mind for aeons, led to the contemplation and deification of Kali in India, as an imperious and ambivalent mistress, both positive and negative, cruelty and killing alternating with loving feelings for her own. There are mathematical permuta-tions, in the grammar: ka(substantive)-li(verbal) versus ka(verbal)-li(substantive): Slaying the Ka versus Striking the life. To kill is from Old English cwellan to quell or kill, precisely to ka-u-ai-lai-an, ka-that-which is-layed-verbal marker. Ka had the meaning of the life driving force world wide, as can be seem from Ancient Egypt to Japan. Slay is the identical formation with the sibilant, the spirit of live-liness, activity, life in place of the Ka. Kill, cull, quell and slay are doublets. With this rationale it became possible for Kali's Thugs to kill with the best of motives as an oblation to their goddess. This ambivalence, with close knit loyalty to the in-group and compulsory hostility to the outsider, characterises the earlier Kali-worshiping expellees from India, now known as Gypsies, after their expulsion from Egypt also, a figment foisted on the goy to deceive them simply in order to please Kali. (Kali is The Ka-layer or Killer as well as the Slippery Actor). Their knowledge of the Egyptian great gods is fragmentary and their magic similarly confined to a few snippets of sympathetic trickery such as might easily be picked up when passing through Egypt, before they were rumbled again and made to move on[2].

Killick (16), is apparently a small anchor. Partridge is at a loss, but cites Ernest Weekley's guess in his Concise Etymological Dictionary of 1952 as possibly from keel-lock. See keel above. For lock in this sense the Lithic appears to be lau-kai, loop/enclosure-making; the same elements as in to close, to shut up, from ka-lau-sai, make-closed-action. Only the Lithic analysis into semantic elements which can then be transposed in order without impugning the meaning but merely changing the idiom (which was pretty optional in early days – as with close and lock) makes any sense of the major metatheses so happily prayed in aid without any explanation by ill informed old fashioned etymologists, who apparently imagine such reversals of order merely result from group amnesias.

Kiln (8) is from English cylen, of the same original form as Latin culina, a kitchen, also akin to Latin coquina, kitchen, from coquere to cook. It appears cooking was conceived at the outset as a tenderising process. Lithic kau-kai-ere for coquere is strike-striking-verbal marker, indicative of the original tenderising technique, raw meat for children probably beaten to a pulp with a stone "hand axe". The Roman culina made the food lai, juicy, tender (yielding) and tasty by cooking instead of bashing. Perhaps it defined an oven, and was also a long reduction process; and that is the usage which has come down to us. The earliest ovens were clay jobs set in the ground. First the fire went in, then it was raked out, the food, meat, was put in and the whole sealed over with sods and left for a relatively long time. The kiln technique is now largely confined to firing pottery. The Lithic la or lai carried, simultaneously if need be, the semantic contents tasty, liquid and a long and slow process. These meanings are separately derived in chapter 9. The statistical probability of these four meanings meeting up in a word where all are appropriate just by happenstance is difficult to calculate, because it is not determinate what degree of correspondence between which ideas is involved. If it were, it would just be a sum. What does seem to emerge is that the witenagemots of naked sages who ruled on language usages in early times were usually impressed when a number of separate meanings converged. With prompts from more than one side, the natural meaning exposed itself; and those not satisfied with one nevertheless gave their same vote for another, with the result that in such circumstances it was usually nem. con. Cooking, it is clear, replaced the beating of the raw meat to tenderise it before the taming of fire and was named for the original process, Lithic kuku, beaten with lots of repetitive strokes.

Kilo (44) is from the Greek, Khilia, a thousand. Lithic Khai-lai-ia carries the meanings Earth (as the hard unyielding element)-slippy/lax/loose. This is soil or sand which equally are marked for the same property: they slide down like water and quite unlike rock. The shifting sand is the classic case. Lithic sa'n-dai is movement-does. Sand is loose and mobile and dunes drift and even rise to present barriers under the influence of the wind. A dune has dau-nai, become protruberant. To the early Greeks, a thousand was a large uncountable number as numerous as the grains in a handful of soil, khilia, Lithic khai-lai-a, chopped-until it flows-one. The old gray beards were guilty of a trifling exaggeration, as we can now see, with our much more precise idea of number. Incidentally million has the same parentage; one of the principal meanings of ma is the massive element, the earth; and mealy earth is soil or marl, which when kept really dry has the same mobility as sand. The Latins indeed used mille for a thousand, including a thousand paces, passus, which made up one of our miles, apparently 63 inches, which is too big for a stride so that attention is drawn to the Lithic elements of pa-ssu-(s). The –ss-u- evidently stands for actions-dual, that is to say steps by both legs, two paces. The legions evidently marched to a Guards pace of 31 inches. Leaving aside for the moment why the Latins should have an m- in their mile where the Greeks affect a kh-, for which there is no overt reason – it is not a common substitution and does not appear to offer any easement or other gain – we can see that the rest of the Greek and Latin words (little enough admittedly) are similar. Since Lithic lai appears in both, it might be that the idiom is the same, in which case the preceding syllables should be in some way equivalent. In Lithic meanings these two syllables do indeed meet in the meaning earth! Lithic mai started out as the perceived downward seeking instinct exhibited by heavy masses, of which rocks and earth are the most notable examples in nature, probably because the phonetic form of "mmmm…." with the mouth closed was perceived as the opposite of the "shshsh…."syllable with the mouth open and the air issuing. Ish was already spoken for as the name of fire, because the burning brand when dowsed unmistakably said ish, see chapter 14, and the flame partook of the rarer and rarified upward seeking instinct, to say nothing of the tall columns of smoke rising over forest fires which can darken the sky. So the opposite kind of sound for the down escalator seems to have been chosen. The syllable ka meanwhile arrived at the rock or earth as terra firma meaning by a different route, starting from the sound of the stone age flint knapper at work, the harsh chink of rock on rock; and so to adjectival correlates or gulls like hard, and from that the hard element wherever it was found like in rock. These bifurcations of meaning may well have taken an aeon or two to take effect. Language evolution on this grand scale has generally been very slow and quite widely spread; prompting perhaps in due season the derivative idea of evolution as a process involving real species. Most good ideas, as well as all the bad ones, arise for off beat reasons, the initiator having a head full of misconceptions through which he (or increasingly she) dimly perceives a useful chink of light. Arthur Koestler was rather good on this.[3]

Kilt (48) the Scottish garment, from kilt, tucked in around the body, with which compare the same word in Swedish which has the meaning the lap. The kilt was originally designed as a stomacher, and is akin to the Gothic kilthei which meant the womb (which the ladies kept there); and even the Old English cild, child, which came from there. So much is from Partridge. There is a passing resemblance to the Ancient Egyptian Khati for belly, the feminine part of the body. Lithic kai-lai-tai can be glossed body-looped-twice. Either the kilt was wound round twice, in place of the fancy pleating affected these days; or else in the Swedish idiom the lai meaning was tai, twice, viz. the lower and lolling part of the body. Jock said to himself as he kilted his kilt "just as one would with one's stomacher!". Then he forgot what he said. He may additionally have been thinking he was shortening the thing, which could take a bit of winding, since curt (from the Latin curtus meaning curt) is suspiciously the same, and there was a kirtle across the sea up north in Norraway whence many Scotsmen came. There is of course the ready alternative it was always the winding which impressed. Lai was always a loop, from the oceans which supposedly circled the globe with the skyline the largest of loops. In that case the Swedes too had hold of a gull, the lap being merely the area lapped by the kilt.

Kilter (7), alignment, originally perhaps a wine press, Partridge says is akin to the Middle Dutch kelter. Perhaps Lithic kai-lai-terai, forcing-lye-through makes sense. It sounds like a wine press, or perhaps the earlier and original process of treading out the grapes. The sense development is not as far fetched as it may at first appear. With a press the difficult mechanical bit is to confine the lid or piston laterally with sufficient accuracy to avoid the fruit escaping out the sides while at the same time squeezing enormously and letting the juice run out. A press which is out of kilter will not separate the juice; it lets the fruit through too.

Kin (22,31), and twenty three other words akin which Partridge lists under the one head entry, with an even greater number of cognates in other Indo European languages, is from the Middle English form cennen, to beget. Another group of ninety three English words are collected under the entry for general, and a further group of sixty under native, from which the initial ge- has been dropped, a process the etymologists call aphesis from the Greek. The central and original meaning which supports this huge group is perhaps kindle in the sense start a fire, initiate, create, make – the ghost of the old flint chipper again – whence incidentally beget, since life was heated and hence from the flame. The male role was ill understood, being first mistaken for entertainment merely, but it had at a relatively early stage (possibly from keeping sows, that most fertile of beasts, which would not farrow unless accompanied by a gentleman pig, the caged sow the first virginal animal on earth) become apparent the male's activity was an essential precursor for parturition. The male had to be in at the start. He provided the spark which lit the life much as he lit the fire when it went out, by grinding away with his chark until the friction produced the heat to ignite the tow, or else by repetitively striking flint on flint until a spark lit the spunk. Generations of wise old birds must have espoused this simplistic theory – not complete or perfect but near enough to be going on with they must have thought. The idea of seed planting came next, by analogy with plant life, and is current in the Jewish bible and still current in uneducated circles today. In reality the seed in its pod is of course the vegetable equivalent of the egg in the womb. The male organ is merely a dirigible pistil or pollenator, saving the worker bee his trouble. The semen of the male he has to learn is not really his semen or seed at all but only his pollen. Science knows now. The public stay stum, wrapped in the language.

Kink (27) is a twist in a rope or anything else, which results in a sharp directional change, a discontinuity or corner. The paradigmatic kink for me is in a watering hose, where it becomes important and must be removed. Cut and corner appear to be akin. Lithic ki'n-ki, with two diminutives, like chink which is a chip of sound or a chip of light, or an aperture allowing the light to chink, is making a little corner shape. Ka as a corner, a join and a break go together in Lithic, as if they were all the same thing just seen from different points of view. One of Walshe's original Indo European roots is ki as in chink, meaning split or crack[4]. Hairy old Homo Faber or Handy Man appears again, cross legged and hacking away at his flints. A kink is also a rigidity where otherwise no rigidity would be, which may have influenced the choice of idiom, the word seeming apposite from more than one point of view. These convergent prompts with two or more possible reasons for an interpretation can be adduced as counter arguments showing that the Lithic hypothesis is unsupported by the evidence proposed; since there is scope for rather too free composition, making use of quite modest correlations of semantic contents too loosely defined and vague to carry the burden of proof. I think the short answer to this is to invite the critic to generate another scheme which meets the evidence of speech already spoken as well, or even at all. Vague speech is the way by which we have come. In any one case a gloss may appear loose; but the consistency of the whole body of psychosemantic contents informing language idioms around the world cries out for recognition. Any scheme devised to pick up all these evidences must have very many chances of not fitting very many cases; and statistically none of achieving any breadth of correspondences; unless, that is, there be some real underlying connection between the instances resumed, which the scheme accesses.

Kiosk (53,22,42) is from Turkish kieushk, a garden pavilion, and Persian koushke a portico, perhaps akin to Persian khush, pleasant: a leisure place. The Hindi khushi comfortable is virtually the same word, and quite like the English cushion, although the etymologists won't have it. The Lithic ka-u-shai glosses as place-where-shai. The Lithic shai can mean warm, comfortable, pleasant, from toasting nicely round the Stone Age hearth, warmed by the flame, ish in Lithic. The derivations in detail are in chapter 14. The completive su-, altogether warmed through, feeling very nice, has given us sugar, from su-kara, a pleasant taste maker, in many languages; to be distinguished from Arabic Iskra, a spark, which makes the flame itself, from Lithic ish-kara, flame maker, rather than what just warming by the flame does in turn. Sweet tastes were harder to come by in the Stone Age. If the Lithic is right the final k of the kiosk is for place, and the Persian portico was a place for sitting at ease and sunning themselves.

Kip (16,22,53) was originally a brothel, then a lodging place, then a bed for the night, then sleep. It certainly looks as if in the bad old days lodgings generally offered company in your bed for the night, no doubt at a small extra charge. This is a difficult one for Lithic but perhaps there is some punning: ka, make or place, pai, roof or cover is a possible origin; compare Egyptian 'per' (probably actually pronounced parai) a house, from the Lithic pa-rai, cover [from] the sun's rays, originally a Bedu goatskin tent. Pai, the thinned version of bai, flesh, was earliest skin, along with the different recension of a diminutive burgeon, a bud or shoot. The Lithic kai-pai from which kip is slovened could also mean kindle-piece, without specifying further which piece, which any schoolboy could probably guess in the twinkle of an eye. So the Lithic allowed a covered place, a lodge for the traveler wanting a bed for the night, as well as cover for the other. Ka pai for sleep is also in the Lithic, since when asleep the ka or driving force (roused by karate) was covered and inactive, as well as the ka or body covered in bed, perhaps by a bearskin if not the douvet expected for the job today.

Kipper (48,12) is from Old English cypera, which Partridge concedes is of obscure origin (o.o.o.). But Lithic kai-pai-rai, body-pieces-rayed or cut-pieces-rayed is smoked fillets exactly. The herring caught for smoking was an army fish because of its shoaling, if not quite so tightly packed together as the sardina which are effectively saa-tai-na, where the saa-tai is one-become and the -na is presenting (chapter 11). The sardines shoals present themselves as virtually one, twisting and turning in a mass which appears as if it were solid. The pilchard is a large fully grown sardine, the same shaa-dai, but with pai-lai, large pieces.

Kirsch (16) is short for Kirschwasser, cherry water in German. The Low Latin for cherry is cerisa, the Greek kerasion, Lithic kai-ra-sai-on, making-ray (in Lithic that means colour, see chapter 13)-flame-one. It appears these earliest wild cherries were the wild orange-red ones today, not the dark purple or cerise cultivated ones you can buy. To address the wasser, there are so many possibilities for the Lithic form of water, it is hard to choose. Wa is somewhat structureless, like water. But world-wide it signifies panic. Wah Wah Wah! cried the naked savages as they turned and dashed for the jungle when our hero removed his glass eye and offered it around. The Aztecs used the same phoneme for their supreme deity, Wakan Tanka, wa-kan-Tan-ka; panic-making-World-maker, ie Awesome Creator. We could indeed still join them in this sentiment, though hardly in the bloody mischief they thought followed from their identification, cutting out thousands of hearts from living victims and offering them up to their deity. Wasser is Ware-the tall one, or dangerous-when-deep. The English -ter in place of -sser is not a put off. Lithic te-rai, or in full as originally tai-rai, has the semantic content become-rayed, and so drawn out, and so tall or in the case of water deep. The original tiroire, with apologies to Mrs Grundy once again, was of course possessed by the fair sex as they squatted fully frontal around the hearth, with their Egyptian rays coming into play as the fire warmed the company, fully explored in chapter 13.

The Brits seem to have spelt it out where the Germanic idiom had used the less imaginative vertical indicator. Of course the conventional wisdom merely treats the change from the German s to the English t as one of those slovened changes everywhere occurring without any semantic significance at all. There is no particular objection to this but the subconscious Lithic elements turn out to be playing their part even in the slovening process. Water is also sometimes glossed as awa-terra, ie fresh water as found on land, as opposed to the far larger body of salt water. Certainly the Latinate aqua, agua, etc, pronounced with a glottal stop, a'wa, merely utters the panic sign, not far from the simple use of the two staccato a'a' which will attract the attention of any infant and give them pause, so acting as a pre-linguistic warning in any language. There are other descriptions of the watery element. In India for example pani from the Lithic pa-nai, no surface, or drink, depending if pina, to drink or pani which is water came first. Pina from pai-na might have been lips open, hence drink or pai'n-a, lipping-one. It seems reasonably apt. The meaning-tree for the phoneme Pa is in chapter 12. There is in fact no reason why our primitive forebears might not have voted for some or all of these meanings together, as a bit of Stone Age punning around the fire.

Kirtle (12) is Old English cyrtel and is akin to Latin curtus,[cut] short. Now both Ka and Ta can mean cut; Ka because the original echoic meaning from flint knapping involved striking off a flake of flint, and so taking a piece off; while Ta, following on from the Ka idiom, meant the lesser and less effortful sound of a snapping stick, and so to snap a stick or break anything in two, including cutting with a flint knife, a rougher process than cutting silk with a tailor's scissors. To break in two was to two it, becoming two. So probably the Lithic form for cut was ka-ta, strike/split-in two; and the Lithic form for curt was kau-ta, struck-in two, or even just made two, and so cut off, short. Our short of course is the same word as curt, mis-spelt.

Kiss (16,28) is from Old English cyssan, the -an being a Germanic verbal marker. The y was probably longer than our modern i, with a pronunciation for the whole nearer Kayi-ssa'n, the ssa being echoic for the light smacking of the lips considered good form. Partridge for instance compares the Hittite kuwass, to kiss. Was a Hittite kiss a wet kiss perhaps? They were not British. Relevant also here is to quaff, apparently from an original quass. There is lip smacking in quaffing and kissing alike, especially if the ancients were pulling on their pints like a horse at water or an infant sucking. Suck in fact reveals an altogether analogous form but around the other way, a grand metathesis reversing the order of two original Lithic elements. Kissing and sucking were equally making a sibilant sound. They are doublets; and only independent elements could afford to be switched like this without mucking up the meaning. There is perhaps a debatable difference of ideas implied in the reversal. To kiss is to make or mouth the sss sound, and that is the end of it; whereas sucking is – well it makes a sucking sound – but the actual job is to imbibe the liquid. In passing, the Sumerian word for mouth was Ka, and ka-tze or spit-mouth, the Sumerian for cat appears to have somehow percolated through to German katze and our cat, just as the Akkadian for mouth was pu (from 'two lips') and appears in pu-tse, spit mouth, Akkadian for cat in turn – they were copy cats where Sumerian was concerned, adopting Sumerian words revised in Akkadian terms – very like our pussy for cat. Kittens have been hissing for a lot longer than five or ten thousand years, and can you blame them: they were probably on the menu.

Kit (48), a wooden tub or basket for fish, may be compared with Dutch kit, a jug, Egyptian khati, a belly, and Hindi Chatti a round spoutless jug or bellied jar for water, Arabic khat (the leaf chewed for the mild drug it contains) meaning bush – the leaf is off a bush, as we say the weed for tobacco, and Egyptian kat-cha, thorn bush or cactus, literally sharp bush, and throw in Hindi kacha, inferior, no good (like a thorn bush?). Given the miscellaneous contents of tubs, fish baskets, jugs, chatties and bellies and finally even bags and bushes, the underlying sense appears to have been something like a belly shape or belly shaped container – of a non specific kind – and then just burgeoning into a similar shape like a bush. A bush is not so far from a baji, the Australian for a go up or bird, while a bird is from ba-arai-da, it does a go aloft. The bush is a burgeon up with lots of stalks rather than a tree with a single trunk. A tree is drawn up in a trunk, a drawn up shape or structure. In the case of a kit bag, the container defined merely by its shape, a sausage shaped bag, has apparently become surrogate for the miscellanea to be found in such. Kit thus becomes a collection such as might be found together in a bag or at any rate belongs together and would go in a bag even if it is not found in one. One feels most confident with the Egyptian which (like the Chinese) retains the archaism of the Lithic idiom, composing words from constituent semantic elements, rather than with the heavily grammaticised Indo-European words. Lithic kai has the early semantic contents hard, growth and shape, so the single syllable can stand for hard stemmed growth, such as a tree, and with the additional idea of diminutive reduplicative items added quite neatly for a bush. But with kit in the tub sense the Egyptian belly container sense is the relevant one. Khati is belly in Egyptian because it is the feminine part of the body. Ti was the feminine ending. In those far off days it was the female body which was bulgy (when pregnant and after repeated pregnancies). Their bodies were programmed to accumulate fat for feeding two. Moreover the belly really presented itself in full fig when pregnant. The men were kept busy loping after game which kept them muscular, with less nourishment left over for fattening them. They had not yet found the leisure, or the brewers, to develop the beer bellies most of them wear in the West today by the time they are thirty, making their sexual antics a depressing experience for their partners.

Kitchen (8) is from Old English cycene. The Latin form cocina is clearly from coquere to cook, from the root (original form) *kokw, variant *kekw, as Partridge has it or as we would say from the Lithic kau-kai or kai-kau, meaning repeatedly struck and so softened, which before the taming of fire was the usual technique for preparing meat. Cooking replaced it. The ending -na is used commonly enough to mean rather generally 'the one that has to do with that'; almost 'and so on', perhaps from Lithic en-a, of that, or an-aaa, meaning an extension. See chapter 11.

Kite (1), Partridge suggests is akin to German kauz, a screech owl, which is clearly echoic. It is akin to the Basque for sea gull which is kaio, which is so splendidly echoic of the seagull's call one is actually tempted to whistle it. It is slovened by the Spaniards leaning over the garden wall to gaviota. It all suggests the Old English cyta, Lithic kai-ta, for kite is echoic in origin too, copying a screech with a stop in it such as the bird makes, which the gull does not. The crow similarly said kraaw; and we pronounced our o as if it were a double a at one time, just as our American cousins with the innate conservatism and frivolity which comes of a colonial past continue to do today. An echoic kite, the bird, makes the children's kite a gull, copying the hovering of the bird but without making any utterance at all, just as a gull wing copies the shape of the wing without the gull's call. So the children just get on with it unaware of the catena at all.

Kittiwake (1) is another bird named after its cry, more accurately rendered hikky-waak. Nobody these days expects to make any sense of what it is saying.

Kittle (22), to tickle, is obviously the same word with the consonants transposed, a trick dubbed metathesis or change of places by the etymologists and not explained any further. Tickle could well be a diminutive of tick, to pat or tap lightly – as does the movement of a pendulum clock, whence tick the sound of a clock or similar light tap. Or, more in line with Lithic thinking, tick is simply echoic, and acquired the later meanings of light tap etc from further deduction. The slang use of ticking like a clock for complaining picks up on the depressingly persistent regularity of the clock's tick – not a character of tapping noises in general. The Lithic semantic contents of the two elements ti-ki are diminutive thing and diminutive strike respectively, so clockmakers appear to have a well developed Lithic sense. The rest of us are no less perceptive. Tik was finger first, the little doer or the little tickler, even perhaps a stimulator, kai, of the feminine ti. I suspect (I am thinking of way back in the Stone Age) the boys put their fingers in first to get the girls in the mood. Finger after all is a phai-en-kara, a pahei or genitals-of-stimulator. But then it must be remembered the term for genital stimulation came to mean just any pleasurable experience, or pleasure, over the millennia. So the finger can be treated as just the gentle operator, for picking out your partner's nits and so on, a comfort utility. The Stone Age may even have distinguished pahai (later ph) from bahei, the grosser male organ in Egyptian, thinking the thinned pahei more apt for the clitoris. But the finger was a pointer also when not in use elsewhere, and so a pointer outer and so an indicator of the correct. Tikh means correct, as pointed out, in Hindi, "tikh hai", "that is correct" sometimes translated as "OK" or "message received and understood" and even "and will be complied with". Teachers make ticks in the shape of little corners, one side elongated – perhaps in an outburst of concealed frustration at the banality of the task. When it comes to tickling lai has one meaning close to light and gentle. Without the lai a kai can be a nasty whack, enough to break a rock.

Note that the order of the elements is immaterial if these semantic contents are the effective ones. One is inclined to add that this kind of grand metathesis[5], where consonants change order, is only explicable where there is an internal structure of semi separate word elements such as the Lithic hypotheses propose, and then only if the sense of the elements allows the inversion. Otherwise etymologists are left without a paddle, either having to conclude that speakers sometimes take leave of their senses or pleading easement where no easement exists; or else they must argue the human mind is in general totally inconsequential and unpredictable – against the evidence and a slander on the human race – just as when they also argue for choosing random word roots, stumps of whatever utterances they manage to reduce to simples. You have to be pretty mad to believe in random word roots after due consideration. It is charitable to conclude there is not often due consideration. Carelessness and inattention is probably the only explanation. It can never be a cure.

Kitty (48,19), Partridge regards as a receptacle, and so a pool of money in it, and suggests it is merely a diminutive of kit above. He also suggests it may be a pun on the French 'faire la quete', to take up the collection in church, where quete is of course from queste like our English quest; but taken in English as Kate and familiarised as Kitty. He even allows himself a bit of smut, adverting to the French slang, la catherine for the female sexual opening, which incidentally the Cathar heretics were accused of abusing. Ka-ta-hei-rai-na in Lithic can be glossed Body-slit-when pleasure-rayed-gapes, which certainly smacks of a vagina, which in turn is from the Lithic Oo-a-kai-na, orifice-that-stimulated-gapes. The Cathars were religious fornicaters, early flower power people, and in unreformed medieval times were burnt for it, along with some skewed theology, until there were none left. The personal name one feels must have left the original meaning far behind, although the sex organs of babies when first born, like their heads at the other end, are exaggerated size for size although both are seriously incomplete.

It is as if coarse speaking Frenchmen somehow had access to a knowledge of Ancient Egyptian and could extract some of the semantics at least from the Egyptian idiom. Is this a bag for a donation? There is some degree of misprision here because the abdomen referred to by the Egyptians had a feminine ending not to restrict the anatomical reference to the female configuration, but more fundamentally to indicate that the belly, as the consort (and the sappier part at that) of the Ka (or body blue print, in space as in time) had for them an essentially feminine gender identity. The low French usage has apparently missed this grammatical point and gone for the literal reading. For that to be possible, some part of the minds of these slang composers must have been able to access a source of language associations common to the metaphysicians of Ancient Egypt and modern vulgarians in France. It reads like a time warp. The Lithic hypotheses have even been criticised precisely on these grounds, by those in a hurry to return to their own scrimshaw from Lithic's unwelcome intrusion upon their established scene. It is necessary to interpose at this stage that this is not going to be of any use for the followers of Carl Jung who may wish to bolster his rather silly idea in his dotage, when stripped of its pseudo psychological brouhaha or psychobabble, that there is a public or common mind existing somewhere out there in a mind space of its own to which we all have access. On the contrary the thrust of the etymological argument is in the other direction. By locating the source of the connections between common human experience and common language idioms in the world lexicon itself, to a larger or smaller slice of which we all have access, without having to posit any kind of private drinker reaching up (or down?) into a world soul, Jungians and such are left high and dry, outside the Lithic hypotheses altogether. This intellectual health warning is there for holists and princes alike who might otherwise hope to find their mystical lucubrations confirmed. Historically there have been wise women and words of power deriving conviction from Lithic phonetic and semantic connections recovered from the subconscious; and treated as mystical and supernatural, since they were not explicitly in the conscious lexicon. But they were guilty of misprision.

Klaxon (16) is akin to clang, which is surely echoic, with the nasalisation copying the reverberation of the sound. The sharp k- consonant is indicative of the sudden onset of the sound. La – as in language and gala – is echoic of a clear note. Klaxon however is merely a made up trade name; but semi-eruditely from the Greek klazon, which is a loud noise, from the Greek klazein to make such, to make a la, or go la, where the -zein bit is grammatical, a fandango for a quite general verbal action marker.

Kleptomaniac (16), from the Greek, comprises klepto- the combinatory form of kleptes who is a thief, together with mania. The Lithic elements appear to be ka-lai-pe-tai(s), make-sly light-steps-be/become, take on tiptoe, stealthily acquire, steal, Lithic sai-tai-lai, action-take-slyly. The dubious link in the string, which critics will wish to pounce on, is tai meaning take. It is all spelt out in chapter 6. Lithic is a subconscious pidgin. Fine shades of meaning are absent. Fine meanings in the Stone Age when we were learning to speak are anachronisms. The elaboration of meanings proceeds in individual minds by imaginative metaphor, taking an idea presented in one context and applying it to another. To use a mathematical metaphor to illustrate what is being adumbrated, we now can grasp the first differential, the gradient, course or direction of the semantic changes, which were gradual in the literal sense, and then we can proceed to individually evaluate the steps or stations in the catena. Similar imaginative leaps are required on our own account if we are to recapitulate the semantic steps in the catenas left by our forebears. We are fortunate to have the very same tool as they had for making the copy. Our minds may have become differently configured and briefed, but the same software is still installed. If it will not serve, the line of thinking must be wrong. But the mind, as ever, is a scrambler, not a mechanism, it even has random cards in it. Its scope is effectively limitless. We just have to dare to follow where our forebears have gone before us; which brings us to the maniac bit below, qualifying kleptomania.

Mania, madness, is akin to Greek menos, and Latin mens, mind; and the Indo-European root is given in Partridge as *men, to think. But that is not the half of it. The Lithic meanings of ma are all in chapter 10. In short mai from ma meaning earth in which seeds gestate, and so the planting, insemination and gestation, led into mental gestation or thinking, that is generating ideas which are internal and out of view, concealed, just as seeds are in the earth. Mania is an unruly excess of this, which is -naia, that is springing up in the mind out of control, a sudden outgushing of thought or emotion – they were not distinguished – a mental orgasm in effect. A mind receiving too many mind rays prompting ideas, which were believed to originate from outside the individual, as indeed they often did from outside the conscious mind, would likely overheat, as a pot boils over, due to an excess of the gestatory tendency. Mania can be defined in these terms as simply too open a mind, an excess of maying or minding, which all came from rays from outside impinging on the brain. The brain is from ba-a-rai'n in Lithic elements, the flesh-that-rayed one, viz the receiver of these rays from outside. In the old days it is clear they all thought they were being lived, whereas now it is the credo of only a few of the madder scientists and their followers. On the evidence of language it evidently seemed good to our rude forefathers. With etymology properly perceived, these rude forefathers of our world hamlet come awake again, lisping in Lithic tones through the mists made by philosophy and the carelessness of time.

Knack (3,11) is akin to knock and means strike and crack. Lithic ka'n-a-kai, striking and cracking; or just repetitive knocking. It is still not far away from the simple echoic, the sound of the knapping and cracking of the flint. It comes to mean of course mastery of the trick needed to make or get something done, as the flint knapping from which it comes did, holding and flaking to achieve the implement intended.

Knap (44), a hill top, is akin to knob. The Lithic is ka-na-pai, land-protruding-surface or piece, or bulge. It is a continual surprise for earthlings to discover these days how much can be expressed in so little. The trick lies in keeping each element so vague as to be of almost unlimited polysemy. The other trick required was the supreme ability to pick out which meaning to precise out of the bunch, in the case of any particular usage. When the Deity was speaking – mene mene tekel upharsin for instance – professional seers might be needed. In China there is still a similar call for maintaining a Mandarinate; and tricky points have to be written down on a scratch pad instead of just being spoken, so that the proper selection can be made with the aid of the calligraphy. Chinese provides the paradigmatic case of polysemy being ridden to death, beyond the resources of mind and ear to analyse with any convenience or utility. It is at the opposite pole from the far richer language idiom of most of the rest of the world, where meanings are over determined and redundantly specified, providing a vocabulary of a higher order of magnitude as well as better defined. The Chinese mind is thus caught up in an endless shimmering silk garment which enfolds the best brains often rather unprofitably. They are in a position not all that much different from our forebears before they spoke at all. Most of the calligraphy is not understood by most of the people. It looks as if that is why their thinking readily takes to the clearer uplands of mathematics almost as a recreational relief and release, where the verbiage is minimal. This was perhaps Mao Tse Tung's only valid perception in a life largely misspent, informed by Marx's deeply flawed math, for which he will be remembered long after the Reds and all their terrible terrible mistakes are lost in the mists of time and forgotten. Perhaps we can take the Lithic analysis of the knap or land knob back further still. Lithic ka-en-na-pai has the unmistakable semantic content shape-of-presented-penis. The schoolboy idiom of referring to the glans of his, or more likely his neighbour's penis as his knob has an early precedent leading up to him, slow generation by slow generation down the ages. We have seen earlier in the chapter the same frankly sexual idiom applied to the head. My old pal (fruit) and my old cock are terms of friendly familiarity. Schoolboys of all ages somehow think in Lithic terms still. Culture is skin deep and has moved us on very little. It is not that human nature does not change at all. It is that it has a depth to it, a keel beneath the surface which keeps it on its old course, as well as a surface structure which is culturally determined.

Knap (2) is to strike and split off a flake or piece. Lithic ka-na-pai is strike-present-flake. Whence perhaps also there is the reading make-open-lips, and so eat, and then what is eaten, provender, for which the knapsack is carried on the march, literally an eating bag like a nose bag for a beast of burden, a food bag mostly used these days for everything else, even bombs. A flint knapper is not just a person who breaks stones, he splits them creatively so as to obtain the flake he is aiming for.

Knave (16), squire, attendant, servant, earlier still just a young man at puberty with everything still to learn, is from Old English cnifa which may be compared with Middle High German Knappe, a young squire and Dutch knaap, a youth, a servant. Anterior etymology Partridge says is unknown. We are on our own again. There is a possible kinship of the Old English cnifa with nymph and nubile. Lithic kai-nai-pahai, made/grown-prominent-genitals with the English specifying the piece as the Egyptian pa-hei or joy piece precisely, newly virile, a young man, and the German version leaving that precision out. But there is the rather duller option also of the reading ka'n-a-pai, working-on-foot or with his spuds, a stable lad learning his trade, lacking as yet the wisdom for higher thinking. Before universities higher thinking was just a matter of maturation, as to some extent it still is of course today. Just the passage of time ensures some exploration of the mind even in the dullest learner. It is probably legitimate to go on to ask if these two versions of the Lithic phonemic sequence making up knave can be coalesced, or even if they were. It is tempting to believe they were, but there can be no proof. All we can say with any certainty is that both were on offer. Who thought which is anybody's guess.

Knead (16), to press repeatedly, is from Old English cnedan, to knead. The Lithic is ka-nai-da-en, make-protruding-does-verbal suffix. The semantic contents of the phoneme na are in chapter 11. The average Stone Age Lothario was probably somewhat lacking in finesse, his lovemaking was hard pounding. Kneading the dough reminded him of it. His knee stuck out just as his kneading did.

Knee (18) is from Old English cneo, Lithic kai-nai-au, joint-protruding-one, the only joint of the human body which bends backwards with the outside of the joint sticking forwards. From knee is derived kneel, from Old English cneowlian, to lie on the knees. Compare Greek karpos, wrist, Lithic kara-pau(s), operator-of paw-substantive ending.

Knell (16) is to make the sound of bells. The Lithic is ka-na-lalai, make-present itself-the lala; make ring out the tuneful sound as we would say.

Knickerbocker is the fictional Dutch name of the author of Washington Irving's A History of New York [originally New Amsterdam] to the End of the Dutch Dynasty, who wore them. They were overlong shorts which he tucked into his socks, a German fashion (without the socks). Somewhat inconsequentially they got shortened to knickers, and the garment simultaneously, now nowhere near reaching the socks but more remarkable for their minimal coverage.

Knife (12). The Lithic is ka'n-ai-pai, cutting-that which-bladed.

Knight (16,31) was originally just a youth, with a similar structure to knave above. The Lithic elements are kai-nai-khati, grown- presenting-lower abdomen, a youth past puberty, ready in that department. The lower abdomen was seen as a bag or container, and this sense is developed under kit above. But this was a gull. The original semantic construct was with ka representing the hard structure of the body, the ka precisely, in Ancient Egyptian terms anyway; and ti in the Egyptian lexicon was the feminine version. This could be thought of as the tapped or drilled version, fitted with a receptor, as we still describe screw threads. Egyptian meta-physics however recognised two opposed principles of being, present in every body: the ka and the ba. Volumes would be required to explore all the ins and outs of this thoroughly bent analysis, on which they spent a great deal of time; but at a first approximation the ka was symbolised by the hard skeleton, the male part, and the ba by the flesh. The ka provided the ruling form and the processes of formation, the ba was hung on these and physically fleshed them out as it were. Needless to say the ideas were all worked out by the Egyptian priests who were all boys, and they left the belly and burgeoning of the soft parts as the feminine part. Critics these days will not miss the chauvinistic element in this scheme of things. The boys were the doers and the girls had to be content with just ba-ing or being.

It has to be said that in this respect as in others, scratch a modern and find the Ancient Egyptian lurking beneath the skin. We can now see that Kha-ti in Ancient Egyptian identified the female part of the body par excellence, the belly including what we would describe as the lower abdomen including the genitalia. Our own good old English belly, which rhymes semantically as well as phonetical-ly with jelly, can be glossed as from the Lithic elements bai-lai, fleshy-sloppy; see chapter 12 for the meaning tree for la. It must surely be of some significance that the word night or nacht, which in its modern usage has very little to do with body orifices, or indeed with knights or nakedness, is akin to the Egyptian goddess Nut (probably actually pronounced by the Egyptians nauti or even naughty), Lithic nau-ka-ti, showing-body-orifices or lower abdomen. In Ancient Egypt Mistress Naughty presided over the night sky and is pictured with her body arched to make the firmament, and her body orifices representing stars which were equated with many breasts or tits, (titi meant breasts in Egyptian, it is not a modernism at all) and the moon which was her vagina or ma-oo-na, her impregnation-orifice-open, the identification prompted no doubt by the fact menstruation matched the phases of the moon (more or less).

We deceive ourselves if we imagine the Egyptians, Ancient though they were, actually thought such a lady literally existed spread-eagled across the firmament. It was merely that these still rather adjectival minds could identify the same prin-

ciple at work in the night skies as they imagined they knew in their personal anat-
omies and relations. The moon was thus the sky's large orifice, since it evidently
presided over the menstrual cycle, and indeed was perhaps even menstruating,
and the stars were little titties, spurting light like milk, and thus making a milky
way. Our own word naked is not the past participle of to nake (to strip off? Na-kai
in Lithic is to expose-body!), but on the contrary our derivative and badly enunci-
ated version of knightly virtue, na-khati, exhibiting our lower abdomens, sexually
mature or not, having shed every scrap of clothing. There is worse. Kati was one
thing. Khati was from kahei-ti, the make-whoopee-teat, his glans. If the knight
was making present his Kahei-ti, he was nubile, he was presenting his knob. Ka
meanwhile in Egyptian could also mean a tree, which has a hard skeleton with
a high rising trunk, Lithic ti-rau'n-kai, drawn up, feminine-raying-kindled, the
vegetal equivalent of the male equipment (spine and penis together – we are in
the dream world). A khati was a feminine tree or bush without the male stiff central spine or trunk. The Arabic khat, the bush is used for the mild drug from its
leaves which are chewed, much as we say the weed for tobacco. Cotton in English
is from Khati en shen in Ancient Egyptian which has got cut down in transit
through the Arabic to khat-en. Shen was hair in Egyptian, probably from the
hairy coat of animals, since the Lithic shai'n can mean warming. Khat en Shen is
the bush of hair or hairy bush. Cotton is a bus, it means bush of. It will not have
escaped our Stone Age ancestors the animal kingdom wore hairy coats to keep
themselves warm. We know this because one of their earliest ploys was to take
them from the animals and wear them themselves. But it is possible the cotton
bush, the khati en shen in turn was originally what warms the lower abdomen,
the belly's coat, the pubic hair, and this was what defined a bush. Schoolboys seem
to have accessed this semantic catena on their own account. If so, knights were
admitted to service when they had grown pubic hair. They were post adolescent
boys. All the other definitions follow.

There is an opportunity here to add in Egyptian thinking on the orb that illu-
mines the day, the sun, widely known as Ra; but also called Aton by one sect later
found atavistic and heretical as benefiting The Mothers – indirectly it led to the
killing of the young Pharaoh "Tutankamun", really Tahutau anakh Amun, Know
All Son of Amun. Young Pharaoh Tuhutau's father worshiped the Aton or Eternal
Birth Canal in the sky, through which light was reborn each day into our world. It
was inescapable the Aton was female and must be a goddess. Aton has in recent
times been translated as the disk of the sun from its glyph, a circle. Academic
wisdom has assumed the ancients thought of the Aton as a disk, not speaking the
language. The argument goes like this: they would, wouldn't they! In reality the
boys, presumably feeling a bit left out, countered with the idea the hole in the sky
was an Eternal Eye, Ra. One is tempted to think they were striking a blow for

men's lib including perhaps straightforward majority heterosexuality – Akhaitai en Aton, Conceived of the Aton, conventionally Pharaoh Akhetaton, the heretical Pharaoh Freud and Velikovsky notably wrote about, thought to have been the original Oedipus of the Greek tale, had a markedly queer sexuality along with a deformed lower body. In any case the boys' version won the day and the mother lovers lost out and the followers of the Aton were eliminated and Akhetaton's city destroyed. The Eye was later credited with seeing, including every sparrow's fall, and even concerning Itself with such mundane affairs, which was another good thing for humanity as it turned out, since it suggested that God had a heart after all, never suspected until then. The ways in which changes for the better actually come about are indeed inscrutable. People with good intentions have to work with the buzz which is going, not against it, diverting it at every opportunity to better ways.

To Knit (15) is to knot with a thinned vowel – the diminutive reduplicative i – making here a lot of little ones precisely. A knot is a protrusion or lump of a thing, either resulting from some extraneous process – of growth for instance – or devised deliberately as an extensive process as a piece of knitting; Lithic ka-nau-ti, shape-lumped up-thing! Comically this can be developed as another genital metaphor. Na is examined in detail in chapter 14. If you articulate with your mouth closed and then open it and let out your breath, naaa or something like it is what comes out. It certainly appears that the naked naming committee at the birth of linguistic idiom, studying the articulation for the least indication of the inherent meaning which could be pointed up and passed on, found the syllable carried the message of a sudden gasp as breath held was let out, and they associated that with orgasm. Psychosemantically, such an utterance in any case suggested a pent up state followed by an expansive one. Like ma, from the other hum, there was tension; but with na it was marked for the release, almost already as an involuntary gasp. No prizes for guessing what sudden release our old billy goats were put in mind of. By sense extension, na then stood for presenting sexually, and then just presenting and eventually just being present. Indeed, in the Senoi aboriginal language of the Malay and Vietnamese hills it means just that: "Here you are, take this!", an essential piece of vocabulary for any medical dispensary. "Nah! do biji ubat" in Malay is "Here you are, take this! Two pills of medicine." Arousal, involves an opening or an erection. We shall find these two constructions deeply embedded in languages all over. In English nau, presenting or presented is the here and now. The navy sails in ships made with bare beams presented, showing like those in the nave roof of a church, from the original Lithic pronunciation na-bai, exposed beams. Barn roofs were made the same, ba-ra-nai, beams-visible.

Knob (15). The Lithic ka-nau-ba, is shape-prominent/protruding-flesh/bit.

Knock (3) is already covered at knack above.

Knoll.(7) See knot under knit above, and compare Dutch knolle, a ball or a bunch, as well as knol a turnip. The lai syllable adds orbital circularity, as in ball and the Dutch turnip. The English turnip is in Lithic terai-nai-pe, drawn out-protruberant or knobby-piece. A nipper has opening and closing pieces. The turnip is male, crabs and lobsters are female. It may be concluded that a knoll was first of all a protruding but rounded sloping shape, not craggy as we are prepared to allow it today.

Knot.(7) See knit above.

Know.(16) Lithic ka-nau, is make-obtrude/evident. Partridge goes for it and has a maxigroup of words associated with can and ken. There is of course the possible sense development from making open and presenting or making manifest to actualizing, can, as well as understanding, ken.

Knuckle (3) is a diminutive of knock, little knockers, probably from the original rattling of knuckle bones in shamanic augury and game. Knuckle bones or rattlers have been found in small collections in early prehistoric deposits. Somebody collected them for something, presumably for rattling, perhaps to distract attention from furtive movement like the gully gully man or conjuror, who "acts slyly" like the Kali men of yore.

Kodak, a trade name for a make of camera of arbitrary formation is recent – post Lithic! What the coiner had in mind is anybody's guess.

Koran (16) is from the Arabic Al Qur'an, (The) Reading, from Arabic qara'a, read. The Lithic language elements and idiom look like ka-ra'a, make-seeing, from ra the eye as well as the ray it was imagined to send out, so to take a look, inspect a text with a view to picking its meaning off the page. Bearing in mind Mr. Rushdie's embarrassments, it can be added that the Deity speaks in human tongues when communicating with the species, in aid of getting the message across. The reverence due to the Word is due to the sense imparted and not to the vocalisations we adopt.

Kosher (16), or kasher, means ritually clean or procedurally proper in Hebrew. The Lithic elements appear to be kau-shai-rai, made-bright-ray, and so clear and clean. There is here a connection with the Djeribal aboriginal language of Northern Queensland; the language is kosher, djeri-, bright or clear speech, djeri-bal, by contrast with the foreign fork-tongued devils who talk in code. Psychosemantically there is a temptation to see the same alienation of the outsider figuring in both usages. We can also see the same thinking in Shanta, the gipsy lingo, where shara means bright spot, a white marking on a dark horse, shara, shiny-ray. The psychosemantic contents of Ish are derived in full in Chapter 14 and those of Ra in chapter 13.

Kris (5,8), Malay for a sharp curved fighting knife, ancient and often ceremonial, is made up of the straightforward Lithic elements kai-rai(s), strike-verbal participle(substantive s). This (-s) is also the Greek substantial marker, giving the sense 'the thing for striking'. Malay has Indo-European words, apparently from Sanscrit speakers. There are Egyptian words also, so they may have sailed there too. The Malays give the impression of being passive linguistic magpies, collecting other peoples' words that have caught their fancy. Of course it may have been the other people had ways of making them speak their way. But I have ended up believing a quite different hypothesis, that the Garden of Eden lies under the South China Sea flooded by the great glacial melt, and Malaya The Garden Land is the hilly hinterland surviving above water. Adam's provincial cousins speaking a patois of the language of Eden retreated uphill, while the metropolitan people went by boat to Sumer as well as northwards by boat to the mainland of China and even out into the Pacific and over the ocean to South America. This is not kosher for the people of the book who are shewn to have captured the story of Adam when they captured Sumer as Akkadian tribal Cains, along with the technique of irrigating padi, the Garden of the East's special skill, which they carried to the Nile. I must rely on the mercy of Allah for forgiveness for revealing the real history behind their records. The padi fields of Eden are under the South China Sea, along with the drowned river courses irrigating them, which can still be picked out on the sea-bed. Malay carries the traces of the Semitic and Chinese languages Adam gave the proto-Semites and proto-Chinese. Was it Eve with her digging stick who displeased a hunter-gatherers' deity by knowing better and inventing agricultural irrigation, enabling the stay at homes to usurp the role of principal providers from their hunting menfolk, upsetting the domestic pecking order? It was Adam, with his external genitalia, who needed a trifurcate fig leaf. Any old leaf would have done for Eve. Adam's spiel about Eve taking the lead may have just been his plea in mitigation, diverting attention from his own priapism. If so it did not work. On the contrary it looks as if it was his sexuality over the aeons which sparked the whole confrontation. Adam's God took the boys' side, but then He was the boys' God. Anyway did God really melt the glaciers to punish Adam's misdemeanours, or Eve's for that matter, or is geological evolution just a matter of blind natural development as Charles Lyell purported to show[6] in 1830?

Krypton (16), the gas, is from Greek kruptos, hidden, whence also English cryptic and crypt. The Lithic appears to have been karau-paitau, with the ke-rau- and the -petau perhaps agreeing in end vowel case because perceived as two semi-independent constituents of the word in apposition. The semantic content is made-rayed one-covered-become one, with the substantive ending (s) again. This builds to visibility-concealed, and so to the full blown Greek sense of concealed from view.

Kudos (8) is simply the Greek, and means glory or acclaim – from akouein to hear – what being widely heard of does. The Lithic elements are a-kau-ai-en, as-stimulated-ai-en, that-struck-air-of, air struck: ai an extensive idiom from the aaa continuum, in this case spatial, space or air, followed by -en a verbal marker; the marker again from ai with en added (for whatever reason) to make up the marker – perhaps a closure coming at the end, just as coming at the beginning it suggested an opening, the other terminus for the continuum. The stimulus in this case of hearing is from one of the audible space rays no doubt, and the -dos adds the idea of English does. Kudos comes from ones deeds being bruited abroad. There is no suggestion of course the Greeks' ai came from the English air, but it may well be air came from the same Lithic perceptions as the Greek use of ai in akouein.

Kuklux is a recent fabrication as the name of a secret society set up with a view to saving Southerners, after they lost the civil war, from the perceived malign effects of negro emancipation. Perhaps from the Greek kuklos meaning circle, as clumsily pronounced by Hodge in the Southern states. See the remarks under kettle above for kuklos. It has also been suggested the sound imitated the sound of a gun being brought into the shoulder and the safety catch released. The clan certainly has a fearsome track record of cruelty and killing, in an attempt to pin down the negro by intimidation, with legal warrant for the policy withdrawn. Since we have no way of discovering what was in the minds of the founders of this insidious American organisation we can only guess and quickly pass on.

Kultur (44) is the German word for culture, a concept a good deal more powerful and insidious in that country than in ours. In the UK it is as often found lying about in a dish as laying claim to shaping affairs. In any case it is from cultivate, which is from the past participle cultus in Latin of colere to till the soil, which we should be clear was first of all a question of felling and clearing a ladang and dibbing in the seed; kau-lau-ere, land-levelled-verbal ending. Its metaphorical use as a measure of civilisation on the continent is fairly far fetched. Weltanschaung is better.

Kummel is flavoured with carraway seeds, otherwise cummin, originally akin to Assyrian kamunu. The Assyrians were Semitic speakers. It is not now known if they cut their foreskins off, nor exactly which gene pool they emanated from. They were hairy men, by all accounts. The Hebrew is Kammon and the closely related Arabic kammun. These formations are perhaps from the Lithic phonetic elements ka-mau-ne. Simple ignorance of the significance the seeds held for whoever it was who dreamed up the word makes it rather unprofitable to hazard a guess at the semantic contents. Perhaps it just meant edible (seeds)? The licquor is drinkable, though not to everyone's taste.

Kurd (44,33) is akin to Sumerian Qarda; but what aspect of the Kurdish people attracted the remark of Sumer is probably impossible now to determine for sure. My guess it meant theHill Tribes. Lithic kara-tai could be mountain born;

or perhaps harsh doers? Or both? The bourgeois Sumerians will likely have looked down upon these rude mountain goatherds, much as the Baghdadi does today.

That ends the words beginning with k that Partridge concerned himself with. Attempting to translate each word into its Lithic elements set a fairly random test of the Lithic hypotheses. The reader is likely to feel at first that the results are inconclusive. Some of the semantic contents suggested make a degree of sense of the material; but others may not carry conviction. On the other hand it must be borne in mind that the semantics as they are written here can not properly capture the rough and ready indeterminacy of the original Lithic terminology, simply because we are having to use the much more precise meanings of modern diction. The modern lexicon can only provide pointers to the original Lithic pidgin. Lithic is a foreign idiom for modern speakers. We are conditioned almost from birth to think in largely random word forms, the internal structures of which are generally overlooked and dismissed, even in those cases where the structure is obvious on consideration. The value of the attempt to rediscover the Lithic idiom does not lie principally in the accuracy of the derivations, or in the degree of assent to them produced in the average reader. It lies in the examples given of what is meant by the statement that meaningful syllabic strings making words up are prior to word strings making sentences up. On reflection the reader will probably agree it would be surprising if it turned out that the human mind had sprung to arms at the birth of language with a pre-ordained format, chatting away in fully formed sentences such as we use today, hundreds of thousands of years of thinking later. There are certainly no grounds for such a belief. This book is intended to show as an important result of the work in it that our most elaborate linguistic constructions nevertheless hark back to the Lithic pidgins still underlying them. We are all redskins under our mind skins. The whole fabric of language is shot through with these very primitive elements, and they can I believe be exposed to reveal semantic patterns which simply could not and would not be found unless they had actually been legislated in in past times by the linguistic practices of our savage forebears.

The grandfathers, our totems, are still with us, though subconsciously, and capable of atavistic whisperings in our ears. That in turn shows that clarity of thought is a late novelty. It comes from a sufficient degree of abstraction and vocabulary building for our logical propensities, and also our mathematical propensities, to find full expression. It is essentially no more than pattern making, from perceived similarities in spite of differences; based upon the adjectival minds of our Lithic forebears. That abstraction in turn starts from mental entification – the precising of adjectival images in the mind and treating them as persistent entities. Words are symbols – expressions merely – of those mental entities. With words we are able to call them to mind, and even to teach others to think of the same things. That way we get responses from our thinking. With words networking begins to burgeon. The rest is history. But there has not been enough of it yet to transport us quite beyond the ambit of our pidgin thinking past. That is how it is that, given the patience and attention, we can still reconstruct the Lithic etymology of language. Subconsciously we still have connection with it.

After wading through the rather uninteresting K words in English above, with the more interesting ones not really English at all, it struck me the words of foreign origin I excluded to keep the list short are in fact a better challenge than the English ones, so I append their Lithic analysis here, at the risk of over buttering the parsnips.

Kafir (16), from the Arabic, means an unbeliever or infidel, later borrowed to mean (contemptuously) a native (pagan) African. It comes from Kafara to be a sceptic in religion,. It is evidently akin to the Persian gabr or gaur used by W S Landor in his poem of 1798 "Gebir", and then rather less accurately by Lord Byron in his 1813 poem "The Giaour" from the Turkish version giaur. Kafara to me smacks of hedonism rather than mere scepticism, indeed I think it means in origin a fornicater, basing my suspicion on the Ancient Egyptian, a Semitic tongue with many Hamitic borrowings. Ka-pahei-ara, make-[with the] pahei or joy piece-infinitive marker is much the same as our best known English four letter word, with a major metathesis which is always possible and to be expected with original Lithic formations. There is one further differential between Kafir and a fucker and that is the final -ir. It could of course have come from arai the Egyptian verbal marker we find making its way over into the Latinate languages also (as –are,-ere,-ire). But it could instead be what is left over from an original aria meaning -that rays, in which case it could be an odour, that stinks – an unkind reference to an African unbeliever's unreformed habit of keeping his foreskin on and the smegma unwashed away.

Kaka (1) is Maori for a large parrot, not unlike the Malay Kakatua or cockatoo which is the Malay for a pair of pincers, the semantics being ka-ka-tua, strike-strike-dual, not a bad sketch for pincers which nip. You really need to know the cockatoo uses its hooked beak as a climbing tool or for any other job it has in mind as well as eating fruit or chumping nuts. You should also perhaps be told there are those, ignorant of that, who imagine it means an old uncle. Tua is old in Malay while two is dua (see Chapter 6) and Malayan uncles tend to be regarded as old wafflers or cacklers, probably from giving unwelcome advice on deportment to the next generation on, including amongst other things, their marital obligations, one of their traditional roles. Kaka has a firm semantic content waste, detritus, faeces from the chips we know as debetage (10) which the flint knappers left as they went ka ka ka tapping away flaking flints. The slang cack handed for anyone with an awkward manual performance is out of the same stable. Of course both the cockatoo and the new Zealand Kaka may have calls something like Kaka too. The kaka is pretty obviously echoic.

A Kalmuk (Turki) (53), including of course Count Ivan Skavinski Skavar, a Russianised Kalmuk who famously fought Abdul Abulbul Emir to the death – they are still at it – is a Mongol tribesman and according to Partridge the past participle of the Turki verb to remain at home. This Ivan's tribe was not one of the Russian empire builders, in spite of his powers with a sword. The final k will be the past tense from kai. This leaves ka-la-mai for the staying at home. I suspect the Kalmuks were Abels, "cultivators of the soil" instead of marauding on horseback, an extraordinary role for a Mongol who were pastoral nomads for the most part, like the Bedu, born on the hoof (literally the bum). La-mai is not so far from the Ma-lai of Malaya, it signified the leaking (of water) onto the marl. The Kalmuks had probably found a river which had enabled them to settle and grow crops. Ka-la-mai-kai is land-flat and moist-soil-making, horticulturalists in short like the Hindustai mali, and the garden land of Malaya. They are stay at homes to keep their crops alive.

A Kanaka (53,31) is a South Sea Islander. I think it is their term for a native, literally Ka-en-a-ka, Country-in-that-made/kindled/procreated/born. If so, they compare quite well with the Guanche of the Canary Islands, from Gau-en-khai, Born-in-the country in Carthaginian, as the aboriginal people described themselves to their Spanish dispossessors. The Carthaginians had probably colonized them a thousand years before. Comically the Kanakas were mostly so termed by Whitey when they came to Queensland as seasonal workers, where they were not actually procreated at all.

Kangaroo (45), Walleroo and Wallaby are lumped together in Partridge's dictionary. They obviously all refer to the kangaroo family's extraordinary gait. Roo or rau is rayed and rays give a fillip to the recipient. They could be raising rays like those which grew the plants or rousing rays which raised your sexual organ or rays of rage which infected your brain, but in this case they clearly targeted the kangaroo's bum, catching the kangaroo in the back legs so he leaped, literally ka'n-ge-rau, going-ge-rayed. The Wallaroo, from ua-lala-rau, was the recipient of a huge one-leap leap-ray. The Wallaby similarly went (bai) with a mighty big leap. The rays were probably held responsible in his case too, they just weren't mentioned, perhaps a common sense. Compare the Australian baji, a bird, which is a go-up.

Kaolin (30) is from the Chinese site where this pure white clay was first mined. It was a high hill. Pekingese kao-ling means high hill. Kao is stimulated and so raised, just like the penis, and ling is level from the skyline at sea. But kao-ling is also ground's-level. So the clay was both: from a ground location at a high level, which we rather more prosaically just call a hill. It has to be said however that hill comes from an Indo European root

Notes

1. Pidgin is from the Hong Kong/Shanghai Chinese attempt at the "business" language from the English busin- via bisin- to bidgin- and pidgin-. The terminal sibilant seems to have gone missing, perhaps because the Chinese took it to refer to the pidgin as an activity rather than contributing to the meaning. A pidgin activity would be just pidgin.

2. I have moved on a gypsy invasion of private land in hours by cursing them in the name of the Egyptian great gods who they knew would not have approved of their deception.

3. Arthur Koestler. The Sleep Walkers. Hutchinson 1959. Penguin Books 1964,1968-75.

4. M O'C Walshe. A Concise German Etymological Dictionary. 1952.

5. To distinguish it from minor metatheses where a vowel is transferred from one side of a consonant to the other, a clear case of slovening to ease pronunciation merely.

6. Sir Charles Lyell. The Principles of Geology. 1830,1833.

CHAPTER 6

THE PHONEMES DA AND TA

This chapter deals with the third phoneme, Ta and Da. They sloven between the two forms so readily there is no point tearing them apart to treat them separately. Or else it is that it appears that way because Da has not received the care and attention it deserves. But I believe the perception is veridical. The Tau is such an age old symbol the phoneme must rank high in the pecking order in the subconscious mind (reinstalled all unawares by every speaker), being inter alia in the old days a feminine sex symbol, as well as a Tao out East, and now just a T in the West, but prayed in aid as a dialectic by Hegel and Marx. It is intended in any case to treat the remaining phonemes more summarily after the marathon chapters on Ba and Ka, addressing the psychosemantic trees straight away and trying to keep the illustrations less copious in aid of simplicity. The important interest is probably more in the examination of the psychosemantics than in the evidential base, although this has to be presented. To me, after living with Lithic more than thirty years – forty years on the linguistic roots – it is the bye ways of the mind I most enjoy, while proving it has become a burden.

The psychosemantic tree for ta and da is on page 181 so we can number semantic contents in brackets as they crop up. Ta (1) is a light tongue tap or lingual plosive. It is less vigorous than the plosive from the glottis at the back of the throat, Ka. Ka was identified in chapter 5 as symbol for the powerful and skillful stroke of the flint knapper, the klink of flint on flint. It is undisputed the klinks went on for over a million years. Ta was thought of by comparison as the echo of a comparatively light natural snap, say the noise made by a dry stick when snapped in two for the hearth, or crushed with a blow from a hand axe and then snapped. It was the symbol for the break (to break or shatter is tar in Sumerian), and the mind invited to dwell on this came up with the effect of it, to separate or divide (5) into two (6). We are trying here to follow the meanders of the primitive mind before it had all that much to think with, remember, aeons before the first mud brick was sun baked for the first building at Sumer. The mathematical school of linguistics started by Gottlob Frege in the nineteenth century and now burgeoned beyond belief via Bertrand Russell and the early Wittgenstein as well as others all the way to Noam Chomsky, began with the concealed premiss language was informed by mathematics, whereas the truth is it was the other way around and math must have developed out of language. Logic is thus informed by primitive grammar and not a transformational grammar by logic. It does not make a lot of difference to the sums you can do, but it has a good deal of bearing on the status of the art and science of language. The firewood snapped left you with two bits – probably one in each hand, and often about half and half in each. The stick, single before, was now two, just as the flint was when you flaked it, come to think of it; but then not so obviously so as with the stick because the debetage was usually lots of little bits shed (sked, skai´d, action chopped off), each one with difficulty. It was a reductive process, not a clean break in two. Day One of math! So the Ta sound symbolised the break (3), and two was what you got when you broke one into two. You were doing a simple division, and not a multiplication as with ka, which was making a plethora out of a single flint. It was not higher math this breaking into two, but it was certainly a math already. The Tau was also what you got with the binary symmetry of the human body, a vertical central partition exposed at the fork with girls, with two virtually identical mirror images on either side of the centre line. Perhaps we are comprehendimg here the slow stages of a master mind of yore. How many plain folk will have known of the symmetrical pairing of their arms and legs before he or she spotted the abstract duality, one wonders? Probably some bright spark quite soon was ready then to do the sum backwards and put the two together again. Then what did you get? Well, the both of them: hardly world shaking, or anyway not immediately, although it would perhaps in a few hundred thousand years play a part in some relatively recent miscalculations over the dialectic, which I fancy to have for the first time finally nailed in chapter 16 on the origins of thinking.

Once our forebears domesticated pigs and learned from them the boar and his pharau was needed if the sows were to farrow – before that procreation was taken as recreation merely, such a commonplace it never occurred to anyone to connect it with fertility – they decided the male role was the key one and the men were the drivers of life, injecting the Ka for the women to clothe with their Ba, the flesh, which was what was going on during gestation. To bear a child was to butter over the skeletal framework or foetus, the rigid male virtuous part, with the relatively feeble (female) flesh. The foetus (15) from the Lithic phonemes paha-u-ai-tau-'s, the male genitalia-what-that which-developed-'substantive marker, imagined as a micro-skeleton. Women's role was to flesh the foetus out and then deliver it into the open air, and it was an ancillary role only. From a scientific point of view it is absolutely bogus. Females lay the eggs internally and males supply the pollen. This is today an exposure of historic male chauvinism over hundreds of thousands of years, and in no way its celebration. Still, they can not be blamed for the scientific

THE PSYCHOSEMANTIC TREE FOR TA AND DA

The Phonetic Tree

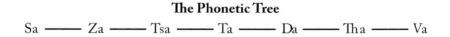

Sa —— Za —— Tsa —— Ta —— Da —— Tha —— Va

The Semantic Tree

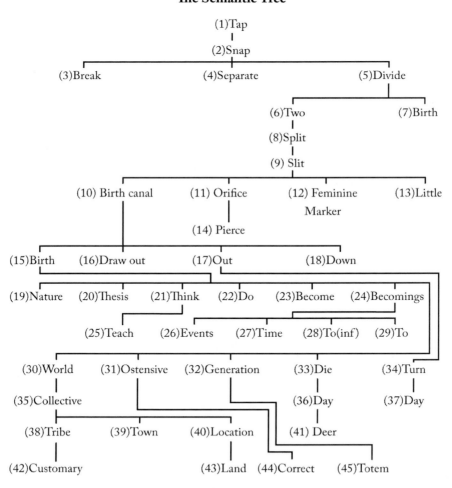

(1)Tap

(2)Snap

(3)Break (4)Separate (5)Divide

(6)Two (7)Birth

(8)Split

(9) Slit

(10) Birth canal (11) Orifice (12) Feminine Marker (13)Little

(14) Pierce

(15)Birth (16)Draw out (17)Out (18)Down

(19)Nature (20)Thesis (21)Think (22)Do (23)Become (24)Becomings

(25)Teach (26)Events (27)Time (28)To(inf) (29)To

(30)World (31)Ostensive (32)Generation (33)Die (34)Turn

(35)Collective (36)Day (37)Day

(38)Tribe (39)Town (40)Location (41) Deer

(42)Customary (43)Land (44)Correct (45)Totem

error, which is a commonplace even today, however well intentioned the scientists. How many men realise their own semen is pollen and not seed? We are just not any good at picking out errors. Science scarcely advances bar the hard way.

Taking the thinking forward from the split following upon the sound of the break, a split (8) as well as a clean break (3) can also be a slit (9). Quite a big jump this. Along with the overall binary symmetry of the human body of both sexes, the female has a slit where the male has a unique tubular protrusion, a little pipe or tap, in technical terms a throttle or strangler, developed purposefully for inserting into the female and squirting the pollen up her vagina. The purpose does not establish all in one creation theory, but the purpose emerged one way or another. It leaves the birds and bees in the shade. We shall deal with this male protrusion fully with all the semantic transmogrifications it has led to in chapter 12 on the phoneme pa, only prefiguring what is necessary in chapter 7 for Fa, which has accumulated some interesting four letter accretions concerning its usage, for explication in that chapter. The psychosemantic penumbra has been surprisingly wide in scope as befits this obsessive subject matter. Psychologists tell us we think about sex every other minute of the day. They may be judging us by themselves: they are lively thinkers. But we certainly make use of sexual language roots just about every time we utter a sentence, and this must come from past mischiefs at least. Only we don't know we are doing it[1], because by now it is all down below in the subconscious. But it is quite doubtful if it gets syppressed as Freud thought; it just falls down there like water flowing down hill as if the ocean is its home, while up top we imagine we have moved on and left all that behind altogether.

The girls, meanwhile, get full coverage in this chapter. Ta, at first the snap but early on the female slit, was thus the birth canal (10), the marvel of marvels of the Stone Age. Its recreational utility was of course well enough known and just as highly regarded as now, as well as in everyday use. But by comparison with its performance at birth (15), the earlier sexual fandango was regarded as old hat. Any fool could see an erect penis would fit in it quite neatly, even was designed precisely for the purpose; but it took actual witness to grasp that a baby's head could be got out of it, and then it was still a seven day wonder. It is not achieved without the most extreme contortion of the human frame, with pain for the mother, to deliver the child. It is still beyond belief for the juvenile today and has to be hammered home. They naturally think of solid discharges coming from the anus. So for our hominid forebears the miracle of birth left sex an also-ran. It may well be that the emotional impact of non-consensual sex, not much anyway, was diminished to match. Hominid sex was probably a relatively coarse affair, a gross indulgence without any play before or after, leaving the female to pick up what she could by the way. The same can be seen today in the all too common cases of gross male promiscuity. Stone Age sex was simply acknowledged as part of daily experience. The Ta was also Tau, and oo meant rounded out like the lips when oo was articulated. Try saying oo without the lips rounded out if this seems far fetched. You can´t get nearer than a force-thinned French u, which was quite outside hominid mouthings. The Tau which started out as a snap and then a magic twinning soon came to mean the vagina with its engorgements, but principally for giving birth; and relatively early on these unseemly imaginings were joined by the twinning that became the two dimensions of human experience, space and time, space along the top of the tau and time the riser. If it was not yet quite a mathematic it was certainly an abstraction, while we were still learning to speak. Birthing led to becoming (23) and the path or progress of becoming (24), and thus to the Chinese Tao. The mix of basic psychosemantics and human whimsy can account for all this, and quite frankly nothing else can.

Soon in Lithic terms really means no more than comparatively early on, perhaps a few hundred thousand years later. When you think earliest speech patterns were established by our hominid forebears probably more than half a million years ago, you should realise hundreds of thousands of years were available for working things out, as it turned out. The passage of time an order of magnitude which is many times greater than the whole of recorded human history still leaves it early, because by comparison the rate of change across the recent history which has been recorded has galloped, until it now has the after burner full on. Although we can still pick out the semantic connections over these long periods in the psychosemantic trees, due to the refreshment of the Lithic heritage from generation to generation, it is surely an impossible problem now to achieve with any certainty any precise and particular course of semantic development. The connections are there. The sequencing is not; unless of course the semantic trees themselves require a particular sequence of development, the meanings leading out of each other but only in the order experienced. On some of the trees dotted lines once indicated cross references where different preceding senses apparently contributed to a semantic trace. It is anybody´s guess how exactly these connections were seen in any particular or in any average case in the old days. But the semantic connections are definitely there.

A notable case of division or separating out into two was parturition, the birth and coming into being of another separate individual instilled with independent life. Not only that, but we are back with the female slit immediately, the birth canal or vagina, especially if you thought about that chain of events quite a lot anyway. Ta, from a light tap, was transmogrified via a slit into the birth canal and the birth it gave birth to. It also became the feminine marker since of all the antithetical aspects of the two sexes, the juxtaposition and contrapuntal nature of the girls' vagina and the boys' penis was the most critical and intimate, as well as a popular subject on its own account, simply because of the pleasurable activity it had to offer, just as today. Then a hole (11) can be verbalised, turned into a verb – "holed below the water line" for instance, or "to hole in one" – and then to make a hole is to pierce (14). The Sumerians had Sag-i-tar for arrow, the Latins only somewhat later (a few thousand years). Sag was the head, the top, from the two Lithic phonemes sa-kai, up or top-of the skeletal structure/body, the sa of the ka, -i-ta, which-pierced. An arrow is a piercing weapon which on arrival simply pierces with its head or point, unlike a spear which has to be thrown or a sword wielded. Admittedly the arrow has been fired from a bow, but that is not taken into account because the bow is a machine imparting a magic virtue to the arrow enabling it to penetrate. We would call it momentum, not magic. Is the bow the very first machine? Probably the spring trap came earlier. But there the spring sapling attached to the spear is seen to be doing its work as the spear strikes. A trap is a tra-pai, a drawn piece. A bow is simply bum shaped when it is bent and not treated as a trap.

The Ta or birth canal was indeed a veritable gulls' nest for ideas. Birth is a drawing out and the baby once born is out (17), from au-tai-, a completed-birth. Is it too fanciful to think of it tobogganing down the very rays the birth canal was already believed to pack for drawing out and up the penis and inflating it. At birth everyone came into being. They had become (23). It was a pre-eminent event (26). Then many births were already aggregable as a generation; and a generation (32) was already a tribe (38). A totem (45), from the Hawaiian Ototoma, from the Lithic Au-tau-tau-ma, all-the generations-dead – you could see them represented on the pole one above the other, often with the tribe´s mythical animal progenitor at their head – was an assertion of tribal solidarity, bestowing identity and worth on every member of the community (35), past and present alike, a chain of being in spite of mortality. Each birth was a pre-eminent coming into being, a happening or event. Many events were also history and the procession of events was time (tai'm) (27) or becoming. Mental births neatly described thinking, while all the events made up the Egyptian world (30), the Ta-un, since oo was the inclusive vowel, the event circle, oo, their encirclement or collective, all the events, feeding back in turn to tribal custom (42) which for some was a measure of rectitude and virtue: Te (from the Lithic tai) for one Navaho Indian tribe of California (the Awani tribe in Yosemite National Park) meant (more or less) good, as well as correct conduct, in accordance with tribal custom and the birth line it enshrined: tribe, tribal, customary, correct, virtuous.

Yosemite, pronounced yose-em-itty, is from the Awani Navaho language ia-ushi-ma-i-tai, it that-our-mother-of the tribe, which the park director believes means "grizzly bear". It is actually the response by his man friday to a miner forty niner, a gold panner who asked "what do you call that one then?" pointing to a retreating grizzly bear. Since the grizzly was the Awani totem it was an indelicate question to put. Her name was a secret, for fear with access she might be conjured against the Awani. We can guess at the exchange later in the canteen: "Sounded like Yaushemity to me mate", later tidied by those that came after to Yosemite. It is of a pattern with the earnest researcher given the name for a finger when pointing to something of interest. On present form it may yet finish up as "José Might", in which case the totem certainly mightn't.

Mata ayer, a source of water in Malay, a well, was first an earth hole (ma for earth, see chapter 10 and ta for orifice). Wells, especially springs, are sources, as is the birth canal. Ma, as well as earth, had a mental connection, also revealed in chapter 10. Mata could therefore be read as a mental source; and the eye feeds the mind with images. That is why mata means eye in Malay, and why mata hari, the eye of the day is the sun (and mata jarum is the eye of a needle, which goes both ways, to and fro and in and out). An eye and an orifice are akin. Hari is from the Lithic i(h)a-u-Rai, it that-one-of Ra: a sun unit, like our hour and year. Ra was seen as the world eye. Darat in Malay, from Lithic ta-ra-tai, rayed-become, means dry (the English is from the same source of course) and in particular the dry land. Drying anything was done by putting it in the sun. Naik darat, ascend dry land, is disembark and come ashore. But dara is the maidenhead or hymen, the birth canal's eye, and anak-dara, daughter-of or with the hymen is a virgin. The eye in the birth canal is evidently seen as a sphincter. Darah however is blood, from dara-hei, the arousal of the birth canal's eye. Dari is out of, from ta-arai, birth-infinitive, to be born, which is to come out (of the womb). In Hindi a dhoti is a loin cloth, a length of cloth wound between the legs, the Lithic a ta-u-ti, a two hole or orifices-both-thing. Chawat is the same minimal garment in Malay. Chawang is a fork (in a bough, road or the body). Chawang appears to be from the Lithic elements sha-u-a'ng, direction-dual-going. The chawat is a crotch thing, and with the aboriginal hill tribes becomes a minimalist item in wide open-weave bark cloth (net), but without which no adult male would be seen dead out and about. They are not monkeys. They are very early Victorians.

To let down a baby at birth was putting it down, and a mental put down is a thesis or proposition, a thought (21), something which happened to you in the mind. Ideas popped up just like babies popped out, but a lot slicker of course. To get folk thinking was to teach (25), from the Lithic tai-ka, to make think. Compare Old English taecan, Old High German zaigon, Latin dicere to show (31), from point out from tikh the tickling finger which pointed out, and so later just to say – was there a disciplinary problem even in those old days and nobody was listening to old soapy any more so it came to be understood he was just speaking without teaching anything? Or else perhaps the birth process was extended to cover subsequent development, making teaching the addition of tiers to your being as it were, achieving your full potential, as teachers still like to think today.

But today there is so much to learn it tends to get drummed in – or left out – without the benefit of much active thinking about it (the fun bit) at all. That is left to further education after leaving school, or it was until skills for earning a living, like carpentry and legal practice and household management, took its place there as well. Now it is native (15) wit alone which has to carry the whole burden. Meanwhile we are all good copyists, without really thinking and making our own rules, but instead just making other peoples rules our own. Too many people live and die like this like zombies through no particular fault of their own, but just by being copycats all their lives. They may not like to hear this, but the phonetics warrant it and the world lexicon is not as dispersed and uncorrelated as is generally presumed, since it is all spun from a human subconscious most of it so general as to be effectively single.

An event might be instananeous but it might also, like the birth on which it is predicated, be drawn out over a period of time. Thus an event could comprise a phase, a turn of events between limits, a beginning and an end. Then the ends in turn are transforms and so events in their own right. The turning at the end was ultimately just a change, in turn, and inter alia a change of direction. So a period of time with ends to it partook of this character, like a day (36) which has a clear beginning with sun up and an end at sunset. With a lifetime, the end was not a sunset but a death (33). But then the day was thought to end with the blood red death of the sun anyway. Dead, Lithic Dai-a-dai, meant both terms were done, since birth and death were the two terms of life. At birth you were fully fleshed and from then on a being until your end, or anyway the end of your beginning and your flesh. Life was envisaged as an upward striving, from the flame which springs upwards which was regarded as embodying the essential life force. Life had fire because animals are warm. Dead animals go cold and death pulls them down. This may all sound like philosophy but first of all it was just linguistics. Purists may like to riposte it was philosophers who made the language, but that is a case of the chicken and the egg. In truth the egg came first, since it hatched a species (a dinosaur) which was not yet a chicken, and the egg came before the dinosaur as well since the evolutionary stages the egg comprises were not at first inside the dinosaur. Similarly language preceeded philosophy and logic as well as grammar, informing them since it was from the linguistic egg that they were born, and not the other way about as Chomsky appears to think.

A deer first meant any animal, and that was the category of those that came into this world by separation (4) from their mothers at birth (7). They were parturients, the species kingdom that gave birth. Animals are by nature (19) wild, and they do not go to school, so a deer came to mean a wild animal, all of whom feared man the tool maker and fire tamer. Then, as a gull, it was applied in particular to the timid species, the deer (41). Perhaps it was then additionally assumed they knew about dying, dyers (33), which made them run away. They were parturients afraid of dying. A day (36) in Sanskrit was dyaus, from the Lithic elements Dai-au-sai, the terms-both of them-of shining: the day was the period of daylight between daybreak and sunset. Dyaus also meant sky, visible by day, day stressing the temporal aspect and sky the shining. Our word for sky seems to have been using the initial s- for top (chapter 14) and the kai for place (chapter 5), but there is evidently a penumbra of making the brightness of the daylight as well: Perhaps the sky was thought to reflect or diffuse the sun's rays to earth, making the shining. If so it was not far wrong.

Partridge has sky from cloud, a cloudy sky. If "sky" is originally cloud, that must mean the semantics of cloud comes from smoke, which reads in Lithic ish-mau-kai, fire-dead-makes, while sky, from Lithic ish-kai, can be read fire-makes, and fire does make smoke. Now clearly fires do not make clouds, although a forest fire can make clouds of smoke. So perhaps a cloudy sky was seen to be a smoke of cloud?. It is not necessary to believe the naming committees ever thought clouds were smoke. But in so far as they shared the opaque aerial character of smoke they would have been thought appropriately bracketed together by the adjectival mind; and they had probably consciously forgotten already the ish and the mau and the kai contributions. The gamuts were just lumped together in their minds. Of course if ish could be characterised as the symbol for opacity it would fit smoke and cloud equally. But it can not – unless of course a fire dampened down with a lot of greenery crackled and smoked reminding the hunkered hominids of the hissing of the dunked brand so that smoke too picked ish as a gull from the hiss, so ish came to mean smoke as well as fire. They must have noticed smoke went up with fire already. The conventional etymology still has to explain why the ancients should have picked on clouds as sky when in reality it is obvious the clouds conceal it. Were the clouds seen as bits of the empyrian which had congealed so they could claim to be more fully sky than the diffuse uncongealed blue variety visible at other times? I doubt it. Then again clouds scud but that hardly makes them sky. Without the Lithic, etymology is at a loose end here. We might try top-place for sky and top-kindled for cloud, but then different formulations would have been used so people knew which they were talking about. Our English clouds come from Lithic kai-lau-dai, made-looped-become, a natural gathering or patch, which describes a cloud pretty well though without any understanding of its real formation. Even better, a lye is cloudy (opaque) unlike clear spring water so a cloud is made-opaque-become. A clout picks up on the patch, a brief breech cloth; while a clod is a natural gathering into a clump or lump. Infidels with no faith in Lithic must nevertheless remark that words do tend to hang together.

The immortals were deos or theos in Greek not unlike dyau/dyo in Sanskrit for sky and day. The day, the period when the sky is lit up and light with terminals at dawn and dusk, sunrise and sunset, is bracketed and contained between these two events. The Lithic analysis is dai-au-sai, the births/becomings/turns-both of them-of the shining. The Lithic is simply the idea that the day is the period of light between sunrise and sunset. It is after all commmon sense that that is the case. So it should be no great surprise the system adopted by speech says as much. In the case of the gods the –sai is not of the shining but of the living. Sai meant both. See Chapter 14. The difficulty in sorting this out today is because expression in the early days was succinct to the point of obscurity – unless you knew the correct interpretation because you had been taught it. The language, as well as the minds behind it, was not fully adequate to uniquely identify the thought. Now of course we are not taught because the original thinking is largely forgotten. The consequence is it requires a thoroughgoing discovery and examination of the original Lithic idioms to enable us to get to grips with the reading of phoneme strings using the correct patterns of thinking. We can still think the same but it does not spring trippingly to mind: if you are on your own it may take forty years. When language was young the philosophy was thin: ideas about ideas could probably be counted on the fingers of one hand. There was the pattern of vowels, into which much was read; there was the criterion and the category (chapter 16), apposition and contingency; the developmental agency of the Tau; and the intentionality and drive of the ka (chapter 5). Emotions were flare ups like the flame. There was no psychoanalysis in those days. There was not much conscious psyche to analyse. Human consciousness was a light sprinkling on top of the secret worships of the subconscious mind, a sprinkling perhaps only born with language and certainly only with language capable of growth.

So it should be no surprise that deos and theos, the immortal gods, should be addressed in the same terms as the day, the two turn shining which was also the day. The day died but the gods continued shining. Sunrise and sunset were everywhere regarded in human terms as the birth and death of the sun, the source of life and light alike. The pattern was at one time universal of basing perception of the world at large upon the inner experiences of man. Infants still recapitulate this error. My grand-daughter at three will hide her eyes in full view and assume the world, which takes in her grandparents of course, is unsighted too. There is an autistic assumption the world around is simply part of one's own personal perception and sensations. It is that, but it actually has an independent existence on its own as well. It is easy to snap out of the autism when there are adults around correcting the misunderstanding. But digging your own way out of a hole you have fallen into is always harder than being pulled up. Otherwise why bother with school! So far as our hominid forebears were concerned, if we began by being born and ended up dying, then so did the day. Even our intimate sexual experience was thought to be reciprocated at large in the environment. Our day was followed by a night but not for the blessed immortals and the gods who lived in perpetual day, both turns illuminated; which must have seemed like Heaven to a hominid – with no night predators or spooks. Their grammar allowed the day two events which started and terminated the light which were expressed in the same terms as the immortals whose two terms were both light. It could lead to indecency amongst the immortals since all their copulations tended to be open to observation and on record.

Visually a change of state was generally a movement, a movement from and to. Thinking positively it was to (29); and since all actions involved movement of some sort active verbs picked up the marker to (28), the infinitive marker in English. Other verbal markers abound; for instance –er (French), -are, -ere, -ire (Latin), -arai (Egyptian), all from those omnipresent stimulants the Egyptian rays; and -an (Germanic), -en, and -ein (Greek), -na (Hindi), and so on, all from aa'n, extension or going. They will all be reviewed in their relevant chapters.

A door which you go through, it could be argued, provides a kind of coming out, a birth but it is not a very notable one. What is notable is early doors were swing doors, usually two leaved meeting in the middle, more or less, rotating on poles one end in the ground and the other in the wall. They swung to and fro. The Lithic elements were tau and arai, the tau was the aperture and the arai was the toing and froing as the leaves were pushed back and then returned to their blocking positions (chapter 13). The Spanish is more explicit: puerta for door is from the Lithic Pu-ai-arai-ta, two leaves-going-raying[to and fro]-aperture. The original ray, remember, was an active radar kind of ray, going there and back, explaining action at a distance involved in vision and attraction, eyes and sun alike. Even Isaac Newton followed the same thinking. His gravity was geraying, the force reaching out from one body to the other and pulling it back towards itself on the ray's return journey. The Latin porta came from pau-arai-ta, dual covers-reversing-apperture, like the English portal.

Two (6), duo, deux, dos, do, zwo, twu, twe is a fair spread of Indo European forms for two, from the Atlantic to Tokaria[2] on the way to Mongolia. But we can do better. It spreads over into Malay (dua) and the Dua Taun the Second World of the righteous dead in Ancient Egyptian. Malay and Egyptian share also hari, the same sun unit, from the Lithic I(h)a-Rai, it that-of the sun Ra, or sun-unit, or is it 'it-that-raying', ie when the sun is shining for the day. Further off, we use it for an hour from the Latin hora, (which in turn is from the Lithic phonemes i(h)a-u-ra) a sun unit too if a rather bogus one made up to divide up the day; while the Greeks, whose language is half Egyptian anyway, used it for a season of the year. This was why the Egyptians had Horus the son of Au Sa Rai whom we know as Osiris in Greek. Au Sa Rai, Our Sarah, was a fellah and was for the Egyptians The World Sun Rise (or Eternal Sun Rise, Immortality) and so indeed the promise of immortality as well as the annual fertility of the crops. Does not the sun rise smiling at the dawn of another day? If the Malay is the nearest we have these days to what it was that Adam spoke in the garden of Eden ten to twenty thousand years ago before it was flooded by the great glacier melt[3], then the Indo European as well as the Egyptian for two could have reached them via the Sumerians and Akkadians from Adam, whose language the humble hill tribes who survived the deluge spoke in a provincial patois. Does our two come originally from the Malay dua? The Sumerians were of Adam's tribe, the sailors, Noah, who emigrated: but the Akkadians were Semites, out of the Arabian lands with their light soils, and in those days still pastoral Cains or hard men ready to fight for their turf as they moved across the inhospitable Arabian hinterland. They defeated the Sumerian Abels who were sedentary, watering their crops; and then in due course adopted the Sumerian way of life. They learned paddi gardening and settled living for themselves, absorbed the Sumerian culture and myth, a good deal of which found its way into their Bible (much as the Greeks absorbed Egyptian culture and the Romans absorbed the Greek) and then some went off on their own to farm the Hamitic tribes of the Nile, teaching them to use their grubbing sticks to better advantage and let the river water into the paddi. Cousinship proved handy later when the Biblical Jewish nation lodged in Egypt.

The totem pole of Hawaii already mentioned, Ototoma in their own idiom, from au-tau-tau-ma, all the become-dead-generations (32), is not a mile away in linguistic terms from the vegetables the Aztecs and their forebears grew in South America. The potato and tomato are both from the same stock originally, bred by painstaking selection over the generations to the stage where they are separate species, one with edible fruit the other with edible tubers. The fruit needed enlarging and the acids it contained purging (by selection of variants year after year for hundreds if not thousands of generations) since the green fruit of the potato are poisonous eaten raw. I have not tried cooking them. The tomato roots make poor eating being tough and stringy and sour to the taste. The fruit and tuber are distinguished in their native country as, for the fruit, tau-mau-tau, birth-death/gestation-birth. The tomato is an annual and you plant the seed for the rebirth. Even in Europe seed is a form of life which is dead or gestating (Semen or Sai-mai'n). The matter still teases the Catholic mind after some ten thousand years. The potato meanwhile is perennial and presents no theological conundrums; since you plant the tuber repeatedly, pau-tau-tau, tuber-birth-birth. The English tuber from tau-bai-a, is a bit which has tau, naturally become bai, fleshy, bulgy. Though with quite different usages, the whole Pacific Ocean gives sanctuary to the very same Lithic elements. Their Taboo, or Tabu or Tapu, originally a Fertility Deity, is the Birth (Ta) or Sourcing of bau, All flesh, everything which is fleshed, and that of course includes the vegetable kingdom along with the animal. It is this fertility deity who sets the tone when it comes to religious observances, if you want to get a good crop. Taboo are thus the rules of what is permissible and impermissible under the eagle eye of this goddess. I simply guess her sex from the birth canal (ta), that fertile slit she rules over and makes her own. Unless of course the tapu is the ta-pipi or bunged piped birth canal of the boys, making Tapu a male fertility deity after all. Tabu can also of course be read as the two testicles. See chapter 4 for bu as those dual fleshy or bulgy bits. This may date the prehistoric fertility religion from the discovery of the trick which underlay the need for a sow to be penned with a boar with his conspicuous bu for fertility to ensue.

In Egypt the sun, before it was declared by the male god Amun to be the World Eye Ra, was taken by the followers of the goddess Au-Si-ti, Supreme Lady, or feminine life source known in Greek as Isis, to be the Aton, the world's Everlasting Birth Canal, giving birth to the light every day. Aton is believed by conventional Egyptologists to be the disk of the sun, but it was never a disk it was always an orifice. The A- of the Aton was extension, the Ongoing or Everlasting. The −ton was the vagina, the female slit, as birth canal, birthing light into the world. The heretical Pharaoh Akhenaton, whose sexuality has never been resolved – perhaps he was bisexual, his body was malformed – returned Egypt to the religion of the goddess, including worship of the Aton. His name was really A-khai-en-Aton, That-created-in-the Aton, Son of the Aton. He claimed to be directly descended from the supreme goddess and not from Amun like his forebears. His son Tahutu anak Amun (conventionally Tutenkamun), Tahutu son of Amun, started out as Tahutu anak Aton, but had to switch religion at the counter reformation on his father's death and was murdered in the disturbances of the accompanying revolution. Anak is son of in Malay today, literally an-a-kai, one-that begotten. This is probably a word come down from Adam speak from Eden in the South China Sea via Sumer and then with the Akkadians to Egypt, which could account for it being the same in Malay today. Also in Malay today Au Siti is Our Lady, the Virgin Mary, Queen of Heaven worshiped in the Catholic church like the Egyptian Isis before her and no longer just the humble mother in the animal stall.

In the West we have carried the idea of birth over into the mind, thinking it a kind of birth when an idea turns up in our heads. As Partridge would put it, it is a figurative birth. First it is not there and then, when thought or become born, it is. Discrimination, which is close to separation and distinguishing, all of which we know from other usages follow on from the idea of birth, has always been allied to thinking as well. To think (21) in Old English was thyncean and meant to appear (23) and so to seem. Methinks meant it appears or seems to me, nothing to do with the mechanism, figurative or otherwise, responsible for the seeming. Nevertheless the Lithic elements of thyncean are t(h)ai'n-kai-en, birthing-makes.

Well it makes a baby, usually loudly declaring its presence shortly after its appearance. The case seems to be established we think we think by giving mental birth to ideas – which of course we do. Of course the birth is just a metaphor for a thinking process which still escapes us in any useful detail. We can even see a further development (dating back perhaps as little as a couple of millennia in Northern India, now Pakistan), the practice of thuggi, the killing by subterfuge by the followers of Kali, the goddess of concealment and deception, of infidels everywhere at any time. Thuggi comes from the Lithic tahi-kai, think-making, ie deceiving by feeding false information and getting your victims to believe you before killing them, originally by strangling them – although it is perhaps worth noting in passing that in the Malay which has claims to being the earliest extant language tahi is excrement, with a different orifice the source. Tahi lalat, fly shit, is their corruscating term for freckles. According to Kevin Rashby[4] thuggi has claimed millions of lives and is still alive and well today, even targeting Islam ever since The Prophet declared war on Kali, weaseling her way into Islam.

Because it sounds the same we might ask here what a thing is, res in Latin, that is to say what is 'rai' or visible in Egyptian, any phenomenon, any visible item, res vista. If in the mind we think, in the world there are things, items, appearances, phenomena. Partridge glosses a thing as "a single object whether material or immaterial", an indiscriminate identification like a thingummyjig, from the separating[5] (in the mind) whatever it is from the rest. There is even more thinking in Malay. Tahu, pronounced more or less tau, means to know, which is the same as having thought it and so having the information tucked away in the mind for recall. If you don't know it is polite to say "belum tahu", I do not yet know, rather than confronting your interlocutor with a blunt negative fully frontal; as if to imply since he wants the information you will now bend every effort to discover the truth of the matter for him. (Nothing needs to be done). It also suggests that the information requested has not yet happened (to you), that is the idea has not yet been vouchsafed to you, but when fate wises you up you will be at his disposal. If you do know, it is because the answer has popped up in your mind, a birth of knowledge, tau, has occurred in your brain. Somehow the Ancient Egyptians had the same idiom: their god of knowledge who people think was Thoth, sometimes rashly pronounced Tahuthi, was actually in the mouth of an Ancient Egyptian clearly Tahu-tahi, the All-knowing. Their h was pronounced ahí or ahu, a cockney h separating two vowels otherwise likely to be slovened together. The South African Archbishop might like to know he is named after the know-all Thoth – some might think he has somehow divined it – and it comes from a pharaoh named for the loving god Amun. But the archbishop is not the son, anak, of Amun the Ever Loving (and the un-dead, and the unburied). Ankh, with many meanings, is dealt with in chapter 11. The glyph is known as the ansate cross and is sometimes used as an amulet by hippies and mystics, the word being a word of power for mystics, probably because of its several different scansions. You can sit and think about it and meditate on different things.

To teach is to get pupils to think, or else to guide their thinking. From the Old English taecan, to think-make, like thuggi above, also the Old Frisian teken to show, which is getting close to tikh, the old word for finger, the tickler which was also the pointer, and so might be expected to easily develop the meaning to point out and show. Similarly dicere, to say in Latin is from the Old Latin deicere to show, more finger work gulled for the pointing out, and then transferred to the full exposition you can provide by word of mouth. It is clear there has been some cross referencing here, and how much by deliberately thinking it through and how much by dreaming it up is anybody's guess. But the connection can be seen.

A tack, from ta-kai again, joins two things, just as a tacking stitch does prior to the full hem, from the Old North French taque a nail and Low German takk a tine, as opposed to teaching and thuggi above. It attaches the two (6) together, and so becomes the ropes holding the sails of a sailing ship, which tacks by changing the fastenings, whence also tackle and tacky meaning sticky, tact and touch. It has prestigious cognates, like attack from the early French attaquer, which joins two [battle lines]; and Italian staccato which is really from a slovened distaccato, with every note sharply detached (4), or untacked, from the previous and following ones. It is a quirk of the primitive mind it sees no inconsequence in equating opposites like split and join, both from ka. In fact it can do it with relish, as with the slayer and the slain. It makes no sense to the modern mind, but to the emerging adjectival mind it is only viewing the same character or event, or the state of play resulting, from opposite ends of the action. Splitting a flint leaves a divide where before there was none present. What now is split (8) was formerly joined, and at the site there is a joint, now admittedly outmoded but nevertheless still recognisable to the patiently enquiring mind, since the flint and the flake still fit together precisely. To touch meanwhile is from an original Gothic tekan to touch, I guess with the tik, the tickling finger. If so it has drifted since to tak instead, perhaps influenced by the joining of two things together above. The Latin is nasalised and voiced as tangere to touch, giving us our tangent. The Spanish have shifted further to the round with tocar to touch, using tangir instead for plucking string instruments, whence the dance to a guitar, a tango, perhaps also influenced by a kindled or kindling ta, and in Argentina a street festival with dancing, a plucking par excellence.

A tadpole is from a toad poll, ie his head only as the tadpole developes. The toad, with this intermediate form is twice born, tau-tai, or anyway enjoys two changes, egg to tadpole and then tadpole to toad, acquiring legs and coming ashore. A frog on the other hand is not identified by its peculiar breeding habit like the toad but by the fact it goes with an ejaculatory leap, pharau-gai, his pahei or joy piece rayed raised and roused. The ukulele is a similar idiom with different phonemes to the toad. It is a Hawaiian grasshopper, an uku, both the two kas, lailai, singing. The musical instrument has a similar stridulent note. We call an uku an insect because it has a thorax and body almost cut in two. The ka or driving soul of the Egyptians has found its way to the middle of the Pacific Ocean. The ka was dual. There were two kas, uku, one for this world and one for the next. The grasshopper, as an insect and profligate in its present avatar in the sublunary world using up both his ka by having two bodies simultaneously, had no prospect in the next. Is that why he rasps away so?

The Greek temnein to cut (in two) is from the lithic elements tai-em-nein, to expose the duality of it, as if the two halves were nestling there side by side waiting for their duality to be uncovered by the knife. Nai can mean exposed (Chapter 10). Tomos, a tome, started out as a single volume of a larger whole work, half a scroll originally, separated masses – or is it perhaps separated mental illuminations, mau-sai representing the work? With the present meaning of a tome the part has acquired the character of the whole it was designed to accommodate. We can glance aside in passing to observe a volume appears to have been originally a roll. Anatomy was originally the cutting up of the cadaver. The up, ana-, is from protruding or pushing up; the -tomy or cutting, dividing the masses, was to expose and exhibit the organs. Now the anatomy is not the cutting up but the organs cut up. It is a semantic bus[6]. Thomas which means the twin is from Tau-mai-sai, Dual-birth-impregnated-once. But an Uncle Tom is not a twin but a toady. Every word is subject to redefinition in use once it has been coined. There is no other true definand in the long term. Lithic does not claim to give the current meanings, nor does it. It provides a fascinating insight however into the way the human mind has worked and is still working, which is a great deal more important than a few small definitions. The Mahatma Ghandi dismissed "a few small bridges" blown up by his followers (as trains loaded with humanity passed over them) as no derogation from ahimsa.

With the world lexicon to pick from it is hard to find a single sequential presentation and the left over notes it is hard to leave out entirely. The Egyptian goddess of the night, Nut, pictured as a nubile lady in her birthday suit, toes on one skyline and fingers on the other, arched over Geb, a prominent boy god flat on his back on the ground with a gigantic rampant penis reaching up into the sky, heading for the moon which the goddess wears between her legs, with the stars a myriad teats dripping light into the night sky. The goddess is named from the Lithic Nau-ti, Presented-orifices. Nut is similar to nacht and night which have the same Lithic elements, Na-kha-ti, presenting or showing-the body-orifices. So Nut lives. We do not see these orifices by day when they are modestly withdrawn from view. Naked has the same base precisely, na-ka-ti. It is not the past participle of a verb to nake; and nude, from Latin nudo, with the orifices exposed, merely leaves it open to conjecture which orifices the Romans (and the Spanish) have in mind, just like the Egyptians. The nearest we get to nake is the snake, Si-na-kai, Brer-bare/exposed-body, not even limbs to break the smooth body profile exposed, and in the bare buff without the coat which most animals wear. Si is from sai, living, life and so life form or phenotype. The brer sense apparently comes via Malay with Kuala Lumpur, Estuary of Mud on the river Siput, Brer penis knob, Snail river. In the West we have the putti, another little plump body with even less excuse than the snail. Not much further off naughty probably encapsulates the same mischief, nakedness in fancy or in fact being for some the root of all evil whilst at the same time for others the source and well spring of life´s pleasures. So naughty can be nice! The underground is speaking. You can watch it doing so on the beach where some at least of the khati are sometimes these days exposed, although still regarded by others as naughty.

The Egyptian world view was all in spades. Princess Nefertiti was in spades. Nefer meant pretty. Titi meant just that: Princess Pretty Tits. It is true -ti in Egyptian was simply the suffix for anything feminine so titi could be read as feminine things. But then what were the feminine things which were found so pretty? Nefer is from nai-pahei-rai, which is easily glossed [when]showing-the penis-[is]roused/raised. Pretty is not so far off, from pai-rai-ti-ti, if you choose to separate the double t: a single t can carry a salacious meaning too. The essence of a titty is a repetitive number of diminutive orifices such as are to be found in the female breast. A single ti, as with the didgeridoo, is a single tubular shape, neat but not so diminutive. The di-dgeri-doo is a tube-with a loud-toot in Australia.

This is written in the lea of Mount Teide on the island of Tenerife, the highest mountain in Spain. The volcano has a conical fumerole on its lip, and the name is Punic or Carthaginian, a provincial Ancient Egyptian from the time when it was the Lingua Franca of the Mediterranean litoral three thousand years ago. These barbarians spoke Berber, which meant speech in Punic, much as babble means chatter in English, and the Greeks found barbarous since they could not understand it. It appears the Carthaginians circumcised too, Pu-nai-kai being Penises-exposed-made. They were in fact Phoenician seafarers, Pahei-au-i-nai-kai-an, Penises-what-they-exposed-made-ones. Circumcision, started by the Pharaohs, was clearly a seven day wonder for those still entire, and it is still a puzzle today often justified on hygienic grounds but probably originally a male chauvinist trick to beat the girls by removing the male muzzle covers, thus enabling the boys to fire first, without having to wait for the feminine rays to peel back their foreskins for them. In this way the Pharaohs could seize the initiative in every encounter, as befitted their divinity, their potential completed with this neat thinking and action to match it, which they represented as a deal made with their male God, Ra (and one in the eye for the Cow Goddess), who bizarrely was actually believed to have approved this quite severe modification of his original design of the male genitalia, and conveniently even the salaciousness lying behind it also. We must accept Father AbaRaham's subsequent covenant with God had nothing to do with Amun Ra.

The Aton is present in Tenerife also. Tenerife is from the Carthaginian Ateneraiphai from the Egyptian: Aton-arai-i-pahai. The A-ton-a-rai is the Everlasting-Birth Canal-that-rays, that is to say the fire coming from the sun, and so a fancy way of saying fire, and i-pahei is which ejaculates. A fire ejaculater is a volcano, and the whole island has indeed come from the crater. It is tempting to treat the Aton in Tenerife as the volcano itself, copying the sun which some thought was a world vulva set in a stone roof which revolved. But the Berber (Carthaginian) language has "The Sea of Tenerai" for the central Sahara where the sand sea is so hot it burns your feet. Sea of Fire makes sense but Volcano Sea does not. The sun's fire rays Aton-arai still warm when they reached earth, drew up the plants on their return journey back to the sun. The ti-rays which emanated from the girls' mini-vulvas drew up and out as well. So any orgiastic outcomes were in no way the boys' fault. That is how we get drawers, trays, drays, tiroires, tractors, etc; even nature, na-tu-rai, for all the different pulls and forces exhibited by nature. Even a tear is drawn out, in this case out of the eye; while to tear a thing in two is literally to two it. What has become has happened and what has happened is an item, so what is tai or tau is ostensive (31) as with the, this and that, or even the Russian da for yes (that's it). The Malay for that one or the is itu, from the Lithic elements ai-tau, that which-become/established/indicated. The Latin is –tus for the past, what has happened. A town (39) is a small world, a collective (35) or community. The tic-toc of a grandfather clock is a repetitive tapping (1), not unlike a snapping. A tapping is from a tap, and a tap is a ta-pai, both an orifice with a blocking piece in it, first probably a spigot, and also a holing piece for drilling holes with. Many readers should be ready by now to take it from here for themselves. The Tao is open for those who choose to see.

Notes.

1.   We will by the end of chapter 16.

2.   The Tokharian A and Tokharian B languages are two extinct Indo European outliers whose speakers went East across the steppes from the Indo European tribes' projected cradle in the Black Sea area. The waters are not so much black as belaked. It is an inland sea, broken into by the mediterranean sea comparatively recently. The Tokharian tribes were hillmen, in the underly-

ing Lithic idiom Tau-Kara-ai or in the Greek Tokharoi, Born-Mountain-ones which the Uigur nomadic tribesmen had as Tokhri, Tau-kara-i in their Turki language. It rather looks as if the Turki tribes were also claiming to be natives, Turai-kai, born-in the country, which is interesting as they were always moving on, and this was probably their weakest link in any claim they might have to the country they were in. The Kara Khorum range is to the South of these peoples' stamping grounds, and do indeed include "the mountains highest risen" the snow covered peaks along the north of India from K2 (Mount Godwin Austin) to Everest (from Ai-u-rai-sai-tai, that which-most-risen-up-become) in Nepal, Nai-pa-lai, the Valleys of the Peaks, the Peak District as we would put it. In Hindi a valley is a nullah, from the Lithic En-awa-la(h)i, of-water-the flowing [did it]. In Arabic it is a wadi, from the Lithic awa-di, water-did [it]. In English valley is from the Lithic Awa-lai, water-flowing [did it]. Kara is mountains, rocks rising up and Khorum from Kau-rau'm is the completive case of these rising rocks, the most mountainous mountains you ever saw – and they still are.

3. The great glacier melt has now been calculated to have raised the level of the seas by as much as 350 feet or over a hundred metres. How long it took is hard to discover now. It was not in a night, but most probably over many decades or centuries, but rise it did, dispossessing the inhabitants of Adam's garden land in the East, at that time it would appear the most civilised on earth. A hundred metres is the depth of the shallow South China sea which covers a flat plain on which can still be discerned the courses of great rivers which Adam and his fellows exploited; or was it Eve who first put her digging stick to such good use – while the menfolk were out hunting game in the age old manner – and first tamed the waters for growing paddi in irrigated fields. Malaya, which means the garden land, is all that is left of the garden of Eden. A mali is a gardener in Hindi too. The Lithic ma-lai makes it clear it is irrigated-earth, paddi fields, which were the real garden of Eden, (Eden is the East, Ai-a-dai'n, that which-that-born, the birth place (of the sun) since it reads soil (ma) leaked into (lai). It had nothing to do with fencing off a bit of real estate to grow flowers and take tea. Malaya today is the hinterland of hills still above the sea, and the aboriginal tribes along the central jungle clad spine are hillmen from Eden who probably spoke a simple patois based on the same roots as the language Adam's people spoke. It was Adam's paddi which supported the first city populations. With wealth and leisure for the first time, at least for those with authority, there is no telling what mischief Adam may have got up to. It appears in any case he was too clever by half, perhaps arrogating to himself dictatorial powers as if he were of divine birth,

as kings and emperors have always found a temptation; and Eves have I fear often been too ready to concede to them, since sleeping with a God adds a smidgeon of enthusiasm over and above the really quite sweaty physical reality of lovemaking in a tropical clime.

4. See Children of Kali by Kevin Rashby, 2002. Constable, London. ISBN 1-84119-393-3.

5. Separating is from se-parare. Parare is part of the pare group under which Partridge lists forty words, prefixes and suffixes. Sai can signify single in Lithic (see chapter 14) and the pare verb can mean produce (as in parent and parturition). Pa is a shoot so pa-are is to shoot or burgeon. To have burgeoned singly is to be separate, and not equal to itself as some have thought.

6. A bus is a word which is shortened without any reasoning so that for instance an omnibus, which means for all in Latin, is reduced to the dative case marker –bus from the Latin. Another example is a pram from a perambulator, where per-ambulare is Latin for walking around. The per- is apparently a bus already in the Latin, from peri-, around, from pai-Rai, the skin of the sun, its periphery. Per- from Pa-ire means through which does not fit. A priam would be better.

CHAPTER 7

THE PHONEME FA

Rabbi Marc-Alain Ouaknin´s Mysteries of the Alphabet – he is a professor and Director of the Aleph Center for Jewish Studies in Paris – provides a classic exposition of the aesthetic version of Lithic appreciation, but without any of the hard graft putting real meaning into any of it. Aleph he declares means ox in Semitic languages. "So in the beginning the ox appeared". But did it? What actually appeared to his vulgar forebears was the animal´s extraordinarily long dick. Cows were tamed early on for their milk and the ox for his contribution to farming pulling the plough. His domestic performance thus came under close scrutiny at a very early date, and his sexual performance was at once a seven day wonder. Just a whiff of a cow and the bull extrudes an astonishing length of verge swinging in the breeze. Aleph, aa-lai-pahei is an endless-long-wowing piece. You do not stand in his way. Aleph can be variously interpreted of course, for instance as having lai-fai, smooth puffing or breathing, but it has nothing to do with a bull. That also leaves out in the cold another seven days wonder the elephant, ai-lai pahei- en-tai, an animal "with long cocks, two of them", one at each end, the one at the front even more tirelessly inquisitive than the one at the back.

Ouaknin´s gloss continues: "The ox is the premier sign because it represents strength, the energy that is so important for living, for agriculture, [ploughing] for transport [ox-carts], the elemental energy that sets everything in motion, which changes from being to existence". But it was not really that which appealed, it was a much more earthbound dimension. He continues: "Some interpreters see the various directions [of the horns in the different developing scripts] as being symbolic between man and the surrounding world. The horns are like antenna directed at the outside world making it possible to capture energy and information". Further: "Where the horns point upward [Shem´s original contribution!] this indicates the transcendental dimension in man´s position in the world. It is the vitality of the finite, drawing his strength from the infinity of the creator, God, or the celestial powers. This relationship can be called vertical or theological. The 90 degree turn directing the horns horizontally to the right or left indicate the change from theological to anthropological [some backsliding here! Turning a full 180

degreee circle [actually a half circle, Ouaknin is a rabbi not a mathematician!]
introduces an even more earthbound dimension [a vulgar one dreamed up by the
goys!]". Now this is certainly fanciful, making Lithic analyses by comparison look
like bedrock science. When I look hard at it I have to say it seems to me to be
interesting but ultimately all fanciful rubbish, however much I admire virtuosity.

You have to ask yourself what exactly is prompting these whimsies. They are
not wholly misguided, it is as if there were something guiding them though at
one remove, and certainly not aiming for scientific rigour. This applies equally to
the Lithic language and to the Oaknin fantasies of course. With the Lithic we
can pin it down to a nascent logic with psychosemantic contents prompted by
the phonemes. Ouaknin´s transcendental dimensions, theological vertexes and
anthropological horizons, per contra, hint at the hypothetic extravagance of the
professional wrangler rather than the word smith. It is free composition on a
ground of psychic perception only, picking meanings out of the blue. Something
is coming through from underneath in the subconscious, but it is by no means
a full monty. The bull´s formidable genitalia have disappeared completely, to be
replaced by a theological fantasy, so that the rabbi deserves high marks but his
linguistics is questionable.

But it would be wrong to write him off entirely. Fossicking in the linguistic confabula there are symbolisms to be gathered. The original meanings of the
Semitic vav (our Fa) apparently includes oar, hook and nail. An oar was first a
rudder over the stern for steering a boat. Water in Lithic is often awa, and the
agua group probably had a g smuggled in to replace a glotal stop, which then
almost replaces the consonant in turn. The awa is because water is without (consonantal) structure, and also because if you immerse yourself in it for a time you
find yourself saying Awawawa, shivering: so in a way it is the cold water speaking
through you. I rather like the idea of a boy Tarzan in the Stone Age shivering
when he stayed too long in the pond under a lowering sky just as I did 600,000
years later. He was the hero, unable to retire to a dry cotton towel and two squares
of Cadbury´s milk chocolate. Were there cow pats and duck lice in his pond too,
I wonder? If he were still around I would hug him whether or not he smelt sweet.
Aua can be "that one [that] go". Vav has the original phonemes awa-awa and the
steering oar has to do with water travel surely. Hooks and nails suggest joining. A
carpenter is a joiner. Carpenter in turn is perhaps from Kara-pai.en-terai, a joiner
of precut pieces. But u is the dual as well as the completive substantive vowel, so
Vav can perhaps be read "one that duals", in the same word family as juga, yoga
and yoke, in spite of coming from different language families altogether. These are
all vowel meanings and they are all in chapter 16.

Ouaknin´s derivative meanings include furthermore (unexplained) phallus,
pipe and finger, all three of which Lithic semantic analysis supports, as well as vo-

ice (think of Latin fari to speak, and a shower of words with meanings to match), illuminate and shine (compare flame and pharos). He comments however "We have found no reference to these various meanings in the classic texts; neither the shape nor the etymology contain anything to justify this theory". But we have. But not in the Kabbalah, that mysterious jam pot to which he repeatedly refers, where the vertical line of vav is "the sign of the descent of divine energy downward, a meeting point between the transcendence of humans and the immanence of God". Vav also, apparently "represents the various conduits by means of which the body can receive from the outside and exchange with the outside, thus the vav may represent the esophagus, the trachea, the artery [which one?] or the spine in which nutritional and respiratory energy circulate [Oh!], as do the nerve pulses. It is also the male genitalia that permit coitus and build life based on the encounter". So he is on to the Egyptian wowing piece, pa hei, phi in Greek, at one remove. A phallus is a pahai which has got lau, roughly that is inflated into a loop shape as in chapter 9. A pipe is a pipi or quail in Egyptian because pan pipes peep like game chicks, and even a dumb drain pipe inherits the configuration as a gull. Finger can be read as Phai-en-kara, for the stimulation of the pahai, a coarse description of its possible use certainly, but quite a good pointer to the primitive mind. It shows where the lewd and licencious soldiery when they get together get their lewdness and licenciousness from. The pahai carried across to the fair sex also. I remember in the Home Guard at sixteen learning to load and then to unload the Bren gun which required a finger under the body of the gun to locate the magazine ope-ning cover and slide it shut. The army corporal instructor´s commentary on this manoeuvre has stayed with me more than sixty years. He had a very similar idea of the prime use for the finger to that of our lisping forebears, while I thought of it, and still do, as holding a pen and lately as tapping a keyboard. Vav also means "and" [Wa in Arabic]. This is also because it is the completive vowel in Lithic, u-a, complete that.

Of course nobody disputes the letter A started out as old long cock´s head with the two horns sticking out of it, nor that its orientation varied as described. His trademark the other end was a refractory glyph because of its shape and orienta-tion. An alphabet needs letters that occupy roughly similar spaces. In Egypt they had glyphed the human phallus, but then it was a comparatively neat job com-pared with the bovine version, pronounced "mai" (the implanter) or "pahei" (the joy stick), the Greek phi (Φ), originally with the verge entering the circle rather than just laid across it, the symbolisation at the outset matching the phonetics and semantics and merely garbled later. This is yet one more case of the explicitness of Scrimshaw man followed up by Wayland's obfuscation. But alphabets represent a major advance in conventional thinking, dumping yesterday´s mental pabulum and freeing the mind to attend to the job in hand, in the case of copyists an easy running hand ignoring the original semantics in the pattern. It was speaking, we must remember which first presented the possibility of this kind of public code. Finding meanings for sounds, propagating these meanings and carrying them forward in the public domain was the birth of convention, which has expanded unceasingly ever since. Now we call it culture and seek to trim up the convention wherever it pinches.

A glance at the psychosemantic tree for Fa opposite shows quite a complex and heterogeneous phonetic tree but a relatively simple semantic one. That is not to say there is not a lot of language using the Fa phoneme. On the contrary it gets more than its fair share of use because of the psychic pull of the male genitalia. The Egyptian Pa Hei is in the top row of the psychosemantic tree at (3) because of its power. It meant originally the orgasmic piece (as laid out in chapter 8) quite like the joy stick world war one pilots grasped between their legs to keep their plane flying straight and level. The orgasm was always amongst the ephemera (17), from the Greek epi-hemera from the Lithic ai-pai-hei-mai-arai, as is-the penis-climaxing-impregnating-verbal. A Greek Ouaknin has tidied the ai-pahei-mai-arai to epi-mai-Ra, on-the dying/sinking-of Ra the sun, or better that which-covered or bounded-by the sinking-of the sun. Hemera is the day in Greek, noted for its ephemeral quality, just like the orgasm. It was probably moot if the sinking sun was dying (the commonly held view) or gestating in the underworld ready for a rebirth over the Eastern horizon the next day, since mai had both semantic contents. Ma-te in central Senoi, an aboriginal language in Malaya, means down onto or into the ground, while mati in Malay means dead. Ask a father's name and be told dia mati: he is dead (and buried), so his name is none of your business to conjure against us.

But first of all Fa is clearly a puff (1), half way to a sibilant. A continuous fff was originally more likely to be recognised as a hiss. It is also quite close to Ba and Bha which was identified ab initio as a lip plosive. There is a lip plosive element in Fa but it uses the top teeth too, and is therefore peculiar to neither. Its analysis as ph, made up of p and h is significant and at the same time quite difficult to understand. Pa and Ha put together phonetically do not make Fa or anything like it. But put together dialectically they do, since Pa is a stop and Ha its opposite: the breath is not stopped and may continue as an aaa ad nauseam. This may seem a silly analysis to us based on a somewhat slender identification of the phonetics involved, but we are dealing with our silly hominid forebears remember, for whom this kind of ratiocination was taxing in the extreme. The dialectical synthesis Fa is a consonantal stop which at the same time is not a stop but a fine filter for the breath and thus a hybrid or synthesis of the two, retaining the semantic undertones of the two supposed prior constituents and a slice of the sibilant phoneme too. That is the dialectic for you.

THE PSYCHOSEMANTIC TREE FOR FA

The Phonetic Tree

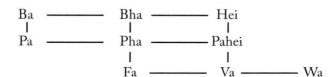

The Semantic Tree

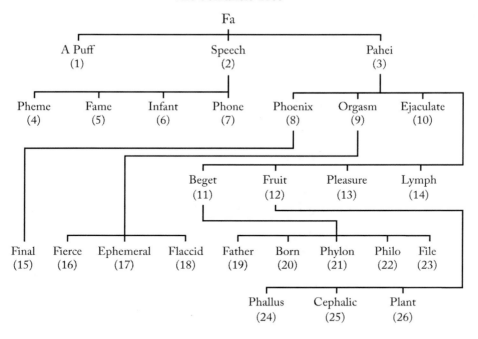

Every utterance comes with a controlled expulsion of breath, every phoneme accompanied by a puff, variously modulated. So in a sense every puff may be thought of as a phoneme; and it is phonemes (7) (and their meanings) which have built into words. It is necessary to say this several times as it is no part of current epistemology. In the same sense every puff may be thought of as a word. Speaking is uttering a sequence of puffs – think of spreche in German – admittedly quite variously modulated. If a sentence has too many words in it you run out of puff and have to pause for breath. So to puff is to speak and that is the meaning of fari in Latin, with the –ari suffix just the verbal marker. You spit out your utterances, a sudden cry is even an ejaculation. In English fate (from the Latin) (5) is what has been decreed for you, a divine statement of your curriculum vitae, like it or lump it. To date it has always included a fated fatality, as if the mortality of human kind were fatal, as indeed it is. The Greek is pheme (4), a saying, from the Doric phanai to speak (puff-present), with the Greek offering also phonein to utter, leading to phone (7) a sound, uttered or other, but mostly uttering as with the telephone over a long distance, and of course a phoneme with the –eme probably just a mass or lump. When we come to look more closely at the phonemic structure of speak and spreche (4), s-pai-a-kai and s-pai-rai-kai respectively, we can see there is another sense in there as well as just fuffing: action-pieces-that-[in a]row-joined and action-pieces-that-[in a]row-makes. Speech is the stringing of pieces – in a row. It is the combinatorial novelty which makes the build up of meanings possible, and it is that which got our hominid forebears thinking to some purpose.

Partridge relates all these words to an original *Bhami, I speak. The asterisk means KV (cave! in Latin: watch out!) he may be making it up. There is no doubt however that lip and tongue, Ba and La, go to make up the idea of speaking around the world while the ph phoneme means to ejaculate or spit or puff. Try Bal in Queensland, an aboriginal coinage for speaking, bolna in Hindi or lingua in Latin. The lips are really just fleshy and the tongue first of all the taster, both around well prior to any verbage. Phone, originally an utterance, is now used for any sound. The –nai phoneme has the very early meaning of to put forward or present, with no prizes for guessing it was the joy stick that was first perceived as pushing forward and presenting, as is fully explained in chapter 11. In English an infant (6) is an under aged person legally unqualified to testify, a non speaker, including the infantry joining as young boys. The Latin flare (1) to puff, where fari (2) is to speak, adds in the la phoneme bringing with it the notion of overflowing and flowing, the instinct of liquids to flow into the lows (chapter 9), flatulence linking with that other puff the fart (1), and inflation to the Latin follis (1), the bellows; as Eric Partridge puts it all "ultimately echoic", like much of Lithic. A flavour too is from the old French flaar, an odour. A flare is a different ray (of light) – it has fa for the puff. Even the finch (4) or spink (2) is an utterer in its own way, and the humble puffball if you press it puffs pollen just like the puffer we are now coming to in the following paragraph.

A puff can convey the sense be off, and you find it in flit and flee and fly and fleet of foot as well as in aerial flight. Birds fly when approached, they flit and take flight or fly away. The fly is fly and can fly so quickly you need to use a mesh to swat him, upsetting his response to the pressure wave ahead of the swat so he leaves too late. Both flow and fly use la for the smooth kind of movement of liquids as their la instinct takes effect and they slip away into the lows: see chapter 9.

The rest of Fa is most readily treated principally under the Greek phi rubric, from the Ancient Egyptian pahei (3). Half the Greeks lived in Egypt in classical times, and most of the educated ones. Perhaps half Greek is closely related to Egyptian, a Semitic tongue. There must therefore be a suspicion Greek philosophy and thereafter Western civilisation received its first major input from these Egyptian Semites who had acquired an African colony – probably on the strength of their riverine agricultural skills which they had themselves learned from the Sumerians who came from Malaya and kept their foreskins (3) on, just as the Akkadians probably did in those days before they got to Egypt. When they captured Sumer the Akkadians were still at the primitive beduin stage, baidau-in, travelling-born-ones, Cains beating the sedentary Abels. The Sumerians were refugees from the South China Sea, the Eden garden flooded 350 feet deep when the big glacier melt raised sea levels that much between ten and fifteen thousand years before the present. It means that Adam was not a Semite after all. The Akkadians borrowed him off the Sumerians after they captured Sumer, along with most else they knew. So for example the Sumerians called their cats ka-tse, spit-mouths. The Akkadians called their pussies spit mouths too, pu-tse in their language. I leave it to others to trace these etymologies over the intermediate five thousand years. The Latins picked up the same feline defiance with felis for cat, a lye ejaculater. The Egyptian term for their cat goddess, or natural essence of cat was Bast, properly BaSiti, girly bum or ladylike gait, a dainty stepper. They clearly entertained pet cats where the earlier barbarians thought of wild ones. They slyly emphasise the softness and gentleness of the feline paw omitting to mention the sharp claws which enable it to tear the flesh. We may note the West has taken up the idioms of the barbarians though without understanding them.

Who the Adamites were perhaps we shall never know. It may be there were not enough of them to have left much mark in the genetic record. There is a smidgeon of evidence that (like the Chinese) they spoke a language closer to Malay than any other. It was markedly different from Akkadian, the earliest Semitic tongue of which we have any record. Research may yet discover Chinese is the nearest tongue to Adam´s, and ten thousand years of Westward migrations, all prompted by the sea level changes which heavily punished the low lying Eden garden, has skewed our historical perspective and kept us looking towards the sunset.

It would be unkind to say the Chinese after starting out so promisingly have lagged behind a bit since then, but it is probably true. There is no royal road to progress, it is a haphazard affair which perhaps can not be planned for at all. A plan could help. But we are proven bad choosers, usually pressing forward firmly in the wrong direction. The Chinese uniquely retain the Lithic idiom of recognised word structure made up of strings of individual meaningful phonemes. The combinations often appear fanciful now due to meaning drift over the aeons, but the surprising thing is surely the degree they still fit together meaningfully. So long as the structure is recognised it holds the meaning in a headlock, retarding the semantic explosion which occurs when words are randomised. You even have to be something of a savant to have all the meanings at your finger tips. In China, when wrangling, you may even have to paint a meaning to make sure your interlocutor has it right.

At the height of the Egyptian cultural dominance in the Mediterranean and Middle East their language was the Lingua Franca for the whole of the Mediterranean litoral. There may even have been colonial places in Britain with provincial Egyptian speakers. Some place names can be read in Egyptian. If so they did not survive the Celtic invasions. The Celts were head hunters with a yen for human brains for dinner, as well as some rather unhygienic habits when it came to displaying the heads they had cut on either side of their front doors. You did not last long if they captured you. You were for the pot. The heads were still outside their front doors when they reached Britain. Of course this was a very long time ago and there is little trace left today of their former predisposition.

Hei as well as extreme pleasure could indicate extreme pain, shock or distress. Hot was a cry of pain on being burned. "Ho!" will convey to an infant, that is someone not yet speaking, the idea that touching something is painful. You put your hand towards the kettle and let out a "Ho!", and for good measure pull a face. For practical purposes you are back in the Stone Age. So it is of interest to us examining the origin of language to find it works. The phoneme really carries the psychosemantic content of sudden overwhelming shock, whether it is a nasty burn or an orgasm or any other shocking circumstance anywhere in between, like hurting or horror. But it is all fully covered in chapter 8. Here we are solely concerned with the genitalia and the ecstacy or extreme pleasure to be obtained from that quarter. The Greek phuein (11) to engender may open the batting. It is related to pu which in Egyptian is the quail chick, a cheeper because it cheeps always in pairs, never a single peep, and u being the dual vowel it is named pu. Then it becomes the glyph for u. Also pan pipes which make a similar sound, pipi, are called pipi and then as a gull any other small pipe such as the penis becomes a pipi, if a dumb one. So a pipi can be a pu. See chapter 12 for the full development of that catena.

There is a well enough known four letter word in English which in Ancient Egyptian is to be read as making (perhaps literally striking as when flint knapping) with the pahei, phai-kai, shortened to pha-k in English (10). So far as I know this is an entirely original etymology for this rude boys´ word which has generally been ignored as impolite, which of course it is, since it covers an area with heightened emotional content with not so much as a nod to the emotional side, instead treating it as a crude physical phenomenon merely. Ka got its creative semantics indeed from the making of flint tools, since the phoneme Ka was first identified with the clink of flint on flint, as the shaping took place. The background is all in chapter 5. In Latin facere means to make, originally from to procreate but that is forgotten. The English make is a special case, originally pounding a mass into shape, like kneading dough, or more likely shaping clay. Homo faber (11)was a handy man and a fabric is what has been made. Further off, a fact is what is composed, a statement put together to give a definite outline rather than a flint chipped to shape.

The Pharaoh of Egypt had a royal phallus (24), in fact Ra´s, and Ra was the supreme god. It was also exposed and visible. The Egyptologists´idea it was his house that was royal is the result of confusing pa with pahei. In Ancient Egyptian a parai, a skin for the sun, a parasol or sun shade parrying the sun´s rays was a house, originally a goat skin tent named for the shelter it provided in the desert in the heat of the day rather than the warmth at night. But a pahei was the joy piece. Sir Wallis Budge apparently started this confusion between a Pharaoh and a Paraoh in 1921. Ra was the World Eye, the sun looking down on His creation, bent at first on keeping everyone in order, but seeding the idea Christianity added a few millennia later that even the sparrow´s fall was of concern to Him. In Egyptian ra meant eye as well as World Eye, and rai seeing or seen. The Pharaoh´s royal phallus was visible because he had cut off his prepuce (from peri-puti). His idea was probably to remove his muzzle cover so that he could project the rays supposedly emerging from his glans at the female and pull the ladies in his harem whenever he felt like it, instead of having to wait for the mood to arise and his piece be readied as a result of any feminine rays around, withdrawing his muzzle cover for him. The −raoh is Lithic −rai-auai, raying everywhere and always, a dialectical verge befitting a supreme being, and a propensity only available if the essential modification of the commoners´ configuration of the genitalia has been effected. Rameses, Ra impregnated the life, Ra´s son ought not to be kept waiting. Who planted the seed in the case of Moshe, the biblical Moses, is not made clear in the record. Probably it was Iau or Jaweh. Joseph, Iau.seph, with a sai pahei, a visible pahei, was certainly circumcised. By his day it was apparently a badge of office at

Pharaoh´s court, like an order of nobility at court today, or anyway a cross between that and the Japanese Yakusa's pinky (severed top joint of one finger as badge of membership). Anyway the British Museum has a splendid statue of a pharoah proudly showing off his circumcised and protruding penis. It is hard to think of his reasoning in any other way than as described. We do not know what relationship there was between him and Aba-Ra-ham the biblical author of the foreskin trick, but now that it is known that the Pharoahs were Semites speaking a Semitic language, if much intermixed with the Hamitic tongues of their black subjects (as were their genes), it is not so far fetched to have their Jewish cousins copying the pharaohs. But Aba is father and hai is rejoicing, so the biblical Abraham appears to have been in with Father Ra, just as somewhat later Johannes was Iau-ha-nai: Iauai (Jehovah the dialectical god now)-pleasure-showing, or shows pleasure – at the birth.

The phoenix (8) started out as the palm tree. Paha-u-ai-nai-kai-s, a penis-one-that is-erect-shaped, clearly refers to the tall smooth trunk, without branches like most trees until you get towards the top. The Latin Pine tree has the same habit. Pliny described the vertical plume of volcanic ash put up by Vesuvius before the gases reached him and killed him, from memory when learning Latin 65 years ago "in longo trunco non aliquem quam pino". At the time I could not see why he could not just have said it was like a pine trunk rather than beating about the bush with his non aliquem quam. But I never had a Lithic thought in my head then. At the top of the palm a tuft of leaves sprouts out, the ejaculate appropriate to a phoenix. The adjectival mind saw the same patterns widely displayed in different circumstances. The leaves were the vegetative ejaculation where the animal one took a different more dynamic form just as you might expect. The leaves when they die hang down in a dead brown mass, where the birds nest. Planted close together and fired they flare up and burn off leaving the trees otherwise unharmed. The birds nests however are destroyed, including any young in the nests. The parent phoenix birds laid another clutch.

The Phoenix was probably any of the game birds with chicks that peep in pairs, never singly. They are thus pipi or pu, and the pan pipes are named after them and so, with a fine gull, are pipes of all sorts, even a dumb drain pipe or the smoker´s receptacle, but particularly the boy piece. The Latin for boy is puer, a piper, his voice unbroken. The Malay for such a one´s penis is a sparrow, puzzling until you know the Malay for a sparrow is pipit or cheeper. The phoenix myth is metaphor of course. Its death is the little death of orgasm, and it recovers and comes to life again to repeat the cycle over and over again. The orgasm is likened to a conflagration, a spark and then a small flame which bursts into a blaze. The patterns were seen as similar. We were easily satisfied when we wanted to be. Nobody thought sexual congress involved the actual burning of anything. It was poetry of a sort.

Phoenicians (8), those intrepid Semitic seafarers, of whom the Carthaginians were the last, were remarked as Phau-ai-nai-koi, because they were circumcised: all the phalluses-that which-exposed-folk. Carthaginians were Punic, pu-nai-kai, Phalluses-exposed-made. The Pount who appear peripherally as a Semitic tribe were central Semites, also one must suppose circumcised, from Pau-nai-tai, with their phalluses-exposed-cut. The Finns from Finland seem to destroy this gambit however. They live far too far North however to be exposing their genitalia and they are not circumcised, anyway not as a rule. Tacitus had them as Fenni and Ptolemy as Phinnoi. We must fall back on a reluctance to drop their trousers to relieve themselves, because of the cold, instead fitting themselves out with flapped codpieces which struck Greeks and Romans alike as in more flowing garb as highlighting their genitalia so they called them exhibitionists when their instinct was in fact the reverse.

A fin is a pai-nai, a protruding piece on the back of a fish, which is from the Latin piscis, which is from pais-kais, from pai-sai-kai-sai, foot-action-body-action: it gets along pretty well by just wiggling its body without any feet. Its fins are related to pins and Latin penna, a wing, an extended surface, made of feathers, which in turn matches quite well the Greek for wing, petera a surface terai, drawn along just as the boys at one time believed themselves drawn out and up by the ta rays the girls emitted. The ta was early on the vagina, a slit or cut emphasising the binary symmetry of the body, seen as the birth canal (rather than the oo-a-kai-na, the orifice-that-when stimulated-gapes/orgasms). It had the propensity to call up the males in aid of parturition from the very day their role was discovered. The conventional derivation of vagina and vanilla are from the Latin meaning a sheath or a pod. The vanilla is a sheathed or podded seed like the pea. The vanilla can be a container-that is-protruding-lengthwise, the seeds in a line, the vagina a sheath too. The Greek wing was called up by nature and acted as a sky hook. The conventional etymology identifying the vagina as a sheath has it back to front. The sword sheath was a vagina. Etymologists may not care for it but the simile works equally well both ways. It is not marked for direction.

We get to finality (15) in quite a roundabout way, starting out with finis a land boundary, first of all a post stuck in the ground to mark the corners. It was a pai or phai which nai or stuck up, just as a post is a pa-u-stai, a piece-what-stands up. Eric Partridge draws attention to its closeness to the Latin figere (11) to push or thrust in (to the ground in the case of a post) and so to fix. Finis transferred its meaning from the post to the boundary or limit it marked out, so far and no further., and so a terminus or ending. That way a boundary post achieved finality, courtesy of Tarzan's penis. That is language for you.

A fine is just an imposed payment, but one to achieve final settlement of a due. You pay and that is quits. A fine day is laughably derived conventionally from the same semantics, since a settlement may be regarded as satisfactory like a fine day. Pahai was always pleasurable as is a fine day. Pahai-nai, originally representing an orgasm, gets watered down over the aeons inter alia to merely any pleasurable sensation. Fine is just about the same as nice, like nai-sai, feeling warm, at ease, from heat-presented. A fine day, incidentally, is probably a warm one. Finance, on the other hand, is back to the payments in final settlement, or indeed about the final settlements or sets of accounts they produce in turn. There is nothing about them which is nice like feeling warm. Here is true polysemy.

In Egypt Nefertiti has left us a fine statuette of a beautiful princess. Nefer (13) meant pretty. Titi meant just that. So she was Princess Pretty Tits. Where I write this is under the lea of Mount Teide, and the Carthaginian invaders, speaking a provincial Egyptian patois, christened it Mount Titty. The volcano, the highest mountain in Spanish territory, has a conical fumerole on its lip. In Lithic nefer is nai-pahei-rai, present-the penis-rises. Pretty is not so far away, pai-rai-tai, the pai-rayed-by the vagina, the same predicament entirely. That is not to say Nefertiti in her day was identified in quite such fundamental terms. She likely saw herself as of pleasant appearance, naiferai. The ending –ti was used as the feminine ending. The preceding -ti may well by then have become tacked onto the nefer and neferti meant just naturally become of pleasant appearance, even -ferai by then just easy on the eye. Tai meant birth from the birth canal and the diminutive ti meant many small orifices such as are found in the teats. Who would like today to pick the meanings which lie behind our English teats? Eric Partridge cites the Greek tit-the, for a nipple, and provides a suppositional *dhei to suck. Any *dhei would more likely come as a back formation from the nipple: if you are sucking you are nippling. Otherwise there is no backing for dhei for sucking. It is just one of the totally random and meaningless roots on which established etymology is based, dismissing the titi as if irrelevant as well as randomly selected.

The English fair (13) appears to be allied to the Egyptian nefer. Its earliest form in English was faiger, which unmistakeably unravels as Lithic pahai-karai, making the penis aroused, penis kindling. The somewhat earlier Gothic was fagrs, with much the same Lithic constituency. Eric Partridge throws in Sanskrit pajras for good measure, which he has found, but meaning in good condition, fit and strong, which looks more like from pa-sh-rai, skin shining, a glossy coat indicating an animal in good condition, rather than good looks amongst the girls. The Latin from which we get our pulchritude uses different phonemes but can quite easily be analysed from the Latin pulcher, beautiful, and the Lithic Pul-kara, as a phallus kindler much like nefer. Psychosemantics seem to rule.

The Arabic fakir (3) meaning poor is allied to the fakir who is a religious mendicant and may still sometimes be seen wandering the streets in India with no clothes on. Both the religious naturist and the abjectly poor with no money find themselves in the same position unclothed, with their genitals rendered visible, pahei-kerai, much as for the Australian aborigine gara is colour, what the (light) rays make. In 1902 in Durban my father reported the Zulu rickshaw pullers going naked. They fought earlier the same way. The Arabic for unbeliever, kafir, was apparently one not ashamed to gaphirai, go naked, pahei visible. In Persian it becomes gabr, going with barai, the flesh visible, and in Turkish giaur, going au-rai, the whole lot visible. Unbelievers across all these languages were simply regarded as bare bottomed savages – or their like: reasoned disbelief was inconceivable. From that came the fkr root for disbelief.

Friable (3) is such that it can be broken up into a grain by rubbing with the hands. It is from the Latin friare to rub. Pahei rai is rousing the pahei. It can in fact be done by rubbing it. So rubbing is rudely defined as penis rousing and applied even to polishing up the handles of the big front door. That is language for you. A finger, a phaien.-kara, can be derived equally vulgarly. It has many other uses of course. But it is sexual metaphor which rules, look where we may. Mostly we have looked away.

Fat (3) is clearly a slovening of pahei. Why pai, originally the diminutive of bai, the flesh, and therefore skin or a diminutive piece of flesh, should come to mean to swell out and fatten is not obvious. But then the penis, one particular piece, is a classic as a diminutive shoot and also when it comes to swelling out and becoming fat. If there is any alternative derivation for this gull I have been unable to find it. That makes the shift from pa to fa- more understandable. A penguin is conventionally derived from the Welsh pen-guin, white headed. But a penguin is not white headed and there is no reason to imagine Welshmen to have ever entertained this misconception, nor to have got to the bird first. It is folk etymology invented on behalf of the Welsh. Latin for fat bodied is pinguis. It seems obvious the penguin is properly a pinguin. A fatter waddler in the avian world is impossible to find. If ever there were a bird fit to be described as penis bodied, plumped up in phallic distension all the time, it must surely be the penguin. The French petite, pai-titi, just the teat, and perhaps the auriole surrounding it, pai, fattened, is another misunderstood Lithic link. Anything else little enlarged is petty by derivation. Partridge adds tone to these derivations by citing Sanskrit payate it swells or fattens. But he lists neither the penguin nor the titi. He does however include the Greek pion for the adjective fat and piar and pimele for the nouns, the former probably just the fat in situ and the latter the mailai or edible liquid after it has been fried. Fry, phrai, or phai rai (3), is therefore from the same source, phai, fat, which has been or is rai or roasted in the liquid fat which runs out. Roast is rau, altogether rayed, sai in the flame, and the tai is just become. Nowadays the literal technique is confined to chestnuts at Christmas or potatoes in boy scout camp fires, along with the twist, dough wound round a stick and offered to the flames to roast as a form of unleavened bread, thoroughly smoked and almost inedible even for a boy scout, but marginally less indigestible than eating the paste raw when it swells up inside you.

Frisky and fresh are doublets, although a frisky horse is not pukkah while a fresh one is. The actions (from the sibilants) are determined by the phrai, an erect penis. Fierce, freh for greedy, fuerte (Spanish for strong) and friend can be lumped in here. All these terms rely upon the male erection as explanation for their tensions. It is absurd, but that is language for you. Greedy does the same, it is what being gerai or made roused does, the effect on the lower abdomen later transferred to feeding. The linguistic metaphor here plumps for the sexual connection even when it is obvious the eating frenzy has nothing directly to do with it – unless of course you prefer to posit a specific heroic eating ray to account for the greed like the bravery ray with which the brave, berani in Hindi, become berau, like the heros in Greece. But were the Greek heros not hei too, their bravery from their erection, perhaps with only the brave deserving the fair. A bahadur is also a brave man in Hindi. Behai-durai, like the Malay durian, a fruit with a hard skin and prickles all over it from the Malay duri a thorn, just differently spelt in English. Both the bahadur and the durian appear to share the same hard on. Durability in general must be a gull from the hardness because the original erection is ephemeral.

A flagon, from which is derived a flask is a huge jug made of hide. It is related to ply which is to fold a skin (Latin pellis, any [flexible] surface, originally the skin of an animal surrounding the flesh) or any other pai. With its exaggerated spout for pouring it had fancifully the form or shape of the phallus, phalla-ka-un, an earlier form being flakon, related to the old French flascon, probably originally palais-ka´n, one made of lapped skin, which the French spotted could be seen as a phallic shape.

Franco (3), now free, was a spear originally, a prong kau, that is a sharpened one like the flaked flint. Any prong it seems was copying the rampant penis, pa-hai-rau, rayed, raised and roused by the feminine raying from the girls. Femina (3) is from pahei-mai-na, the penis-impregnating-presenting, the fair sex labelled the agressor and initiator of every sexual encounter since na meant drawn out and offering a rounded vagina equally. These spearmen were the Franks, and the army spear carriers were the only freemen of the day which puts a new gloss on freedom's roots. They were probably lancers fighting on horseback, the cavalry of the day, already the nobility able to afford two horses and a stable boy apiece and free to offer their allegiance to the military commander of their choice, not just fighting for their feudal masters. A free man was a mercenary.

A brother or Latin frater was brau- or phrau -terai or born (20). Phrau has the dual vowel, indicating the same pahei in both cases. Brother is thus a doublet with boy, from the closely akin bwoid for penis in Celtic tongues. The Celtic bau-dai is a bunged vagina in Lithic, which indicates the strangler on it making it unfit for serving as a birth canal. A buoy is just the same bung in general use as a float. There is an alternative reading for brother, Sanskrit bhratr, Avestan brater, Tokharian A procar, Tokharian B procer with derivative old French fradre whence fredre and frere, Englished friar. Joel Chandler put Brer on the map, American slave slang for brother. Lithic barau-therai can be fleshed out both-womb raised or born, both raised in the same womb. Either the same father or the same mother marked you out as brothers, in one case fraternal in the other brothers. In Stone Age terms the brothers will have preceded recognition of fatherhood.

Fraud (3) is from the Latin fraus. The pahei is clearly rau, a cheeky chappie, but there is more, fraus is closely related to frustra, one of Eric Partridge´s o.o.o. words (of obscure origin, ie he does not know what). Frustra is in Lithic pahei-ish-tai-rau. The penis is ishterai, roused by the warmth of the hearth merely and not a genuine vaginal ray at all, that is when there are no girls around or worse when they don´t want to know you. Frustrare in Latin is to drag things out, to render an action vain, to circumvent or deceive a person. The arousal is in vain and under false pretences, as these days from a hot bath.

The frog (10) goes with an ejaculatory leap. Leapfrog, the children´s game, picks up the same psychosemantic content unawares. In Latin the frog on the other hand is rana. It comes via the Greek from the Egyptian and ra is eye and na is pushed forward and presented, the action originally of the rampant penis when rayed, the "Na!" originally it seems perceived as the sound of the expulsion of breath at orgasm after holding it as the tension builds up. Rana is rampant eyes, they are on the top of his head so he can, like the crocodile, a more formidable water borne predator, lie doggo with only his eyes above water ready to snap up any insects dancing over the water surface, or tackle cattle in the case of the crocodile. In passing the crocodile from the Greek kroko-dilos (or –deilos) is skull bodied or hardened bodied (kroko)–and born or become by nature (dai)-lau or run down, like the instinct of water to do the same. He lurks in the water as the water itself lurks in the lows, just rana only, like the frog waiting for his prey. In Celtic the frog started out a puit, but they obviously did not know the difference between a frog and a toad since it is the toad whose body becomes puffed out when challenged. It may impress a smaller passing toad but hardly anybody else. As children we used to prod them to see them do it. The English pout with the mouth is a straight copy of the pau-tai: the lips appear to copy the plumping to make the pu sound. The original derivation will have been left behind long ago (or anyway passed down below into the subconscious, but tagged to the Lithic language prompts to resurrect it generation by generation). It can still be read from the linguistic record nevertheless. It is as if the sexual generation of species has preserved a virtually perpetual linguistic stasis where the semantics are concerned – quite outside the Darwinian curriculum, half way between life and entropy.

There is ample scope for continuing through the dictionary picking up and deriving all the words in f- and ph- as well as all those with either phoneme within them. But it would lose readers one by one. We have so far covered the meanings from phi which include orgasm, pleasure, ejaculate, beget, make and present. The tree for fa has also fit, fetch, fruit, ferrites, flow, front, and feelings. The psychosemantic tree is confined to one page but could be made to cover several. Some meanings are left for readers to turn over for themselves. The book is too long already.

A fit (3) is one thing going inside another, a square peg in a square hole, but originally a pahei or phi in a tai or round one. It came eventually to be inter alia a canto of a poem, a piece from inside a whole work. In German a fitze is a skein, a single strand of a number twisted together. The paroxysm of the epilectic fit had the same character as the orgasm (9) when the phai is tai. The necktie involves a dialectical synthesis joining two sides of the collar together which before were parted, apart. Old English fitt, strife or conflict resulted similarly in a dialectical conjunction along with the paroxysm leading to a fight. To be fit for a fight you had to be matched, suited, ready, in this case strong and vigorous. To keep fit certainly seems overly ambitious, even inhibiting action. A fitter is fitting others together. Fitz for progeny seems to follow along. Was a follower originally a stalker, perhaps an unsuited male in old English fylgan, following, from the old High German fola gan, phaulai-kain, his phallus kindled, following a family, a group linked by phai-mai, the mai or impregnation of a single phai, the pater familias, in the hope of gaining access to a marriageable maid? The fola gan became ful gangan in English, confusing gehen, ganging along with a cockney h, with geheien with a fully semantic hei. From all the above we may perhaps conclude the fit Charles Darwin had in mind when pondering the role of the fittest was the later sense of suitability and readiness for the struggle of existence; and it was Mendel with his generations of peas who harked the biologists back, no doubt subconsciously, to the original fit.

To fetch or bring forward is from old English fecan (3), a clear enough sexual metaphor. A ferry brings you across a river. Fs and Ps are virtually interchangeable. F, if it does not say puff, says sex. P says one piece or another. It may be the one which says hurrah! Or just a flat surface like the skin which encloses the flesh. A plate is clearly flat by nature. Pro, pointing forwards, clearly a gull from the penis when rau, informs a prow as well as a Malay perau, a boat with a rampant prow, while froward and forward go in the same direction for the same reason. Fore! For the golfer is look out in front, not down at his own front. We get to front with the final t, here a side, while side explains the thinking further, sa-i-dai, one of the twins, a single side of a slit or divide, with divide a parting into two.

The words for fruit around the world suggest that for primitives animal genitalia are regarded as the equivalent of the fruit carried by the vegetable kingdom. Animal and vegetable were not so radically differentiated to start with. The adjectival mind saw characters as universals. It must be borne in mind it was the male genitalia which received attention, since the sexual organs in the male are worn outside the body and are active for all to see and admire. The females of the species offered no more than a receptacle and a passage for viewing. All the rest was secreted within the body, and was largely overlooked at first. Early speakers will have been largely if not entirely ignorant of any of the inner workings of the fair sex. Fruit (12), Lithic ph-rau-i-tai, apparently comes from the rayed (and grown, swollen) genitalia which have naturally developed or become (tai). The fruit swell from natural development (tai) while the genitals are kindled (kai) by sexual rays emitted by the genitalia of the opposite sex. The fruit are not kindled, there is no bodily heat involved in their development, nor is the process to be likened to a spark followed by a flickering (10) flame (10) and then a sudden final blazing up. Amazingly fruit were regarded as male. This dialectical comparison of the animal and vegetable fruiting is probably responsible for the otherwise puzzling use of frigidus (Latin) for cold, when the animal sexual arousal can hardly have struck our forebears as frigid in any of its senses. This frigi (12) was dau, not kau, it was the vegetal fruiting and its principal distincta were its leisurely procedure and its absence of either the furor or the hot temper of the animal orgasm. By contrast heat, Latin calor, was seen as exemplified by kau-lau-a, the sexually kindled variety of enlargement of the organ per contra. Other terms support this quite difficult analysis. We talk of animals coming into heat. Frigidity is coldness but also the total absence of what is already identified as coming into heat. There is thus a link between sexuality and temperature independently established and one may suspect prompted and arising from a common source in the subconscious mind.

Fruit in Hindustani is phal, close to phallus. The phallus was regarded as the male fruiting body, fully alive and therefore capable of fruiting repeatedly under active control, not rooted in the seasons like the fruiting of the vegetable kingdom. There are fruit clearly named after the genitalia. One is the fig a leaf of which Adam used to cover his genitalia when God disapproved of his going naked, na-kai-tai, showing kaity, his bodily orifices. Fig in Lithic elements is pa-hei-kai, pahei-shaped. The fruit is much the same shape as a testicle in the human scrotum. It is moreover a hermaphrodite fruit since when fully ripe it splits open revealing inner surfaces reminiscent of the tumescent vulva, both in shape and colouration. It is the testicles of course which phai kai, kindle the phallus, as stated in the Lithic for the fig. If you cut them off potency is lost, fattening occurs, and as well there is a significant reduction in the male aggressive instincts. For these reasons bullocks were castrated as soon as they were tamed and bred. Human castrates were cut also for harem servants; while other boys had the whole of their male external genitalia removed in order to simulate feminine physiology, a procedure not without life threatening risks of infection which is still killing boys in an unregenerate India today.

The Vatican even cut boys at one time just to keep them singing treble, with a fine disregard for their human rights which include the pursuit of happiness, wickedly telling them they would go to heaven more easily if they shed their testicles. It is true the promptings of the testicles can lead to mischiefs, and without them you probably have a better chance of a clear run in, but it must be moot if you acquire virtue for resisting temptations you never experienced. Eunuchs can sometimes achieve erections but they can never breed. Some may even have been in demand in the larger harems for their safe sexual services when the turn for the pater familias came round comparatively infrequently. There is the final murderous absurdity of Wahabi suicide bombers sneakily worshiping the black goddess Kali instead of Islam, expecting to enjoy Kali's seven virgins in heaven for killing down below. One can only cogitate their disappointment on catching site of these compliant ladies at the pearly gates when looking down they discover that in the after life there are no genitalia: they were meant to be used up entirely in the here and now instead of killing, and they seriously messed up this divine provision. Lithic promptings from the subconscious appear to have somehow not got through to them in any timely way, so that it is likely that there was some simple physical inadequacy responsible for their misprision of their sexual role on earth. Terrorism is at root a sexual perversion and not a call to martyrdom at all. There is a dialectical antithetical misprision in it too, killing instead of giving life.

To return to Adam's fig leaf, it appears it was testicles which were the source of Adam's offence, calling for a leaf, which has liberal foliation allowing three separate fronds to be draped over the offending equipment; and since in the highlands of Eden there are aboriginal tribes who cover their phalluses but leave their testicles exposed, wearing penis sheaths which extend above the navel, this may quite possibly have been the Adamites' style of adornment too, even while Adam was thinking up names for all the animals as his tribe gave birth to language. In this way the male fantasy of his own virility receives a public and unhidden boost. How much of the sheath is occupied by the phallus within is left to the imagination of the bystander. Borneo is the land of boars, and the boar, unlike any other animal, wears his testicles high up on his rump and with his tail held high they are prominently visible from behind, as any farmer's boy will tell you. Not only that but in Borneo the pig is treated almost as human. Piglets are suckled by human mothers and on ceremonial occasions they are eaten as pork. Human flesh, occasionally also taken in old days at least, is known as long pork, long because we carry our legs in extension of our bodies instead of one limb pointing down at each of the four corners. It is our badge of humanity after all, as any anthropologist worth his salt can tell you. An-thro-pos, the Greek for man(kind), which he studies, is in Lithic elements A´n-tirau-pous, that one-[with] drawn out-limbs, old long legs. The tirai or ti rays were originally supposedly the rays emitted by the vagina which brought the boys out and into play. Who wrote the nursery rhyme Georgie Porgy pudding and pie? Greek aner (the male) from the Lithic an-nai-rai, the one who rays (in turn) once he is nai, that is protruding and presenting with his muzzle cover withdrawn, bringing the female to fruition. But for the species of both persuasions it is just the legs that are drawn out, although it could be argued that homo faber´s arms are also brought into play.

There is an alternative reading of anthropous where the pous is really pus, the genitals, both of them (boys´and girls´together) and not just the limbs (pous like Greek bous for ox, with the big strong haunches). It is peculiar to humanity that both sexes enjoy copulation and actively seek it. The Latin offers some support for this reading because humani, humans are hei-u-mai-nai, enjoying (hei)-both (u)-the impregnation (mai)-orgasm (nai). It certainly seems to make better sense than other suggestions like earthlings, from humus, soil, in spite of the fact human in English is usually derived from homo in Latin. Homo readily enough translates into the Lithic phonemic elements hau-mau, enjoying both-impregnation both. Humus, which Eric Partridge follows through off at a tangent in the absence of any Lithic phonemic meanings, has a cockney h quite unlike homo. There is no heightened emotion in the earth. Humus reads in Lithic a(h)u-mau, that all-milled, mashed or ground up, referring to the granular structure of the soil. Ma is fully treated in chapter 10. Similarly soil is sau-i-lai, all its action is to slip down, it has picked up some of liquid´s instinct as the size of its particles approach the infinitessimals of liquid. You need a dry sample to show it is the instinct of the soil and not liquid´s instinct coming from the wet, when you can get serious watery characters breaking out in quick sands and bog (travelling ground). Sand in turn is drifting dunes paradigmatically, saen-dai, it moving does, as the wind whips it over the crest of the dune and down the far side. Soil per contra only slips if you stack it, and in bogs where on a slope they can slip.

The ti rays drawing out our legs are the very same ones in language that it was supposed drew out our manhood in the Stone Age, the ta rays from the girls´ vaginas, tai ta-ing, or better tarai, ta-raying, which all unawares we pray in aid every time we use a tray or open a drawer, and nature, from the Latin natura and the Egyptian Naturai (sometimes written neter), uses whenever the tura na or present themselves, as when the wind blows or any other natural force is seen at work. The boar in Lithic elements is Bau-arai, the dual bulbs or bulgy bits visible. The penis sheath may well have been adopted in simulation of the pig´s anatomy, and the testicles left out as witness to man´s pigginess. The Malay, which is closely related to the lingos of Borneo, with common words alike, for instance fish in Malay is ikan and across Borneo it is ika, a single body (no arms or legs), has buah for fruit, just like the dual fruits the boar wears behind. In all the circumstances we might have expected the terms for fruit and testicle to be linked, and this appears to have been the case. A bull, in a different language family altogether, perhaps comes from this same use of bu, in his case linked. Unusually his testicles are rolled up together in a single sausage, with a unified outline just like the bullrush, as any farmers boy can tell you, the bull hanging down the rush raised up. But the animal and vegetable kingdoms were always in dialectical opposition, and the genitalia always a source of fascination it seems, and especially so in the Stone Age when even the grandfathers were still just boys. If you want to access the Stone Age mind you should expect to meet up with boy talk once again. A natural vulgarity and a fascinated engagement with the emerging genitalia ensued.

There is also the avocado which in Spanish is pronounced abocado, and is commonly believed to be named after the testicles because of its shape. It is a fair size for a testicle but that is part of the jape. Some outsize ones rival the papaya or pawpaw even, which was spotted as matching a size D cup. The Lithic phonemes seem supportive: a-bu-kai-do, those dual bulbs that do the kindling. Unfortunately, as Eric Partridge points out bocado in Spanish means a bon bouche or delicacy and the avocado which would be pronounced abocado in Spanish may have seen some reshaping as a result. The fruit is actually known as aguacate in Spanish, pronounced ahuacate, from the Aztec language Nahuatl, where it is ahuacatl. The –tl is little more than a substantive ending in Nahuatl, which translates to nauaho in California. It must be remembered here that these forms are traditional renderings from some time ago. The question seems to be whether ahuaca deserves to be regarded as testicle in Nahuatl. We can readily enough accept –ka as meaning create or make because their supreme deity is Wakan Tanka, which neatly enough translates in Lithic terms as Terror-making-World-maker, The Awesome Creator. A-hu-a-ka reads quite well as that-hei in the completive (u) case-that-makes, that is that makes the ecstacy or orgasm. You might think it is the phallus which sends the ecstatic signals to the brain, and indeed there can hardly be any doubt our primitive forebears started out under that presumption. It was only when they tried cutting off the testicles they found out they made all the difference. The testicles´ role was then at first a seven day wonder and worthy of remark. You might also think enlisting of the vowel u both as the completive sense of the hei-ing and then again as the dual form to register the two hyers is stretching Lithic meanings further than is justified, but this is by no means the case. Such double usage was for the Lithic mind confirmation of the soundness of the construction of the meaning string. We are not yet allowing them to be words in the full sense of codified strings with overall meanings semi-randomly picked. All the same they were not stupid. The enlargement of the testicles at puberty which accompanies the awakening of the procreative instinct must surely have been noticed long before anyone knew how to say what they could see. The mystery will have received powerful confirmation when they got round to the castration of live animals. The more ideational links to their line of reasoning that could be spotted, the more likely it was to their minds that their thinking was veridical; and there was no professor of grammar around to forbid them doubling back on their tracks when they saw an opportunity. Human castration will have been for a purpose, as with the Vatican: which means after the need for the testicles for breeding was known if not their actual role as pollenators.

Ferrites are made of ferrous (iron) metals. Metals, mai-ta-lai, are born as lyes from the earth, earths become liquid, just as stones are ish-tau´n, fire born ones, from volcanos. But iron is the rayed one. Ferrum, iron, phai rau´m (3) is the source of magnetism, an attractive force just as the phallic ray supposedly attracts the female. A magnet is from he magnesia lithos, the Magnesian stone in Greek. Magnesia is a district of Thessaly, the source of the iron ore. Magnesia as a local name might mean anything. Is it named for its most notable product the ore from which iron is obtained by heating? Ma-genai-sai-a can be read as earth-indicating-direction, probably the centre of mass of the local ore bed rather than north, the centre of mass of the whole globe or else the axis of rotation of the electrically charged magma at the earth's core. Readers of Velikovsky will be aware of the possibility of the orientation of this liquid's revolutions being distorted by resonant visiting astronomical bodies electrically charged. Indeed the meaning of direction for sai comes from its upwards directional semantic content from the flame which determinedly springs upwards – see chapter 14 – and it may have been the vertical tip of a suspended metal needle, now known as dip, which the ancients first discovered. It is in any case a classic example of the way the meanings become generalised as they are abstracted as metaphor: the more abstracted the more general. In this case the upwards direction becomes just direction, just as a lye, a bitter taste becomes just taste as well as the taster the tongue or langue and then the language which comes from its wagging.

To feel (3) is to have an experience phai-like, like with the phai, if less intensive. It is natural enough to perceive the pahei as the source and centre of sensation where its most intense and pleasant avatar is to be met with, and then to abstract and generalise that meaning. Lymph (14) started out as water, the lai-em-phai, liquid of the phai; but also that other discharge, aahei, and so any mucosal body fluid, from the spine or brain for instance, supposed by primitive butchers to be all of the same kind as sperm. In India you still find some of the same confusion today, much like rabbi Ouaknin´s nutritional and respiratory energy to be found in the spinal fluid, and related to the phallus, and all resumed in the phoneme fa. Religious meditation in the Stone Age can be seen to hark back to Lithic language roots, interpreting the subconscious phonemic messaging as intimations from the gods. Did religion start out as grammar? If so Noam Chomsky is going home.

Of course in retrospect it can be seen you need to have as full a knowledge as possible of Lithic protocols, even at the risk of it becoming slightly obsessive, to follow through the semantic twists and turns we are heir to. It is a language of the mind, only accessible at one remove from the page, and it is in the subconscious mind it lives. You have to learn to let your subconscious sensibility lead, picking up the sense of sounds in a manner ultimately quite poetic. You join the fuzzy-wuzz-ies without bothering about their hair. That is no bar to rejoining the logic of the classroom as necessary and at any time whenever the hat drops. Much of the fun is to be aware of the two worlds and to flip six hundred millennia when you feel like it. It is the only way I know to get Chancellor Gordon Brown, that Treasury poodle, out of your hair The case for Lithic can probably rest there.

CHAPTER 8

THE PHONEME HA

When addressing the aspirate there are really six different sorts of h, some of them just huffing and puffing others seriously using the glottis. First there are the aspirated consonants like bh and dh best dealt with under their parent consonants. Then secondly there are the gutturals kh and gh, in English sometimes spelt ch as in loch, the aspirated consonants which so frequently lapse into plain aspirates that they need treatment in this chapter as well as with ka and ga. These are really cuckoos in this nest, but they are dealt with here because they often get eroded and turned into plain h, and it is with these we are now concerned. Then thirdly there is the cockney h, half way to a glottal stop, separating two vowels otherwise adjacent and liable to elide. Perhaps this was at one time the commonest usage. In Ancient Egyptian it was probably pronounced ahi or ahei and where it appeared in front of an a it could make instead iha, even slurring straight away either to ha or to ia. There is a trace of this usage in our pronunciation aitch from ahi, akhi, aikh and aich. Fourthly there is the sudden gasp with involuntary expulsion of breath. The glottis is locked and then suddenly a scream emerges. I liken this to the last cry of a boy in the age of the Pleistocene caught in the back of his cave by a sabre-toothed tiger without his burning brand. Fifthly there is the jocular expulsion of breath expressing jollity or sudden humour as in Ha! Ha! Surprisingly enough, a sabre tooth and a joke both evoke a Ha! The jocular ones are lots of little ones. The sabre-tooth ones are single and long, the gasp leading straight into a scream, sometimes terminal like the parachutist´s farewell when his parachute had not opened – in the old days before he had any reserve chute and he knew he was going in.

But then a long gasp of the happy Ha turns up as another meaning. The semantic pattern as meanings expanded and in the process became more generalized is important. Once established as an involuntary gasp, like when a careless boy, or else a girl, hunkered around the hearth when language was beginning, picked up a white hot stone mistaking it for an ember to toss back into the fire and let out an involuntary "Haa!" recording the error as he or she shook it off, the meaning will have been generalized gradually from "Hot!" to take in any sudden emotional input (or output) like "Ha! Ha!" denoting hilarity, or a "Haaa!" at orgasm translating to the happy aspirate, which comes to occupy an important key to human understanding of Lithic language. It was apparently the one that pulled them in the Stone Age. It is a constituent of the Greek phi and has already appeared in chapter 7 on the phoneme fa. The Ancient Egyptians represented tehei (their letter th) with a glyph of the mallard drake in hot pursuit of the duck, wings fluttering. The drake is single minded enough in his pursuit to sometimes drown the duck while mounting her, so intent is he on impregnation. The semantic content of this high is whoopee! or wow! from the expression of ecstasy at orgasm, when the breath held as the tension mounted was suddenly released at ejaculation. The millennia have not succeeded in eradicating this original quite blunt semantic identification for the hedonistic aspirate from the lexicon. It is still in there, somewhere in the subconscious mind, directing the shaping of language as it changes and is remoulded, from whimsy or simply from lack of conscious attention. These phonemic meanings, now no longer consciously relied upon are nevertheless picked up in the subconscious as every child has learned their language for the last 600,000 years. That may seem some way from the thrust of our English composite letter th today, as indeed also from pahei or ph now pronounced f. But it can be seen to be readily copied by every generation which rediscovers its four letter words. What is conclusive is the Ancient Egyptian usage of hei in the composite pahei, meaning the joy piece (akin to the joy stick pilots in the last century named the steering stick they waggled between their legs) with an uncompromising hieroglyph of the human penis, otherwise read as mai, the earther, planter or impregnator. The psychosemantic tree for ha is on page 224, starting with the aspirated consonants kh and gh (2) which have often been slovened to h. The columns are numbered (1) to (6). The examples which follow are in no way exhaustive which would involve printing most of the entries in Eric Partridge´s excellent etymological dictionary. The original Lithic derivation of every word in the lexicon it is not now possible to resurrect, because of the slovening over the aeons. The surprise is how many words in how many languages can still be derived from the original Stone Age semantic contents.

At the beginning of language the original natural meaning of the aspirate was no doubt a matter of considerable discussion, in so far as any discussion was possible. In those early days natural meanings, what you could reasonably conclude from the sound itself, as well as the occasions of its natural expression, must have been the touchstones for communicating. That must surely have been the way inarticulate folk thought: look for the 'natural' meaning from the occasion of its expression. If the shock of a burning hand evokes "Haa!" the natural meaning of the phoneme is 'hot!', just as the burning brand when extinguished in a puddle with an "ishsh!" makes it clear the 'natural' meaning of the sibilant is flame or fire.

The aspirated consonants which do not sloven into a plain aspirate h are covered under their own phonemes, bh in chapter 4 for ba for instance, dh in chapter 6 for da and ta. It is proposed here to deal with the cuckoos first, the echoic words which copy a sound heard. The simplest is hard, which is from khard.(2). Ka was taken to be the clink of stone on flint when flaking the flint to make tools. The Greek for skull is kara, the hard part of the head. Khara could be read in Lithic terms as baked, from made rayed. Clay responded to heating in that way to make earthenware: made rayed it became hard and you got a pot. Ceramic is from the Greek keramos, earthenware, which in turn is from the Lithic phonemes Kai-rai-ma-u(s), made-rayed-earth-one (Greek substantive marker), baked earth. Horn is next door, originally khorn, akin to the Latin cornu, which in Lithic phonemes is kau-rai-nau, the dual raised protruding bits (of the skull). Nau's several meanings include protruding, the original protrusion being, I am afraid, of the male organ when copulating, see chapter 11. The skull was kara (in Greek) because it was supposed it had hardened from the same causes as the baked clay pot. Pot is from caput in turn, the Latin for head, the skull cap, suitably sawn off, having stood in for the earthenware pot before the baking of clay was invented. Ka-pu-ti in Lithic is body-penis-teat. The cap is from the first bit, the pot from the second. A hot oven won't do, or the heat of the hearth, it has to be a kiln with a much higher temperature if you want to have a pot which is not porous, pa-u-rau, piece-un-rayed. The horn which toots is of course either an animal's horn or else at least a spin off shaped like it. The corn on the foot is a callus, hard like the horn, from the Lithic ai-a-rai, that which-is-rayed (heated and hardened). Field corn is hard too if you try to eat it as it is grown (just like sweet corn too). It is said to make an ear, which is a hard head like the skull, and the grain is at the head of the stalk – close to a horn or cornu, but not quite so uncompromisingly hard. That is why they got ground to a flour; and because they were ground they were grain. Our English heads are cuckoos too. The Latin caput and the Greek cephalos start with ka, in these two cases the hard structure of the body, the skeleton which forms and supports it, but used here simply for the body; followed by puti and phalos. These are both terms for the glans of the penis, like it or lump it. Both the Greek and the Latin say body-knob, much as we might describe the glans as the head of the penis. Magritte would have recognised the Lithic here. Our head is from heafod, which surprisingly has the same pedigree as caput. The transmogrification of the phonemes in caput from ka to heia and puti to phaudai is not a wit less sexually prompted, if anything more so, emphasising it is the engorged glans the head is likened to. Our chief and chef follow along.

A "hammer" (3) is really a downer as well as a striker-marrer or smasher, see chapter 10. Here (2), from khai-rai is place which-visible, the immediate environs. It is also iha-i-rai (3), it that-which-visible, a powerful confirmation of the

THE PSYCHOSEMANTIC TREE FOR HA

The Phonetic Tree

The Semantic Tree

Ha

Echoic (1)	Kh & Gh (2)	Cockney H (3)	Hot H (4)	HaHa (5)	Happy H (6)
Huff	Habit	Halcyon	Hack	HaHa	Hale
Inhale	Haggis	Halo	Hackle	Hilarity	Ham
Halitosis	Haggle	Hammer	Hades	Humour	Hammock
	Hair	Harangue	Hemorrhage		Hand
	Halt	He	Hag		Happy
	Hamper	Hear	Hallo		Haunch
	Hang	Hebe	Hand		Haw
	Hard	Hebrew	Harakiri		Heart
	Harrow	Hegira	Harem		Hearth
	Hat	Helios	Harm		Heaven
	Have	Hear	Hawk		Hedonism
	Hay	Helot	Harmony		Hello
	Head	Heron	Haste		Hemp
	Heap	History	Hate		Hen (2)
	Heave	Horizon	Havoc		Hermes
	Heckle	Horus	Haven		Heyday
	Hell	Hospital	Heath		Hi!
	Helm	Hour	Heed		Hie
	Hem	House	Hideous		High (2)
	Hen (1)	Huge	High (1)		Hip(py)
	Henna	Hydro	Heinous		Homo
	Hide	Hyoid	Hinder		Honour
	Hill	Hypodermic	Horror		Hooray
	Hit	Hysteria	Hot		Horny
	Hold		Howl		Hug
	Hole		Hump		Human
	Horn		Hurry		Hymn
	Hunger				

appropriateness of the attribution, as well as perhaps accounting for the elision of the k-. Hear (3), at the same time, is it that-which-is audible: since rai is one of the Egyptian rays which were everywhere about us, accounting for sensations and influences arriving from a distance, including both visual and auditory prompts, even in some cases for thinking rays wafted in from outside, or better registered by the brain, from the Lithic elements be-rai'n, be-rayed or the flesh rayed, in passing, since they probably predate any clear identification of our own individual identity or full sense of self. Partridge here relates hearing to akouein (2), the Greek for hearing, which gives us our acoustics. The trouble is there is no r in akouein, which is from aa (vacuous extension and so air as we say it)-kau-ein, air-strike-verbal marker (from ain, extensioning, and so going), a rather serious omission for the Lithic ray interpretation just proposed for to hear. But audibility actually results as we all now know from an air strike, a modulated puff, on the ear drum, which seems to be the Greek semantic idiom, so rather unusually we have to give the Greeks top marks above the Egyptians here.

A hammer is perhaps from kha-ma-arai (2). Kama, the Old Norse word originally just meant any old piece of rock, ka-ma or hard earth. But the Lithic Ka-ma also means strike-down. A hammer started out as a stone strike-downer, a smasher or smiter. All those hand axes we made for a million years and more (two million year old chipped stones) were actually mostly for macerating raw meat, which is why when cooking was discovered it was called kau-kau, the exemplary maceration and tenderizing had simply been achieved another way by heating instead of beating. Khamar was not so far from camera, a dark place, which was one which killed or suppressed (kama, made dead) the sun´s rays (ra), and so a vault or room (both originally windowless) and so a dark chamber including the one provided in photography to hold the light sensitive film, and so as well a comrade just sharing the same room. It comes as a surprise to a Northerner that a room, from rau-mai, should be derived from the suppression of the sun's rays since in Northern climes it is regarded as a warm shelter from the cold and wet rather than as a sun shade, but the language goes back a long way and was invented in a hotter climate. A maul was a heavy hammer, from the phonemes ma-u-lai, damaging-when-swung, which was swung in a loop (lai). See chapter 9. It was allied to Old Celtic maca to strike, particularly to strike ma-, that is heavily down. Norse kama and Celtic maka assemble the same phonemes but in reverse order. To me that suggests confirmation of the independent meanings of the phonemes which can be used in either order. Linguists call it metathesis, a putting after. Meta- was originally after in time, from m'-ai-ta, him-that which-become, and here as after in space.

Hide (the animal skin) (2), Latin cutis, is a long derivation from the Lithic ka-u-tai, struck in two and so cut out. The hide was the skin after it was cut from the animal,. Compare Old High German hut, Germanic root *hud, Indo European root probably *kut"(uncommonly like our cut) but pronounced nearer coot. It was used as a coverlet or to cover the body. To hide, the verb, came to mean to cover, and cover to cover from view and so to hide, with the substantive hide as a place to observe from unobserved. Compare Old Persian keuto, hide and even Latin cutis, skin, and Latin scutum a shield (made of hide) and Sanskrit skauti, he covers (all cribbed from Partridge). Then there is Greek keutham to conceal, and probably even Serbian kuca a house, and English house from Old English hus, the basic idea being a covering or shelter, which is sai, or warm with a hearth with a fire (ish) in it. A covering is of course a concealment. Partridge quotes Sanskrit "kukara" conceal, Lithic kau-kara, covered-make. Thuggi, (Hindi) (Lithic tha-kai in place of Kha-tai for hide) meaning concealment, was the practice of Kali worshipers (Kali was the goddess of concealment and deception, her followers ka-lai, acted-slyly) of joining caravans representing themselves as bona fide fellow travelers in order to strangle the others while they slept. A thousand years before Mohammed she offered a tariff of seven virgins in the hereafter for fifteen kaffirs (infidels or unbelievers) killed. Her religion has been cobbled onto Islam, the religion of Peace and Mercy by extremists over the years, with the offers of virgins much inflated. In Kali's day it was not widely appreciated spiritual beings have no genitalia. It was perhaps the ultimate deception even in Her day. The virgins are outmoded Kalian carrots for killing, and have nothing to do with The Prophet or genuine Islam. A hat (2) (Indo European root perhaps khat) was originally any old covering for the head, including a hood, from a khat and a khud, perhaps originally fur caps against the cold. A hut did the same job on a larger scale as a khat. In Arabic khat is a stimulant leaf of a bush, chewed as a mild drug. The Arabic khat has nothing to do with a hat or a house, however. It means the bush much as we refer to tobacco as the weed. The bush is from kha-tai, with a bifurcating trunk unlike a tree, much like the English twig, a forked stem, which Partridge relates to the Sanskrit dwikas, double: clearly from Lithic two-make or dual shape.

Hay was khai (2) originally, close to hacked, like the flint knapper's original ka, echoic from the clink of flint on flint as they struck, flaking flints, making flat flakes. A harrow was from ka-rau, make rows, just like a rake, from rai-kai, ray or row maker, which after all is just a hand held harrow. Hoe and hew are from an original kau (2), chopping actions both. The Latin incus, on-struck, from Latin cudo I strike (well, do a stroke) which Partridge quotes, is the anvil on which the striking takes place. I have likened Wayland's tactic, mauling the hot metal into shape to our linguistic habits where elision and elipsis have been universally adopted for smoother pronunciation regardless of the original form or meaning. To harry is another kh- derivative. The Old Frisian was here, and the Old Norse herr (pronounced hera or herer, the short e or schwa on the end) both meaning army, a strike force. But the Old Prussian was kara and the Indo European original root kar-, strike, which Partridge suggests was "ultimately identical with kar- strong", anticipating the Lithic semantic tree in chapter 5 for the phoneme Ka. Armies until quite recently, when they were usually too busy, or too improvident, to find the time to provide their own foodstuffs,, were inclined to live off the land, "harrying" the inhabitants, stealing their goods.

Perhaps we should have 'have' (2) next, akin to Latin habere to have. The Spanish is tenere to hold. To have and to hold (2) are similar in meaning. Holding is one form of having, which has a much wider spread of meanings. The Latin tenere is in chapter 11, another vulgarism. Habere, if from khabere, is certainly close to capere in Latin, to hold or take, capture, etc, the Lithic ka-pai-are, make-covered-verbal marker, that is put under your protection, just as you put yourself under the protection of your coverlet of skins at night, or even to seize. Partridge says of capere that "Walshe[1], voicing the opinion of every reputable scholar, says that the resemblance to Latin habere which extends to terminations, can only be fortuitous. But to postulate fortuitousness merely because Latin h normally becomes Germanic and Celtic g (as in Irish gailim, I take) is to go perhaps too far; there may have been either conservatism or persistence or recalcitrance". The Indo European root is apparently *kap-, to take. He is kicking over the traces, half way to Lithic.

The cockney h (3), separating two vowels which otherwise might elide, is a world-wide phenomenon by no means confined to Londoners. For openers I can not forbear to bring up once again the Ancient Egyptian usage, where the cockney h in Ptah turns out to be pronounced ahi and mean that-which, and so our. It is one of my minor triumphs of etymological investigation which still gives me a kick every time I rehearse it, because it breaks new ground in the accurate reading of the hieroglyphs as the language was actually spoken, instead of being content with a stunted transliteration filling in between the consonantal values with minimal vowelisations which is the best that the academic Egyptologists can manage. That way you get absurdities like Ptah Renpit as a title of God. We are here exposed in flagrante teaching the senators wisdom. Sorry guys! Also, lest it be thought vanity only, the string of meanings available in this one short sentence properly read is a fine example of the fine texture of language, so that the skeins of meanings are tightly intertwined with the phonemic structures. Starting with Sir Wallis Budge´s Ptah Renpit, which he glosses in his magisterial and still unrivalled Dictionary of 1925 "apparently a title of God from a late Coptic text", it can be read with the full Egyptian phoneticisation as Pata ahi arai en Pai Taun, loosely translated Father-our-who art-in-skin-of world (Heaven) which Christians will immediately recognise as canonical. The arai conveys activity, which is slightly off centre today. Pai is skin or roof and Taun is the universe or world. The academic recension of the Egyptian for Heaven is Pet, but the glyphs were not primarily just alphabetic. They were really syllabic. P was pronounced like the Greek pi, which copied the Egyptian. The semicircle, identified as a bun (sic!) by academia, the glyph for T, was really the flat earth with overarching Heaven and was pronounced Tau – the Taw or Tao – or Taun, the Cut in Two or top half, since the underworld was the other half, called by the academics the Duat, but the Egyptians actually called it Dua Taun, the Second World of the dead: the dead were reborn into it and lived there when they died out of number one. Death was like going through a doorway out of number one and into number two, just as Christian belief still copies. So much for the Duat. Tau also meant all the happenings, a temporal universe rather than our purely spatial one. These derivations are all derived more fully in chapter 6.

The Egyptian god Ptah, one of the oldest, nevertheless was not vouchsafed before his glyph the neter or pointed axe of divinity like all the other "gods", however minor. This neter was really a pennant blown out in the breeze, not a pointed axe at all (a pretty useless implement) and neter was really natura, na- presenting or showing and -tura the draw or pull, showing a pull or natural force, the same word we use for nature. The pointed axe of divinity was really a pennant blown out in the breeze, exhibiting a natural force, in this case the wind. It was the Greeks who made the Egyptian personifications of all the natural forces into godlings like their own mischief makers. It can now easily be spotted Ptah uniquely had no neter because he was really Pata-ahi (3), Our Fathers, the Egyptian ancestor god, and not a force of nature at all. Egyptologists will be interested in this because until now they have been unable to solve the problem of Ptah´s missing neter. Egypt is from hoiku-Ptah. Hoiku (3) in Egyptian is similar to ekoi in Greek, loosely translatable as where begotten, and so home. The Greek is in economics, ekoi-nomoi, home rules or household management. Egypt is supposed to be Land of Ptah. Actually it is home of our fathers or the fatherland. So I don´t think my identification of Pata Ahi as Our Father is all that far fetched after all, and the rest follows along without much difficulty.

The Copts were early Egyptian Christians. Knowledge of Egyptian (Coptic) was lost when the Wahabi (6) marauders, masquerading as Muslims, killed or castrated every Egyptian who failed to speak Arabic and was caught speaking Egyptian. Reconstituted for religious purposes with the aid of Greek (which is half Egyptian) Coptic is now a mix of Egyptian and Greek, and written in Greek letters. It is probably true both Christians and Jews had much greater connection with Egypt and owed much more of their thinking to Egyptian traditions than either religion now cares to remember. The Pharaohs (6) were pre-Jahweh (3) Semitic imperialists who brought the priceless gift of riverine irrigation technology with them to the African tribes, and then went native: the cross-cultural influence of their native African subjects, darkening Semitic skins as they came to share Hamitic (6) genes, led to one of the greatest leaps forward in civilization the world has ever known, perhaps even to be compared to the taming of fire in the first place and then the establishment of the first consensual civil society around the hearth. It was an essential precursor of all modern religions which recognise a God with a personal relationship with individuals here on earth. Previously religions just preached resignation to a harsh natural order, while pagan (country bumpkin) beliefs remained immersed in primitive magic. The personal God started out a harsh disciplinarian, although he was supposed to be Ever Loving (Amaun), but the interpretation of His mind has become more liberal over the millennia. Nowadays His liberality is such He is thought by Christians to welcome even those malpractices He was previously declared to condemn. But the point in this chapter is simply that ahi, the h of the hieroglyphs, can sometimes simply be separating a from i, or marking the final demise of one of them; since the further observation needs to be made that the first of the separated vowels may still in time be lost, leaving a somewhat redundant h as the only trace of the lost preceding vowel. We are dealing with thousands of years, remember.

He (3) is a case in point, originally ahi. The underlying ai, which is fully explained in chapter 16 on the meanings of the vowels, meant something like that which, and the same phonemic sequence has contributed also the pronoun I, (pronounced ai) where the h has completely disappeared. Halo makes sense as ia-lau, it that looped, a circular glow surrounding the head.

Hebrew (3) according to Eric Partridge is from the Hebrew 'Ibhri, one who comes across (the Euphrates. Better is goes across, and comes back, since the i is he, -bhai is going and −rai is there and back, like the Egyptian rays, and like Aberdeen and the less well known Brandon in Suffolk, where the aber means crossing place, from the Lithic a-bai-rai, that/where-going-verb (where the estuary of a river spreads and shallows). It does not fit so easily the sense of the tribe coming from the far side of the River Euphrates, unless of course it referenced the fact they had been carried off captive there and were now returnees (with a historical claim to the lands they were repossessing). Hebrew, apparently from the phonemes Iha-i-bai-rai-u could just be the speakers from the Lithic He that-which-speak-verbal-ones. Considering their cousinship with the Phoenicians (6) and Carthaginians who were also circumcised and their names record the fact (Phoenician is from Pahei-au-ai-nai-kai-n (6), penis-that one-which-exposed-made, and Punic is from pipi-nai-kai, penis exposed-cut), it is natural to just take a look to see if Hebrew has the same distinguishing phenomenon in mind. Hei-ba-rai-u can undoubtedly be read as (6), ecstasy-bit-visible-ones. Rai, as well as seen can also mean rayed and roused, and indeed the aim of the Semitic Pharaohs in cutting off their own foreskins in this radical manner appears to have been in recognition of their duty as Pahei-Ra-au-hei, bearers of the Phallus-of Ra-always-virile, to be ready at all times to fire first and not have to wait like the ordinary run-of-the-mill males for rays from the female genitalia to pull out their penises and withdraw their muzzle covers before they could ray back and arouse the females in turn. When the run of the mill lot copied the divine penis, they too made it into a deal with their Deity. It would be quite wrong, an anachronism, to think this kind of nomenclature would be taken as an invasion of personal privacy in those days. Indeed it was a religious boast then for those who had been cut that they were chosen for the afterlife and the uncircumcised were dead men. It was a claim which must surely have struck everyone, whether Jew or Goy, as a defining belief. In Pharaoh's day the fact the glans of the penis had been artificially exposed was what gave identity to a Jew, and they and their neighbours recognised this equally. Folk etymology today is less liberated and it is not correct to harp on these genital mutilations. Crossing the Euphrates is safer territory, although it was by comparison with the other (which after all they brought with them and loudly declared was their guarantee of acceptance by their God) a remote and little known circumstance by which to describe a race. Leaving captivity was perhaps worth celebrating, but hardly the fact that they boated to freedom – across a river. It is these considerations which persuade me the genital mutilation is the most likely contender and the river crossing can be binned as false folk etymology. There will I am sure be those who will wish to contradict this appreciation, and some who will reject everything in the book in order to rid themselves of this pesky conclusion. Nevertheless it should appear. They should be asked where they got their initial h from, because we can point to whence it came.

Also under the Cockney h rubric (3) are, as a suitably mixed bunch, harangue, hasan, hegira, helios, helot, Horus, hour, Hebe, halter and Egyptian hua for water, (really ahua, like the Lithic awa, as well as all the agua languages), as well as hupo in hypotenuse and hyoid, which is from the Greek huo- and weidein to see: u shaped, weidein from the Lithic uai-da-ien, everything-does-verbal marker, or going both ways-does. Seeing was supposed to be a matter of sending out rays from eyes which went out and came back, so the going both ways was seeing. Then everything was what you saw; and it could be with the mind, just as we say 'I see' when we mean we have it in our minds, in which case an idea could be a concept, a mental appearance which had come wafting in from outside on a ray like vision. With hyoid which is from the Greek hueidos, meaning u-shaped, it all comes down to ah-u-eidos, that-u-become/shape or idea. It is perhaps a nice example of the complexity building from original simplicity, discouraging Sapiens Sapiens from working backwards up the tree to trace his verbal roots. With hypotenuse, from Greek hupo (3), under and the Latin tendere to stretch, the Lithic for tendere is taien-da-erai, birthing-does-verbal marker: there is a lot of stretching required to give birth. The Greek was the simpler tenein, to stretch, Lithic tai-nai-ein, giving birth-presents or shows-followed by the Greek verbal marker -ein. The Lithic elements of hupo are ih-au-pau, it-that one-skinned one, that is to say one that is covered, and what is covered is underneath. The hypotenuse turns out to be the one which stretches under (the right angle of the triangle under discussion). At least the stretching points to the length of the hypotenuse, in the case of a right angled triangle, being proportional to the other two sides. With triangles other than those with a right angle it is a mess, because the angles are variables too. We can note also the Lithic agreement of the au with the immediately following pau. In so far as the pau, skinned or covered, is the completive case or past tense, the au can be understood as in agreement, also in the completive (substantive) case – not necessarily to be transliterated as that one, perhaps just that with case agreement with pau.

Harangue (3) has a convoluted derivation which shows up the original meaning of the Old High German hari for army, which in turn produced the German Herr we translate as Mister, really a warrior or brave. The Old German hring (3), a ring, is read in Lithic phonemes easily as ahi-ra-en-ga, that which-Ra-of-shape. The h preserves the only trace here of both the preceding a and the following i. The shape of the sun was paradigmatically circular. General Montgomery was accustomed to call the soldiers into a circle around him when he wanted to harangue them. It was a trick nearly as old as speech. So large a body of men as were to be found in armies in the past positively required making a ring of them if you were to be heard. There were no microphones in those days. The harangue followed once you had got them in a ring. Otherwise you tended to have them in ranks, linear like the sun's beams, for doing the business, Lithic rai-en-kai, ray-of-shaped. The sun was round but its rays, sometimes caught in a sunbeam when dust in the air shone, were as straight or straighter than the skyline at sea, and with no other natural rival for exemplifying a row (from rau) or line. Shoulder to shoulder is best for hand to hand battery, but vulnerable to cavalry or missile attack, which is the history of warfare and armies in a single sentence: shoulder to shoulder makes for morale but it makes for carnage too – and this is true – from Agincourt to Waterloo. Fire and cover from fire always wins. I was a gunner and remain one. Hari (3) originally appears to have started out as an army by definition lined up in ranks ready for the fray. But the rough behaviour of armies when not engaged in battle, unranked, led to the interpretation of the cockney h as the fourth horrid one instead, which we still have to deal with, because of their harrying (4).

There is another possible root for hari, an army, in the Early French har (4) for a horse, Lithic the frightener, with hari horsed ones, horsemen sweeping down on the fold. But the Germanic tribes did not generally derive their speech from the French. Their word for horse is pferd. But the Old Frisian was hors, and Frisian is perhaps the nearest continental language to English. Horse could belong with the

fourth horrid h (4). Horses are hard to handle and they were a hectic ride, probably partly from rough handling, and one ridden at you was alarming. The Lithic
hau-rai-sai or si could be frightening action, or brer frightener. But I believe on
balance it records the horse's own joy in its own action (6). But then why not all
three together? Hasan was, Partridge records, related to hare (another animal that
rejoices in its speed and agility), the Old High German for gray. Hares are not
notably gray. They are brown. The hare was really a soldier – in flight, not so much
a frightener but frightened: flushed they run a mile and as fast as a horse. The Old
Frisian, a good guide, was hasa for hare, the fourth h, the one of horror or despair
accompanied by –sa, active or action. That signifies: gone with the wind.

Hegira (3), Mohammed's departure, flight from Mecca is the Arabic hagara to
depart, hijra departure or flight. Mohammed was forced to flee, but the hegira was
politely put, a departure. A haji is one who has made the pilgrimage to Mecca. The
h is a Cockney h. The original phoneme string is ahi-ga-ra, with ai in its primitive
form, extensioning or setting out (it would become just going)-go-verbal suffix.
Helios (3), the sun in Greek, is from the Lithic ahi-a-lai-u-substantive ending,
that that-which-looping or orbiting-one. The sun as orbiter. Helot (3), a slave, is
chiefly built around the lau phoneme, uncommonly looped in the sense bound,
tied up. The Lithic string is iha-i-lau-tai, it that-which-bound-become, with a
cockney h. A harlot (6) per contra, is with the hippy happy h, a slave to pleasure,
the same h as makes up the Egyptian joy-piece. The Norman French given-name
Herlot (6) – William the Conqueror's mother was so named, not as it turned out
a happy choice – requires a slightly different reading, a lasting hooray, expressing
parental delight. That did not stop the King of France, a spin master who found
Normandy an overmighty subject, declaring William's mother a harlot, and the
media copied, inventing a tanner's daughter. Tanners were the untouchables of the
day, since they worked with the raw hides scraping off the stale fat so they stank.
To allege a duke had consorted with a tanner's daughter was meant as a mortal
insult, which the history books have copied; and William (who was in fact not a
very loveable fellow) is generally believed to have been illegitimate. Duke Robert
may of course have had his wicked way with Herlot and bedded her before getting churched, but if so she hung on and he wed her after. Anyway spin wins.

Horus (3) is the Ancient Egyptian son of Osiris. Osiris, the Greek name,
was Au-sa-rai, Everlasting-sun-rise in Egyptian. Like the sun which set and rose
again smiling, Osiris guaranteed the annual growth of the crops. He himself had
demonstrated remarkable fertility, since he succeeded in fathering Horus even after his genitalia had been cut off and thrown away by the wicked Saitan (the grim
reaper, from the Lithic Sai-ta'n, vitality-severing, thought to have been called Set
by the academic Egyptologists who remain unaware of the proper pronunciation
of the language). Our Satan is credited with even worse mischiefs. Osiris beat him

by actually managing to grow a new penis – some say it was a graft provided by his mother-wife Isis who badly wanted a kid – and exposes it through his mummy shrouds as firm evidence of its regeneration. So he rises smiling although mummified. The horizontal angle of his protruding organ, clearly intended to be erect, raises the question whether that was the best the Ancient Egyptians could achieve due to poor diet, etc; or whether his was horizontal from excessive use. The issue must remain moot, although there is the further possibility the priests stuck it straight out as an attention seeker so it should not be missed. It was after all for them the symbol for resurrection, for life after death, the principal dogma they were peddling. Horus is from the Lithic Iha-u-rau-sai, He that-one/who-raised-alive. He was born from the dead as it were, thanks to his father's remarkable powers of sexual resuscitation. He was however, in accordance with the Egyptian whimsy, anything else as well that his name of power bestowed. So he was also U-Ra-sai, Unit-of Ra-movement, which is why our hour is so named from the Latin hora; while the Greeks had hora for a different sun unit, a season, and later we got our year, another sun unit, from the same Lithic phonemes only garbled a bit. Partridge debates if the Latin ire to go, Lithic ai-are, semantic content simply extending-verbal suffix, contributed to our year, German jahr. The fact is Year itself had ia in front, which enabled generations of folk etymologists to pronounce year as a unit denoted by the travel of the sun, (without calling upon the final r for Ra), probably from mid season to mid season as measured in stone circles.

Hebe (3) was the Greek goddess of youthfulness and strength. Now ba (chapter 4) meant flesh, and of course flesh is muscle and fat, but mostly muscle. To be bai was to be with bulging muscles. Some of the bulgyest are in the bum or butt. In youth your body (Lithic bau-dai, fleshed) is still building and burgeoning also, indeed putting on muscle. With bai we have youthful musclature all in one. The He- therefore appears to be merely another Cockney h, with the Lithic Ai-ba-i, That which-ba-ing. However you may like to consider this was a goddess and it may be she was rejoicing in the youth as he established his manhood, and that was why she was adopted as his champion. In this case Hebe should be moved into column 6, rejoicing in the musclature. Partridge just jumps to Lithuanian jegiu meaning I have the strength, and concludes the Indo-European etymon or original root was iega, ignoring the switch from g to b. But g does not flip to b. Why should it? If you can ignore the consonants etymology becomes impossible. Language as we understand it, as opposed to calls sung out in vowels before speech, came in with the consonants as we learned to sound them (and label them with meanings) along with the mere vowelisations of our previous communicating system. Admittedly we say befall and the Germans say gefallen, but they are not equivalents. Be- is present tense, ge- is past. It is not a case of one changing to another.

Halter (2) by comparison is a bit of a damp squib. The la phoneme looks at once like the one shared with helots, since they share an element of confinement. Lai can also be lithe and sinuous, a character it picks up by being in antithesis to the phoneme ka, which is hard and rigid, gulled from flints. Helots (3) vary somewhat in their agility and this aspect is inappropriate for them – unless servility can be counted as emotional sinuousness. Partridge sends us off mischievously to the entry he has for helve which he also finds akin to helm (2) (the rudder you steer with, from ai-lai'm, going-in a line/at sea-'m), in turn akin to the one you wear on your head (3) (ahi-lai-mai, that which-surrounds [the head] and lowers the hammering [aimed at it]), and probably also related to the Lithuanian kilpa which means a stirrup and is from kai-lai-pa, making-a looping-piece for the feet, while the English stirrup is composed of the phonemes stai-rai-pai, stand-raised-feet. You stood up in your stirrups swinging your mace. Lithuanian, by the way, has the distinction of being the extant language most closely related to Sanskrit which (with Avestan) is the earliest and most fully recorded forebear of the whole Indo European family of languages. So here is quite a pie. In the case of the rudder, the helm which ships answer, I fancy it is from the Lithic ahi-lai-mai, which is that which-aligns-below, hidden under the water, in contradistinction to the helmet's that which-limits-the damage, or lays the marring. The helve must surely have started out with a b in place of a v. May I write he for ahi and ai, that which? If so helve (3) is from he-lai-bai, he-linear-bai, he the business end of a linear tool. I think also it referred originally to a linear tool which you swing, (the sun, helios (3), is from he-swings or loops above) and was the end where you apply your muscles (ba), the handle you grasp. Perhaps the stirrup is a foot steering mechanism too, you steer with both feet, horse willing when riding, as well as tugging on the reins. If so the stirrup's terai is the steering as well as the drawing up. The Lithuanian stirrup (kai-lai-pa) similarly may have been making the alignment as well as a convenient loop to put your foot in. The halter is now clearer. The Lithic is ia-lai-terai-a, it that-loops-and pulls along, a loop for pulling along. It is clear to me Eric Partridge was diplomatic in what he revealed. What was too much for the senators he did not present. But it certainly appears he often knew more than he wrote. Not only that but he was of course still confronting the prejudice, still observed in powerful places in the linguistic orbit, that the meanings to be attached to word roots are all random and not to be attended to. His dictionary usually omits the meanings altogether, unless they are positively required as some part of the etymology, as inevitably occurs.

The fourth Haa! is a sharp shock, as when you pick up a white hot (4) stone. In the absence of sabre toothed tigers, put your child's hand on a steaming hot plate on the stove and the first reaction you will get may well be a Haa! I have not tried it. "Hot!" is rather easily understood, if accompanied by suitable hand withdrawal gestures. A "Haa!" is even better. It is an involuntary sudden expulsion of breath which accompanies a sudden sharp pain or extreme dismay. In the absence of such a warning my elder daughter (when still young) once inadvertently backed her bare bottom onto the element of an unguarded electric fire. What she said as she did it was a cross between an Aou! and a Hou!. It was a cross between a wail and a howl (4). The source of her trouble was immediately apparent. Now a matron, I imagine the evidence of this misfortune must still be recorded on her tail. At one time you could make out the outline of the coiled electric element quite clearly. Her private Hell, just that place (2), is now a distant memory. Greek Hell was Hades (4), where Hai prevails, a hideous (4) hateful (4) place of harms (4), often made out as hot (4); so that Wayland Smith with only a little exaggeration in his own mind will sometimes use the expression "as hot as Hell".

A heathen (4) is derived from the heath (4), an infertile area which has hai-tai, heat (4) dried-become, with nothing much but heather growing on it, which can also be read as from ai-a-tai, that which-first-inhabited, or really where we were all first born, with only a little obliquity meaning inhabited, and none for Wayland. Because of the light soil the trees were stunted and easier to fell, so they got felled first to clear the land for cultivation. These areas were those first exhausted in turn, and so became Breck or broken ground abandoned as infertile open plains, colonised by heather and bracken and gorse (ga-u-rai sai, grow-where-heat rayed or dry); but eventually barren, the sandy soil by the eighteenth century blown into shifting dunes. But a heathen (hei-a-tehei-en) is also akin to a hoyden, a bold lass not waiting for the boys to make the advances; and it may well be both may have become known for their lack of morals, not infertile at all but on the contrary bumpkins, regarded as inadequates left behind on the less fertile ground or even pushed out onto it, with an eagerness for the simpler pleasures, hei-a-tehei-en, enjoying-copulating, and thus jumping so far as the etymology is concerned from the third h to the sixth, leaving out both the horrid fourth and the hilarious fifth altogether. Horror and hilarity incidentally make strange bedfellows in the same phonemic quiver, and their discovery points to the earlier overarching semantic content from the pain of a burn, which only the Lithic hypotheses can provide. Partridge has the gorse commonly found there akin to hearse and earlier hirce (a harrow (3) from Latin hirpex), as well as hirpus (3) for wolf, an enthusiastic (6?) foot traveler, fircus a he goat, hirsute and even Greek kher (2) for hedgehog. But then he had no Lithic. Gorse is certainly prickly and so is a hedgehog. But wolves and goats are not definitively hairy. All animals have coats. The hearse and the harrow had ray shaped pieces, in the case of the hearse sticking up, sai, (as ornaments), although it may originally have been just a raised platform of strakes. The wolf rejoiced in his (fleet) feet, running his quarry to death, the goat had the same pleasure nimbly skipping from rock to rock, hairs are rays, and the Greek kher for hedgehog from the original Lithic Khai-rai has hard sharp rays as does the Old English hedgehog, herrison from French hericon, from original Lithic ahi-rai-kaun, that which-rayed-both all hard and all over his body; which also gave the Latins their ericius, Lithic ai-rai-kai-u-s, that which-hard-rayed-body-altogether and whole body (but otherwise much like our rake which has only a single row of hard rays) the final s of ericius just being the Latin substantive marker.

Hurrying (6) was first perhaps away from the sabre toothed tiger. Partridge suggests it may be related to hurr, an echoic snarl (we can compare khurr with tigre, with the ti- readable as mistress, mistress growler) and so a sound generating horror (4) and swift evasive action. Compare the Old Frisian (very close to Old English) hurrein, of winds, to blow in gusts. That suggests a hurricane, but hurricane is from Taino huracan, an evil spirit of the sea in the Caribbean, for which the original Lithic phonemes appear to have been I(h)-wa-ra-ka'n, He-terror-ray-makes, because it chimes with Wakan-Tanka, the Central American creator god, Terror-maker-World-maker or Awesome Creator. Tan-ka in turn picks up the Ancient Egyptian taun, all the births, becomings or events, the universe – as in the Lords prayer in Coptic: "Pata ahi are en pai-taun", Father our art in heaven. Hurly-burly and hullabaloo clearly each carry an emotional h with them, as does to hurl (4), to launch with great effort. Emotions were believed to arrive from outside, heroic (3) or (6), and cowardly, raging and charitable alike, arousing the emotions concerned. Charity set out without any h at all, from Latin carus, Lithic ka-rau-s, body-aroused-substantive ending, a state of arousal affecting the whole body, indicating the one of the original concupiscence. A happy h seems to have volunteered itself as an additional guide to the meaning. Carus denoted endearment. The Germanic root for whore, spelt hors in the earlier Gothic, denoted an activity of endearment. These were rays from the outside like most if not all of the others. (Well the eyes were active emitters like the sun but fielded the reflected rays on their return journey). Even a whore was in a sense acting out her allotted role in receipt of signals from the environment, which in a practical assessment she probably was, since payment for services enabled her to live. With the arrival of a tiger the idea of hurrying away was about right, in this case prompted by the visual and or the audible signals similarly from without. A harrier and a hawk made havoc amongst their prey. Crying Hawoc (4) and unleashing the dogs of war has both the fourth h for horror and wa for shivering in fear (chapter 15) and ka for strike: it was actually shouted on the rampage by Wayland, who probably fancied words had the power to impose their meanings on the enemy along with the phonetics. Without getting too political, the Wahabi (6) tribe of Saudi Arabia, Wa-hai-bai, fear-rejoicing-habitually (as long as they remain bai, fleshed out, that is in being), were a fierce warrior race, using terror tactics over millennia, named by their long suffering neighbours as terrorists but proud of it. To hate (6) is the emotion which engenders these practices. The Gothic hatis meaning hate (4), from the Lithic Hai-tai-sai is horror-become-sensed, a response to threat, real or imagined. The French elision hair (pronounce hai-eer) to hate seems to be semantically taking the initiative and anticipating hurt (4), and French haine (4) is showing hate or hateful, to be hated, whence the English heinous. Haunting (4) puts the frighteners on believers. Malay hantu an evil spirit does the same.

Yet Partridge links haunting to home, with the meaning dwelling, much like the Spanish finca (6) from the Lithic pahein-ka, a pleasuring-place (compare the Egyptian pahei, (6) the pleasuring piece or penis), nowadays just a fine (sic) villa in the country. A haunted house is in the traditional etymology just one frequented by spirits, and a haunt is a place one frequents, perhaps a club or a natural beauty spot or any other resort. Of course if you read haunt with a Cockney h (3), then you just have a(h)u-natai, it-where-born, a bear's haunt or home range or hide for instance, or a gentleman's club. Home (3), with a Cockney h, from iha-u-mai, it that-where-begotten (mai = earthed, planted, impregnated, begotten), and has a wide following in Germanic tongues, often including the surroundings as well, such as a farm or estate. But inevitably home becomes an emotional tie as well, the third h picking up additional meaning from the eighth. Home economics has a degree of redundancy since economics is from the Greek ekoi-nomai, home rules or household management, home in this case from ai-kau-i, similarly that-we-kindled/begotten-we. Egypt (3) is from hoiku pata ahi, Lithic iha-u-kau-pata-ahi or it that-where-procreated–fathers-our: our fatherland. In Egypt it was the boys who counted, just as today. Home, like Egypt could appear with humus for soil under the cockney h (3), since it is iha-u-mai, it that-where-engendered, but it clearly has acquired some of the semantics of happy h (6). The German heim shifts towards hei-i-mai, with affection for where you originated, leading perhaps to powerful patriotism, even right or wrong. The Malay hantu (4) is a horrid spirit to be kept away. It has of course nothing to do directly with an English haunted house, although in England there are those who would keep away from such a place as if it were from the horror h (4). And this particular haunt probably is. It has everything to do with the common Lithic underground promptings world-wide, informing meanings from the subconscious mind. The mixed meanings of the phoneme ha, sometimes appearing together in a single word string, if not common, is quite often to be found. A hideous (4) countenance however – one thinks inevitably of Dorian Gray – is a horrible one that clearly gives one a great fright or feeling of repugnance and horror. Partridge nevertheless relates it semantically and phonetically to hairiness, from the supposed horripilation (4), your pile or hair (or fur) standing on end from horror. The Lithic however clearly suggests the hair, which stands on end when horrified, is just a pile (long pieces), and hair has a Cockney h only, and the hair is just seen as ahi-rai, that which-raised rays, or else khai- (2), grown (rays). After all the hair is raised from the flesh; it sticks out and comprises very thin strands like rays, but above all it grows. We do not feel horror with our hair all the time, nor did they in the Stone Age either. Perhaps animals use it more to express fear and hostility, as well as to keep them warm, paradigmatically the porcupine, which is the spiny pig, from Old Provencal Porc-espin. The porpoise, in passing since Partridge adds it in for good measure, is called a pig-fish, apparently elided all the way from the Latin Porcus-pisces. A pig is a fat body, pigs can be fattened, and pai gulls fattening from the painai(s) or pahei, the penis. A penguin is a piggy bird, with fat naturally selected against the cold.

A porker is akin to farrow, which is a plural, a lot of young pigs, a litter, from the Old English fearh (8) for one little pig, from the Lithic phai-are-hai wearing an h from the second column of the semantic tree, from kh, and then treated as a k and a cockney h, kahi, whence kai. The little pig is pahei-are-kai, procreating-verbal-made, a new- born litter. Pigs always have a litter with a lot of young, so they must have been continually at it, one go one piglet like everyone else. They all come into the world that way in a litter, and they can do it twice in the year, so it is a suitable distinguishing marker and a powerful argument for eating them. To polish off the pisces also before going on, a fish is legless: the Lithic pai-sai, leg action, the pis- bit, is replaced by kai-sai, body action, the -ces bit, slovened via pais-kais: that is originally the same as fish (completely hashed in English). Perhaps a good deal of this major slovening only arose with the birth of alphabetic writing. Fish flit through the water by wiggling their bodies in the absence of any legs to wiggle: a whole body mover, which perhaps appealed to early Christians who must have sometimes felt legless and ill endowed in face of Roman power, and forced to rely on soul power instead, their whole body capacity.

The Japanese have an irrational habit of committing hara-kiri (6) when the shame of living gets too much for them. It comprises a ceremonial slitting of your own belly with a sword which is stuck in and then drawn across with fatal results. It must be pretty painful too. The hara is the belly, because like the heart in the West it is regarded as the seat of the emotions in Japan, so hara is the emotional organ for the Japanese (starting with a stomach ache?) while kiri is the cutting of it (refer to chapter 5). The power of the custom is locked within the words. Hara-kiri cuts the belly and cuts off the emotions both at once. True, it extinguishes life as well, but that is just the other part of the deal, to show you really mean it. The emotions to be cut off are of course the bad ones, chiefly the horror (4) of being shown up as failing in a code of honour (6), like losing a fight for instance, that fatal loss of face which all over the East is taken so seriously – almost as if it were a public castration. Honour (6) there is a question of how to handle the horrors (4). Westerners accept the contempt of others better, having thicker hides (2) and perhaps a more built in self belief, with less consideration for the opinion of the others. It seems the kowtow (ka-u-tau, the ka-u-become, that is bent down, prostrated – the physical body and the spiritual ka at the same time) is taught and not inherited. Surprisingly it is the wimps that take to violence like ducks to water.

English honour (6) however employs the happy h, indeed it shows it in the Latin honos, an honour awarded, an office of honour or the quality of honour, Lithic hau-nau-s, admiration-shown-substantive ending. Here Wayland has picked up on the oblique stem of the Latin as we see in the accusative case, honorem, when picking the English, probably just because it gives him that little bit more to get his mind round. The priests of Amun of Egypt used "Hei" as Halelujah (6), with arms raised (in lieu of the penis?) in appeal and praise of their Deity above. Hale-luya might be read as a Heil-and a high level one, I suppose. It was not in English of course. In Hebrew it is read as Praise to Jaweh (3). But the semantics of hail (6) a high (6) one is incorporated in the semantics of the phonemes in the idioms of other languages too, including hale in good health in English. Hare Krishna, hurrah (6) for Krishna is from the same source. I have not followed the theology of Krishna but kare-ish-na in Lithic phonemes carries the semantic content perhaps, inter alia, of creating-life-meaning or some such. Or it could be glossed as representing the creation of life. Naming gods could, I suspect, often be an entirely subconscious exercise, as if the deity were declaring himself by name as you mostly thinking as he prompted you. That meant it did not have to mean anything in particular, only to incorporate phonemes in high regard within the subconscious mind. Krishna appears to hint at creation, the flame, and exhibiting understanding.

I have always found it a matter of astonishment that readers of the proofs have not found the Lithic idea at all easy to understand. I have been accused of losing sight of chronology and linguistic distances by cherry picking in different languages. Of course there is a significant nub there. I invoke the historic subconscious accumulation of traces in languages, which brief the learner to think in these terms, regardless of the other idioms of the language that he or she has consciously learned. There is a subconscious keel attached to the web of words we learn with our conscious minds, and it is in the form of phonetic meanings which underlie the words we use. They lie there because that is how originally we spoke, and it is from these meaningful phonemes our speech is composed.

The fifth ha is shortly disposed of: Ha! Ha! Hilarity (5) gets its meaning from the human reaction to a humorous circumstance of whatever kind. It is outside the scope of this study to consider what all these circumstance might be. The suddenness of the perception must take one by surprise, for which purpose it is usual for comics to lead their audience up the garden path thinking they have understood the story line, only to be overtaken by the sudden denouement, breaking the mould, and the realisation they or the character in the tale had it all wrong. The

Greek god Komos, kau-mau, personified a flaked mind or broken line of mental thinking, leading to comedy. However hilarity has not spawned much in the
way of collateral ratiocination. This is probably partly because the sixth ecstatic h
has monopolised the field. Laughing and procreation often come close together,
indeed the Eskimo is said to offer his wife to a visitor with the suggestion they
should laugh together. It is surely a matter of some regret that the human mind
should prove to be so thoroughly soused in sexual metaphor, dating back to their
earliest mouthings to each other, since it makes the whole of the Lithic hypotheses that much harder for academia to accept. But there is resignation too, since
sexual metaphor is comparatively easy to identify. Sex is simple – we all know how
to do it, it is a conservative tradition, and Wayland is thoroughly at home with it.
"Hie thee to a nunnery" I hear; and Partridge offers the original mission of folk
who hied. It means to get along in a hurry. In the case of the Lithic it is surprisingly complex. Since aaa was just extension before it was worded up and specified
more fully, ai, amongst a good many other things according to context meant to
extend your position, and so to go. The Latin ire to go can be read in those terms,
from ai-are, just extensive–verbal ending. With a Cockney h (3), hie is ahi and so
ai, just plain going. But now we learn that it has the additional meaning to strive,
to hasten, and in Dutch to pant, to be eager or desirous. This has clearly picked up
the sixth and highly sexual hai, which has come to be spelt hei in Egyptian and
which must now be dealt with at some length. There is an element of humour in
hieing of all places to a nunnery. The Middle Dutch was higen. G could be pronounced like y. But it started out g, so there is the going in the Dutch along with
the hieing. They evidently hied and then went – eagerly and in a hurry.

The Egyptian pahei meant penis, sufficiently like the Latinate term for reflection. Else they used mai. Ma is covered in chapter 10. It meant in this case earthing, inseminating, planting the seed just as if you were earthing it up like vegetable
seed. Animal and vegetable functioning were much closer together in everybody´s
minds in the Stone Age. The whimsy can be seen when you consider it was the
women who later had the digging sticks and did the planting, usurping the male
role and possibly enjoying the mischief. Was that why Adam shopped Eve for
using knowledge (of irrigation) to improve on natural growth, outsmarting the
deity, a rash and risky business? God said "You want water for flooding the fields,
then? Try this!" and melted the glaciers raising sea levels 350 feet and driving
Adam and Eve from what is now the South China Sea. The Malay aboriginal
version of the flood myth is it started when a dog (khok) barked (khurl) at a tree
(khruing). The Senoi for tree means a hard growth, which could be read also as a
completive or superlative, even forced growth like irrigated padi.

The Lithic pai-hei, if you read the glyphs alphabetically – the Egyptians generally didn`t – was conventionally p-h. The Greeks had their conjunct letter phi

for this dual sound. The symbol was originally a circular orifice with a straight line entering it on the slant, but later it was extended so as to cross the circle, formerly more like our Q which was probably kau in Lithic terms, where the tip of the line is only just entering the circle, perhaps providing the stimulus which rounds out the kau circle in turn. The Greek phi thus appears to have been a penis in flagrante, while kau, our Q, meant struck; and striking could be a figurative strike, a kindling or anything with a sudden strong effect. It would certainly include the impact of an Egyptian ray such as were supposed to emanate from the sun (Ra), the eyes, (ra) – and by a corollary assumption likely to be emanating from all rounded objects, orifices and puff-balls alike – which rode forth and then returned with their booty. In the case of the sun the rays pulled up the vegetation on their return journey, so that Egyptian pictures of the sun's rays had hands on the ends so that Wayland might understand their function. It must however have been worked out by Egyptian science by way of the two eyes, weak suns only, incorporating the sunny instinct capacities only weakly, so that they brought back only pictures, mere visual phantasmagoria of what they had encountered on their outward journey, which could sometimes be caught sight of deposited on the iris or irradiated part of the eye.

The male response to sexual arousal was taken as the effect of another ray originating it was supposed from the female presence, and where else than from the orifice she had at her command. Puff-balls by the way have an ejaculatory habit when struck which may well have reassured some old soapy in the Stone Age his thinking was on the right track: the male organ after all is a puff-ball on a stalk, the phallus being the knob or fruiting body on the top. It meant fruit in Sanskrit[2] male genitalia being regarded, quite perversely of course, as the animal equivalent of the fruiting bodies of the vegetable kingdom. The phallus (6) was the glans, but the Malay buah, dual-fleshy bits, means testicles and fruit. To avoid too much confusion the testicles were further marked out as buah pelir, with batang (meaning stem) pelir meaning the penis, with pelir the piece that leaks or flows (compare hilir (3) to go downstream and lareh to pour). Malay paha (6) is the hip (6), the joy piece in Malay and English alike. Sex (sai-kai-sai, pleasure-making-life, the making applies both ways) uses the hips to obtain the reciprocal motion stimulating the genitalia. The hip that is a haw (6) meanwhile bears an albeit modest similarity in appearance to the glans in arousal – making allowances of course for the differences in detail to be expected between the vegetable and animal kingdoms. The English ham (6) from hai-mai identifies the haunch (6) as the actuator in copulation, mai being planting or impregnating in Lithic. Kunchi in Malay is a lock or keyhole. Kunchi paha is the groin. The kunchi is an actuator-khai, of the join, a lock in the form of a great bolt slid across two swing leaf doors) A key, which operates the lock is anak kunchi, son of the lock, but the

Lithic elements of anak are an-a-kai, one-that-kindled or begotten. But an-a-kai also means one-that-actuates. The keyhole then becomes ibu kunchi, mother of the lock. As for kunchi, it is from the Lithic ku-en-kai, the ku is the completive case of kai, actuating, and the kai which follows has the earlier semantic content of joining. The idea that the male genitalia, glans or testicles, can be regarded as a fruiting body today seems just silly, after all sperm is just pollen; but it was the adjectival mind´s attempt to validate the idea every character, if it was true, was to be found popping up everywhere. It was a common feature that was seen, not a complete equivalence, the terms in which we tend to think today when we think of an equivalence. In the Stone Age minds were easily persuaded. The slightest indication would do. While vegetation was incapable of locomotion animals moved around. There was therefore the less cause for surprise to find animals fruiting and unfruiting with their genitalia at will. Given what you knew about animal and vegetable behaviour you might almost have expected it. Half the population of the world today (or more) probably still regard the male semen as seed rather than just the pollen which it really is. Pollen, the lexicon tells us, was just ground flour or powder, from the Greek pale meaning dust and the Sanskrit palala flour, no doubt ground in a pestle pounding round and round, -lala (compare Lithic -lau, looped like in Apollo, that-go-loop-loop, the orbiter) which was how to get powders, including dust which must have been ground in nature´s pestle (which more or less it had been) just like the ground as well as grounds. There is nothing about flour or powder or dust, all insignificant and feeble, blowing in a puff of wind, which would encourage a male chauvinist to welcome it as in any way equivalent to his own pride and joy, his sperm. Nor has he. But there it is.

We can see the Sanskrit ph was pronounced as an aspirated p, more like the Egyptian pahei than the Greek phi or our f, because phani was a snake, from pha-nai, with the meaning skin showing or bare just like our English snake, from si-na-kai, brer bare body. There is a kinship with our naked, Lithic na-ka-ti, expose-body-orifices. However phana is the hood of a snake in Sanskrit, such as the cobra inflates when roused, and phakka means to swell, from pahai-kai, to actuate the pahai, not a mile away from our own four letter f-word. Moreover phanda, Lithic paha-en-da, pahei-ing-does, is a trap, noose, gin, snare, or trick, all with a snap if not exactly an ejaculatory action. In Arabic as in Hindi a fakir is a naked mendicant beggar still to be found on the streets in India. It is supposed to come from the meaning poor but the Lithic suggests it means naked, in his case with his pahei made -rai or visible. The poverty is derived from his ownership of nothing at all, not even a strip of cloth for a dhoti, a dhau-ti, an orifice thing, the standard modesty garment when engaged in manual work in a hot clime. Derivations often have the cart before the horse like this when they have been worked out on the assumption the phonology is meaningless. Phatkana in Hindi is to give a cloth a violent shake, to shake it out; whence to scold or rebuke, a dressing down. Whence phatakana is to winnow. Kana in Hindi is to make or do. Phatna is to burst or explode. Pharakna is to throb. Pharapharana is to throb, flutter or flap up and down. All these semantic contents seem to be able to claim kinship with the Ancient Egyptian joy piece and its behaviour world wide.

Anyway we can guess straight away that the hei which appears in the name for the Egyptian penis has the sixth and happy h in front of it. The hieroglyph for hei is a loop of string twisted three times, much like the twitch still used on a horse's lip to take its attention away from a worse mischief being performed upon some other part of its anatomy, stitching a wound for instance. Surprisingly it works. You keep varying the squeeze on the lip by twisting the twitch with a flick of the wrist. This makes it clear however the happy h was not the original one for hei, the hurtful (4) one was, such as eventuates when pressing the bare flesh against a live electric element. It can hardly be challenged the pahei is a source of vehement pleasure. Ha, except for the Cockney version, comes always from such a sudden burst of sensual or emotional response, shock or horror, pleasure or surprise. Hilarity combines them both. Ha was the gasp in all these cases. By now this should be clearly understood. There were no ice creams in the Stone Age. Their pleasures were few and relatively far between; but we can tell from the lexicon if we pay close attention that they gasped at orgasm. At other moments of ecstasy – the all male Amaun priesthood for instance let out the very same cry when standing arms uplifted in adoration of their God – Hei was the most ecstatic greeting tone available: Glory! Glory! Hallelujah!. The Hebrew for praise here is halle, the -lle- is tongue work, as in our laud and loud: intoning hei. Hallelujah is Praise to (The Lord) Yahwe. Al hamd al Illah in Arabic is praise to Allah. Hail to thee blithe spirit, bird thou never wert! Heil Hitler! Good health! The American campus greeting of Hi! falls shorter. The Scots when they spoke Gaelic would astonishingly address their wives as hen, but they were not the clucking sort. The hale and hearty are in conspicuously good health. Malay hati for heart, unconnected in any direct way with English heart, identifies the organ as crucial to liveliness and the emotional liveliness which goes with good health. "Banyak suka hati sahaya berjumpa lagi dengan inchek", Very sugar hearted I ameeting again with you, or Very nice to see you again. All these words take their meanings from the sixth h for happiness.

The hips provide the pumping motions required in sex, which is why they were so labeled, hei-pai, the copulatory pieces. Hippies picked up the idea quite quickly, and wore their trousers low on their hips to give them the extra freedom for demonstrating the movements in public as a tease. I have sometimes wondered if the boys at Rugby public school in the days of Doctor Arnold, now a hundred and fifty years ago, who legislated plenty of cold showers for teasing growing lads, were not somehow subconsciously influenced when they decided to handle their ball to redesign it in the shape of a rose hip rather than just the round one they had been kicking about before, to tease the Doctor in turn – although perhaps not fully aware of what they were doing.

Humanity has already been touched on. It is from the Latin humanus, and must surely be related to the Latin homo, but not to the Greek homo meaning the same, where we have a Cockney h and au-mau, dual masses, two equal masses, two the same. The Latin Homo (6) has a strongly pronounced h, and is ab origine a happy h, indeed it is the happy h like the Egyptian hei. The Lithic hau-mau, both in the matching dual case, is both enjoying impregnation. To think that our forebears were unaware of the differences between their sexuality and the animal sexuality in the wild, which was nearer to a capture than any embrace, is surely absurd. The carnivor's embrace is with his teeth. The popular perception of the shaggy alpha male in the Stone Age dragging his females into the cave by their hair is a chauvinistic absurdity. If only it were thus! But it never was. Or at least not since the hominid taming of fire so all those unwrapped around the hearth, after a tenderised meal cooked in the embers round the edge, were good and ready. The heat will have brought both male and female on together. If the girls took longer, their job as mistresses of the flame will have leveled the playing field somewhat. All humanity springs from this evolution. We live in the latter stages of the fire age, still trying to catch up, and now the information age has overtaken us. The academic view we are earthlings and chose to call ourselves as much, from humus, is ludicrous. Why on earth? Humus has a Cockney h like the Greek homo, ia-u-mau-substantive marker. It named the soil which is granular and (naturally) milled, the ground, grinded. The meaning of humus is that which-altogether-mashed, according to Wayland Smith. Ka, the basic hard structure of the world, which included of course the rocks, the rau kai, roasted like ceramics and so hardened. Witnessing volcanoes had taught mankind that much at least. Rocks could be pounded to bits, anyway the sedimentary rocks could. Flints were quite different, they shattered: you never got a granular structure, only smaller and smaller slivers which cut you. Try moulding that and you would be in ribbons. We do not know why the Latins picked homo. Quite possibly neither did they. But it comes from far back when folk did know, and if it had survived for a few millennia only under the surface in the subconscious mind, that is no great cause for surprise. They used hemo for a single homo, as if the h were Cockney, anybody; whence nemo for nobody. Partridge has one paragraph on homo and the remaining thirteen on the earthlings. Since impregnation was regarded as the planting of seed (in the earth) we should expect to find the ma phoneme doing duty in both cases.

The haunch is like the hips, hau´n-khai, doing the business. A hammock (6) however is from the Spanish, but they got it on their punitive expeditions to South America (America is from the Lithic Aa-mai-Ra-ka, Far-sinking/dying-of the Sun-Country, the Far Western Land: discovered and named – it is in Carthaginian, a provincial Ancient Egyptian – by the Carthaginians), where it is recorded from the Yukuna (a central American language) hamaca and the Taino amaca, and from Haiti. The hama (6) surely refers to copulation, orgasmic planting; and if Lithic applies there amongst the aboriginal tribes the ka has the semantic content of country, land and place. The hammock was the Yucuna finca or pleasuring place. Sai, warmed, comes to mean comfortable and at ease, which is what warm is. A shared hammock is a cosy nest. Kau-sai in English is made-warm, or place-what-warm. Warmth was sensed flame from the hearth, because ish was what fire said when dowsed. It is all spelled out in chapter 14. No doubt the tribes slept in them as well, to stay clear of the creepy crawlies as well as flash floods, as I did at one time. But I fancy a certain cheerful eroticism will have led them to name the equipment for the facility it provided for their principal interest in life, as if that were its sole purpose.

A hand can be used for most manipulations. We do not know our Stone Age forebears´ predilection. Perhaps number two, chipping flints, kha´n-da, chipping does or making does makes sense. But mischief may have prompted boys in the Pleistocene however, just as today. We may be using the sixth ha here. Nobody had thought as yet to tell them they would go blind; and there is the finger too which looks remarkably like from Lithic pahai'n-kara. Pahei had likely come to mean the principal erogenous zone of either sex. There were no civilised standards as we understand them to be defended by fair (6) means or foul.(4). The heart is taken, quite wrongly, to be the emotional seat. It started out just the thumper, Greek kardia and ker, Latin cor from ka-u-are, strike-one-verbal ending, the striker. With h instead of kh it is in column 6 in place of 2. The stomach, as the Japanese have spotted, with their hara-kiri, is nearer the mark; and even they need to go a little lower to pick up the hormonal centres of the happy bits. Compare ish-kara (iskra) a spark in Arabic, a fire maker like our (obsolete) English chark, sha-rai-ka, fire-maker, the swizzle stick used to light fires in the Stone Age. With exemplary economy suka also means in Malay to desire, overheated almost, covetous, a very human sentiment. Then it is used with more cool to mean just to like, and figures in the phrase above for pleased to meet you. Alternatively if you want anything you use mau, it means to want, but not to lack but to desire. It comes from the baby's stressed cry when it is hungry, see chapter 10. In Malay that can stand in as wanting to plant your seed as well (because ma is the opposite of sa, and human whimsy has worked it up to mean as much, see chapter 10 again).

The hearth (6) itself betrays some of the thinking surrounding it. Hei-arai-tehei is a rozener for sure. The German herd and heide discourage treating the th in the English as original. Hai-are-dai from hearth however suggests joy-verbal marker-gives, enjoyment giver, the hearth makes you feel warm and comfortable at least. But it may nevertheless be an elided kh after all, as Partridge thinks. Lithuanian kharstas is hot (although the rs offers rays and flame), Latin carbo is coal, carbon in English, and the Greek keramikos for ceramics is fired in a kiln. The Lithuanian from Khara-sai-ta, made rayed-by the flame-become, is certainly hot. But sai, hot can be just warmed through. Coal, science now tells us, is hard compressed vegetable matter, and the Greek pottery, ceramic, kera-mai-kau's is hard-earth-made 'substantive. It does not mention the kiln, but who needs it? I believe we are entitled to stick with the Lithic. It is in fact quite central to the Lithic origins of speaking. But were any of this shown (after publication) to be a misunderstanding of the derivations, the Lithic mechanism proposed for bursting into tongues would not in itself be impugned. Our hominid forebears would merely be shown up as having missed a point I could have shown them.

Hymen (6) was the Greek goddess of marriage. To marry was to do the business, the planting of seed. Hei-mai-en is ecstatic procreation which She epitomised, in praise of marriage (the planting): ma femme, femme from phai-mai, my delightful sexual partner. The hymen is the membrane broken in the process. Our hymns (6) started out as bridal songs from the Lithic hei-mai'n, celebrating-the impregnation. Not many parsons know that their hymns originally celebrated the rupture of the hymen. They will wish to argue it is outmoded as a derivation, and it is a fair point.

Hemp (6), from Old English haenep, belongs with the sixth h, in Lithic a hei-nai-pai. Chewing it appears to have given folk a high over the millennia, if not an actual orgasm apparently an ecstatic elation – hei-nai or hei-mai – to match it. Hemp is named for the utility of its leaves. The -pai may even refer to its leaves, but the word in German appears to point elsewhere. The Old High German hanaf, German hanf for hemp embodies the Lithic ha-na-pahei which seems to pick on orgasm precisely, since each one of these phonemes can stand for as much on its own. Certainly the fibre, which serves to weave stout canvas and strong hawsers gets no mention. Cannabis, the same plant as the canvas plant, clearly also refers to its narcotic effect. It is akin to kannabis in Greek, and copies exactly the Latin term. The Old Bulgarian or Old Church Slavic was konoplja. The Lithic from the Slavic is Kau-nau-palu-a. It appears to have given the Old Bulgarians an erection at least – they weren´t picky – or else they were footloose about the way they handled similes. For the Poles it is konop, while the Lithuanian is kanapes, going back before the Greek. It has a more convoluted origin than hemp. At least it provides an ecstatic feeling. In reality it does nothing for virility, but it provides a substitute or simulacrum, a kind of ecstatic swoon accounting for its hold on those addicted, most often inadequates. Walshe´s Concise German Etymological Dictionary of

1952, which Partridge quotes, cites similar Cheremiss and Zyrjan words from the Finno-Ugric family, "a wandering culture-word of wide diffusion". Cannabis has had a widespread pull. Our canvas is hempen cloth, cannabaceus in Latin.

The French canapes, light aperitif snacks eaten before a meal or in its place, actually mean sofas or divans in French. The original piece of furniture seems to have been what we would now call a chaise longue, because a canape-lit is a sofa bed. The idea apparently was canapes were to be eaten reclining comfortably, not at table but in the classical Roman style. The question then presents itself why canapés is sofas in French (and a preprandial snack taken on them before sitting down to the main meal) and the narcotic herb in Lithuanian. The established answer is of course these sorts of coincidences are common since all or most words have been randomly selected, so that it is a waste of time to bother with reasons – and only a mug would try. The divan allows you like the Romans to put your feet up. The Lithic is thus ka-na-pai, make (or place)-stick up-[your] feet. The drug in turn had the same result. You reclined under the influence of the drug, probably imagining yourself in a yellow submarine and quite unfit for work. But it may have made your penis stand up too, at least in fantasy. It is a misfortune the feet and the penis both answer to pai, both thinned diminutive derivatives from bai, the flesh, the limbs compared to the main body and the penis compared to the bum, the principal fleshy, that is muscular part of the human body. The polysemy results from the very general meanings the original phonemes originally had and the consequently numerous derivative meanings they acquired. It was this polysemy indeed which led to the abandonment of the system of stringing phonemic meanings to make a composite meaning by a process of ratiocination – of a sort – and led after the taua or tower of Babylon to the acceptance of the phonology and memorized composite meanings, regardless of the structure of meanings by means of which words had been built up over the aeons.

Notes.

1. M O'C Walshe. A Concise German Etymological Dictionary. 1952.

2. Sanskrit phala meant fruit, and thence consequence, result, reward, recompense, retribution, punishment, loss, disadvantage, gain, enjoyment, compensation, result of a calculation, product, quotient, interest on capital, and finally arrowhead, like the penis head. It is a nice example of the polysemy which arose from using the phonemic semantic contents in an ever widening metaphorical series of senses.

CHAPTER 9

THE PHONEME LA

La, with a curled tongue, when our hominid forebears began learning to speak, was the first consonant or stop between the tones alone we used at the chimpish level, before we spoke. This was because la was the natural break between two tones or vowels, which were the only utterances we had to express meaning before we spoke. With the addition of the consonants, five with the tongue eventually – la, ta, da, ra, and ish – language began. With a twist of the tongue it all began, tra-la! The trail is open for anyone who cares to pursue the matter to piece together the sounds we uttered and the senses the hominid mind picked for them. There were howls and cries with semantic contents before speech but they were all vowels, plus perhaps a few growls from the back of the throat, more of a khkh-aaa then a grr. There weren´t that many vowels so the tonal qualities were in demand. Recent research with recorded audiographs of chimpanzee cries has revealed chimps are better at distinguishing tones than we are and have an extensive vocabulary of them for different foods, etc. The Hamitic Chimpanzee, its anglicised form, in Lithic can be read as Si-m´pansai, brer-him-limbs-up, brer stander or climber. In Malaya a friend had a tame pet Siamang ape. They have very long arms and swing around the place at speed. Louis could be twice round the room on the picture rail in half a dozen swoops. Si-a-ma-ang is Brer-un-heavy-one or Brer-weightless in Lithic phonemes. The llama from South America is pronounced in the native tongue yama and the Lithic is Ia-a-ma, it that-un-massy, another Brer Weightless or Mr Lightfoot. They have long legs and their hind legs appear to be only lightly fastened to their bodies. They have a fair turn of speed from a few hours old to escape the coyotes. The original wild llama or guanaco is called simply the origi-nal 'wild species', Lithic gua-en-a-kau, country-in-that-begotten We still keep la as a separator between notes in tunes, without any meanings, along with do, ray, me, etc to make a scale. To go-la is to make a la, to sing; and a gala is a sing-song in origin. Ma and La were an oppositional pair because Ma meant massive and heavy (chapter 10) while La came to mean light and floating.

The semantic contents of the phoneme la, once the hominid mind got to work on it, as well as what Sapiens Sapiens has contributed since, are in the psychosemantic tree on page 250 under some forty subsidiary heads with columns indicating some of the English usages. The contents are to some extent arbitrary. The pursuit of meanings, which started out as a very large crossword puzzle with a myriad clues and solutions came quite soon to resemble instead an outsize jigsaw puzzle with even more pieces, a compact texture rather than a bare loose network of meanings with stops between. Not only are the phonemes and their meanings strung into words, a historical development without end, but their ambient other meanings make a field around them like the residual fields around protein chains of radicals which make them twist up into irregular lumps instead of lying out straight in a simple line. A phoneme emplaced in a word often exhibits a meaning from column n in a psychosemantic tree with a whiff of column m as well. That surely is a sign of the subconscious mind at work, maybe mine but equally possibly the mind of man in earlier days. As I age I find myself a wandering troubadour trying to retrieve meanings everywhere, occasionally becoming disoriented and springing from one percept to the next like an athlete skipping across a stream on a very few stepping stones, sometimes led astray by footholds out of the intended alignment. The correct Lithic language roots are not easy to discern, but the facility grows gradually, and a bit of guidance is a great help.

With a curled tongue la picked up its first widespread semantic content as Nasty taste! Like Yuk! See lye (3) in the psychosemantic tree. The Stone Age mind moved from a brackish taste to the liquid responsible, and so to liquid with a clear cut Stone Age science to go with it: it is the instinct of water to go downhill and to taste nastier as it does so, starting as clear as crystal in a spring and ending briney in the sea. The purity of the water became polluted in the rivers on their way to the ocean, even in the Stone Age. Dead creatures fell in them so that they picked up off flavours even in the haunts of coot and hern. To defecate in Malay is pergi ka sungei, to go to the river, where we say we attend to our toilet. The function is by nature distasteful and we do not directly foul our lips unless we really must. At the estuaries the water was brackish and salt. Whence indirectly there is 'Lat!' in Arabic for no, don´t [drink it, it is bitter and will make you sick]. The negative in Arabic otherwise is ma – the opposite of sa, so and si. In English there is lye for any bitter brew or other suspect liquid not clear as spring water. Moreover the Germanic etumon (Lithic ai tau-maun, as it-born-minded or meaning, but now perversely taken to mean its original phonetic form instead) of our English lye appears to have been lauga, slovened to Old English leah, but the Dutch have kept the g of the earlier form with loog. The Lithic will have been lau-kai or -gai, made lyed (3). Kai, originally echoic from the strike of flint on flint as the stone age knappers shaped their butcher´s and kitchen cutlery, meant made by human intervention – including the sexual intervention; knocking off a flake seems to have suggested it – whereas tai, (parting into two, or twoing into parts,

THE PSYCHOSEMANTIC TREE FOR THE PHONEME LA

The Phonetic Tree

Ra – La – Ra

The Semantic Tree

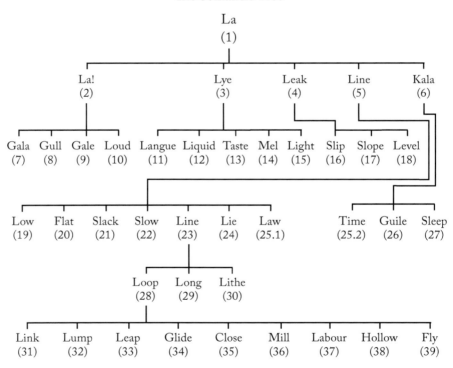

and so parturition) meant born, separated, distinguished, discriminated and become, whence natural occurrences, and for Ancient Egyptians Taun meaning all the occurrences and so the universe – a race evidently with a fine historical sense and not mostly limited to spatial patterns with the rise of science like us, so that we are inclined to dismiss the temporal and historical approach.

The Pharaohs at least, of all the Ancient Egyptians, were Semites, the people of The Book (in which they recorded their history as an ethical record). So here in Egypt is liquid being given an intentional status, because it exhibited downhill movement of a sort, half way to the animal kingdom, unlike vegetables anchored to the soil in one place; as well as with a preference for (nasty) tastes, going low and going lyey as it goes. Water apparently liked the land and would lie itself down on it if given the chance, so that it was evidently taken to be possessed of an instinct for that pattern of linked behaviours: going low and becoming lyey. Of course it could be it only wanted to be just off downhill and had to endure the off flavours in the process: in which case the offing would be kai and the off flavours tai. But in any case the –u vowel was the completive and dual (which is why we say two, and why one is a mispronunciation, it comes from Latin unus via French une, so there is little excuse). U was one of the only three vowels recognised: a came first, the natural unmarked general vowel, followed by í (ee), the thinned diminutive, and u (oo) resuming the other two as the completive (and so dual, embracing and complementing the other two and thus also indicating the substantive). It is as if we counted one, two, both of them, instead of one two three. It even seems it was a big leap to three, since two was seen as a Tau or T, a distinction rather than a numeration, and three was in due course derived from the (three) rays of the Tau or T. Try T upside down and you have something quite similar to the coat hanger concept implicit in the dialectic as developed in chapter 16 on thinking. The three vowels formed a primitive dialectic (or Tau), examined in painstaking detail in chapter 16 on the way we came to think with the new equipment of linguistic crutches.

It is good to be able to make Karl Marx out as an intellectual recidivist in passing, as well as a moral recidivist and renegade historian. His dialectical materialism introduced a moral puppetry based ultimately on the idea macht ist recht (might is right) hiding behind a declared democratic morality, with awful consequences both for Communism and the German spin off of National Socialism. Marx was a renegade Jew and Hitler was out to dump his dialectic. Hitler was an evil maniac and the German people disfigured for all time to have followed him. To hear a tape of him ranting, almost foaming at the mouth, is an education today. But he was clever with it. He was a nihilist in so far as he supposed he could make up his own agenda as he went along without inhibition from anything, including external reality. He would today be classified as autistic. That was the fatal flaw in his character and it killed him, but not before he had engineered the death of very many millions. He was by no means the first of these mad magisters and may not be the last. The majority of folk are enthusiastic simpletons when it comes to spotting one of these plausible lunatics and badly need inoculating against them – starting with the German people, but even the so called freedom loving people are not auto-immune, and the rest of the world is peculiarly vulnerable. Sorry world! No offence intended. The point here however is merely that both the urge to slip away into the lows, which follows, and the predilection for off-flavours were seen as instinct in liquids. It was all rubbish but at in the Stone Age it passed for science and common sense even. If there were any Pleistocene Einsteins no doubt they were firmly told to shut up, or ignored altogether, as sometimes can still happen today as punishment for stepping out of line and not being intellectually correct (IC) or academically correct (AC), sub categories of the better known Politically Correct (PC). The totalitarian streak is in every polity and in every mind.

It quite soon becomes apparent that, foraging for water with no portable containers – we are at a very early time while still learning to speak – hominid scientists concluded water sprung fresh but lapsed into lye as it slid into the lows or ran in the rivers sloping down to the sea. Sea is from the Lithic sai-awa, active water, attracting a Neptune, since its active waves and sea horses made it a half-way creature, half way to the independence of the live state, often showing bad temper with it, in raging storms and homicide. Anthropomorphic imagination influenced our early ratiocination. The patterns we spotted at home base from our own interests, promptings and behaviours we naively transferred to nature at large. By the time river water had hit the beaches it had got as low as it could get in this world, it had hit the ultimate depth, it had gone home and it had also turned completely briney and bitter. It made Neptune an old buff. Partridge has him originally a god of springs, Nai-pa-tau-nai, protruding-surface-river-birth, (who must have got caught up in the liquid bind, and so carried off out to sea). Salt, sel in Latin, is from the Lithic sai-lai (3), heated and dried-lye, dried sea water. Compare the English sere from sai-rai, originally flame-rayed and dried, see chapters 14 for Ish and 13 for Ra. The sea is lyr in Old Celtic, probably pronounced originally approximately lua, and it is laut in Malay, from the Lithic elements la-u-tai, altogether run down and altogether bitter (the dual case)-become. Liquidity for the ancients comprised those two linked instinctive developments and they were due to lack of fibre. Liquid is from Lai-kau-i-dai, lai´s-dual drives-which-does. Water has no sensible structure, it is yielding and accommodates itself to its surroundings by going low and lying flat. If you walk on it, it betrays you and down you go because it has no surface. Its apparent surface is a sly fraud. Pani, from Lithic pa-nai, surface none, is the Hindi for water today. You could read it as no feet in-

stead of surface too, since it travels without them, but the surfaceless reading wins
hands down. Pinica pani is drinking water. The drinking is to make with water.
You could argue the pini is the act of drinking and the pani is the drink which is
drunk, but the Lithic prefers the water was identified first, the surfaceless element
with no skin. Compare Greek panorama, Lithic pa-en-au-ra-ma, surface-of-all
that-see-solidity. Everything solid has a visible skin, its surface. Their pa-en referred to everything. Greek pan was (inter alia) everything or all. That is Stone
Age thinking, surely.

Babylon, which is customarily taken as either Bab-El-One, El's-Gateway-
One (where El is the Lord God); or Babble (because of the misunderstanding of
whoever it was that wrote that bit of the Bible), really meant Bab-I-laun, mouth
of the lawn, the flat salt marshes, now the Sha'at äl Arab, the spread of the river
at its estuary where the water has risen level with the land, Sha'at from the Lithic
Sha-awa-tai, up-water-become, flooding the delta inhabited by the marsh Arabs,
with channels and lagoons now networked by the hand of man, but a poor copy
of the riverine irrigation upstream at Sumer five thousand years before where the
super crops were being planted, because the lawn is sour, soaked in salt. London
like Babylon was at the estuary of its river as it arrived at its Lon-, its salt lawn at
sea level. En-don is of-the river, as with Donbas in Russia and all the other rivers
Don (and Deen and Dee), all originally birth canals which have been transmogrified in the human subconscious into just natural topological canals or channels.
Flow (19) down, Oh London (19) River! Then there are seagulls as well with their
silver wings[1] which this chapter sorts out next.

La (2) was the original separation of the pre-linguistic tones of which our cries
and howls were made up. It was an articulation with the tongue curled, which
came naturally. For speaking, the tongue (ta-un-kai) was the divide-one-mak-
ing, the divider and its use was first to divide the tones uttered. A miners' gala (2)
was originally a sing-song before they got around to politics. The lays of Ancient
Rome were short poems to be sung. Ballads [ba is lip and la is tongue, from the
taster (11)] were also sung by traveling minstrels, telling stories which were usually more or less fanciful, of courtly love. For ballad, the Lithic ba-la-dai is what
lip-tongue/sing-does, a tale to music. Ba and la were compiled as the elements
of utterances in several widely separated languages, one of the most telling the
North Queensland Djeri-bal from the Lithic ba-lai, speech. Then there is bolna
in Hindi, to speak, one of the most widespread usages. To lay an egg or lie down
are both by way of lowering or letting down (23). A melody in turn, Lithic 'm-ai-
lau-dai is him-that which-song-does, and it comes from the Greek melos a song,
Lithic 'm-ai-lau's, him-that which-sung (2). The seagull is a sea-go-la or sea-call-
er, and the nightingale is a singer in the night. The curlew says curlew in the night.
Actually it does not have any consonants in its call. It really says her-whew just

as the owl really says erwhee' erwoo without any t in it at all. We fool ourselves because of our own speech habits. In Egypt the owl said "a'-maoo", which could be read as all the ma's, so the owl was the glyph for m, ma, mai, mau, etc. The lark is a singer too and the Old English was lawerce. The Low German lawerke and the Old Norse laervirki provide the opportunity to demonstrate to some effect the art of expansion to expose the Lithic. We have from the Old Norse laervirki the original Lithic form la-ai-rai-u-kai, singing-as it-rises-when-making. The fact is a lark flies up higher and higher in arching spurts until it is so high you can lose sight of it, and the song goes with the spurts in its flight. Nobody knows why it should do this. Eagles similarly do not appear to be looking for prey and never swoop down from their soaring flight, just making use of thermals for their fun soaring. Eagles are silent gliders, ai-a-ge-lai, Lithic that which-that-ge-lai, makes a loop or goes flying, in a smooth flow like liquid slipping away. Or else perhaps the a-gelai was originally a-kai-lai, un-powered-gliding. Eagle and glider are perfect semantic and nearly perfect phonetic doublets. The ge- could be just going, but it is more likely from kai, meaning a kind of kindling, from struck (by a ray) giving them an oomph (or a sky hook) which enables them to slide up rather than down without flapping their wings. Thermals were way in the future. Both the lark and the eagle appear to be just having fun going up, which is why when we get up early it is said to be with the lark. The lark itself goes up in the middle of the day, particularly when the sun is shining brightly. It is rejoicing. None of these four calling birds have any speech in their songs, they are just tunes. A gale of wind is one that howls and sings in the trees and is akin to the miners' gala, both at bottom just going la, or making a la (a wordless lay, a tone).

La, with curled back tongue indicating distaste, was the natural precursor of "Yuk!", which relies for its effective semantic content on the final –k, a gagging. The build up of Yuk, with ya- or eeaa (ia)- is vaguely deliberative, but otherwise adds nothing to the meaning, unless perhaps the constriction of the glottis for the final k is symptomatic of retching. From the truly aboriginal minds of hominids learning to speak, the bitter taste of the lye (3) shows today in words like sloe, from Lithic sai-lau, sense or taste-very bitter (3). Countrymen, with fresh sloes on the blackthorn in the hedgerows to taste, will bear witness to the cogency of the name. Piccalilli and pickle are from the Lithic pai-kai-lai, pieces-made-lyey, or in the case of piccalilli lyey-lyey, very much so; and in the Dutch version meaning briny. One principal source of all the lai meanings undoubtedly comes from lye (3), the nasty taste. There is also blasphemy where the Greek precursor is blasphemein, to blaspheme. Phemein is to ejaculate in Greek, the sexual meaning the original one. The Lithic is quite specific: pahei-mai'n, the joy shoot or phallus-earthing, planting or impregnating; but just as in the English it was used also for uttering an ejaculation, making a sudden outburst and so an outcry. "God's boots!

he ejaculated, as he realized the canoe was sinking" is clearly a statement. "I am coming he ejaculated, as he picked up his pack and set out after his friend" might cause some confusion over the punctuation, like the Panda which eats shoots and leaves, or eats shoots and then leaves, or eats and then shoots and then leaves. The blas-, as Chambers has it, is "probably with the meaning false"(which has a similar set of phonemes). Actually Lithic suggests something more like bitter and full of bile, a simple spin off from lye (3). If you blaspheme it is not a matter of making a mistake from a false apprehension. It is heretically to speak mischievously and slightingly (which is taken to be from bitterness rather than from ratiocination) of a religious tenet. Blasphemy has been punished by death.

The bitter taste of the lye was parlayed to just taste, an example of a widely used idiom of generalization and expansion of meanings over time. Taste was identified as from the tongue, so that the tongue is Latin lingua, the taster, Lithic lai'n-ka-u-a, tasting-makes-one-that, which is paraphrased for the English idiom quite precisely "the one that does the tasting", the tongue; whence also the Latin lingere to lick, which is tonguing. The Latin lingere, to lick, is from lai'n-kare, to make [of or] with the tongue (originally in order to taste, most likely). Chambers has it the other way about: lingere is to lick and the tongue is the licker. But there is then no reason offered why the li- in lingere or lick should mean what they do, for which Lithic is needed. Partridge curiously thinks lingua is an alternate form of dingua, which is another Old Latin (Sabine) word for tongue. Any convincing etymology for the Old Latin dingua is lacking. Partridge just derives it from a guessed Indo-European root for the purpose *dingwa, which he then exhaustively compares with Old Persian hizbana, Persian zuban, Sanskrit jihva, Avestan hizu, Old Slav jezyku, Lithuanian lezuwis, Old Prussian inguwis, Old Irish tenga, Gaelic teanga, Manx chengey (with Breton and Cornish cognates lacking the n), Old Norse tenga, Gothic tuggo (pronounced tungo), Old High German zunga (meaning both tongue and language), Old Saxon tunga, Frisian tunge, Middle English tunge and tonge, whence English tongue. He adds "The 'tongue-language' dualism is as widespread as it is natural". This is true but which came first, the chicken or the egg? Or are there two groups, one putting the chicken first (the taster) and the other the egg (the speaker) and each deriving the other from their original. We can add to Partridge's philatelic collection Basque hitz for word, and miin for tongue and iskuntza for language, Albanian gjuke (tongue and language) and ton (tone), Chinese sketou (tongue), yuyon (language), Japanese shita (tongue), gengo (language), Malay lidah (tongue and taste) and bahasa (language, idiom, manners). Which of these words are variants of the same Lithic idiom, and what were the original semantic contents? The Old Persian hizbana, Persian zuban, Sanskrit jehva, Avestan hizu, Old Slav jezuko, Old Russian inguivis and Malay bahasa are clearly an aberrant group. Old Persian hizbana appears to be from the Lithic ai-sai-ba-na, that which-action-of the lips (mouth)-presents, that is it defines the tongue as the ancillary speech organ rather than the taster, and the rest of that group probably came round that way too. The Chinese and Japanese shai-tau for tongue appears to be using shai- as sensing in place of lai, tasting, or else shai- is acting or active and the -ta element is as in the Norwegian storting their parliament, a talking shop, which comes from the primitive idea that thought (and its expression) was a kind of tau or giving birth in the mind. That would make the Chinese tongue the teller; but it looks as if it is the sensor however on balance of probabilities. The etymologies of Chinese and Japanese yuyan and genko for language are obscure. The Malay lidah for tongue rather convincingly belongs in the lingua group, using –dah, does, in place of ka, makes. It is then a fair bet language is from the other approach, in the Malay case bahasa being made up of the Lithic elements ba-a-sa, mouth-that-acts, mouth action, that is to say speech. But it also has a meaning more like idiom or habitual behaviour, even procedure. This perhaps refers to the alternative Lithic semantic content of ba which from the fleshy lips which pronounce it transfers to flesh and other fleshy, that is muscular bits like the haunches and their role in walking, German bein, leg for instance, whence going and thus how you act physically – reinforced no doubt with bai for being, since alive you are fleshed but dead the flesh perishes.

The tongue group is open for bids as to the proper etymology. It is not to be found in etymological dictionaries, anyway not under tongue. Lingua is the taste maker so perhaps *dingwa is the din maker, whatever the din- bit is. It varies to ton-. In fact Partridge's den- is guesswork, a fabrication on theoretical grounds. We are on our own and it is not easy. But ton- suggests tone and tune. Tone is akin to Latin tonus, and Partridge has identified it as within the group which is principally identified by the Latin tenere (to grasp, hold) and tendere (to stretch) and includes the Greek teinein to stretch and tonos a stretching. Partridge rather absurdly derives hold from stretch by suggesting it originally meant to hold at a stretch. He should perhaps have been asked to actually do some holding at a stretch so we could see what it looks like. He also suggests a stretching means a tone because it is a raising of the voice. Perhaps we stretch (our vocal chords) to sing? It may not be very inviting for the modern mind which by Stone Age standards is moderately refined, but it has to be faced the stretching and grasping may have been the respective contributions of any two parties tai-nai, become-orgasmic. Boys stretch out in a remarkable manner, and girls have a surprise reaction too: their vaginas grasp the penis. They stretch too in an even more remarkable manner in childbirth (nai) or nee in French, nascere, natus (or genascere genatus) in Latin. The word stretch itself is a sexual metaphor, from the Lithic elements s-tai-rai-khai, actual-vagina-rayed-makes, and strike is from the same source as make. Perhaps the clincher is the Greek strephein from s-tai-rai-pahei-ai'n, actual-vagina-rayed-phallus-action, which means to twist. It was evidently an Elvis twisting motion, hip waggling, nowadays presented on TV at every opportunity by hedonist producers in pursuit of permissiveness. Their sexuality is living them rather than the other way about, unaware of their own underlying Bonobo Chimp psychology, indeed shying away from it. Lithic goes back a long way. Perhaps its only virtue is it does explain thinking otherwise inexplicable. But that is a big gain. The semantic content has moved to the effects of stretching, and here we leave the marriage couch and drift off to the heights of Parnassus, with a stretched string, probably a sinew in origin (on a string instrument) which – quite surprisingly in fact – produces a note or tone when scraped. Has it gone orgasmic as a result of the rubbing, our rude forefathers may have wondered. Now a tone is a finely graded sound, which varies with the length of the string and the amount it is stretched, and that leads in to a tune, which is a sequence of sounds with an appeal to our senses, because of its rhythm and pleasing fluctuation of tones. A note is a tone spoken the other way about, putting nau first stressing it in its sense made clear, remarked, marked, a mark or a collection of marks in a written note. Your author is unfortunately virtually tone deaf, and in old age moderately deaf to sounds in general, particularly the high notes produced by the high frequency vibrations of a stretched string, or the vocal chords when they sound the consonants. But composers and conductors have that preoccupied look which suggests they are experiencing some of that same access of emotion from which their lexicon derives. Anyway it does appear that tongues are the talkers and language is a tasting. In forming our lexicon we have switched them about in a typically dream world manner, such as we should expect when our subconscious thinking comes into play. For some the discovery of this subconscious layer of living can be disconcerting. You are not being lived, but you are living beyond your expectations with the submerged part of the iceberg unrecognized.

Speech is a sequence of tones, interspersed with consonants which allow the mind to identify each segment in turn and refer in turn to each segment's semantic content or meaning. At once a lexical plethora is introduced. Where before speech there were only tones – a few finely differentiated howls at best – now it was possible to string these consonantal beads of meanings indefinitely. Crisp sentencing enabled the first words to be compiled. For words as we know them are Lithic sentences or at least phrases with the whole simply committed to memory with any amount of slovening over time in order to ease pronunciation as the constitution of the word is forgotten in conscious thinking and allowed to fall back into the subconscious part of the mind. With the development of linguistic thinking the tones produced by stretching strings rang a bell with the stringing of phonemes to provide composite meanings. The tongue was the maker of these segmented semantic tones, as if the mind itself had been stretched to utter, as

indeed it had. The phoneme la was a tone which had been singled out as exemplar
of speechifying (because speaking started with the la consonant). The tools for
talking are the lips and tongue. Bab were the lips (chapter 4). So ba and la both
together make an uttered tone, whether it is a loud (la-u-da, la-completive-does)
and unspecific bellow or the even less specific bell which merely chimes; or else
erudite speaking as in Hindi bolna to speak or the Danish taler to speak, or the
bans before marriage when the ba is an announcement, or a ban which is a ba-
nai, a say-nay or proclamation of prohibition. The Queensland Aboriginal tongue
Djeri-bal is Bright or Clear-speech, as perceived by those who speak it, by comparison with foreign tongues which are in code.

Just as bitter taste gave rise to taste in general, undifferentiated, so the lye,
a bitter liquid, gave rise to liquid in general and undifferentiated. Latin liquor,
liqui, is to be liquid, to flow, from Lithic elements lai-kau-ai, lye-shaped-that is.
Greek gala, milk is Lithic ka-la, body-lye, and Latin lac, milk, comes from the
same Lithic elements in reverse order, la-kai, lye of the body. Indeed you could
regard the reversal of these elements as evidence of their independence as individual semantic elements. Milk is from mai-lai-kai, drinking-lye-of the body.
All these phonemes we use when we speak stand for their semantic contents,
slovened in articulation and somewhat similarly sometimes slovened semantically
as well. That is the genius of language. The Milky Way is our own original galaxy
seen sideways on from within, with others seen from afar without the milky appearance but given the same name as a giant scientific discovery. Blood has the
following elements: ba-lau-da, flesh-leaked liquid-does. The grammar may not
fit Noam Chomsky's scheme of things precisely but the substantial elements are
clearly germane. When the skin is broken the blood leaks out of the flesh within.
That is a sound scientific perception, if not one calling for profound perceptive
skill, just hominid level thinking.

The slipping down slopes (16) semantic content has informed a host of words
using the letter l for that meaning in English: slip, slide slant slop sleigh sleep
slouch sleet sluice slump, slink, launch, lacquer, blain and bleed, plain and plead,
etc, etc. But lame is from lai-mai, smoothness marred (20) and to lead is from
loop (23) and link (31). The river Lune in Lancashire is slipping down to the
sea. Lune means river, since it comes from the Lithic elements lai-awa-n, leak-
ing-water-one. Lancaster is the fort on the river, but by then it was taken to be
the name of the particular river, as indeed it had become. One can read into some
of these elisions a conqueror's enquiry (perhaps before cutting a throat) "What
is your name for this one then?" "Lune: (it's a river, you coon!)". I have for long
nursed the suspicion these unfortunates were colonists speaking a Mediterranean
patois, with their brains picked out by the primitive Celts. To slope is to have an
inclination as the ladder (16) does, as well as the clinometer. For reasons to be

explained in chapters 10 and 14 the sibilants (s, sh, j, z, and dj) went up, the hum (mmm) went down and la sloped just like a ladder between the two, a diagonal for the figure of which the other two provided the sides. You could follow round it in the mind. Liquid Partridge derives from the Latin verbs liqui (12) to flow (or fare low a back formation from flood), and liquere in Latin was to be filtered, to clarify and so be clear, just what a lye is not; and later on to melt (to become liquefied). These verbs are back formations from liquid, the noun. If you attend to the structure and semantic contents carefully you can get the correct meanings. The lai they had in mind in the original Lithic was the slipping or draining away and not the lye taste – perhaps a tease. Filtering was achieved by lai-kai, making the liquid do its stuff and drain through a cloth, probably a bark cloth only but it will have got out some of the soil and bits at least. Much, indeed most of our linguistic repertoire today, is achieved with a somnolent tongue, but we still think of a language as a tongue. This is because the uttering of consonants with meanings allocated was what discriminated language from prelinguistic cries, and the first was la with a wag of the tongue. As a matter of history the phoneme la introduced language with the first consonant, and all the rest came later.

The bitter taste (2) is also found in honey (Greek meli, Latin mel, French miel, and Greek melita and melissa for the honey bee, giving birth and issuing the stuff respectively) perhaps another tease, but an indication also honey was used mai-lai, masking (negativing, canceling out) a bitter taste ab initio. We don´t know if they already ate baked apple, perhaps in a pie or pai with a pastry lid or cooked topping, from the Lithic pai-ish-tau-rai,surface-fire-become-rayed. But they had been working on their hearths for some time and could have done so. Crab apples (or apples kara-bai, strong fleshed, or skull-fleshed in the case of the crustacean), those available in their day, needed more than a spot of honey to mask the lye, in fact to kill it. Wild apples were bitter fruit. A peach (Greek melocoton, a melon kau-tau'n, a mask-lye-one-completively strong-become) was a very sweet melon indeed. The meanings of ma are covered in full in chapter 10, but it is not possible to confine any chapter to a single phoneme since we find them in use in strings which need explaining. The burning brand which said ish when dunked, or anything else which accidentally caught fire and was put out with water and hissed (said ish) as it died, had flames which leapt upwards. Fire was warm (very) like live forms which clearly all had some of its spirit, warm, active and lively, symbolic of life, which is dowsed in due course also when we die, though we don't hiss when we go, probably because we are somewhat less imbued with the flaming element than fire itself, so that any propensity to hiss in extremis would be proportionate and therefore minuscule. Ma was the opposite of the sibilant, because a sibilant and a hum were the only two consonants capable of being continued as long as you had breath which made them a pair; and whereas the sibilant clearly involved an outrush of breath, a hum needed none, or so little it was disregarded – you can even hum while holding your nose with only a trifle of inconvenience, as if the note were reluctant to have its true nature dragged out of it. Ma was a distress call from babies, when their stomachs were stressed and they were hungry, and their babbling turned to "ma!" Mothers the world over imagined it was a vocative (as indeed it was, or at least a natural expression of need – the little darling is calling for me, and named themselves as mothers with a ma. Mammals, Mamalai, lai from leakers (4), had two (or more) down hanging feeders aboard exuding lye. If sai was up and lively, mai was down and passive. Things which fell to the ground – with varying degrees of damage if landing on your toe – had a bundle of instinctive ma qualities, massive as well as malign and capable of inflicting mortality, dragging you down with them. That was how honey was able to kill or neutralise the bitter taste of crab apples baked in a pie (or roast in the fire for that matter). A melon was a sweet fruit, doing the job itself when ripe (ripe is from the Lithic rai-pai, a rayed piece, the sun's rays causing it to grow, from ge-rau) a mellow one (3), edible (mai) and tasty (lau), ripe and sweet. Marmalade was evidently first made from quinces, maramelon. Here is a turn up for the semantic somersaults the subconscious can accommodate. In the same word there is ma contributing, by masking the lye, to the sweet taste while in the opening mara- (compare French amer, bitter) ma is serving the contrasting semantic purpose, as the opposite of sai used for sweet, and so sour. The quince is bitter sweet, a bitter melon (sweet when cooked). A melody (7) goes further back to the Greek melos for a song, m-ai-la-u, him-that which-la-one, from the original use of la, probably originally just a hummed tune, with lau all the notes of the tune. La (1) was the first stop at the birth of speech and since the Arabic Lat is a semantic stop (it means no, don't), it may have contributed to the nasty taste rather than the other way around: Stop! Don´t drink, it will make you sick: a kindly intervention.

As so often with the oldest Lithic meanings La is not so well represented amongst extant meanings as those derived from it, the tail or root being lost in time as it were, with the meaning chain broadening as it develops. From Greek we may perhaps exhibit melancholia, from mela- black (masked light, rather than masked lye. La is light (from lai-kai-tai) too because oil, or fat, both lye, when kindled (kai) caught fire and gave off (-tai, became) – well light! About this masking: readers should think of the idea involved, that is to say the covering up, as with masking tape, rather than the article to which the idea has been applied (the mask covering over the face). Ma-sa-kai is making a contrast (situation) and so making a death of the sight – not a literal death but a defeat and an elimination or suppression. We are in the world of ideas and they are very flexible and fluid when not constricted by verbage. Greek khole (body lye) meant gall or bile (fleshly lye), where the l's are lai (lye), in the English gall and bile (Lithic ka-lai and bau-lye, body lye and fleshly lye) as well as in the Greek. The historic slovening is from -lai to -le to -l alone. A bale, for instance of hay, Lithic ba-lai, is a loop (28) of vegetable bits, while the bails on a cricket wicket are other (wooden) bits lying (23) flat (20). A bail meaning a pail is from the original item made of skin, pellis (28) in Latin, pelt in English (since the skin encloses (28) the flesh), and to bail out is to empty water out with a pail, or in an aeroplane to empty yourself out, not in this case in a pail but on a parachute – which could in fact be identified as a pail of a sort, a bowl for air rather than a bucket for water. A bailey is a castle's outer encircling (28) wall, originally an outer bank, a ba-lai or encircling bund of earth. It became a walled enclosure and so a prison, whence at its entrance The Old Bailey – you passed through the portals of the court and into the gaol on conviction. Eric Partridge makes out a bale is a ball, but the ball like the balloon is looped in all directions, blown out all round, while the hay bale was held together with a circular twist of straw before binder twine took over. Is that why the ball has two ls? A bailiff comes from Latin bajulus (pronounced baiulus) a travel- ing indentured labourer or porter, later a professional indentured steward with legal responsibilities – his indenture appears to have enabled him to come up in the world, but still with an obligation to complete his stint. To bail cattle was to confine them behind cross pieces, larger versions of those to be found on the tops of wickets. Bail money is paid by a person undertaking, like the bailiff of yore, to confine an accused and produce him to the court when required, on pain of con- fiscation of the bail money. The Latin for a book is liber from which the English library derives. Books were rolls of parchment first, lai-be-rai, lengths (29) be- rolled. Liber in Latin also meant free, from which the Statue of Liberty derives. It had nothing whatever to do with book learning. It was the individual's links (31) (shackles) which were be-raised. Any rai reversed any lai because raising was the opposite of lowering. Without the psychosemantics, the diverse meanings can not be comprehended, so they have been dismissed and phonetics declared random. It is the apotheosis of ignorance – which sometimes seems to be grinning at us.

Flavours come in good and bad; and a Lithic element at first strongly marked for one pole of a presumed dichotomy (or spectrum if you attend to the sequential nature of the distinction as a continuum rather than its categorical differentia- tion) in course of time diffuses with a fine inconsequence to assume the character of the whole. So nasty taste by a natural progression becomes unmarked and signifies merely taste. The nastiness highlights the taste, and its effect is then al- lowed to be spent. Lithic lai (lye), at first marked for bitterness, by a like process assumes the larger character of just liquid or fluid (12), especially if not wholly clear (clear from Lithic ka-lai-a-rai, a form-of-lai-that-rai, visible or translucent) as we find already in Greek gala for milk, (as in galaxy, the milky way, originally with the Lithic elements -ga-la signifying body and lye, ie milk, and the following

−ka or ga-sai of galaxy, go up, the sloping stripe lit up in the night sky, at one time taken to be a ladder to Heaven for the souls of the dead – night, black, death, see the next chapter 10 for ma. We English, with eloquent pragmatism, have added in our word milk the prefix mai- (mi-), drinking or eating, edible, for consumption – perhaps to distinguish milk which is drinkable from other bodily secretions which leak from it which are not. Do not be bothered by the common origin of eating and drinking, as if they were both the same. They were: just ingestion. In India you drink a cigarette (cigret pina), in Malaya you eat a cigarette (makan rokok). In neither place is the smoke in fact ingested but instead passed into the lungs and so as a pollutant into the blood which carries it to the brain as a mild drug with long term physical debauch to pay for the immediate soporificity. We need to reflect here to ga-lai, go lye, often resulted in clear water acquiring an off colour as well as an off flavour. A colour is a ka-la-au-rai, a form-of the lye pro-cess-that one-visible.

It is not a great semantic step from taste to taster, the tongue, and so from lye to langue (French) (11), also the tongue; and the tongue will wag as well as taste, so we still talk in tongues. Language is simply tongue-age, the speech that comes out of our mouths, as babble and ballad, bellowing bawling and yelling do; where the b's are from the same Lithic source as bab, which is indeed precisely mouth in Semitic tongues. The two b's are the two lips which we use to say b, and head the semantic tree for that letter in chapter 4. Much of our utterances around the world we describe as tonguing and mouthing, or using both lips and tongue. Hindi has bolna with conventional root bol- for to speak. As already mentioned (in the opening chapter as an example of meaning diffusion with the Queensland aboriginal djeri-), the Djeribal folk say "-bal" for speak/speaking (speech)/speak-ers (12). Of course an Indian expedition could just possibly have quite recently tipped them off to use the Indo-European form, but one feels that in that case they might have given them a bit more as well, and there remains the difficulty of timing. It is either Lithic or sheer coincidence. With the whole gamut of vocal sounds to pick from, to have arrived at such a neat fit by sheer chance is not very likely. But then if you accept that, you have let in the tip of the Lithic hypotheses at least, because if it was not chance it will surely have been some kind of causa-tion. The vulgar Germanic languages, by contrast with the Australian aboriginal, make a spirt: or in other words ejaculate their speech (from sprechen). Whereas ejaculate merely means throw out and refers almost equally well to speech as to the male orgasm, it has to be said (with the usual nod to Mrs Grundy) that the prime reference of the German metaphor must surely be to their sexual perfor-mance, because there is so much of it in our speech; which is then prayed in aid as analogous to utterances from the mouth. The sounds sputter out.

As between ba and la, the latter is all with the mouth open. We mean business.

We are either going to bawl or sing, tra-la (2). Thus a miners' gala (7) was evidently originally a sing-song before by a kind of progress it turned into a political demonstration. Similarly a gale of wind was originally a howling (or whistling) one until it became just a strong one. Then there are the four calling birds. A sea gull, already mentioned, in the context of a gull wing, as a mnemonic for a type of semantic transfer from one aspect of a named object to another prominent one to which attention has drifted, is a coastal caller, or a squawk-mouth, ghulbean, for the Celts. Here, as an aside, is a simple case of multiple meaning (polysemy of a kind) from a pair of Lithic elements. Gala can be parsed 'go La' or 'earth-ocean', with the two elements providing double duty as 'coastal caller' as described above and island, which we find doing duty in Shri-Lanka or Holy Island in Sinhalese. The simple coastal caller (using the la twice) was all too abstruse for the Germanic races, who added a sea- in front so the point was adequately made. The second calling bird is the nightingale, which obviously enough is a caller in the night, since that is when it delivers most of its song. Goodness knows why! The third might be the less well known Stonegall or yeller (from the) stones, perhaps our forebears even humourously implied the bird was in some sense the voice of the stones: 'stones calling!' The fourth calling bird, the curlew, another night caller in fact, has a call that is readily rendered 'curleeoo'. Their blood curdling screams in the night I heard through my open bedroom window scared the living daylights out of me as a child brought up on the edge of the Breck, which I still remember vividly from seventy five years ago. Now they are hardly heard, modern farming practice having damaged their habitat and the Forestry Commission with their shallow rooted fir trees and the War Department with their tanks between them having sterilised most of the Breck formerly cultivated and providing habitat. Cultivation is essentially to till it, to make it flat and clear of weeds. Cultivate is from Latin colere to till. Cultivation is from the past participle, coltus. Partridge suggests it meant to move around with the root *kwel to move around a place, which makes sense in Lithic *kau-a-lai, place-that-circled. He was no farmer. Just moving around butters no parsnips. Lai (20) is required, not lai (28). To crop the land you need a harrow. Still it suggests he had some idea of lai.

The oceans were presumed to be encircled by a containing lip, (a lip is an orbiting (34) lai-pai or diminutive piece of flesh, it surrounds the mouth) – compare Latin pellis, the skin, a diminutive of flesh surrounding the flesh – since a body of water outside of a natural saucer was a denial of the science of the day. Except in such a fix, it must have seemed obvious that the oceans would have splashed over the edge of the universe and slipped down and away into oblivion. So the inarticulate scientists of the Stone Age knew at least one thing: it was the mission of liquids to settle (19) (Lithic sai-tai-lai, action-become-low) and slip down to the sea. Liquid was the element of default, liquids lacked, they lacked the stiffening

264   On the Origins of Speaking

of solids. It has to be said that as far as it went the science was sound. It required many millennia, perhaps aeons, for science to add much of substance to these original perceptions; and meanwhile language was being built around these original ideas and a few more like them – as can be shown from careful study of the vocabularies of today which contain within them these elementary fossils (some of them coprolites) left behind by the earliest inhabitants.

Of course, for language, fossilization is merely metaphorical. We are only concerned here with the metaphorical usage. There are the two processes: the ossification of a mould, the shape of an original perishable body, by infiltration of the space; and then also the encapsulation of the original molecules; and we should be clear which we mean. With fossils the ossification is common but the encapsulation is rare to impossible. But with language it is the encapsulation which counts. This is because with language the internal structure is the semantics, and it is the semantics which are the hard interior elements for the human mind, the meanings are the bones compared with the phonetics which correspond to the soft tissues. It is thus not without irony that science in approaching language study has dismissed the semantic elements in favour of the phonetics because they can be more readily and reliably accessed in the living species (speech) – and one might add the phonetics on their own can be arbitrarily subjected to schemes of evolutionary process (such as Grimm's Law) which in reality successfully accounts for barely six penn'orth of the whole.

For the idea of down flowing and overflowing of fluids related to the Lithic element la we have a plenum or plethora of percolating metaphors in the English language, as well as others all round the world, many already linked by the truffle hunter type of linguist to the earliest times. To resume them all would be a Herculean task requiring many volumes. But many lazy readers meanwhile will look at Lithic as merely an unlikely fairy tale; and yet perhaps later slowly learn to believe in it. To leak (4) is to make a lai or a draining away. A blain is the flesh leaking, and blisters contain lymph. Lymph is physical lye[2]. Blood, blut in German, is another flesh-leak when the containing skin is cut. Oil (13) is from au-i-lai, which we find clearly in the Greek elaion, that which or in the Latin that one which-lyey-one, (3). The olive tree is the oil tree, Latin olea, Greek elaia, and it was olive oil on which the language formed. The refined petroleum is petra-oleum, rock-oil pumped from under the rock (not having to be pushed up naturally by the natural gas with it). The Latin olere to emit a smell is a gull from the oil which comes to the surface naturally in places and emits a nauseating rotten smell from the natural gas with it, betraying its biological origins in earlier world catastrophes. Oil when kindled lights. Light is from la-i-kai-tai, oil-which-kindled-born. The Latin lux, light, is from la-u-kai-s, lye-what-kindled-flames. The flame (the -s) may just be the substantive ending: the kindling may stand for the enflaming on its own. Translucency manages without the flame; the c was originally a k and smoothed for easier pronunciation. A lamp refers to its wick, a piece or pai, at one time floating em, in lai, liquid, in this case the oily liquid. Lapis, a stone in Latin is a liquid which has developed a skin or surface on it as it cools. It is a derivation which does not spring to mind today. But pa, as surface, pertained to all solids, which after all conspicuously have them, and indeed was the aspect perceived by the rays emanating from the eyes, as in panorama (Greek), the surface that is the eye's capture or target, of everything in view. Pan in Greek was used for everything, and thing in Latin is res, the rayed, the visible, the phenomenal. Pa in Ancient Egyptian was used as the ostensive, as we would say for the.

A snail is from si-nai-lai, brer-presenting-lye. It leaves a slimy trail. Slime is from si-lai-mai, actual-liquid-solid like wet earth (mud, which must, it appears, have originally been pronounced mood, the dual ma of earth and water). For ma as water see chapter 10. A leech (4) is a blood sucker, lai-kai, leak-making. It makes a leak. Lithos, the Greek for stone, is liquid-born (12), with Greek substantive suffix –s, whereas stone is from ish-tau'n, fire-born'one: both from observing the flow of burning lava from volcanoes, cooling to stone. The time which needs to be spent on individual analyses in Lithic elements strung together to make words is not critical to the perceptions which the Lithic hypotheses sketch. If it requires time it just requires it. It becomes a chore when demanded, though a continual delight when allowed to present itself. Evidence is collectable indefinitely, but it makes more sense to examine the hypotheses themselves for credibility. Do they hang together and give an adequate explanation of how our language has been built?

The ocean meanwhile added other ideas, once it was accepted as the repository of the dual instincts of liquids to slope down, go flat and become polluted in their flow to the sea. The skyline at sea is the only straight line in nature apart from a ray of sunlight when dust in the air shows it up; and a liquid surface compared with the land is the only flat. Water goes low and flat together. So la has the psychosemantic contents also of flatness (22) and level/depth (18). Moreover from an island such as an atoll (Maldivian, from a-tau-lailai, that-born-ocean-loopy) the skyline is not only linear but runs all the way round in a loop (28). The same can be seen in a lake, la-kai, an ocean-on land, (if not so regular and seldom actually circular but at least the edge is always continuous and always comes back to where it begins, and dead level). It is the skyline at sea which shows the pure case. To the Greek circle, kirkos we have added the l to make a circle, the original (Greek) version kirkos is akin to krikos, a ring. *Ker, the conjectural Indo-European root recognized by both Partridge and Chambers is akin to the same phonemes we find in church, which in turn is from Greek kurios (Lithic kau-rai-au(s), powerfully-rayed-one (substantive marker), meaning master or lord. Ka-u-rai is also ka-urai, the ka-upraised, the soul beseeching, prayer. Kirie-ka, kirk or church can thus be read as prayer-place, The ecclesiastical Kirie Eleison, properly Kurie Eleeson, means Oh Lord have mercy [on us]. Lai-sau'n is gentle action. Refer to Allah, Al Lahi, The-All Merciful. Ancient Egyptian, as so often, may be summoned in support in this thicket. Khu-t, properly kahuti, in Lithic the superlative of Ka, strong, powerful-become, meaning in Egyptian power. You need force, power, to bend anything, say a willow withy (note here the Indo-European root wei to bend or turn, going in an o), and Chambers at least puts the Indo European *ker to bend first. So the Greek for circle, kirkos, from the Lithic karai-kau(s) is all the bends or bending to completion – until the two ends meet. Our circle then is in Lithic terms bend-bend-loop. What lay behind Egyptian khu-t meaning power? Alas it was another sexual motif. Kau-tai in Lithic is – well, cunt-struck, in receipt of those powerful rays emanating from the vulva (tai) which have the power to make the male stand up, and rant and become aggressive, forcing himself upon the ladies. Gentle readers will be horrified like the gentle author.

With the idea of a natural circular loop or ocean saucer rim it soon got stood up vertically as an orbit. Apollo, the personification of the sun, is Lithic A-pa-u-lau, that-foots it-oo-looped, or goes round in a circle. The sun was assumed to repeat life cycles and die in the West and travel under the earth at nights, as if subjected to gestation before arising in the East in the morning as if new born. The pollo, strictly Apollo, which the Spanish eat is the sun bird because the cock crows at dawn celebrating the sun´s resurrection. Typically, the bird was credited with an intentional motivation – since it crowed at dawn it was greeting the sun, which made it wise, a thoroughly anthropomorphic interpretation. In reality it simply crowed at sun up because the light triggered this response. The Greek goose, anser, from the Egyptian, the one of the sunrise, an early cackler, was Osiris's bird. Osiris, in his original Egyptian avatar AuSarai, was the universal and eternal sunrise, anthropomorphized to make the concept more easily recognizable. With all the rising He acquired a permanent erection, but – perhaps because it was so incessant – it only reached the horizontal, or else as the sunrise he was wed to the horizon, and the horizontal was his signature even in bed. Apollo was being gulled to name the bird. The sun was seen to fly through the sky in a looping line. Birds had the same trick too.

Locality, from the Latin locus, was a circumscribed area (lau) of the earth (kau). The mathematical locus redefined the phonemes – lau, linear one from the skyline (22) and kau in this case go – hence the route or transit (going), with the linearity regarded as involving a continuity rather than a straight line. An enclosure, from to close, combines the Lithic phonemes ka-lau-sai, make-looped or encircled-acting. A sailor is an ocean actor (in reverse order). A galleon, from ga-lai-un, is a go- ocean-one (19), a sea going ship. A keel, on the other hand, from kai-lai makes level (18) a ship, required for ocean going in the swell.

With to limp (16) la picks up its opposition to ka, the driving force, the decisive splitting stroke, with an injured leg causing a shuffling gait. But also it means flaccid, lacking, the opposite of kai, which is hard and strong like the flints which the ka phoneme was supposed to echo. In the same way since the light of day is in opposition to the dark of night, light red and dark red treat red as a continuum with light at the unemphasised pole and dark at the contrary emphatic end; whence by analogy light is similarly opposed to heavy in the spectrum of weight. The Lithic analysis of dark is ta-ra-kai, become-sun-cut. The light has got the chop. The feeble slippage which liquids express appears in rivers. Malay hilir is to pole downstream, to go with the current slipping away downstream. The Australian billabong is an oxbow lake formed when a sharp bend in a river bungs up with silt. Lithic bai-la can be read as going liquid (water) and so river. But billy (bai-lai) is just water in Oz and the idiom is likely the same as the ber- in Malay berbaling, a wind driven rotating (bai-lai'ng going-looping) bamboo sail mounted at the top of a tree with bamboo pipes at the two ends of the blade to whoop all night as the wind blows it round driving off any marauding evil spirits. Ber- has the same meaning as the English be- in becalmed, besotted, etc, merely to be in a continuing state (as after all water is), with the –baling of the berbaling being to go looping as well as baling, uttering, lip-tonguing, la-ing with a ba in it and therefore with a message for any unwelcome callers. What, we may wonder, is the message of this whooper in the night? Is it indeed precisely "Ba la!": "Bum off to the far horizon!" uttered in howling banshee tones, speaking their own fearsome wailing and addictive tongue – in tune with the panic waves of the insane brain? For Senoi boys and girls without a night light it is comforting music, whatever else. The rest of us just have to get used to it, as with the brain fever bird, and sleep through it as best we can. At least we are not likely to be troubled by evil spirits as we sleep! Bili in Oz is continually in a state of being lye, the state of liquid, namely slipping away into the lows and turning lye as it goes like the brackish water often to be found in a billabong, finishing up in the salt sea: just water in fact, not in motion. A billabong is bunged or trapped water, but as it happens from a river altering its course.

With a mixture of water and the solid, heavy element (ma, by contrast with ish the flickering flame which flies upwards) we have lime and slime. The lime was originally glue like bird lime and only later the caustic mix. Try analyzing glue in Lithic elemental meanings. Latin limus, mud, comes from the same mix of liquid and solid elements. English mud has gotten slovened from ma-awa-tai, earth-water-born. Greek leimax, a snail, from Lithic lai-ma-ka-sai, a slime maker – with brer on the end, or is it his habitual action? Greek leimon is a moist meadow, we would call it a water meadow; and limne is a marsh, presenting mud. Our own lemon meanwhile is bitter when eaten, the -mau'n is a definitive suffix to make clear which aspect of lai is to be taken into account: lemons have a sharp taste rather than making off downhill and unless you are thinking in those terms you are not going to be reminded of the fruit, the acidic taste one.

Ships are launched on a slipway (16), and launch is slip down-made (16) from lau'n-khai. A launch is a (small) sea going vessel which may be carried on a ship for launching to take passengers from ship to shore. Chambers notices Malay lancharan, a launch, from lanchar, agile, swift, in turn from Lithic lithe (30) and considers the Malay as entering English via the Portuguese who spoke Indonesian at an early date. But the dates don't fit. With Lithic we have no problem with Malay words having similar phonemes to English ones, across conventional language families. Launch is a doublet with lance, the semantics originally embraced any leap (33), by a thrown lance, or a French arrow (fleche), or a ship on a slipway. A lance is launched through the air in a looping flight like Apollo, the sun on his daily course across the sky, a line (22) and a loop (28) together like the skyline at sea. A sling-stone has a similar trajectory, a sling has a looping action, sai-lai-'n, an action-looping-one. With a leap the loop is described with the feet (or anyway the limbs), pes in Latin and in Lithic pai meaning a lesser-flesh-piece like a skin or a small shoot or minor spur or appendage or any protrusion from the main body like a limb. With bellies and pillows it is merely the looping outline which catches attention – unless with the belly, which gets the b- because it is part of the main body and not an offshoot from it, there is some early butchers' lore there too, the belly organs tasting bitter, lye (3). With labah-labah, the Malay for spider, he is legging it round and round in a loop (33) making his web, the web-maker. It is worth repeating the h originally was a break, like the Cockney h still, between two vowels otherwise liable to elision, and its original pronunciation was ahi, of which our letter 'aitch' is a reminder. The Lithic for the Malay spider was clearly la-bahi-la-bahi, loop-going-loop-going – guess who? There are no other contenders[3]. Gulled from the spider in Malay melabah means to be in a state of agitation, as we would say in English in a spin like the spider. The English spider, much slovened, is from the Old English spinthra, the spinster from Old English spinnan to spin, Lithic sai-pai-en-na-en, action-piece(thread)-of-present-verbal suffix or its original birth. A spinster brings the thread into being. In Old England spinsters, those without husbands, were spinning for their rations (in central accommodation in each village) and presenting thread, in their case by twiddling up the wool by hand wheel, not being blessed with spinnerets themselves. Partridge relates spin also to span, a pair of animals fastened together or the distance between two points like the pillars supporting a bridge, in both cases a linking element, Lithic sai-pa-nai, single-piece-presents/gives rise to. With spinning the single piece comes by way of twisting the strands together. Chambers also raises the meaning for span of the measure of the outstretched hand (between little finger and thumb), found by 1560, but this is probably from the preceding Old English meaning to grasp, fasten, join, and is just the grasp. The law (24) is a collection (of rules), Latin leges, Lithic la-kai, loop made, looped, collected, originally a gathering or harvest, making a loop (28), a sheaf tied with a twist around it, or just a collection of nuts for instance. Partridge and others think it comes from what is laid down (23) metaphorically speaking. Who knows what the subconscious may put together, but the principal prompt is from loop (28). The law is essentially a composite of rules, like the Commandments, of which there were a collection of Ten. It does not prevent other derivations being added. The law lays down a line (22) of conduct (not to be overstepped). The more prompts for meanings the more likely the Lithic will get adopted.

The skyline at sea is shewn in the psychosemantic tree at the head of no less than eleven subsidiary meanings. The ocean as well as very salt is also low (19) and flat (20) viewed from the land (19). Land comes from a special kind, suitable for living, flat cleared land. Compare Malay ladang (20) a jungle clearing for cultivating crops. Cultivating is from Latin cultus from colere (20) to till the land, and till from the Lithic elements tai-lai, to become-level (20 again). The Latin colere is from kau-lai-are, ground-flat-Latin verbal suffix. Compare Latin lamina which Partridge declares of obscure origin, o.o.o. in his jargon – he had no Lithic – "perhaps Chaldean". A lamina was originally a metal plate hammered flat but came to mean any thin plate, sheet, scale or layer. The Lithic is therefore most probably la-mai-na, flat-hammered-presenting, showing a hammered flat surface. Slow is from low, low in speed by metaphor, as opposed to a high speed.with the initial sa indicating the following phoneme lau was to be read with reference to action rather than a nasty taste or any of the other meanings not to do with action. The Lithic is sai-lau, movement-low (19). Low is from lau, the action of water, run down, from its liquid instinct to leak out and away into the lows. A slug goes slow. To lie (23) is to be low and below is the state of being low – compared with what is above! Most surprises lie in the duplex derivations of line (22) and loop (28). A line is long (29) and so is any linear extensive like a lane or a life, physical extensions in space and time. A millennium is from the Lithic massive-length-showing-one, like the grains of the earth (mai, chapter 10) which have been milled – perhaps by those mills of God which grind so slowly and surely, but if not by Charles Lyell's natural geological evolution[4]. A good deal of grinding has been involved in producing the grains of the earth which make up the grounds or ground. Sand is broken stone and sandstone is reconstituted rock grains. The grains may have been produced from slow weathering with water getting into the cracks and freezing and crumbling the rock. Our own domestic efforts have been achieved with grind stones going round crushing grain, and latterly coffee too. Round is another originally sexual metaphor, it is from rau'n-dai, rayed-does, and it just means rayed by the rays supposedly emanating from the genitalia, male and female, which could both be seen to be rounding out their targets, a trick they likely had in emulation of the sun (Ra), a notably shining round in the sky, imagined to be the world's birth canal birthing light into the world afresh every day, and rounded out for the purpose just like Mrs Homo Erectus. It may not be table talk today, but to Homo Erectus it was just common sense. These perceptions, with their astonishing naivety, should surely be sources of delight for anyone without emotional hang-ups about their sex, which after all they can in no way be blamed for having. The grain of wood is from the tree rings marking annual growth which simulate the scratches made by the upper upon the nether grindstone as it goes round. But cut longways wood grain appears longitudinal instead of round. To grind is to go round. Ground and grounds result from the going round. A per-egrination is a going round, with peri- from Lithic pai-rai, the skin of the sun, it's circumference, and so around the outside. Now jump to Peri-Taun-i or Britons – the Greeks called these remote islanders Pretani, Circumference of the World Ones. The Greek was borrowed from the Egyptian. It is all in the book elsewhere but merits a few repetitions.

To clear land is to make it flat (20) but then to make it visually clear as well, from Lithic ka-lai-rai, make-long-visible (chapter 13, Ra). The –rai is there to indicate which of the 40 semantic contents (and there will be many more) of la is intended. Malay lilit, is a turn or twist (28) and tali (22), is a string or cord, from the liana, the long lithe one Tarzan swung on. When it comes to tracing Lithic word formations in other languages it is important to escape from the Indo-European family where borrowings and modifications of an original common stock makes the case for a truly world wide, because psychosemantic, relationship less convincing. In a book in English addressed principally to English speakers, of all ethnic origins, the work involved is formidable, and Malay is picked as a language unconnected with Indo-European, apart from a few recent borrowings, mostly from Dutch, and I happen to have had a year or two in the country at one time trying to learn it. The correspondences of Malay words beginning with la- in Sir Richard Winstedt's excellent two volume dictionary having caught the eye, a list follows with Lithic elements shown for a hundred and one words to indicate the degree of correspondence from Lithic origins which can be shown in a small window beginning with la- and going to lantin, a judge's take, a few pages only of the dictionary. Each word is listed with its dictionary meaning, followed by the relevant column of the psychosemantic tree (from 1 to 39), and then its Lithic elements and the meanings of the elements in English. The Lithic meanings given are meanings and not particularly well represented by the English words used, but they do indicate the original semantic structure of the Malay words for an English speaker reasonably well.

Laboh, trailing, too long, of curtains, sleeve, shirt, from la-bau (16), long-become.

Labu, bottle, calabash, gourd, cucumber from la-bau, long-fleshed (29).

Laban, to chatter, gossip (11), la-ba-un, tongue-lip-one.

Lachak, abundant (of fruit) (16), la-sha-kai, low-height-making, weighed down.

Lachar, abraded, (20), la-kha-a-rai, flat-made-a-rubbing.

Lachi, a drawer (in furniture), (16) (22), la-khai, slip-making, a slider.

Lada, pepper, (3), la-da, lye-does.

Ladaian, riverine fish trap, (16), la-dai-an, flow down-does-one.

Ladam, horse shoe, (20) (28), la-da-'m, loop-does-one.

Ladang, (jungle) clearing, (20), la-da-ng, flat-become-one, land.

Lading, curved chopper, (28), la-dai-ng, loop-become-one.

Ladong, batu ladong, plummet or sounding lead,(16)(29), la-da-un, level-does-one. Batu = Stone.

Ladun, opera singing, (7), la-da-un, la-do-one, sing-do-one.

Laga, clash, collide, (31), la-ka, link-strike.

Lagi, more still, still more, (22) (29), la-gai, linear/long-going. (Linear implies extensive).

Lagu, tune, air, intoning, (7), la-ga-u, la-go-one, sing-make-one.

Lahan, melody, (7), la-iha-'n, la-it that-one. (Something one meets with when singing! Got it?)

Lahang, palm sap, (3), la-ahi-ang, a leaking/lye-one. Compare Senoi 'kruing' (growing) a tree, the kru- carries the semantic content not merely of growing but of growing superlatively, the big hard plants.

Lahar, mere or forest pool, (12) (19), la-iha-a, liquid-it that-one.

Lain, other, another, different, (31), lai-nai, linked-negative.

Lejeng, lejang, unmarried person, (21), lai-gang, slow-goer, low ka one.

Lajor, a long strip of land, (29) (20), la-gau-a, long-land-one.

Laju, fast, (29), la-sha-u, distance-speedy-one.

Lak, a sealing wax, (12) (31), la-kai, liquid-[when]kindled.

Laka, a liana, (30) (31), la-ka, link-make.

Laklakan, gullet, (12) (11), la-ka-la-ka-'n, liquid-make-tongue-make, the glugger.

Lalab, cold vegetables eaten with curry, (15) (13), la-la-bai, light-taste-vegetable.

Lalah, gluttonous, (29) (13), la-la-hai, many-tastes-enjoying.

Lalai, dawdling, dreamy (of lovers), inattentive (of workers), (21) (21), la-lai, slow-slowy.

Lalang, tall grass (growing after jungle felling), (29) (20), la-la'ng, long-long 'one.

Lalat, house fly, (39) (39), la-la-ti, fly-fly-little.

Lalu, pass by, and then, (29) (16), la-la-u, long-slip-past.

Lama, long time (past), ancient, (29), la-ma, long-dead (time).

Lambai, to wave (one's hand), (28), la-em-bai, loop-of-limbs.

Lamai, brother- or sister-in-law, (31), la-mai, link-[of] marriage.

Lambak, pile, (confused) heap, (31), la-em-ba-kai, link-of-bits-made. Compare pile, pai-lai.

Lambat, slow, (21), la-em-ba-tai, slow-of-pace-become.

Lambong, flank (of body), (22), la-em-bau-'ng, line/side-of-dual-fleshed-one (ie of the body).

Lambut, bulge, (28), la'm-bau-ti, loop-of-flesh-thing. Compare belly.

Lampai, slender, graceful, (30), la'm-pai, lithe-of-limb (the 'm or of is either prefix or suffix).

Liok, liompai, swaying, (30), lai-au-em-kai, lithe-that one-of body, lai-au'm-pai, lithe-that one-of-limb.

Lampan, to wash for tin, (16), la-em-pa'n, leak-of-pieces-verbal suffix.

Lampas, polish (furniture, etc.), (16), la-em-pa-s, slippery-of-surface-action.

Lampias, flow, gush, (16), la-em-pai-a-sai, slip-of-surface-that-action.

Lampin, baby's nappy, (28), la-em-pai-'n, loop-of-covering-one.

Lampir, enclosure to letter, annexe, (35) (31), la-em-pai-a, link-of-covered-one.

Lampit, a (rattan) mat, (20), la'm-pai-tai, flat-of-cover-thing.

Lampong, floating, (12), la-em-pau-'ng, liquid-of-surface-one.

Lamu, seaweed for making jelly, (12), la-ma-u, ocean-edible-one.

Lan, nauseated by food, (13), la-nai, taste-negative.

Lanang, manly, (29), la-na'ng, long-orgasm-one.

Lanar, lanau, (ooze, slime) (12), la-na-a, la-na-u, liquid-ejaculate-one

Lanchap, tapering and slipping out, (17), la'n-kha-pai, sloping-shape-piece.

Melanchap, to masturbate (of males) (4),me-la'n-kha-pai, a-leaking-make-penis.

Lanchar, swift, fluent (reading), (16), la'n-khara, smoothly-to make/go.

Lanchok, a large puddle, (12), la-en-shau-kai, liquid-of-deep-of the ground.

Lanchor, gush (as out of pipe), (16), la-en-sha-u-rai, leaking-heightened-verbal.

Landa, wash for gold, (16), la'n-da, leaking-does. A sieving action lets the water drain out of the pan.

Landai, shelving (of shore, horses back), (17), la'en-dai, sloping-does.

Landak, porcupine, (28), la-en-da-kai, coiled-become-sharp.

Landasan, anvil, (20), la-en-da-sa'n, flatten-does-fired.

Landoh, long, trailing, (29), la-en-tau, long-ing-become.

Landut, sag, (28), la'n-dau-tai, looping-down-becoming.

Lang, eagle, (16) (39), la'ng, gliding, glider.

Langah, agape, wide open, (28) (29), la'n-kahi, looping-shaped.

Langcha, rickshaw, (22), la-en-sha, unenergetic-action – for the passenger.

Langgaian, drying platform (for fish), (20), lang-kai-an, flat (or slat)-shaped-one.

Langan, subscribe (for newspaper), club together to buy, (31), la-en-ka'n, loop/linking-to make.

Langang, tungang-langang, head over heels, (19), la'ng-ka'ng, low-one-head-one.

Langas, free, without ties, (31), la-'n-ka-sai, linking-cut-action.

Langeng, eternal, lasting, (28), la-ng-gai-ng, linearly-ongoing.

Langir, leaves used to ash the hair, (3), la'n-kai-a, lye-make-one/that.

Langit, sky, (22), la'n-kai-tai, skyline of-land-thing, land above the skyline.

Langkah, a pace or stride, (29), la-en-kai, length-of-going.

Langkai, slim, graceful, (30), la'n-kai, lithe one-of shape, lanky.

Langkan, latticed verandah, railings (of bridge), (29), la-n-ka-n, long-shape-one.

Langkapura, Ceylon, (19), Lan-ka-pu-ra, Ocean-land-Holy, Holy Island.

Langlang, to globe trot, (29), la-en-la-en, far-going-far-going. (also eagle-eagle or glide-glide in Malay)

Langsar, tall and slim, (30), la-n-sa-rai, lithe-and-up-raised.

Lansing, log brake on a bullock cart, (21), la-en-sai'n, slowing-of-movement.

Langsir, hangings, curtains, (16) (21), la-en-sai-a, slipping-vertical-one, hanging-one.

Langsong, very far or soon, last, (29), lau-ng-sau-ng, long-one-action-one, (long=extensive=extremely=very). "Terlangsong perahu boleh balek, terlangsong chakap ta' boleh balek", "Boats that have gone too far can be brought back, but not words".

Lanjai, slender, fragile, (30), la-en-kai, lithe-of-body.

Lanjar, long, stretching far (as lianas), next, forthwith, (29), la'n-gara, long-one-goer, (=langsong).

Lanjam, plough share, (28), la-en-ga-mai, linear-go-earthing.

Lanjut, too long, (of breasts, life, etc), (29), la-en-shau-ti, length-of-very-thing. Dan sa lanjut nya, and the length of it = etcetera. Nya is from en-ia, of it or of him (or her).

Lantai, decking, floor, (20), la'n-tai, flat-become, flattened, made flat, a flat (surface).

Lantak, ram in (pegs, powder, food, etc), la-en-ta-kai, low-in-to-strike. Pelantak = ramrod, pestle, or male lover. (sic!)

Lantam, loud, conceited, (9), la'n-tai-mai, entoning-become-great.

Lantar, outstretched on the ground (corpse, etc), (23) (29), La'n-tai-a, lying-become-one.

Lantek, launch, install (ruler), appoint, (19) (39), la-en-ta-kai, slipping/fly-become-strike/make. Pelantek, spring spear trap for game, a launcher.

Lantin, payment to a judge additional to a fine, (3) (12), la-en-ti'n, bitter/oily-thing.

Selangkang is the perineum. Selang is to let slip (from between the fingers?) and so intervening. Selang dua hari is let slip two days between, and so every third day. Similarly selang is a (narrow) passage between two buildings (you can let yourself slip through), a line of passage or a movement line (sai-la'ng) or alignment. With the perineum, it is by no means clear if the slippage for the Malay idiom is between the two limbs or the two orifices. The Greek, peri-nai-u'm, is clearly around the two orifices. With the Malay probably the reference is to both, an inter-regnum par excellence, both ways on.

These constructs are clearly tentative, playing with syntax from the time when speaking was new, and we were only gradually accustoming the mind to the idea of a grammar. The 'it-that-one' and '-do' or '-does-one' are almost redundant fillers, but they are understandable mind games, given that the methodology was entirely new. The idea of grammar was slowly developing in the mind, a new mode of thinking, a construct without precedent before speech – and somewhat prior to any transformational potential.

Notes.

1.   Silver is probably from Assyrian sarpu, from surrupu meaning to smelt (Chambers). The Ancient Egyptian is hetch (Partridge), Lithic ahi-tai-shai, that which-born-fired, smelted, not unlike the English stone. Silver was just another metal (Lithic mai-ta-lai, a solid-born-liquid) extracted from a (different) ore. It was also notably shiny (sai) like the flame.

2.   Physics is from Greek phusis, Aristotle's term. It actually referred to the action of life forms, particularly the biological nissus or drive for change seen in growing, burgeoning, the oomph which was (paradigmatically) also exhibited by the male pahai (the joy piece) in action, which grows in short order when rayed. Phusis is from the Lithic elements pa-hai-u-sai (s), shoot-joy-one [when]-active: the rampant penis in short. It exhibits the yen for growing to an extraordinary degree, embarking on another trip at the drop of a hat. Anyway it has virtually nothing to do with the mechanical concepts of modern day physics, to which it has been transferred.

3.   We once (about 1930) had from a turkey mated with a chicken a brood of churkeys given us, but their brains had got mixed up and they spent their whole time circling obsessively and died off young. They had brown feathers but long bare necks and purpled heads. They were ugly ducklings.

4.   Sir Charles Lyell, The Principles of Geology, 1830, which demonstrated the

evolution of the rock strata by vulcanism, erosion, glaciation, etc, based on the temporal sequencing of the strata by means of the microscopic shell collections included in all the sedimentary depositions. Lyell assumed the shells had evolved and guessed those with more pronounced features were posterior to those which were less developed. Much of Lyell's book was worked out using my great grandfather's shell collection on visits to Merton. They were barristers together in London. Lyell's book also includes the Merton Stone, the largest glacial erratic in Great Britain, weighing (at a guess) some 25 tons, which we dug up in the seventeenth century when digging for marl (at fifteen feet below the surface) to strengthen the soil later in aid of Coke and Townshend's Norfolk four course rotation. Marling was done as early as 1664. Species evolution was dangerous stuff in 1830 and although the book (which Darwin took with him on his five year round the world cruise on The Beagle) was full of the heretical conchology (since shells are species) it could not be mentioned, so that in 1859 when Darwin finally came clean, under the duress of losing any claim to his life's work if he did not publish in face of the young Alfred Russell Wallace's paper on evolution by natural selection addressed to the Linaean Society, he claimed it was his idea and not Lyell's. Darwin was concerned his book might lead to insurrections and more head lopping – the French Revolution was recent history – and had opted to publish posthumously. His fib about species evolution, pretending he had thought of it, was so his old tutor would not be sent to Coventry by Queen Victoria, and dons in dog collars. Darwin's espousal of natural selection was all his own. The media and then the history books followed his misrepresentation, now the received version of events. Lyell's book was recently republished so the evidence for this demythologizing of the history books is readily available, with the evolving shells on almost every page. It was a risky guess, since the convolutions of the shells might have been getting less. But it worked, because biology and biological evolution are anti-entropic, a kind of teleological impetus neo-Darwinism overlooks, and is not readily explicable.

CHAPTER 10

THE PHONEME MA

As the reader ploughs through the book chapter by chapter there is bound to be some impatience with any repetitiousness, but it is hard to avoid. Any points missed on first reading can easily be picked up by referring back to the relevant chapters. Wise virgins will have already annotated the margins in pencil as they read for easy reference later. In any case, this chapter will endeavour to deal with new stuff only. The psychosemantic tree for Ma is on page 279 and 280.

Just mmm without any articulation is a hum. Only Ish and mmm, s and m, the hisses and the hums, can be sounded continuously as long as you have breath. All the other consonants are stops[1]. This is not regarded these days as in any way significant, but there appears to be evidence that when the search for natural meanings of our first articulations was on, at the birth of language, the fact was regarded as highly significant. Nowadays a hum is used as a filler in a sentence while the speaker searches for the next word or phrase. Most recently a similar use is made of an articulation which can be represented phonetically as Yn-O, a slurring of "you know", but stripped of any semantic content and used simply as a meaningless hum or filler. Anyway as a first perception the hisses and hums were paired. Then came a search for semantic contents. To utter a hiss there is a clear expulsion of breath whereas with a hum there is not. Indeed you can hold your nose and still hum with only some minor inconvenience, but you can not even begin to utter a sibilant without the expulsion of air. It was therefore natural enough for the adjectival mind to pair off and then to oppose and contrast these two sounds and their semantic contents and that laid them open to dialectical thinking, given that dialectical thinking was around[2].

The phoneme Ish (with the vowel element in front because that is how the flame articulated its name, ishshsh, when you dowsed your burning brand at dawn in the nearest puddle) is examined in detail in chapter 14. Whereas Ish was, as a sound, lively like the flame and positive like the breathing out, Ma was therefore identified as lifeless and negative, and as the flame springs upwards, Ma was taken to go down. Moreover because the hum was regarded as a filler with a vanishingly indefinite semantic content the sibilant came to be regarded as having a precising function. Well it stands to reason, if you see the phonemes as in opposition. Because for convenience of reference the chapters dealing with original phonemic semantic contents are arranged in alphabetical order (with some elisions as with chapter 6 which lumps Da and Ta together, and chapter 14 which lumps together ish and z and j, because they have been lumped together over the aeons by the human mind; the clear differentiation between voiced and unvoiced consonants was a comparatively late development), Ma´s derivative and subsidiary role in this relationship has been reversed and the semantic contents it picked up from contradistinction with the sibilant are examined first in this chapter. Readers have a clear choice here. Either they can flip to chapter 14 and then flip back, or they can take the chapter 14 meanings of the sibilant on trust for the time being.

Simply because they were taken as opposites, at the two ends of the semantic spectrum, or more accurately at the two ends of various semantic spectra, the mid positions could be called up by linking the two of them together, a bit of a muchness neither the one thing nor the other. The synthesis equally had the elements of both with the meaning of a combinated dish in accordance with dialectical thinking. You can relate this equally to the scientific notation giving a result and its accuracy as a value x plus or minus y. The x is then a middle value. This was not terribly good math because positives and negatives should refer to a single criterion and not with whites positive and blacks negative; but it was Lithic thinking precisely. In Albanian mesit actually means middle today, which suggests the dd in middle comes originally from the sibilant via th. This is confirmed by the Aeolian Greek messos and the Attic Greek mesos (the single s is more like our z) – whence our Mesopotamia, the land intermediate between the two rivers, the vehemently flowing Tigris, the tiger river at one end of the spectrum, and the well flowing Eu-phrates at the other. A tigerish river is a gull. The tiger is mistress growler, but the river never growls, it just flows fiercely. Similarly the technical term mesocephalic means with an intermediate shape of head, cucumber at one end of the spectrum and pumpkin at the other. Yet Eric Partridge[3] curiously prefers to refer back to an original dh for the sibilant in meso, in spite of Armenian maj and Gothic midjis also, both relatively ancient languages in the context of modern historical linguistics although only recent arisings in the context of the six hundred thousand year history of language – since first it was spoken, according to the Lithic hypotheses. The aspirated consonants in Partridge's day were taken to be typical of the rough pronunciations of our rough forebears. Assuming that it is true, it is no reason to dismiss the sibilants.

Rather more imaginatively, shamanism was the exploitation of intermediaries between the living and other worldly states. A sham is the one thing representing itself as another significantly different thing, often an opposite, for instance an untruth represented as the truth. A shampoo, from the Hindi, is in origin a head massage, a kneading up and down, rather than just a hair-wash. The -poo was probably from the Lithic elements pa-u, an indication it was to be done with both hands, an up-down two-handed; now transmogrified into a bottle of soap suds: quite a nice example of semantic drift by means of gulling. When we look at Sanskrit (originally Shamskrit) and Prakrit, it appears to suggest the grammarians behind Sanskrit were the inheritors of the Shamanistic tradition, high priests of learning and linguistics, while the common folk who preferred the easier Prakrit dialect for everyday affairs were locked into the mere physical sensational every-day world despised and even shunned by the intellectual elite. The pra- is from the Lithic pa-irai with the -krit the speech bit. The pa-irai compares quite well with the phi (Φ) in the cognitive spectrum which is sketched in chapter 16, page 505.

The psychosemantic tree for Ma is opposite, with numbers in brackets in the text of this chapter referring to the numbered entries in the tree. Many of the meanings are illustrated in the text with Chinese phonemes, as well as others. Chinese really requires a chapter on its own like several other historic languages, but owing to the exigencies of space it has been necessary to postpone these chapters to a subsequent volume, in preparation and already partly written.

Reviewing the hums, apart from the ums (2) which are plain fillers with no meanings, represented in the chart by mm, next are the 'ms, m's or thingumybobs (3) or items of one kind or another, quite common across Africa in the Hamitic languages but with a fair representation world wide. The Hamitic 'm is easily memorable – if a trifle inaccurately – as him (5.2), a substantive prefix as in the Swahili mtu, a person, human being, individual, man, Lithic m-tau, one-born, down the birth canal. Mtu mume is a man, a born person him who plants/im-pregnates and mtu mke a woman, a born person whom made pregnant. Then there is mtoto, a child, young person, offspring, offshoot, descendant, from the Lithic one-born-born, that is just born and so in an early stage of development and subordinate position. Mdache is a German, a straight copy from Deutsche with a him in front (and an imprecise ear). We can however think of the 'm in our English him (and in me) in much the same way. 'M can clear away a lot of confusion where a hum otherwise defies analysis. It amounts to a cockney m, a bit like a cockney h, which is used to avoid elision of consecutive vowels (and then in time the h survives after the first protected vowel has dropped out). The cockney m adds a hardly necessary qualifier on the way to precising the meaning.

Psychosemantic trees have achieved a complexity over the millennia which leaves analysis a juggling trick, because potential meanings abound. For every phoneme there is a network, a whole texture of meanings in which the structure of every word is caught up; and perhaps unsurprisingly many words appear to be caught in the net at numerous points. In English a mare was originally just a horse, pronounced not so far away from the Chinese 'maa which also means a

THE PSYCHOSEMANTIC TREE FOR MA

The Phonetic Tree

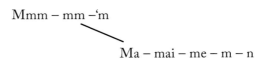

Mmm – mm –'m

Ma – mai – me – m – n

The Semantic Tree

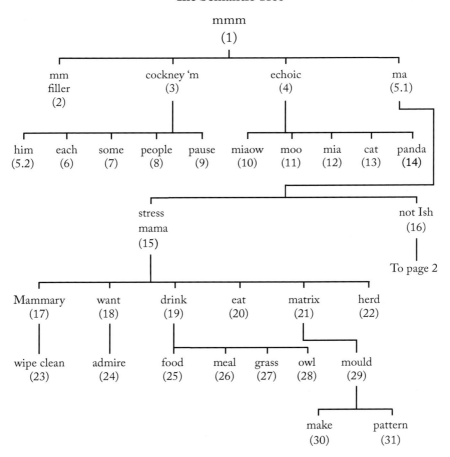

THE PSYCHOSEMANTIC TREE FOR MA

Page 2

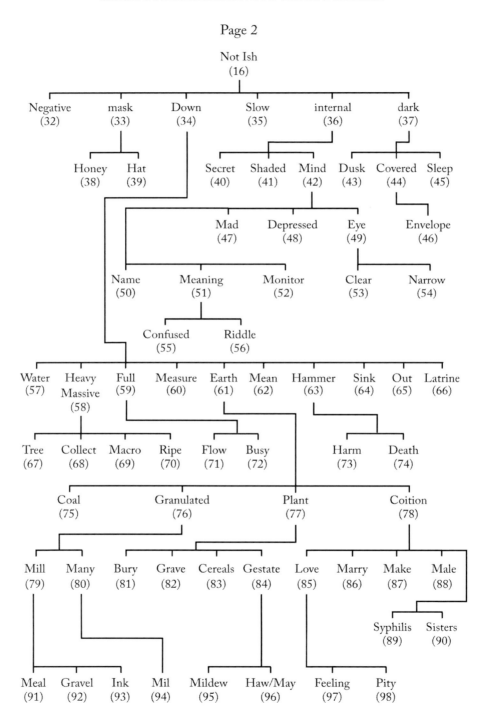

horse (inter alia!). But then the mare got identified with the female animal, probably because it began with a ma- and that triggered the idea of gestation; although
it might as well have triggered impregnation, the planting of the seed, and that
could have made a mare into a stallion. Since it just meant horse, the 'm started
out as a cockney 'm. Yet it still might have been a full blown ma-, because the
Lithic semantic contents include heavy (58) so ma-are could have been a heavy
goer. Moreover ill treatment of a horse, when breaking it for instance, could make
a horse spiteful and dangerous, and there will surely have been some of this in the
stone age, so that a harmer (73) perhaps came into the equation. The gustatory
facility is then kept for the mother, which in Chinese is maa too, while we say ma
or, on the far side of the pond, mom (pronounced maam). It is worth repeating
from time to time these psychosemantic promptings arose spontaneously from
the subconscious mind in the age of the Pleistocene when first we were lisping
in linguistic mode, as they do so still for anyone attentive to the poetic muse.
Readers other than the poetically inspired may wish to query this, but even the
most bovine will undoubtedly catch themselves out from time to time, if only
responding to music.

Meanwhile in Maori, to ring the changes, motu, from the Lithic 'm-au-tau,
him-that one-severed (two-ed) meant – well, severed or cut. But from severed
the Maori meanings proliferated via the idea of cutting off, and so to separated,
to making a separate thing, and so anything obviously separated such as an island alone in the sea, and then also a grove of trees, probably planted for ritual
purposes, in a wild wood. The island separation was an act of nature, the grove a
copycat procedure for human purposes. Both the island and the grove come with
a cockney 'm, and chasing after any meaning from the semantic tree seems otiose.
The meaning flow of Maori thinking is instinct with original Lithic thinking like
many tongues undefiled with overmuch modern ornamentation. To the Maori
mind maroke spells dry, with the Lithic 'm-a-rau-kai, him-that-rayed-makes. It
may not seem exactly like dry to the modern mind, but then we are not any longer consciously composing with Lithic phonemes and their devious meanings in
mind. That leaves out whether our primitive forebears were either. It may be they
were not as yet fully conscious as we understand consciousness to be, but that is to
wander into fascinating realms way beyond the remit of any linguistic study.

Meanwhile if the rays were the rays of the sun, the paradigmatic ones, what
does the raying make? Surely it made the washing dry just as it does today. It
makes the observer dry too, even today, come to think of it, many millennia later.
In Maori again maro means stiff and hard, and the Lithic seems to indicate another cockney 'm. Ma, weight (58), pressing down, grinding yields soil and grains.
The grains were mankind's contribution. The soil and sand were nature's. Both
were nothing stiff; and other semantic contents are similarly contra indicated.

The rest of it makes perfect Lithic sense if we treat the m as a cockney'm: maro from 'm-a-rau, him that rayed, roused and raised, the male penis in receipt of the feminine emanations, rays, causing it to stiffen and harden. Maro is a straight gull from the genitalia. Tarzan knew nothing of the circulation of the blood, nor of the spongy tissue of his genitalia. Sex was for him magic. It was a powerful and generally disastrous juju, but that is beyond linguistics again. Primitive perception had no other theory for the process. Perhaps stone freezing after ejaculation from a volcano – eruptions were likely commoner in the Pleistocene – will have added to the science of the Pleistocene couch. It will surely have fallen under the same rubric, the old men adding their sixpennyworth of understanding, and rounding on any young shaver who demurred. The sequencing of the volcanic eruptions is not precisely the same as for the animal penes, but then nature and the animal kingdom were already regarded as in some degree at least in conflict. In place of the cockney 'm however it is possible to follow a different route again. Suppose the rays which caused the hardening and firming were to be defined as planting or impregnating rays, the 'm instead of him would be from mai (78), impregnating – eroded admittedly. We would perhaps more readily expect mai- with a resultant meiro or some such rather than plain maro. None of this means a Maori speaker, quite as gentle and refined as any other, using maro to mean stiffen is conscious of the derivation. It is a fair bet he or she is not, any more than an Englishman using the word stiff derives it from siti-pahei, feminine action-of [on the]-phallus; or using hard derives it from i(h)a-rai-dai meaning it-that-raying-does, with a cockney h to separate the opening vowels i-a. H was originally pronounced ahi whence our vestigial aitch in English. As a separator of two juxtaposed vowels it could separate i from a following a as well as a followed by i.

Immaculate, without spot, is derived from the Latin macula which means a mesh, the Lithic perhaps 'm-a-kau-lai, him-that-joined/crossed-lines (or in linear directions), which would make a net. Maculate is thus become gridded and enmeshed and so marked, and so blemished, whence immaculate is unblemished. Psychosemantic contents can not be derived against the grain. You can get from a mesh via a mark and a blemish to the meaning of unblemished for immaculate, but you can not get from an impregnation to a mesh. The impregnation is a rational development of opposing ma to ish: from down to weight, from weight and down to earth – it is heavy and down below your feet, having settled there in accordance with its instinct. To earth seed is to plant it and planting seed is impregnation. The cockney 'm, him, meanwhile is merely a matter of articulation, and Lithic is understanding the utilization of the process by which human whimsy put together meanings by metaphor, and gulls. Gulls fly only in one direction, like the hypnotic fluttering of papers across the screen in one direction which Microsoft offers when downloading data from the internet courtesy of Bill Gates, as nice an example of the anthropomorphisation of information technology as you could wish for. That unidirectionality provides some framework of restraint when discovering the correct derivations from the Lithic idiom. A match, 'm-a-shi-kai, is a thingumybob-that-fire-makes. Originally it meant a torch (a burning branch) or a lamp wick and so in due course the match that comes in a box, shortened in military slang to a BOM or box of matches. The Lithic applies to torches, wicks and matches with equal aptitude, which is why the meaning has slid effortlessly from one to the other. Compare the Arabic iskra, a spark, from ish-kara, fire maker. The spark is the source of the flame as well as scattering from it. Making originally meant putting together or building, perhaps from 'm-a-kai, him-that-making, but also ma-kai, earth-kindling (61), that is planting, planting seed, procreating (78) and so making. Making was also making cakes, from kneading or moulding (29), pressing the mass (58). The builder probably started out a joiner or wood worker, since quirkily but authentically ka as well as signifying the flaking of flints by striking them also acquired the semantic content of joining them together again as well – not a practical exercise but a logical one. You can fit a flake back onto the core and that is the joint between the two, where they meet and join in perfect fit. The ka which is the echo of the flaking survives to identify the interface of the pieces put together, the joint, where they join. Kare could mean to join as well as to flake and to kindle. The semantic catena could not pass for logic today but it could for our earlier forebears, accustomed to big fuzzy categorizations in the absence of any large lexicon. The verbal form to match or make a match, to join or bring together gives us a love match and at one time, obsolete now, a spouse akin to Old Norse maki a spouse (86). The Lithic 'm-a-kai can even be read as him-that-joined. But it could have come too from ma-kai referring to the earthing or planting (77) of seed involved in espousal. Ma-kai, as in our English make, is also derived from earthing, impregnation (78). The earth-mother springs to mind. But it has also at the same time been derived from moulding, striking the mass, pounding the dough or the clay slip. Immaculate conception makes a baby without any human impregnation, the planting of any human seed. It is not really germane to enquire which derivation is correct because both intimations arise from the subconscious semantic lexicon, and are not mutually exclusive but on the contrary mutually reinforcing, and that is what deriving making teaches us. We are living in a dream world and it is not a mathematical one. More is the pity perhaps. Matins, from the French matin, morning, is from the Lithic 'm-a-tai'n, him-that-is born'one, and so him that is just born, namely the sun. When the sun is just born it is morning. There is the additional gloss of the ma, dead (74) sun returning to life, the sun coming over the horizon shining light.

A mattress was originally a sleeping rug you wrapped around you to sleep, a douvet more than an underlay, 'm-a-ta-rai-sa-sai is the Lithic analysis which can be read as him-that-drawn/pulled [around you]-is-cosey/warm (Chapter 14). Me and mine as well as him all have a cockney m. Ai is I. Me is from 'm-ai. Mine is from 'm-ai-nai, 'm-ai plus adjectival marker –nai. See chapter 16 for the vowel meanings. Nai really means showing or presenting here, and so representing, whence the adjectival usage (chapter 11). Him is the plum example of the cockney usage. It has a cockney h at one end and a cockney m at the other, as well as the initial vowel missing, the middle letter being the only surviving one with much in the way of semantic content, and that from a vowel with very early meaning attributes, and it has to be said very general ones. The letter in the middle is i, relict of the ai the h was put in to protect, but later losing the initial a of the original ahi. In Ancient Egyptian the hieroglyph for h was actually pronounced ahi. In The Lord's Prayer in Egyptian "Pata ahi" was "Our Father". The thinking appears to have been a-i, that-[of]plural[we]. But as pata could be plural also it meant Our Fathers too; and it was thus the name of their Ancestor God, commonly (but quite erroneously) treated as "Ptah". Egypt is from Hoiku-Ptah or better A-u-I-kau-Pata-ahi, That-where-begotten-Our Fathers, or as we would say it The Fatherland. You see much the same in economics, which is from the Greek. The Greek in turn is closely patterned on the Ancient Egyptian whence actually came most of the Ancient Greek philosophy the West prides itself on. The Egyptian was a polyglot lingo formed over generations of Semitic colonial conquerors farming the local population and gradually acclimatizing and going native, chiefly because of concubinage. Pharaohs got darker not from the tropical sun but from the Hamitic genes. The scribes however kept the language for the most part Semitic meanwhile. Our aitch bears traces of the Egyptian style ahi. Our –tch is probably from kh, and the articulation as it has come down to us through the generations probably started out as ai-khai, joining a and i or making ai, an elaboration compared with Egyptian ahi, which simply articulates a followed by i.

Mete and meed, both now a little passé, concerned with right action and our bounden duty, are akin to measure and so come to mean to apportion also. The Old English was metan to measure, originally to be weighed (66). Further back the Gothic was mitan to measure too, suggesting the proto Germanic (Nazism's Ur-spreche) was metanan to measure, and the prototypical measurement was weighing to discover the genuine quantity (58). Meed meaning recompense, reward, payment, rent, hire, which are all from ma to weigh (66) had nothing to do with the cockney 'm or m'.

As a medial intrusion or as a suffix 'm the attribution is sometimes troublesome. With the Thai word lom meaning wind for example the Lithic lau can represent the soughing of the wind in the trees as in the Old English gale, leaving the 'm as simply a terminal substantive indicator, thingumybob or thing. But there is always the thought that the real semantic content is simply being overlooked, and the thingumybob 'm prayed in aid to get rid of it. In our own broom cupboard meanwhile the broom is a utensil for beraying the rubbish, the Lithic is berau'm. Both the completive-substantive -u and the 'm or thingumybob on the end apparently are serving here merely as noun markers. In fact there are even traces here of the same idiom as the Ancient Egyptians used with their unpronounced determinant glyphs which they put at the end of a spelling in hieroglyphs, to give you a clue. A similar termination is in a boom, a reverberating sound beginning fancifully enough in a b- because our own utterances started out that way, and ending in a cockney 'm because when we end the air flow accompanying the oo vowelisation it produces that closure. Neither consonant actually features in the sound we hear yet the oo bit is clearly echoic with a clear cut commencement and a reverberating terminus represented by a hum. A bomb potentially makes the same noise, but it is not as emphasized as the boom being only potential rather than striking the ear. The bang or boom will come later. The entirely silent anti submarine boom meanwhile adds a semantic content to the initial boo-, a blockage or bung, from way back in chapter 4; with a little help from a beam by way of a berm, and actually first cousin to our English boys and the even more directly insistent Irish bwoid or penis (both with bunged urethras). The Chinese mind appears to treat bu- similarly as a no-go area but desexualized as a simple negative, or not. Perhaps we should look at the Malay bukan here which means on the contrary and so not, and gives us an important clue to the thinking behind the Chinese bu. You have to put it together with the antediluvian propensity of the human mind to think in terms of contrary entities, a fanciful whimsy responsible for every kind of philosophical absurdity (especially Marxism); so that just to voice the dual vowel, as with bu, prompts already for a contradiction. Bu could of course just mean bung: your thinking amounts to a blockage. It could even refer to those dual bits the boars in Borneo so rudely expose to view behind. Were the Mandarins, consciously or not, saying balls? A brim, like a broom, is compiled around the ray but in this case it is be-rayed from the fully frontal sun with a clearly marked circular periphery, a metaphor fitting a hat or a bowl quite well, in the latter case at the top at the same time as round the periphery. That is why brimming is up to the top. A broom, from be-rau'm, has many rays to do the work.

The Greek omphalos, the navel or umbilicus, has a marginal cockney 'm in a medial position. Severing the umbilicus in the stone age, with a flint or with your teeth, left rather more attached to the baby than we are accustomed to expect today. Greek models of the omphalos or world navel were humped like a straw beehive; because the tummy button of old was of the pouting variety, not the impressed version so conspicuously studded in the streets of the West today. To be fair to the Greeks, their statuary makes it clear they had mastered the neat depressed job by then. The beehive effect was a traditional idiom for representing the world navel, usually in stone, carried over from ancient times. The Lithic is a-u-em-paha-laus, it-orifice-of-phallus (the fruiting body). The pattern of the protruding navel was seen as closely following the pattern of the glans of the other phallus, the penis, which capped the birth canal, the urethra just as the navel capped the umbilical tube. Their functions were not confused of course, but it was supposed the similar physiological circumstances evoked similar responses, and so what was common to the two bits was recognised in the language. We can conclude at the same time that the phallus actually referred to the engorged glans of the penis and not initially to the erect penis entire as is commonly assumed. This is supported by the use of the same phal meaning fruit, the male organ in the animal kingdom being seen as fruiting occasionally and repeatedly, while in the vegetable kingdom the seasons dictated the regular periodic fructification – the vegetable kingdom not having broken free from natural rhythms which was the human achievement. The glans was an animal berry in this analysis, and it is indeed the word for acorn, the oak tree's berry, from the Lithic gai-la-en-s, grown-circular-ing-substantive. The acorn was merely described as a rounded excrescence. Whereupon the metaphor failed, with the penis glans having no edible nut within, although it was supposed to discharge seed. The testicles however were also regarded as the fruits or seeding bodies, after all quite like plums, and with more justification (except they dispense pollen only and not seeds at all, which the females monopolise); and they are still regarded as choice tid-bits in primitive societies, carrying the essence and virtue of the bearer, animal or human, which can be acquired by ingestion. To be frank and come clean it is not a very nice idea, but it is where our forebears come from. Not many Westernised citizens today, accustomed to sanitised readimeals, would look kindly on testicles for supper (although surprisingly some would).

With omphalos it appears the -m- is either a shortened em, which in Egyptian would be a genitive (em is of in Egyptian), in this case a suffixed one, or else it is just 'm, a substantive marker after the oo. In favour of the genitive is the close copying of much of Egyptian in Greek. With umbilicus, the Latin for the navel, we can trace the same protrusion, at least originally of the Roman navel, since it is a diminutive of umbo, the boss of the Roman shield. This boss, a hollow metal bowl-shaped bit at the center of the shield accommodated the hand of the shield bearer behind the shield gripping the bar across it. The Lithic elements oo-'m-bau can stand for a hole-him-bulged, which describes the umbo on the Roman shield quite well; and a little one, umbili, fits the protruding navel too, with the -cu-s or -kau-s coming from -shaped-substantive. The Sanskrit, the language closest to the source of Indo European, has nabhis for navel, with the Lithic elements nai-bai-s, protruding-bulging-substantive, and is copied by the Old Persian nabis, and at one further remove by the Old English nafala, picking up the fala from the Greek phalos – whence our modern day navels, with the protruding bulge and the phallus or fruiting body mixed, nowadays anachronistic with neither any longer related to the remnants of the cord as worn today. Nai could mean pushed forward, presenting, protruding. It is an originally sexual metaphor, since "na!" was identified as the expulsion of breath at climax after holding it as the sexual tension built. It is all in chapter 11, one of the naughtier bits which nevertheless needs to be understood. Finally, the m in omphalos is still only doubtfully either the Egyptian genitive or a cockney 'm serving as a substantive marker as just proposed, because there is also open the interpretation derived all the way from mai, the gestation (84) for which the navel string is designed. In reality the subconscious may well have thrown up all or any of these variant representations simultaneously, so that the Greek editor of Tarzan's legacy was in no doubt of its applicability.

A cam shaft has a hump on it so it lifts a lever pressed against it as it rotates, for instance on the cam shaft opening the valves of an internal combustion engine in turn. It is a ka'm, a driving thingumybob or driver. Ka in chapter 5 is amply supplied with pointers to this semantic content. So the 'm really does appear to be a classic cockney 'm. But it is a doublet with a comb, German kamm, which has a bunch of teeth, gomphos in Greek for a molar tooth, from kau-em-bau's, the chewing of flesh. The Sanskrit is jambhas for tusk. In Sanskrit kh- appears in many cases to have migrated uniquely via gh- to j-; and it may be the original Sanskrit derivation was khai-em ba, the hard growth of (or from) the flesh; after all a tusk is not a chewer like a molar. That is of course why elephants are named jumbo; it means tusker; and it sounds jumbo, meaning big, blown up. Boomerang, in many Australian Aboriginal tongues, is composed from the Lithic elements bau'm-ai-ra'ng, gone (or go dually)'m-coming-backing, it goes [under muscle power, ba] doubly, coming-backing. We would just say it goes and comes back again. If we had actually had the job of naming the contraption we would probably have called it a Kumbak or some such.

A hum at the beginning of a word is commoner – particularly in Chinese as we shall see shortly. Meanwhile in Tupi, a Caribbean language, not Chinese, a macaw is the name for a parrot. But according to Eric Partridge, the word may have been imported from Africa by Bantu speaking slaves of the Portuguese. It is echoic wherever it comes from. 'M-a-caw, him-that-says Caw, is first cousin to Jim Crow. The initial 'm is the common Bantu him. Macaws feed in great numbers on the palm fruits of the macaw palm, which is probably called the macaw palm, maca-uba in Tupi, (where u-ba is tree in Tupi, the 'super-burgeoned' genus), just because of the macaws seen in it. The macaque monkey similarly comes from the Portuguese macaco meaning just monkey, but again probably from a Bantu word used in Angola, Lithic 'm-a-cacau, the cackler or him-that-chatters all the time: all the time is from the –cacau, repetitively -caca-, and absolutely from the

–u. Monkeys have numerous calls and tones and use them frequently, whether they mean anything much or not, in a way a cow or other main quadruped does not. Even birds call to each other more than the larger quadrupeds, who are old sober-sides. Chambers Dictionary of Etymology, with a distinguished panel of editors, helpfully adds "ma is a Bantu prefix". But is it not really from 'm or 'm-a, him that?

The Chinese ma (pronounce maa) as well as meaning mother also means a horse. Mother is from her mammary gland (17) as already explained, named from the infants cry for it. The double toned maa (down and then up) marks the extension of the cry. It is treated as the dipping and then rising tone, but it is really just a double aa with no stop between. For the horse meaning the aa, extension, is taken to mean going, and the m is a cockney 'm. A horse is noted as a goer. It has no horns. Its only defence is flight. It relies upon its alertness and speed for getting away. The Chinese idiom is neatly indicated by these additional words: maena is a saddle, for going on a horse. Mabian is a horsewhip, ma che (from khai, driven, ie pulled) is a horse-drawn carriage or cart, maku riding breeches made, designed for riding horses, mafu a groom, majui a stable, male horse power, mazhang a horseshoe, literally a horse travel comforter, zhang having the Lithic psychosemantic content of warm and so cosey and comfortable, as well as movement (see chapter 14 on Ish). Compare an egg cosy in English. At the same time ma shang just means at once or immediately from 'm go and fast, see chapter 14 again, in this case divorced from equine activity, and not a fast horse after all. Or is it in the Chinese mind "fast-horse" and thence at once or "lickety spit"?

The Greek prefix meta- (as in metaphysics or metalanguage for examples) means something which happens afterwards, or afterwards, beyond, from the Lithic 'm-ai-ta, something (7)-that-become. What we need however is an indicator of the after, which puts us in a posterior relationship with what has become. Ai-ta the extension or going or action is fine, but how do we make after out of 'm or ma? 'M, a pause (9), is a period of time, and since it is only a pause it is at the end of the pause over. It hardly needs a Chinese mind to get from just a pause and it is over to when it has happened, after or afterwards or even beyond; but however it was devised it was in fact a Chinese mind which did it. A metaphor is a carrying beyond, a transfer [of meaning]. Meteor however, from the Greek meteoros, high in the air, Lithic 'm-ai-tai-au-rau-s, him-that is-become-altogether-raised up-substantive marker, also gives us our meteorite, meteorai-tai, born high in the sky, as well as meteorology, the logic or discourse of what is high in the sky, the atmosphere.

Ma as the infant's, cry for the breast has imprinted the phoneme in the human subconscious as marking an utterance, giving us a lot of dodgy echoisms, starting with the cat's miaow (10) and its description as a mew (10). It really just says iau which combines the three ancient vowels, which may have been why the Egyptians had the cat as a goddess conventionally transliterated Bast but actually pronounced by the Egyptians as Ba-Siti. Bum-of lady, or Ladylike-gait. Cats walk daintily. The God of the Mosaic religions, Jehovah, from Yahweh (really just I-a-u-a-i), possessed the same secret dialectic vowelisation thought to reside in the tetragramaton of Adonis, really Adonai with vowelisation A-au-a-i, not a perfect match but then what is; and it saved having to mouth out loud the sacred formula Iauai, from I-a-u-a-i in Lithic phonemes, it-that-all-ongo-ing, or better The Universal and Eternal. Jahweh was not the first monotheist creator God as is sometimes represented, but is probably the first and only dialectical one, with the Christian Tria Juncta in Uno, Three Joined in One (Father, Son and Holy Spirit), copying the dialectical framework with modified terminology. Students of Marxist religion will spot the relationship with Thesis, Antithesis and Synthesis, copied unawares from the very same pattern of thinking the Egyptians saw in their vowelisations five thousand years ago.

The cat's miaow (10) as we have seen is shortened to mew (10) – to save twisting the mouth about. A Chinese cat's mew is mimi (10). It is not that Chinese cats make dual mews, they do not; although if they are like the Siamese ones they do mew somewhat repetitively. The duplication indicates a general meaning rather than a particular utterance or one of occasion. Compare sa (one) orang (person) in Malay and sa sa orang, anybody or somebody. Sa sa kuching China is any old Chinese cat in Malay, just as sa sa orang China is some Chinaman or somebody Chinese. (Is this the place to interpose again the similarity of Sumerian ka-tse, mouth-spit or spit-mouth for cat with Malay ka-u-tschai'ng, mouth-what-spitting?) The logic of duplication appears to be this one or that one, one or another one, with the little helper prepositions Indo Europeans use left out. In the case of the Chinese mewing, it is this mew and that mew, and so mews in general. It may not fit in too well with Noam Chomsky's universal grammar, but it seems that is how the thinking has gone. An actual Chinese cat is a mao (13), clearly echoic like the Vietnamese cat, meo (13), a mew. After all they may well have traded cats, perhaps from Siam. The French dialect maraud, pronounced maraau is a very clearly echoic tom cat from the noise it makes when out on the tiles to see off a rival, before the fur starts to fly. It has given us the English to maraud, to act like a tom cat on the warpath on the tiles, along with the agential marauder. Merrill's Marauders however had nothing to do with tom cats (so far as is known), they were Americans who fought with Chiang Kai Shek in Chungking during the second world war, and after with the British Fourteenth Army in Karachi on their way home by air, flying the long way round. The Chinese Panda, the bear with the black and white face, is known in China as da xiongmao (14) or da maoxiong, a nice disregard for sequencing reminiscent of the Lithic idiom like so much in

Chinese. It is a strong (da) powerful (xiong) cat (mao). Every Chinese attribution is time consuming because of the polysemy of their syllables, another relict of the Lithic idiom, even after differentiating their four vowel tones, up, down, level, and repetitive (down and then up). A Panda is of course a bear and not a cat at all, which the Chinese must have known when they dubbed it a strong cat. The Lithic idiom with cat includes every meaning which can be gulled from the feline. The Chinese designation contrasts the panda's size and strength with its gentle docility, the Chinese cat too having the delicacy of gait the Ancient Egyptians noticed. There is surely some common thinking here, widely separated in time and space, the commonality being provided by the cat, common to both scenarios.

Our cow is from ku, horned, duals. It has two horns you need to watch. With horses, donkeys and even goats you don't. It says moo (11). To be fair to the cow it does say something very close to "mmmm" but when it is worked up it is more of a raucous "rrerrm". It is never really a moo but human whimsy has picked on moo, because of its phonemic value (semantic content) in the subconscious; and in the case of the cow we can not deny its echoic base. It is the Egyptian hieroglyph of an owl that is used for their letter m. But what it actually said in Egyptian, and other things being equal (which usually they are not) how it should be pronounced, is "Aa-maoo" (14). This is a much better shot at echoism than the rather pathetic "Ter-wit-ter-woo" we have. Hoot-er-woo would be better. Also the Egyptian actually meant something. The aa, the extensive vowel, including spatial extension, either as a dimension or even a progression, movement, meant something like "Here I go!" Mau is ma in the dual case: in this case both darkness (37) and murder (74). Owls hunt small game in the dark. The most you could extract from the Egyptian is perhaps: "Here we go! It is dark beyond a peradventure and I am an exceptional hunter a-hunting!" All that from so little? Certainly.

Latin flies and certainly mosquitoes and midges also get their names from their signature sounds. The Latin for fly is musca. It makes a sound both a hum and a hiss which we call a buzz, as if it spoke English (where speech starts with a ba, as in chapter 4). There is a rival school of thought that the fly was believed to be generated from dead and decaying matter, for which it consequently had a yen in life: Lithic mu-sai-kai, very dead-life-created, a magical reversal of the normal natural process. It may sound silly today because we know flies feed on rotting matter and procreate much like us, laying their eggs in organic waste so the heat of decay will gestate the eggs. But flies do strike us as odd. It has only recently been suggested insects arrived lately from outer space with comet debris. The mouse meanwhile gets its name from an original mus or something like it in Old Saxon, Old High German, Old Norse, Armenian, Albanian, Old Slav, Latin, Greek, Sanskrit, Old Persian and even Luwian an early neighbouring language of the Hittites who copied with mashuil for mouse. All this is in Eric Partridge's

Origins on page 418. He adds Greek mus also means a muscle – as if the Greeks thought it looked like a mouse. Compare Latin musculus for muscle, a little mouse seen rippling under the skin of an arm or leg. What made a muscle like a mouse is a muscle spends its time hidden (36,37,40,41) under the skin.

A mouse, far from making its presence known with any kind of buzz like a fly (mus, with a hiss which is more like a hum) or mosquito (a diminutive fly in Italian) passes its life (sai) living mau, hidden (37 and 40). Mice are notoriously timid creatures (although they can be tamed). They have little defence against larger predators. Their name has in turn triggered some absurd conjectures they are a form of life generated in the earth, like the fly, the other mus, by decay. Timid in turn is from Latin timidus, fearful, akin to Latin timor (fear), and comes from Latin timere to be afraid, to fear. But that offers no very obvious guide as to how the semantic content is derived. Eric Partridge boldly claims Latin timere is akin to the Greek deos to be afraid, which he derives from an original form *dweios, with an original root dwei- to fear. As only a single letter is common to timere and deos the kinship must surely be treated as dubious at best. However Lithic helps. In cases like this it is open to surmise Eric Partridge half knew more than he ever declared, perhaps because he thought it too way-out to gain acceptance, perhaps because he thought it would damage his reputation as "Word King". Did he have an inkling of any of the Lithic hypotheses? Lithic Timei- and Dewei- beginning with t- and d- respectively are akin to Malay ter- which in Malay is a comple-tive prefix roughly translatable as become, from Lithic tai-, born and so become (for this derivation see chapter 6 if you have forgotten). If we then relate ter-mai and ter-wai we do uncover a startling kinship. The Latin is using –mai where the Greek is using –wai, and with those becomings we get the meaning of fear in both cases. Wai is easy although the Lithic is ahead in chapter 15, analyzing the semantic contents of the phoneme Wa. From the echoism of shivering (wewewe) human psychology derives water because prolonged immersion in it, so that you get taken over by the watery 'fluence, cold water, which makes you shiver; and fear because that makes you shiver too. It has to be fairly severe alarm but it has to be remembered learning to speak started in the Pleistocene age, in company with the sabre-toothed tiger. The 98 psychosemantic contents charted in the tree for Ma do not include fear. But this may just be an error of omission. Mind (42), Depression (48), Water (57), Harm (73) and Death (74) coming together lead to fear, without too much imagination. Fear should probably have appeared at 42(a) or (48a). It is taking Lithic to an advanced level to be composing meanings from multiple semantic contents of a phoneme, but it is a subconscious process actually going on all the time in the dream world of the subconscious mind, where the conscious mind dips unthinkingly into a mélange of closely textured meanings.

A mouse displays lifelong timidity, its life is obsessed with death, defenceless against raptors if seen. Its defence is to remain hidden (37,40 and 43). The Anatolian Luwian language now extinct had mashuil for mouse, with the -shuil in place of the simple sibilant, which offers some reinforcement of the attribution of life and living to the sibilant phoneme (see chapter 14) in this case. The Lithic string Sh-u-i-lai reads shi-completive-of it-length, life- over the whole-of it-length, over the whole length of its life, coming after ma- for hidden (37,44). Also in Sanskrit Eric Partridge points out muska also means scrotum and vulva, two rather different bits but both to do with procreation, ma (78). The Lithic 'm-a-u-sai-ka, them-that-together-life-make. You can compare sex itself which appears to be from sai-kai-sai, or in modern terminology life-making-action: factual, unsentimental, shameless and correct, all the way from the Pleistocene? My grandchildren, still young, tell me in primary school it is now a transitive verb in itself and not the noun which the previous generation would have had it. They contemplate sexing their partners – in due course – and report meanwhile of the stars of society, principally footballers, etc: party x sexed party y. The vulva which Chambers describes as the external genital organs of the female are not in fact all that external. The Latin vulva or earlier volva was the womb, where gestation actually takes place, why is hard to work out. Partridge refers the enquirer to voluble, under which main heading he groups no less than 74 words with the same derivation – from vulva to willy (a large basket) via convolvulus, revolution, helix, walk, weld and whelk; while Chambers refers to volume and relates it to Greek eilyein to wrap around and elytron a cloak, so that the vulva is a sheath – for the fetus as well as for dad. A volume was originally a roll when (in Egypt) lengths of parchment of one kind or another were stored in pigeon holes in libraries wound on spools. For those who imagined the scrotum held two fruiting bodies which produced the seed they and the womb which held them while the seed matured were quite properly described as the two essential genital attributes. The testicles, of which all warm blooded animals have two, are the dual bits hiding under the skin of the scrotum, just like the biceps muscles under the skin of the arms for instance. In so far as the act of coition was taken to be a planting of the seed of life (actually of course only pollenation), with semen the Latin for seed, muska, from Lithic m-u-sai-kai, dual skulkers-life-makers or him-what-life maker is an undoubted pointer to the scrotum and womb respectively. Then in Old Persian we find mushk, a substance obtained from a sac hidden under the abdominal skin of a male musk deer and when dried used as a perfume – now only as a base, the smell is genital and aphrodisiac like the his-and-hers attractants sold as cosmetics discreetly by post today. What can Lithic make of this pot pourri? The musk comes from mu-sai-kai, seed planting (61,77,78). It is a scent the male deer discharges when mounting Mrs deer to get her in the mood. We borrow from the stag. The mush-ka is akin to Moshe, Englished Moses, it makes moshe, planted the semen or seed. In Egypt the Pharaohs Rameses and Tutmose were claiming divine descent, begotten of Ra (Ra-planted the seed) and Tut or Tahuti, literally Tahu-tau, Tutu, or the great god Know-all, widely believed to have originally bestowed hieroglyphs and any other knowledge on the human race, planted the seed. Moses has omitted his progenitor, presumably Jahweh. If he was an Egyptian (Semitic) priest of royal blood that may have been a matter of some discretion. The establishment sun god of his day was the Aton, or Everlasting Birth Canal from Aa-tau-oon in Lithic elements, birthing light into the world each day, now traditionally regarded as the fully frontal disc of the sun. Akhenaton the heretical and probably bisexual Pharaoh with strangely malformed lower body claimed to be A-khai-en Aton, That-begotten-in-the Aton, Born of the Aton, viz of divine descent from the sun. Japanese Emperors have the same hang-up. It is a common fantasy of hereditary rulers to make rather more of their descent than is warranted by their actual performance. That is not to dispute their ability at equestrian events including polo, or the street cred their patronage gives to horse riding etc. The Holy Roman Emperor Charlemagne, with divinity off the menu with the Pope blocking that opportunity, had a pedigree done for him which traced his lineage back to Adam, perhaps just for PR, there is no telling if he really believed it.

Next to the hums (1, 2 and 3) in the Ma tree, and the standard echoisms (4) come the mammary group of meanings (15 to 31). These all started out with the infant's anguished cry when hungry. The stomach is stressed and the child's neutral babble, ba-ba, changes to a wailing ma'a! It means I am hungry, but doting mothers world-wide have interpreted it as a vocative: "The little darling is calling for me"; and they give it their breast. It is for this reason that the word for mother has a ma in it world-wide. At one time adult boxers were not above letting out a "hm!" with a heavy blow as they tensed their stomach muscles to deliver the punch from the back leg. It was a natural reflex and not a vocative at all. Utterances naturally arising were taken to have natural meanings – and indeed they did – only to be interpreted variously. The mammary ma is a gull's nest with meanings 15 to 31 on the tree. Latin mammare to suckle provides a duplex format for what, for the ladies, is a duplex function. Our own Ma and Mama are exemplary. Albanian meme for mother follows the Latin perception. The Sanskrit was ma, the Chinese ma or mu.

The Chinese ma'a requires a falling and rising tone difficult for the Westerner but easily explained as arising simply enough from repetitive a'a, two a vowels one following immediately after the other, when the correct pronunciation is automatic. In the case of the maternal semantic contents it springs from the long drawn out wail of the infant seeking the breast. The very same word, similarly pronounced, can also mean horse in Chinese, a language which neglects no opportunity of extracting every last meaning from every phoneme, their mandarin class having spent many millennia leaving no semantic stone unturned. With four tones, respectively up, down, neither (flat), and repetitious they have managed to eke out the Lithic conventions long after they were past their sell-by date, often with helper syllables added after the fashion of the Ancient Egyptians' determinant glyphs coming after the uttered word, themselves unpronounced but prompting the class of meaning involved. The Chinese similarly have numerous glyphs pronounced exactly the same but nevertheless each with its own meaning. It is said you sometimes need a paint brush and paper to explain exactly what you are saying. The horse meaning is arrived at, it would appear, by way of ma-aa, elided to ma. In this case the ma prompts for big (58) and aa as an extensive, in this case spatial extension and so going in place of the infantile wailing, and defining the horse as the major goer, the galloper. With the other tamed beasts oxen and donkeys, the horse stood out as the speedy and temperamental one, just as it does today. The Latin equus, from the Lithic elements ai-kau-s, suggests going-strong-acting in the original Lithic, or even going-strong-fast. You probably have to be Chinese, addicted to their kind of word games, to pick up the meanings at all easily. In Chinese mama – both a vowels flat – is a wet nurse displaying both of her mammary glands, an interpretation confirmed by the alternative term mu, a substitute mother, relying upon the dual vowel in place of the mama repetition. We see the very same protocol in Ancient Egyptian where pu replaces pipi (chapter 12). Ma in Chinese also carries the semantic content of the other motherly function to wipe clean, an obvious gull. The Ancient Egyptian mentiti is the breast, the nippled feeder; -titi like our tit or titty meaning teat, with the –ti ending in Egyptian, teated, being also used as the feminine marker suffix. The Malay for mother is emak, pronounced in practice more like ma', the e- being vanishingly present and the –k being effectively a glottal stop. The Navaho, a native tribe in California amongst the oak trees say ma' for mother. It is hard to believe it comes from the Sanskrit ma. The Zulu is umame, where m' is him and um' is perhaps them, in which case um-a-mai reads in Lithic elements them-that-breasted or feeding, meaning full breasted for feeding. The Vietnamese is the same as the Sanscrit and Navaho: ma. With all these ma words cropping up all around the world, meaning mother, it is hard to dismiss the underlying psychosemantic promptings from the subconscious arising world wide. The mothers of the world are indeed the principal supporters of the Lithic hypotheses; because if ma has a psychosemantic origin, why not anything else? So Doubting Thomases must first of all ask themselves what other explanation for maternity around the world is there? When they have found it out they should write it down, and not keep it to themselves. Everyone will be waiting to know.

After the stress (15) group of meanings in the ma tree are those characters springing from opposition to Ish (16), namely first of all and most tellingly – instead of leaping up like the hissing flame – the contrary instinct of silently falling down, falling (34) not rising, instinctively going down, as philosophers later had it of things pulling themselves towards the centre of the earth – still at it even down a mine. But in the Stone Age these were simply properties of matter, their natural behaviours, inbuilt like their hard surfaces. Mass, Lithic ma-sai, what activates the falling action, stands in contradiction also to liquid (La, chapter 9) which likes best the interface between earth and sky, running down into the lows but also sometimes rising up in springs to regain the surface when some other force has apparently carried it below. The reality has not yet been accepted by the British Ministry responsible (at this moment DEFRA) which believes water runs downhill in the underground strata from hills around to make artesian springs. In reality the pressure of the overburden (300 feet of boulder clay hereabouts) floating on the aquifer (chalk) 300 feet down forces water up where there is a crack (or bore) in the overburden. These hominid "instincts" (just as good as the current Ministry view) come from what would now be labeled a teleological approach to science, and psychologists would regard it as an anthropomorphic world view – that is interpreting the world about us as if it were endowed with the same psyches and wills as we have. Undoubtedly this was the opinion of humankind as we emerged from the prior hominid darkness of subconscious thinking (like dogs), into the full light of recursive thought, which mental symbolisation enabled us for the first time to grasp and retain in memory in clear-cut terms. Whether the symbolisation preceded, accompanied or resulted from speaking is a separate issue much debated at present, which makes no difference whatever to the resultant clarification, as all agree. Before speech, you had to be an Einstein to get your thinking act together. How many mute and disregarded prelinguistic Einsteins will have wasted their sweetness upon the desert air, unable to communicate except in the most basic terms must always remain moot. It was their frustration, no doubt, which provided the pressure needed to crack the mould and led to the revolutionary outburst of symbolic communication in language. The improvement in internal self-expression and understanding, the mental clarification which will have accompanied intercommunication, because of the sheer memorability of symbols or labels for identifying ideas, so that they could be recalled at will and mulled over, has prompted some folk to claim we spoke to help ourselves first of all; but it is a non sequiter. We spoke to express our own state of mind and impress it on our neighbours. It eased (but did not altogether remove) a nasty dose of claustrophobia.

The words for measure (60), starting in Biblical times with Mene Mene Tekel Upharsin, use the going down instinct (34) in the tree. The Lithic phonemic elements of mene, mai-nai, showing (chapter 11, Na)-the ma-ing, are repeated for emphasis in the quotation above and to indicate repetition of the measurements: weighing, weighing: i.e. you have been repeatedly weighed in the balance; and been found wanting, literally the weights (tekel,shekels, from the Lithic be-come-make-level) u-pha-rai-sai´n: oo-paha-rai-sai, un-pushed-upwards-action, from the original pushing up action of the pahai or penis when rai or caught by the feminine rays of the Stone Age ladies squatting opposite around the hearth. By Pharaoh´s day the reading of language in its original (already old fashioned) Lithic phonemic elements (God Speak) required the services of a soothsayer who could discover the underlying significances of phonemic strings, disentangling their polysemy. The pha-rai-sai Lithic phrasing is to be found in the English word phrase. It is from the Greek phrazein to indicate or explain. In this case it is a case of pushing forward (pha-rai) pointing up or presenting the illumination (sai), sense or meaning, not the John Thomas. The sense or meaning of sai here is also of course from warming by the hearth, how we (pleasantly) sense or experience it physically, and so of course how we experience or sense things mentally as well. Sense thus comes to mean how we grasp the import of a word or sentence. That is what a meaning is, like an etymon – before it was hijacked by the experts, dealing in phonetics in place of semantics, who have declared it to be the original phonetic form merely, where etymon (42), Lithic ai-tai-mau´n, as it-born-meaning (or thought), is clearly to do with the original semantics.

Weight belonged to solid things which if you dropped them fell on your toes. The flame per contra was insubstantial (actually incandescent gas) like wind, thinking and spirits which all supposedly partook of the flame, as did indeed all animals in some measure in so far as they were warm blooded. The Greek marmaros (in phonemic terms ma-ma-rau-s) meant first of all a large boulder, in Lithic terms a mass of solid matter (ma) raised to an ultimate level of massiveness (marau), almost a big marrow. As Eric Partridge puts it, "influenced by marmairein (gleaming from the Lithic 'm-ara-mai-rai-ai´n, him-visible-matter-raying-verbal) to gleam or shimmer" it signified a shiny rock like marble. Marble is "dissimulated" by the French from the Latin marmor, according to Partridge. Pars pro toto (part of a word taken up as standing for the whole) mar- stands for marmor. The French boulder has been given a ba-lai, lithe flesh or smooth texture from polishing. We may however prefer to put the thinking the other way about, because the boulder marmaros gleamed and shimmered when polished the word used for to shimmer was gulled from marmaros: to large boulder, marmairein. Then since water's surface too was seen to mimic such a large boulder or shimmer under a slight breeze it was described as moir, a string with an awa in it as well as shimmering – see chapter 15 on Wa and its meanings. But the m- could just as well be a cockney 'm, him-awa-raying, cold like winter or the English water.

As the sun sets and shines obliquely through the earth´s atmosphere its coloured rays are striking. Ra, the source of the raying has been known as a term for the sun since Egyptian times, particularly to the Greeks who had acquired their civilisation largely and perhaps even chiefly from the civilisation of Egypt, a civilisation arising from the empire of the Semitic Pharaohs though with some Hamitic accretions from their subject African races. To a degree the Pharaohs went native. The Carthaginians, who spoke Punic with exposed penises, like the Pharaohs were already circumcised and a Phoenician seafaring race (theirs exposed too) when Rome was still a pig-sty (a sty is a standing or stay, from the same root as stable). Their Punic language was a provincial Egyptian at a time when it was the Lingua Franca of the whole Mediterranean littoral. But ray is older by far and its placements in languages around the world presents it as a product of Stone Age thinking at the time we learned to talk

The Carthaginian occupation of the Canary Islands off the African coast – (Canary is from Carthaginian Kan-aria, Rocky coast, and not from Latin for dog at all, as Pliny the Elder pretended, which as a third declension Latin noun, canis, would have yielded Canery Isles) – heavily influenced whatever it was that passed for language there amongst the Guanche indigenous folk beforehand. Guanche, from Ga-u-en-kai, land-where-in-begotten, simply means native born in Carthaginian. The genuine aboriginal substrate of the language of the Guanche people, now lost as a result of the Spanish conquistadors´ religious aggression, can be taken to have been related to any one of hundreds of Hamitic tongues spoken in the great African bite. The Greek marmairein was a gleaming in the gloaming. The Lithic is fairly easy. Ma-Rai-mai-rai´n, Death-of the Sun-dying-raying. But it is also hard to spot because neither the gleaming nor the gloaming really belong to ma, but on the contrary more straightforwardly to the flame, ish. But the sun's death rays are brilliant, redeeming the darkness of death. There is often a whimsical element behind Lithic determinations, rabbits are sometimes pulled from hats to astonish the onlookers. Similarly we find in Tenerife the small hilly island of Gomera just off Tenerife's Western coast, over which the prevailing trade winds sweeping up the African coast often produce a tuft of cloud which gives Tenerife the most magnificent sunsets over Gomera. Gomera is from Ga-u-mai-Ra, Land-where-dies-the Sun, Sunset Island – certainly in Lithic, but also in Carthaginian. Watching these from the balcony of the apartment in which this book is largely written it is a thrill to think five thousand years before somebody else was watching and naming the phenomenon. It follows as day follows night America is Carthaginian also. The Lithic phrasing Aa-ma-rai-ka is easily read as Far-death or sinking-of sun-land, the Far Western Land, a tradition passed down the millennia from the heyday of the Carthaginian Empire. The vowel chapter, number 16, illuminates the use of the general vowel aaa as an extensive: you can keep at it as long as you have breath, which is generally not the case with the stops, the proper consonants. Doctors ask you to make the same continuous sound when they want you to keep your larynx open so they can examine it.

The Carthaginians beat Christopher Columbus, as also Brendan the Celt, by thousands of years. The myth America is simply the name of the cartographer Amerigo Vespuchi can be explained since he must have been named at birth by parents well aware of the fabled land and keen to give him the stimulus to explore. That century the novelty of sailing to distant lands to discover the globe had the same fascination as space travel today, and there has been no count as yet of American boys named Buzz. In a few centuries it will probably be averred they were all named after the busy bee which generates so much sweetness. Meanwhile there are many hundreds of millions of folk on the far side of the pond who remain unaware they are talking Carthaginian and imagine the American continent is named after a sixteenth century European cartographer. But Vespucci carried the name of the continent, much as babies are now christened Buzz. "Amerigo!" was the buzz when he was born. Columbus too could have disillusioned them but preferred not to do so. The New York Times has been informed as well, but has not regarded it as newsworthy either, perhaps waiting for one of their own Guanche or natives to break the news, instead of having it borne in on a haughty wind from the wicked world across the water.

A hammer, as already explained in chapter 8 under the phoneme Ha, is a tool for making heavy downward strokes. Administered to any live species it is harmful, a hurtful marrer. It tends to mar whatever is struck. Maccaroni is from the obsolete Italian verb maccare to break up into pieces, one must suppose by a sequence of heavy chopping blows from a hammer or some such. The Hindi makhana to harm or injure, to make ma, and so punish is surely related to maccaroni. Murder and massacre (6) make use of the same ma as maccaroni. Murder or murther is from morthor the Old English noun, with the verb myrthrien. Mur-, it appears, is merely a slovening of mor- which brings the English into line with the Latin group based on the verb mori (Lithic mau-are) to be deaded, to die, the opposite of living (sai). Eric Partridge appeals to cognates in Sanskrit, Armenian, Old Slavonic and Lithuanian. The English group includes post mortem, really just Latin, mortality, the morgue, mortgages, to mortify, to amortize, moribund, morbidity, even a murrain and check mate in chess. The mate of check mate is from the Arabic mat which looks like a borrowing from the Old Persian Shah mat, the Shah is dead. Mati in Malay is dead too. It might be taken as a borrowing from Arabic but the Aboriginal Malay gives that its quietus: the Malay Aboriginal term ma-te for dead means in the ground. We can work this out because where Malays say buang from bau-aa-ng for muscle-away-ing, throw away or sling it. Aborigines say bus-ma-te, which is throw-ground-to, chuck it down. Living sparsely spread in a virgin jungle they can afford to just drop things as they go. So Malay mati means in the ground (buried), with the reasonable presumption the body was dead before burial. But of course mati can be read also as from the Lithic ma-tai, dead-become, a birth into the nether world in fact. Lithic is happy with multiple routes/roots, indeed they may have been regarded and so should now be regarded as reinforcing indications of 'natural' meanings. Massacre is from the French and related to macher to crush, but the Lithic analysis of the phonemic string suggests the ma-sa is demolish-life and the –crer is from –karai to make. Yet massa appears also to have suggested a killing en masse at the same time, although the stress appears to be on the action rather than its widespread nature. The semantics of a single syllable or even a string of them can be read by the subconscious mind twice with two different meanings without any discomfort. It is a sleeping dreaming state.

If a body goes on going down it finishes up on the ground, made up of all the rest that has settled there. The earth is the solid element, solidity being next to weightiness. But the earth is also the place of insemination – where you plant seeds – and germination and so of fertility. Dead (inert) seeds are planted in the ground and come to life. Latin serere is to plant (seeds), bringing them to life in the most unlikely place the dead earth. To earth them, that is to bury them, is to bring them to life. Burial became popular because of this linguistic reasoning. Indeed to bury was to plant the seed, to propagate, to gestate in the earth, and ma came to carry the meaning of seed planting in the animal kingdom as well. In Egyptian the (more clinical) term for the penis is mai, the earther, planter or inseminator. To marry was to go a-planting. Amare, Latin to love, is as planting (your seed) when it is a common experience to feel an access of goodwill towards your partner at orgasm, regarded in the old days as the source of affection; and not without reason at that. Just the anticipation can turn heads. The Egyptian god Amun, A-ma-u'n was supposedly The Ever-Loving-of all-one, just like everyone is when engaged in intercourse. Amun is from the same phonemic roots as amare to love. From serere to plant in Latin comes semen, the planting and so what is planted, the seed. That is the etymological derivation, but the subconscious can handle multiple meanings, and sai-mai´n is a live thing which is dead, so it means life-dormant. Indeed there is no real reason why semen needs to be derived from serere to sow. Sowing seed is bringing it to life by sprinkling it on the ground, what seed does or becomes in fact. But serere also carries the meaning of action-raying, akin to spray, which (like sprin-kle) has the p in it, which was the paradigmatic sprayer for the Lithic unconscious. These roots have a common derivation from a common Lithic substrate, rather than being connected daisy chain style. They all draw their inspiration from the subconscious under-layer of language, the very same one that Noam Chomsky has prayed in aid for his universal grammar, as if the genes actually carry ideas rather than just structural programming.

His deep structure is really linguistic structuring of the mind in the languages consciously learnt by each speaking phenotype in turn. Babies have no transformational grammar at their command, any more than their legs are programmed as to what walks they will in the course of their lives choose to take. Chomsky thinks children could not learn language without it being inbuilt because he can not see sufficient guidance offered. That is because it is subconscious. It does not register with the conscious mind. It has to be accepted we can think at a low level without knowing of it, just as we can dream without knowing how we do it. Our conscious thinking has a subterranean keel to it. Lithic abandons determination for whimsy when it comes to thinking. It is neo-Darwinism that has got it wrong here. Natural selection is fine. It has provided us with brains but it does not determine the thoughts we put together. From that point of view we are post-natural, able to survey our prisons though not to escape them. It does not mean our thinking is right, indeed it means much of it, if not all, is likely to be askew – as history, the record of performance to date, seems to affirm.

The sibilant is redolent of life, liveliness and activity – not because you can extract any such significances directly from the sound itself, but solely because that is the way human whimsy has chosen to regard it, the thinking simply following on from the original identification of ish with fire, a classic example of Lithic ratiocination such as it was. The idea was utterances (like all sounds) must have natural significances or meanings, and learning to communicate by uttering sounds depended on discovering what the natural meanings were and then using them. That way young Tarzan hunkered next to you, unselfconscious in his birthday suit, might get the message[4]. Once a natural meaning was identified you were locked on. One way or another we kidded ourselves we had correctly identified natural meanings for all the phonemes and used them accordingly. Of course it was a little mad, but then we are; and after all it has worked quite well, although nowadays the original 'natural' meanings attached to phonemes are buried in the subconscious, as keels below the surface languages we learn as infants and use for communication. We subconsciously recover the phonemic semantic attributes, generation after generation, at the same time as we consciously learn to speak. Ideas are not inheritable, any more than individual walks are when we learn to walk. We inherit the facility but not the performances rendered possible. Those we have to learn afresh, by means of self education.

Notes.

1. If communication before speech was by means of cries, as in Chimpish, what we would call song, without any stops (except perhaps a La, the odd halloo or two to break up the tones, see chapter 9 on La), what originally made the

difference and introduced speech as we understand it was quite simply just that, the introduction of the stops, or as we call them consonants. Hisses and hums were half-way houses, old friends as it were, not so very different from the clear vowelisations with which cries were made. All the other stops by their very nature were not singing notes at all. So hisses and hums were cases for early study. The distinction between mmm and nnn, which is minimal so far as the phonetics are concerned was apparently generally not made.

2. The dialectical thinking of the Stone Age, as well as Hegel and Marx´s re-vamped version is examined in some detail in chapter 16 on thinking.

3. Eric Partridge. "Origins. A Short Etymological Dictionary of Modern English". A glance at the 364 "Indogermanic" word roots at the back of WW Skeat´s Etymological Dictionary of the English Language of 1879 – 1882 reveals his predilection for the aspirated consonants as originals in the first few paragraphs of his introduction. It also provides a succinct synopsis of Grimm´s Law and its implications. All Skeat's roots are at Appendix B.

4. On the front cover he has already gone to bed under a skin inside the cave leaving grand dad still at it, the mums having to listen to the puzzle.

CHAPTER 11

THE PHONEME NA

Knapping flints has been going on for a million years and more. It was clearly a trick learned by our hominid forebears, and indeed we likely would not be prepared to count them human at all if we were to come face to face with them today. At "Grimes' Graves" in Norfolk, England – Grimes is the Devil, kara-mai(s), who makes all the mais, the mayhems and harms – a few stones' throw from where this is written, the mines were dug in the sandy soil to recover the undisturbed flint nodules, with no faults in them to spoil the flint knappers work. They provided perhaps the first industrial complex in the Western world, with a network of tracks to send them far and wide. These mines with their crawl tunnels from the base of the shafts, with notched tree trunks providing access, were probably old when Stone Henge was young. In the centre of the chamber at the foot of the main shaft of one of the best preserved and renovated mines was a fine phallus in clay the height of a man, which was removed to the store rooms of Norwich Castle Museum half a century ago before the site was opened to the public, and has not been seen since. It was put there by our local forebears to fertilise Mother Earth to do her duty and give birth to a plentiful supply of flint nodules for the miners to find. It is a delight to think of these simple souls happily patterning nature upon their own sexual experience. After all how could they possibly know that what they had learned in the hard world of experience was no good at all for decoding everything else. It is a lesson still to be learned. Dating before any known religion the flint mines naturally attracted the fear of the Devil in times when he was believed to actually exist.

Stone Henge has been out of use two thousand years but at Brandon (Bara-en-don, crossing-of-the river in Ancient Egyptian), the town beside the mines astride the river, the Flint Knappers Arms was providing refreshment for the current generation of flint knappers shipping flints for flintlocks to West Africa for their muskets when I was a boy. Here was an industry which probably went back some fifty thousand years, before the last glaciation, which led to Noah's flood when it thawed some fifteen thousand years ago. We do not know if the Egyptians shipped their flints from Ultima Thule but there does seem to be some

linguistic evidence they were here, the surviving evidence thinly spread after the
Celtic invasions, but otherwise hard to explain. The Celts will have mopped them
up when they called since they were in those days head hunters with a partial-
ity for the brains of those they killed, and they probably even killed them for
the table, and so quite shortly used them all up. Egyptian geometers may well
have been responsible for the straight tracks across England and the ley lines
supposedly involved, which fossickers so enjoy retracing and marvelling at today. Civilisation has been set back more than once by barbarian invaders. The
Romano-Celts would later themselves be swamped by the Saxon tribes flooding
into the country, so that the fens which were drained before the Saxons came were
flooded for another thousand years until Dutch engineers fresh from draining the
polders were called in in the seventeenth century.

To knap a flint is to strike it in such a manner as to produce a flat plaque or
flake, which comes away with a flat surface and a sharp edge. The strike presents
you with a piece with a surface which can be used chiefly for the sharp edges. We
shall see before the end of the chapter that the Lithic elements on which the word
is based, ka-na-pai, the first syllable slovened to a single letter, the last slovened
to -pe and then a bare final -p, carry the semantic contents strike-present-flake,
which is precisely what knapping is about. Nothing could be further from the
current linguistically correct view that words are formed from randomly selected
roots which have no intrinsic meaning, a view which is patently false, although
it saves a lot of thinking. Every other word in all the languages of the world, if
sufficiently examined, and sufficiently unslovened or reconstructed, will teach the
same lesson. Language is built from meaningful elements assembled slowly from
phonemic roots, first of all our only media of communication. Words are constructs made up of meaningful pieces. The same process continues today. UNO
does not mean the United Nations Organisation for no reason. It comprises three
phonemes each carrying the meaning of the words they have been chosen to
represent. If you do not know that you can still use the word in a meaningful way,
you simply lack its etymology. It is just the derivation of the meanings which is
different in this case from the original methodology which was a bit more basic.
As a result it takes a whole book to get folk to think in these unaccustomed ways
and so to understand how language was made.

The psychosemantic tree for Na is at page 305. Eric Partridge's second entry
– the first is nab – under the letter N is nabob which is a nice example of the slovening of navab from an original nawab. W is not v and v is not b, but Wayland
is not that bothered. The Arabic nawab is the plural of naib, an ambassador or a
provincial governor, officials sent in subordinate positions with the role of presenting the views of the ruler. Now in the Indian army a naik is a corporal of foot
representing his sergeant. This chapter has as a principal task to show that the

phoneme na originally meant to present or show. Chapter 4 already attached the meaning of the haunches and their movement, going, to bai. A naib is from nai-bai or explicator bum (16). The same applies to nabbi which the Moslems use for Nabbi Issus, Jesus the Travelling Prophet. Nabinabi in Malay however is the seven limbed starfish, show-bits-show-bits (probably the bi started out bai and conveys burgeons), remarking his astonishing accumulation of limbs when most of the rest of animal life makes do with only four. The prophet is travelling, the star fish is burgeoning. They can both do their things because both spring from the underlying idea of flesh, fleshy bits, and so in the case of the prophet the haunches which provide the musclature for perambulation, and in the case of the starfish the burgeoning which is the habit of the flesh.

Na is the sound of the expulsion of breath after holding it. Such a breath holding with a sudden release is typical of orgasm (1). Much of the semantic contents of this phoneme spring from this identificarion. When we were learning to speak we had little in the way of inhibition as we know it today. Our forefathers, as well as their mothers, were shameless when it came to working out how Tarzan next door to them around the hearth might be thinking. You have to locate yourself like them in your birthday suit squatting together, even scrummed up together around the welcoming blazing hearth. It does wonders for your civilised prepossessions, with which of course they were in no way encumbered. It is an education to follow them into their linguistic symposiums, whatever it does for your morals. We know from our exploration of the other phonemes already that the orgasm was going to be gulled for its concomitants. The early mind was tyrannised by the eye, much as today. Once you have Tarzan thinking like you, you know he will be rehearsing the scene as it unfolds (nightly) to the eye. He is enjoying a sexual bonanza and we are going to have to follow him at least in outline, to see what arises for science. Were you today in a fix like your Stone Age forebears having to invent speech, you too would be grasping at sexual activity like a drowning man grasping at a straw. Moreover "Na!" even today is a natural expression of sympathetic delight which my elderly spinster cousin, a horse breeder, emits when a new foal prances out for the first time. There will be others expressing the same sentiment similarly with other stimuli. So there were hundreds of thousands of years ago. It is a shame to denigrate so natural an expression of pleasure. Ternahak in Malay however means to be overcome (ter-) by desire (the -nahak bit), much closer to the original meaning. There is a further reason, perhaps, why this phoneme depends so widely upon the sexual motif. There was no competition. Hums were spoken for by Ma. Na was an opening sound, and an a closing sound, with nothing much to offer in between.

The negative (5) presents perhaps the most daunting challenge to Lithic analysis. To explain the semantic content attached to ne- or nai calls for a radical ex-

THE PSYCHOSEMANTIC TREE FOR NA

The Phonetic Tree

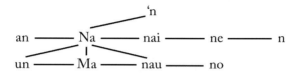

The Semantic Tree

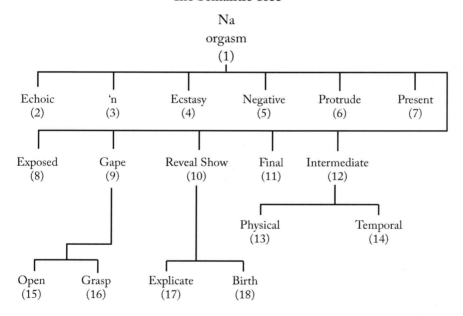

amination of the thinking which accompanied linguistic origins, and all without any contemporary guidance or input whatever. In previous chapters frequent reference has been made to the role played by the way the phonemes are produced by the human mouth parts in attributing semantic contents to them. So, for instance, ba is uttered by pursing the lips lightly and then releasing the general vowel aaa, and the meaning attached to the sound is from the lips that uttered it, the fleshy surrounds of the mouth, the fleshy bits, and so flesh and all the characteristics which can be gulled over the millennia from lips and flesh. Ba is also a relatively gentle and gradual utterance without the sharp, even explosive impact of a ka, a pa or a ta. It does indeed have a character which really does suggest the characters of the flesh from which it comes: soft, bungey, bulgy, adaptive, perhaps spreading etc. Similarly pa, an unvoiced ba, is a thinning of flesh and so the skin or another diminished diminutive piece of flesh (animal or vegetable) such as a flower bud or shoot or any minor part of the body by comparison with the torso, like a limb or foot, or indeed in the classic animal case the male organ, budding and shooting expresso at will. This is pretty basic stuff and needs to be understood. Then there is echoism, with the psychosemantic contents obtaining derived from the characters that can be gulled from the phenomenon echoed. Ish and the sibilants for the flame for instance comes to stand for heat, warmth, flickering, activity, liveliness, life, etc, because when Tarzan dunked his burning brand at dawn it told him "ishsh!". Whether the sibilants (hisses) have of themselves any character related to the flame is moot, but by now they are honorary members of the flaming class in the human subconscious mind. Ka is taken as echoic of the sound of flint on flint, and a great deal flows from that. All these echoisms are somewhat approximate. There is also the stress of aiming and striking precisely which the ka contributes as a hurrumph. More whimsical still, ma opposes ish because of the way it is pronounced, a continuous tone ish with the patent effusion of breath while the hums are virtually without. So if the flame springs upwards, as it does, a hum goes down, which is why science has mc squared, and when I was a boy P = mf. It stands to reason! Breathing is an in and an out, opposites of course! Ha means hot because it is an involuntary sudden expulsion of breath resulting from the trauma of a burn. It is said the Inuit of Alaska voice Ha! rather than Na! when mating, and in the old days hospitality demanded visitors be offered the opportunity to share a laugh with the lady of the igloo – apocryphal no doubt but life on the ice makes one concentrate solely upon the really important thing in life, a diet of raw fish. But anyway Ha stands for a breath catching sensation, whether just nice, funny or hurtful, and by extension indicating emotion, an internal mental sensation like an affair of the heart. The Malay for heart is hati, the emotion teat, regardless of what Malays may think it stands for. Ta, too, is echoic with a bit of fanciful interpretation, given the fanciful psychosemantic treatment was proving so successful in getting Tarzan to learn his language. It was taken to be the sound of snapping in two, presumeably firewood for the hearth, prompted no doubt by the flint on flint success with ka, but not so hard and sharp in the case of wood.

So how does this all translate to explain why nai is negative? Na has been identified above as the sound made when holding the breath as emotional tension builds, with a final sudden release at orgasm, ending the tension in a few pulses of sweet sensation flooding through the whole nervous system. In chapter 15 on the vowels meanwhile there is a somewhat more prosaic examination which identifies the vowel aaa as extensive and unrestrictive. You can go on with an aaa for as long as you have breath, as you can not with a p, or a d, or a k for example. The consonants, which came in with speech, and indeed provided the articulation (separation) which enabled us to string our thinking in separate bits where before we were unable to sharply terminate one thought and start another, now act as restraints partitioning the flow of sounds uttered just as they do the semantics. This should probably be taught in schools, immediately after the letters and their phonemes or sounds; but not before. Now it remains to demonstrate why, of all the consonants, the na phoneme should have been chosen, should have presented itself as the classic stopper. The hums (chapter 10) can be sounded for as long as you have breath, unlike typical consonants. When the doctor tells you she has seen enough of your throat you may not articulate an -an, but it is a fair bet your tongue will impact your palate, which gets an n. If you just shut your mouth you get an m. The Chinese use bu for the negative, probably because they take their lips as blockers too. If you shut your mouth in China you get the reverse of when you open it. The vowel u is picked up in China for its inclusive and conclusive character uncovered in chapter 15. Semitic tongues use m. The Indo Europeans all go for the palatal stop, the n. The phoneme na is the signature of this closure. You do not have to be a senior wrangler to understand that when you terminate anything then there is none. True the vowelisation of an with the −n actually terminal is on the hither side of the consonant whereas the phoneme na is exemplified with it on the far side. But this is a common dual phoneticisation which applies to every phoneme and was evidently regarded with indifference.

The vowels are open, the consonants are closures. There is a degree of opposition already involved in this circumstance. So it actually follows from this that if aye is positive, its closure terminates it and implies its absence. The semantics of ne, is n-ai, the closure of ai, even though it opens it. That is hominid thinking for you. Of course we do use un- as well as a negative. Chapter 15 on the vowels provides some more indications as to the meanings attributed to ai. It came to mean that which or that is, really the same idea, a positive position. Its closure therefore absents the positive. The absence is not an opposite. But it was thought to be so. The absence of existence is taken to be the opposite of existence. It sounds sound.

But is the absence of red the opposite of red, its negative? Is it different for an adjective and a noun? You can read more about how this came about in chapter 16 on the origins of thinking. The conclusion is that because when you stop saying aaa you can finish up with an n, na becomes a negative marker. To decide meanings in this way may seem like bordering on insanity, but that is how it has been done. There is no guarantee we have not, ever since the forebears of Erectus first rose onto their hind legs, been certifiable; and a good deal of evidence we have. The mania has for the most part been homicidal, often with sadistic accompaniments. But that does not mean we can not avoid it in the future, only that it is not guaranteed. There will be academics who will seek to dismiss this thinking, anxious to show the negative is fortuitous with words all selected at random. But they can not win. The evidence is against them. As a species we may not have been all that clever. But we have been thinking, and for a very long time indeed. To think is to make things become, not in the real world but in the mind, the hidden invisible world of mentality. Mental space (the metaphysical) exists in a sense, but not like the real (visible) physical world we see, which in reality is only visible, a spin off from whatever lies behind what we see. Mental and physical spaces are thus distinct but not so far apart, both constructs of our minds like scribbles on the wall paper trying to sketch the wall behind. We are not gods. Everything we know and understand including maths and science is fantasy, although some of our doodling is very creditable to the species.

However it is necessary now to leave the wall paper on one side and to explore the human genitalia, to see what psychosemantic contents we can find therein. Much of the nomenclature comes from the Egyptian. The schoolboy pee which comes, in a long slow meander, from the Egyptian quail chick is in chapter 12. The rousing raising rays which invade our sexuality come at only one short remove from the Egyptian sun, Ra, in chapter 13. At the precise juncture na, the male member is raised upwards and forwards and is presenting strongly and there is an outflow of fluid. Indeed it will have been well known to all ranks in those far off days that this was the posture of the male member even in the introductory stages. The chosen target may well have been still squatting on the far side of the hearth warming up. What is more, behind the piece the carriage is in generous mood too. The Egyptian God Amun, the ever earthing, planting, fertile, impregnating, sowing his seed, was the ever loving too. Latin amare to love comes, it would appear, from a-ma-are, as when-planting-verbal suffix; and this was no agricultural chore but mating. It is not intended to suggest couples in the Stone Age were incapable of the generous sentiments of love at any other time, but merely that was the time when even the thickest proto farmers boy will have registered the emotion most strongly. Indeed elsewhere it is suggested that to be truly human is not (as the etymologists have imagined) to be an earthling, from the Latin root for humus, but on the contrary to be hei-u-ma'n, enjoying-both-the mating. It was the taming of fire and the superheating of the swains which led to the humanity of human mating and thence to human mutual recognition and communication and so to civilisation. Strike a match and see the world of man explained – by an adult route. We are still living in the fire age. Animal copulation is both violent and often short, and neither participant betrays anything other than vehement effort, and in the case of the female utter subjection. This may not apply to the lady praying mantis who apparently makes a gastronomic bon bouche out of the opportunity provided of getting really up close to her partner by eating off his head. This is apparently prior to orgasm as the performance of the male is not inhibited but on the contrary appears to be concentrated on the job in train by the removal of any alternative call centre. Does the headache come after? Anyway Stone Age wallies did not study the mantis.

The earth does not mate and has no sensibility at any time. Humus benefits from the overflowing polysemy of the Lithic cornucopia, so generous with its meanings because the rules of composition as well as the root meanings in the first place were so little exercised, so generally phrased and so casually manipulated. Humus, i(h)u-mau-s, with a cockney h concealing an opening vowel since lost, it-one or what-most down, heavy, and milled, the soil, ground by nature to a granular texture: the ground, the earth precisely. Whence to earth seeds is to plant them and propagate a plant, so ma adds mating to its meanings. The seeds were sprinkled on the ground, and the male member seemed to be trained to do the same. It was regarded as a fruiting. Animals could fruit and unfruit repeatedly. The glans was a seed head and the acorn was a glans. Malay buah is fruit and testicles and the testicles were dual fleshy fruiting bodies. The boars in Borneo had bu, dual fruiting bodies, arai, raised and in view. Pigs do in fact carry them up behind, as every farmers boy knows. In Borneo where pigs are totems the men exposed theirs to view too with just a penis sheath as a roister doister surety for good conduct. If they could have moved them round behind they probably would have too.[1] A bull, and here is the clincher, in English, some way from Borneo, has his testicles unusually in a scrotum which shows them strait laced in a single long tubular (looped) shape, and the bulrush has the same configuration, though it houses very many flying seeds, the bull's scrotum none whatever. That is why the males were supposed to be the seed bearing sex, they fruited – absurd but true. Pollenation was terra incognita. Who was to tell Tarzan oranges and lemons were female? Vegetables could only burgeon, they had no locomotion and with their inferior only partial vitality they could only fruit once a year in season. It all fitted together sufficiently well to keep simple minds happy, just as today. What is presented, nau (7), is present, and it is not so far from there to the present, where we are in time, now (14), in French m-ain-tenant, him-extensional(temporal)-

tai-nai become presented, the present, or alternatively being held (Latin Tenere to hold).

It comes as a surprise that na can breed a series of echoisms. To snore (2) is the sound of snoring, which can vary a lot; this is a sniff in followed by a -narr out. When asleep we pause between the in and the out just enough to introduce a na. A sniff, snuffle and snuff are barely echoic but pass as such. There is not really any n in a sniff. It is tempting to think the n has sneaked in as an indicator (17) and it is just the s-ff which is the sniff, the nearest we can get without actually talking with our nose instead of our mouth. A neigh is an equine na. It expresses equine recognition if not actual delight. A snicker and a nicker express strings of them, and a whinny is a whole lot of loud ones. A horse's nearest to no is a snort. Come to think of it my Shetland pony stallions snorted when mating too. It was an understandable expression of triumphalism just as when it indicated rejection. It could indicate what they would have as well as what they would not, an expression of what the philosophers would describe as the will to power and what in Ancient Egyptian was pronounced Ka, the skeleton, the key, the guiding principle for life, effectively the soul – it had the same character as the soul in so far as it came in two portions, one for this world and a second bit for the second world – and in Modern Japanese it is pronounced the same. Maybe we all started by snorting too: but chimpanzees don't. A snap is thought to be echoic of a sharp break, for instance of a dry stick. If so it is the final p which provides the echoism. The sna- is just the run up, "here it comes"; and indeed the initial s- which conventional etymology regards as an Indo European common "vaguely intensive" prefix, in Lithic analysis often suggests that what follows is an action, an actor, such as an animal, or at least something phenomenal from the world of human action. Snap can be read as action-present-pop or crack. It does not say that. But that is a fair representation of the semantic content that went into the string that makes the word. Anima (Latin), the soul, has long been accepted as echoic from an original breath of air, and so the breath of life and so the soul. After all when you are dead your breath disappears. Eric Partridge sets out to analyse the echoism and starts out well: "a- a slow moving in-breathing, plus ne- a moment of relaxed breath-ing plus -ma a strong out breathing". If you try to reproduce this sequence you will find yourself faced with three breaths instead of the usual two, an in and an out, and you will have to open your mouth for the third and final out breath, the strong one, to get a ma. In reality it is possible to recognise a light click in the gullet as the direction of breath changes from in to out but that is some way from a nasal tone and even further from ni, and following it with a third stage open-ing the mouth for a ma does not echo reality. Breathing with the mouth open we can recognise an a and a na. The -ma in anima looks like an additional semantic suffix in Lithic, and can be read as m'a which can only be verbalised as him aa:

the semantic content is 'that extensive' in other words the meaning refers to the continuity of the breathing and it should not be taken to refer just to a single breath as echoed.

The principal virtue of the soul which is here an entified breathing process (air is rather insubstantial) is that it is the insubstantial element making up life which continues, while the substantial part is mortal. These echoisms have clearly been taken from sleep patterns when breathing reveals its tonal values. Normally when awake we breath silently. So we have flatus from fla(in)-ter(out), and spiritus from spi(in)-ri(out), both Latin, and atmos from at(in)-mau(out), Greek, and atman from at(in)-man(out), Sanskrit. Readers will recognise the anemometer, the atmosphere and the mahatma from these breathing exercises, which are well worth grasping in order to experience the power of the echoic, such as it is. It has been enough to set Sapiens Sapiens off on his poesy. Animals are breathing species (with a recognisable nose) but are not usually taken to be further blessed with the Latin anima or soul, nor yet with its masculine version, animus the thinking mind. Since thinking was taken to be insubstantial – it is – it seemed reasonable to relate it closely to the insubstantial spirit which informed and indeed provided life, the elan vital of philosophy.

Nay (2) negatives aye, just as never negatives ever. Rather more esoterically no negatives au, which means the totality and can therefore be written o. No means none, and so not at all, pas du tout, full stop. We don't have au in our English vocabulary. We have o and treat it as the same as no and call it naught, from no wiht, nothing, as a blank o instead of an inclusive one. Negare in Latin means to deny, to say no, or nay-make in Lithic; and negro in English, now taboo in the West for fear of causing offence to Africans, means not gerau, that is not rayed by the sun and therefore as black as night. Nether negates ether, the upper air. Ether, ai-ta(h)i-rai is become rayed by the sun, ra, which raises the plants so that they gerau or grow, and the same raising has apparently given us the upper air, or so our forebears assembling language evidently thought. Nought negatives aught (or wiht?). Somewhat more controversially, in- negatives ai; and sin negatives sai, although ai and sai do not appear on their own in English (as going and comfortableness/existence); narrow negatives arrau, that rayed again but this time not raising anything for the boys but instead rounding out for the girls. We have always personalised the way our world behaves, and much of our personal perception has been based on our own sexual experience. The Egyptian rays in chapter 13 on the phoneme Ra were prayed in aid to account for any action at a distance, and our physical sexual responses, like our thoughts and mood swings, were taken to result from invisible rays of one kind or another arriving from without. The sun was first recognised in Egypt as a world vagina birthing light into the world.

Since the male member rises when aroused the feminine member must therefore be the source of the rays which draws it out and up, just as the sun does the same for the plants. With a bit of hindsight and a slightly more critical mind set today we can see that the transference of performances was really the other way about. Since the male member rises, the crops are doing the same. Since the vagina rounds out when roused it acquires the same facility as the sun and in turn signals to the male. It starts out narrow and finishes arrau or round. It was a laughable corollary that the feminine vagina started every sexual encounter since the male organ was sheathed and unable to ray back until it had been roused by a feminine ray. There may be some sense in this but if so the process takes place in the minds of the participants and not by means of any physical rays, which leaves open who is the initiator and who the initiated, and in reality the circumstances will be as various as circumstances usually are. It was certainly taken as no laughing matter by the Pharaohs of Egypt, who reckoned as Ra's sons they were entitled to take the initiative in every encounter, as royalty are apt to do, and cut off their muzzle covers so they could fire first. It has not been explained as yet why Ra should not have thought of the rearrangement of the male member in the first place for himself, had he wished male members to wear foreshortened foreskins. Perhaps unsurprisingly this particular piece of thinking has been banished to the subconscious dark room down below and does not feature any longer in the language with which we choose to communicate today. The arrow we recognise is not rounded out but instead flies through the air 'as the sunray does', up and away on its return journey to the sun. The name may even be echoic of the sound made by a flush of a few hundred well fledged arrows as they are discharged from the bow in battle. In Sumerian, as in Latin, the arrow is sag-i-ta, sag is the head in Sumerian from Lithic sa-gai, the top of the body, and i-ta, which punctures. The arrow was a weapon which penetrated at a distance like a bullet, when most weapons were wielded.

For a phoneme supposed to have originated in the ultimate pleasurable sensation there is little enough in the linguistic record at first sight to confirm the sense. This is perhaps because orgasm does not play much part in polite conversation. Or else we do not feel ourselves in full control at this instant in time and therefore lack confidence when adverting to it. The Old English cennan meant to beget, kai-nai'n with forms akin in Old Saxon kunni, Old High German cunni and Gothic kuni. If kai- is kindling, kau- is kindled, the male and female aspects of copulation as imagined by our forebears (in reality the perceptions are awry). Cunni suggests kinship with cunt, originally from Lithic kai-nai-tai, the kindled-orgasmic-birth canal. Comparable is vagina, Lithic u-a-kai-na, the orifice-that-kindled-gapes or orgasms. Compare the shameless Hindi sacred symbol in Hindu religion, the yoni, a close up worms eye view of the engorged vagina with exposed clitoris, Lithic ia-u-nai, it that-orifice-orgasmic. In Malay naim (4) means delightful. If the final m is the result of slovening mai via me to m, as commonly occurs, then it is highly significant: nai when mai, orgasming-[when]copulating. Moreover Malay nahak means desire from the Lithic na-ha-kai, what makes for the joy of sex; and ternahak, become desirous is described as overcome by desire. The ha phoneme (chapter 8) contributes a shock element, as in the Egyptian pa-hei, the joy-piece which we describe more prosaically as the penis, the pe-nai(s), the protruding piece(4), showing the preoccupation of the owner, and so even perhaps the witness piece. But come to think of it, it is the penis which plays the principal part in the original orgasmic na (4). It could be the orgasming piece. Yet we know it meant originally the protruding piece because it was used in Latin to refer also to a dog's tail, which when wagged may register delight but does not carry the nerve endings to allow stimulation to register an extremity of sensation. Indeed Chambers´ estimable Dictionary of Etymology represents the genital meaning of penis now as merely copied from the Latin penis meaning tail, the protruding piece, with the description simply brought round in front to refer to the male member, the little tail the boys carry in front. Of course Chambers has no Lithic; and that is all very well, but then it does remain to be explained why na should signify protruding in the first place, which in itself may present no problems for conventiomal etymologists who have decided to eliminate any such enquiry from their agenda by declaring all symbols randomly selected in the first place. But it is a view by now so palpably foolish as to need no further contradiction here. Na appears where its sexual credentials are fully established and the only character common to penises and tails, after all, is their orientation. The penis must surely win on points for emotional impact, tails maybe for greater public exposure when worn. But tails have no pull.

Eric Partridge is more ambitious than Chambers but he is also astray, heading the penis group with penates, the Roman household gods akin to the Latin penetralia, the innermost and hence the most secret parts (of beliefs for instance). Now there can be no doubt the penis is a penetrator as Partridge maintains, but the question which has to be confronted is whether the Latin penetration derives from the action of the penis or whether the penis is named from a previously established meaning for penetration to do with the household gods who were ensconced within, so that the penis during copulation was perceived as a copyist of these godlings, perhaps nipping in to present compliments to the penetralia, the innermost and secret parts. With the issue spelt out like this, the conclusion seems inescapable. We based our perception of general manoeuvre upon our private (bodily) experience and not the other way about. The Latin penetrare to penetrate is made up from the Latin elements pene-trahere, and trahere means to draw or pull along (and within), based upon sexual analogy. These are the feminine T-rays at work. The Lithic for trahere is quite clear cut. Ta-rai-hai-are is vagina-rayed-joying-verbal ending. The male organ is supposedly being drawn in by the (completely imaginary) active radar type of ray the birth canal emits which on its return to its source pulls the male genitalia back in with it, just like the vegetation which is drawn back up towards the sun by the sun's rays. In fact we can see that the transference of the idea was in reality from the genitalia to the sun, perceived by the Ancient Egyptians at one time as a world birth canal birthing light into the world every day. The basics are in chapter 13 on the phoneme Ra. The hei inserted before the final verbal suffix -ere in trahere is not fortuitous. It comes from the pleasurable sensation accompanying the original sexual exercise which framed the concept. The conclusion is obvious. The penis was the orgasmic protruding piece, the protruding aspect only also applicable to a tail. It supposedly got drawn within by the rays sent out from the opposite sex. The orgies around the hominid hearth were judged by the linguists to be initiated by the womenfolk, who were enjoying a new found humanity, that is they were were hie-ing the mai-ing just as well as their mates (the meaning of humanity), and initiating the copulation.

The cart is often put before the horse like this where conventional etymologists want to have the penis a tail because they have no knowledge of Lithic psychosemantic contents to guide them and are quite unaware of the Egyptian rays in chapter 13. The dog itself in Latin is canis, which confirms the perception of the penis as the protruding piece since the ka was the male contribution to the human body, the skeleton and all-important framework (on which the fair sex was judged merely to hang the dependent flesh in the womb). With the dog, canis from ka-nai(s), here was the end of its backbone (ka) acting as its witness piece.

At the same time hei and nai have a lot in common. The ha syllable is analysed in chapter 8. It adds vehemence traditionally derived from Latin vehere to carry, now vehicular transport but originally in the days of human porters u-ai-hei-are, when going strenuously, ie under burden, for instance under a forty pound pack which after a mile or two you know well you are carrying, and then with the usual –are verbal suffix. Anyway in Malay nak or na' is to desire (3), usually taken to be a short form of hendak, from hei'n-da-ka, copulate-do-make, and for the most part reduced to a prediction, not what we want but what we will, we will it, or perhaps better in the Malay idiom it is willed, we have been struck with that desire so that that is what we intend to do. There will be other cases of the na phoneme meaning enjoyment, but English mostly passes them by. There is only nice and it has such a troubled etymology it is hardly worth the effort disentangling it. As well as pleasing it also means precisely accurate or discriminating, a curious mix. It comes via protruding, presenting, showing, making explicit and clear, discriminating, and so finally precise accuracy. These semantic contents conventionally are supposed to originate from (the meaning of) the Latin nescire, not to know, to be ignorant. Eric Partridge demonstrates the supposed semantic catena thus: "ignorant, innocent, whence....foolishly, whence shy, hence discriminating...hence agreeable, pleasant". He seems easily pleased when meanings have to be got to run in a single straight line rather than the Lithic reality of whimsical cross currents and polysemy in every phoneme. Ignorant and foolish string well enough, and perhaps innocent and shy with agreeable and pleasant, if barely. But discriminating seems to be well out on a limb. Shyness does not arise from a hyper discriminating mind as Partridge seems to require. Most likely it comes from the subconscious dark room hinting at realities the conscious mind does not wish to entertain. It typically afflicts teenage girls not yet ready to plunge into the sexual jungle opening up before them but beginning to recognise its pulls. It comes from confusion and lack of understanding as well as a refusal to face up. It is a long way from nescire.

But then Partridge also derives science from scire which he thinks is "probably originally to cut through, hence to decide, quoting Sanskrit chyati he cuts and Irish scian'a a knife. These are really from ka, via kha, the flint knappers' ka from the sound of striking off a flake. Lithic suggests scire is from sai-kai-verbal suffix, sai-making, making illuminated, clear; in which case the nai in nice is not a negative (5) as Partridge imagined but is the same as the Malay nah, which comes from show (13) and means 'here you are, take it', as in "Nah! Do biji ubat": Nah!, here you are! Do(pronounced doe), two, biji, little bits, ubat, medicine: or 'Here take these two pills'. With the Malay ubat ba is to burgeon or bloom and u-ba-tai is altogether-blooming-becoming, a make-you-well or medicine. The nicety is nai-sai, understanding showing and also showing comfort, as originally around the hearth; or delight such as sugar makes on a purely tasting scale. Nice gets some of its pleasurable niceness from its first phoneme nai, it is not unreasonable to suppose, but it is the dual meaning of sai which yields a nice, that is to say warm and comfortable, whence a pleasant taste, but also a bright and clear and so a precise judgment. You need the Lithic analysis in chapter 14 for ish to identify these meanings which are gulled some way from the original flame. Without Lithic you take your fragile mental catamaran up the semantic creek without a paddle. A catamaran is fom the Tamil and the Lithic is ka-tau-m'a-rai'n, join-two-him'that-rayed'one. The -m'a-ran, the him'that-rayed-one bit, is Tamil for a tree, Lithic ta-rai in English, in both cases the sun's rays being the agency for drawing the trunk out and up, and appearing in the linguistic symbolisation. All vegetation is subject to this universal processing but the trees are evidently the dab hands with their responses which explains how they grow so strong and tall. In fact ma-ra'n could be massive-grown'one rather than him'that-rayed'one. The catamaran, two (dugout) trees tied together – kattu is tied in Tamil – is a design which has led to the trimaran design ("three trees") which has the solo round the world sailing record today – probably fibre-glass trees. Its mental avatar has made its way just with its Lithic paddle over the generations around the world. With random word elements you would not get very far.

Canabis, the hemp plant in many languages, including Sumerian the oldest language known, where the name is read as kunibu giving a Lithic analysis of kau-nai-bau, what makes-ecstacy-of the flesh. What pleasure (4) of the flesh is intended is open to debate; as indeed is also the Lithic analysis – like all Lithic analyses; but particularly in this case because of the extreme antiquity of the source and the limited understanding of the Sumerian phonetics involved. But hemp seems to clinch the matter since it reads as hei-em-pai, where the em means of, where the pai closely resembles the Egyptian pahei or joy piece the glyph for which is an unmistakable penis in arousal. Moreover the Old English version was haenep from hei-nai-pai, while the Old saxon was hanap, the Old High German hanaf, from Lithic elements ha-na-pa-hai, Old Icelandic hampr, from ha-na-pa-rai, Albanian kanap, Lithuanian Kanapes, Persian kamb and Greek kannabis, these citations being from Partridge and Chambers. The halucinatory drug made from hemp is mildly addictive and can provide a high which is usually extremely pleasurable though sometimes horrific. The ancients appear to have associated it with sexual arousal (4). How the moderns find it today is moot for oldies who have not indulged, but the young will keep taking it, with a persistence usually associated with the sex drive. Canabis leads in Latin to canabaceus, hempen, and so to Old Northern French canevas and current English canvas, made from hemp. Walshe's Concise German Etymological Dictionary of 1952 also cites Cheremis and Zyrjan words, both languages from the Finno-Ugric family. Knowledge of the drug seems to have travelled widely. There was certainly something powerful going for it. There is some black humour in the reports of the brewers' droop which follows its use. Droop goes with drip, drop, and dribble. Curiously the drai- or drau- which mark the drawing up and out also function as drawn down and out, pendant in fact: erect or flaccid depending on context. Lithic is like that.

Both Partridge and Chambers go on to record canvassing as tossing in a canvas sheet and seek to relate this to canvassing for votes which seems a rather far fetched semantic catena. Partridge has it to be by way of sifting through canvas, hence sifting thoroughly, whence examining thoroughly; which is still some way from canvassing as usually conducted. Chambers finds tossing in a canvas sheet and canvassing for votes "seemingly unrelated", after reporting the supposed trace via shaking out and examining carefully. More likely canvassing is from unscrupulous wooing of the electorate by providing the pleasures of the flesh, food and drink, while speech making, now democratically confined to offering promises of future pleasurable improvements in voters' fortunes in return for their votes. Canvassing in the form of tossing in a canvas sheet or sifting through canvas goes back to the sixteenth century and is best ignored. A canvasser is offering voters, at several removes, promises of the pleasures of the flesh the party plans to provide for him. Of course he does not know what his terminology implies. The subliminal effects are unknown, but apparently modest.

A snipe is a small bird of the open heath with a very long bill. Victorians would serve it spatchcocked with its long bill stuck through its body as a skewer. Si-nai-pai is brer-protruding-piece (6) in Lithic. The snipe also drums in flight, a celebratory diving wing flutter which makes a sound which has to be heard to be appreciated: zze-zze-zze-zze, lasting about ten or twelve zze on end, faster than you can easily say them, a bit like the flush of feathered arrows. When flushed from cover it escapes in jerking zig-zag flight making it hard to hit. Shooting it is a shame, it is only a mouthful. A drum is ta-rau'm, a ta-rayed or stretched out-him, a skin stretched on a frame which vibrates when struck, with a booming sound which puts the snipe to shame. There is perhaps some bucolic bawdy in both the snipe and its drumming. A sniper is a snap shooter picking off fleeting targets (like snipe), single enemy who expose themselves often at extreme range, a badged infantry skill. Snipe (6) is from si-nai-pai, brer-protruding-piece, also with ecstacy in his wings. The protruding piece however is actually his beak, which is almost as long as the bird, for poking in the mud for creepy crawlies to eat, and was used as a skewer stuck through the body with its head twisted round when these birds were served as a dish. As a boy on the Norfolk breck I would wander off to the heath behind the local mere to listen to the drumming, and hated the world for eating the birds.

A banana, like the seven armed star fish nabinabi (with a plethora of protruding bits) in Malay, fruits in a bunch of protruding upturned pieces. It is from the Taino, a West Indian tongue and is akin to the Arawak prattana which says the same with perai-ta-nai, raised pieces-become-protruding. No doubt the nudge-nudge linguists who named the fruit enjoyed the similarity with the relevant human performance. But the appearances will have been taken quite seriously to indicate a common reality: the banana was bananaing because nature dictated the performance just as the human genitalia behaved as they did. It was a game of spot the common pattern, no different at all from the way scientists practise today. It was to take hundreds of thousands of years to knock them into shape. Whilst with the fruit, we can notice briefly buah nanas in Malay, the pineapple, with a fruit on it the shape not of an apple (which means fruit, like the phallus) but a pine. The Pine tree has a tall upright trunk without branches, another protruding piece our elders remarked, with a cone for which the tree was really named. Apple, with seventeen cognates in Indo-European languages, is akin to phalos in Greek which actually referred to the knob or fruiting body on the end of the penis and not to the whole member at all. In the old days boys had three balls, one above and two below, a very early trinity; and indeed the foot type of ball may have been named after the testicle rather than the other way around as is commonly imagined. Buah in Malay is fruit, and the pineaple fruit is like an outsize acorn or oak corn, or glans in Latin, when pai-na, in arousal. Buah pelir in Malay are the testicles or penis fruit, since pelir is Malay for the penis. This is akin to the Greek phalos, although unrelated linguistically – other than from the Lithic. La, chapter 9 embraces liquids, flowing downhill (an instinct in all liquids), looping like the line round the ocean where it meets the sky, and the orbiting of Apollo the sun, and inflating or ballooning in an enlarging loop like the phallus. The Greeks refer to the pa-hai-lau(s), the inflated ecstacy piece, the Malays more simply to the pai-la-ire, the inflating piece. The anti-Lithic lobby have to explain how the minds of the Greeks and Malays got together, not a congruent couple of words but close enough, if their minds were really not informed at some level by similar sounds having similar semantic contents, so as to need some other explanation. They should perhaps concentrate on that and leave aside any reservations they may have about the subject matter not being in the best of taste or leaving them out in the cold. Our forebears had not invented the idea of good or bad taste and sailed ahead with their word formations as their thoughts prompted them. As early humans, hei-u-ma'n, their joint enjoyment of copulation is writ large in the linguistic record. In half a million years the physical pattern still pertains in language at least.

Nibs, nebs and nabs are all three prominences, and a nipple is a little one that leaks liquid. Even the belly button or navel protruded originally. The Old English was nafala, the Sanskrit nabbhis, the Old Persian nabis. They had to get hold of the navel string in clumsy hands before they could get a flint to it or maybe their teeth, so there was a bee hive effect rather than the sexy dimple now embellished in the West with studs and ringlets. The umbilicus or Greek omphalikos, the hump, or him-phalus-shaped was for the Greeks a symbolic centre of the body and therefore also a symbol for religious centres, which they marked with stone navels like bee hives or acorns. The acorn is an ak or oak kara nai, or head protruding. Kara is skull in Greek. Latin cornu (the horns of cattle) are skull-dual-protrusions, kara-u-nau, as indeed they are. The corn grows a prominent seed head. A bead is a bai-a-tai, a bit with a hole (drilled in it). But the bead on the foresight of a firearm is also a barley corn. It has no hole in it but stands up, a tiny knob for aiming with. A knob is ka-nau-bai in Lithic, the shape (ka) of a protruded bit. Naik is an ascent in Malay, from nai-kai, an up-going, and kenaikan is to rise, to make an ascent. A knot in wood is a protrusion from a cut side branch, and a gnarled trunk is one with many knots. Canis, Latin for a dog, is the one with the waggly tail. The ka resides in the spine and the dog's spine protrudes at the tail end, whereas the cow (kau) has dual skull protruberances, its horns, cornu, karau-nau, in front. The gnu has two horns too but it is named by the South African bushmen n'ku like the cow and only altered to gnu by whitey. With ka a corner and a joint the knee (ka-nai) is the protruding joint. Elbows, wrists and ankles do not present their corners in front. In France the knee is genou, -nou in place of −nai. Both are in Lithic protruded and presented, the -nau rather more forcefully than the merely −nai.

A canopy comes from the Latin canopeum and the Latin is from the Greek konopeion the neuter of konopeios the adjective from konops, a mosquito, and the Greeks had it like much else from the Egyptians. It is widely suggested the etymology is influenced by the Egyptian city of Canopus, though it is intrinsically unlikely the city name had anything to do with mosquitos, however many were around. The citizens will not have welcomed them. Lithic can offer Ka-en-nau-pu-tse for the Egyptian city, if it was mosquito city: body-of-exposed-hot-mouth or stinger. A mosquito stings any bare flesh. The Greek konops is from kau-nau-pai-sai, body-exposed-picker-firey; and the canopy is from a body-exposed-cov-ering-one(substantive). The pai-tse is like the pussy cat which in turn quite sur-prisingly is from Akaddian pu (mouth)-tse (spit), the cat being known as a spit mouth. Cats spit. Mosquitos bite. The Akaddian is echoic. The mosquito is more like the Hamitic Tsetse fly, another hot lips. It is the same s as in sting, which meant to prick, but a firey prick, a sai-tai-ng or sting, a hot puncturing, which is what you get. It is perhaps necessary to repeat from time to time that Lithic is a semantic study and when words in one language are suggested as indicating the meaning in another, it is not the words offered which are supposed to provide the indications but the meanings. Critics often forget this and object to connections claimed between wholly unrelated languages because there can not have been any linguistic contact. The Lithic hypotheses per contra claim that the human race has been thinking the same − if you dig deep enough − all along; and these correspondences of meanings when the phonetic record is looked at with proper perception demonstrate as much. The correspondences come from the common human stock of psychosemantic (now mostly subconscious) identifications. There is no suggestion English words, for example, somehow influenced Inuit, Navaho, Malay or Chinese words. They did not, unless by some remote and improbable borrowing we know nothing of. Indeed assumed borrowings have been used, all unawares, to cover up Lithic correspondences, and only become absurd when they involve prehistoric travelling beyond belief. Malay, the classic magpie language under this rubric, turns out to be related to a very early source language now lost, spoken in the Garden of Eden, the plains East of Malaya, the present Garden Land, which are now three hundred and fifty feet under the South China Sea. That is how Malay provides a conduit to Lithic meanings so readily. Inheriting on the periphery an advanced civilisation of its day, there has been the less impetus for change and the more respect for tradition.

Malay jankal mankal means sticking up irregularly, a bit of jankal and a bit of mankal as it were. Malay jongkang is sticking up, up-shape in Lithic, or perhaps ups-making. Jan or jong is up. The Chinese copies. Shang-hai is On-sea, strictly above the ahai or awai, ocean with a cockney h to separate the first a- (now lost) from the -ai. Ocean, incidentally, akin to the earlier Greek okeanos appears to be from the Lithic au-kai-a-nau-(s), from an original au-kai-awa-nau-(s), that one-strong-water-presenting(in the same case ending as the one)-substantive ending. The idea is one of powerful waters. The sheer force of an ocean swell will certainly have impressed ancient seafarers venturing to sea with dugout canoes or trussed bamboo rafts. Canoe (Taino canoa) from the Lithic ka-nau-a, means hard-hollow-one or dugout. The hard hollowed was a tree trunk. The English cannon has much the same Lithic elements, as does the Spanish cana or cano, a tube, as well as Spanish canyon a large tube or hollow, and so also a deep high sided valley carved out by rushing waters. A cane is hollow like a canoe – well not all that much like, but semantically out of the same common semantic stable.

Mai on the other hand is the opposite of shang-, jan- and jong-. Sticking up irregularly involves some sticking up and some dipping down. What we finish up with is a zigzag horizon like a line of mountains in the distance. Geology can be almost as good as sex when it comes to identifying the Lithic origins of words. So in Malay we have nusa an island, from the Lithic elements nau-sai, protruded-up. An island sticks up out of the surrounding water. Nu- with the completive vowel u even suggests the protrusion is something which has taken place and is now a done job, as if historically islands have done their arising. In fact this is what was widely believed and forms a significant part in creation myths, particularly the Ancient Egyptian ones, since one or two submarine volcanic eruptions had shown it happening. Similarly stone was considered to be sai-tao'n fire-born 'n, since volcanic eruptions had shown fiery lava turning to stone. It was common sense for anyone who had seen a volcanic eruption. From nusa an island we have Nusantara the Indonesian archipelago, that string of islands federated today as the Indonesian Republic, a corrupt nominally Moslem empire held together with violence and with island guerillas fighting for independence. The Lithic is nausa-en-tara, 'islands-of-drawn out': a string of islands, the archipelago, using a metaphor originally sexual (see chapter 13 on the phoneme Ra) but in this case naturally disposed rather than by the fanciful sex rays from the girls playing upon the male member. Our chest of drawers has the same semantic pedigree, and the underwear is such as you step into and pull up too. A drawer is pulled out and drawers are pulled up, both like the male member when tau-rayed.

To ransack Malay still further we have the nibong palm, with a straight naked trunk (a trunk is from tai-rau'n-kai, a drawn out shape; and a tree is similarly drawn up above ordinary greenery) and there is a burgeon, a tuft of greenery protruding at the top of the palm. Ba is flesh (chapter 4), or foliage in the case of vegetative life forms. An elephant's trunk is of course a protruding proboscis up front and one suspects the elephant comes from ai-lai-pahei-n-tai, them-long/flexible-penises-of-dual, except that the earlier Greek elephas has no –nt, ending instead with an –s. But we are perhaps entitled to ask why the -nt got added later. The indication is somebody was thinking in terms of a proboscis at both ends and using a metaphor originally sexual. The Greeks seem to have thought "what a long member!", leaving it to their countrymen to decide which one to consider. The Aryan mind added the consideration Mr Twococks, with a tail at both ends. The nibong palm is also used to describe a brindled dog. But a dog does not have a tufted head. Nai-bau(ng) can be read as showing dual flesh. The brindling is an intermixture of hairs of two colours in its coat, brindled being from the Middle English brinded, finely branded or streaked. A streak is like a string, but perhaps the s- in this case indicates the mark was originally burnt; although in chapter 14 on ish the initial s- which occurs in many English words making s the biggest section of any letter in the dictionary, which is often described by conventional etymology as vaguely intensive (whatever that really means), is derived from the existential character of ish, like is for example. It means the word originally referred to a phenomenal item, and was not an abstract term. That is why there are so many of them. That was the common pattern of initial (Lithic) symbolisation. With the palm the final u is completive. With the brindled dog it is dual – from the prehistoric dialectic in chapter 15. No Lithic, no comprehension.

Finally for the protrusion sense (6) of na there is the Roman frog: in Latin rana. Frogs have eyes mounted on the top of their heads so they can observe when submerged in a pond with just their eyes above water. Ra is eye or eyes in Egyptian. Ra-na is eyes protruding, or "Old Pog-Eye". Disappointingly the Greek, the common intermediary between Egyptian and Latin, has batraxos, and Aristophanes had his frog chorus singing "Grek-ek-ek-ex coax-coax", a croaking song, fanciful perhaps but we can follow him. They called the frog a croaker. Cold climate frogs croak less, it is a sex call, and if deprived of the sun's rays they can not copulate. The croaker may have displaced rana, which if you don't know your Lithic is a bit dull, although if you do it is delightful. Ba-tra-ks-aus, behind the Greek, is twisted mouth, and it is also echoic of a raucous croak. Frogs as well as gnomes are modelled for the garden, and the frogs all have exageratedly prominent eyes to appeal to the comic muse, showing this character is well established. In fact frogs are prestigious leapers as well as croakers and the bull frog leads in all these fields being hefty and muscular like the bull. Frog is from pahai-rao-kai, his leap makes a movement which is ejaculatory like the rayed and roused penis The common fircone (6) is akin to Latin conus, a fircone (which has a protruding shape), and to Greek konos from which establishment linguistics derives Greek konikos and French conique, and we have the far more precise conic sections. The Lithic ka-u-nai-kau-s means made-protruding- shaped-substantive marker, or shape-when-protruding-kindled-substantive marker. In either case it is the acorn shape or glans, viz the shape of the knob of the penis when aroused. (Sorry folks!) The geometrical shape is a little more precisely described. It is rounded and comes to a point, and it has a place in higher mathematics with conic sections and the equations for them. But that is where it comes from and that is the message of Lithic.

Now we move to meaning 7, to present, which is a straight gull from the action of the penis which, in times before trousers, presented itself in public when aroused so that it has been described as the witness piece, its angle of attack being a fair indication of what was occupying its owner's mind. For presentation there is of course an element of metaphor involved, that is to say it involves the impact on the beholder, already at one remove from the bare perception of protrusion, but that is a fine distinction it is not important to understand. Under the same rubric comes the shift from presenting to the present. The switch is highlighted by comparing a Christmas present with the present time. Probably not one English speaker in ten or even in a hundred makes any conscious attempt to relate these two meanings. Nevertheless they can quite easily be related. In the case of the Christmas present we are closest to the penis. We can envisage the actual process of presentation, holding the present and then extending the arms, pushing the present forward to put it within the grasp of the recipient, proffering the gift much as in a relationship the penis is proffered. The present time, now or nau, what is presented, (using –u in the substantive mode), relies upon the prehistoric view the world was presented in consecutive snaps of the state of affairs to human view, much like the early cinematograph machines which flickered from frame to frame. The one which is presenting itself is the state of affairs in the here and now. These ideas are picked up chiefly from the Egyptian language, a relatively recent language compared with the origins of speaking, our records of it only preserving at all precisely the form of the language some ten thousand years at the very most. But it is argued elsewhere that most of the divergence from the old ways of speaking has occurred only recently (since Babel). Nothing of course is certain when addressing a period so long ago. But then nothing at all is nearly as certain as most people imagine, including the whole body of science which only approximates reality at best. The one which is showing (10) is also nigh, spatially present or near (originally the comparative of nigh). Other Indo European languages have ni, nei, na, nah, nahe, nach, nehwa, etc. It is hard to distinguish anything other than the phoneme na as contributing anything to the meaning, and it means presenting and therefore presented and being present. New (14), akin to Latin nova, Greek neos, Sanskrit navas, Hittite newas, Tokharian A niu, Gothic niujis, Old High

German niuwe and finally Old Irish nue, to pick examples from Partridge again, is the same idea applied to the temporal dimension. All these cognate words in numerous Indo European (and some other) languages are all in Eric Partridge's etymological dictionary, but there is little point in wasting space and readers' patience quoting them extensively. The origins of speaking effectively form the second volume of Eric Partridge's own 972 page on origins.

Partridge has a nest (Latin nidus) "a place in which to sit down", presenting a perch as it were, although almost a hundred percent of all sitting in the last million years has been hunkered akimbo on the ground. Egyptian Isis, properly Au-Siti, World Life-Source, had a seat as her glyph, a throne. On it she sat suckling the infant Horus, a pose transferred later to the Virgin Mary, Au-Siti in Malay, Our-Lady, but also the Life-Source-sedentary on a seat, up become and at ease. The correspondences are compelling. In the Stone Age the women stayed at base camp with the children and keepers of the hearth. They were sources of the flame and warmth as well as of life – they fueled the fire, empathised and gave birth. Sai was warm, and so comfortable, and so pleasurable. To be sedentary was to be keeping the flame. Nowadays we put our tail ends in a chair. A nest presents a seat. Partridge treats nether as from a root ni meaning down where Lithic has nai as pointing up. But Lithic shows nai as a negative also, here the opposite of plain therai, drawn up. Under reinforces the Lithic, in this case un-drawn up.

Sand in Spanish is arena. The Latin is harena. Our arena had originally a sand covered floor. Sand is from the Lithic sai'n-dai, movement does, the shifting sands of the desert, where the wind blows the sand off the top of the dunes and deposits it in the low, so that the dunes move slowly across the landscape, sometimes invading living space, as in the British Breckland in the eighteenth century and drifting all the time in the deserts in the tropics. The surface of desert sand gets hot enough to burn bare feet. In sand the first phoneme sai as well as movement can mean hot. Sai'n-da does heat and movement both. Arena for sand is from the Lithic a-rai-na, that-(the sun's)rays-presents. Sand gets hot. The Latin harena has a cockney h, separating an initial i (since lost) from the a next door, i(h)a-rai-na, it-that-(the sun's)rays-presents. It is not such a bad description when the sand gets so hot it burns your feet. The Hittite seems to confirm the analysis of the Latin and Spanish, their word for sand being koraiz, Lithic ka-u-rai-ish, land-what-rayed-fire, a land surface which heats up under the sun's rays. The Latin introduces an ish too in an alternative hasena as a variant of harena.

A noise, being auditory, presents problems for semantic analysis but in the event the Lithic proves easy: nau-i-sai, presentation-of which-moving. Most natural noises are made by a movement of some sort. With speech on the other hand the movements are not what catches the attention, it is the sounds uttered and the meanings which can be attached to them. If you wanted to mime a noise you would I suppose make a variety of noisy movements. You would not include any utterances, like a roar or shout for instance, since that would mislead the guessing into searching for meaning or emotion. In the jungle a noise indicates movement, perhaps of a predator, or nowadays a terrorist. Wild pigs rootling are a pest in the jungle at night. It is best to just ignore noises in the dark concentrating merely on not making any. Not many tigers are left and terrorists can't see to move in the jungle at night.

The Arabic for a lighthouse is menorah. The Egyptian is pharos, ejaculate-rays-of light. The Arabic says much the same but in a different idiom, mai-nau-rai, planting-nau-rays[of light], copulatory-orgasmic-rays, sudden bursts of light. The Malay is rumah api, house of fire. But a Malay house is defined in terms of the activity which goes on in its shelter: rau-ma(h)i, rayed planting, warm begetting. It may sound far fetched. Just two phonemes are hard to be sure about. But then look at the Ancient Egyptian: hoiku, i(h)au-i-kau, it-that-where-they-be-gotten, and the Greek ekoi (in ekoi-nomoi, home laws, household management, economics. The original light houses had a fire in them. A railway train is a kareta api, a fire chariot, with api from a-pai, the flame being un-surfaced, without a solid surface like water, pani, in Hindi, surface-none.

The Latin genere means to procreate, and the Lithic elements are kai-nai-are, making-orgasmic-verbal suffix; a fair indication in itself of the meaning of the phoneme na even if additional evidence were wanting. As Partridge puts it at the head of 25 paragraphs on this group of no less than 95 words akin, including general, generator, genius, genes, genitals, jaunty, gendarme, genuine, germ, gentility, genealogy, gentile, progeny and even the genitive case, none of which are particularly orgasmic: "the relationships between Greek, Latin and Sanskrit are strikingly numerous and intimate". Sanskrit ajananta, they were born, matches with Greek egenonta; and Sanskrit ganus with Latin gens, a clan. It is important to give Partridge's research work an occasional airing like this to draw attention to the relatedness of words within a language family which is already fully established. Lithic relates the families in turn, a task which has so far defeated phonetic researchers, by pursuing the semantic connections, a pursuit which offers up a different set of congeners. Immediate examples of the different phonemic strings used in different languages to define the same things by way of the same meanings are sand and lighthouse above.

Ignis, the Latin for fire, compares with Lithuanian ugnis (often particularly close to Sanskrit) and Sanscrit agni-s and is from the Lithic a-kai-nai-ish, that-making-show (10)-flame. This is quite interesting since it seems to suggest that the idea of fire was of something lying behind the flame, which might manifest itself in the fully expressed burning form of the flame or perhaps less forcefully in the heat of the bodies of all animal species. If so it was not good science, but it was certainly science. It may even throw some light on the nature of the magic bird the phoenix which burnt to death and then arose from the dead, which we will look at shortly. The ichneumon, an Egyptian weasel or mongoose means the tracker or hunter in Greek. Ichnos is a track, akin to Lithuanian eiga a walk or course. Lithic ai, extending, and its semantic cognates including going are explained in chapter 15 on the vowels. The Lithuanian eiga, a walk (and so a track made by an animal or person going), is clearly from the Lithic phonemes ai-ka, going makes, and relates English go and Latin ire (from ai-are) to go, to extend (your distance from your point of origin). Partridge relates the Greek ikhnos, from ai-khai-nau, go-ing-makes –shown, to a supposed "Indo European root *eigh to go, an extension of ei to go (as in the Greek and Latin verbs)". Lithic does not subscribe to word analysis by cutting them down to "roots" of a single syllable. Tracking is following a traveller from the traces of passage left, which is the track. The Lithic in the first phoneme does indeed validate Partridge's guessed "root", but he misses all the rest out, which is what makes sense of the word as his "root" can not. The ichneumon's eating, ichneu-mon, tracked-mau'n, is by tracking down its prey, often apparently by smelling out the nests of buried crocodile eggs. The ichneumon fly which lays its eggs in caterpillars which hatch and eat out the catapillar while still alive, leaving the vital organs until last, is a tracker for the purpose of the plantation (mau'n) of its eggs. In point of fact the Egyptian for ichneumon appears to have been kha-tarai[2], make-ta-rayed, drawn out, or here along. Either it was supposed to send out an attractive ray and follow along the ray as it returns (which guides its search) or else it picks up and follows up the ray emitted by its prey, which seems the better idiom. It is an originally sexual metaphor like so much in Egyptian hieroglyphics.

The Japanese art of flower arrangement meanwhile, ikebana, is from iheru which means to arrange from to put in a row, and bana which is flower. Bana flower is interesting. Ba in Lithic is originally flesh or foliage. What is it about na which picks out the flower from the remainder of the foliage? The flowers attract attention because of their colours; and the pollenating insects (that some say are colour blind) are attracted by their scent. Is it possible von Linné's discovery in Sweden in the eighteenth century that flowers are the sexual organs of plants was old hat to the Japanese when they were dreaming up a name for flowers? But on the other hand flowers present the seed and fruit in due course, and with ani-mals ba can mean testicles as well as fruit. That is unsurprising once it is realised that they were taken to be seeds in a pair of fruiting bodies. The Japanese Stone Age naming committees' biological knowledge may well have extended that far. Linaeus in Sweden in the eighteenth century brought shame on his father, a pas-tor, and was driven off his head by the condemnation of the Swedish church when he suggested flowers were the plants' sexual organs. On the other hand flowers are foliage which present themselves to the observer and to the pollenating insects whether the attractants are associated with sex at all or not. The young ladies in the West pressing flowers to preserve them found them attractive because of their colours and delicacy alone. There is no obligation to suppose Japanese perceptions were any different.

Now we can deal with the Phoenician Phoenix group which Partridge was unable to crack. It involves Greek phoinix, a date palm, and Egyptian Pount (really Puntai), "a collective name for the Semites of the Eastern Mediterranean hinterland", Latin Poeni, the Carthaginians, the magic phoenix bird and the Greek phoinos for blood red or purple. Partridge says "The semantic succession and interaction are obscure. The date palm, the bird and the colour purple or scarlet senses of Greek phoenix all follow naturally from Phoenix a Phoenician; and phoenix could be an –ix derivation of phoinos blood red, purple if the Phoenicians were so named because they wore purple or scarlet robes. Probably however Greek Phoenikes, Phoenicians represents, as Boisacq suggests[3] the influence of Greek phoenos, blood red, purple upon Egyptian Pount, a collective name for the Semites of the Eastern Mediterranean hinterland". The Queen of Sheba, it may be remembered, allied Sheba with the land of Punt. We have a Phoenician tree, a Phoenician bird and Semites labelled Pount, and some purple as yet unallocated.

The date palm like the pine has a bare trunk with the leaves and dates in a bunch on top. It was a Phoenician tree only in the sense that its growing habit matched the habit of the Pount, in Lithic analysis Pu-nai-tai, the Exposed-glans-tribes, the Semitic circumcised tribes of the Eastern Mediterranean hinterland. The Lithic embedded in phoenix, a Phoenician is paha-u-ai-nai-kai (s), paha-one-that-is-exposed-made (substantive ending). Pahai or pa-hei is the ecstacy or rapture piece, pleasure organ or penis in Egyptian, or otherwise mai, the earther/planter/inseminator. These tribes were not dressed in red or purple. Far from it! Phoinos, blood red or purple, was the colour of their pahai or glans when nai (orgasmic), which invited ever so slightly snide comment in their case because of their comical custom of cutting off their foreskins exposing the glans as if wanting to show it off. It may even have referred subtly to the belief behind the practice, borrowed from the Pharaohs, that it gave them an edge on the girls by enabling them, with muzzle covers off, to fire their imagined sexual attractant rays first. That would surely raise a few smiles from amongst the powerful Jewish Momas. Indeed it may have been the conceit of the Pharaohs' belief that they were the divine penises on earth of their father the sun (Amun, aa-mau'n, for ever ejaculating (light) and so for ever loving, and so with some claim to starting off the perception of an ever loving God who valued even the sparrow's fall) which the Semites were judged to hanker after, and which got them their phoinei sobriquet from the pagan goys: who themselves were happy with what nature provided them, and enjoyed orgiastic revels on a regular basis. It is hard not to side with acceptance and turn against mutilation, for whatever reason. The "circumcision" of women, which involves cutting out the clitoris or feminine penis altogether, rather than merely cutting round the male penis, and then stitching up the vagina to prevent penetration is a scandal like genocide but leading to longer torture, a savagery which can not be excused. It is atavistic pagan male savagery and in a modern civilised world must be stamped out and its proponents heavily punished. It is hard to believe it has anything to do with Allah the All Merciful or with Islam. Punishment should perhaps fit the crime.

The word purple is of similar slightly off colour derivation since the l started out an r. The Old English was purpure and the Old French purpre, with the earlier Latin purpura, a purple dye from a fish called unsurprisingly purpura, the purple fish. The derivation of the colour and of the fish is "of obscure origin" according to Partridge. The Lithic elements when identified say pu-rai-pu-rai, that is to say penis-roused-glans-raying, where the second rai can be read as indicating colour, since it was supposed to be conveyed to the eye by a ray. (It is). The glans at this time is flushed red with blood and indeed purple round the rim. There were not many other purple coloured phenomena to direct Tarzan's attention to when the naming committees came to pick a name for purple. The fish was named the purple fish, since it supplied the colour, and the colour is not, back to front, taken from the name of the fish which had already been named purple on a casual random basis. The fish joins the sepia or cuttle fish which when pursued jets away behind a sepia cloud it squirts out and in this case is named for its performance and the colour is gulled from that. The Lithic is si-pia or brer pisser, and the colour is the gull. Fisher folk enjoy a joke – the bawdier the better. This one may be a very old one indeed.

The story of the magic phoenix bird is clearly an allegory, that is the story is otherwise than what it appears to be on the surface and has a concealed meaning, mutatis mutandis teaching a moral lesson or truth, or even being presented as a riddle to be solved. Chambers Dictionary of Etymology describes the phoenix as "the mythical bird that burns itself and rises from its own ashes. It is from the Greek phoinix; compare the Egyptian bjn: of unknown origin. The Greek word can not be related with the unrelated word phoinos red with blood and phonos murder". What sense can be made of this? Their bjn is better transliterated bai'n or ben and elsewhere benu, akin to Venus, the planet known as the Visitor but also with a hot line to orgasm and these days to venereal diseases and the viruses which attack the imune system. Venus's visits are supposed by some to date from a time when the planet was a short term comet not yet captured in close orbit by the sun's gravity, but the astronomical sciences are beyond the scope of the present study. The hieroglyph for Egyptian j is actually two feathers, better read as ai. One feather is a, the extensive vowel, but misidentified as e. A feather is probably used for the extensive vowel because the feather presents the extensive principle par excellence. Each single strand which stretches out from the central spine seems to be expressing the extensive instinct. Moreover the whole feather contributes in turn to the wing, which is extended and then (they thought) caught up and itself drawn up into extensive mode to fly into the sky. Look at the Greek pteron for wing, pai-tai-rau'n, surfaces-tau-rayed'one, drawn up one. It was supposed wings had ethereal sky hooks so that when they were extended they were snatched up into the sky. A helicopter is a helico-pter, a helical sky hook. Strictly petra is a surface (wing) or piece (stone) drawn up, and the meaning rock comes from the idea rocks are a piece of the earth's skeletal core (ka) drawn up to the surface – which of course geologically speaking they are. Rock, from the Lithic rau-kai actually says as much: raised-solids – kai is hard to capture in modern language because its meanings were so wide. Peter, the boy's name was perhaps magically to ensure his virility. Today he would be spammed on a daily basis with offers of a rock hard erection. Were Mr and Mrs Tarzan thinking along similar lines when they named their son and heir? If so, Simon Peter's parents will have missed the meaning by a hundred thousand years and more.

Lithic suggests that the phoenix bird the ancients had in mind was the pip-pit or better the Egyptian quail chick the Egyptians farmed for the table. They discovered the quail chicks always said pipi, and never a single peep. In point of fact the young of all game birds have this habit. Shepherds playing their pan pipes in Arcadia made a piping noise like a chick, so their pipes were known as chicks (pipi). The Egyptian genius fancied every animal and bird had as part of its heritage a knowledge, or was at least an illustration, of some natural principle – all their hundreds of animal headed 'gods' were really personifications of natural forces and had a 'natura' symbol before their glyphs (chapter 6), a triangular pennant blown out in the wind, Lithic na-tau-rai, showing the tau ray, the pull or natural – originally sexual – attractive force (in this case of the wind which draws air and pennants out together, the pennant exhibiting the force) which for reasons never explained the academic Egyptologists have identified as a pointed axe of divinity (sic).

The chick since it cheeped in twin cheeps was supposed to be equipped with one principle it acknowledged and displayed, namely that everything came in pairs. Really they don't. But this was already the belief of the Egyptians who had worked up a theory of a vowel dialectic presented in chapter 15 which comically enough, as we can nowadays see (since the collapse of the Marxist dialectic), they thought was a law of nature. It appears the original dialectic was an invention (misconceived as it happens) of the Ancient Egyptian mind, with the three vowels a, i and u (see chapter 15), the original vowel dialectic, later revised, by Socrates or else by Plato who attributed it to Socrates, as the Socratic Method. How far it actually went back before that is quite unknown, but perhaps hundreds of millennia to when you could get away with counting "one, two, both of them" in place of a legitimate third term in the series: tria juncta in uno. Of the three vowels, a and i were the first and second, parents if you like; and u was the resultant completive, the child if you like, which grew up to out-top its parents as the dual or completive and substantiating vowel. Replicating this pattern provides the Marxian pattern, like a chain mail of coat hangers: his dialectic.

Much of these matters is in other chapters but it all has to be brought together here to explain the phoenix group. This 'vowel oon' or dialectic was the reason for the quail chick which said pipi being named pu and then used as a glyph to stand for the vowel u. Pa meant 'that' or 'the' in Egyptian, and there was at the same time some uncertainty whether the second and third vowels, i and u, should be treated as new sounds or glosses on the 'original' and basic one, aaa, the daddy of the three; and so whether the i was really to be regarded as ai and the u as au, now the dipthongs e and o. So pa-u said the u in Egyptian, and consequently the quail chick glyph, from its piping pipi, was used for the vowel u. You need to have your wits about you to keep up with the priests of Amun, who made up the hieroglyphs. They seem to have invented human whimsy, positively rejoicing in poetic polysemy; but this is only because before them there is no record readily available. Academic Egyptologists seem to think that the quail chick uttered "Wai!" rather than pipi and so was used for w. But it is most likely that since they saw no need for any reason for the use of any sound to represent any symbolisation, because the selection is supposed to be random, they just accepted what appeared without putting it to the torture to see what they could discover. Anyway it was a miss by a mile. A pan pipe could be gulled for any similar sized and shaped item and it is not hard to guess the organ they picked upon, which does not pipe or whistle at all, just as a gull wing is not a sea caller's wing but an aircraft wing the same shape, which does not call at all. The Latin penis is from pai-nai-s(substantive) the protruding pan pipe or witness piece, and also in Egyptian the pa-hei or joy piece, the male phallus (for pa meanings see chapter 12, for hei meanings see chapter 9). In passing, it is pertinent to reflect upon how Peter Pan came to be named, the boy who never grows up, content with his little pan pipe, pipit in Malay meaning sparrow and a male child's genitals (diminutive pipe) together.

We are now in a position to explore the allegory of the phoenix. It reads in Lithic, still probably semi conscious in Egyptian times, pa-hei-au-ai-nai-kai (s), the penis-that one-that is-orgasmic-when kindled (substantive suffix). To substantiate this you also need to know something of the Egyptian rays of chapter 13, based on the rays of the sun (Ra) which were taken to be emanations of fire. It is unfortunate this precedes the chapters in which the background of some of the elements involved is explained. It may well become clearer and less presumptive later. It really involves reading the whole book through twice, but that is asking a lot. Getting rayed could be from the flames of the hearth at night as well as from the greater flames of the sun by day. Sex rays were inflamation by the fire element in animals including man. It was not that the sexual experience was actually thought of as burning but it was identified as an avatar of what it was to catch fire, flare up and burst into flame. It was an element of fire which provided the normal warmth of the body. Orgasm was a flare up. It was that simple. From the ashes of last night's experience the pipi or pahei, the phoenix was reborn, again and again, ready for another flare up.

The Pount were really pu-nai-tai, the glans-exposed-tribes, of the Eastern Mediterranean hinterland. The Carthaginians were Poeni, their language Punic, they were Phoenicians, kai or people with Phoenai, bared glans, circumcised folk, Semites bidding for imperial conquests based upon their undoubted skill as seamen. We can judge they discovered America from the Canary islands (like Columbus a thousand years later, following a folk memory of a Far Western Land) because of the Lithic traces they left there on their way. America is akin to the small island of Gomera twenty kilometers due West of Tenerife. Because of the prevailing winds coming up the Atlantic ocean along the African coast line a tuft of cloud over Gomera often provides stunning sunsets seen from Tenerife, in view of which blood red but never purple displays much of this book has been written. The width of the island still just about matches the movement of the sunset between the equinoxes. In Carthaginian, a provincial cousin of Egyptian, Gomera is Ga-u-mai-Ra, Land-where-dies-the sun, Sunset isle or Western land. In Carthaginian, never mind the Lithic, America is Aa-mai-Ra-ka or Far-dying-of the sun-land, Far Western land. It provides a frisson to realise that three thousand years ago Carthaginians were marvelling at the same sunsets from the same window on the world and that in the local language is the evidence of their voyaging so far in the past. The inhabitants the Spanish found in the fifteenth century called themselves Guanche, or in Carthaginian Ga-u-en-khai, Land-where-in-begotten, or the native folk, as they had been taught to do three thousand years before when they had had to learn to speak the Carthaginian of their Phoenician overlords.

In Carthaginian also Canary comes from Ka-en-aria, Coast of rocks or Rocky coast islands. Petra a rock is a piece of the –tarai or arai. The idea was of a piece of the core of the earth which has risen to the surface where it is exposed[4]. It was Pliny the Elder (who foolishly insisted on stopping behind and was killed by poison gases when Etna erupted and buried Pompei, and his son fled by boat without him) who made up the tale about the dogs, from Latin canis for dog. It was spin to conceal the Carthaginian achievement. But canis is third declension and doggy islands would have been Canery Isles. The pooches on the island are nondescript and insignificant in size. His fib lasted two thousand years until the Carthaginian origins of the topographical nomenclature were recognised. The canary is a bird first found in the islands. It was a dull grey green but sang well. In the eighteenth century in Germany they were able to breed from a sport with yellow plumage, and now they are pale yellow to tangerine in colour. They still sing but after two centuries kept in small cages perhaps less than in the wild.

Meaning 8 for na is exposed, which is not so far from protruding but does not require the same sticking out or up. These are both gulls from the behaviour of the male member, preceding meaning 9 (open, agape, empty) from the female sexual response. There is no significance in the order in which they are put other than the closeness of the meaning of 9 to the meaning of 8.

It has been suggested naked (8) is from a lost verb to nake, from na-kai, to expose ones whole body to view, the full monty. But the Lithic suggests it is from na-ka-ti, expose-body-orifices. In Egyptian khati is the lower belly where they lie. Nude, from Latin nudus, is surely from the Lithic nau-tau-(s), exposed-all the orifices-(phenomenal suffix). A snake (8) is si-na-kai, brer-bare-body. It has no coat. A snail is brer-exposed-lye line. It leaves a slimey trail. In Malay a snail is siput, brer-penis-teat. Chacun a son gout! Akin to naked is the earlier form nacod. A cod, like the –ked above, could be read as the genitals, and the plural cods were certainly taken to refer to the testicles, perhaps because they were known to be the source, originally tai, of virility, the male drive or ka-, and there were two of them -u. A ti was a source as well as a teat, from tai the birth canal. The Tudors wore cod pieces, trouser flaps over the genitals enabling them to urinate without removing their trousers.

The iguana is a Caribbean Taino word for a large lizard. Like all cold blooded lizards it does a lot of lying in the sun's rays, lai-zai-rai-dai, to warm up and so gain the energy to catch a lady lizard and copulate. It is not being lazy, which is lying in comfort, originally warming yourself around the hearth when you should have been out hunting. Like brer-bare-body the snake the iguana is from ai-ga-ua-na, that which-body-one that-bare, the bare bodied one without a coat. Taino perceptions, at the Lithic level, are remarkably similar to those entertained at some distance by the Romans and others. Snake and iguana make a doublet utilising different idioms but the same elements to string together phonemic meanings to the same end or sense. They are obviously related by way of Lithic alone.

Knitting is to be knotting whereas a knot is the done job, with many Indo European cognates, as Partridge says "another puzzling word meaning something hard prominent and lumpy". Kai is hard and grown, nau is protruding, prominent, and ti is thing (from tai, what has become). His generation were perhaps more strictly brought up in the colonies where the manly virtues were to be accepted without too much introspection. But it must now seem a trifle imperceptive of him to get no prompt at all from this description to help him in his etymological analysis. Admittedly metaphor provided something of a screen. Adjacent words on the same page of his Origins are knave, knee, knob, knocker, knap (the noun meaning a knoll and the verb to flake flints), knoll, knuckle and knurl, only the first, knave, much immediate help with knot or knit, and that well developed from its original form and meaning. It is from the Old English cnafa or cnapa meaning boy or youth, "anterior etymology unknown" according to Partridge. The Lithic suggests a cnafa, from kai-na-pahei, was akin to our four letter word beginning in f., a young man with grown-protruberant-genitalia, past puberty and capable of procreation, no longer a puer or piper, his voice broken, but still in his youth and with a menial job and the congenital lack of sobriety and morality which often accompanies the teen-age years. Contemporary definitions were rogue, rascal, male servant, attendant, squire. Did they have a teenager problem in the middle ages? They certainly respected maturity, a respect which has been buried altogether in the past half century, to the scandal of the nations though not without some reason. The playing card shows a young man past puerility, a prince because of the other royal cards. The cards have no princess. The knee is the protruding joint; a knob is a shaped protruding bit; to knock is from the echoic strike [stone on flint] present make; knoll is from ground-protruding level; knuckle is another outwardly protruding joint shape, a little one; and to knurl is to make show ray lines

The Egyptian goddess Nut, probably from the Lithic Nau-ti, Exposed teats or Open orifices, is represented as the night sky and is pictured with her feet at one side of the earth and her body bowed over with her head at the other side, stretching her body out a bit, with a trifle of the whimsical artistic licence modern art has accustomed us to. The moon is her vagina and the stars are her teats, of which she thus has a ridiculous surfeit. At times like this the appropriateness of the dual vowel also being the completive must have been brought home to the priests of Amun as they struggled to match up the universe to their anthropomorphic schemes. Perhaps this bizarre perception of Nut helped to name the milky way and the galaxies from the Greek from gala, from ka-la or body-lye, milk with its genitive case galaktos, of milk, milky. With her torso studded with breasts like this she was sometimes represented as a cow with stars stamped all over her underside. She was certainly displaying all her orifices with a vengeance. Our own night, German nacht, appears to come from na-kha-ti, the naked sky showing its body orifices at night. Naughty has a somewhat similar pattern suggesting the mischief it originally denoted was sexual frivolity of one kind or another, probably flaunting nudity or perhaps just exposing the breasts, acceptable in some hot countries but not in the West – until recently sunbathing on some beaches.

However there is a copious alternative etymology for the aught, nought, naughty group which seems to have everything going for it since Old English has nawiht contracted to naht, naught and nought in Middle English; all it is proposed from na-wiht, no thing, since wiht is a thing or a creature. The Lithic in wiht is u-ai-tai, one that is born (the creature, a wight) or one that is become (the thing). In Middle Dutch and Dutch today wicht is a child, which appears to suggest cognisance at some level of the one that is [recently] born etymology. With this na-wiht etymology a naughty person is a nobody, worthless rather than mischievous. It would be easy to omit the sentence introducing naughty, which is contradicted by the above, for a quiet life. But it is deliberately left in to exemplify the conflict between Lithic analysis and conventional (phonetic) etymology. It is a perfectly tenable position to argue the subconscious mind has adapted na-wiht to nought and applied it to the O symbol, altering wiht to ought prompted by a Lithic recollection. Otherwise it is simply a coincidence the two analyses are on offer. It does not diminish Lithic. A hundred percent discovery of original Lithic word formations is a Will-o-the-whisp. The challenge will no doubt cite gw changing to w. But there are not many cases of w changing to gw, and anyway the change is from h to gh.

Canada is conventionally supposed to be from some huts mistaken for the name of the place the local tribe reckoned they lived in. We can imagine the interpreter told to ask what is the name of the place in which you live, and reply-ing they say huts. It is of a par with the interpreter pointing to what he wanted to know the name of and being told finger. Or compare the national park in California named after a complete sentence in Navaho "That is our mother of the tribe", when a miner forty niner asked his Man Friday what he called a retreat-ing grizzly bear which happened to be the totem of his tribe: "Ia ushi ma i tai". Thinks (in balloon): "I am not telling you her name for fear you might use it to conjure her against me". It sounded he thought like Yosemite, bear. Undeveloped languages are nearer to the Lithic than languages much built up and make use of long strings of short beads easily slovened by a lazy ear to a single word with what seems like a normal number of syllables. Reminding ourselves of the Canarai islands with their exposed rocks – the Carthaginian was Kan-arai, core-visible, exposed rock, rocky coast – and adding the area below the rim of the Mount Teide in Tenerife, above the tree line and with bare rock reaching to the lip of the vol-canic caldera, which is called on the island maps las canadas, it seems to be saying land-exposed or bare-become, tai being a natural development as opposed to kai which is made by an agency other than the natural ones. The Canadian caʻn-a-da, land'of-that-born is akin to the Carthaginian Guanche from Ga-u-en-khai, land-where-in-begotten. On the West coast of Tenerife is Las Americas, now the site of a bustling tourist resort, the Far West of the island. It at first appeared that Las Canadas in Tenerife might be land-no-use, but the country Canada is not infertile. Better is land laid bare or open. A lot of Canada is open country you had to mush across. It rather depends where these misbegotten huts were exactly. The phonetics may have been misapprised as well, like the case of the grizzly bear misnomer.

Meaning 9, open or agape, takes in hollowed out and hollow as well. A canoe is from the Taino canoa and Carib canaoa or canaeua. They all point to Lithic ka-nau-a, a hacked-hollow-one. The original canoe was a hollowed out tree trunk. A cane is hollow and tubular. So is a reed, but it is named for its habit of becoming rayed, growing up like a tree, though on a smaller scale and without any branches, and in fact its structure is tubular, its interior filled with pith. A bamboo is tubular, but it has bungs at every joint so a cut section makes a container which holds water, and it is named for that and for the impenetrable forest of single shoots (boo) it puts up which leave the banana far behind. They simply have to be circumnavigated in the jungle. The bamboo's instinct was clearly to bung things up at every opportunity, practising it both internally and externally, a bad mannered plant but handy when cut for utensils. When growing it is also brittle when sharply bent and sharp and poisonous, and a parachutist unable to steer clear of bamboo must expect to be put through the equivalent of a bacon slicer, reduced to boo himself. A cannon and a canyon are the same in Lithic. A canyon or valley is cut or shaped hollow, and a cannon is cast or drilled the same. A valley is a shallow canyon from awa-lai, water leaking down, which is what washes the soil away. The Arabic Ouadi, a valley Anglicised as waddi, is from the Lithic awa-a-dai, water-that-done. It has nothing to do with the t in water as Partridge supposes. The -ter in water is to show it is fresh and is drawn up, a bit like the rocks from down below, in springs which then revert to type and flow down again to the sea, the instinct of all liquids being to lapse and slip away whenever given the chance. That is what liquid means. Water is just fresh water, not lye. The infernal forces pushing water up against its natural instincts were perceived as powerful spirits to be got on your side. So springs were holy and prayed to. In Tenerife the dry water courses which have cut through the volcanic tuff are known as barranco. They are slovened, with a w tidied into a double r, from ba-awa-en-kau, going-water-of or by-carved, a scientific statement of the day. The going water is not unlike the bila for water in Australia, with whitey waiting for his billy to boil, and it does not have to be a river to get the name. Water goes by leaking away, in rivers or out, because of its instinct to la, to slip away down and sideways, slopingly, unlike the ish or fire instinct which is straight up and ma which is straight and deep down. See chapter 9.

Anatomy is from Lithic a-na-tau-mai, open-cut-dead, and Greek ana-tomy, from ana which means up (the boys' meaning, as when in arousal, or open for the girls' meaning. We do not know who had which in mind), and Greek temnein to cut. Curiously a tome was a piece cut off a large papyrus roll, so it would fit in a pigeon hole in ancient libraries of scrolls, and so a volume of a large work and so also the large volume needing dividing, whether actually divided or not. The anatomy is what-shows [when]-cut up, and so refers to the cadavers cut up to show their bits and pieces. Gyne, female in Greek, refers to the sex which kai-nai, kindled gapes as with the vagina above, which may at one time of course have been read as oo-a-gyne, hole-that-feminine, but kai-nai is better since it analyses gyne as well. In Malay nyak is a prostitute, Lithic nai-a-kai, one who causes the nai (9) for which she is employed, she initiates the encounter, soliciting.

Meanwhile a nose, with the two nostrils or nose-terai-lai, the nose's little draw holes where the air goes in, is itself from nau-sai, and is the dual openings-upper, not to be confused with the dual openings lower. At the same time the Lithic can also be read as the dual openings sensing, since sai can mean both upper and sensing, see chapter 14. The sensing is by way of smell, from sai-'m-ai-lai, sensing-him-going-floating. The perineum per contra is the area peri, around (but actually between) the naiu, the two [nether] orifices. The anus is significant because it has a sphincter which opens and closes the orifice, which suggests the meaning of nu or nau has taken on this meaning from the fact the girls like the boys have a sexual phoenix function in that the nai for them can be remarkably repetitive too, first engorging and rounding out and then returning to the flaccid state, but then arising from the ashes and repeating the performance indefinitely. Indeed modern research by folk (like the Doctor Comfort who wrote "The Joy of Sex" in 1963) mascarading as scientists, but actually flower-power ideologists, has shown with pile-on sexual orgies in California that the girls are still going long after the boys have dropped out. This is in no way surprising in so far as the male is dispensing pollen which has to be replaced, while the female is merely receiving it. Her hard stint comes later. It is however somewhat at loggerheads with the etymology of girl which associated forms indicate is of Celtic origin where the two phonemes kai and lai alone are always present shewing the untrilled r in the English word is a cockney r merely misrepresenting a schwa. The ka was the aggressive male drive, and a girl is perhaps recognised as by comparison with ka lowered, that is to say a gentle person, perhaps even naturally subservient, which after all the fair sex were liable to be in the Stone Age since they were not as muscular as the males of the species; and at the same time giving birth to babies and having to rear them selected for the caring type in Darwinian terms, since the less caring reared fewer progeny successfully. The girls may therefore be said to be at the Darwinian coal face. It is also noticeable in the case of Latin puer, a boy, which originally meant a girl or a boy but was given a feminine form of puella as an after thought to distinguish the sexes, that the la phoneme was thought suitable for the job: as any parent of both sexes can tell you, the girls are born with a gentler temperament and habit, more la and less ka. Conventional etymology just dismisses girl as of unknown origin. Puer started out unisex since it meant piper: children having high voices.

Malay najan is a star. It is presenting (7) an orifice (9) through which fire (sh) is showing (13), the flaming (-jan) of the upper fires which were supposed to exist above the stone firmament of the sky so that they shone down through holes in the night sky, the moon and stars, which our primitive forebears attempted to relate to the orifices of the human body. Quite often there is a surfeit of Lithic meanings available, so often in fact that it suggests a double analysis was taken as confirmation of the appropriateness of the phoneme string, when language was largely a matter of composition. It also suggests the Lithic meanings of the phonemes, as they spread by means of metaphors and gulls, became so meaning rich as to present a conundrum in interpretation. It may seem madness to us today but that is how they thought; and the way the words are put together is the evidence for it. In a few hundred thousand years there is no reason to suppose we will not appear just as silly to our successors.

The tenable-tendency group which Partridge has assembled – which includes a few surprising plums like continue, impertinent, retinue, tenet, tenacity, tenant, abstinence, continent (noun and adjective both), detention, entertainment, maintenance, pretend, tenuous, hypotenuse, tonic, thin and dance – is one of Partridge's largest groups in which he has collected 205 words. It needs special attention. The Lithic derivation of any one should probably apply to them all. The single examples explained in these twelve chapters which are dedicated to phonemic meanings stand in for sometimes hundreds more, some identified and some not. The tendency sub group of 124 words is epitomised by the Latin tendere to stretch out. Here, it would appear, are no sex oriented T-rays to do the stretching out since there is no trace of an r, relict of a ray, in any of them. It is for this reason they come rather late in this chapter. It had not immediately struck home that an n, relict of a na or nai (via ne), might be doing much the same job as a ray. But in fact ta-nai or tai-nai can mean virtually the same as a ta-rai or tai-rai. Nai is as powerful as rai. The effect of the rays caused arousal in turn. An engorged or nai vagina, ta or tai and in modern slang twat, originating from the two-ing or splitting of the flint knapper, is as powerful a sexual operator as the wholly imaginary rai or ray. The Hindu religion of natural instinctual perceptions is ready to proclaim as much, as with their yoni above, which is quite outside the ethos of the West. Indian religion and Christianity are poles apart, the one descriptive the other pejorative and ethical. The psychological cover-up however comes merely from the erosion of nai via ne to plain n. Hinduism is close to the Egyptian religion of Amun-Ra which deified natural forces rather than morality. Ra did acquire a part to play in moralising however, since as the world eye he observed even the sparrow's fall, while Hinduism remains short on any action involvimg morality. The Hindu gods stand for the psychological pie in which we live. Even Mahatma Gandhi, the maha-atma, the great soul, nominally wed to ahimsa, non-violent-action, a-hei-mai-sa, un-rejoicing-[in]harming-action, was not above justifying blowing up "a few small bridges" (carrying overloaded trains of hundreds of Indian civilians). But then most men have feet of clay. Sapiens Sapiens uses it fraudulently to conceal the truth even from himself. Latin tendere to stretch out is from the same Lithic elements tai-nai as tenere to hold. Tendere to stretch out comes from the Lithic tai-nai-dai, what the engorged vagina does, it draws up and stretches out the male member. At the very same time tenere is from tai-nai-are, which means vagina-engorged-verbal suffix, to grasp, seize or hold. The two meanings must come as metaphors from the sexual performances of male and female on arousal. Boys stretch out while girls admit and grip. Mrs Grundy will not like it. But the two base meanings from the same elements are hard to explain in any other way. Stretching out and grasping together apparently suggested nothing at all to conventional etymologists. But then they have no Lithic, and their words are all supposedly randomly formed, except those that are echoic when a Lithic plan obtains.

Partridge's nimble group of eighteen English words plus 97 foreign and former forms includes a fair spread of words akin: nimmer (thief), numb, nomad, nemesis, number, numismatist, and numerous, and they are all derived from the three base meanings of na displayed in the Old English nomme meaning numb and Old English niman to grasp, seize or take, and Greek nemein to distribute or spread. The Lithic easily deals with grasping, nau-mai, orgasmic-[when]impregnating, when convulsive constrictions of the vagina occur, grasping the penis. It is not polite, it is bawdy; but it is a Stone Age idiom long before Mrs Grundy. Nor is it fanciful. That is the exactly the way we thought in those days long ago. That is where we come from, and it is quite important we understand it if we are to master our thinking today. Hundreds of thousands of years of gradual civilisation have modified the original vulgarities by means of metaphor on metaphor, but the atavistic traces remain in the lexicon, learned and preserved and understood by everyone who learns to speak but only in the subconscious mind, that submerged part of the mental iceberg which informs our thinking still, although at one re-move from consciousness. The subconscious forms part of our thinking, it is the aboriginal dream time and our dream world that we enter when we dream, where ideas flow freely in an uncontrolled stream without strict logical control[4], largely in pictures with meanings implicit, and usually without expression in words, the way we think when awake. Our dream world closely resembles the waking world of our forebears before they learned to speak and thus to order thinking and al-low the development of phonemic structure and reasoning to monitor the flow of thought. The unconscious, on the other hand, as opposed to the subconscious, is wholly unconscious, inaccessible directly or indirectly to the mind (anyway in normal states, ignoring the claims of yogis). It is thus quite unlike the subconscious, which can be summoned on occasion to give evidence, and may sometimes prompt the conscious mind uninvited from the wings. We can not control the promptngs of the subconscious mind. We can only deal with the consequences when they emerge into consciousness. We do not think about the unconscious or with it at all. It is not part of the mind. It is involved with the autonomic system looking after the housekeeping jobs like keeping breathing going, regulating the beating of the heart, recording the protocols for interpreting the raw input to the eyes and ears, for reporting pains and other sensations, and operating the functions of all the other organs of the body. It is simply the biological control room and has nothing to do with thinking other than the maintenance of the brain. It is located in the basement and ground floor of the brain while our consciousness lives (together with the subconscious mind) appear to operate from the cortex on the attic floor. Biology and psychology have so far failed to distinguish adequately between the autonomic system and the mind, virtually denying the mind any independent role and even making it a metaphysical figment. For all that, the discovery of Lithic is a poison. You can play mental cats cradles for ever, but the message of this book is that linguistics is a subject matter sui generis for study without any remit to sort out the scientific mess of present day psychology.

When it comes to spreading and distributing from the Greek nemein, from ejaculating, we can perhaps relate the meaning of Onanism, from Onan (a back formation) the eponymous ancient, who spread his seed at orgasm upon the ground, away spreading or wasting, au-na-naʻn, everywhere na-na-ing, spreading his male pollen (not seed) around everywhere, in place of channeling it properly: an extravagance – like a banana. The Greeks may well have also taken into account the meaning of the extensive vowel aaa, which has also been used for going (extending your position from your point of origin) as well as spreading and even a spread of time, for Greeks an aeon. Lithic allows both these meanings, the aaa and the na, to present themselves as contributions for the adoption of word structure. Nomme, however, meaning numb, is the most interesting since it comes from nao-mai and surely means sensation-dead. Orgasm is the acme of sensation and would have been used metaphorically in that sense. Numbness implies sensation has been suppressed (mai), or even killed off. The –b got tacked on later to show it was referring to the flesh in general to distinguish it from the other meanings of na and ma.

A further meaning of Lithic na-mai is in the English name, which has nothing to do with lack of sensation, grasping or pollen spreading. A very widespread idiom occurring in Old English as namian to name and Old English, Old Frisian and Old Saxon nama a name, Lithic showing-the meaning, a symbol. The Old Saxon is identical to Malay nama as well as, closer to home, akin to Hindi naam, Old High German and Gothic namo, Dutch naam, Albanian emen (the phonemes reversed, a metathesis which underlines the independence of the two elements which can be read in either order), Latin nomen, Greek onoma, Sanskrit neman, Tokharian A nom (slovening the -ma like the French), Tokharian B nem, Lapp namma, Finnish nime, Turkish nam again, and Old Persian emmen like the Albanian, with (slightly garbled) Old Irish and Gaelic ainm, Manx ennym. There is a further group of languages suggesting a name was widely regarded as a symbolisation simply representing the phenomenon symbolised, and so leaving off the ma, the mental presentation of the nama group. So we have Danish navn, Old Welsh anu, Cornish honua, Armenian anun, Hungarian nev.

Perhaps we should also look at the Chinese ming zi meaning name, where the zi is merely a noun suffix sometimes appearing to denote agency. The Chinese idiom of stringing phonemes with minimalist grammatical inflections is close to the original Lithic pattern. It is as if their language congealed early on and never had a Babel revolution like the rest of the world. The result is it is too difficult for anyone but a mandarin (or master, compare Malay mentri or minister) to master, which tends to make the mandarins good at mathematics and the masses inarticulate. Not being a mandarin it is difficult to guess how ming zi comes by the meaning name. We can see it has the same two phonemes (one nasalised) as the Malay nama – in reverse order like the Albanians and the Old Persians, which is probably insignificant. You have to ask if the Chinese ming can be analysed as from mai-nai in Lithic elements. If it can, then ming is equivalent to nama. This is an example of the symbol as a tripartite concept, as in Appendix C (on the philosophy of language): the symbol, the word and the symbolising mind.

Then perhaps the Zulu iligama for name is also relevant, from the Lithic ai-lai-ka-mai, it-linked-make-minding, perhaps a long shot but symbolisation does exactly that: it relates the phenomenon to its mental recognition, the name conjures up the phenomenon, the referend, in the mind. Then the Chinese ren for man (mankind, both sexes in origin anyway) much like Malay orang (this time the Malay version is the nasalised one and the Chinese not) is from Lithic rai-nai, exhibiting rays, taking them in from outside, the rayed species, with reason. The name claims that mankind is uniquely the rational being, in this case by being the recipient of mental rays lower life forms are incapale of receiving, untuned to reason which nature therefore is piping only to us. Not much sense can be made of ren and orang without the recognition they are based on the general belief amongst the ancients that attitudes and their mental correlates in humans result from rays which enter the mind from without triggering emotional responses. It may have been reassuring, removing any feelings of guilt as receivers of these teasers from outer space over life lived in a violent and confrontational world red in tooth and claw and hand (which does the ha-ing, the horrific things as well as the pleasurable ones). What was actually happening was probably the rays were prompts from the subconscious, as yet unrecognised other than as part of the other. Anyone unprepared to recognise the subconscious which influences their thinking today can not possibly accept the Lithic language hypotheses and should put the book down. (They should then go on to re-examine their own personal psychology and get with it, or seek help).

So far we have progressed to meaning 10 in the psychosemantic tree meaning to show, as far as to explain (17). Birth too (18) was an epiphany. Partridge refers us to fancy where in Greek epiphany means to show to, a showing, exhibition or manifestation, the -phany clearly from pahei-nai, the rampant piece. Rampant is from ra-em-pa'n-tai, the ray/raise/present-of-the piece'ing-become. Note the ra-em-pa- is on the way to becoming a verb which can have the –ing at the end oif the string instead of following the ra- Similarly we have Noel for Christmas where Nau-El is birth or Birth-of-El or the Lord, as the angel did say: "born is the king of Israel" (Israel is from Ish-arai-El, Burners or Warriors of the Lord). Christ's mas, meanwhile, is from ma-sai, plant-seed or life, conception rather than birth. In Ancient Egypt life was supposed to begin at conception, a belief inherited by the Pope along with the Pharaoh's hat, putting the Catholic church in the Pharaoh's debt. Nau, birth (18) as an epiphany is reinforced by the circumstance the birth canal, rounded out at orgasm, is ten times more so to pass the baby's head. Semen, sai-mai'en, life-planting, is also up-and downing, the reciprocation leading to ejaculation. It certainly must have seemed to the ancients their linguistic prowess encapsulated reality. Native is from the Latin nasci, from nai-sai-kai, to be born, in Lithic to exhibit or presenting-the life-kindled [at conception]. Compare sex, from sai-kai-sai, the initiating action (sai means both, see chapter 14) [for] making- life. The semantics of sex and six can be related if you know five in Indo European refers to the points of the body (panch for five in Hindi, is from the Lithic pa-en-kai. The Punjab is thus from panch awab, the five rivers, with awab from awa-bai, water-moving, not unlike the Australian aboriginal billabong for an ox-bow lake, a bai-la bunged, travelling liquid, a river blocked up). When called upon to think of a sixth point of the body to add to the head and limbs our forebears were forced to fall back on the rather minor male member, and maybe for a seventh, the two life bits sai-bain, switching from the penis to the testicles because there were two of them, an opportunity too good to miss, overlooking the protruberant criterion they had been counting upon until then.

The Latin natus has the past participle –tus ending, like all the other Latin verbs, from the Lithic tau (s), the birth canal and so born and thence become, and so the past participle quite precisely, with a substantiating –s ending. The semantic content is present-become or born. Either phoneme, na or ta, on its own can signify born, na perhaps to some extent as a result of a semantic bus from its use joined with tau, and in Latin souped up with kai making gena-. Tau can be further analysed as ta-u, with the ta- being the original division in two of the human torso which like all mammalian bodies has a binary symmetry, the two sides being mirror images one of the other with the female exhibiting the crucial slit or division between the two. The -u or oo is then the orifice, the form it adopts for sex. At birth the baby comes out from between the two halves of the bisymmetrical human frame – a seismic fault, or else like a seed from a pod. The Spanish nino for child is a nai-nau, a newly-born. The French just have née from naitre to be born, which can also mean to arise (6), as well as puisné for later born, younger or subordinate, coming after. A cobra in French is a naja, a riser upper, spun off from the Indo European naka or bare body of Hindi nag and English snake, while the cobra comes from Spanish from the Latin colubra, referring to its locomotion, Lithic kau-lau-bai-arai, body-looped-go-verbal suffix, but bai-rai doubling as large, compare Hindi barra big. Snakes coil along, and a king cobra is supposed to be able to overtake a horse, probably an exaggeration, but it will certainly catch up with you if it wants to. It stands a good five feet tall with a vicious temperament. It will attack man or beast in its way unprovoked, probably the only snake to do so. Flushing a king cobra you stand still and pray, offering it your shield to attack if you happen to have one. Partridge derives the Latin natura, nature from the Latin natus, born, but the Egyptian semantic derivation is to be preferred. The aboriginal Malays' name for themselves is Senoi from Sai-nau-i, First-born or present-ones, making their claim to be the original stock – and the present Malays to be the usurpers of the land, a historically fair assessment. Malays retaliate by calling them Sakai, Sa-ka-i, Single-Ka-folk unlike dual Ka folk (one for this world and one for the next), and so animals in effect. The insult is understood and resented: the Senoi are not Moslems and wear their foreskins in full.

We have so far used a terminal 'n (11) without comment. Hums tend to be used as fillers: speakers in Indo European languages use mmm while thinking of the next words, and these days in Africa m' is often regarded as semantically him- and the 'n in Indo European languages is similarly thought of as short for -one, an unspecified one because as a hum 'n carries no very obvious meaning at all, making it suitable for those constructions where an itemisation is required without any additional semantic baggage. But then there is the Germanic usage of -en as a verbal marker; and for the Egyptians en or em is of, prefixed or suffixed. In all these cases the vowel e is from the dipthong ai, since for most or all of prehistory there were only the three vowels recognised, a,i and u. As a verbal marker ai'n makes use of the vowel a as an extensive and the i vowel as the diminutive reduplicative to indicate a spin off from the preceding one, so the semantics of –ain or -en is on-going and so a verbal marker. There is a similar semantic relationship in the case of the genitive in Ancient Egyptian, ai having the semantic contents quite generally of that-which, or one-that, the second term being as it were a spin off from the first, a subordinate rider or addendum, and the n merely indicating closure to separate it from what follows. It follows the a in ai is much the same concept as 'n, meaning one or even one that or the one that. Aa is a vacuous vowel as well as an extensive one. That gives it its semantic suitability for air and water, ever and aeon (extensions in time), far and away (spacial extensions with the intervening space empty), numerical extension or summation as add and all, continuity like and (which as a concept is empty) and anything else which like mere continuity, more of the same without end, strikes the imagination as abstract, insubstantial and unbounded, paradigmatically like the Jewish Deity Iauai, sometimes transliterated in English as Jehovah; with the Egyptian God Osiris, really Ausarai in the original Egyptian, World-sun-rise, as runner up. This is Lithic thinking at a secondary level, trying to pick up some of the implications for thinking of the fuzzy original semantics obtaining at the birth of linguistic competence, rather than merely trying to identify the pieces of the original semantic lexicon. At this distance we are dependent upon discovering the implications of the Lithic lexicon from the reconstruction of the Lithic lexicon itself, from the traces left in linguistic usage today; and in both cases we are in turn dependent upon assessing the validity of the thinking by way of such subconscious promptings as we can access, at least to reject what does not carry conviction.

Another snake is the anaconda which is probably first from the Tamil since it appears in Surinam too, rather than from the Sinhalese, the language of Ceylon, from Kai-lau'n now Shri Lanka, Holy Island, La'n, Ocean'in, and ka, land. The Lithic elements are a-na-ka'n-da, that-no-striking-does (2) or that-convulsively gripping-does. The anaconda coils round its prey and squeezes the life out of it and eats it whole, it is not poisonous and has no fangs. Or perhaps both prompts from the subconscious combined to suggest the same string of phonemes with both semantic contents, one appealing to some folk and the other to others, or even both to them all. It is sometimes tempting to believe such a coincidence of prompts is a reason for the word being formed.

The word manual, from Latin manus, a hand, deserves a paragraph or two on its own. Prelinguistic communication will have been by expression when close to, or otherwise entirely by gesture, mostly by hand signals: when hunting, for instance "You creep round to the right" pointing to a hunter and then in the direction he should go – precisely as in the jungle when hunting terrorists today. And another twenty or thirty signals much the same, including in the Stone Age signs for the different species of prey sighted. Terrorists are all of the same species but the number observed is of immediate interest. "Take cover and prepare to engage" must surely have been the handiest, and probably still is. The idea we had no ideas before we spoke is by now rendered absurd. How then could we have formed the concepts which issued in speech? African bushmen have hand signals for every species of prey which they can use when hunting, as well as directional hand signals, even more essential when the quarry is an animal rather than a terrorist because of their more sensitive hearing. A dog, a horse and even a cow has ideas but they are formed from their experience, which does not include symbolisation: they are simply reminded of past experience by envisaging similarities with what they see (or smell, or feel). Their feelings are largely to do with feeding, sex and predation. In origin we are no different.

The hand might therefore be from Lithic ma-na-u, mind-show-er, what shows the meaning strung the other way about: meaning-present-one. Hands were prized as signallers. Of course they were the active agents for every kind of activity as well. But if you can not speak you value the ability of signals to communicate the highest, because at human level you need to relate to your peers and you are already beginning to build up claustrophobic tension. So the hand is probably named for its communicative potential, next to facial expression which is only available at short range, and is less specific anyway. Hand signals are half way to language. After all they are already symbols. But compared with the squiggling available to script, or the phonemic strings which can be uttered, bodily gesturing of every kind is an impoverished medium – which is no doubt why human mentality spilled over into language. But Eric Partridge moves half way to Lithic with his analysis of masturbation. He has "*mas [paragraph 4 under male, page 374] male seed (cp. semen) and thence masturbate to turbinate the male seed, or stir it up. Masculine might then be from Lithic masai-kau-lai'n, gestating-life [maisai is dead or gestating life, which describes a seed]-make-leaking'one, which distinguishes the male from the female as the sex which supplies the seed. (Of course it is not actually correct, but it is the well established historic belief of our benighted forebears and the belief of plenty of folk still today. The reality is the boys are mere pollenators of the female seed, as such contributing half and no more of the genes and less of the foetal influences – except many genes appear to be sexually linked so that male linked genes appear more in male babies and female linked genes more in female babies). With these semantic contents the hand (manus) is not disclosing a mental state but instead presenting the seed. In short hand is the masturbater; down the middle but bawdy for nowadays. But for six hundred thousand years ago? The English hand is from ha'n-da, the pleasurer. The very ancient word for finger, tik, comes from Lithic tai-kai, the tickler, vulva-kindling, stimulating the vagina. That goes back a long way. A finger is from pahai'n-kara, a pleasurer again. Both hand and finger come under (11), the final position of the 'n in (3).

Now tikh means in India – from pointing, pointing out, indicating – correct; which is understood across a number of languages, and it is even the source of the tick teachers make opposite correct answers in schools meaning correct. Indeed at my school some years ago now when manners were taught in school, pupils when passing teachers were required to tick them, a salute made by raising the forearm with pointing finger extended to make a tick. In thoroughly democratic manner the unfortuate teachers were required to reciprocate, as with a military salute, so that passing boys in a school corridor they were wagging their forearms with their books clasped in their other hands, and many learned to progress with hand raised in a continuous response. It became a game. Why the V shape with one long arm should have been selected to represent correctness remains moot, o.o.o. or of obscure origin in Partridge speak. Perhaps or indeed probably it was the arm with the pointing (or tickling) finger on the end of it. The arachnid tick is a puncture maker, though Partridge says a nipper. The German has zecke, like the tsetse fly, the sting from a hot mouth (or tail). Compare Armenian tiz for a tick. Ticking off the answers was a spin off from the ticking of a clock according to Partridge, to tap lightly or lightly mark an answer – no semantics given and so lightly. An earlier reference found noted says "ti-ka" was originally the digit or pointer outer and is the oldest Indo European word – with the oldest traced history, from Lithic tai-kai, making a division, ie discriminating and so indicating: "That!", "That's it!", "That is correct!" As a finger it may have been described in soldiers' slang as the tickler or titi-kindler. In 1941 my Home Guard sergeant instructor would become ribald as he instructed us boys to feel for the Bren light machine gun magazine opening cover on the underside of the weapon with our index fingers. You had to strip and reassemble the gun in the dark. Little did he know, any more than we did, he was repeating a psychological pattern over half a million years old.

No doubt Stone Age culture had far more numerous more prosaic manipulations for their fingers. But the language brightens up perception with references to sex. As a species we have been a rather naughty lot from day one. Not even MrsWhitehouse would have any finger trouble today, but long enough ago what is a finger but in Lithic pa-hai'n-kare, a genital stimulater or pleasurer. Aphrodite, per contra, the Greek fertility goddess, is a-pahei-rau-da-tai, all-the penis-arousals-does-her vulva, a potent lady without a kai, the male kindling, to her name: a very busy lady. This is really powerful world-wide juju. Launching a thousand ships or so is by comparison rather small beer. The Greeks also had Orpheus and Euridice, as the classic romantic couple. Orpheus is from Au-rai-pahei-u(s). He appears to have been in a permanent state of erection; while Euridice similarly is in Lithic Ai-u-rai-tai-kai, That which-always-rayed-vulva-kindled. She was evidently in a state of permanent response: altogether a couple Kinsey would have

been pleased to include in his survey of modern day sexuality. Indeed one sometimes wonders if in fact he did so. Was he perhaps a throw back to classical times
when love and lust were hardly distinguished? Or are we? The regular weekend
multi-coupling sexual orgies in California amongst the flower power generation
smack of Pompei or even of Gemorrah. Partridge surmises however that finger is
merely akin to five since five fingers are on each hand. But the kinship might of
course equally lead the other way, five referring to all the pleasurers on the hand
(the hand which hei-ing does, or is it a cockney h, relict of that-which-does, leaving out the sex?).

A map appears to have started out as a breech clout, a broad strip of cloth
wound around the crotch to cover the genitalia. (Mai is Egyptian for earth, planting, impregnating, and so the penis the impregnator, with an explicit close up
of the aroused male organ as the hieroglyph, which is alternatively pronounced
pahei. That glyph at least is a logogram and not a letter, it symbolises two words
with the same rebus (or referend). Latin gets it through the Greeks, much of
whose ideas and language were simply borrowed from Egypt where civilisation
was thriving when Greeks were still just simple Celtic tribesmen – though in this
case it seems it may have come at one further remove via the Phoenician languages, with the identical word in Carthaginian). Such a cloth was thrown into
the arena to start the Roman games. Competitors were probably naked so perhaps
it was a discard from one of them used for the job. A similar piece of cloth was
used for the mappa-mundi, "a napkin or small sheet of the world" as Partridge has
it. By the time the term is used for a canvas for drawing the geography on it, its
original function of covering the genitalia has obviously been forgotten, and will
have been residing in the subconscious among the Lithic derivations there.

The hums (mm and nn) can be exchanged. "The Old French mappa is dissimulated first in Old French nappe and then nape, leading to English napery
and the diminutive napkin This is the terminal 'n, (11), simply a coverlet. The
Middle English nape is the flat part of the neck accoording to Partridge, akin to
a napkin. But the neck is not flat, it is the na-pai, the protruding (6) piece of the
spine between the shoulder blades, much like the tail the other end of it (canis
from ka-nai). The apron too has quit the crotch and covers the body, nowadays to
protect clothes from splashes in the kitchen. It comes from a misperception of a
napron, 'n-a-pa-rai-un, one-that-cover-ing-one, as an apron, just a covering.

Having dealt with nib and nab, both with meaning (6) protruberance, originating in male arousal, nip (whence nibble) and nap now refer to the feminine
aspect of arousal, or perhaps even to both aspects together. Malay comes to mind.
Ketam bersepit is a pincered (binary-action-pieces-two) crab (kai-tam, hardened-
become in Lithic, the crab is hardened all over, and English crab is similarly
kara-bai, skull-body), or in abusive slang a Sikh, widely if unfairly regarded as the

Shylocks of the Far East, because bersepit can be read as hairy as well with a bit of poetic licence, and Sikhs are not supposed to cut their hair (or drop their pants in public). Malays and Chinese can enjoy that calumny together. My informant in this was my friend and one time Sikh colleague with the SAS, one Santok Singh who had mastered Cantonese as well as English, and made blachan just for the two of us (in my piala, to save flavouring his tea – beggars can't be choosers!). There are many Santok Singhs so he will not mind being mentioned should he by chance happen to be still alive fifty years on. The ber- is also much like the be- in besotted. A nip from a crab's pincers is a grasping with the two protruberances, girls' and boys' sex together in an inimitable conjugation in a single phoneme nai for nip. A nap is a short sleep, a momentary covering (of the eyes) just as a nip is a short pinch, where pinch in turn is from pai'n-kara, to make with the pro-truberances, and the original climactic nai is short also. Nowadays we say rather more tastefully instead in the wink of an eye. In Norwegian we have nippe, to take a nap, a snap, a quick closure. The nap of cloth, or of the earth, is its protrud-ing pieces or surface irregularities, or in the Dutch even a tuft of wool. Probably conclusive is the Old English ahneopan to pluck off, with Lithic elements a-khai-nai-u-pa'n, away-cut-protruding-ones-[of/from the]surface-ing, a mouth-ful and head-ful of Lithic semantic beads in a string. Attending to all that, what else have you head room for?

The ankh is a symbol from Ancient Egypt otherwise known as the ansate cross with a history of mystery. It is still worn as a talisman or good luck charm by silly folk. It is roughly an egg sitting on a T. It is certanly old and hard to de-cipher. Moreover like many amulets it can be read in more than one way, which was taken to indicate magic power; perhaps you can look at that as representing for the ancients the kind of assurance that they had it correctly, much like the as-surance that today you get when filling in a crossword puzzle when the letters for words across match up with those you want for a word down. We should probably think of it in terms of seven or eight thousand years before the present. That is only 5000 or 6000 BC. The hieroglyphs are by no means fully understood. You would never think it, from Sir Wallis Budge's phenomenal hieroglyphic diction-ary with more than a thousand pages of scrupulously cut glyphs at the cutting edge of printing technology when it was published in 1925, three years before the first edition of the Oxford English Dictionary was completed. Budge's volumes were not printed again until one of the three copies extant was stolen and spirited away to the United States half a century later where photogravure produced a two volume paperback edition. This was an indispensible benefit for scholarship if a trifle disgruntling for the University of Cambridge whose volume it was that was pirated, leaving Oxford and the Victoria and Albert Museum in London probably sole surviving possessors of original editions in the UK. One wonders how many copies were ever printed, and their fate, perhaps burned as mixed up in black magic by inheritors? Serious scholars of Egyptian can probably be counted on the fingers of one or two hands.

The Egyptian hieroglyphs were always difficult. The very monks who produced them made mistakes themselves. Since the library at Alexandria was burnt in the seventh century AD by barbarian Wahabi invaders in order to rubbish civilisation, with much of three thousand years of philosophy and history lost for ever, there has been the additional problem there is nobody left who can speak the language. The original speakers were killed if they spoke other than Arabic. Only in far away Abysinia some monks may have clung to their religious, though not their mother tongue. But if so they forgot their hieroglyphs and had to restore the reading of their religious texts with the help of Greek scribes so that their Egyptian was reborn as what now counts as Coptic, a mix of Egyyptian and Greek. That way it was hoped the Deity would be content and the Wahabi fooled. Copt is a slovening of Egyptian which in turn is a slovening of Ahu or Iha-i-kau-pata-ahí, it that-which or that-where-begotten-fathers-our (and note the grammatical idiom); which we have slovened again via Haiku-Ptah to Egypt, instead of The Fatherland.

The ankh is believed to have mystical meaning, chiefly because nobody to date has understood what it really means. It is an attribute of the Pharaohs. Aa-en-khai, Eternity-of-khai, where the Ka was the male soul, the hard structure, symbolised by the skeleton, of the otherwise female body, and the driving force, the male life principle. It came in two parts, one for this world and one for the next. Equipped with the Ka for eternity you were immortal. The Ankh glyph thus means Eternal Life. Pharaohs claimed to be sons of the immortal gods, ascending into Heaven when they died. Their titles ending in -meses or -mose (Ra-meses, Thut-mose) named the god that they supposed had planted their seed. Ra was the rumbustious sun god while Thut was a know-all from tahu-tau, now Tutu. The usual symbol, the hieroglyph for the ankh comprises three parts: the egg on top with an upright on which it rests with a horizontal stroke cut across, perhaps giving it a platform to sit on. With a little bit of slovening it could mean a-oon-a-khai in Lithic, that-vulva-that-kindled, which could account for the egg shaped bit on top: The Mother and Source. One even wonders if the Egyptians had Americanised their pronunciation of the oo so that it sounded more like an aa, as with American Mom pronounced Maam. But then what is the Tau doing underneath? Is it perhaps the eternal seat or Au-Siti, Our Lady, Isis, the symbol of the eternal feminine Sai-ti, Life-source, making the whole the Goddess's vagina, as a Source of inspiration for contemplative souls? Perhaps! But the Lithic might be a'n-a-khai, one-that-begotten, son. The Pharaohs Akhenaton and Tutenkhamun, really A-khai-en Aton, That-begotten-of the Aton (the sun as eternal birth canal birthing light into the world each day), and Tutu-anakh-Amun, The All know-ing-Son-of Amun (Amun Ra, the sun). In Malay anak means child, an-a-kai, one-that-begotten. So either they learned from the Ancient Egyptians or else their Lithic thinking found the same meaning string from the same Lithic se-mantic elements. On this interpretation putting an ankh in a Pharaoh's name signifies son of, probably in a trinity of godly avatars – copied elsewhere! Why a trinity of avatars? Because of the vowel Oon (chapter 15) the original of the dialectic, which both Hegel and Marx dug up out of their subconscious minds from the Lithic constituents in residence there, which had been borne along by the linguistic heritage of the human race, individually relearned and refreshed generation after generation, since we first learned to speak.

The symbol, however can also be read in a different metaphor as Na-tau, remi-niscent of the flag of divinity blown out horizontally by the wind, na-tu-ra or na-tau-rai, Show-tau-ray or showing the natural draw or pull, perceived as a ray. The Egyptian ray scheme was hostile to practical aerodynamics, which was con-sequently not a strong suit in Egyptian understanding. If Tahu-tau, Know-all in Egyptian, with tahu also to know in Malay, was Thoth's or Tahuti's strong suit, na-tau, show-all makes a universal symbol for natural science. Tau'n is Egyptian for the universe, as we can devise from their symbolisation of Heaven, Egyptologist-speak Pet, but actually Pai-Taun, Lid of the Universe, a square for a surface, bird's eye view, followed by a half circle sitting on its flat side for the over-arching sky. The square is a pai, a skin or surface. The Greeks transposed it to a view in eleva-tion, their Pi with two plain supporters and a wavey surface or lid seen side on to show that that is the bit to be taken on board. The half circle, believed by the Egyptologists to be a bun (sic!), is the waking world of the living, a penny covered with the bowl we call the sky. The underside of the penny was for the Egyptian mind the Duat (in Egyptologist speak), in reality the Dua Taun, the second world of the souls of the dead around which the dark sun circled during the night before reappearing gloriously reborn to the world of light at dawn (which means the birth, the tau-ing or dawning). Why birth and universe together? Tau is the birth canal (ta = cut or slit, oo = round hole, and the birth canal is both in turn) and so birth and so becoming, and so ta-oo is the becomings-all (oo the completive vowel, chapter 15), and so the universe conceived as the totality of what happens as opposed to the totality of all locations in our own idiom. Simple really, it all fits together; but you do need a bit of Lithic to start you off. Na-Tau is Lithic Presenting (7)-Totality, The Tau (and even the Torah?). Or else and as well Na (17)-Tau is Explicating-All, all you need to know on earth.

The Ankh is first of all eternal life, immortality, and then the son (of God), as well as the Goddess's vulva as fertile life source, Source of Life of the World, God the Everlasting Mother, the Aton. The Ankh is thus a dialectical trinity, The

Mother, The Son and Immortality or The Holy Ghost: and that is all you need to know on earth. Did Jesus learn anything from Egypt?

This is the end of the forty sixth page of this chapter on Na, time to nail the chapter down and move on. Nail (6) is from the Germanic nagel, the g commuting to y and then to i quite easily. A y is a gentler contraction of the glottis required for g, so the pronunciation of the g and y at any time at all distant in the past is always open to debate, the gutteral g shading to y. Na-kai-lai, a protruding-making-linking, which is germane, related (originally by germ or mai) to the humble nail. Or else it is simply 'n-a-ge-lai, one-that-makes-linked, a jointure. Or both!

Notes

1. It should be made clear, to avoid causing offence to present Borneans that the original Borneo tribes are now to be found only in New Guinea, some still sporting penis sheaths, the Borneans replaced by Dyaks who took their heads and wear chawats and then by Indonesians who wear sarongs or trousers; and so far as is known neither of them ever wore penis sheaths at all.

2. See Budge's Egyptian Hieroglyphic Dictionary, Dover 1978 Edition, Vol 1, page 534, column b.

3. Emile Boisacq. Dictionaire Etymologique de la Langue Grecque. 4th Edition. 1950.

4. Sir Charles Lyell validated this perception in 1830 with the first of his three volumes entitled The Principles of Geology. He taught Darwin evolution.

CHAPTER 12

THE PHONEME PA

The root meaning of Ba (chapter 4), from the fleshy lips, which come together to articulate it, was flesh. We are asked to believe our hominid forebears, when they were learning to speak, thought of that as the natural meaning of the sound they were making hundreds of thousands of years ago; and then that their perception has been passed down from generation to generation for four or five times as many generations as hundreds of years, or two to three million generations in six hundred thousand years: a game of Chinese whispers all through twenty to thirty fair sized football crowds – but you must remember each individual had a lifetime to get the idea across to his neighbour, and there were a lot of them all at it together in each generation. Not only that but the perceptions will have been reinforced because they were incorporated in the construction of the languages people were speaking, so that the meanings of these basic phonemic elements presented themselves in the subconscious minds of every speaker while their conscious minds picked up the language. That anyway is the Lithic hypothesis, based not on surmise but under the compulsion of the linguistic evidence. They learned their language and picked up the basic meanings behind it unawares. That is surprising but there seems to be evidence that that is what happened. It makes better sense than the evolutionists who have no history and posit a blind process for language development based on physicality. Hindi speaking people still tend to say ish for the sibilant, showing them to be a very old historic folk.

The psychosemantic tree for Pa is on page 352. Pah! (1) like Bah! indicates contempt. Pooh! does as well. The unvoiced expulsion of breath from between the lips is a puff. Pff! can be added to the other expletives, and Pish! is out of the same stable. It is sometimes thought to derive from piss, but the derivation probably went the other way around. They are all expressions of spitting out and so of rejection – a Stone Age gesture when something edible turned out to taste nasty or even poisonous. To spit, from ish-pai-ti, is to issue from between the two pai, the lips. Ish meant issue amongst other things, see chapter 14, but also matching pish and piss. To piss is similarly to issue from, in this case, the nether pipe (16), lipped or unlipped varieties equally. The colour sepia (Spanish) comes from the cuttle-fish which when pursued by a predator emits a cloud of fluid of that colour as a bitter smokescreen behind which to jet to safety. The cuttle-fish was probably so named by some ancient jolly Spanish jack tar quite possibly of Basque extraction, Si-pia, Brer-pisser, with the colour as a gull from the conduct of the fish[1]. If it is not Brer-pisser then it is just plain pisser, with the Se- signifying the action (one of issuance). Perhaps equally ancient is the origin of the cuttle which is from the Old English cudele, akin to cod which is the pouch of a fishing net, bag shaped, and so the scrotum and by confusion the testicles it contains, so that as a plural cods it has been used for the testicles. The sepia is a pouch (15) shaped fish. A pouch is a swollen shape. The urethra had evidently been traced to the bladder, capable of filling and blowing up. Cuttle is from ka-tai-lai in Lithic elements, body-become-loopy. The Lithic elements are not of course in English. They are in Lithic, and can not be directly translated into English. Ka-born-lyey is an alternative representation, better if you know your Lithic.

Joe Public quite often has it his way even when he has got it wrong. Here he is known as Wayland. The Tudors wore cod pieces, which flapped down when they wished to urinate and meanwhile could be exaggerated in shape and decoration to draw attention to their supposed genital achievements nestling within. Some sixteenth century models were stiffened to project with a flat table top (10). King Henry the eigth who had seven wives in spite of being syphilitic was an afficionado, but it is unfair to pick on him particularly as they were all at it in those days if they could afford a pair of fancy pants. Nowadays Lotharios are reduced to putting a pair of socks in their underpants, or professional entertainers buying a padded pair from a sex-toy shop in order to keep the dolly birds screaming. The fact remains the cod was the pouch (of a fishing net, which ka-u-da, gather-all-does) and the cuttle fish has the shape of a little pouch – containing sepia dye – and back in the Stone Age pouches were pau-khai, made out of skin (5), as well as pouch shaped. Bag at the same time, from ba-kai, simply means belly shaped, the belly being from ba-i-lai, the sagging flesh, just as liquids sag down hill. It could be argued you sag when you lie down, but at the same time you straighten out in a line and lie low. Certainly when you stand you become upright (sa-tai´n-da, up-becoming-do). The syntax may seem strange to us. To examine the Lithic semantics more deeply, sa is up or upwards, tai is coming into being, or come into being or become. The ´n is a filler of uncertain significance, perhaps "of" or "pertaining" or a kind of verbal marker before verbs were generally distinguished. The final da or dai shortened to d is out of the same box as tai, to be about, to be becoming or be doing. When you are static you are merely upright, whence it follows you are staying still and not loping off. The cod is a fish which defies etymology, but as a large shoaling species is, or in old days was, probably harvested by the bulging bag full, fishermen thinking the cod made a full bag. That is why the cod has been

THE PSYCHOSEMANTIC TREE FOR PA

The Phonetic Tree

Wa – Va – Ba – Pa – Ba – Va – Wa

The Semantic Tree

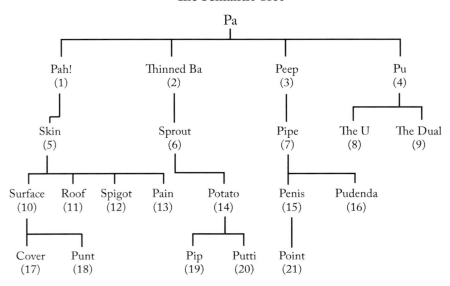

fished near to extinction, prices falling and then rising. Predators go for the easy option.

Pa (2), as the thinned diminutive of Ba, suggested the skin (5) (on the outside of the flesh), or a diminutive piece of flesh, like a spike or sprout (6) or leaf or petal (Lithic pa-i-ta-lai, a sprout which has become flat). The small piece of flesh which attracted most attention in those far off days was the male penis (15) – much like today. The name came indirectly from the cheeping of game bird chicks, which sounded as if they were saying pi-pi (3). If you wanted to start off your fine vowel-elisation with a consonant in the modern manner of the day you started it with a p. That may have been just a whimsy. The sound of the quail chick was started with a p because it starts its notes sharply. It actually produces a note like an eee, and not a howl like an owl. Pa starts sharply and so is used also for a sharp sound like a tapping sound, and so a tappet and a patter (3). A tap has a further semantic construction: ta-pai is a certain orifice-covered or stopped up – with a spigot. The earliest tap was perhaps in a barrel and the spigot stopped it up, it was a (wooden) piece. Today we quite like peep-peep or even cheep-cheep for the game bird's pipi, which is perhaps over egging it a bit. The Ancient Egyptians studied quail chicks and liked pi-pi. They were probably rearing them for the table. The quail chick always chirps twice – never a single peep. It says "pi-pi", "pi-pi". As a matter of fact all ground-nesting game bird chicks do the same. Now for the Ancient Egyptians (and all the other ancients we know of as well) the vowel u was the dual vowel. (The reasoning behind this is in chapter 15 on vowels). They believed every species had some special characteristic which went with the species, and gave their many gods animal heads to point up their identifications. The quail chick's specialty was to be wed to duality. So the dual pi was a pu; and since pa in Egyptian meant "the", "pu" – with only a little imaginative elision – could be read as "the u"(8). Accordingly a charming hieroglyph of a quail chick was used for the vowel sound u. It suffered like all hieroglyphs from one big disadvantage: it was far too complex and took far too long to draw for a single simple symbol where sentences were to be recorded, especially if you were having to cut it into rock. But the Egyptians had far more time on their hands than we do, and they liked the artistry that went into their script and the punning that had gone into the shaping of it. You must remember too that recording thinking was at the leading edge of technology when we were learning to do it. Nothing appeared extravagant. We can note in passing the quail chick is supposed to be wa by the academic Egyptologists who have no Lithic – as if it barked like a dog. But as all syllables are supposedly randomly selected throughout the world it presents no problems for them: the quail chick's use needed no justification. A priest of Amun had a sketch of a quail chick the others thought neat; so they popped it in at u as that was where they had got to. But we live in a much more closely textured world than that.

Then came the jolly herdsman a-playing on his pan-pipes (7), making piping noises – the lazy puss, instead of hunting – just like the quail chick. His pipes were called quail chicks, "pipi". Notice his were not dual, there were a number bound together and blown in turn. The pipi vowelisation suited them quite well as the i vowel was the diminutive-reduplicative and the u vowel meant the inclusive and so all of them not just two(chapter 15). Otherwise our drainpipes and the pipes we used at one time to smoke might have been called poops instead of pipes since our pipes are learned from the Egyptians through Greek, etcetera. Pan´s pipes are not the only musical instruments to be called after the creature that makes a similar sound. The ukulele is named after the Hawaiian grasshopper which makes a stridulent sound by scraping its thighs together to attract the female. (You need specialised thighs for the job). Boys use their hips instead, which they gyrate hippy style, and the music has to be provided as an accompaniment. The hips are from hai-pai, the ecstasy limbs or hams because they are needed for sex. The bright scarlet hawthorn hips are ecstasy pieces as well because fancifully they resemble the glans of the erect penis; and the haw with greater economy is just from a ha-u, the ecstasy-one.

It has been widely believed from Egypt right across Asia and the Pacific Ocean that the Ka was the driving force or essential soul of the body, often thought to be resident in the spine and skeleton. In Egypt you had a Ba as well, presumably resident in the fleshy bits. The ka and the ba were respectively the boys´ and the girls´ contributions. Honest folk (anyway if they were male) had dual Kas, one for this world and one for the next one after death. Feminine claims to an immortal soul were uncertain. Aristotle doubted it, as Ba (flesh) decays. When I drew attention to this in a tutorial at Oxford fifty five years ago a fellow undergraduate (male) walked out in disgust as if it were my fault. Some time later he committed suicide. He seems to have got the message he would be all right. Insects were taken to have deployed both of their ka in the present world, many of them going in for dual births as well, from egg to larva and then again for their final form with thorax and body or belly both on display in the here and now. Their prospects after death were thus seriously compromised by their profligacy in this world. That may indeed have been why some of them rasped away so. Anyway in Hawaii an uku was an insect, a dual ka life form with both ka on display. Lele in Hawaiian meant la-la, singing – see chapter 9 for the meanings of La. The Aboriginal Malays living in the jungle are unkindly called Sakai by their Malay cousins around the coasts, single Ka folk with no better prospects in the afterlife than an insect. They are not Muslims and they do not mutilate their genitalia as Semites and their converts do. They do not bother with much in the way of clothes when at home either – just like Adam and Eve who were plains folk from right next door, the Paddi Gardens (Malaya) of Eden now under the South China Sea. They prefer to be referred to as Orang Asal, the first or original folk. They are probably the genuinely nicest people to be met with these days, unspoilt by the competitiveness of progress.

The penis (15), a single pipe, one which nai, presents itself and stands upright and engorged (rayed) when doing the business (see chapter 13) does not play tunes like the pan-pipes, any more than the gull wing sings. A penis can thus be described as a double gull (see note 1) since from the quail chicks´pipi the pan-pipe is gulled because of the similarity of the sounds each makes, and then the pan-pipes are gulled again because of their similarity in shape to the choke or pipelet on the male urethra (from oo-rai-te-heira, the orifice-roused-become rayed, the vagina, oo-a-kai-na,which kindled gapes; said to be a little sheath, but with proper metathesis the sheath comes second and lies open to receive its blade. The two perceptions which largely shaped language are both represented in chief by the penis: first echoism and secondly metaphor based on shape. Echoism was the easiest to understand, it pushed itself into consciousness, as it still does today. Shape was perhaps the most important – it has been described as the tyranny of the eye – since it packed an additional punch: shape was either static (remanent) or mobile (elastic). The inert bits of the world like rocks and even rivers stayed very much the same, and the vegetable kingdom changed only very slowly and never got up and ran; growth after all is a slow and almost imperceptible process so leaves and fruit burgeon and the plant gets bigger and bigger but only slowly and always controlled by the due seasons. But animals move about all the time and their limbs come into play in any number of different and striking ways, and their most astonishing trick of all is they can change shape – in part – enlarging and shrinking before your very eyes. This ability admittedly is confined to the genitalia which also show every sign of being in many ways at the core of the life form of every phenotype. The males can fruit and unfruit time after time, putting the strawberry to shame[2]. The Malay for fruit is buah and it also is used for the two testicles, as well as for a bobbin, a little bob, a plural ba, originally a pendant bunch as with a plumb bob, perhaps at first a pair as with bub, and then only one needed for taking soundings. It is only a guess but it may well be the testicles were regarded as the receptors of the energising feminine rays. They are egg shaped like eyes, after all, which were supposed to receive the returning rays they had sent out, bearing pictures of the world outside back irradiated onto the iris. Hominids must surely have noticed if they removed the testicles, or when they were undeveloped before puberty the feminine rays were ineffective. Egyptian for the male genitalia is ba, bits of flesh, of which the dual form is bu. Comically the Ba was the feminine part of a man, which is no doubt why his genitalia so desperately sought the female all the time and the female in turn packs such a powerful pull on them.

Abu for father appears to be using the A in place of a long Aaa, an extension, outgoing or outcome of his testicles, and so he with the source testicles. The females meanwhile can open up from the merest slit to round out and accommodate the male organ and then even the head of the baby at birth as well, reverting to standard slit after. It may not be teatime talk, but our hominid forebears had no teatimes – they never took tea – and an appetite for understanding at almost any cost, as ideas piled up in their heads. Much of language will have built around the hearth, where the encumbered matrons had all day, along with the unencumbered girls when they were not out with their digging sticks grubbing up tucker for the evening meal. Indeed it is arguable what triggered language was the women staying in the heat of the hearth all day working up an interest in pulling the boys when they got back to the hearth with the meat. How did they work it? They made themselves available. More curiously, how was the biter bit? The ancients reckoned once the boys´ muzzle covers had been withdrawn by the female rays pulling out and plumping up the acorn nestling within, it sent out its own retaliatory rays rounding out the girls and attracting them towards their sexual nemesis. Pharaoh, who evidently supposed the royal penis was of divine parentage, had his own cover cut off so as not to have his god Amun-Ra, the Eternally Planting or Ever Loving god demeaned by having to wait for rays from any passing houri to start him up. Or else he thought by exposing it to Ra – the sun, the light – He would come for his acorn and draw it out. Pharaoh is conventionally translated House of Ra or Royal House. But that would not be a Pha-rau but Pa-Rau, a roof or skin covering (5,8) against the sun's rays, a sun shade, originally a goat skin tent in the desert; whence the Greek polis, where the pa is still the skin roof as shade against the rays of Ra but the -lai is a loop indicating a collection of them, the city and thence the city state with police. We can not easily distinguish ray from raise since Egyptian rai meant both. Pahei (15) is unquestionably Egyptian for penis and "Pharaoh", from Pahei-Ra-au-hei, can only be translated as Royal Penis or Penis in which Ra rejoices, or even Penis-[of]Ra-Ever-Orgasmic, a Royal Super Stud. Anyway he wasn't waiting for his muzzle cover to be withdrawn. The proactive monarch cut it off. He had no proper job to keep him out of mischief. The Semitic races have joined in the party ever since, as if it were their divinity and not Ra with whom the original circumcision deal was done. Abraham from Aba-Raham is a trimmed and tidied up translation of Pha-Raoh with Aba as genetrix, father.

Pa, as a thinned (actually unvoiced, which makes a finer note, voicing is comparatively gravelly) version of Ba, is a thinned diminutive of flesh, a shoot or sprout (6), hijacked by the quail chick (3) above, echoism taking precedence over mere metaphor (which requires reflection). The quail chick, all unawares, identified one small protruberance of the animal (human) form, because it was quite like a pan pipe, which in turn was called a chick because its notes were similar. That is the way metaphor works. The Pan pipe picked up an echoic icon, followed by the penis with a shape similarity, and so a pee from a peep, although the penis never peeps. But the limbs in turn are diminished protruberances (6) of the corpus, which in turn is the core (ka) of the limbs. The haunches are burgeons, bottoms with bilateral symmetry. But the feet are thinned diminutives as in Latin pes foot, and pous leg in Greek including the haunch. The Latin supinatio means regurgitation, to which we are all liable when supine, especially after dining too well, (Latin supinus Eric Partridge translates as overturned backwards, and the verb supinare as to lay backwards, no reasons given). The Lithic can be read as su, all upwards, pai, limbs, and nau presented, pushed upwards or protruding, much as the quail chick's second derivative does in fact, or like a playful puppy or kitten on its back with its legs in the air, a perfectly useless posture which comes through in the penumbra of meanings attached to the supine position as passivity in the face of circumstances calling for action. The Romans, who spoke the Latin, were inclined to overeat and drink supine with their feet up on chaises-longues. The pai in this case are the legs, only thinned diminutives relative to the main body. We can see much the same semantics in the pupa or chrysalis, with all the limbs, pu (4), pa, covered (10), just like the pod does, paradigmatically with peas in it, the little plumplets (19) covered (17), legumes like the bean, faba in Greek, which some Greeks refused to eat as pahai-ba or testicles – of nature and the gods? In Malay the mouse deer is si-pelandok, brer dainty toes, picking its way timidly through the jungle leaving only the lightest of tracks. It is little bigger than a fox terrier, and apart from two top teeth like darning needles which it will use to slash if cornered it is defenceless against predators. Its pai (feet in this case) la'n-do', smoothly do. It is credited with sly cunning, the brer rabbit of the jungle. It slips along slyly. It gets caught and eaten nevertheless by the still slyer aboriginal hunter with snares set in holes in hedges made of undergrowth on the way down to water sometimes half a mile long or more. The origin of pedestrianism is the Latin pes for foot, from pai-sai, motion pieces (6). The meanings of the phoneme ish are in chapter 14. With pes the s could just be the Latin substantial (noun) marker. In Malay again si puti is brer shell. Kuala Lumpur the Malayan capital is on the Sungei Siput or Snail River. A shell is a hard coat or covering. Siput (15) was principally a snail, for which the term was coined, Si-puti being Brer penis-teat. The resemblance is somewhat fanciful. It is metaphor of course. That meant a common facet of nature spotted, a natural pattern shared. With Malay pintu which is a door, like the Spanish puerta, we have two surfaces (10): the old fashioned door was of the Wild West saloon door kind with two swing leaves. They could be closed so they could not be kicked open by John Wayne with good solid beams across them as bolts. Neither a mountain pass nor a sea port, from the Latin porta, have even one swing leaf between them, the derivation is purely a semantic gull, the pass is a gateway enabling travellers to pass through the mountains and the seaport is a doorway or point of entry and exit for ships reaching or leaving land.

The Hawaiian for a sea shell is paua (9,10), and u is the dual vowel as well as the completive, so pa-u-a is a dual lid one, as well as being a completely covered one. The completive was also the dual, since for the primitive dialectic mind any completive state was the product of two preceding states – just as two peeps made a pu, and two pigs make a piglet and two people make a child (and two Latin people a puer (3), which picked up the piper sense with voices as yet unbroken).

In India prayer (which in English is composed from pai-rai-a, arms raised one) is poojah, from pu-sha, the both arms-up, just like the Egyptian priests of Amun-Ra (when praying), with elbows in a right angle making it clear they were praying to the divine dialectical scheme of the Tau, the two dimensions of the world, the up-down (time) and the sideways (space), as seen in Egyptian tomb art. It is only a short hop – a convulsive move – from there to the colour puce, supposedly the colour of the flea – we have pea green so why not flea puce – from puce which is flea in Latin, but with a derivation far from the colour, from pu-khai strong legs, enabling it to jump over the moon (above its weight) and if tethered to pull a cart a hundred times its size as a circus trick. The Latin is pulex irritans, the pulex from the Lithic elements: pu-lai-kai-sai, an irritating legs-leaping-strong-acting, spelling out in elaborate detail just pu-kai, legs-strong, French puce. Our King Charles spaniel, investigating a dead hedgehog in the greenhouse, incarcerated overnight for the children to see – out in daylight they are usually discommoded – was struck on the snout by fifty flees jumping simultaneously like a single black pellet and sprang back as if struck by a stick. The colour puce is a gull from the flea. It has no legs and does not jump. The Greek phulla remarks the flea's leaping like our English frog's as ejaculatory.

In Africa lives the chimpanzee (6): si-m´pan-sai, brer-him-limbs-lively/active, or else, more likely from the activity of the limbs, pa´n-sai, a goer-up, not unlike the Australian go-up, baji or bird; but in the chimp's case not a flyer but brer climber. They climb nimbly through the trees. In Sumatra, on the other side of the Indian ocean, they call a smaller local species of monkey chipai, lively legs, or another goer-upper. The nimblest, with long arms and prehensile tail, is the siamang, or si-amang, brer-weightless. The Sanskrit for a man is puman (15), with a pipi ma´n, an earthing or planting (impregnating) pipe. In chapter 10 for Ma man has already been identified as the planter. It is tempting to read woman as u-au-ma´n, the passive version from the completive (passive) vowel u, making passive-that one-planting, that is the planted (impregnated). The same pu as in the Sanskrit is in Latin pubes which means first of all adult, the pu- bai(s), the genitalia burgeoned, sexually mature, even the penis-bits, the testes may be meant, and thence the pubic growth of hair which indicates as much. Eric Partridge relates pubes directly to puer (7), a Latin boy but puer was originally a child of either sex, a piper with unbroken voice. In reality this pu goes right back to the quail chick, with a nod on the way to children´s high piping unbroken voices

Curiously the Malay for the human groin is kunchi paha (15). Kunchi is from a kau'n khai, a join-maker, a closure or junction, used also for a lock. Ibu kunchi, the mother of the closure is the keyhole (sic) and anak kunchi the son of the closure is the key, an incestuous etymology fortuitously arrived at. The paha looks like the Pharaoh´s pahai, identifying the fork as the one with the genitals attached. Anak, son, from an-a-kai, one-that-begotten, is quite like the Egyptian ankh, variously translated. Tutu-anakh-Amun, transliterated for English readers as Tutenkamun, means Tahu-tau-son of Amun in Egyptian. Tahu-tau, Know-all, was another god Englished as Thot or Tahuti still leaving a certain amount to be desired. It results from reading the hieroglyphs as if they were alphabetic. Curiously tahu in Malay also means to know. A thing in English is an item, something distinguished from the surrounding texture or panorama, visually or verbally. Tahu as to know is perhaps semantically to distinguish and so to identify, just as in English thinking.

Another significant elision by the Egyptologists is to write Set for Sai-tan, the wicked god who bit off Osiris´s genitals and threw them into the Nile, where they were quickly gobbled up by the fishes and lost. It means something like the actions of the world, perhaps the ways of the world, so that we are asked to renounce the ways of the world the flesh and the Devil. The flesh is in SaiTan, since it is the sensing of the birth canal, the way things happen, as well as Satan being the Devil, because the world was, for the Egyptians, everything that happened, all the becomings, and they used for that idea all the birthings from ta the birth canal, so that tau meant all the births or happenings and so the universe, Taun in Egyptian. We can see this in their use of Aataun, the Eternal Birth Canal, Englished as Aton, the sun´s "disc", fully frontal, the sun which was seen as giving birth to the light each day. It was identified as "the disk of the sun" by the early Egyptologists, as more acceptable than the sexual orifice the Egyptians saw it as. In Ancient Egypt the boys felt left out as if the girls were hogging the Divinity with their Aa-tau´n and declared the sun the eye (Ra) in the sky instead. The sexes share the visual facility, but it appears in hindsight to have been a declaration of independence by the boys no longer prepared to have goddesses in charge. A quite unlooked for spin off was an observant deity could be seen to have a purpose other than just sending out rays willy nilly like a world vagina. At first no doubt His purpose was seen as simply a disciplinary inspection to punish any conduct found deviant from the divine will, sending down floods and droughts as well as murrains and even volcanic explosions when things went wrong. But later a seeing god proved capable of approbation too, of love and care for sparrows' falls; none of which was really possible from a vagina in the sky. So the boys have it on a technicality.

There are those in similar competitive vein who have tried to make out that Apollo was the Eternal phallus, the glowing glans ejaculating light, but A-pau-lau, Eternal-traveller-in a loop, the orbiter, is better, the traveling from feet, pedestrian, (6). Egyptians could get away with this idea of an eye in the sky without any inconsequence since the eyes we have were supposed to be active radiation sources rather than merely the passive receivers of the sun´s rays reflected from the panorama we now know them to be. The Egyptians drew Ra´s rays with hands on the ends to teach the ignorant peasantry that the rays of the sun came down and then went back up again pulling the plants back up with them: whence to grow in English, ge-rau, ge-rayed, from kai-rau, made rayed. Ignore the spelling, even the words, and think of the meanings merely. Our feebler eyes returned only with a simulacrum of what they had encountered, reflected on the iris of the eye, the irradiated or more precisely it-ray-show, for the manikin to read from behind the eye. As we now know, it would not be long before people would come to ask what this eye in the sky was doing, and the first belief it was keeping an eye on disciplinary matters would come to be superceded by the idea it was concerned even for sparrows´ falls. For this we have the civilization of Egypt and the lost Egyptian language to thank

From the skin, the surface of the flesh, came the idea of a surface (10) and thence a roof (11) or lid or top, the Greek pi., and so, via the skin or periphery of the sun a circular measure, 2 pi d. The subconscious appears to have chosen the pi. The Beduin´s roof is made of skins in any case, to provide shelter from the sun, and this predicament of escaping the sun´s rays must have been around since savanah conditions prevailed in hominid days. Sa-u-a-na reads in Lithic heat-what-that-present. There will not have been enough cool caves to go round. Whereas the pa that was a vegetal shoot or sprout (6), a small burgeon, would push upwards just like its fleshly cousin, if rather slowly and relatively insignificantly, a surface could slope any way or even be circular like the surface of the sun, the boundary of a tube seen end on, whence the Greek and Latin peri (5), from pa-i-rai, skin or surface of Ra. It was the idea of anything going or being around the edge of something, a periphery. The -phery is from the Greek pherein to carry. The carriage was originally from impregnation, the pahei did not stop raying until it had triggered the pregnancy. It was the Greeks who started Britain as a name. (Our "carriage" is from putting it on the head, kara, just as a pair of horns, cornu, were the two protrusions of the skull). Britons were called Pretani in Greek. It came from Egyptian Peri-taun-i, periphery of the world ones, that Ultima Thule or Tahu-lai, the Ultimate World loop or rim, beyond which you ran the risk of falling off the edge of the world. There is some linguistic evidence Egyptian speakers once colonised the place. Taun was Egyptian for all the birthings or becomings or happenings, the universe as experienced, as already explained in chapter 4. Similarly Egyptologists believe the Egyptian for Heaven was pet (sic). Akin to a spit? But the glyphs were not usually read alphabetically. Pai, a surface, was drawn as a square in hieroglyphic, a surface in a bird´s-eye view. The Greek pi (10), was the same in elevation with two supporters and the top surface in the shape of a curlicue to direct attention to the top surface as the bit intended. Top can also be read in the same Lithic terms since the Tau or Tao (a T) was believed to represent, amongst other things, the two fundamental extensions or dimensions of all hu-man thinking, namely the extensions of time and space, whence inter alia (for the Chinese) a lifetime path or way to follow, amounting to a religion. The vertical dimension was the temporal one and the horizontal cross piece on top the spatial dimension, seen sideways on with a flat earth. The tau-pai, the surface or space dimension of the tau, is the top of the T. Time can be seen to be coming up here, offering progress.

A pie (10,11) is lidded, that is surfaced with a pastry top, unlike an open tart. It is made of pieces too. Eric partridge, without the benefit of any (elaborate) Lithic semantic contents, declares a pie might be so called because originally made of magpies. The children´s nursery rhyme meanwhile plumps for four and twenty blackbirds. The semantic catena in reality goes the other way. The magpie (10) is named for its contrasting patches or surfaces, black and white. A plate is a similar flat, and circular (like the skyline at sea) surface, from the French plat (10) mean-ing flat, a surface-smooth-become. The Latin penna (10) is a wing, a protruding surface (in flight). The Greek pan (10) as in pantechnicon and panorama, mean-ing everything, is a more difficult one, being the combinative form of Greek pas which is from the Egyptian pa-sai, the surface as sensed, in this case seen, that is everything in view – after all you do only see the surfaces of things and it is no great leap to see the panorama as a single surface as presented – the world as sensed, and therefore every-thing. Panorama (6) spells it out with –orama which means that what-eye-ment, all-seen, a sight. In Egyptian Ra was the sun and ra was an eye as well, with rai meaning seeing or seen as well as rayed by the sun[3]; and much of Greek is closely akin to Ancient Egyptian. This is because for many centuries so many educated Greeks lived in Alexandria and studied at the library there, forerunner of modern universities, until it got burnt when the Wahabi in-vasion occurred in the seventh century, the thirteenth BP. There will have been extensive looting and smuggling away before the library books were burned by the fanatics, some of its greatest treasures surviving to kick-start Arab culture. In Greek horan meant to see. The h seems to have been a cockney h, from the Egyptian one pronounced more like ahi – even hinted at in our "aitch" – dividing (any) two vowels to prevent them eliding (chapter 8). Greek horan is thus i-a-u-ra-en in Lithic terms, roughly it-that-one-eye-verbal, to eye or see.

The Greek for eye, and thereafter face, was ops (6), in Lithic expansion au-pai-sai, that one or what-pai-senses. It is the eye which lets you know where the material boundaries are, saving your shins. The pa is the same pa as in panorama, the surface of things in view, after all the surface is all that you see, so you get a superficial view. That is how the Egyptian pa came to mean "the" for them, denoting particularity, by way of the one in view rather than any old one that might come to mind. The au is also an oo or o or egg shape. The eye is defined as a sensing egg. However the pai-sai can also be read as the surface sensed or seen, and so the front of anything, and in particular the face. Our face or front is from the Latin facies which adopts a different and somewhat ruder definition based on paha-kai. The pai has been exchanged for fai or the pahai. P can of course become f under a law like Grimm's which finds consonants being switched on a regular basis between related languages as if by a (subconscious) fashion in pronunciation. However for the -s in pas to change to -k in facies (15) under such a dispensation is hard to swallow, and the Latins appear to have followed a different tradition. The Egyptian nefer (15) as in Nefertiti meant pretty, and it can quite easily be read in its Lithic precursor form as nai-pahei-rai, showing-the-pahei-is rayed and rises. We can all be influenced by a pretty face, and its expressions provide the entrée for relating to the personality within as well. It does not make the world go round but it certainly plays its part. When we say pretty we are somewhat similarly saying the pee-raised-becoming, what a pretty face does for you. We don't think in these rather blunt terms today but when we learned to speak it was in fairly brutal terms. Today a pretty face is pleasurable but that is all, anyway so far as we are prepared to admit. But I remember a boy at school who looked like an angel and because of the glances he attracted concluded he must be the reincarnation of Jesus Christ, finishing up with his frontal lobes cut off to disillusion him. He was sacrificed because social etiquette decreed he could not and should not have the truth explained to him.

With facies, face, ka can mean to strike or kindle (chapter 5). A pretty face can arouse passion in a beholder, rather more than a shapely arm or other part of the body not a secondary sexual character, like the foot or ankle. If he is male it can probably be said it will. As a boy soldier at seventeen I once followed a pretty face I saw when traveling by bus in Aberdeen – it was heavily chaperoned by an older woman – all the way to its home with a view to striking up an acquaintance; but then funked doing anything about it. Human whimsy is such that just about any body part can become a fetishist fixation, along with its usual covering. But the face is always seen uncovered because it carries the owner's eyes – unless a fetish makes it taboo and requires it to be covered at all times for fear of the lascivious-ness that, facing, it might otherwise arouse. Romans went around clad but not yet constrained to wear any yashmak or visual dowser. It is indeed possible to go so far as to derive the front from the missionary position. The Latin Facies comes close to the four letter word, with striking understood in the stark physical thrusting sense rather than merely as kindling. In Albanian, that maverick language next door, para means in front, the surface visible. They were clearly talking to the Egyptians long before they got caught by the Turks. The Latins used para to con-front and so to oppose, to be against, surface presented to surface, two parties up against each other. Pugna in Latin means both fist and battle: fist from pa-u-kai-na, the inflated end (of the arm in this case)-made-protruding (4); battle from dual surfaces-made presented (10). The two battle lines in those early days simply confronted each other, locked shields and bashed at the enemy line like a rugby scrum getting down. Opposition is confrontation precisely.

Another maverick language along the Mediterranean litoral, Basque, now confined to the top end of Spain, has pipi for moth. The moth is notably silent with nothing in common with the quail chick, so it is clear immediately we have here a shape metaphor, with two little surfaces (10) or wings, with a flapping action. Moths, and more particularly butterflies are conspicuous flutterers. A butterfly in Albanian is Flutura, a flitter or flutterer. I have found it used as a girl's name. Greek used pai for wings too. Their word for wing is ptera (10), the plural of ptron a feather, which we only commonly come across in helico-pter and ptero-dactil, that which circle-makes-wing and winged-fingers. P is pronounced properly here of course: pi. For the Greeks (far enough back) wings were surfaces, pai, which were tai-rai, subject to Egyptian rays, in this case the vaginal rays (see chapter 5 for ta as the birth canal) which pull things out and up, like our chest of drawers which we pull out, or our drawers or underwear we pull up; and nature which for the Egyptians exhibited (na-) a quiver full of pulls, tura, to be propitiated. Wings can be seen as sky hooks which have the facility to get you pulled up into the empyrian, an ability mere human propensities, not even the ladies, can aspire to, lacking the natural pullers necessary to grab the wings. None of this makes any sense today, but is it not quite fun? The Latin for a feather and a wing is penna, our pen we write with, originally a goose's feather with the end cut into a nib (a protruding bit). The Latin penna for wing is a protruding surface (10), but the feather makes better sense if the pai- is a piece (16) like the penis. The feather offers a surface, admittedly, but not one which is notably protruding. The individual piecess of the feather however all protrude in a remarkable fashion from the central quill or spine, in so far as they have minuscule hooks along their length enabling them each to join their neighbours on either side to make a waterproof and airtight surface. Birds preen (16) (Lithic pai-rai'n, arrange the pieces) their feathers with their beaks to rehook joints which have become separated. It is the protruding pieces of the feather (a feather is from phai-a-terai, pieces-that-tai-rayed, drawn out: not shy of revealing the original sexual source of the metaphor precisely) which make up a surface, which is not itself protruding. The wing then makes a surface which is protruded in flight, supposedly hooked up in turn by the rising rays of ancient fancy, but actually providing lift by beating down upon the air.

A bishop or overseer is from the Greek epi-scopus, Lithic ai-pai-sai-ka-au-pau(s), that which-covered-see-make-all-surfaces, a doggerel which means ai-pai, on top or over, see-make or as we would say just seer, which is because ops in Greek is eye and skopein is to view. The –pau– here is the same as in the pa- in panorama, the visible surface which we see. In Latin palear is the dewlap of an ox. The Lithic, pa-lai-a, is piece and surface-slack or flaccid (10)-that or one. Palla is a long cloak worn by Roman women, and the Lithic is pa-laila, surface-long and flaccid. The pallium worn by men – including now the Pope – is a mantel or a coverlet: which shows the idea is a surface which can be put to use to mean equally either an item of clothing or a furnishing, including also a pall in English. A pane is a surface like a panel, both surface ones (10), though a pane hammer is one with a knob behind (instead of a claw) and is a protruding piece, although its use is to beat panes (10) or panels flat, its rounded profile avoiding making weak places with a sharp edged hammer. Then there is a palus in Latin which is a long piece (16) meaning a stake, whence the English palisade, and the phrase beyond the pale, akin to the English pole, another long piece; whereas a pile is a (looped) collection of pieces, shape unspecified. In Latin again a pilum is from the Lithic pai-lau-mai, piece-long-heavy and is the heavy javelin carried by Roman infantry. Or else the lai, as in javelin, is looping, flying in a loop like Apollo, meaning it is hurled. Latin pilus is a hair, another long piece like the English pole, but small scale by comparison, and pilosa is hairy. A caterpillar is therefore defined by Partridge as a hairy cat, apparently accepting a caterpillar is a cat (sic) because a caterpillar is sometimes hairy and that seemed to fit, leaving him with the cater- to deal with. The Lithic however is ka-ta-pai-la-a, a ka-two-[with]feet flowing-one. Caterpillars have numerous sucker feet, no legs to speak of, which they use in an undulating manner, their bodies rippling as they lift pairs of feet in turn. The two ka is explained, like the Hawaiian uku for insect, by the caterpillar using up both ka in this world by being born twice, once from the egg and again from the pupa. Stylised butterflies were drawn in the Stone Age, probably as intimations of immortality, because of their ba-ta, two ba, two flesh embodiments or beings. The hope was that death would prove to be a pupation with a rebirth into a far more ethereal form like the butterfly to follow. I have read that children awaiting gassing in the holocaust left stylized butterflies on the walls. Chambers' committee of expert linguists will have none of this, recording merely of butterfly "the origin for this name of the insect is obscure" while Partridge leaves butterfly out altogether. Since keeping puss moth caterpillars and poplar hawks in cages at school the name has bothered me – the headmaster was a nut who required it in order to bring his pupils into touch with nature, and there were batteries of gauze covered compartments which, on visual appearances anyway, may have formed the pattern for the baby batteries made for the kibbutz rising generation in Israel, while their mothers toiled politically correctly in the fields. A schoolfriend, one Greville Adrian Cavendish, of seventy years ago (scion of a noble house, unfortunately killed in action in his teens a few years later) who had reinforcements in a cardboard box awaiting allocation of a hutch wrote on the box so it would not be rubbished "Pillars" – he could not spell caterpillars, and it was not even very well written. The headmaster, on discovering the ruse, told him he would be Dish. And Dish he was from that day forth – instead of Gac (off his underwear) We were friends because we both were teased. For seventy years I have been dissatisfied with the spelling, until only recently I cracked its code. I doubted all along they were cats. In Greek pagos means frost: pa-kau (10)is surface-hardened and covered-ground, and frost does harden the ground as anyone who has tried to dig a latrine in winter above the forty eighth parallel will be aware. You find yourself hacking out thumbnail sized pieces. The Koreans, in the bad old days, confronted with this problem would equip themselves with very large earthenware pots at their front doors as receptacles until the thaw, when the ground would open up to receive its dues again and the pots could be emptied. A second pot held kimche, a local pickle. It was japed American forces, Waylanders, could not tell one from the other.

The Potato (6), from Central America, is from the Taino language via Spanish. Originally the same species as the tomato, it was bred for its root tuber while the tomato was bred for its fruit. Today, if you irrigate a potato crop as it is flowering you get a crop of small green tomatoes. They are mildly poisonous, which shows the breeders were persistent, breeding the tomato for larger sweeter fruit. The potato in Lithic phonemes is pau-tau-tau, plump ones (tubers)-birth-birth. You replant the tubers (14) and get another crop, a second birth. The potato tuber is a shoot (6) which has become burgeoned. The tomato by contrast is from tau-ma-tau, birth-death-birth. With a tomato, an annual, you replant the seeds each year. It is closely related to the totem pole, a garbled Anglicisation of oto-tema (Hawaiian) which in Lithic phonemic elements is au-tau-tau-ma, all-the-born-born-dead, all the generations of ancestors: and there they are one above the other on the pole, sometimes with the mythical original progenitor on the top. Of course they are only a symbolic representative selection since to show them all your pole would have to extend into the heavens.

Water in Hindustani is pani (10), and nahi is nay or no: with no surface, if you step into it you go straight through to the bottom where there is a surface. On the other side of the world the Guarani in Paraguay for water is apan (10),

unsurfaced. In England a pan (10), now with a lip for frying with fat was originally a flat griddle for making baps. It is simply a surface. Bread was cooked
that way once, which is why in France they still call it pain, and in Spain pan. A
Spanish frying pan however is sarten, from fire-ray-become. With English bread
the emphasis is on the action of the yeast in making the dough rise, bai-rai-dai,
ba-i-rayed-become, as it did also with beer and any other brew. Ba was flesh, but
dough was similar, more like flesh than the vegetable matter (vegetable flesh) of
which it was composed. Rays were supposed to work at a distance to raise crops,
penises, visions fetched back to the iris of the eye, anything raised or roused itself
in fact, just as when crops grow (see chapter 13 on the phoneme Ra), so yeast had
this facility too.

Just as the nature of the flesh (ba) was to burgeon, so the pa on a smaller scale
swelled or puckered up. The penis did. Pimples did. The lips would pout, become
swollen. A pudding is doing the same, from the Germanic root pud- to swell – as
the pipi or penis does although the catena is forgotten. A paunch, pau-en-kai, is a
swelling of the body. To poke is to make with the pipi, picked up by colloquial vulgar slang. Pandi is Telegu for a pig, it has become fat, just like the boars of Borneo,
or indeed the English pig, which was pai-kai, waxed fat. In that he shares the hon-
ours with the penguin, which is much more closely related to the Latin pinguis or
the Greek pion meaning fat than to the folk etymology of white head from the
Welsh pen-gwin. Apart from the improbability of the Welsh getting there first,
the penguin does not have a white head anyway. Linguistics buffs, saddled with
this absurd etymology, have twisted and turned to propose it perhaps first referred
to another bird which did have a white head, no suggestions made, and then got
transferred to the penguin in a fit of inconsequential ornithological inattention
– an ornithological error rather than an etymological one, anything rather than
an admission of foolish error. The French petite, which is taken to mean anything
small at all, comes in delightfully French fashion from pai-titi (15), a swollen teat,
a breast or pap with only the nipple (from nai-pipi-lai) or teat protruding, little
more than a pimple, and used precisely and with fine Gallic humour for any lass
only modestly endowed. A pea in its pod is a small plump piece become covered
or skinned. A broad bean is much the same but being that much bigger (baraud,
flesh-rayed-become) unfortunately picks up the semantic connection with those
other fleshy bits the boars in Borneo carry out the back in full view, their testicles
or fruit. Probably in emulation of the pig, which they hold in high regard, the
natives wear penis sheaths which greatly exaggerate their genital achievements as
well as keeping them tied up, but leaving their testicles in view. Prince Phillip on
a visit was presented with a bramah model for his personal use, but was diplomati-
cally not required to actually put it on. Partridge lists thirty one words along with
prince, all semantically from in front and forwards, which he presents as pri-. The

Lithic is pai-rai, or visible surface with which you are visually confronted and anyway represents the front – for you – of whatever you are looking at. At one stage it appeared to come from the pai-rai or rayed-piece conspicuous in front, congener with proud, prow, pro-, prance, prank, prink, forward, and even proof (from probus with Greek baino meaning I go – I show a leg – going forward, proudly, confidently, honestly) etc. The prince is from princeps a front or first ceps, taker or performer, from kai-pai., making covered, and so to seize (in the hand?). It looks as if as principal warrior he got the first slice of the booty. It is not altogether clear that a prince was not originally making with the pa-rai, claiming droit de seigneur From the same stable is to press, from pai-rai-sai, piece-raised-acting, thrusting or pressing in. The Latin to press is premere. The Latin action is one of mai, planting or impregnating, or even (in Egyptian) of the mai or penis. The price of anything on the other hand is soberly estimated. The Latin is pretium, declared by Partridge to be o.o.o. (of obscure origin – he gives up). Pai-rai is the observed surface again, the perception, the perceived value, the estimated worth of goods for sale. It was a superficial calculation, and perhaps still is.

Notes.

1. As a reminder a gull is used throughout for the way a gull wing is derived from the seagull which has a wing of that shape. The seagull is a sea caller or singer, like e gale of wind which is one that sings or howls, just as you can have a gale of laughter. The wing does not sing or howl. Its connection with the singing or howling is indirect, just sharing a wing shape.

2. Linguistically the strawberry name, if traditionally treated as from the strawing of plants to keep the fruit from the ground, has a Lithic structure relating it to the glans of the penis, which takes up a shape and even an enrouged colouring which with only a little whimsical over egging can be regarded as both shaped and coloured like the strawberry. Straw is from sai-ta-rau., of the flame (or the sun) become rayed, that is to say dried (corn stalks). But siti in Egyptian was the female. In Malay Siti Maria is Our Lady Mary. In Egyptian Au Siti, in Greek the goddess Isis, who was the mother and wife of Osiris, Au Sara in Egyptian. They were respectively World (or Universal) Sunset and World Sunrise. Between them they produced Horus, the day. Well they still do, every day. The sunset does not seem a very positive role for the ladies, but you have to understand what it meant in earlier times. The sun died but to be resurrected next morning at sunrise. Now the dying was at the same time the necessary stage in nature before being reborn, gestation in animal life, propagation for vegetable life like the seed which falls down and enters the earth and gestates there and is born next season. Siti, as well

as the female life principle was also feminine sensitivity, and at the same time the sedentary female, tending the hearth and nurturing the children while the men went hunting. The sunset was thus the mother of her son, the sun which was born next morning. It meant all of these things and confirmed the philosophers and scientists of the day no doubt that with such a concatenation they had got it all correct. The reality was of course the concatenation had been shaped by their own whimsy.

3.   The Egyptian rays are fully covered in chapter 13 on the phoneme Ra. They were not really Egyptian rays but part of early science, it is just they are extant only in Egyptian hieroglyph. Ra, like the Tau, is one of mankind´s earliest symbols, the circle to add to the T.

CHAPTER 13

THE PHONEME RA

Most of the meanings of the phoneme Ra are best treated as gulls from the Egyptian sun god Ra. It does not mean that the Egyptians were the source of world-wide meanings, but only that they were thinking largely in line with the original Lithic semantics. But it makes sense to start by asking why for the Ancient Egyptians the sun was Ra in the first place. As a consonant Ra has the peculiar character it shares with the hisses and the hums (Ish, Ma and Na) that unlike the other consonants it can be prolonged for as long as you care to keep your tongue vibrating against your palate. The late Peter Ustinov as a boy maddened his parents by pretending to be a motor car, accompanying his movements with a "rrrrrrrrr"... in imitation of an internal combustion engine. Ra undoubtedly stands for repetition. Before the motor car there were the growls of the feline and canine families and the croaks of corvids as well as the frogs and toads. Woodpeckers too string sounds with their beaks and even a snipe drums. But the sun, like Old Man River just keeps rolling along. So why should the repetitive consonant be chosen as its symbol? Perhaps because sunlight shining through trees may extend multiple fingers of light reflecting motes in the air, which suggested a string of tiny bits of light following each other down the ray. That will certainly have been noted as a rare give-away of the nature of the sun's rays.

Perhaps also the sun's rays were seen as repetitive arrays because the arising of every blade of grass was ascribed to a ray from the sun pulling it out and up, and there were an awful lot of them to pull. We say grow from ge-rau, from that original idea of the rays making the grass grow. For that the sun must surely have a myriad rays to be able to address so many clients. The Egyptian priests drew the rays of the sun with hands on their ends to make it clear to the uninformed populace that that was how it went. There was another prompt for repetitiousness where the sun was concerned. The sun was regarded as a world eye in the sky. Our own much feebler eyes sent out rays which reached the panorama confronting them and returned to the eyes whence they came, not pulling back their targets like the sun but only a picture of what had been encountered, which you could sometimes see from in front painted on the iris, the irradiated surface of the eye. The picture was taken to be pointiliste – like the grass – and that obviously pointed to a vast army of individual elements of rays for the job. We do not know which idea came first, the case which accounted for sight, the action at a distance which we all enjoyed, or the action at a distance we could all feel and see when the sun shone. It does not make much difference to the ideas involved. Rays went out and then came back to their source with their mission accomplished, we would say like radar beams. The sun and the eye were active radars. We now know of course our eyes are passive and merely receive and register the light rays from the sun reflected from the surfaces of whatever is in view. We can see that although to the Egyptian mind these rays were purely physical with a mechanical action, their conception as active seeking agents with a role to play actually reflected an anthropomorphic imagination. But that is only the beginning of the Egyptian rays, just what is needed to make the case for the Ra trills to represent the motes of light chasing each other down the sunbeams.

The rays from an animal's eyes, also ra in Egyptian, came back to their source just as the sunbeams supposedly returned to the sun. How else would the crops grow? Or we see at a distance? It will no doubt have ranked as a wonder a few hundred thousand years ago when we were learning to speak. Previously, when the world was ruled by goddesses, before men became bold (or rebellious) enough to shed their reliance upon their mothers, the sun was seen as a World Birth Canal, birthing light into the world each day. In Egyptian it was Aton, from the original Lithic elements A-taun, Universal-Birth Canal seen fully frontal and transliterated by the Victorians as the Disc of the sun. The hieroglyph was just a big O. It usually had a dot in the centre. For perspective? Even as late as in Ancient Egypt there was still a recollection of this earlier religion of the goddess. The hermaphrodite Pharaoh Akhenaton, in Lithic A-khai-en-A-ton, That- begotten-in-the World-Womb, a divine birth, led a religious reaction against the chauvinist priesthood of Amun Ra. But the priests eventually defeated the Pharaoh and his name and his capital city built for the Aton were deleted from the Pharaonic records. Sigmund Freud even made him the original of the Oedipus legend, partly because of his deformed and bloated thighs shown in statues of him, on which Freud based his Oedipus Complex; and the late polymath Emanuel Velikovsky more recently revamped much of the same material rather better. But he was silenced by the astronomical establishment for heresies in the field of astronomy.

Egyptian Pharaohs were expected to copulate with their mothers, a kind of ancient droit de seigneur exercised by the dame from whom legitimacy appears to have descended, a relationship from which AkhenAton, with his impaired sexuality appears never to have escaped. Tahu-tu anak Amun, AkhenAton's son (vulgarly known as Tooten-car-moon), started out Tahutu-anak-Aton, All-Knowing-Son-of the Aton, but changed his name when his father was defeated by the priests of

Amun to Tahu-tu-anak-Amun (Know All, Son of Amun this time) perhaps in the hope of retaining the throne. But it appears he was murdered while still a boy, perhaps a triumph for the very first bureaucracy. We can imagine the trauma if these transferences for the populace. It will certainly have been argued no Eye in the Sky will have cared to be misidentified as a vagina, any more than a goddess would care to be mistaken for a male.

With the sun the eye of the world, what made the difference was it was open to wonder for the first time for what purpose it looked down upon the world, a whimsy which could not have been prompted in any way by a sun seen merely as an everlasting light supply, the purpose of which was simply to let the light into the world. Admittedly Amun Ra – Amun is Ever Loving – looked down upon the world with a rather severe affection, not uncontaminated with self love, in order to punish evil doers who challenged His will as God; as indeed did Yahweh, the God of Ancient Israel, in Lithic I-a-u-a-I, He-that-Universal-Eternal (secret vowelisations identifying perhaps the first dialectical deity), especially when His subjects hankered after earlier cow goddesses. The cow was supremely female because of her extended lactation, and the Aton was supremely female because she was so busy giving birth on a daily basis. It was Christians who first thought God's oversight might be due to His concern even for the fall of sparrows, a truly compassionate deity who would show mercy to all believers. It was of course a dangerous heresy for anyone who laid claim to represent His authority on earth, and much blood was spilt before a compromise was struck with authority, and the church made an uneasy peace with the state, the Papacy with the Emperor. Mohamed too held to this belief in Allah the All Merciful, in deliberate and even violent opposition to the harsh chauvinism of his own Wahabi tribe. Wa-ha-bi in Lithic is Terror-rejoicing-being, or in Proto Arabic simply terror-enjoying-all the time, or in short "The Terrorists", the judgment of their neighbouring tribes in prehistoric times. On Mohammed's death, after his jihads (or vigorous actions) against his own Wahabi tribe who expelled him, his religion was infiltrated for a time by the very tribal leaders he had sought to defeat. The Moslem religion with a Wahabi slant was then carried by the sword all across North Africa into Spain, before The Prophet's true message could reappear and the old unreformed Wahabism be replaced by those who believe in Allah the All Merciful and genuinely profess the true Moslem faith.

It appears some Stone Age Einstein abstracted the idea of a sunbeam and put it to work illuminating a whole galaxy of Egyptian rays, mostly invisible, but some even physical like rain, and including the ray sent out by the ordinary animal eye to feel over the panorama and bring its simulacrum back to the eye. In Egyptian to see was peterai, from the Lithic pai-tai-rai, the surface-drawing up. Ra was the eye and rai was seeing, visible; but vision was drawing up the surface (back onto the eye, the rays' source). The surface (pai) was like the Greek pan, the surface of everything seen. You fielded a superficial view of the whole panorama brought back to your eye. Panorama (Greek) is from the Lithic elements pan-au-ra-ma, surface-that one-the eye/see-matter, all that the eye sees. The final -ma is hard to translate. It was the opposite of ish which as the flame was light and airy, flickering and insubstantial. Ma could feature as such an opposite even in an abstract composition such as the insubstantial mechanism of vision. It should perhaps here be translated just as thingumyjig, with an inconclusive meaning, almost just a substantive marker. It means what the eye sees. The Greek pteron, a wing, was another pai-tai-rau'n, a surface-be-rayed-one, and so drawn up, in this case drawing the bird with it into the sky. A bird's wings were sky hooks. A helico-pter has helical wings or sky hooks. Anyway, whatever the reasoning, it can be seen from the gamut above the growl phoneme came to stand for Ra, the sun, and rai for its rays, bringing with them as a gull what was already worked out for the growl, its repetitive nature, with audibility as action at a distance courtesy of one of the rays around.

The psychosemantic tree for Ra is opposite, with semantic contents 1 to 25. A dozen different arrangements could easily be drawn and no doubt many more meanings formed around the world are missing. But the overall pattern is clear. Words are in origin strings of independent meaningful phonemes and it is only a comparatively recent trick to treat words as singletons rather than strings; and this in spite of the universally recognized fact we go on adding to the strings as a matter of course, calling the additions prefixes, suffixes and even infixes (in Arabic). The academic stasis in linguistics involves dismissing psychosemantics and treating words as randomly composed and the elements strung as themselves meaningless. The loss of grasp is only felt when it comes to trying to understand our linguistic heritage and what that has of interest about the way the human mind has worked and works.

The sabre toothed tiger was simply "Grrr!"(1) in echoic proto language before we learned to speak. It can be counted as a cry. But ti-grrr is speech, meaning mistress growler, which gives us French tigre; and English tiger is just an ignorant mispronunciation of the same. There are plenty of similar echoic names for crows and ravens, etc. They are not only in English. In the jungle along the central spine of what is left, since the last great glacier melt, of the Biblical Eastern garden land of Malaya from which Adam and Eve were expelled by the rising sea level ten to fifteen thousand years ago – quite recently in the age of tongues – the Senoi aboriginal hill tribes copy the growl of their faithful hounds. A dog is khkhauk, (spelt in the guide books chok!), the final k from Lithic kai: growl-maker. It suggests the Latin canis for dog comes from Lithic khkha-nai, which would mean growl-showing, or growler again. Our own rather tame dog perhaps started out

THE PSYCHOSEMANTIC TREE FOR RA

The Phonetic Tree

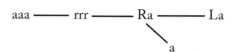

The Semantic Tree

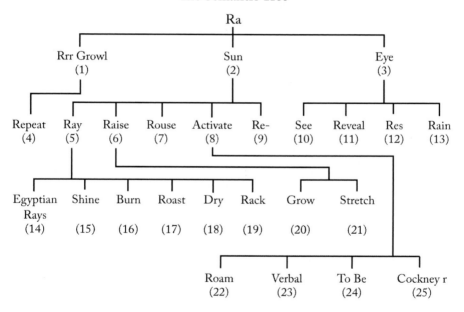

from the Lithic dau-khkh, it does-growling, another growler. They all do it. We
have our own cur, surely from krrrr or growl. It comes via the Old Norse kurra
to grumble from the Middle Low German kurren to growl. If the trace is not
found precise we are still triangulating the meanings in these words for the prior
semantic content of the underlying Lithic phonemes. The original nomenclature
can now only be surmise. But I have no difficulty with it. Growls were likely mim-
icked for as long as it took, say khrkhrkhrkhr (1,1,1,1), to get Tarzan on board to
start with. Once he had it, it then became economical with spit to cut the sound
down to size to chok or cur or canis or dog. Raw is a quite different semantic
structure, although the phonetics are much the same. It comes via crudus, in Latin
bloody, from red, sunset red from Lithic ka-rau-tau. Karau is make-rayed and so
coloured, and rau-tau is Ra when terminal. You can compare mai-ra, the death of
the sun as it goes down. The French saw the sun go down in the sea, so they call it
mer. We have adopted a mere, neither the sea nor where the sun goes down, and
badly pronounced it at that. Gomera, in the Canary islands, is the Western Isle
from Ga-u-mai-Ra, Land-where-dies-the sun in Carthaginia. America, also in
Carthaginian, is from Aa-ma-rai-ka, Far-death-of the sun-land. The NY Times
have been told, but judged it not newsworthy, though very many hundreds of millions of folk on their side of the pond happily use the word all unawares they are
speaking Carthaginian, and Carthaginians beat old Christoph to it by a thousand
years. If that is not news I do not know what is. We may even suspect the Gallic
tribes got their sea from the Punic speakers living in France before eating them.
It seems a long way round to raw but it gets worse. Rau by itself could mean red,
the sun in its extremity (-u), that is going down, when the sky is bloody. The adjective crudus was applied to red meat and even to gore, so that is how raw came
to mean uncooked. When cooked the meat is sealed and the blood is browned.
The classic rose meanwhile was rau-sai, light red. They were mostly rose coloured,
that is pink, although modern plantsmen have succeeded in ringing the changes
since. Lithic suggests raw's reinforcement directly from Ra the source of sunrays,
with raw being like the Greek agora in the open air, as animals are when grazing,
from grass (20).

   Repetition (4) can be recognized in our English ritual, which comes from
– or anyway is closely akin to the Latin ritus, a rite. We have to ask what exactly
was a rite in the mind of whoever it was who made up the term, or whoever they
were, because words are generally adopted by acclamation not by single coinages.
Eric Partridge compares the Greek neritos which means numberless, where the
ne- is clearly the negative so that the -ritus must be the numbers, in Lithic terms
rai-tau(s),: we could say growl born (1) but repetition-derived (4) is better. What
else is number than iteration? Well in Greek it is arithmos which is where our
arithmetic and math come from. The Lithic is a-rai-ta(h)i-mau's, which meant, I

am fairly sure, that-in a row-become-a mass or bulk quantity: a sequential measurement of quantity. Earlier I had the Lithic for arithmos analysed that-repeti-
tion-derived-meaning'substantive marker. In Lithic terms they are both the same,
although I prefer my second go. That surely makes a ritual a repetitive drill or
procedure, which is what it is.

It perhaps throws some light on reason too, from the Latin ratio, which comes
from ratus, the past participle of the Latin verb reri, to be counted (4), to count, or
reiterate, whence to calculate or reckon and hence to think. But also just to count
out a ration or calculated share. It suggests that thinking was originally perceived
as the deliberate rehearsal of points in turn, one by one, maybe even repeating
them out loud, a skill dependent on a language of course, in order to arrive at a
balanced judgment based on all the relevant data. Certainly it suggests the fanciful virtues of reason developed by philosophy are rather over-egging the reality,
which only claims to be rehearsing what seems relevant, as anyone reasonable
would do before coming to a conclusion. To do less is reckless, from Old English
reccan to take heed, to take into account, in original Lithic rai-ka'n, to count-
make. To reckon turns out to mean at base to put in a row (like the motes in a
sunbeam), to put in order, which is what regulation is about also. You don't have to
be counting the motes but you may be. A mote has just mau-tai, become a mump
or mound, a little accumulation. You would not expect such a mump to move and
you would be right, since move, from Latin movere is from mau-bai in Lithic and
it gets the movement (of the mass) from the bai, those muscular burgeons, the
buttocks, which do the leg work. Movement is also derived, like going, from a,
the extensive vowel, incidentally already sketched top left in Figure 1 for chapter
3, illustrating diagrammatically the semantic input of the vowels. In addition the
sibilant phoneme (chapter 14) has action and so movement amongst its semantic
contents from the supposed liveliness of the flame which says ish as it dies. All of
which makes the Greek ameusasthai meaning to become displaced quite relevant.
The monarch meanwhile generally just takes an overall view, as sole archon, the
one making rows. He has ministers for doing the detailed counting and costing in
the rows he makes, currently in the United Kingdom a Mr Brown.

Eric Partridge adds the Sanskrit racayati, he regulates. Our English kings, if
we help ourselves by looking also at the German one, konig, are supposed to be
kau-nai, strength-exhibiting or exercising power, in the Latin version their potes-
tas recognized, their ka here standing for their political potency or power. You can
compare the Arabic (and Aramaic) nabi for prophet and naib for ambassador (later governor of a province) both from the Lithic syllables nai-bai, expositor-bum,
a traveling informant: one a mendicant preacher the other a pompous emissary,
a representative of the supreme power sent to explain what that power requires.
They don't intrinsically mean anything else other than their Lithic origins. What

else we understand about their respective roles are merely add-ons in practice from usage over the aeons, which often outmode the simpler and blunter Lithic meanings – in the process making the underlying psychosemantic structures much harder to spot or even concealing them entirely. Lithic research is not primarily to find out what we really mean or at one time meant, but to study the way ideas and their expression have expanded, been modified, drifted and changed. We are not looking for evolution to rule, a process which starts by random variation followed by natural (unplanned) selection of the fittest variations, which is applicable only to blind biological change, including particularly, as Darwn had it in 1859, speciation. We are on the contrary dismissing this protocol from language studies altogether. It has nothing whatever to do with language development which proceeds by human whimsy and circumstance, which have shaped the way we consciously think, a derivation driven by human thinking itself, a meta-physical phenomenon however much it may emanate from a natural source in the brain. We are no more controlled by the structure of our brains as to what thoughts we may think than we are controlled by the structure of our legs as to what walks we may take. We can not fly and we can not step outside the powers of human cerebration. But in our own gardens we can wander where we will. Will the Massachusetts Institute of Technology stop crowing from the top of their big hill and please note their cognitive researches in terms of the brain scarcely impinge upon language and certainly do not warrant belief in Chomskyan hard wiring of ideas, our ephemeral mental actions in life. The Chomsky-M.I.T. alliance is misplaced.

From ra as an eye (3) come the obvious meanings to see (10), and thence to show (11) from seeing, like the rabbit which shows its buttocks or bottom (Lithic ra-baba-tai, its visible twin bulges) as it flees, by flipping its white skud into the air as it runs like the antelope, another one-that becomes-with looped-feet, as it bounds along; or else with its pe-nai or protruding piece, its white tail rather than its feet which describes such elegant curves in the air as it goes. A bunny is one that presents its bum. Were there wise women in the nursery with unacknowledged knowledge of Lithic underpinnings of words giving them a feeling of words of power? If they coined bunny, could they also read rabbit? Or coney, kaunai, which addressed the rabbit's tail as a spinal extension which has protruded and exhibits itself, apparently immediately from the Spanish connejo pronounced conneyo, the –o on the end simply a substantive ending: from au, that one. The rabbit's skud is from ish-ka-u-da, show-spine-that-does. The spine here is of course the bit which sticks out the end. The spine is for most of its length embedded in the flesh for which it provides the support and frame., but where it has an exposed end or tail (severed linearity) it has a modicum of independent and visible action. It can wag and flick flies, for which it was hardly designed but comes in handy like much of blind anatomy. The ka is a widespread term for the skeleton (an upright-strong-flexible-job, it has jointed vertebrae), particularly the spine. As such it is also the male soul which provides the structure and also the drive and will-to-action of the male. The female soul is the ba or flesh which is draped over the ka in life but perishes at death., leading males to confirm their pristine belief they possess immortality while women (like animals), lacking the male soul – and presumably possessing only the simulacrum of it in their spines – were mortal. Should it be necessary to add that these beliefs, although still traceable in the lexicon, ought not to be followed in civilized society, since they are merely fanciful and extremely bad mannered? Such ideas are now so distasteful it is hard to find them recorded but Aristotle is on record and for the etymologist coyness over our past misdemeanours and ineptitudes is inappropriate, since understanding Lithic semantic contents requires this kind of honesty.

While on land the bunny rabbit is presenting its tail as an escape tactic, in the pond next door the frog is presenting the other end, his eyes only above the water line. That is why the Latins call him rana, protruding eyes, brer pog-eye. He has managed to redesign his headwear so that his eyes are on the top of his head. When it is submerged he still has a a full view. Na is to protrude, originally gulled from Tarzan's penis, and thence to present, to present oneself, to be presented or present, a presenter or exponent (an ex or out pu-nai-ing one precisely – hard not to see Tarzan's penis resurfacing here again); and finally the present, nau, now. The retina of the eye is another case in point. It is from the Latin. The Lithic is rai-tai-na. An intermediate translation is rays-tai-presented or showing. To extract the meaning of tai here we need to refer to the prehistoric meaning of the Tau, the symbol we call T. It represented the two dimensions which make a surface, as well as the two dimensions representing space and time, and then the two dimensions representing the world as we know it, and so even the world as we know it, since tau also stood for all the events, happenings, originally from all the births, with birth from the ta or birth canal, from parturition, dividing into two. Thus the Egyptian for Heaven, conventionally transliterated pet but actually correctly pronounced Pai Taun, skin or roof (Semitic desert dwellers' roofs were goat skins against the burning sun) of the World. The hieroglyphs are just a square (a birds eye view of a surface) and a semicircle on a horizontal flat side, conventionally described as a bun (sic) but actually of course the image of that day which was of the flat surface of the world and the upturned bowl of the sky under which we live and move and have our being. The Greek pai, spelt pi, (and known to school children the world over as chosen to represent the ratio of the diameter of a circle to its circumference) is drawn in elevation, the surface with a curlicue as the main feature and the two supports plain as only helpers. Will there still be those who think I am making all this up? The rays tai or in the two directions made a network precisely for the Latin rete. A reticule adds the –cule, in Lithic -kau-lai or joined or crossed lines.

A thing in Latin, res (12), Lithic rai(s), was anything visible, as we would say pertaining to the phenomenal world. Of course it is open to argue that what we see is not immediately real, and this is argued exhaustively in Appendix A on the philosophy of language. So far as the history of reality is concerned in the human mind we may note the semantic catena from the visible to thing to chattels to goods and wealth, so that the Vedic ram meant riches and the Sanskrit rewan meant rich (with lots of things). Eric Partridge picks our Middle Welsh rai meaning precisely goods or riches. Riches itself has obvious kinship with Old Frisian riki and Old Norse rikr, where Norse final r was pronounced a (25). Both are variants from the Lithic rai-kai, meaning powerful, but from the idea of having possessions: wives, chattels, cattle, etc. In the Stone Age you had the possessions you had the power to hang on to. Partridge supposes that *re (the speculative original root) meant property, arguing reification, to invest with reality, is literally "to make property of". There was really something of the repeating, numbering and counting of items under meaning (4) in Latin res and Welsh rai, as well as seeing (10) via rays (5). The psychosemantic trees drawn to demonstrate the descent or perhaps better the sprouting of meanings one from the other in fact misrepresent to some extent the dream-like cross-referencing of prompts from the subconscious. The root Partridge was seeking is *re to make real or realize, given of course reality rests with the visible, which of course it does not.

From the rabbit with its tail end showing as it runs it is a short semantic hop to rain (13) which shows a pattern like a series of watery rays, leaping over the obvious difference that the visibility comes from sunbeams and the other from substantive watery beams; and from there follows the idea of a stream, although the Egyptian lingo makes it clear the sequence tr had a special significance from the earliest meaning streams passed down in the subconscious mind from our hominid days, and re-accessed from generation to generation as every generation consciously learned to speak and subconsciously – as Chomsky would say at a deep level – identified the phonemic meanings from which words are built – just as it still happens, more or less, today. But it is the lexicon which is our first tutor, and not any transformational grammar. In our subconscious minds we learn to recognize the bricks while upstairs with our conscious minds we are learning to construct the building.

A ray from the sun (5) was gulled by the priests of Amun for all they were worth. The sun's rays raised the plants, acting at a distance. In similar fashion anything else which was raised from a distance must surely be being rayed in order to raise it. Tarzan said it wasn't him doing it. It must be a ray coming from the outside. Not only that he had a very good idea whence it was coming, because whenever he was sitting facing the fair sex. – around the hearth for instance – he found his member rising. So it made sense to look for whatever might be emitting rays like the sun, and since the sun had for long been identified as a world vagina in the sky (the Aton) it was easy to see the little tau the girls had between their legs was the likely culprit when rounded out like the Aton above. The males were in thrall, it thus appeared, to the feminine nature which was to seduce the male. Such an imaginary pull, a magic force, was and is still recognised in every kind of application such as in English trays and chests of drawers which get pulled out. Even the underwear we wear are pull ups, drawers, though the original sexual gull may no longer be on the wing. The Egyptians marked out the forces controlled by their gods with a glyph before their titles which the Egyptologists have called a neter – the glyph is of a pennant blown out in the wind – but the vowelisation is just guesswork, since it is usually not marked in the glyphs, as with all writing in Semitic tongues (unless added with superscripts or subscripts afterwards). The glyph is misidentified as an axe of divinity – since it precedes the glyphs for the numerous gods of Egypt. In reality the figure is of a pennant blown out in the wind as a symbol of a natural force and should be pronounced natura with the meaning na-tau-rai, showing the tau ray or natural pull or force. Their many gods were at one time anyway not gods in the Greek style but symbols of the natural forces over which each presided. In case this is not concise enough to convince the senators, reluctant perhaps to be taught wisdom by a rank amateur, it can also be shown that one of the oldest gods of Egypt Ptah nevertheless is uniquely denied any neter. This is because he is properly pronounced Pata ahi, which means Our Fathers. Since he was an ancestor god he did not represent a force of nature but a source of advocacy and consequently he was not described as natura. Egypt itself is from Aui-kau-pata-ahi, and is not the land of the god Ptah but on the contrary That where-begotten-of fathers-our, The Fatherland. Father is from pa-ta, or piped-urethra, the male organ described as a strangler preventing childbirth. The Irish bot, Manx bwoid is their word for penis, indicating a similar blockage, and boy in English, it must be suspected, has a similar origin. A buoy is a similar bung or fleshy bit but floating free.

Latin has the same semantic content in the tra- root as the Egyptian pennant of divinity. Trahere is to draw out or along, no doubt with the sexual origin of the gull forgotten. Our English farm tractors are exhibiting at several removes the power of the feminine pudenda to draw out the male organ, but this is of course to be disregarded in common parlance. Yet it is needful to remind the reader of the whimsical and vulgar provenance of the term because it illustrates nicely the mentality of our hominid forbears, who after all had no television and only one entertainment; so that the greater part of our original lexicon can sometimes appear (as already touched on in chapter 1) to have been largely hammered out on the anvil of our own genitalia. To track is to follow the traces, drawn along by them indeed, for a hunter-gatherer the second most thrilling experience of his life. The noun is the trace left by the tracking. The Latin trans, across, with fifty main compounds in English alone, is from the same semantic root, to be drawn across – from the boys' side of the hearth to the girls'. A trance is a fixation whereby the victim is locked into an attractive ray.

A tree is a plant of the variety which has notably been drawn up with a hard-ened trunk, just like the male organ in receipt of the same ta ray, though a job which in reality has been carried out by Ra, the eye in the sky but nevertheless given a connection to the old belief in the uplifting feminine rays

Now we can see three is from the rays of the T, while quattuor, Latin for four (four is from the Lithic phau-u-arai, the protrusions-what-activate (8), the four limbs) was perhaps in conception joined Ts rays, one upside down on top of the other, counting four directions. It makes a cross, in Latin crux apparently from the Punic, a provincial Egyptian. It is a curiosity the Lithic phoneme ka, with its semantic content from the identification of the sound of flint knapping strike, flake, split off should here be used to mean join. If you put together a flint matrix with a flake just struck off, it fits exactly with a barely detectable seam, highlight-ing the perfect fit or join. From that point of view a joint between any two items, to be a fit, was where they had been split apart. Ta, which was the lighter sound of the snap of a stick broken in two, which meant to make two from one, to give birth, to be born, to become, and so any transference from one state to another, to die to become dead, similarly came to mean to join together to twin, to tie. Like the slayer and the slain, a discontinuity, once perceived, could also be seen from the near side of the event as well as the far side. It is one of our more splendid inconsequentialities that we can have the same semantic content with two quite opposite interpretations.

To try is to be in receipt of a ray which drives us to make an attempt. It dates from before the persona as an independent or reasonably independent agency had been put together. To tremble is to be drawn, terayed em-be-lai, as-be-liquid, that is immersed in cold water, suffering from hypothermia, when the body tries to generate heat by shaking the muscles. These supposed rays (14) are in fact seen as omnipresent. To rehearse them in any firm order is hard. If the reader has suc-ceeded in wading through the first twelve chapters a good deal of understanding of the Lithic hypotheses will have been gained. Rays were supposed to be around which could affect the mind. It was supposed an individual's brain was be-rai'n, the organ where these influences were received and registered. It was the play-ground for outside rays or influences beyond his personal control. Indeed the idea of an individual personality is a comparatively recent fabrication which has grown up with the expansion of language and the capture of more and more human thinking by the conscious mind. You can see some relics of this belief in the idea of spiritual possession by good or bad spirits. A dream came into the mind as a ray drawn in. As such it might well carry a message from an outside agency such as a god. A hero for the Greeks was in receipt of hai rays so that he performed heroically. Bravery came that way. Berani in Malay means brave. Ber in Malay is much like our be- in benighted or begotten or beware. The rani is from Lithic ra-nai, ray-showing, a clear case of inspiration from an outside influence. Or else it may have been the –nai ray was intended, via presentation to suggest confrontation. In so far as nai came originally from sexual presentation it could easily have slipped into confrontation. The Malay has also berahi with a Lithic hei on the end in place of the nai. Hei we find in the Egyptian pahei, the ecstacy piece or penis. Hei, as with the American greeting Hi! conveys pleasure (or else pain, but always a sharp emotional response, as in hot). The Malay berahi means amorous and lustful, in the modern American slang hot. Berahman in Malay, Brahmin in Hindi, is lustful of the mind, actually meaning an ascetic. In Hindi brave is bahadur, from bai-ha-tau-rai, be-hero-tau-rayed. Rage is simply a ra-kai, a ray kindling or stimulus. A veranda is from the Hindi baramda via the Portuguese. The Indians appear to have got it very early from the Persians. It is essentially a protruding roof from a building providing a place to sit in the open air but out of the sun. Ba in Hindi is in use as a bung of one kind or another. A veranda acts as a blocker of the sun's rays. The hums m and n are both in use as fillers but also as meaning fillers too, where we would now use a preposition to guide the relationship between two nouns. Modern syntax calls for an of after ra, in accordance with the postpositional idiom of the Hindi tongue.(which now uses ka). Ba-ra-'m-da in Lithic meaningful phonemes is Block-sunray-of-does. In Malay we find an opposite gloss on ba, from the haunch to going to be ongoing, as in our own benighted, to be in a state or even in motion. Beraja for instance is a planet, from Lithic ber-raja, be-shine-rayed, sending out a shining ray, or is it that the planets were recognised as illuminated by the sun without any luminescence of their own, just like the moon, Silene, presenting reflectd light, ra-ja meaning sun-lit. One wonders if the Hindu raja was claiming to be God illuminated too, rather than just a regulator. The Sultans next door, after all, Su-al-taun, fancied themselves either the Delight of the world or else its Illumination, the Light of the World. Or take the aboriginal Malay berbaling, a pair of bamboo tubular, deep throated whistles, mounted on a rotating shaft hoist to the top of a tree. It is ber-ba-lai-ing, going in a loop all night in the wind, making a whooping sound keeping the evil spirits for miles around at bay. Every well appointed ladang or leveled clearing should have one. Then there is bera, be-sunning, which can mean changing colour, a light bright colour, inflamed, blushing or swollen, all conditions the sun can be held responsible for, the swelling really most applicable to fruit, but since a swollen poisoned limb feels hot the rays get blamed for that one too. Berai is scattered, much as we say sprayed, from the sun's radiating rays in all directions. Spray is perhaps at one remove from Ra, the sun. It is ish-pai-rai, the action or even the issue-of the piece-which is rayed – with no prizes for guessing which piece or pipe caught the imagination of our cheery hairy forbears. A spray is an ejaculation in origin.

The ray was thought of as a stimulus or prompt to almost any unusual degree of activity. This was how your fortune was taken to be determined by your fate, what rays might come your way. Folk saw themselves as puppets ruled by superior forces. Smitten with an angry ray you experienced a rage, ray kindled, shaped or made, and proceeded to rant and rave. Even a grin was prompted by a humour ray, from hei-u-mau-rai, a joy-one-minded or happy-thought-ray, a haha ray. Later a new and classical analysis of the psyche made out the humours were liquid elements. Hei was of course at bedrock a shock stimulus of pleasure or pain. Ha! came out for hot as well as humour. Gerai and ragai are from kai which means struck and made or kindled, from flint knapping in the first place. In Malay an amok is someone whose mind is kindled by the original hacking spirit. So he rushes around inflicting it on whoever he meets. He has to be cut down. It is an extreme form of nervous breakdown leaving the subconscious mind in charge to discharge its tensions on the world at large. Unsurprisingly asylums are full of folk who imagine they are in receipt of rays from outside, which in fact they are sensing from their own subconscious minds of which they are wholly unaware.

Fifty years ago, after an operation to fillet a cauliflower ear, for which I was admitted to Shenley Military Hospital, at that time specializing in head injuries and brain surgery – I never really lived it down – I was approached in the ward by a young officer who had had the misfortune to fall from the roof of his Cambridge college while trying with accomplices to lift his tutor's car there in the dark. The task was successfully completed after his fall and for some days he went about his business as usual apparently unaffected before his friends began to notice peculiarities in his behaviour until he had to be hospitalized for his own safety, where he had a substantial benign polyp removed from inside his cranium. Now a year later he was back in for final check up for a medical board to see if he was fit to continue in Her Majesty's service. I was studying for a post graduate qualification in a hotch potch of scientific subjects thought suitable for anyone aspiring to assist in the design of ordnance, and had a book open on electromagnetism, which when he saw he became immediately animated and enquired about electromagnetic rays. While recuperating he had become aware of rays which carried information directly to the brain. He sought guidance on how the common or garden rays were propagated to see if the ones he had found conformed. I told him I could give him the formulae from the book but I strongly advised him not to mention his discovery to the board members the following day. He readily agreed it was the safest course. So I imagine he has by now retired, full of years and honour with his helper rays intact but unexpressed, as a full colonel or higher. He was a personable youngster and had already shown exemplary initiative at university. He just had to control his rays and keep them in order. In Tarzan's day we were all having to do it.

It is a sobering thought that some part of the mind can be dreaming while the conscious mind is wide-awake. How else do we know to recognize our Lithic origins of speech while learning our language today, when no part of it is in the extant script? Before speech our thinking was probably for most of us for the most part unconscious, with kaleidoscopic prompts and inconsequential takes of every scene, as the mind meandered or raced away, just as everyone experiences their thinking in dreams today. What we have built with the tagging of ideas by means of speech is an intellectual crust we can promenade on a day to day basis for practical affairs. Our bodily functions, heart beat, circulation of the blood, digestion and all the rest not specifically captured remain part of the autonomic system, wholly unconscious, that is to say they are not generally within the purview of the conscious mind. Yet there is a degree of mind over matter as well as matter over mind. A tumour can lead to delusion, sometimes of rays, and the rays to maniacal behaviour. An emotional depression can depress vital functions. A physical disorder can make one cross. The unconscious mind can inform our waking state. As well as a deep unconscious we do have a layer of subconscious thought not immediately available to our conscious minds, unless by a specially directed effort probably prompted by emotional discomfort which forces us to dig deep into our mental facilities. It is while exploring to get out of an emotional hole that mental illness is said to have occurred. In asylums folk can be seen sitting in corners, bodies rocking, as they confront the same mental knot over and over again with an inadequate and inappropriate approach, because of their emotional bondage, with reason in an interminable stutter. Compared to the careful way we go about our waking calculations it can be said we all have someone too close to a madman for comfort in the dark room down below; and far from sending down our painful thoughts for safe keeping out of the light as Sigmund Freud supposed, we mostly keep the madman within securely chained as simple common sense.

Without an element of rational protocol there is no way our minds can motor in a continuous straight line. It is a facility the human race has had to build as it has gone along, and it has to be said we have taken our time about it: hundreds of thousands of years. We might have done better if the mind could have evolved like the flesh instead of whimsically weaving itself a frame for thinking largely on its own. But that would have taken longer still; and the end result would have left us with tunnel vision, unable to think for ourselves because our minds were driven by our genes. This is indeed where some over enthusiastic biologists have thought we are at already. But the brain does not determine the terms in which we think any more than our legs determine what walks we will take. The legs will not enable us to fly. The brain will not enable us to master everything we wish. But within their preordained purviews when deciding their particular actions they are supreme. Charles Darwin had no wish to dragoon all knowledge within his one evolutionary idea. He was aware of its dangerous potential in the hands of less thinking folk. He actually believed it might, if misunderstood, release the flood waters of bloody revolution upon the streets of London, and was disposed to leave his work for posthumous publication (after he was safely gone!) Only Alfred Russell Wallace's paper he sent to the Linaean Society in 1859 announcing his discovery of the evolutionary mechanism (Darwin's old tutor Charles Lyell its president) persuaded him to break his silence to avoid being deprived of the kudos of his discovery. Papers from both Wallace and Darwin were read and Lyell declared Darwin's the better of the two. Else we should have had Russellism. Ideas are only virtual things. They have no existence except when they are being thought. They leave no particular impression on the brain which survives the phenotype, any more than the particular walks the legs have taken leave any particular impression on the legs. Their legacy is by transference from one mind to another, quite unmediated by the genes. We have sidestepped evolution by means of speech. We talk so much our legs would probably by now be slowly getting shorter, since today it is no longer the most successful lopers after game who carry off the most brides. Only we are getting longer because of our optimal feeding (those of us who are optimally fed). But the lexicon enlarges itself every day quite without regard to biology. It is a metaphysical reality, along with scientific theory and everything else in the realm of ideas transmissible directly from phenotype to phenotype by means of speech. We have talked our way out of the slavery of the genes, never mind blind clockmakers who take an opposite view. That does not mean that with this new found freedom most of what we have thought has not been rubbish because for the most part it evidently has.

The rays which were perceived as impinging on and registering in our brains (ba-rai'n), the flesh rayed – or was the brain eventually perceived as perhaps itself not just rayed but raying, a sun itself, a source (of ideas) itself? In any case these brain rays were evidently taken to be a peculiar and privileged acquisition of mankind, suitable for distinguishing man from beast. In Malay we have orang for man, from au-ra'ng, that one-raying, either in receipt of rays which are raying or else himself emitting rays, like brain waves, although the former is the most likely as the original form, since the brain has no need of rays to itself and they do not reach anyone else. The Latin vir, from uir and Lithic u-i-rai, one-which-rayed is semantically much the same although superficially quite different. It is as if rai meant rational, gifted with reason, straight up thinking. It may have been what the brain rays supposedly vouchsafed. The Chinese for man is ren. It could be akin to orang. Apparently from Lithic rai'n, it means the rayed-one. Lithic has a remarkable ability to pull widely disparate languages together at many points. It would take a master spirit, or more than one to hunt down all the instances, and a lifetime or two each at their disposal to complete the task or even get anywhere near it. You start to think of monkeys sitting down to type the Bible a randon, as the sun does, scattering its rays all around without discrimination, firing its rays at random. But we do all seem to have been proud ab initio of our ability to reason, even if the conception of how we thought it went seems askew today. When conscious thinking was a novelty that need be the cause of no surprise. It is nevertheless a temptation with more recent dissimulations to rename proud Sapiens Sapiens simply Homo Fraudster. Reason is a malleable instrument of use for many purposes other than explication. Business alone calls for playing cards held close to chests. It even calls for concealing science when needs be to win a deal or sell an environmental poison.

In India where the sun sets over the Western Ghats in a glorious blaze like over Gomera, merah means red. Carmine and crimson are out of the same vat, but complicated by to-ing and fro-ing between the Semitic and Indo-European tongues. Kermis or something like it is the word for the cochineal insect which when crushed produces a deep red dye[1]. In the case of carmine the word from the Latin mixes together the kermes insect and the Latin minium for red lead to produce a deep red. Skipping the minium for the moment, the kermes just meant insects, the Lithic suggests kara-mai-sai, maker-of-earth-ups. They were probably white ants which build irregular castles many feet high from the dry earth by gumming the grains of sand together. Their cousins the cochineal insects, ka-u-shai-nai, body-what-shine-presenting, had the colour. Kermes certainly can make of the Lithic elements ka-ra-mai-sai, body-sun-dying-shine, loosely translated as body the colour of the setting sun or red body. The Sanskrit krmi, pronounced keremi, from the Lithic kara mai, an earth worker, was both an insect and a worm. The worm is easy. The insect was presumably one which lived in the soil or close to it, as many do, most of them scuttling away when turned up. Our worm on the other hand, from the Latin vermis from uermis, although capable of being described as a soil turner, appears to have originally been a maggot usually found living in rotten matter. Mai means both soil and dead.

Tales of the mythical Aamairiga were around as a Shangrila when Vespucci senior named his more famous son Amerigo, and the mythical land will have been known to Columbus when he set sale to prove the land actually existed. His idea of the size of the world allowed him to believe it would prove to be the land the valuable East Indian spices came from. In this he was disappointed, but Spain found silver in abundance instead and lived on the booty for over four hundred years. There is no other possible explanation for the two oddities, the pyramids in central America and in Egypt, than a common dispersed source. We can conceive of a common psychosemantic linguistic connection – taun for instance in Egyptian and taan in Aztec mean the same, but a cultural artifact dreamed up from the lexicon by two separate civilizations is a bridge too far. Only ignorance could allow anyone to believe the contrary. The contact must have been many years ago, but probably after the great glacier melt raised sea levels around the world by three hundred and fifty feet. Most probably the transmission was from Adam's Malaya going East and West.

Rock is from rau-ka. Ka (chapter 5) is the knapped flint, gulled for its hardness. Most places you come to it quite soon if you dig down, and much of it sticks up bare of much soil. In 1830 Charles Lyell demonstrated in his epoch making book The Principles of Geology that it had indeed been thrust up, not once but repeatedly from down below. The ancients used ka for the earth, and so for land. That was what was in there, just as bodies had bones as hard structure to hold them together. The samples which stuck up above their natural covering of soil, it was clear even to the ancients had been raised – more rays at work. A rock was an expelled bit of the core. Had they not seen it often enough in volcanic eruptions? Stone is from sai-ta-un, fire-born-one. Metal is from mai-ta-lai, earth (the ore)-born-liquid. The Canary islands are supposed to be from the doggy Isles in Latin. This canard was invented by the elder Pliny a couple of thousand years ago and has had a somewhat longer run than it deserved. Before speaking in the Roman senate he would begin "Carthago delenda est" (Carthage must be destroyed) and he would repeat the slogan again before he sat down. Fascism came from Rome and re-emerged under Mussolini only recently. To be fair the Carthaginian foraging general Hanibal had made a mess of the Roman campania and had only been defeated by the Fabian tactics of the Roman general Fabius who finally slaughtered the Carthaginian force hemmed in on the shore of lake Trasimene (spelling approximate, only recollected from secondary school). Nevertheless the genocide of all the Carthaginians in the metropolis and environs of Carthage which followed in due course can hardly be excused even by a Fascist. The language is all but forgotten and is now spoken only by the Berber hill tribes who escaped, a provincial patois based on Carthaginian which was itself a provincial version of the Ancient Egyptian language (which was destroyed in turn by the Wahabi Arab invasion nine centuries later under the Islamic flag). Pliny's fib was flawed from the outset: canis is third declension and would have given us Canery Isles. The Carthaginian was Ka'n Aria, the Araising Ka or Rocky Isles. The Carthaginians can be shown on the linguistic evidence to have watched the sun go down over Gomera from the West coast of Tenerife, which means volcano in Carthaginian.

The whole island is tuff from the volcano which likely started as an under water vent. Holidaying there it is an unrepeatable experience elsewhere to reflect as the sunset paints half the sky in red and gold that three thousand years before Carthaginian visitors watched much the same scene and recorded what they saw for posterity with their name for Gomera Island. Unlike Pliny they spoke true.

An anorak and anorexia are widely separated in origin but come side by side in the dictionary. The anorak is Inuit from Greenland, and simply means clothes. Like the Malayan aboriginal tribesman asked the name of a growing timber tree who replied at once it was a tree, and the Australian aboriginal asked to name a budgerigar who replied it was a bright coloured bird, the Inuit asked to name his anorak said it was clothing. The Lithic appears to be a-nau-rai-kai, that-present-rays (may we guess warm ones?)-[to the] body. Strictly the Lithic says rays of the body but the prepositions all come from the position of the second phoneme, which carried the sense 'of' initially. It could be referred back to the first phoneme, so the pattern A-of B could also signify A-B of. It is no more surprising really than putting the adjective before or after the noun. Girls with anorexia are on a different tack, but they answer to the same original Lithic phonemes with the same meaning trees. Orexis is appetite or desire from the Greek verb oregein to stretch out and desire. The stretching out is evidently from au-rai-kai'n, to be ray kindled. These are clearly Egyptian rays like those which have already been found to stretch out the male organ. The au- here is either an introductory that one, as the Stone Age mind wound itself up to a positive identification, or else it is an oo or orifice which is getting stretched out. It might be either, since the boys were supposed to have reciprocal rays for the job once their muzzle covers had been pulled down; but it seems clear it was the boys who were the paradigmatic and original stretchers out, since before trousers their ostentation was conspicuous enough to spot the desire even at a distance. The anorexia is a classic loss of appetite for food, but linked at some deeper level with a disinclination to copulate, a distaste and denial of feminine sex, and even of sex altogether. It usually cures itself in time, the Dawkins genes being so strong, but can be traumatic and even life threatening while it lasts since the victims starve themselves for their greater good and to save themselves from having to confront their own natures fully frontal. The intellect is so far the only effective curative known. Humanity is not usually silly for ever; just for rather a long time. The anorexic have really forgotten how to laugh.

While every schoolboy knows about the antics of his own organ he knows very little about a girls vagina, which appears to be from the Lithic u-a-kai-na, an o or orifice-that-kindled-presents [itself]. For the girls the presentation is by rounding out. Indeed round itself is from rau-en-tai, rayed-of-the ta, or ta-rayed, cut, division or slit-rayed. These are feminine rays. If it were rand instead of round

it could be sun-become, the round shape gulled from the sun, which is conspicuously round; and little reliance can be placed upon vowelisation over the years,
so rand originally is not impossible. But all the rest we have gleaned about the
Egyptian rays points us in the direction of feminine rays in this case as well.
The conventional wisdom pays no regard to the phonemes involved and derives
vagina from the Latin meaning a sheath. In their book the vagina is simply another sheath. However it is open to a Lithic speaker to respond that it went the
other way about: the swordsman's sheath started out a vagina in which he fleshed
his sword. The sheath would after all need to be designed reasonably na for the
sword to slip easily in and out. In Malaya I had a parang ground out of an old
car spring for felling trees which went in a sheath made of two hollowed pieces
of wood bound together so as to be sufficiently na to hold the blade which had a
thick blunt side the original thickness of the spring. Inside the sheath the clitoris
is a miniature residual ill-formed penis which inflates and obtrudes in order to
catch the stimulus of the reciprocating full sized male organ when admitted. It is
formed from the Lithic phonemes ka-lai-tau-rai (s), which readily read as makes-
liquid-[when]the vagina-[is]rayed (substantve marker). In arousal the vagina becomes lubricated. The clitoris probably plays no part in this but the simultaneity
makes the Lithic string veridical. It also provides the sensation, which is why it
is so wicked to cut it out. Female circumcision is a barbaric male chauvinistic
mutilation, often accompanied by stitching together the vaginal labia to prevent
penetration, leading to chronic infections. It is the mark of barbarism at work. It
is no part of Islam. Formerly pagan tribes pretend it is. The punishment should
perhaps fit the crime.

   An orifice is from an o-rai-pahei-kai in Lithic, a hole-rayed-phalus-kindled.
It is a round hole in short. It is true the –fice part is from the Latin verb facere to
make, but facere is from the same derivation, the making being begetting in origin, just as making too started out as making an earthing, planting or inseminating. With making itself the ma- has been ascribed to kneading the mass, apparently preparing dough to make a cake or else the clay to make a pot "by pressing
repeatedly with the hands" (Partridge). There is however no mention of the supposed hands. The other is to be preferred. The other rounding out of the uterus is
at childbirth to allow the passage of the baby's head. Jaweh is said to have inflicted
this painful passage on women, apparently withdrawing his own rays which would
have helped at this juncture and replacing them with others that make the pain,
to punish them because Eve had upset the divinely instituted balance of nature.
Eve in future was left to do the pushing on her own. Apparently she had used her
intelligence to improve on the divine dispensation with her digging stick, leading
the water from the river to the padi fields with their much improved yields – from
which the deity drove our forbears by drowning them under the South China Sea.

We are having to rely upon Adam for this analysis of where the trouble lay. He had presumably been innocently killing game for a living in the time honoured way. He said he had simply accepted the food he was offered. We may suspect the tree of knowledge was really the ta-rays which Eve had picked up with her brain when working out her hydraulic plans.

From growth there is grain, but grain is from grind. To grow is to be rayed and rise. On the grind stones which go round there is in due course inscribed a grain, the round scratches from the grit which gets between the upper and the nether stone, along with the corn. Wood grain on planks is not round, but that is because the timber has been cut lengthwise. In nature the tree rings add to the girth as the tree grows year upon year and can be counted to tell the age of the tree. The ground has supposedly been ground, since it is generally covered with soil, which has a granular structure, like the coffee grounds at the bottom of the pot. The grit is gerai-tai, born of going round, grinding. If it is put between the stones it is not born there; but sufficient was rubbed off the stones to suggest it all came that way – as indeed it does, by erosion one way or another. To erode is from the same root as a rat which is a rodent, a gnawer, but the gnawing is only one kind of abrasion from abradere to wear away in Latin and radere to rub. We have here a fleet of Latin buses. From grinding, the ra phoneme has been put to use as if it is the essential phoneme for abrasion, whereas that is the wrong bit to borrow since it only provides the rounding; it is what goes round, namely the grind stone, which really provides the abrasion. However in Malay a thorn is a duri, and a local prickly fruit is a durian. It gives the guide to the meaning of the English thorn, a holer, from tau-ere'n. It has a puncturing action, represented by the verbal –ere- (8) like the Sumerian sag-i-ta with a head-which-punctures. The colour gray is the colour of the rye and emmer wheat flour. Wheat flour is white. Flow and flour are akin. The powder flows as if it were a liquid. You have to hold it in a solid container like liquid if you do not want to have it slip away. The r in flour is a cockney r, untrilled and pronounced like a, with the same meaning as if it were a – one or that, in the case of flour just one, a flowing one. It is interesting that by milling the flour right small it begins to acquire the character of a liquid, confirming our forbears' belief water lacked a solid element and that is why it was so slippery and elusive. By abrading the solid elements by milling them you got them moving towards a liquid state. A flower is a fe-low-er. It is a shoot, fa, lower [its petals], lau, actor (8) –er. Or else we have in the –er another cockney r, and the flower is a shoot-with lowered petals-one, just as the flour is one with a fluvial habit, a dry powder in effect, although the powder itself is simply one that has been pounded, with a pestle (from the Sanskrit pinsati, he pounds) rather than with a fist, and the fact it flows if it is dry is not covered.

It now becomes possible to discuss the derivation of the English adjective rare.

It means these days to be uncommon. Partridge as usual has some good stuff[2]. It is perhaps well at this stage to remind ourselves of the character of the sun's rays, or indeed those of any light source, as they will have struck our hominid forbears when they were teaching themselves to speak. They shine (15), they heat (17) and they can burn (16). As terrestial fires send out similar rays to the sun it was assumed that the sun was a fire source, and a volcano was a terrestial sun which only worked occasionally and often half heartedly at that, while the sun was burning at full bore all day. There is of course no direct evidence of this ratiocination hundreds of thousands of years ago, but we can see that reason provides that it went that way. Fire will actually cook food put near to it but shielded from the flame. The rays will also dry (18). They are straight (19), as observed in sunbeams when the motes reflect the rays. The motes lit up were mistaken for the rays, detectable as a string of microscopic particles, suggesting the repetitious rrrrrr. The rays raise the crops so that they are gerau and grow.(20). The effect of rays of every sort is always to stimulate and bring to action at a distance. In any case they seem to be the activators that provide the action. But perhaps more fundamentally they radiate in all directions around their source, with an instinct to spread themselves around, which in turn perhaps gives them their universal application. Anything that is spread around becomes sparse and rare. To ray is to radiate (14) and so to become opened out or spread out, individually to gape and collectively to have gaps between, separating the pieces. What is separated with gaps between is the eremite who lives alone, from the Greek eremos, Lithic ai-rai-mau(s), going-spread-into-one(singularity), which means a solitary, a unitary entity, from both au (chapter 15) and the reri from earlier in this chapter, to itemise and count.

A hermit, from an eremite, is one who has become a solitary, from the Lithic a(h)i-rai-em-i-tai, withdrawn from the inhabited world. The Greek eremia is a desert, an uninhabited part of the world. Rare meat on the other hand appears to be contradictory, since it appears at first sight to have been getting a lot of raying. In origin, all the words leading to rare meat in Germanic languages come originally with a cockney h in front, originally pronounced ahi (to separate the vowels a and the i). Rare from rai-rai, a reduplicative, emphasizes the raying but nevertheless means only lightly cooked. Roast is thoroughly cooked over the flame, literally become flame rayed. But the Old English was hrer, the h later shed as redundant. Like the hermit, which glossed the Greek eremai, the h in hrer is a cockney h, originally separating an initial a vowel from a followng i. In Egypt h was pronounced ahi, and our aitch is relict of the same pronunciation. In Middle English the meanings of component phonemes was disregarded and ai had become pronounced as her, so the difference between hrer and rer was not regarded. Rare meat which was un-continuously rayed was spoken of as continuously rayed, the absurdity unnoticed because the meaning of the word was well established and its dependence upon its original string of phonemes was forgotten. This is only one case of such slovening which just happens to have lost the original meaning thread. There will have been many others. It would be sweetly reasonable to tick off every word which is not immediately responsive to analysis in terms of the Lithic psychosemantic trees printed as further cases in point. It may not strike those who do not want to acknowledge their random roots have been discredited as a reasonable sequitur.

The roster that allocates shifts comes from a roaster or gridiron and so a grid and thence a table allocating jobs or duties, etc. There is certainly some lateral thinking involved while for the most part simply following a chain of metaphors. This is not evolution of meanings. It has nothing to do with Charles Darwin will Neo-Darwinists please note. This is how the mind works and how the languages of the world have been built. The liberal transferences of meanings has no doubt been much prompted and assisted by borrowings from languages akin or merely rendered adjacent. When you translate you allow yourself a good deal of leeway, which is missing in your own language where meanings are clearly established at any one time and not to be tampered with so freely. It is however not only the crops that grow. Time itself in the old days was measured on the same yardstick. A crony is a person who attended the same institution synchronously, at the same time. It is assumed cronies will be on friendly terms, from their earlier shared experience, or drilling by the same team. A crony, instead of a contemporary has become just an intimate or friend with no overt reason for the friendship, which may therefore be found sinister, as working behind the scenes together, exercising inappropriate help or assistance one to the other. To be chronic is to accompany the passage of time, to be of or for a time and thus to be continuous like time itself. A chronicle is a historical record in the form of a strictly time ordered tale. The Greek god Chronos was exemplar of what kerau-nau, in Lithic semantic terms what growth-presented. What growth marks is the passage of time, and thence the aging process. Anyway so our forbears evidently thought. Chronos meant age, time passed, and so just the time that passed. He is called Father Time and represented as an old man with a gray beard and a stick to lean on. The Lithic handles it all.

To roam is to wander around. It has been derived from pilgrimages to Rome. But this is absurd, since the Holy City is precisely targeted by pilgrims from the outset; and nor would there in that case be any call to change the spelling. It makes more sense to link the name with Romany or Roumany gypsies, who perhaps gave their name to Roumania, or else acquired theirs from Roumania. Rouman sounds Hindi, the original Gypsies' language. The Egyptian connection was only fleeting before they again got expelled for anti social behaviour like the Jews some time before them. Their later pretence to be Egyptians and to possess

Egyptian magic was just that, a pretence required by their black goddess Kali when having intercourse with goys and unbelievers. Deception is imperative to keep faith with the goddess of concealment and deception. Kali can be read in several ways. In Hindi it means time and tomorrow, probably from an original ka-lai, go-looping or make-orbit like the sun god Apollo, from A-pau-lau, the Ever-roofed-looped: that is daily orbiting in the world's skin or roof. But the Hindi also has the meaning black, from that part of the sun's orbit which ka-lai, goes low, that is the night time transit under the earth through Tartarus by the dead (but gestating) sun, before its rebirth relit at the Eastern horizon. The English black has the same phonemes and no doubt the same semantic source with a metathesis of the constituent meaningful phonemes, benighted. Also ka-lai can be read in Lithic phonemes Act slippery or slyly. That was what the goddess had in mind. She was convinced like President Bush that those who were not with her were against her and adopted a proactive policy of eliminating them all. She wears a necklace of fifteen skulls, from the goys her followers have bagged, which change to a necklace of flowers when she comes out and makes a public progress through the streets. Sometimes she switches from black to a jollier blue. Already in prehistory she was offering the faithful who killed fifteen infidels seven virgins in the hereafter. Her followers who have infiltrated Islam, the religion of peace on earth, follow her rule of thuggi, killing travelers by joining their caravans pretending to be innocent fellow travelers and then murdering them by stealth while they slept. The Prophet's message is negatived, so far unnoticed. There are other confirmatory evidences of the abuse. In Baghdad assassins have put out the eyes of their victims as the thugs did in Pakistan in the eighteenth century, a final triumphant gesture to mark their successful deception.

Anyway we can compare the Sanskrit bhrama, roaming, to roam in modern English. If this is a cockney h originally separating an a and an i the Lithic elements appear to have been ba(h)i-ra-ma, going-raying-of the mind, going as the rays of the mind guide you, as the spirit moves you, everywhere and anywhere indiscriminately like the rays of the sun, spreading yourself like the rays do. It only appears far fetched because we have lost the facility to think in terms of meaningful Lithic phonemes strung together ad hoc to convey complex meanings, before language had adopted the post Babel scheme of learning words by heart with their meanings attached by rote. We no longer compose words on the hoof as it were. A Chinese scholar will be more at home with Lithic. Their words are still seen as made up of meaningful phonemes strung together. Like Indian roaming, bhrama, is the English witch's broom stick, used wandering through the sky at night, na-ka-ti, flights of fancy with their secret sexual proclivities to the fore, something of the night about them. At one level a broom is merely a besom with a raking action, at another like the Indian Brahmin it can mean those in a state of spiritual exaltation, which may be dried up asceticism (as Brahmins claim) or otherwise of the night, wikka, an awesome (fear-making) mental activity forsaking the established paths of knowledge in the light of day in pursuit of enlightenment. These old crones had probably stumbled on a spot of Lithic language which gave them the impression of words of power, capable of summoning into full cognizance a hidden protocol from the past, as they would put it spirits of past life now reaching us from the rays they left in their tracks. That is not to say they were not effectively quite mad, because of the use they imagined they could make of their perceptions, nor that most of those punished for witchcraft were not innocent of evil.

Now surely it all seems obvious straight away, once you have managed to hook up to the Stone Age way of thinking, shedding our more recent and more sophisticated pathways in the mind. Straight away is a long way round. Straight is from the Lithic syllabic analysis ish-te-rai-ga(h)i-tai. The sibilant is up, vertical and straight (like the ash tree trunk). Terai is drawn out (like Tarzan's penis) and gai- or kai-tai is shaped-become, and all of it is straight beyond a peradventure. Moreover a straight route is the shortest way between two points, which is how straight away, an away on a straight route comes to mean in the shortest time, while that time may in fact be taken up with no wayfaring at all, but only with an instant's reflection or even a reflex response for fear of unwelcome correction. A string is strong enough to take the stress and withstand the strain and all these words come strictly from stretching out (21). Compare Greek oreigein to stretch out, from au-rai-gai-en, that one what-ray-kindled, from which comes also our erect and erection, drawn out rather than vertical. The verticality has evidently been picked off Tarzan's penis, his contemporaries having spotted the gull perching there. Then once straightened by the ray required, things can be seen to be in a row, rau for all to see. A run comes from arousal. Else you would walk. But it can be in a row or series by a semantic leakage from straight, like a run of bad luck. These rays arranging visible (real) things in a row are really all the same. Rails are straight lines and may have a train on them, and a train is a string of carriages getting drawn along – or else a bridal train drawn along by the bride, towed behind her. A ruler for drawing is from the Lithic rau-lai-er, or rayed-linear-verbal marker. A line is straight (from the skyline at sea), but a ruled one is straighter, eliminating altogether the looped one seen from a coral atoll running all round the skyline in a circle. A rafter is a long (drawn out) straight load bearing beam, modeled on Tarzan's penis again. A raft, made of rafters, in Malay is a rakit, traditionally made of stout bamboo lengths tied together with rattan (a liana, a long lithe looping vine) which has become rayed, extended in shape and quite like the ones Tarzan would swing on. A rakit fits almost too nicely: straight-trunks-tied. In return for an hour's work at the riverside you can get many miles downstream with your rucksack rakiting beside you. A rug on the other hand, ray shaped, has the rows going in the other direction, originally a fur (gulled from Tarzan's penis again) sticking up like the hair on a shaggy dog. Hair is from a(h)i-ai-rai, that which-one which-rayed, or else i(h)a-i-rai, it that-which-rayed. Hair is ray shaped and also it rises. A rag, from ra-kai, is all tattered and torn, into bare warp or woof. A rake, also from ra-kai, certainly makes rays on the surface raked. Ranks have the same shapes, they make rows. A range as well as a ring, like anything else which is round, has been rounded out, and not only by the rays of the sun, but also (alas!) by Tarzan's penis again. What price an engagement ring?

The human mind has had to accommodate a round sun radiating rays which on the other hand fly straight and true, though you do not have to go straight to be true (attracted and so faithful) including as a further gull faithful not merely to one's master but also to an ideal of a reality which can not be denied, and so to be true in the way we mostly use the word today. A very small rake is a curry comb for combing a horse's coat and leaving it nicely arranged (14), also achieved by brushing which makes it shine (15). The curry you eat also leaves you arranged or rayed, these rays making not alignment but heat (17). A curry is simply a hot dish (17) like a roast one which is cooked (17).

A plate rack (19) is a set of bars like a barbecue, from the Taino barbacoa for a raised rack. You could cook on it or dry your fish in the sun. It will have been a slow bake because it was made of wood. To bake was to tenderize the flesh, just like the hand axe pounding in use for a million years before the taming of the flame. Cooking (kau-kau) was a repetitive pounding and tenderizing in its new guise of heating over the flame. A hat rack however is a rack of hooks. The racking function has taken off and abandoned the straight rows it had. Or else the rack's function all along was to raise the items racked, hats, plates and meats equally, holding them on hooks or on rows of bars as appropriate. A stack on the other hand makes a stand from the same Lithic s-ta which is up/vertical-become. Wine too is racked to separate the rack, the skins, pips and stems and also the sediment from the wine. These solids may first of all have been raked off after the pressing. The lees that slipped through the rack on which the grapes were pressed would then have to be passed through a filter to clear the wine, and this secondary process appears to have inherited the same name, in spite of the fact the final process is effected by drawing off the wine from above and/or draining through a filter.

Raise and rise (6) are gulled from the sun's rays, no doubt afforced by the sex rays which Tarzan suffered from so regularly. A ramp is a rising surface. A rampant figure in heraldry is one with raised fore limbs. Or else the general posture is simply copied from Tarzan's predicament. A ripe fruit is one that has been rayed and swollen accordingly – precisely the same process as that suffered by Tarzan's fruiting body. A berry has its flesh in a similar rounded out condition whether it is as yet ripe or not. In some ways it has jumped the gun. You may have to go by the colour to see if it is ripe. If it is still green, the colour of growing, it is still growing and unripe. In Latin, the kidney, somewhat the shape of a pear (fancifully the same shape as Tarzan), is ren with the plural renes, of obscure origin as Partridge puts it. But from the Lithic elements rai-nai, rayed, presented or showing an internal organ was nevertheless taken to have been rayed and filled out like two joined berries – or from the English kidney, kai-dai-en-ey, a joined duality or pair of eggs (Old English aeg, pronounced aey as well as aeg). A thorn has been drawn out into a hard point, and so has a Malay one, duri, with a durian a fruit with a skin covered in raised protrusions, though not actually sharp. Sharp in English is gulled from spike so far as the ideas are concerned,. A spike, ish-pai-kai, is an upward pointing stake probably with the blunt end stuck in the ground like the Japanese panji of razor sharp bamboo to spit unwary attackers. Sharp is probably gulled from the spike.

Re (9), our usage, refers to the Egyptian rays' habit of going there and back again, a pattern we have not entertained in historical times until the discovery of radar. If you go back then you will be back and back is behind. The back is really the behind, the ba-ka, fleshy [part of the] body. Malays use balek, which is like our black, the lower circuit of the dark sun when it goes back from the West where it set to the East where it is relit and rises the next day – reculer pour mieux sauter? At the back is in the rear, where the second r is most likely a cockney one (25) untrilled, pronounced and semantically just a. Old Norse writes -r where we would write –a. It can be seen elsewhere that rai as well as to go back means to go over the same route again, to repeat. When we redecorate a room we do not do it backwards or back to front the second time, but rather we set out once more after we have reversed to our initial starting point. When we are done the room has recently been redecorated, with recent really meaning freshly, the Latin recens coming from the idea of a new arrival, originally from rai-kai'n, of the sun the kindling, the sun at sunrise, recently come forth bursting with light and energy ready to climb the skies. A blue rinse has much the same import since it has muddled through via the French from Vulgar or Low Latin recentare meaning to become or be fresh. This is taking liberties with the rays of the sun but it is well within the range of a semantic gull or metaphor.

At the other end of the spectrum of rays and their meanings is Latin rasicare to scratch often, a frequentative version of the Latin radere to rub, a simple semantic hip-hop from the Lithic rai-dai-are, ray (or rake)-doing-verbal suffix. When in English we rub we are ra-bai, sunray-going, that is going backwards and forwards, or more correctly forwards and then backwards. A rascal identified himself as a member of the great unwashed, lousy and for ever repetitiously scratching the rashes on his scurvy skin. Today he is just suspect of mischief, especially if only a bit of a one. Radere is just doing the same as the sun. From that comes the school eraser or rubber, abrasions and even the razor with a rubbing or rasping action. To be rash however comes from the German line with the Old High German rase and the Old Norse raskr (pronounced raska), from the original Lithic phonemes rai-sai-kai, rayed-action-causing. This is one of the insidious Egyptian viral rays spitting the brain, injecting a yen for action regardless, leading to a lack of proper premeditation and precipitate action. It must then be asked what a rasher of bacon must be. Is a thin slice of ham instinct with wild ideas? Eric Partridge opts for a variant of rase to cut which will hardly do because rase is really to scrape or rasp. The sober truth is a rasher is simply echoic. When ish-rayed it says ish almost as impressively as the brand when dowsed, it is a hisser when rayed in the pan. It comes from the fat which rapidly melts, which already gives it its streaks, the straight rays it makes before it gets near the flame. Whether you roast or fry you get the fat running out as juice. The Latin frigere which means to roast, grill or fry, Partridge says is akin to the Greek phrugein to grill. He adds "perhaps echoic". The g could be pronounced g or y, which enabled the French to spell it and pronounce frigere as frire. Partridge was probably thinking of his breakfast bacon here. But even phr is a poor echoism for a rasher. The fact is fat, the juice (which originally meant the gravy or even broth, fruit juice being added later), used with a wick for a light like a candle, was perceived as just one avatar of the organic lymphs which exuded from the body or were to be found in it, for example in the brain and spine. It was for this reason supposed until quite recently the semen was made in the spine, and the flame (of life) was supposed to be connected with these juices as language suggested already, ish for flame and sai for life. These were the equivalents of the juices which are to be found in the vegetable kingdom in fruits. That is of course why the term juice was found suitable to represent both the animal and the vegetable varieties together. The conclusion is inescapable that far enough back bodily lymphs were regarded as fruit juices and the male genitalia were regarded as animal fruits. That was Tarzan's view anyway. A fry up produced the life juices from the meat in the same way that sex produced the life juices from the fruit. Look at lymph, lye-em-pahei. Is it going to be argued this phonology is random and accidental? Frigere and frying was a form of frigging. It may put you off an English breakfast but you do not have to follow the thinking of our hominid forbears just because their memo pad appears to have survived in the phoneme strings we use in modern languages.

The reciprocating action of the piston (from Latin pinsere to pound, which is from the Lithic pai-en-sai-ere, the p-of-action-verbal suffix, which means to pound (repetitively) by way of the action of the p, as with a pestle or little pilum, akin to phallus and itself a pestle or a javelin – where the –lau or lai refers to the javelin's length and its looping flight. In a mortar, which is a pila, the feminine version of the pilum, the pila's loop is in the bowl shape. Tarzan rudely saw the mortar as a mau-ta or planted vagina, a gull from the shape. The re-cipro-cating Partridge has from a supposed *recos, backwards and *procos forwards. Recipro- then becomes an overlap or amalgamation of the two supposed roots. We can certainly see re- and pro- there, each with a kai suffixed, and making or going-back-going-forward probably does the original string justice. Re is from rai as already demonstrated. Pro it is naturally tempting to relate to Tarzan's penis like so much else, since an Egyptian ray seems to be involved. It is akin in that case to prow and proud. However it may be the eye's ray, which is involved here because the panorama which the eye reveals is a surface, pai, and pai-rau can be the surface-seen. The surface seen is the front surface and it is in front of the viewer. You take your pick. My pick is for Tarzan's penis on the grounds it comes forward while the view sits passively in front. A nice case of polysemy ends this rudely radiant chapter. With so few phonemes and so many meanings and so general allocated to each you can see Babel was predicated and the need for words with fixed meanings was only a few hundred thousand years away when first Tarzan lisped his first few meaningful phonemes to his mate.

Perhaps we should end with a bon bouche to clear the palate. A raisin is a dried grape. It is dried in the sunshine – or else it dries quite well hung in a cellar, but the classic idea is drying from a ray, and a ray is taken to be responsible for the process willy nilly. But the etymologists will have it otherwise. It is said to be from a raceme, a bunch (of grapes), from the Latin racemus, a ray-shaped-mass (of berries). Pull all the grapes off a bunch and you are left with the ray shaped mass, a collection of stalks which supported the bunch. But a raisin is not the bunch but a single grape. Its claim to its special identity is not that it is a grape but that it is a particularly treated grape. We might therefore expect, before ever we come to examine the etymology that the nomenclature might have been chosen to reflect this character. Without Lithic the blind watchmaker working on etymology goes by the phonology alone. He knows the semantics are not of prime consideration. Given there is a raceme and it has to do with grapes and the pass is sold and the raisin abandoned to its neighbour without further ado. But it is the ado which is needed in every case if sense is to be made of the way we learned to speak and the way we speak today, which after all comes from it.

Notes

1. In Arabic the cochineal is qirmiz, in Early French kermes, in English kermes, in Sanskrit krmi, in Persian kirm, in Lithuanian kermis and in Byzantine Greek khermezi. The Spanish, from this hotch potch, introduced their creme-

sin from which English distilled crimson. They were all really white ants, no good for togas or red dye at all. Take your pick.

2.   I have often thought I am really only writing Volume 2 of Eric Partridge's Short Etymological Dictionary of Modern English. I had for this reason added an appendix C entitled "What Eric Partridge knew". Included are some less charitable exposures of what he did not know. For instance he believed that pies were called pies because originally made of magpies, whereas they are called pies because a pie meant a skin or covering or lid, and pies, made of many things but never of magpies, have a crust on them, usually of pastry but sometimes of potato, etc. I feel after forty years studying his book I know him well enough to rib him when Homer nods. Just when I thought to call on him and show him some of my work he died. It is arguable he had discovered some Lithic at least but did not care to publish it because it seemed in his day too way out. That is what I wanted to ask him. Now we shall never know. The appendix has had to be adjourned to Volume 2.

CHAPTER 14

THE PHONEME ISH

If you approach the question of the beginning of language and how people were thinking then, or if they were thinking at all, with a mind emptied of preconceptions based on the last few hundreds of thousands of years of more or less articulate ratiocination, there is nothing much left to think about. Nevertheless it seems obvious enough folk were thinking before they were speaking, for how else could they have had the brilliant idea of setting up a means of communication. In reality it was not a single or sudden decision of course, but a long drawn out process we can hardly hope to reconstruct in any but the most cursory fashion today. There were many pre-articulate noises which the mind had learned to interprete: whoops and shrieks from fellow individuals of the species, the peak of hominid comprehension, and also of course a plethora of natural noises from the patter of rain on the surface of water or on your leafy roof to peals of thunder and the crash of falling trees, or just the splashing of a stream and significantly enough the hiss of a burning torch extinguished in a puddle of water. If a twig snapped the quick witted got used to asking themselves who goes there, and the less quick ones had a less turbulent life but quite often a shorter one, just as today. So there were natural noises like the snap of a twig which betrayed a semantic content and there were other noises made by active agencies, and some of them could be predators and others prey.

A silver-back gorilla is quite good at reading these symbolic indications and a chimpanzee even better. A gorilla slow in the uptake is at home in the forest habitat without much to fear. His physical strength alone will probably get him a progeny in Darwinian terms. In the gorilla´s environment you don´t need superlative intellectual performance to make your way, so nature has not selected for brains but rather for strength, which is surely why the gorilla is bigger than the chimp. The chimp is less well placed environmentally and the evolutionary pressures have selected for brains. The same can be said for hominids although it seems there have been times when hominid size was being pursued for its own sake, for else why should we have grown from chimpish size to six feet and more, and much of it recently at that. First of all there was probably a time when hominids fought and ate each other – until only one species was left; and since then we have just kept on going for the winning physique which worked well for us in the past. Or else the brainless ones were just beaten to the food, and better feeding got us our size. In any case in more recent times we have been able to afford a few luxuries, including foods and size increases, as our brain power has given us domination over our fellow animals. You might think stature is a telling factor in hand-to-hand fighting, and at one time no doubt it was; but weaponry, which is brain power in action, cancels that out. David whacked Goliath, when hacking each other with metal weapons was the presumptive standard procedure, a technology well developed already when the Philistines confronted the Israelis on the plain of Esdra-elon some three thousand years ago.

So far as linguistic ability was concerned we can imagine eloquence will have been admired regardless of its utility when language began, simply because it was the new cool thing. Did hominid lasses swoon when Tarzan turned out a well composed sentence as teenagers do for a pop star today? They probably did, since much of their time they worked around the fire and kept it fed, while the boys were afoot out hunting, and will have filled their time practising their phonemes and trying out different tunes with them and guessing their significances. They do that with much greater acquiescence than boys even today and it shows up in their examination results. The boys dream of shooting goals as a displacement from bagging bush bucks. They are not significantly stupider than girls, and their determination is greater; but their attention is adrift when it comes to any kind of filigree, whether requiring mental or physical dexterity. They hammered flints in the age of the Pliocene. Any hominid boy in those far off days when speaking was the latest wonder, a sedentary accomplishment requiring some fine tuned fancy thinking a bit like the nimble finger-work required for sewing, who was nevertheless prepared to face the brain damage and join the fireside circle and its discussions on girls' terms was already half way to their affections. Older alpha males may well have been these former ladies´ boys; because, if the testosterone is up and running, access to female company is a powerful instinctive priority, encouraging even attendance at chat shows of no intrinsic attraction. "If you can sew with phonemes – I can do it better!" "No you can´t!" "Yes I can!" "Yes I can!" "Yes I can!"

Be all that as it may, it is obvious echoic utterances must have been the first symbolic communications, long preceeding speech as we understand it. The paradigm is "Grrr!" for a tiger – which with language assumed substantiality, identifying the brute present or otherwise, whereas in prelinguistic days it meant more like: "Leap for the tall trees, I see a tiger!" Language put a Ti- in front, probably because felines have always been regarded as female from their slinking, even graceful and dainty motion when creeping up on prey; and with domesticated cats from their gentle gait and care for their kittens. So "tigre" means "mistress growler", from the immitation of the tiger´s growl by our hominid forebears from say a million years back. Rock formations will have weathered away in that time scale, but semantic formations have survived because of the repeated refreshment of the semantic patterns by successive generations, the triumph of reproduction over inert nature. The ten chapters on individual phonemes from chapter 4 on Ba up to this one on Ish, have revealed that the etumons or original meanings were phonemic, before morphemes; or in layman´s terms each single sound itself was given meaning and the original roots of words were not random but carefully thought through, leading to further derived meanings when stringing more than one phoneme together became the norm. It is the Chinese idiom precisely, and to be half way successful today it needs to be afforced with numerous tones to distinguish meanings, and even then it leaves a good deal of polysemy to be sorted out simply from context. This is still brain damage for Westerners, and any old mandarin could probably have seen off Plato, Aristotle, Thomas Aquinas and Saint Augustine all together when it came to mental wrangling. At least it is good for mathematics, and the Chinese nowadays take to math like ducks to water, because their language idioms retain the semantics on which they are based and do not encourage inconsequential memorisation like the languages of the West.

From the mewing of chimpanzees, with finely discriminated tones way above our abilities, they must think "pity they haven´t mastered our tone language!". It enables them to build quite a substantial vocabulary of sorts. It is clear that vowelisation preceeded speech as we understand it. The tongue is used already when consecutive vowelisations are discriminated, but varying tones come from a long way further back, in history and in the throat, than the linguistic expertise requires for consonantalisation. The physiology is otherwise immaterial when writing a book on semantics.

Some of the apparently original phonemic meanings adopted, which still show up in the languages of today, and more still in old dead languages frozen in time from before literacy and spelling blurred the significances of the sounds themselves, come from the way the utterances were (and are) produced. So for instance in chapter 4 the sound Ba is found to be made by pursing the lips and then uttering the most general vowel sound of aaa from between them. The meaning attributed on those grounds was lips whence the sound came, it was their signature tune; and from the lips which are the fleshy surrounds of the mouth Ba was taken to symbolise the mouth and fleshy bits, and so just flesh. It became the signature tune of the flesh and the fleshy bits. From then on Ba acquired, by the process identified for Lithic as a ´gull´ because there is no other term for this mental step and this term simply appeared an easy mnemonic for it[1], all those characteristics which can be attributed to flesh, bearing in mind flesh could be applied in those days to vegetable tissue as well as the animal variety, so that the lips were seen as exfoliations as was the phallus also, which was classed as a stalk with a fruiting body – phal means fruit as well as phallus – and the ancients imagined the sperm was the seed, whereas in reality of course it is only the pollen. The girls keep the seeds tucked away inside.

Then, secondly there were of course, from prelinguistic symbolism, utterances which were echoic of natural sounds. Wa is perhaps the best exhibition of this linguistic development because it does not go outside the range of our own natural human behavioural responses to find its meaning. It required no natural philosophy of the external world. It is the sound of shivering, from prolonged immersion in cold water, or indeed any hypothermia. The body is trying to generate heat by tweaking the nervous system to generate muscular contractions[2]. So Wewewe, the sound of shivering, meant water; and for the full justification for the identification of a meaning half a million years old try the next chapter, chapter 15 on the vowels. It was as if the water were speaking through its victim, captured as a result of going too far in surrendering herself (or himself) to a natural element which had dubious intentions. Only a mug would do as much. Does not the water find expression in water sprites like crocodiles with less than friendly intentions? When you shiver perhaps the water is also telling you "You oughter be frightened!" Fear brings on uncontrollable shivering as well, when the teeth can involuntarily chatter in a truly astonishing manner indicating a similar nervous breakdown.

As a third mental step it is possible to go still further afield and pick up symbolic echoisms from impersonal natural phenomena. Cuckoos and Cockneys or cock-en-eyes, Cocks´ eggs, spring to mind. But the paradigm here for echoisms derived from nature must surely be the phoneme Ish, the sound made by a burning brand when Tarzan extinguished it in a puddle when the new day brought relief from the threat of the sabre-toothed tiger. It was identified as a clear symbolic sound for the flame and, gulling again, all those characters deriving from the several characters of the flame to be covered in the present chapter, particularly the instinct of the flame to spring upwards when most other things went down. If you drop a flint it may well hit your foot. To drop was first of all the instinct of what is dropped. It is pulled down (by gravity, in fact). Our forebears thought the pull was instinct in pieces.

Fourthly there is the phoneme La, which paradoxically was quite possibly the first consonantal stop phoneme to be used and indeed may have served as mental trail-breaker for all the others in turn. If you are intoning, using singing notes without words like the chimps do, and you are looking for a break between them – Oh Paleolithic Einstein! – a flick of the tongue is the easiest one to pick with minimal diversion from the tones. So it was probably the first tongue movement to be added to tones. Consider the difference between m´-i-a-u and m´-i-la-lu[3].

The m´ is scarcely even in the actual pussy cat vocabulary. We put it in because we like consonantalisation and where there is none we are inclined to choose a hum. The true comparison is between iaw and ilalu. With the tones just eliding as in iaw there is only the whole to consider. Even at that, the tom cat´s catawaul can take on a gamut of quite reasonably explicit statements, though confined to his frame of mind: from lust on the lookout for the female to slake his passion, to furious challenge on the approach of a competitor standing in the way of his quest. You can hear the change of tone as lust gives way to aggression. It is an unfortunate character of the male psyche, and not only tom cats, the two lie far too close together for comfort, and still present a formidable test for holy matrimony many millions of years after our forebears parted from the feline branch of the physical tree. The semantics of the La phoneticisation may not have obtruded initially; but if the consonantalisations were to be expanded to include other sounds and their meanings – and they did so expand – we have lift off when the first vowel had a La in it. All that was needed was the son of our former Einstein of the Pleistocene, or at least someone who understood what he did and how. With hindsight it is clear such a one must have been born, and all the other consonantalisations were adopted and their meanings hammered out. The result is a language with a depth of texture nowadays unrecognised. We have learned to skate over the surface using merely the derivative meanings we have memorised for words. It is only the subconscious mind which still picks up the old constituent phonemic meanings as we each in our turn learn to speak, and keeps the original structures alive although unseen.

Chimpanzees sometimes seem to have reached an appreciation of the use of the tongue, perhaps their tongue wagging (which produced the tongue movements of "La" at least) meant "Discriminate! Discriminate!" or "Communicate! Communicate!"; or else they are natural tongue waggers for no particular reason. Their tonal vocabulary of mews will certainly carry no other consonantal values. For hominids bursting into speech La was identified as taste simply because the lingual grimace followed a nasty taste – see chapter 9. The tongue is the taster, so wagging it meant taste; and since water tasted fresh from the spring and became increasingly brackish and lye as it ran down to the sea, the deteriorating flavour and the sloping-down-to-the-sea syndromes became regarded as the two natural debasement instincts of liquids. La received those two psychosemantic contents, compounded of the way the phoneme was uttered and the phenomena it was judged to give rise to. Following upon these two combined perceptions, all the gulls along the sea shore came to life, as explained in chapter 9.

Pausing here, we should perhaps reject simple echoism as just prelinguistic cries, we might say as just signs of the nascent human mind, with parts of speech wholly absent. But with firstly our own utterances as meaning sources as with Ba and secondly environmentally prompted personal utterances as meaning sources as with Wewewe (shivering), and thirdly environmentally directly derived meaning sources as with Ish (the sound of a burning brand when dowsed), innocent of any psychic input, and finally mixed utterance and environmental meaning sources as with la, we can say that language was up and running, if still with rather modest pretensions. It comes from the turn-over from the nominal to the adjectival mind, a change examined in chapter 16 on thinking. With that, the introduction to this chapter is complete and we are in a position to elaborate those meanings which derive from this original echoic symbolisation of the sibilant as fire and flame.

The psychosemantic tree for the phoneme Ish is opposite. It is a wide ranging one. It makes sense to study it before continuing since it is not further referred to in the text. However the headings are numbered, and references in the text have numbers in brackets to help readers follow through the positions in the tree. The sibilant phoneme is first of all a hiss. In chapter 10 on the phoneme Ma, hisses have already been paired and opposed with the hums covered in that chapter, because they are the only two consonants or stops which can be voiced continuously as long as you have breath; and they also have opposed characteristics. By contrast Ba, Ka, Da, etcetera are proper stops, uttered once and spent. Continuing them merely extends their accompanying vowelisations. But you can hum or hiss without an accompanying vowel at all. Nevertheless they are lumped with consonants because, like the proper stops they do act as breaks between consecutive vowels. A stop is a better term than a consonant which means they are ´sounded together with´ an accompanying vowel. Hums and hisses are not necessarily so accompanied, but they can be. It also suggests the accompanying vowel in some way has priority, since the stop is described as sounded with them. This is of course precisely correct from a historical perspective, since we sang before we spoke, that is to say hominid hoots and cries were prelinguistic and comprised sequences of tones only. Perhaps the phoneme La was the mother of all languages because curling the tongue between notes in the musical scale was the lead-in to all the other stops. The discovery of the ability to consonantalise and then to symbolise such sounds was what led in turn to the origins of language, and the sea change in thinking which it brought with it.

Apart from the word hiss, from the Lithic a(h)i-ss, that-which-ss, there is not much else to be said about the sibilant on its own. It means nothing unless it comes from a snake – when it soon comes to mean hai-ss, 'horrors! – like picking up a hot stone – hit it or quit, and be quick'. However hisses crop up elsewhere where they can be seen to carry a semantic content, and there seems little doubt our hominid forebears will have been alive to these meanings. A kiss not only makes a hiss (chium in Malay, clearly echoic) but is also a gesture of comfort or

THE PSYCHOSEMANTIC TREE FOR ISH

The Phonetic Tree

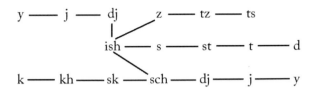

The Semantic Tree

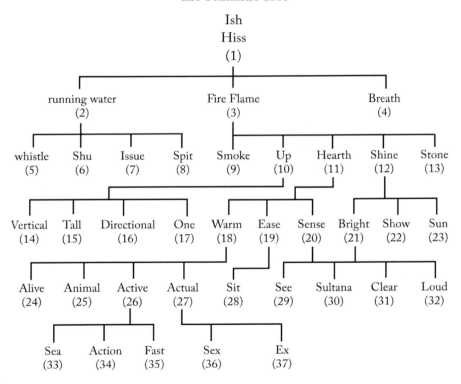

pleasure (19). Then there was in nature the sound of rushing water; and even the trickle of a stream had, perhaps fancifully, the same sound. The roar of a mighty fall of water, or a raging flood, has the character of white sound, heard as a loud hiss, widely used to disorient and brainwash prisoners nowadays. It dominates the mind, blanking out meditation and together with sleep deprivation makes a potent psychic mix. But for just a bite size hiss the snipe is a good example. Its whirring noise as it flies is well known to shooters, something like "thirer-thirer-thirer-thirer", but quicker than you can say that, and commonly described as drumming. One assumes the snipe does it by swooping and vibrating his wings, and it surely must just be for the fun of it. With "snipe" the Lithic phonemic elements involved are si-nai-pai, semantically brer-protruding-piece. In his case his protruding piece is his bill, as long as his body, for poking in the mud for prey. Tarzan could easily spot which bird was meant because of the metaphor used. Which having said, an alternative reading of the Lithic construction of snipe is sai-en-ai-pai, zizzing-as-going-winged: his drumming and his bill competing for recognition. He makes good eating but is rather small. You could use the facility with which the phonemes can be manipulated to provide different meanings as an argument Lithic is a fancy. But in reality it is too extensive and comprehensive for that; and it is important to introduce these simple and unimportant semantic constructions based on phonemic meanings to try to get the reader to start thinking in phonemic terms in place of the word meanings he or she has grown used to since learning to speak, so that words may seem by now the only and mandatory way of addressing the world. It should not be too difficult to make the mental flip, because there is an ally beneath the surface of the mind, the subconscious element, which has been doing it all along. Just give it a chance by letting it free, by letting the mind free to roam in a dreamy way without thinking in structural terms at all. Never mind if some of your reveries are rude: you do not have to pass them on, and you can shake them off again when your reverie is over[4].

A whistle (5) is echoic, like wind: if you blow out you get a whi-, with a bit of a hiss thrown in, and the telai at the end of whistle is become lai, that is uttered in singing tones, because La was the singing stop, no stop at all really in those singing times, just indicating a change of note in a continuous howl (or yowl). A syringe is more difficult. The Greek syrinx was a tube or channel or shepherd's pipe or whistle, whittled from the hollow tube of a syringa shoot. But the syringa bush was named from the whistle made from it: the whistle bush. The syringa, Lithic sai-rai-n-kai, starts with an echoic whistling sai-. The rai is the sound ray, which carries the sound to the ear, the organ which gets rayed, so that you hear. The hiss of the extinguished flame has come to stand for sounds in general. Not many things in Stone Age inanimate natural science had a characteristic sound, but the flame when dowsed had this remarkable articulation. The n in syringa is perhaps just a verbal marker, while the kai is making: whistle-raying-making, ie the tubular shoot from the bush you use to while away the time while watching over your flocks all day by cutting and trimming the finger holes so you can get a tune from it In Chinese you get Shu (6), which is the whistling wind. Back in England you get an issue (7), an expulsion of breath suggesting a flowing out. It is a sound which appears when you spit (8). Lithic analysis perhaps can explain the choice of the unfortunate shepherd, probably happily playing his pan pipe, named Syphilis, chosen to name the venereal disease. I believe he was named an innocent piper. But his name could be read, sai-pa-hei-lai, either sai-pai hei-lai, piper pleas-ing-lay, or sai-pahei-lai, issue-pahei-lye, the venereal discharge from the penis. Syphilis was Niobe's eldest son in Greek myth, born near Mount Sipylus from Sai-pai-lau's, a high-flat-surface'substantive marker, a plateau, and since it seems it had a flat top, maybe even suitable for grazing sheep for Syphilis to herd.

The mouth has already been identified as bab (chapter 4), because it has two lips, and the lips are the fleshy bits which utter the ba sound. Its duty as fleshy bits has led to the bum the bubs and the breast and even the legs (bai in Ancient Egypt, which included the whole haunch or buttocks; bein in German) and arms, baah in Hindi, which are burgeons off the main body. The lips, in retreat in face of these big bits of the body, have been transferred to the thinned and diminutive pai in place of bai, which still loop around the mouth, lip from lai-pai. The issue of the two lips is after all a spit. A pout is from pau, lips pushed out. A spout has much the same Lithic structure. The spurt from it is potential rather than actual. Curiously the Sumerian for cat was katse while the Akkadian was putse. The Lithic for these strings are respectively ka-tse and pu-tse. It may not seem much unless you know the Sumerian for mouth was ka (the cut) and the Akkadian was pu. In Ancient Egyptian pu could be read as pa-u and since pa in Egyptian meant the, pu was read as the oo or u, and the quail chick or pipi was used as the hiero-glyph for u. It appears the Akkadians too read it as the oo or hole[5]. Compare the Egyptian kati for a different (feminine) slit with a vulgar nasalised English term for the pudenda; which may even be related to the Akkadian in turn.

A slug is a slow goer and moreover leaves a slimy liquid line which slips or slurps down behind him as he goes along[6]. The Greek limax with Lithic elements lai-mai-kai (s) slime maker, is a snail. A slug is in fact a snail with an ill developed shell, which shows up as a thickened saddle on its back. The lai-mai also can be read as liquid-earth, as in the Greek leamon, a moist meadow and limne a marsh or mire, a mixture of liquid and earth. Both these English terms require explana-tion. As well as slipping down slopingly on any reasonably hard surface, water sinks into soil, especially in dry parts of the world. There it can be perceived as en-tering the soil and going on down as if there were no tomorrow. That presumably is why Semites put an m in front of their awa for water, and we now have moya for

water, sometimes spelt moir with the final r a cockney r, untrilled and synonymous
with a, with water's downward-seeking weight in register. A marsh is soil so wa-
terlogged the water appears to be rising, shai, upping; and with mire it appears to
be rising too (rai) like the vegetation which naturally grows, from ge-rau. A well
is water which lies there, from awa-lai. A spring is where it springs up and breaks
surface. This was why Aristotle fancied water had a yen to get to the surface, so
that if on top of it it ran down along it but if under it it popped up instead in a
spring – and then reverted to its more usual running down, clinging closely to the
local declivities of the surface. We may interject here that water was described
as surface-less, pani in Hindustani, where nahin is no (as a complete statement
on its own), just as Latins have ne- as the negative and the Scots still say nay as
well as aye. With such a serious shortcoming in the fraternity of natural elements
perhaps water reasonably went in pursuit of any replacement surface it could find.
The switch in behaviour from up to down evidently appeared to Aristotle to be
brought about at the threshold of the surface of the earth.

Oranges, really naranjes, are from 'n-a-ra-nai, one-that-sun[colour](Ra)-
shows (22) or else 'n-a-ra'n-shai, one-that-sun-shines (12): the golden sun of
midday, not the dying sun at dusk which glows red. A lemon is described as lye or
acid tasting, an orange as golden coloured. There is of course a bit of poesy in the
orange, but the lemon is right down the middle. Shara is a Gypsy term – Gypsies
come from India originally, expelled for their thuggery some six hundred years
ago and then again from Egypt where they sojourned like any other refugees
seeking asylum in those days until their reputation as tea-leafs came to the attention of the Egyptian authorities. There was no system of social welfare to pull
them then but the country was a real land of milk and honey because of the Nile
padi. As followers of the prehistoric black goddess Kali, in those days their treach-
ery and deceit in all their dealings with non-believers was mandatory. They were
actually required by the goddess, whose thinking had become somehow turned
upside down, to indulge in criminality whenever dealing with infidels in order to
acquire merit, while to deal fairly with a goy was a crime. Some still pretend to be
Egyptians to avoid telling the truth to goys, and there is a spin off: the Egyptians
had the reputation of magic words and powers, including screwing their hands
around their eyes to make goys think the evil eye would be upon them. They were
originally convicted of garotting travellers in India (now Pakistan): thuggi, joining caravans pretending to be innocent fellow travellers, already promised seven
virgins in the hereafter by the black goddess in prehistoric times – black for darkness and hence concealment and deceit – for fifteen unvelievers killed. Just like
modern day religious fanatics you may think, now pretending to be Islamists, the
ultimate deceit. There is a concealed premiss here, which seems quite doubtful,
that martyrs will still have their penises with them on arrival in the hereafter,

since the etherial world is generally believed to be insubstantial and their genitalia are therefore likely to be gone past recall. What would one not give to see their faces fall (if they have any of those either!) For far from having gained access to the delights of the flesh in abundance, apparently a different lady for each day of the week, they will instead have been cruelly robbed of any such possibility with fraudulent promises from professional fraudsters pretending religiosity: the ultimate deception, which is Kali's delight. The British, when they got to a position of power in Northern India, followed an uncompromising policy of putting anyone guilty of thuggi, or ritual killing to acquire merit with Kali, to an ignomineous death by hanging after the briefest of trials. It greatly reduced belief in the Black Goddess since when it actually came to it She just abandoned her followers to their fate and none of the revenges promised followed. Meanwhile in the here and now amongst the remaining Gypsies Shara, the light of day, is no longer hazardous, just a bright patch, a sun ray in effect. So for the modern gypsy Shara is my daughter's black pony with one white sock, whether the Black Goddess, the deadly nightshade amongst the deities, likes it or not. It may not be politically correct but the truth is Kali was worshiped across the desert lands of the Arabian peninsular for thousands of years before the Prophet Mohammed rescued the Arab tribes from her embrace, preaching a truer religion against the worship of malice. Kali's revenge is by infiltration.

To shrink is from ish-rai´n-kai, fire(3)-raying-makes, which drives out the liquids and reduces things to their dried up shrunken states like dried up sticks. It also causes anyone exposed to such scorching to withdraw from the flame, and so from any other challenge. There are the two meanings of shrink explained from the Lithic elements involved, otherwise inexplicable since getting smaller and withdrawing from action are not themselves connected. The Arabic iskra (3), a spark, ish-kara, is a flame maker, as is the obsolete English chark (3), the device for making fire by drilling with a sharpened stick in a wooden socket with fluff around it for ignition. The friction of wood on wood generates heat until the fluff ignites. What it ignites, ignis in Hindustani is the sibilant ish, i-genai-s, the generated flame. To char, from ish-arai, is to burn, flame rayed, by rays of the flame; while a spark, from ish-pa-rai-ka, is a firey speck which makes a flame, with all the same phonemes as the Arabic iskra. A speck is itself from a spark, and a speckled hen is one with markings which are spark like, that is with little spots or flashes of colouring. Roast is from rau-sai-tai, rayed-of the flame-become. A fry is fa-rai, rayed in fat. Fat and fry both have the f- in place of the p- of Greek pion, fat. In chapter 12 for Pa the case is made for the semantic contents of this phoneme including fattening. It could certainly be argued that fa- is a better original for fat, in so far as the Greek phi comes from the elision of the Egyptian pa-hei which is the penis, the ecstasy piece (chapter 9 for hei). It is a clearcut gull from the penis which is addicted to swelling, so that it is taken to have the fattening trick to a T. But by now it is an embarrasment to be always harping back to the genitalia, so that wherever possible an alternative derivation is to be preferred. Nevertheless it is absolutely inescapable we started speaking in idioms we gathered to an astonishing extent from our own genital performances, simply because that occupied our minds to an overwhelming degree; and anyway we generalised outwards from our own personal thinking about our own uninhibited personal sensations and reactions to the world around. It was naive but it was frank, and even half a million years later it still shows. Remember we were only hominids when first we learned to speak. The human mind can only have got around to the consideration of any relatively complex questions of propriety well after language had been around long enough to have established a tradition of coarse reflection upon coarse behaviour. To go back even before that, our world was a semi-conscious or even an entirely unconscious world in which what bubbled up got expressed, and autism was the rule. There were no prisons or prison reformers then, only the punishment handed out by the outrage of your peers, if outrage it was. Sexual aggression in itself was perfectly acceptable so long as it did not intrude upon anybody else´s territory, which almost inevitably it often did. If you were caught jumping the local talent belonging to someone else it was a matter of course you were in trouble. You just better choose wisely or act secretively so as not to offend the alphas. That was all the morality there was. You can see the same behaviour in our cousins the chimpanzees today.

Then the flame leaps upwards (10). In Chinese shang is up or upwards, and shan is a mountain, an up-one, an upland. The English mountain has just become a superlatively massive one. In Ancient Egyptian sa'a is to go up, while saha is to set upright, to erect, and sash is to prick up the ears, from the Lithic sa-shai, sensers-upped (20,10). Sa-arai is to bring up, with the arai meaning to bring (from the extensive a for bring, in Latin meaning go, ire to go from ai-re, going-verbal ending). Thence we have sariu, bearers, carriers, porters in Egyptian, where –u did duty as a plural. At the same time sasha meant shine (12), actually sa-sha, sun-shine, or anyway like the sun. With no grammar to speak of, up, upwards, on top, and the top or summmit all fall under the one semantic head. In that sense, thinking at the beginning of language was fuzzy by our standards. In fact it was worse than that. The mind could elaborate further from there, in spite of the fuzz or even because of it. The inclination was to relate the idea to its expression in human terms: it was as if the mind said to itself 'and how does this Ish reflect upon us, how does it find expression for us?'. In Old Persian Shamash is the sun. So we have to ask ourselves why. The sun in those days sprang up shining and then it sank down and died, often in a blazing blood red series of splashings across the Western sky – precisely as it still does today. Upping, and at the same time shining, sha (12), the sun then descended to die, ma, but encouragingly to gestate below the horizon (ma again) and arise gloriously the next day, resurrected, sha, again. "Does not the sun rise smiling at the dawn of another day?" Shamash, Lithic life-death-life, has much the same semantic content as the tomato, an annual which blooms and the seed must then be planted to germinate and come to life, be born again. Osiris, in the original Egyptian really spelt Au-Sarai, World Sunrise, promised immortality; though not like the God of Christianity does as a salvation but as a natural occurrence like the vegetation which renewed itself each year.with seeds planted and germinating in the ground. Seed is from sai-dai, living-becoming. The Latin for seed is semen, the living dead but germinating life – when planted. For the Persians, at one time fire worshipers, Zara-thustra shared the phonemes Shara- with Osiris – as well as with a pony with one white sock in Romany. Shara seems to have been a shiny white ray (as opposed to any other sort); or else the shining sun or the seeing eye, or indeed all three together. To stand is from sa-ta´n-dai, upright-becoming-does. The does is little more than a verbal marker indicating a natural process, or one which results from the nature of things, as opposed to ka which is often indicative of making from human agency, like the knapping of flints. When the idea is universalised Ka still retains the forceful nature of the original activity. To stand is hijacked as the state of standing too, a stand, as the syllable ai did duty for our syllable ing as well as our syllable ed. Stood makes the past sense clear from the au (oo) phoneme that it is a done job, oo being the completive-substantive vowel (and therefore also dual, but not relevant here). See chapter 15 for the vowels.

To score or scratch is to chip out or cut an upright stroke, sa-kare, to upright-carve – the original scoring, or anyway an early one, was to form a number of upright lines for counting (10). Or with scratch the same phonemes contributed, with a confirmatory –tch, probably from sa-kara-ta-khai, a scored vertical cut. The upright scores can be counted, and of course they were: that was how numerals were first recorded, just as they still are on cricket scorers´ pads, and on prison walls, where a diagonal stroke is used for the tenth stroke if the sentence is a long one, representing the digits of the two hands. We count in tens. In Malay, often the language with the most direct Lithic understanding, sa, an upright and a single line, is the word they use for one. It is an elision of the form satu, an upright which has been cut or scratched. The Malay sa could be treated as a bus from satu, but at least it is a bus using the right end of the word instead of the wrong one in the case of the bus taken from the ending of omnibus. They go on to use sa-sa as any-old-one and so any. In Hindi one is ek, just any old cut, from ai-kai, that which-cut, a cut. The Aboriginal Malay for one however is a surprising Mi, which can probably be read in its original Lithic form as 'm-i. The 'm was most likely just a hum and doing service as such, as the Senoi mind braced itself for enumeration.

An initial 'm is used similarly in Africa, sometimes translated as if it were him, which is the semantic content more or less. The Senoi are using the vowel i in its original role as the diminutive-reduplicative vowel, which serves quite well as the base for enumeration, a singleton in a reduplicative series of many. Four is another maverick for the Senoi, 'm-pon, all the (four) limbs, from them-limbs. In Selangor the fourth child is often named Uda, which makes four from both-twos, while in Perak, which is more jungly, we find Pandak for four, which in derivation of meaning follows quite closely the Senoi since it can be read as the points or limbs the body develops, including the legs of animals and so number-four. Jumping to the Punjab in Northern India, now Pakistan, which comes from Panch-awab, or the Five Rivers, where Panch is from pa'n-khai the points-of the body (four limbs and the head); or else the points joined, fingers five. Note Awa-bai for rivers in Punjabi, water-legging it, on its way down to the sea. Although the British rivers are supposed to derive their nomenclature from the Latin ripa for their banks, this has always seemed dubious etymology. The phonemes arai-bai-a'a, now slovened to river, seem better: travelling water. Arai was used already in Egyptian days for going, and so a verbal marker, where there were no legs involved.

Language did not spring fully fledged from anyone's head, it built over the millennia. Language is now a strait jacket, but not quite in the way Benjamin Whorf imagined half a century ago. We first of all dreamed up the lingo by dividing the world to shape it. In other words we had been thinking over millennia before we spoke. Then we forgot how we did it, so it now appears as if it was the language which framed the world. But the opposite is the truth. Of course it was the world as we apprehended it at the time, rather than the real thing, which we analysed. The straight jacket today comes in the form of the secondary meanings we have developed using the phoneme strings we now call words. Breaking that crust releases the genie or genius beneath. We get back to our original perceptions and symbolisations. Meanings come to life again, a mile away from the arid syllogisms of the linguistic logic compiled as transformational grammar. Meaning is back where it belongs, in the teeming lexicon built over the millennia around the world.

The tally in turn started out as (Lithic) ta-lai or cut on the slope, from the instinct of liquid to slip or slope away into the lows. Of course liquids really go straight downwards like anything else with mass whenever they find the opportunity, but our hominid forebears who framed our speech had not got that sorted out, and an irregular sloping surface (or even a river) appeared to them to support the slippery protocol. A tally was sharpened like a pencil with sloping cuts to make a sharp point for use as a stake to stick in the ground. But it got taken up as anything purposefully cut along its length, whence restricted in application to the split stick recording numerical contracts including those legally entailed. The earlier idea of cutting to shape is where we get our tailoring from, and a toll was a share of the goods exacted at a border, trimming the load to size and taking a cut. But the medieval tally was a split wooden stick like the stake, the original stick, which refers to the vertical posture of the stake when stuck in the ground, sta-kai, made standing, indeed struck on the top in all probability to get it to go into the ground and stay upright, with the very same Ka phoneme which came from the striking of flints at the time of our most primitive echoisms. The tally was cut with numbers of strokes to record the numbers involved in a deal (sheep so many, cash so much) then split longitudinally and half given to each of the parties. If they tried to cook the books they would not match. They were vertical cuts, not cut on the slope, but then ta-lai could mean split lengthwise. All this only took a few thousand years to emerge, or if we start with the original psychosemantic meanings perhaps a few hundred thousand. In that length of time, given human whimsy it is remarkable there was not greater semantic drift or development, whichever way you care to look at it. We are picking up a pointer to subconscious refreshment over the generations as they learned the language.

The tally has nothing to do with a pony tail at any rate in origin, since the tail comes from the sense of lai (length) derived from the sky-line at sea (chapter 9). A pony´s tail has long hairs which lie down in linear array, and it is swished or switched from side to side with lithe movements like the liana. It meant hair or a rope´s end (frayed like hair) or in Gaelic a ply of rope and in Cornish a lock of hair. It could be spelt tagel, but g was pronounced y as often as not, or more correctly the y sound was spelt both ways. But it makes one think hominid hair was usually tangled, ta-'n-ge-lai, composed of joined lengths. Combing came later.

To put some body on the psychosemantic tree for ish, the hissing (1) is to be seen in the Malay chichak, a little house lizard skittering about the walls with pads on its feet enabling it to grasp the ceiling if needs be, simply by clenching its feet and making use of the vacuums they form. It makes a high pitched cheep amounting to a hiss. The h in hiss is a cockney h (chapter 8) showing the word started out a-i-ss, that-which-'ss'. The cicada, (Latin) a grasshopper, cheeps too, in Spanish cicaria, pronounced thicaria, the 'ss' or 'th'-maker. To cheep in Malay is chiap, the cheep from the pecker and not from the lips. You can hear the soughing of the wind. The English sip is from the sucking sound of the lips. If you say it drawing breath in instead of out you get the sound of a sip so exactly you can use it to tease your children when they are learning a noiseless sip.

The babbling brook can be found in gush (2) which goes 'sh', and in splash, ish-pai-lai-i-sh, action-surface-liquid-which-'sh'. Note two different semantic contents for sh in the same word, (35 and 1) suggesting some degree of fluency in the phonemic meanings, consciously or otherwise. Lai registers the instinct of liquids to spill, in turn the action of going lai or flowing downhill, ultimately to the briney ocean where the water has turned into lye (lur for ocean in Celtic and laut in Malay). To wash is to splash water, and a flash or flush was originally a splash, as a flush still is. Splish, splosh and plash are just whimsical variants, the first two evidencing the use of phonemes with the stops mostly regarded rather than the vowels. Plash, without the initial s-, leaves nothing critical out. Plush on the other hand is not an action and has no initial s for this reason. It is a hairy or long piled material. There is a nice conjugation of semantic elements involved here. Pellis is a skin in Latin (though perhaps from Homeric Greek where it meant a milk bowl, the lai in that case being the bowl shape rather than the enclosure of the flesh), from which we get our pelt, and a skin of course may be ours or an animal's. Skin is from ish-kai'n, it warms (18) the body. If it is ours, most of it without significant hair, the pai-lai is simply the surface-looping (surrounding) our flesh within, pa being the thinned diminutive of ba which initially carried the principal meaning of fleshy or flesh because it is pronounced by the two (fleshy) lips. But animals have pelts with conspicuous hairy coats. Gulling therefore allows the surrounding surface (pai) to acquire the meaning hairy. A sheep's coat is thick and keeps it warm, shai-pai is a warm coat, a character it acquires from being so shaggy or long haired. Brer Warm Coat is a sheep and plush is a material with a shaggy pile. It is also soft and pillowy but that is another connection, kushi (Hindi) like a cushion. The simplest translation of kushi is soft and comfortable like a cushion. It relates to sai, at ease around the hearth, nicely toasted (18,19), made comfortable or a comfortable place or placement.

Washing was mostly done in a stream if you go far enough back. They were urinating and defaecating in the same stream too, so it is no surprise as you went down stream the flavour was less bland. Each village had strict rules ensuring defaecation was down stream of watering points, but of course the next village downstream was unable to benefit from this dispensation. Only the natural breakdown of vegetable matter in the pleistocene provided a degree of purification for those living downstream. Under this dispensation the hill tribes tended to be the hardier even though on shorter commons. There is still the same problem in so called civilised countries today where water boards discharge "treated" sewage into the rivers. You would be ill advised to try to drink it. For that it needs further treatment. Father Thames is supposed to be drunk five times before he reaches the sea, each time after treatment which was entirely lacking in the Stone Age.

For the Turks ush is a penis, u-shai, what shshs, that is to say it is what water-squirts. Stable lads talk to their horses thus. Before putting down new straw they intone shwsh- shwsh-shwsh until the horse, quite without benefit of Turkish or linguistics of any kind, nevertheless eventually pisses, so the new straw goes down after it has drained away. It is a clear case of psychosemantics, which evidently goes back a long way. Even potent grave and relatively rational seniors are sometimes instantly put in mind of the need to urinate when they turn on a tap. A spray, starting out a distribution of liquid and only later a buttonhole, gets its initial s- from the gushing sound as well as the active semantic, the p probably from the penis (a squirter), and the ray from the jet formation.

The sudden "sally", before bickering down a valley as the poet had it, was not in origin a slipping down but a leaping up as a loop, in Lithic from the skyline at sea which runs all around the horizon, and then from the similar orbit of the sun which runs all round the sky, and so from the Latin salire, to leap up: sa is up (because the flame springs upwards) and lai is an orbit or loop; and so a looping action is sa-lai-ere, up-looping-verbal marker. Sala the salmon is a leaper up while the -mau'n is in aid of plantation of the seed, for which salmon in their hundreds leap up river rapids in a mad scramble to spawn and die. The Chinese evidently have in mind the whispering breezes in so far as their word for wind is shu.

But ish as a phoneme is largely given over to the flame (3) and all the meanings that are derived therefrom. There are not so many words today in English with the sibilant meaning fire precisely, so it may be thought the original identification is wrong. But in reality the scarcity is precisely because it is the thirty or forty subsequent derivative meanings which survive. However the Basque for fire is Su and the Arabic for a spark is iskra. It was the name TE Lawrence, when he was not in the Arabian desert urging Saudis to rebel and throw off the Turkish yoke, gave to his Cairo news sheet to get the Arab masses thinking the same way. The paper survives in Cairo to this day, though under quite different management and with a sharply revised editorial policy. The red chequered tea towel Lawrence bought in the Cairo sukh and issued to Auda Abu Tai (Auda Father of his Tribe) and his fellow Arab rebels as an identifying uniform for those fighting for an autonomous Arab fatherland are now worn by Arabs across the Middle East, by kings and commoners, as badges of autonomous pride. To char is treated by Eric Partridge as a back formation from charcoal, with char like chore meaning a turn as evidenced by the turn of work a charlady performs. But work comes easily in Lithic from chipping flints, productive labour, u-a-kai, what-that-makes roughly, suggesting the charlady was originally a khare-lady; while the char in charcoal comes just as easily from the same source as the chark: ish, the sound of the flame hissing as it dies. English also has ash. Ash is the modern much elided form. The Old English was aesc from the Lithic ai-sai-kai, that which-fire-makes. The Old Norse is aska, with exactly the same Lithic elements as Old English. The Gothic was asgo, fire-made, and the Sanskrit was asas. Sanskrit routinely had sh in place of an original kh, and here the sh has additionally become an s. Partridge simply guesses the Indo European root for a turn was as or az, as a terminal conclusion with no reason given, but of course he was under the Skeat illusion that words are composed from random morphemic roots, not phonemic meaningful ones at all.

Lithic sorts out the mess. The Old English carried the nearest reproduction of the Lithic. A char lady is a worker (from khai-are) and charcoal is burnt wood (from shai-are) which glows hot like coal. Simple really.

The ash tree on the other hand is a tall one (15). It goes up. The English ash penetrates the woodland canopy largely branchless and has smooth tall trunks in established wooded areas around my house today. Without the Lithic psychosemantic tree nobody can explain the two meanings of ash, so they pretend there are none, which certainly saves thinking. In the Pleistocene such woods (as well as Lithic meanings) were bog standard. The oak by contrast spreads its branches to suppress rival growth, and it is named for the superlative hardness of its wood. The Aboriginal Malay kruing for a (hardwood) tree has much the same semantic content There is also the aspen tree, originally just asp, an up shoot or tall piece, a tree not conspicuously tall but simply tall as a tree compared with undergrowth, herbage, etc. Here we can include also arbor, the Latin for tree, which gives us the Nularbor plain in Southern Australia, an infertile region with little enough herbage and nil trees. It is still a surprise to find a Latin speaking digger in early days but there must have been one. The untrilled r is a cockney r replacing a. Arbor comprises the Lithic elements arai-bau-a, raised-burgeoned-one, ie a tall growth, a tree. Tree is quite similarly from the Lithic te-rai, originally tai-rai, rayed by the feminine rays issuing from the ta, the female pudenda, which were found to draw out and up the boys squatting opposite around the hearth, and so meaning from time immemorial drawn up, raised, stretched tall (tall is from ta-lai, born and so become-linear or long). Our chest of drawers has drawers which are just drawn out rather than raised up, but it is clear where the idea comes from. In ancient Egyptian it was the cedar which was called ash or shai, the tallest tree in the Lebanon. The cedar is in Lithic terms Sai-da-are, much the same, that is up-become-verbal marker, a tall grower, the tall tree. Or else it is from the earlier Greek kedros, with initial k-. The Lithic from which it comes is then kai-terau-sai, trunk-drawn-up-tall. While looking at trees, all remarkable for their height compared with the undergrowth, we can include the American sequoia capable of a hundred feet and more, a giant pine in the American Cherokee tongue, from sai-kau-ia, a tall-grown-it that or one. Right next door is a sequin, originally zecchino, a Venetian gold coin, from zecca, a mint, which in turn is derived from the Arabic dar as sekka, a mint where the metal is melted and poured in a mould. Dar is a house. Sekka is from the Lithic elements sai-ka-ka, a fire-making-place. Metal, melt and mould are closely akin in Lithic. Metal is from earth(the ore)-become-liquid, melt is ore-liquid-becoming. Mould is from ore-that what-liquid-births, the mould forms the melt. The Malay Senoi aboriginal word for a tree, kruing, is from ka-rau-i'ng, hard-raised-one. The sapodilla reveals its own original logic after some unwinding of the Aztec lexicon. The dilly, a tree found in the West Indies, is aphetic (a shortened form) of sapodilla, which in turn is a Spanish diminutive (-illa) of the Aztec tzapotl. The –tl is simply the Aztec substantive marker. Tzapotl in turn is short for the Aztec cuauhzapotl, of which the first element is from cuahitl which is their word for tree. The Lithic elements are kau-a(h)ai-tl, grown-extensive-noun marker, or grown high (chapter 8). The u vowel is the completive one (chapter 16). The h can therefore just be a cockney h, and the -a'ai a reinforcing extensive. The Spanish diminutive -illa in sapodilla is actually from the Aztec –tl, their substantive marker taken from the bus tzapotl or tall piece. There is no reason why different languages should not have parsed their words differently, which has obscured the commonality of Lithic and provided the astonishing diversity of the six thousand languages currently on earth, along with as many more really numberless languages which have perished, all from a common phonemic starting point. Of course there may well have been diversity in psychosemantic terms ab initio as well. You would surely have expected it. But the surviving evidence points to uniform Lithic thinking as extremely widespread if not universal. Rather depressingly we seem to have started out thinking all in very similar terms, with common phonemes, and ended up at loggerheads.

The Latin os for bone is from au-sai which is the unburnt. Bones are burnt up in modern cemetery furnaces but in the prehistoric funeral pyre they were not consumed. Instead as the hard masculine part of the body – the fleshy parts were seen as the feminine contribution and so as ephemeral – they were collected and given reverent burial, supportive of male chauvinism, where they might germinate and lead to reincarnation. It is perhaps pertinent to remember here that Aristotle believed women were mortal, having no intellectual souls. Their contributions to the world were confined to the sins of the flesh, fleshing the male seed and rearing the next generation. It was the women who, hunkered round the hearth in considerable deshabille, with the feminine rays which emanated from their genitalia provoking action at a distance, who drew out the male phallus, seducing its owner. Since the flesh was mischievous in this way, women with their fleshly orientation, including their bulgy bits, were the mischief makers and it was therefore not surprising they were not going to benefit from the after life. It may even have prompted Adam's report to Deity which landed Eve with childbirth. Some sixty years ago when I drew attention to Aristotle's chauvinistic position on these matters in a university tutorial a fellow student got up and left the room in indignation, imagining I was recommending the posture. So it is perhaps wise now to include a disclaimer. The posture, should it reappear, needs slapping down. The fathers of Western civilisation need to be stood in the stocks. Their mischiefs should not be overlooked as our Victorian forebears overlooked them. Only lawyers now care much for Aristotle's syllogisms. Karl Popper has moved the rest of us on.

The classic case when it came to raying was the sun, whose rays the Egyptians drew with hands on the ends to symbolise their propensity to pull up the plants on their return journey to the sun. The Carthaginians who spoke a vulgar Egyptian tongue, Punic, had tenerai for fire. It came from the Egyptian Aton-a-rai, with Aton, their word for what the Victorians translated as the "disk" of the sun, actually the sun as orifice, Aa-tau'n, the eternal birth orifice in a firmament of solid rock, the busy sun birthing the sunrays into the world every day. By comparison with a volcano, the source of the sunlight was taken to be fire; so atonerai, the eternal sun that is raying, shortened and slurred to tenarai, became the Punic for fire. The island of Tenerife, colonised by the Carthaginians while Rome was still a pigsty, is named for its volcano from which the island came. Tenerai-i-phai is fire-which-ejaculates in Punic: Volcano. The whole island has come out of the crater, Teide, at one time an active birth canal itself. Or else the lava was a male earth's ejaculate. You could not expect the natural world to discriminate precisely between the sexes. A hermaphrodite performance was even to be expected, predating animal division of sexuality into two opposing forms. It was an achievement of a sort for our forebears to have picked up these correspondences between human experience and the over-arching natural world. Maybe the world was hermaphrodite. It is probable gay folk were always with us, like the poor. Punic speaking survivors of the Roman genocide when they captured Carthage are the Berber tribes in the Atlas mountains. In the hinterland of the Sahara is The Sea of Tenerai where the sand is so hot it burns your feet if you step on it. A television programme recently revealed the local Arabic speakers in their simplicity think it is named after an unknown Sheikh Tenerai who owned the place at one time or another (and the television presenters evidently knew no better). Many pre-Celtic place names are similarly treated as named after phantom Sheikhs in Great Britain also. We are into Lithic thinking here. None of it was entirely veridical, while some can now easily be seen to have been absurd. But that does not mean it did not obtain at the time. The flame as ish can be finished off with a sizzle, sai-zzi-lai, "like the hiss of the flame" (when extinguished) for anyone who speaks Lithic.

Asbestos, as well as causing cancer, is also unconsumed because it is incombustible. It is from the past participle of the Greek verb sbennimai to extinguish, composed of the Lithic phonemic elements sai-bai-nai, the burning-of organic matter-negating. Asbestos is from a-sh-bai-sta-u, Lithic that-burning-organic matter-halting (standing)-one, fire extinguisher. For some reason Eric Partridge – who although the word king of his day had no Lithic (or did he?) – took the initial a- to carry the semantic content un- from a- as an absence, which it often does, as well as 'that', and read asbestos as inextinguishable in the face of the physics. Asbestos is incombustible and puts fires out. If it were inextinguishable it would burn furiously. But then Homer himself sometimes nods. Meanwhile in Malay salai is to heat over a fire with lai indicating continuity, by way of linearity.

Salaian is a rack over the fire for smoking meats, the lai picking up fresh relevance by way of the linearity of the racking, and the -an (pronounced long, more like arn rather than ann) being a substantive ending in Malay, which can be read more or less as if it were one in English. The Malay prefixes and suffixes are a quite lengthy and important study on their own account but not germane to the argument here.

Brazier, Partridge has worked out in his book, is from braise, originally breze, that is embers or live coals; and we can add the Lithic analysis ba-rai-sai, flesh, tissue or organic matter-rayed-of/by the flame. The point about the embers was they glowed red as live coals at the seat of the flame before fading when burnt out to ash. The Primitive Germanic had brasa as is found in Swedish today meaning fire (or a burning log), and cropping up also in Old Provencal brasa and Italian brascia, bracia, braga and brece. In English we have braise, "now only in cookery" as Eric Partridge puts it. To braise is to cook with live coals. But the live coals glowing red led to the South American country Brasil, like the embers, named for the hard redwoods of the country at one time the principal export, named for their redness, named for the red embers, named for the Lithic phonemic and semantic elements above.

There is also in English combustion, with the sibilant on offer as indicating fire. But the word is from the Latin comburere of which combustus is merely the regular past participle. The Latin prefixes co- and –ambi- as prefixes (co- is joined together and -ambi- is 'as the flesh': that is with bilateral symmetry and so on both sides) so that the word actually has the original core construct –urere, Lithic u-rai-ere, where the u- is as the completive vowel ("all done gone finished") and also the passive, and rai- is rayed, by the fire, ish in fact but not stated because the fire's rays had already acquired some of the semantic content of the flame which uttered the rays. The final -ere is just the Latin verbal suffix. Rays (re) acted upon their targets, having effects; and so they were activators, and so makers of activation, and so verbal markers.

Breath is akin to breeze. Compare Latin susurrus, the whispering of the wind in the trees. A hiss (1) on breathing in, followed by a parting of the lips and a puff when breathing out has given us our spirits, from the Latin spirare to breathe, the spir- (Lithic sh-pia being, as Eric partridge puts it, "as clearly echoic as one could wish". The s- is breathing in and the pia is breathing out through the mouth (compare spit). Halare in Latin, also to breathe, is also echoic: the ha- is the sound of breathing in and the -la- of breathing out, with the usual -are verbal suffix. Note the -la- separating two vowels, and the fact the vowels are both aa (see chapter 9 on La). The Greek pneuma for breath, air and wind is also supposed to have been echoic breathing again, the pneu- is breathing out and the -ma breathing in. It does appear our forebears were rather an asthmatic lot. The Latin tussis for cough is also supposed to be echoic, leading to tos for a cough in Spanish; as is whistle, a bit of a wheezing sound originally, rather than the clear notes produced by professional whistlers today, some even capable of rendering classical tunes by mouth. A whizzer acquires his speed from the sound of rushing air, and a whisper is sibilant communication, or for poesy just the sound itself, as when the wind is alleged to whisper in the trees or even green grass to have the facility. Whether the Chinese derived their shu (6) for wind from the hissing involved in breathing or from the susurru of the breeze is moot, but it is clearly echoic in Lithic terms.

Issue (7) is generally judged to be directly from the Latin ex-ire to go out, but if so its slurring is psychosemantic, from the puffing and hissing of breath (4) and wind. The breath issues and the wind blows. Ex (37) is itself the result of major slurring in turn. The out of its meaning was in origin a rising out, ex is from ai-kai-sai, going-makes-up, like a cork out of a bottle[7] – neither of them invented when language began – so perhaps from the sun coming up and out of the horizon each morning, indeed 'as it-begins-to shine', which is as good a reading of the Lithic elements ai-kai-sai as the other. The Latin ire to go is from ai-ere, ai-verbal marker. Ai is aa-ing and so going, the distance gone an immediate extension of meaning from the extensive vowel. All vowels are extensive in so far as they can be continued for as long as you have breath, and a as the general one was picked to exemplify the characteristic precisely, as a psychosemantic content of the phoneme. The extensiveness of the vowel is then gulled for going. It is a semantic gull. The legs are borrowing a character from the glottis. Issuance probably accounts for quite a number of the initial s- prefixes treated conventionally as general intensive prefixes in the Indo European tongues. It is not clear in any of these cases why an intensive marker should be required, but certainly the s- prefix is often there. As will emerge, it has several roles which the Lithic reveals. Sparse, spray, spurt, spout and sperm, all related to the Greek speirein to sow, strew or scatter, probably in ugly origin all from the performance of the male penis which does all these things and also links up with the Greek peos for penis, pai-au-sai, piece-that what-issues or spurts. Compare Sanskrit pasas or sapas for penis, where there appear to be two quite separate secretions on offer, as indeed there are.

A hose (cockney h), i-awa-u-sai, it-water-what-issues, passes water too. But curiously the original hose were the ones cladding the legs, and they were tall (15) like trousers, terau-sai-a, also a garment pulled-up, pulled up ones. They also covered the lower legs, a novelty when introduced since the lower legs were formerly left free for loping after game. The original chawat in Malay, a loin cloth merely covering the crotch, actually meant crotch piece, since chawang means a fork in Malay as found with a branching bough as well as the body. Now a fork is a bifurcation from one point of view and a joint from the other. So the chawat is probably from Lithic ka-u-a-tai, joint-dual-that-divides, a joint of two pieces is a fork or crotch and the chawat divides it by passing between the haunches. It is made of cloth, bark cloth originally. The tailoring also is not of a high order, being a single length of material long enough to encircle the waist and then be twisted behind and the two lengths passed between the buttocks and up in front of the genitalia and then over the belt piece, so that when tidily arranged it is brought down fanned out in front to cover the male profile more or less sufficiently. A tailor is really a tai-lai-a, a cutting-joining-one, from two-ing or dividing in two and then linking the bits together with needle work to make the tailored shape required. The original chawat is not cut, since it would come undone, but it is shaped in a woven strip, which distinguishes it from natural materials like bunches of leaves or gourds which formerly served the same purpose, and so entitles the chawat to be described as tai or trimmed. There is no long flexible material in nature suitable. Fur trousers might do in Northern climes but not in the tropics. Adam's single fig leaf from the genus ficus was never more than a scribal alsurdity. The lightest of breezes, or even a single stride would have rendered its purpose nugatory. The fai-kau of the ficus or extended (central) part of the petal may have struck the scribe as fitting for Adam's profile, or else his subconscious was prompting him for the Egyptian pahei from the fai- of ficus (chapter 7).

A TV team and its well known leader recently appeared on our screens ber-chawat, wearing this skimpy attire, having withdrawn to a hut to throw off their clothes and wind local chawats around their persons, imagining it would ingratiate them with the local folk. They will of course have been regarded as mad whiteys to discard their superb garmenting for the wretched local equivalent. Moreover their embarrassment was readily discernable in their gauche movements in deshabille with pale bottoms, which the locals will have much enjoyed though too polite to show it, maintaining a discreet deadpan for the cameras. Aboriginal folk are not simpletons. They certainly know their psychosemantics better than whitey. They are completely comfortable with everyday exposed bodies, only preserving a powerful tabu on exposure of the genitalia in public, which probably never occurs after puberty. Washing in the stream gets the chawat a wash too. White soldiers washing without chawats in the local stream in the jungle would bring every boy in the jungle clearing out to watch the pornographic show, dead pan but open mouthed and agog, while the women were apt to take to the jungle until they were done and the male genitalia safely caged again. Here was civilised permissiveness battering at the doors of tribal culture and the boys were immediately fascinated – hooked was not too strong a word for it. It was a nice example of whitey's assumptions about the primitive savage being all awry. The aboriginals were not uninhibited. On the contrary their belief in standards were stronger than us moderns. The garden hose therefore has no obvious connection with the stockings, although they are both tubular.

The garden hose is probably related to ooze. Ooze in turn probably comes by way of spit. There is a cross current which enters the lists here, deriving from the spitting, from the Latin spuere and sputare both meaning to spit, producing spittle and sputum. The classical spit was preceded by a thorough-going hawk, and the phlegm spat out was supposed to be akin to all the other mucosal secretions and slimey things like white of egg, sperm, brains and bone marrow, even frogs eggs and snail trails. Slimes were all ish-lai-m, live-lye-matter It was not yet quite science, but it was classifying by appearances which preceded science by many hundreds of thousands of years, and may sometimes still stand in for it even today. Ooze is from Lithic awa (the emphasis is on the w with the a prefix and suffix approaching an indeterminate schwa) for water or other liquid; and the -zai gets its semantics from the slimes, the liquids formed by life forms – which are oozy. A virus, originally Latin uirus, from Lithic u-i-rau-s, liquid-which-is rayed or roused (and so oozing out), originally just meant the sap or juice of plants which runs out, including the notable ones which were poisonous. The –s in uirus is probably merely the Latin substantive marker, but wi-raus certainly attracts the psychosemantic content from the sibilant we see in issue (7 and 24), a liquid which has arisen from life forms, a live juice like the plant sap and the disease carrier. Animal and vegetable were taken to be closely aligned, as indeed in some respects they are. Animal flesh and vegetable tissue were accepted as equivalents. Both were implied by the phoneme Ba, simply because the lips which make the sound are fleshy. The poisonous sap, Latin uirus, Lithic u-i-rau-sai, liquid-which-roused-issues, was 'wos' from aw-au-sai, water/liquid-which-issues, in Old English matching a similar Middle German wos. Old English 'was' meant mire or dampness – compare German vasser, water, another fluvial liquid – so the poison gave a new meaning to virus, a poisonous agent quite unconnected with either spittle or mire, but deriving its semantics from the poison of some saps, by way of a semantic gull, sidestepping the tyrannical eye. Sap is merely a sai-pai, an issue (7) of the skin or surface or bark. It flows out of the plant, for instance when the bark is cut or the plant picked. A virus is a poisonous agent which turns out to be a class of microscopic semi-live macro-molecular cells capable of interfering with the genetic makeup (DNA) of the phenotypes of the macro species introducing diseases; and nowadays under human control even modifying them to order as agents of beneficial genetic modification under human control.

To spit (8) is echoic too, a puff with a liquid element represented by the initial sibilant (2). Spit has a phonetic relationship to part, Lithic pa-tai, pieces-divided, as well: the pai or lips are tai, divided, two'd, parted so the spittle issues. Compare Latin potare to drink – by parting the two lips. The group is closely akin to the Latin sputare to spit, with English spew and even water-spout, which in turn give us the shaped pourers or spouts on our pots. To spout originally meant to vomit. Splash and splatter are other variants. Eric Partridge contents himself with the initial s- as the "Indo European intensive prefix". But then he had no Lithic and needed a general intensive prefix to cover a quiverful of meanings, like for instance the other spit or spike on which meat turns over the fire, the turnspit. The first s- here will have come from the spike, originally a stick stuck upright (10) in the ground, probably as a marker, and the -t at the end of the spit probably comes from an s or ts or tz as in the Germanic tongues, with spitz meaning sharp in German today. The meat is spitted over the fire (3) on a sharp stake (10). The psychosemantic contents sharp and flame (3) combine seamlessly to indicate the use of the sibilant. That is how the subconscious mind works, pulling discrepant recollections together linked by incidental connections outside reason.

The flame Ish (3) gives us smoke (9) from ish-mau-ka, the flame-put down/de-pressed/ marred/maimed/morbid/dead-makes: quite a good definition of smoke even today. The dying fire smoulders and the flame moulders. In the introduction, chapter 1, attention has already been drawn to the cigar, from the Central American Maya tongue yet astonishingly like the Arabic Iskra (3) for spark above, and simultaneously compatible with sugar, from the Sanskrit Su-kara, in this case making a pleasant sensation (19 & 20), from being nicely toasted (18) around the hearth (11) instead of making a flame. Cigar is from the Lithic sai-kara, fire (3) maker or burner which after all is precisely what a cigar is. Perhaps it has overtones also of the same sensational element as sugar. Smokers certainly think so. Cigar is immediately from the Spanish Cigarro which the Spanish took to be a fair transliteration of Maya sik'eh to smoke and sik tobacco, the burning material which you light and smoke. To smoke is to make smoke if you are enjoying a cigar or cigarette, or just to emit it if you are a bonfire, but both are making it. In Hindustani you drink a cigarette (cigret pina) while in Malay you eat it (makan rokok), and a Tamil cigar is a cheroot, from the Tamil and the Lithic shai-rau-tai, fire-rayed-become. It is lit.

Lexicological research across six thousand languages is inevitably an ongoing enterprise, which will require a regiment of volunteers working to establish Lithic language roots beyond a peradventure. But there certainly seems to be a remarkable community of perception where dowsing burning brands is concerned. It is evidence in itself that the dawn of the fire age, which we still live in, dates to the same period as the dawn of language. We can hardly go back before the Sumerian, only a few thousand years ago. Their word for fire was izi (3), not widely divergent from ish, the title of this chapter. The Akkadian was isatu, Lithic ish-a-tau, flame-that-become. Compare Malay satu (one), an up[line]-cut, a vertical mark (10,17). In Chinese shihuo is to catch fire or be on fire (3). The -huo (chapter 8) can include a sudden pain and suffering. The shi root in Chinese appears to mean to lose nowadays, but when one comes to check over its combinatory forms it turns out to be not so much to mislay anything but to suffer a loss (such as in a fire?), or to lose one's grip, to let slip, to lose one's bearings, that is to slip or melt away like the evanescent and insubstantial flame (3). Shiling in Chinese is not to work properly – here one sees the active sense (25 and 35) of the sibilant phoneme – shipei means "I must be leaving now", the idea is perhaps that my feet will be slipping away. Shiwong is to lose hope or confidence, a slipping away in the fright department. Chinese appears to be a language retaining elements so old it preserves Lithic idioms of composition: words are still recognised as phonemic strings with meanings derived from the phonemes. In Sumer sweat was izutu, heat generated. It occurs to me the victorious Akkadians entering Sumer will have been confronted by sweating Sumerians declaring themselves on fire. They will have compromised on sweaty hot, what the English sweat (18) means precisely, along with sweet which has the su- one step further metaphoric (19). The Lithic in this case appears to have been izi-au-tau, using izi as the heat of the flame and reading the whole as heat-that what-born. When you get hot you sweat. Pay attention, Tarzan: what happens when you get hot? Right! You sweat! The word sweat in English is from the same construction, ish-au-ai-tai, heat-that what-that is-born; and the French sueur has a final rai in place of tau, raised or roused, in effect drawn out, in place of born or become. Professor CG Gostony of the Sorbonne, of Hungarian extraction, has traced words akin to the Sumerian in a variety of languages, but mostly Hungarian where many correspondences are striking, and he does not shrink from drawing the net quite wide when it comes to semantic correspondences[8]. So, for example we have the Sumerian word silim which Gostony translates as to be intact, perfect, or in good condition, en bon etat, which we could perhaps stretch in English as in favourable circumstances. It smacks surely of Lithic sai hunkered around the hearth, warm, cosy, comfortable, at ease (19) Interestingly the Akkadian translation he records as salamu. He then prints for comparison the Hungarian sima meaning lissom, sleek, favourable or easy (19 again), followed by selyem the Hungarian for silk, comparable with Latin saeta and serica, Italian seta and French soie, with English silk, German seide and finally Chinese sunn which as well as silk can carry the meaning of law as well as soft and docile, following their universal practice of milking every last metaphor from every phoneme. If you consider the Chinese meanings a moment it should appear that silk exhibits the exceedingly soft and supple characteristic which it can be argued are to be found, in their own spheres, also in the law which supposedly is a smooth procedure lubricating social intercourse, as in softness of texture and in docility of temperament. The same character is not hard to find similarly in the Hungarian sima, lissom; and silk is soft, supple, smooth and claimant to a certain perfection (where wearing apparel is concerned). Is the same hangup reflected in lawyers' outmoded dress sense today?

Sumerian, Akkadian, Chinese, Hungarian, English, French, German, Arabic, Maya, and Tamil are amenable to the same psychosemantic phonetics and semantic contents. Coincidence? Surely not! Eric Partridge, treating the s- as simply a further case of an Indo-European emphatic prefix, has little difficulty attributing other words for smoke starting m- and without the s- like Armenian mux, actually from the Lithic mau-kai-sai with the burning removed to the far end; but with Old Irish much, Welsh murg, Cornish moc, mog, mok, Breton moguet, all not unlike English murk, to a primitive meugh or meukh, all meaning smoke. But he had no Lithic. The s- must have been dropped long after the Tower of Babel, when words broke free from Lithic phonemic structures at the conscious level and words became simples rather than strings of phonemic meaningful elements and the initial s- became sidelined as a less than useful emphatic or intensive marker. The mental shift from phonemic composition to words as we know them was a paradigm shift greater than the later parallel shift from pictograms to letters in writing. Both demoted reason, the original semantic content, prefering system and simplicity. Slovening and slurring of the old forms became acceptable. The wonder is so much survives, and this can only be accounted for by the work of the subconscious mind which prompts for the old patterns of thinking, and is repatterned in every child's subconscious when consciously learning to speak their mother tongue, all based on these Lithic whimsies, to refresh the thought patterns of the first speakers with each generation.

The flame springs upwards (shai), while everything else goes downwards (ma) if unsupported and can easily damage bare toes. Hot air and gases were closed books to the ancients. The flame was magic, alive yet consuming life, devouring the flesh of animals and vegetables alike, omnivorous. The vertical, the instinct of life to shoot upwards, was the vegetative miracle, culminating in fruiting and seeding. It still is, and attracts generations of gardeners to this day. So much thinking is reducible to this original identification of life with rising, and following from that identification the corollary identification of death with going down, that it is a waste of time to try to arrange the whole gamut in any kind of schematic arrangement. A piecemeal approach presents the evidence in its entirety without any preconceived ordering. Half a hundred examples should suffice, taken in any order. An island is land which arises, springs up (ish, 10) out of the ocean (lau, chapter 9). The -land in island is a doublet with plain land in folk etymology already. But the laun is not originally land. In the original Lithic it refers to the ocean from which the island arises as land: is-lau-en-da, up-ocean-from-born. The Celtic for the ocean is laur, the Malay is laut. Both mean the briney, the cumulative final state when all the liquid's slipping down is done. Ceylon, is the Holy Island or Shri Lanka, where La'n-ka is from the Lithic Ocean-in-land, and the Shri is spiritual (4) from heavy breathing and many of the meanings of

the flame. The English Ceylon is from Silan, the Hindustani name for the island, from the Lithic Sai-La'n, arising-ocean-from, much like the English island
above. Malay selah is to lift up a curtain, which on its own has the natural habit
to be slack and lapse or hang down. The Malay sayap is a bird's wing, an upping
pai or surface. However the vertical can also indicate the stationary. The vertical
| is contrasted with the horizontal –, as in the Tau or T, the two directions | and
—. To stand (English) is from the Lithic sai-tan-dai, vertical-become-does, or the
vertical [line]-of the Tau-does. The Malay sampai is to arrive, the limbs standing
upright and still after travelling, working their way sideways in a line or sideways
extension – like the skyline at sea. Jalan, Malay for travelling, is going linear.
Compare aller in French which also means to go, a spatial extension a going linear
process again. Admittedly you do not leave a slimey thread behind you like the
slug, but there is a viritual thread or linear trace marking your journey.

For the French, sauter is to jump as well as to cook. In the first case you
become sa-u-tai, both acting (34) and vertical (14), in the second you become
heated by the flame (18). It is no coincidence the genitalia have come to enjoy in
language both erection, upping (10) and heating (18) together. It is inbuilt in the
psychic encyclopedia of the subconscious mind which gleaned its lexicon from
its psychic highs, as is already remarked in previous chapters. The ash tree has
nothing to do with the unburnt residue in the grate. It is the tall one (15) which
grows up (without side branches) to get to the light through the forest canopy.
It has a strong instinct to go up like the flame from which it gets its name. Its
long upright shoots made strong straight spears. An oak on the other hand has a
strong completive spreading instinct, as indicated by the vowel u, and its wood is
the hardest (in temperate climes), au-kai.

The sacred from Latin sacer, Lithic sa-kara, is the uplifting and life enhanc-
ing comforter, with the same Lithic elements as the Arabic iskra for spark and
Sanskrit sukara for sugar. Compare Tamil shri for holy, the spiritual flame. Eric
Partridge makes great play with Sagamore, which he has from Mitford Mathews'
Dictionary of Americanisms (1951). In the original Lithic it is Sag-em-au, top of
the (skeletal) body (from sa-kai), ie head, followed by –em-au, -of-all. It meant
tribal chief, whence in America the Grand Sachem or head of Tammany. The au
for the all could be the community or tribe, or a town, or even the whole world in
Egyptian. But Sagamore is from the Algonquin languages, specificly Naragansett
Sachimau, whence the Abnaki dialect Sagamore, tribal chieftain. For sag, head,
we need to go all the way back to Sumerian, which it is hard to believe directly
influenced the Naragansett or Abnaki tongues. It meant innards guts or heart in
Sumerian, but that was because these were thought to be the seat of the sa-kai or
life drive. The head was also recognised as such a one as well. So it meant head too,

reinforced by the reading of sa-kai as up-of body, the top of the torso. In Sumerian sag i ta meant head which pierces.

The Latin sagitta for arrow, from the Lithic sag-i-ta, the head or point-which-pierces, as opposed to the common hand bladed weapons you swipe with, is thousands of years later than the Sumerian sag i ta, where sag meant head. Eric Partridge offers no derivation, but suspects it might be from the Scythian or Parthian, a deal closer to Sumer than Rome. Or sagitta could also be read in Lithic as sa-i-kai-ta, action-which-makes-a hole. But it does not fit so well with the phonetics. The arrow was the precursor of the bullet. It travels like an angry ray. The two reinforcing readings probably ensured the adoption of the no-menclature. The bow, which is bent (bau) is something else again. The spear is a sharp-pointed-one, sai-pai-a, or it could just be action-pointed-one, the business end with a cockney (untrilled) r standing in for an a or schwa. The sword is from sai-u-arai-dai, action-both-ways-doing: you could swipe both ways since both sides of the blade are sharp along its whole length. A dagger too has both sides of the blade sharp but it is a ta-kara or hole maker, like the sagitta, but it does not have just a sharpened head for the job like an arrow, it is bladed its whole length like the sword. Yet you punch it in, it is not a swiping weapon, being too short. The Saxons' seax or broadsword, sai-a-kai-(s), action-that-strikes, was a striking action weapon. They may have got it from the Romans in Gaul. They beat the Celts who had heavier picks or celts, axes with long handles which were kai-lai-tai, cutting by loopy striking, swung in a looping overarm stroke, to strike at the head. A hit was curtains but the Saxon sword with a shorter swing most often struck home first. Certainly you could recover and get a second blow in quicker if you missed with the first. The best tactic was probably to dodge the first whack from the celt and then lunge forward while your assailant was rewinding, and cut the side of his neck. What usually settled the matter, then as now, was how many weapons could be brought immediately to bear. Saxons were stodgy and fought close to-gether like the Romans; Celts were wild and swinging their celts kept them apart. They were a collection of individuals. Lai was swinging, from the orbital action of the sun, Apollo, that goes in a loop, swoop or orbit. The celt had been shown to be vulnerable to the Roman short sword or gladium, gai-lai-dai-u'm, with its go-looping-does-one, a snicker-snee, and the Roman close battle formation; but the Celtic temperament appears to have rated the traditional pecking order over reason. They had the Irish in them.

A summit has the Lithic phonemes sa-am-ai-tai, top-of-travel-become. There is the implied contrast at the same time of up (sai) and down (mai) as if to say "would you believe it, the down element has now become an upper one: surely you can guess what I mean". Tai, becoming, is originally from birthing, from the birth canal, from parturition, from division, one dividing into two, and from the division which is the female genital slit, from twoing, the tau, from snapping in two, from a snapping branch, by borrowing a similar echoic pattern to that of Ka, the sound of the flint knapper flaking flint, see chapters 5 and 6. Birth was taken to be the paradigm for happenings of all sorts: first you don't see it, then you do, events being born, appearing, in consecutive takes like a slide show or the frames of a cinema performance. This is not as way out as you may think when you get down to brass tacks and start to question the way we think – mostly by metaphor: all sorts of correspondences begin to bulk large and count for more than the lay- man would readily believe. Zenith, the summit of the sun's passage across the sky, is from the medieval English cenith, senyth or cenit, spelling was variable in those days, and is thought to have arisen simply from a scribal error misreading the Arabic samt (summit) as senit. For prior etymology see summit above. A sum, which sounds a bit like a summit, is from the Latin summa which meant the sum total (the top amount) and came from the highest amount when you totalled a column of figures, probably traditionally starting from the bottom and adding up, not down. But semantically, however added, the totaling up was thought of add- ing individual amounts one on top of the other. A total is an inclusive singularity of course. All sums were just adding up originally. Long division, and worse, came rather later, as it still does.

A squirrel has a very fine over-arching tail. Understanding his name involves knowing the Greek, where a shadow is skiouros, literally as Partridge has it "the shadow tail". He has not got it quite right. The Greek for tail is ouros, probably because the sun's rays made the vegetable kingdom sprout and shoot, and in an animal the tail was seen as a kind of surplus shoot sprouting from the far end of the animal. What kind of ray? Well there were other rays which made the penis sprout and others again which shot ideas into people's heads goading them to ac- tion like rage and distress. The eyes' rays meanwhile were believed to return from feeling over the panorama and paint the picture of what they had closely felt upon the iris (the irais, the rayed bit)of the eye. Rays were the explanation for all action at a distance without direct physical contact. That is how the Latin –are, -ere, -ire became verbal (action) markers for instance. The tail was frisky – against flies? – and so must have been the receiver of rays, the Greek auros, Lithic a-u-rau-(s), one-what-rayed. It is a Lithic hypothesis that these linguistic structures were put together before full consciousness, when it was assumed we were for the most part being lived by outside environmental influences, forces or circumstances. Only later were these forces, or some of them at least, adopted as part of the persona. You can not very often make much sense of words without understanding the thinking behind the Lithic phoneme strings. The shadow was a tail made by the light, s-kau-ouros, a light-made-tail, emerging from the back side of the light like a tail. Latin carried the Greek skiouros to sciuros leading to scurius The shadow then got hijacked as an ordinary tail and was used to describe Brer Tail. But did the squirrel's tail at the same time seem to (over)shadow its owner as well? Perhaps it was an additional prompt for the nomenclature.

In precise contrast to the squirrel whose name hangs by a single convoluted thread, the Egyptian god Osiris rejoices in a quiverful of interlocking associations, as any good god should, in the semantic contents of the sibilant in his case. Osiris is the Greek mispronunciation of the correct Egyptian pronunciation Au Sarai. Our Sarah was a fellah. He had the misfortune to lose his genitalia in a fight with Set, who evidently fought dirty. The Egyptologists' Set is correctly pronounced Saitaun or Satan. Osiris in Lithic phonemes is Au-sai-Rai, that universal/eternal-upping-of the sun (Ra); the Eternally Rising Sun, The Sun-rise, Life Arising, Universal Reincarnation, The Comforter[9]. You can see that with this lot of indications it is no surprise to find his birth was celebrated each spring in the households of the faithful by planting mustard and cress, "the fast grower" – or some such – which germinated and shot up in pots in the house, showing the resurrection of the apparently dead seed. That was why the Egyptians mummified their dead. With the right ritual and glyphs in the tomb it was going to ensure their germination and resurrection if they had not offended the gods while on earth. We may laugh; but we look too to the same end, albeit in more sophisticated ways. Should we pause to consider that we come from simpletons? Have we learned?

The French for sky, ciel, and the English rather more prosaic ceiling, are both probably akin to Latin caelum, the heavens, and so have suffered a transmogrification from a hard c, really a k, to a soft c like an s, the letter c permitting the transfer. This kh/s shift is common enough in Sanscrit. It comes from the fact the sibilant, the expulsion of breath from the half closure of the teeth and the palate, can be quite closely copied by the expulsion of breath from the half closed glottis. Anyone can try it. The Semitic tongues with hacking and hawking glottal consonants which have none of these gentle features have no difficulty keeping ka and sa apart. It has to be said they are well advised to do so, because semantically they are poles apart. To address ciel the sky we should perhaps notice the Greek kuklos for circle, in Lithic kau-kau-lau(s), each and all the corners-looped, that is to say a smooth line going through all the turns required to get back to where you started out. The caelum is this looping of corners of the over-arching dome of the firmament. This requires no upper loop from ciel with a sibilant, it is about smoothed corners and the upturned bowl we call the sky, and not in origin the location of the firmament up above. But then again the fact that the sibilant c can offer an upper loop may have assisted the slurrers. As for our English sky, we may be mixed up with the squirrel, since sky comes from Middle English skie from Old English skua, skuwa, cloud, akin to Old High German skuwo a shadow, which certainly seems to have something of the Greek light tail about it. But to suppose sky comes from a cloudy sky from a shadow seems far fetched. Clouds surely appear as superimposed moving contrasting items, with a degree of solidity and consistency and a different colour from the blue of the empty sky. The tail is a foreign body caught up with the Greek for shadow, and is found in clouds as shadow making. The sky however is from the Lithic ish-kai, light made, made of light. When the light goes the sky disappears. At night Nut appears instead, the black night-time goddess with the stars as her teats expressing jets of light, the German nacht, Lithic na-kha-ti, showing the body's orifices, and accounting for the spelling in English. Naughty is perhaps from the same Lithic string, a mortal with the same mischievous propensity, which gives us our naked also, not in reality a past participle of a lost verb to nake, although a snake is probably from si-na-kai, brer-bare-bodied, that is to say without fur and also legless. In Hindi a snake is nag. Kipling's fans will remember Kala Nag the elephant, Black Snake. He probably got his name from his trunk and his mean temperament, or else because elephants have no coats, like the snake.

The budgerigar has already been made an exemplar of Lithic semantics, ba having the semantic content to go. Lips don't go, but by way of fleshy, flesh and the other conspicuously fleshy bits of the body like the buttocks which muscle the legs, the legs can leg it and go. Ba-ji or go-up (10) is the Australian aboriginal for bird. The djeri-gara or bright colour of the budgy (from baji-jeri-gara) shows the Australian aboriginal mind was never so far from the Western mind as folk have imagined. The djeri is sherai in Lithic, brightness (21) being what the flame rays. The -gara, from the Lithic elements ka-ra, is colour because colour is what determines the appearance of anything, it makes the ray which the eye recovers. It opens the possibility our colour comes originally from kara too. The ray as well as being the sun's ray was also the eye's ray – also ra in Egyptian. In fact the sun was perceived as the world eye. It is tempting to see the sun presented as the world's eye as the boys' counter attack to displace the girls' representation of it as the world's birth canal, birthing light into the world on a daily basis, which rather left them out. But why was ra an eye in Egyptian in the first place? Because it rayed. Then why was a ray? Because r was a trill, like the late Peter Ustinov's habit as a schoolboy of accompanying himself with a loud trill mimicking a motor car noise, the rapid firing of cylinders, to the distress of his parents. The eye's rays had the job of going out and returning with a whole panorama in great (pointillist) detail. It was supposed they must be very numerous indeed to bring so much detail back. Compare a flush of arrows from an army opening its attack. They achieved nothing like full coverage. A trill seemed to match the detailed repetitive nature required to pick up the whole panorama. In Egypt the sun's mighty rays were supposed to actually pull up the vegetation on their return journey to the sun, explaining vegetal growth, and they were therefore drawn with hands on the ends to symbolise this. Our feeble peepers could only manage to carry back a simulacrum which they painted on the iris, where a reflection can sometimes be seen even today, so obviously in the Stone Age and before.

The Sumerian for bird was gesh, also a go-up, with gai meaning going just like the Australian aboriginal ba (which also features in bird with rai, raised, in place of dj, up). The Sumerians were displaced persons from the Garden of Eden it is now believed, when the great glacier melt drowned the Eastern plains of "Malaya", the Garden Land, its cultivated lowlands whence Adam and Eve were expelled, now under the shallow South China Sea, about fifteen thousand years ago. It was padi gardening, not flowers. The Sumerians were Adamites who came from the East in boats, the first citizens recorded, Sumer being the oldest known city, based on their riverine irrigated rice padi gardening which their women folk had discovered with their digging sticks while the men were engaged in tradition-al hunting trips in the wilder lands around. Their menfolk, Adamites to a man, attributed their misfortunes getting flooded out to the hubris of their women who had used their heads to displace the natural order, which Adam assumed to be displeasing to the Heavenly powers, since it put his nose out of joint too. They had irrigated the land multiplying the yield. What more natural than that Nature and the gods should riposte: "You think more water on the land than naturally supplied will be good, do you? Then try some of this!" raising the sea level three hundred feet and fifty feet. It was bound to give Adam pause. The "Senoi" ("first-born people"in the Senoi tongue), aboriginal Malay tribes living in the jungle of the Malayan spine, speaking a proto-Malay, still today with a slash and burn agriculture moving every few years when the tapioca yield falls off, have their own version of the flood. It starts like this: "Pada suatu masa dak mi ikor chok churrl delong kruing", "Once upon a time, there was one tail of dog – my guess is it was a bitch – which growled at a tree"[10]. This was not the tree of knowledge of the Bible. It was probably intended as a plural, ordinary jungle trees, representa-tives of the wild wood and the primeval ways, which were to be cleared to make padi fields – without any divine planning permission at all. The trees were to be replaced by knowledge, we would say cleared to make way for technology. It was bound to lead to trouble, and indeed the padi fields were destined to become drowned in salt water. Much later the Akkadian beduin who conquered the city of Sumer, Cains killing Abels, then adopted much of Sumerian culture so that the Adamite story as first told by the Sumerians has come down to us from Babylon the Akkadian capital. – including Adam and Eve, the Garden of the East, and the flood story, all borrowed myths. These were not Semites but Adamites speaking a language closer to modern Malay than Hebrew. Adam certainly wore a foreskin, if little or nothing else, and it is a virtual certainty he and Eve added a navel apiece in spite of Genesis suggesting the contrary. The Jewish Old Testament remains a very creditable compilation for its age, though imperfect in parts like most human compilations, even those dealing inter alia with divinity. Locating these Sumerian antecedents actually from the old Eastern Malaya in the hills to the North of Iraq subsequently was a late pious figment, thousands of miles out.

The Albanian for a bird is zog, the same as the Sumerian gesh ten thousand years ago, with the order of the phonemes reversed. The Lithic sa-u-gai, up-what-goes, seems perfectly clear. Nobody can deny the most noticeable character of birds is that they have mastered the art of flight. Who else? A few bugs, including butterflies, (named for their ability, butter from ba-u-terai, limbs-what-terayed or drawn up, like the greek wing pteron, from pai-terau'n) while the French papillon was evidently named for its pair of flappers. The Egyptian[11] for bird offers seventy nine different strings of glyphs (names) for birds of one kind or another, of which of course there are very many species. However the fact is it is only the post-Linnaean ornithologists who have concerned themselves very much with species other than those that stand out because of some visible peculiarity. In earlier times small birds were probably just sparrows or pippits (rather than bowls of porridge). Egyptian definitions turn out to have a lot in common, with the variety of terms largely down to scribal whimsy. The phoneticisations which follow are not all precisely as favoured by the academic Egyptologists, who generally leave out the vowels since they do not know how to determine them, or put in neutral sound-ing ones. T for instance, supposedly a bun or half a loaf, was actually pronounced Taun, with the meaning world – the glyph representing the dome of the sky over a flat earth – unless the vowelisation were modified by a following glyph, when the au could drop out and be replaced by the vowelisation of a follower. Hieroglyphs were far from straightforward writing as we understand it today. They originated as compositions made up of art work representing actual phenomena given mean-ings. The chapter dealing with Egyptian matters in detail and in chief has unfor-tunately had to be postponed to a subsequent volume owing to the exigencies of space, along with several other difficult languages, including Sumerian, picked for their difficulty. The deep historical evidence for the deep historical semantics must await publication of a further volume. The Lithic hypotheses and the demonstra-tion of their efficacy must have priority. The problem is one of size.

Of the words for birds, the Egyptian gashu is not unlike the Sumerian gesh, particularly as the –u ending is most likely to be the common Egyptian plural case ending. For f/e, as Partridge would put it, for further etymology, see gesh above. Moreover it is likely the Sumerian sibilant was pronounced shu anyway, like the Chinese who probably got it from the Adamites from the submerged plains of Malaya, just as the Egyptians also probably did, via the Sumerians and Akkadians. There is also siasha in Egyptian for a bird, from si-ash-aa, brer-up-goer. Shang is up in Chinese. Then there is Egyptian sikama, another bird, from si-ka-a-ma, brer-go-weightless; followed by an alternative recension sahaisahai with a cockney h to separate the consecutive vowels, sa-ai-sa-ai, up-go-up-go, a compulsive flyer just like the budgy. Similarly we find haihaisai, repetitively going up; and araishau, being around aloft[12], or rising aloft like our birds; and awanhei, an air lover; and 'mshaira (using the Hamitic idiom, starting with the personal marker m-), 'm-sha-ai-arai, him-up-go-er. Finally we have arai paitaun, around in the heavens, or perhaps ascending there, perhaps an eagle or vulture; aarai, go-rising-[into]pai, skin, surface lid or roof-of the taun, of the world. In Ancient Egyptian the arai could alternatively mean a lion, not habituated to flying or flight. In his case the name was echoic, arai, the roarer or snarler. As the lion was the king of the beasts, perhaps the eagle was the lion of the skies. Finally there is aasaiu, the air rising one; and aapaida, the air traveller. It certanly appears not only were the Egyptian scribal classes, priests of a sort, allowed a good deal of freedom in the way they strung their glyphs together, the spelling, but this whimsical attitude extended to nomenclature also. They had fifty different ways of saying bird. It accounts for the large amount of polysemy uncovered in Ancient Egyptian, as well as a lot more not identified no doubt, to add to the many words with the same meaning. Egyptian texts are jigsaw puzzles to decrypt and disentangle, and much of the tentative reconstructions are indeed still tentative, and some of them doubtless wrong.

Looking at words for birds certainly suggests a lot were noted for their ability to fly. The Latin avis appears to be made up from awa-sai, air-rising, or rising in the air. English birds are closer to the Australian ones. Ba-arai-dai in Lithic is go-arising-does. Like the Australian budgy they have the frustrating ability to spring into the air and take off when you try to catch them. The budgy seems to have prompted the invention of the boomerang, bu-em-ai-a-raing, a bent bat-for-going-and-returning. A sparrow was any small bird originally, like the pippit, named for its piping notes, but in Malaya (as later in Egypt) associated with pipes other than pan pipes, just from their tubular shape, and particularly the penis, so that the prepubertal penis is in Malay a pippit, a little pipe, rather confusingly translated as a sparrow. Here are Lithic associations and misassociations aplenty. The sparrow was any small bird. The Spanish call all birds sparrows, pajaro; and on the other side of the Atlantic ocean parrots may have been just birds rather than parrots particularly, the name vouchsafed on challenge to show they knew a bird from a bowl of porridge. It makes better sense than their being named from pierots because of their clowning as Eric Partridge suggests, or from a parish curate as Bloch and von Wartberg suggest[12]. A pierot was certainly a clown, but what was it about a curate which suggested a parrot? Copying his rector parrot fashion? Moreover if they were named pierots why are they called parrots? In that case they would surely be pierots. Also there are no pierots in South America, but there also birds were indeed supposed to be blessed with sky hooks, with pai-a-rao-tai, surfaces/wings that drawn up-become. A parrokeet would then become a small screeching parrot, as indeed it is, screeching as it flies. A macaw appears to be named for its caw, 'm-a-caw, him that caws, from a Bantu dialect with the Hamitic m' for him, transferred by the Portuguese to central America where it became associated with the macaw tree in which macaws were to be found congregating eating the fruit, the tree in Tupi being named maca-uba, the macaw tree. Uba is tree in Tupi, from the Lithic completive element u- and –ba for burgeon. Trees are superlative burgeons compared with the rest of the vegetable kingdom, the undergrowth. That provides some slight confirmation parrot just meant a bird since the Portuguese were able to name the macaws in the land of the parrots, borrowing from Africa.

Mountains are high, often with a series of peaks on the skyline, in Spanish sierra, up and return, serrations of the skyline. Latin serra was a saw, and here we have sai, movement (34) and rai-ra, its reverse, as well as again and again like the serrations of a saw (from sa-u, ups-all, all the ups, which trace out an up and down series of peaks and troughs. So back and forth and up and down both appear. It led directly to the serrations on a postage stamp. Sere in English – "with ivy never sere" for John Milton – is parched and dried out, from sai-rai, sun rayed or fire-rayed, scorched even, like a deciduous tree in winter, but ivy is an evergreen. Scorch in turn has an initial s- and the –ch was originally a k, with the Lithic elements ish-ka-u-rai-kai, the ishka- is the effect of the flame, viz to burn, but in this case uraikai, one-ray-made, a burn from radiant heat as opposed to the flame. The redundant repetition of the ka element, at first suggesting the flame made the ray and the ray then made the scorch, is rendered needlessly complicated because we approach the analysis with preconceptions about parts of speech. Ishka, firemake, can be an action or a substantive state of affairs or both at once if necessary. The fire (or other heat source) makes the ray and the ray makes the scorch, as science now confirms. The grammar discloses a prior pairing of ishka and raka and their use together which effectively transposes the ka's as common elements to a joint function qualifying the fire and the ray as a one-off. You would not get away with it today if you were to propose any such arrangement; but Stone Age fuzzy logic could fudge a lot better than that without blinking an eyelid. You had those two pairs already, both with the same second element, and when you wanted a fire ray you were in no way disturbed to find the structure of the next bit needed was already prefigured. This was not thinking in strict linear fashion as we know it; but then it was not writing, it was a first lisping step towards compiling a protocol for speaking. In the mind the two pairings were viewed one behind the other in immediate succession when the common contribution of the two suffixed elements was obvious. Now it makes a nice exercise in rethinking the way our forebears thought at the outset.

Parched by contrast had none of these signatures. It was straightforward: pa-rai-kai, a piece of any sort made rayed and so dried out, with no mention of the sibilant Dried is from dry, Lithic te-rai, which is easy in Malay; and tai-rai in Egyptian, become-rayed. Rays could dry – from the sun or the flame – or be a pull – originally from the rays supposedly emitted by the female genitalia, whereupon the males responded with their own attractant (chapter 6) – such as we see in the English chest of drawers, Lithic terau, or as in Egyptian Natura (conventionally transliterated neter), which meant showing the pulls or [natural] forces, whence nature in English, from Lithic na-tau-rai, showing the tau ray. The drawers are only gulled from the genitalia, they slide in and out under hand control. The ones you wear you do pull up, while a sarong, a brightly coloured cloth like the brightly coloured budgerigar, you wind around your waist. It is just that pulling out (or up) was a function of the sex rays of the Stone Age, and the function is still around after hundreds of thousands of years, long after the original sexual imagery has wasted away with only a subconscious trace capable of keeping the derived mean-ings going generation after generation.

A snout, sai-nau-tai, looks like an up-presented one-of nature. It ends with a plain –t which is generally an end product from tai, to te or ti, to t, which can be shown to follow one another from sequential slurrings over the millennia. In India when the soda water is being poured into the whisky the cry is bas, pro-nounced like the English omnibus precisely. The water has ba-sai, gone to the height (required). Bas means enough! Or else, with a Chinese ba it means block or negative the rising. Perhaps stop in English is out of the same stable, since sta-u-pai, stand-where-surfaced fits quite nicely pouring water into a drink. But pai is more likely to be footed, and the whole is stay where your feet are, or stand where you have gone, ie cease to advance: although pai always carries traces of skins, and so tent roofs, other roofs and surfaces, and lids as well as petals and plant shoots and pipes and penises. Lithic will sometimes remind the reader of a dogs' dinner; but that after all is the human mind. The soda itself in the water is more difficult. Medieval Latin had sodanum, a headache cure, apparently from soda a headache which may in turn have come from Arabic suda, a splitting headache, with sada meaning to split. Sada makes sense as the sense (sa, 20) of splitting (ta) in Lithic, since sa is one and da from ta, at psychosemantic base, is breaking (or splitting) in two. However it is some way from a split to a headache, which might as well be a scorching head, the sada, Lithic sa-da, giving birth to the burning (3) sensation (20). Sodium, which is the chemical name of the metalic element comes from the earlier soda. Sodium bursts into flame when removed from under water, sa-u-dai-u'm, fire-what-born-of water'neuter ending. But this is a relatively recent concoction from the earlier soda, coined an aeon before sodium was discovered. The relation to the metal is from sodium carbonate, an old headache cure. Sau or su could indicate the completive term of sai, nicely warmed (18) from the hearth (11), and so comfortable or even pleasurable, like the termination of a headache. Sodanum was a pain reliever. The headache cure sodanum is after all more likely to have been phrased to pick up the easement of the affliction, than to record the pain suffered with the headache.

To soar is to sa-u-arai, activity(26)-which-arising, to sail up (10), on thermal air currents in fact. The sailing, sai-lai, itself is a maritime activity (26), maritime because lai is the instinct of waters to run down to the sea, so that when lau it is the ocean. But a sore throat is a sensation (20), in this case a painful one. It hurts. Typically the sensation may be positive or negative, probably starting positive and then inheriting its opposite along with a neutrality, generalised to a sensation of either kind. Sai starts at ease, even pleasing, from being nicely warm around the welcoming hearth and progresses to pleasurable and, in the superlative case (su) delightfully sweet like sugar which tastes delicious and negatives bitter tastes in turn just like honey in Latin, mellis, masking the lye. Lithic mai-lai does not have the words masking or lye but only the semantic contents we have in those words in English. Sheer, without any change of spelling in this case, can mean straight up (10), and since it is cliffs and declivities which have this appearance the up can be confused with the straight down; and it can also mean translucent from shiney (12) and bright (21). To surge is to rise up. The Lithic elements are clearly su-rai-gai, up-raised-go, closely akin to the later Latin surregere whence it probably comes. Resurgence and insurgence are out of the same tub. The Latin regere to rule from which these other Latin verbs are compounded introduces a semantic element hardly germane, but its core meaning was merely to go straight and thence after a great deal of constructive thinking to guide (keeping folk on the straight and narrow?), and so to rule – the ruler's own perception of his role of providing wise and straightforward guidance. The Lithic psychosemantic content rai-kai, is just make a ray or make like a ray – a ray is a straight beam. A ray of sunlight, in reality a reflection of incident light on motes in the air, is an appearance of a straight line visible in nature to add to the only real one, the skyline at sea. All the rest is fancy, and here the fancy is peculiar to the thinking which has gone into the Latin language.

With sheer (10) we can group steep (Lithic ish-tai-pai, vertical-become-surface) and scarp (Lithic ish-ka-rai-pai, vertical-made/shaped-surface); and after some further thought the Latin castrum which means a camp or fortified enclosure, in England a Roman cantonment originally fortified, some cities still with bits of their Roman walls still standing after seventeen hundred years, none in very good condition but a credit nevertheless to the Roman "brick", a curious conglomerate which would not pass muster today with the bureaucratic inspectors thrown up by government. The original fortified place made use of a natural hump. The Lithic elements are ka-sai-terau'm, which are readily legible as land or place-up-drawn'm. The 'm appears to be just a primitive (Lithic?) substantive. In Africa you find it in front of nouns, where it has the semantic force of him but without the ungrammaticality which is often taken to go with it in translations into English. There is nothing irrational about its use. The meaning of –terau- is illustrated frequently in Ancient Egyptian where ray theory was well established, so much so that The Egyptian Rays have provided me a significant entree to Lithic thinking. The ta-rays were from the ta or feminine birth canal, which were supposed to act at a distance and pull out and up the male organ. Any resultant orgiastic behaviour was of course for the Egyptian patriarch all the girls' fault because of their inflamatory proclivity. Stone Age ladies were all taken to be whores. They needed meat, after all, and could not hunt with infants hanging off them. A castrum made use of a quite generalised sense of this remarkable facility, which had burgeoned into a pattern to be found everywhere, as the human mind built by metaphor on its favourite fundamental underpinnings. Sai-ta-rau meant raised up beyond a peradventure. Ka, chapter 5, originally the chink of flint on flint, included the semantic contents hard and the hard part of the world, the solid ground (rock if you dug), and then particular locations on the ground in its tree of meanings, a place, an acre, a land, an island. The Roman castrum was an artificially raised defence. You dug a ditch and threw the earth inwards making a glacis, in which you stuck posts, tree trunks, to make a wall. Wherever possible it made use of a naturally defensible position such as a natural mound or a loop in a river. Sheer, however has other revelations. It can also mean so fine that the light shines through a fabric so you can see through it. This is from shine (12) and ray, which for the Egyptians again had the meaning of see. Ra, the sun, was the great eye in the sky observing its creation, with our individual lesser eyes emitting their lesser rays enabling us to see. There is more. Earlier sheer meant bright or shining too. Shine and sheen have an –n from nai (chapter 12) meaning showing. Old Norse skirr meant bright, and the Norse speakers invaded with their bright-making-rays. What is bright is also clear to see. What is clear to see is obvious. What is obvious is absolutely obvious, and thence absolute. Sheer stupidity is absolutely stupid. At sea ships sheer off when collision threatens, and, less well known, the sheer of a deck or bulwark is its upwards sweep. Sheering off has action (34), direction (16), and a ray which goes there and back and therefore bends around. But with all these sh terms it is sometimes hard to avoid believing that there is in there a k, via c, which has got slovened to a soft c and then engulfed in the preceding sh- or s-. Shears or sheer legs lift heavy loads. They are lifters or uppers. A bedsheet is not sheer but it is of the same texture, namely a fine weave, and its thinness

transfers to paper, metal, glass, etc, and even to rain when it falls in a continuous
sheet rather than in individual drops. Sheep shearing has lost a ka for cutting, as
has the plough share which cuts a furrow and turns it over. And ka for cut appears
in a score cut in a wooden tally or scores written as a tally, a shard (a bit of broken
pot) and even an apportioned share which is divided up if not exactly cut, and a
shore marking a boundary between land and sea. Eric Partridge adds in short and
curt, both cut to size, sharp and shred, and even cortex and cuirass, remarking:
"behind all these words lies the idea to divide or separate by cutting". Lithic adds
to that "just as the first flint knappers struck flakes from a flint with a clink which
struck them as sounding like ka".

To jam on anything is to stamp on it, an up down motion from the Lithic sha
(10) and ma. A mash or mush is the same as a jam in the reverse order. To smash
anything is an action (35) originally up and down, a good pounding, but by generalisation any action with the same effect like throwing a glass into the hearth or
a plate across the room, or hammering a china vase. A hammer has a cockney h,
and is named for the heavy downward motion in use, i-a-ma-are, it-that-strikes
down-verbal. Or else the ha- is a memento of a painful blow which glanced off
its target and smote the carpenter's thumb? With the taming of fire, cooking
was discovered, tenderising the meat and making it more palatable, which previously had been done by the repetitive pounding, kau-ka, of the raw meat with the
handy stone tenderisers conventionally called hand axes. The repetitive strokes,
like the flint knapper's, kaka, gave us cooking, the new technology with the same
effect. The flint knapper's repetitive strokes, kaka, also gave us the debitage of
waste flakes which accumulated around him as he worked, and from this idea of
shed waste came human waste, cacca in several languages. Surgery meanwhile is
transmogrified (s- for sh- for kh-) from the earlier Greek kheirourgeia or hand
work, from the Lithic khai-a-au-rau-kai-a where the hand is named as the maker
(khai-a) and the work is 'all that what is makery' in Greek as in English. It looks
as if the ancients proceeded to surgery when massage failed. Both were physical
interventions rather than juju. The hand in English ha'n-da, apparently 'does the
pleasuring'. Were our forebears connoisseurs of foreplay, or is the h- relict of kh-
and our hands utilities for doing things merely, like the Greek ones? It is simplest
to think so, but the oldest word for finger is tik, a tickler or kittler, where tai-kai,
kindling the ta, smacks of foreplay. Doubtless the finger was used for pointing
things out also, which is why we tick a correct answer and in Hindi tikh actually
means correct.

The spine is the vertical piece. In Latin spina was first a thorn, a sharp piece,
protruding rather than vertical. Lithic allows for frequent polysemy by analogy.
A spine of hills may run sideways but it is a raised ridge. A spike, like the thorn
is sharp and in origin was knocked into the ground and stood upright. It was

vertical and sharp together. Now it is any polar piece sharpened at one end like the handspike gunners used to use to swing the trail of a light field gun. A stick, like a spike, was pointed, since you could stick it into a body. Indeed the Old English stician meant to pierce, not unlike the Old Persian tigra and the Sanskrit tigmas, pointed. The older Avestan tighra meant pointed and tighri an arrow Eric Partridge has them both from a root ti or tei meaning to pierce. Admittedly he has stripped away half the Lithic phonemes which spell out the meaning in order to get down to an original random and meaningless root just conventionally adopted without thinking, which was the favoured procedure before Lithic analysis. Ti-kara can be read in Lithic phonemes hole-make, viz to pierce. Ka covered both making – as when the flint knapper made a hand axe – and kindling as when his knapping made sparks. Tikh for finger was not a piercer so perhaps it was an orifice kindler. Or else it could have come later from the generalisation from pointed to the verbal form to point, making the finger a pointer rather than a piercer or a tickler. The Latin instigare meant to stick a stick into someone and so to goad or incite, instigate an action; or get your donkey to pull harder.

Stiff and Latin stipes, a post, are from virtually the same phonemes in Lithic, sai-tai-pai (or phai), up-become-piece (or phallus). Lithuanian, a conservative tongue close to Sanskrit, has stiprus, firm, si-tai-pai-rau(s), up-become-piece-raised/roused. Which piece provided the original motif is not too hard to guess. It was the male organ. Firm starts off phai-rai'm, it is from the Latin firma, phai-rai-ma, (as) phallus-rayed/[when] raised – for planting – and so firm, much as with Latin amare to love, a-ma-re, as planting, or impregnating, in origin just a physical action not a state of mind, unless you read the a in amare to love as "as when" rather than just "when" planting seed. Eric Partridge describes the Latin stipes as a round stake stuck in the ground, a stock, a post, without attributijg any semantic content to the s-. Post in turn is from pa-u-sai-tai, a piece-that-vertical/sharp-become. Partridge's stock is from the Lithic sai-tau-kai, with sai-tau meaning up-become, viz upright, and the kai made. It made a stockade of upright posts dug into the ground. The stocks secured head and hands in upright posts, or a single one with a hinged crosspiece with three holes in it.

A stop is an event, often an action (34), and is from the Old English stopian to close an apperture or a gap, the idea we would convey today with to stop up, rather than to come to a halt as used now on roads across Europe. Latin stuppa is tow, stuffing, later a stopper or cork. With stop the s- indicates action (34) the signature of life forms which share heat with the flame, and the -tau-pai is a –hole-bung, a tamp, tamper, tampion or tampon, just as a tap started out but has diverged to emphasise its ability to be turned on and off. When the tap is turned off the flow is stopped. From the blocking of movement of the other comes the blocking of one's own movement, as an intransitive verb, the object of the stoppage abandoned or turned in on itself. For the French to stop is to stop oneself, a relict of the stopping or stuffing which needed an object. With stand the s-ta'n dai is vertical-becoming-does, an active verb.

Examples of the vertical (up, 10) semantic content for the sibilant because the flame springs upwards begin to become repetitious and tedious even for the born again linguist. Some might perhaps be listed for readers to try to analyse in Lithic elements for themselves. A spire is easy after a spine. Any reasonably short words from a dictionary should suffice. But to sink is to go down rather than up. The pattern here is nevertheless recoverable. Ka is the sound of the knapper's strike. If ish is up, ka is down. After all ka is the sound of a sharp and intentional downward stroke, a forceful and impressive blow. You can consign sink's initial to movement (35) merely, making it the action of striking (flint on flint) which is downwards; but the real semantic composition is probably the chopping off of the levitation. Sinking was a loss of flotation rather than an active seeking of descent. A jig, a jink or a jog illustrates the same pairing of elements; an up down would serve, but short interrupted rises is better. The pattern is repeated in jig-jig, a specialist term used by the Bombay pimp with little or no English when plying his trade in Grant Road, sixty years ago keeping the medical officers in British regiments busy. "Jig-jig Sahib?" is politely translated "Would you care for an up-go-up-go job, Sir?" The psychosemantic content is clearly for repetitive thrusts. It is quite doubtful the pimps had any Lithic theory in their conscious minds nor the medical officers either, but nevertheless there was an undeniable immediate meeting of minds. Curiously jijian is Chinese for sodomy, the very same movements this time round the back. Shanghai, the Chinese port city, in Lithic elements is 'above-the waters', the Walmington-on-Sea of the Orient, though without any Captain Mainwaring to lend it tone.

The hearth (11) is a word which is an unusual construct. It is essentially where a fire is kept alight. A clue to its derivation comes from the Gothic hauri meaning coal, with a cockney h and Lithic elements ia-u-rai, it that-one-raying, ie glowing. Coal glows red when alight. Now a hearth also glows on the floor of the fire where the red hot embers are the hottest part, plenty warm enough even when dying down to cook potatoes in the ashes. Red hot ash behaves like coal. It glows. The Latin carbo for coal looks as if it may have first meant glowing charcoals, kara-bau, deeply burning wood in the hearth at the bottom of the bonfire, and then was extended to cover the natural 'charcoal' when it was found in coal strata. Both produce burning ash and look the same once well alight. Stone Age man went by appearances. Glowing ash and glowing coal were both the same. The hearth's cockney h is moot, and so are the Lithic elements i-ai-rai-tai, it-that which-the rays-are born/become/come from. It might have originally been hot-that-etc. The glow is revealed; the combustion, the flame, is over. The hearth does not mention the flame, but it was the site of the family fire for much longer than the whole of recorded history, perhaps fifty times as long. We live in its shadow.

The sibilant as shine (12), whether the flame's flickering glow or the sun's bright rays, shows in the English shine and sheen, star and mist, Australia and Austria – both Eastern lands – from the fact that the East is where the fiery one (the sun) is born each day and rises above the horizon, the skyline at sea. A stone (13), Lithic ish-tau'n, is fire-born-one, from the volcanoes which were observed by our primitive forebears; and the lava was seen to harden into rock. Volcanic activity was widespread when we were learning to speak due to repeated asteroid strikes, or even after just one biggy. Who knows? Stone is static of course, and we have our standing stones at Stonehenge, where the –henge is supposed to share the root of hanging, referring to the capstones. Nobody has convincingly disclosed how they got up there. Probably sloping earth banks were built, the stones dragged up, displaying the high tech of the day, namely twisting fibre to make rope and the massing of manpower possible from the population increases following from farming; and then the earth ramps were dispersed again. It was an apotheosis of co-operative action following religious community, recognised with the usual mix of human sluggishness and solemnity. It was significantly the very same technology used building the pyramids, encouraging the view, attested on independent linguistic grounds, that Britain was occupied by Mediterranean colonists speaking an Egyptian patois before the Celtic head hunters invaded in turn and ate up their predecessors, retaining only some Egyptian place names attached to the terrain. Pyramis in Greek and pmr in Egypt where the pyramids are mostly to be found are from the Lithic phonemic elements pai-mai-rai, viz surfaced-earthen-raised – the Greek has a revised order. If you were playing a verbal dumb crambo, as original speakers were, what is earth (rock), raised, and covered with a layer of carefully trimmed stone, filling in the steps in the structure and producing a smooth surface. These slabs have since been largely removed so that the popular perception of a pyramid is with giant steps. We have a purely mechanical description of these astounding artifacts. The language offers no indication why they were built. There is by now plenty of evidence they had highly important religious and cosmological significance, but it would be wrong to suggest this nut has as yet been properly cracked.

The vertical (14) is merely the substantiation of up as a direction or action. The Malay seluar, trousers, are up sliders, just as trousers are drawn ups. The ash, as already mentioned, is a tall (15) tree, its habit being to extend a single branchless trunk to penetrate the forest canopy. The same applies to the Latin silva, a whole wood of tall trees, vertical long ones that have struggled up through the competition, drawn to the sunlight. The u (then v) may suggest the lai are dual: not only long but also at the same time a loop or group of them, making a wood. The sa-

vannah, a treeless plain, from Spanish zabanna, is originally from the native West
Indian Taino tongue zabana, tall-burgeons-none (15), treeless precisely. A savage
is a jungle dweller, supposedly untamed and cruel, slurred in the Romance languages from the original Latin silua-ticus, forest-dweller. Tai-kau is made born
or given birth in Lithic. The tai, born, can of course be read as living or become
or even just being; and all from the original ta, the sound of a snapped branch,
two-ing, partition, the slit dividing the two bilateral halves of the human body, the
birth canal, birth, becoming, and so on. Just stir in a few hundred thousand years
of ratiocination of a human kind with the subconscious sector of the human mind
recording it all in the dream world for each generation, and you have chapter six
before your very eyes.

In accordance with the usual Lithic linguistic pattern the vertical direction
becomes generalized, the direction abstracted without its original orientation.
The sewing motion is up and down through the materials being sewn together.
Sai-u is just both directions. Old English spelling seowian to sew hints at the
original vowelisation now slurred: sai-au-ia-'n, directions-dual-go-verbal marker.
Similarly the seed sown in the fields by hand was broadcast to right and left, but
there is a double entendre: the seed was being brought to life. Semen, the seed,
from sai-mai-'n, is a living form (sai) but dormant or better apparently regarded
as actually feigning death (mai'n), certainly inert and without the ability to come
to life and grow unless brought to life by being sown, put into the earth, that
magic element apparently cold and dead but harbouring the seed, propagating
life, gestating the plant and bringing it to life. A seam is what is sewn, and also
in a straight direction. A sow, on the other hand, the lady pig, Old English just
su, is super fertile, kitted out with maximal life (24) seen as an invisible adjunct.
While to cover another neighbouring root commencing with the sibilant, a sewer
or drain is from essever, in Medieval French, with the Lithic elements ai-sai-awa,
going-high-water, or getting rid of high water, viz lowering the water level, which
is what drainage is about. Eric Partridge, without benefit of Lithic and therefore
looking for water in a suppositional Latin root, offers a guessed Latin *exaquare,
to take water out of, to empty of water. Sewage in origin includes Evian spring
water, and indeed excluded waste which was not drained away but deposited in a
hole or in a stream, or in the fields for fertilizing the crops. A side was first a surface, from Old Norse sitha, from the Lithic elements sai-ta, the directions two or
two dimensions (up-down and sideways) which define a surface. The Tau or T is
one of the oldest symbols in the human mental cornucopia, indicative of the first
two spatial dimensions, or indeed of the space and time dimensions; and there is
no need to be shy of finding such thinking around and forming symbols even at
the dawn of speaking.

But before abandoning the restricted meaning of up (10) there is a further derivative semantic content to be uncovered from it. Long before any idea of writing a script had dawned upon our forebears they found scratched marks could be made on wood or stone. A single relatively straight scratch suggested just that: singularity. Two scratched side by side suggested two; and as the mind built on that, repetitive scratches came to suggest increasing divisions or numbers, showing an amount (which is actually what number means, Lithic na-em-bara, presenting, exhibiting-of-bigness, while the Latin, numerus says the same, nau-mai-rau-us, presentation-of mass-raisedness-substantive marker. It may be timely to compare ramai in Malay which means crowded, from rai-mai, raised-amount, with orang ramai the public. Orang is persons (from thinkers – thoughts were supposed to enter the head as rays): different phonemes but counting vertical lines just as Malay counts them with sa, a single upright). Sa, an upright, is one in Malay, aphetic for satu, an upright cut/carved /scratched. The Chinese for one is su, it is the inclusive unity, with su also meaning all. Perhaps this is where the –s for plural comes from ultimately – not from Chinese of course but from a Lithic semantic content shared with the Chinese subconscious. English also has single, sai-'n-ge-lai, one-ge-linked, inclusive one, as well as same and similar. Same is from sa-mai, a single amount, while similar is from sai-mai-lai-a, same-linked-one, one like the same, similar. A sum must be originally an additional total from adding up. If you think in terms of adding by putting one amount on top of the other, as we do when we think in terms of adding up, and as most folk confronted with a column of figures will start at the bottom and arrive at a top or upmost amount when they have the total, it is the topmost total which represents the sum. We use sum for the process and the result. But now the Chinese have suan pan, totalisator board, for the abacus, originally with counters on a board rather than the modern device still in wide use in Eastern lands with beads free running on wires. The Chinese hand is shu, perhaps the totalisator of the digits or the shovers of the counters, and the Lithic for counters has slurred a lot. Old High German has scioban, ac-tion-make-going; while the Sanskrit is ksub for a push, Lithic kai-sai-bai, mak-ing-acting-going. Shove, shovel and shuffle and scuffle are all from the same root. Near sum in the dictionary is the sjambok, Afrikaans for a whip, which the Dutch copied from their Indonesian lands. The Dutch spelling is peculiar. It is cambok in Malay with a soft c, which they appear to have got by nasalisation from the Old Persian chabuk. The Lithic emerging is khai-em-bau-kai, striking-on-the dual burgeons-of the body, or in Old Persian kha-bau-kai, strike-dual bulges-of the body, a bum striker or whip. More recent whippings have generally been across the back avoiding the genitalia with the victim allowed his trousers on – unless he is under age of course! It certainly appears in origin the whipping was in the bare buff and aimed at the bottom as the best area to make a mess of. The cat o'nine tails had metal jags on each tail. Kati was the tapped feminine (fleshy) part of the body, the rump, which may have prompted the cat, otherwise inexplicable. You enjoyed a rump with nine trails of the tails. Or else the whip was recognized as a cutter, with or without tails.

Malay selampit offers simultaneous insights into Malay grammatical prefixes and their lexical semantics. It means a single long flat braid or plait. The Lithic obtrudes. Sai-la-em-pai-tai, a single-length-of-surface-become. It may not be perfect in English, but it is in Lithic. Berselampit is in English terminology be-braided, while in Malay terms it is ber-selampited, wearing a single skirt length "twisted between the thighs as a loin cloth". The definition is from Sir Richard Winstedt's trail-breaking and thoroughly erudite Malay Dictionary in two volumes of 1953, now in a class of its own, with much fascinating detail which native Malay speakers learn from too, all totally lacking from modern pocket dictionaries churned out for birds of passage, in predictably hurried passage, from the IMF and such like international advisory bodies. Winstedt was a professional Malay imperial civil servant whose devotion to the country of his employment shines through every page of his books. I never met him but I was fortunate to arrive in Malaya when his first edition had just hit the streets and I carried his two volumes in my back pack during the two years I lived mostly in the Malayan jungle sleeping under a piece of plastic tied between trees, worn during the day folded at the back of the belt – housed piggyback like the humble snail. The selampit is of course the aboriginal chawat in new guise, and no doubt with a finer and less see-through weave. It was the traditional and entirely suitable attire for those at hard labour in the heat.

Heat or warmth, sai (18) comes from the flame, ish. A sheep, with Lithic elements shai-pai, has had a warm covering or coat ever since the Pleistocene. This is a simple piece of Lithic analysis which can be quoted to doubters to consider. If it is countered the original forms actually had an initial sk- that just makes it a whole body warm coat. So far as Chambers and Partridge are concerned a sheep is a sheep is a sheep, no reason why offered. Partridge adds o.o.o. his short for of obscure origin. Lithic analysis clears up this obscurity once and for all. Chambers says no definite connections are known outside Germanic. However the ever nosey Partridge has found Egyptian sau, sa, sua, st (proper pronunciation sai-tau, in the happy state of become warmed) for sheep, which shows in Egypt too the sheep were well known for having rather cozy coats. Aestus, in Latin, is a burning heat, a-i-sh-tau, that-which-fire-born, viz heat. Our oast houses also were a-u-ish-tai, that-where-heat-applied to the wetted barley seed on the way to producing beer. Whisky is often recorded as fire water, and it is: Awa-ish-kai is water-fire-kindled, a water with a shot of the other ish element in it, a change of state resulting from the heat of distillation. Of course the native American description as fire water referred to its burning quality when swigged neat for instant effect. In Zululand to be on fire is sha, firewood is izinkuni and a firebrand isikhuni, Lithic i-sai-kau-nai, which-fire-kindled-shows. To fire or burn down is shisa, probably from the Lithic shai-sa, flaming-action (3,26) and hot is ashisayo, Lithic a-shai-sai-au, that-heated-fired-that one. Ancient Egyptian throws up sa for flame or fire, with sam to burn, to consume by fire, Lithic sa-mai, flame-consume. Samtau is a conflagration, a fire. Samu is incense, which gets consumed when burned for the scent given off. Tcha and Sa'n are fire drill sticks, flamers. In Hindi a cup of tea is cha, from the Chinese tcha, a hot drink and nothing to do with an Egyptian fire drill, except that both cases are gulled from the Lithic ish for fire. Tea is just our mispronunciation, resulting from incomprehension. Malay teh is also from the Chinese and not much better than the English. Juice in English was initially a hot drink too, and a savoury soup at that, and only later used for fruit juice; indeed it likely referred at the outset to the juices running out of the steak on the fire, Lithic djai-u-sai, issuing(7)-when-fired (3). The Sahara probably prays in aid the heat, Lithic sa-ha-rai, heat-horror-rayed/raised, a desert (also from the Egyptian: dsrt in this case, probably with the semantic content land-dried out-become, dai-sarai-tai).

Warmth, vouchsafed to sheep with their fiery pelts, was often missing amongst our early featherless biped forebears. They borrowed his coat out hunting, as well as for sleep, but the core facility for getting warm in cold weather was the hearth, classically at the entrance to the family cave, tended by the womenfolk and children while the braves were out hunting. The warmth of the hearth, as well as its security – it frightened animals off, and the smoke repelled biting insects – was the exemplar of ease (from sai), comfort, the pleasant sensation and pleasure. With full bellies from the cooked meat, attention will have turned to sexual concourse. Indeed the heat from the hearth will have triggered it. Animals are said to be in heat when sexually receptive, as if they had benefited from hearths too. The sense (20) comes from our experience living outdoors in the Pleistocene and then registering the changed sensation, even perhaps its recovery in the extremities, around the hearth. Sugar (19) can be added to sheep as a classic Lithic analysis. Lithic su-kara is pleasure-maker (19): su, an extreme sensation (around the hearth) being a pleasurable one, just as Arabic iskra (spark) and Old English chark (the fire drill) are fire-makers. Suave is a straight copy from the Latin, "sweet to taste and smell, gentle or soft to the touch, agreeable to the eye" as Partridge puts it. The older Sanskrit has suadus, sweet, suadma sweetness and suadati, he takes pleasure in or is pleased to. Like sugar is the Hindi thank you: shugria, [your action is] a sweetness-maker, a pleasing sugary one. The Malay equivalent suka means to like; it makes a feel good factor like the sugar. It can refer to your taste for marmalade or your desire to bed a pretty girl, or just conventional content: "Banyak suka hati sahaya, berjumpa lagi dengan inchek!", "Very sweet hearted I, bemeeting

again with mister!", in other words: "Very nice to see you again!" The sibilant can
certainly have a sexual connotation, as in sex (36), at a hazard from the Lithic
sai-ka-sai, action(34)-making-a pleasurable (19) sensation (20), or a life (24), or
both at once. In Malay sulbi means the loins, in English hips haunches and ham,
all three with the sudden sensational h-, hip perhaps the pleasuring pieces since
you work your hips when copulating, and ham, ha-mai, when impregnating; but
now of course almost entirely used for the smoked viand. Hai is in chapter 8. The
su- in the Malay sulbi can therefore be read as pleasure just as in sugar, and the
lai perhaps as linking, with bai referring to the ischeral protruberances (bum), or
the movement (going) of them, or just those bits of the body. In Latin jocus a joke
was anything enjoyable, for instance a pastime or sport. In Malay kaseh is love
– perhaps from kai-sai-hei, making-life-ecstacy, or even what sex makes. Anyway
in Ancient Egypt the God Amun was the ever loving, like Allah later, and the ma
syllable (see chapter 15) meant earth and so planting and so impregnating. The
Latin amare to love is as or when planting or impregnating. In English to marry
is taken to be a ceremonial matter, but the consummation is in the meaning, to
impregnate. The Malay jimah is (from the Arabic) coition, apparently from the
Lithic elements shai-ma(h)i, action-of impregnating. Kasi is to give or to cause
to happen, for instance kasi makan is to give food, and alternatively to cause to
rust because makan carries the meaning of eating as well as what is eaten and
rust eats metal. The sense of giving – without any price – makes for contentment,
and settles or eases any dispute over ownership by conceding, giving in. Give
is perhaps from kai-phai, making pleased (see chapter 7 on Fa), the pleasuring
originally provided by the genitalia.

So the warmth of the hearth was an agreeable sensation. Heat covers the full
range of sensations from comfort to acute pain. Sai came to represent that range,
namely sensation or sense (20). Latin sentire to become sensible or sensing, to
feel, has the past participle sensus, used for the substantive term sense, feeling or
what is felt. Feel is from the Lithic phei-lai, copulation-like. Just as the sensation
of warmth was taken as typifying physical sensation, so the sensation of the pahei,
in Egyptian the penis, was taken as the sensation of the life force, the source of
life. The physical is from the Greek phusis, Lithic pahai-u-sai, life force-what-ac-
tion, in this case growth. Aristotle described phusis as the nissus or natural drive
which exists in all life forms to expand and grow like the fruiting of the vegetable
world. His idea was really closer to biology than physics as we understand it,
which is more mechanical (and lifeless). To see (29), the visual sensation, which is
san in Egyptian, is the most important everyday sensation of all, and determines
much of our mental outlook. It is indeed regarded as in some ways more than just
another sensation in so far as it presents us with a mass of information already
processed in the mind as we become aware of it. So a sudden burning sensation

prompts recognition of extreme heat and immediate withdrawal action, never mind why; but the sight of the hot poker, cigarette end or retreating scorpion is fully informative, allowing understanding immediately to flood in. In the Stone Age we only saw properly when the sun was shining, which immediately explains why sun and shine have some of the same elements as see. Chinese shimang is to go blind. We can parse it in Lithic immediately: shai-mang, sense (visual)-marred or murdered or submerged. A sore is a (painful) sense-arising. Or the r may be a cockney r, with the Lithic really sau-a, a sensed-one. The Chinese is important. We can only attribute the same Lithic semantic contents as we have worked out mostly from the English lexicon if Lithic applies to Chinese as well as English. But that is one of the Lithic hypotheses.

The sense of bright (21) really belongs with shine (12) and sheen. The Australian aboriginal budgerigar, djeribal and didgeridoo where the -djeri- means bright, clear and loud respectively, has already been used to illustrate the diffuse semantic contents of single syllables in early language strings. We do not have any word of such generality and must therefore use djeri when thinking about this ancient language usage. A shrimp is related to the budgerigar, because the elements we can identify here for semantic analysis are shai-rai-em-pai, nothing to do with its small size, as might be imagined because this meaning of insignificant size is in fact gulled from it. When cooked the shrimp turns pink, just like other crustaceans. A shrimp was indicated to the Lithic mind as a bright-ray-of-the skin or surface, sh-rai-em-pai, much as the budgerigar was just a bright coloured bird, but in the case of the shrimp flame coloured, sh-rai when cooked, fire rayed in both senses, both cooked and coloured simultaneously. Then we can also relate the aboriginal dje, bright, to shima in Australia which means good, probably by way of a bright or clear thought. However in California, shi ma' in Navaho Indian means my mother. The ma' of course is mother. The my is probably from shai meaning of number one, that is of the speaker, me; while ushi in turn is the completive case of shi, my, and means our in Navaho.

A scone, sai-kau-nai in Lithic phonemes, fire made protruding or drawn up, from the rising of the dough to make the bap, rather curiously turns out to refer to the nature of the flour from which it is made when you would expect to find it referring to the method of cooking it. A clue is the Middle Dutch for scone: schonbrot, clear or bright bread. Scones were evidently made of white flour as a party piece when ordinary bread was generally brown, probably made of brown rye flour. Surprisingly it does not refer to the griddle on which it is baked. But perhaps it meant both simultaneously – a bit like three dimensional chess. Schon in German has many meanings. None follow the aboriginal djeri, but they have an even wider spread: fair, beautiful, fine (arts and words), splendid, a nice (mess), perfect (order), the fashionable (world), kind (regards). On second thoughts all those might conceivably have come in a chain of gulls from an original identification of a blaze, given a sufficient number of millennia. The Greek selas is light, brilliance, perhaps originally from sai-lai, burning-oil, but a glow rather than a blazing light since Selene was the moon, Lithic sai-lai-nai, brilliance-low-showing, showing a dim light. Or else the lai has its semantic content from its usage in the word light, which is from burning lye, as a marker to indicate it is the light of the flame which is relevant here and not any of the other thirty or forty derivative connotations. Indeed for Selene, the moon, the lai could mean circling, in orbit, or even wandering, the moon's course being comparatively irregular, moving around in the night sky with no easily recognized pattern. Refer to chapter 9.

Showing (22) is not so far away from shining (12) and bright (21). In Lithic terms they are one. A sign, sai-ge-nai, the sense-made-presented, is showing the way or more generally the meaning. The Latin for a sign is sema, showing the meaning, a mental indicator, which is a different gloss on the shima of the Australian aborigine or the Californian Navaho Indian above. This degree of diversity in the interpretation provides cover for Lithic, making it harder to crack – so it does not get noticed – and challenging belief. A semantic content is what the sign is indicating or showing. A symbol is a sign of an other to which it has been referred. A Semite is a descendant of the Biblical Shem, he who shares the patriarchy with Ham and Japheth. How these tribes acquired their names is at present quite opaque. It is tempting to hazard a guess at the Lithic semantic contents. Shem, shai-mai, might be bright (white) and bright minded. Ham is perhaps from Ha-mai, rejoicing in-impregnating, ha being already associated with the more immediate physical forms of sensation prompts for a similar sense of mai. If by any chance this is right then the Semitic race is claiming intellect and dismissing the African races as over sexed. It is a pattern which unfortunately whitey is apt to follow even today, in spite of it being clear by now that what determines character traits like these is the education, cultural as well as intellectual, which obtains; and the genetics of the race hardly counts at all. The fact is with widespread impoverished living standards, sex is the only readily available source of pleasure and religious inhibition is absent. The Lithic resonance with sexual motifs is evidence of this. Hundreds of thousands of years ago we were all as sexually active as the bonobo chimpanzees. The goy, meanwhile, is from the tribe of Japheth, a difficult one. Ia-pahei-tahei certainly evokes hedonism, initially by reference to the enjoyment of male and female sexuality, but so anciently it probably stood just for a simple pagan enjoyment of the good life in even the earliest Biblical times. Pagans were not plagued by ideology so much and were not banging their heads and prophesying punishment, nor handing it out personally meanwhile like the Old Testament folk, to judge them by their book. Paganism was a cheerful acknowledgment of the fundamental value of fertility, and sex was a propitiation of these powers.

The sun was anciently universally assumed to be a fire source, but a brahma one compared with terrestial hearths and even volcanos. The sun is the shiner (12), it shines, from Old English sunne, the sun, Lithic elements su-nai, where nai means precisely presenting or showing. The su- means all or any of the characters derivative from the sibilant's identification with the flame. Indeed the sun might have been the original identifier of all the sibilant's fiery characters – except the sun never hisses like the burning brand as it is extinguished. Anyway not yet. There is a very early record of the Avestan xveng for sun, pronounced roughly ksueng, with Lithic elements kai-su-en, the making-shining-one. This can be set beside the Sanskrit (and Malay) suria for sun, Lithic su-rai-a, shine-raying-one. Malay also has bintang suraya, the suraya star, namely the su-rai-a, ultimate-shining-one. With this can be put the country Syria from the Greek Suria. Su-rai-a can be read as light shining or rayed and rising (chapter 13). Syria is thus in origin the Sunrise or Eastern land for the Greeks. Compare Gomera, the island West of Tenerife, ga-u-mai-Ra, the land-where-dies-the sun, Sunset or Western Isle. Then there is in Old Persian shamash, up-down-up or shine-dark-shine, or life-death-life, with reference to Apollo's habit of A-pa-u-lau, Ever-go-one-looped, the orbital traveler, rising (10) and shining (12) and then setting, and then rising and shining again the next morning. The pattern nicely matches the semantics of the Central American (Aztec) tomato, Lithic tau-ma-tao, birth-gestate-birth, the variety which you plant annually from seed, in neat contradistinction to the potato, the variety of the same plant bred by the Aztecs for its edible tuber, pau-tau-tau, tuber-birth-birth. You plant the seed potatoes which give birth to new plants. If you irrigate potatoes as the flowers die back you will get a crop of small green tomatoes, unimproved and mildly poisonous. In Egypt, where they tended to have half a dozen different ways to describe anything of considerable interest, the sun, as God, was Ra, sending His rays throughout the whole world each day. Simultaneously She was for others Aataun (conventionally written Aton), the Eternal and Universal World Birth Canal, birthing light into all the world each day. But there was also Osiris, Greek for Egyptian Ausarai, Eternal Sunrise. He was born of Isis, Greek for Egyptian Ausiti, Eternal sunset, (since the sun after setting was supposed to gestate the new day while orbiting the underworld), and married to Her too, making more cosmological sense than domestic, since they then went on to give birth to Horus, I(h)-au-Rau (s), the sun's rays. You could say the day came from between the sunrise and sunset. In a curious primitive dialectical sense the day was the product of the two opposites it stood between. Horus was also a sun unit, and so the day, hour or year. The relationships are clearly metaphorical. Looking with hindsight at the thinking we must say could do better. In

China the sun is jih, the bright shiner. They favour single phonemic meanings there. In Japan they add a demonstrative ni-: the sun is nichi or nitsu.

As the flame springs upwards and never ceases flickering as if it were alive – compared to a stone – and as animals are warm, and so it appeared partaking in some degree of the element fire, and as they are also lively (they run about, just as the flame without benefit of any legs can race through the forest if it is well ablaze and fanned by a favourable wind. The idea of life can easily be gulled from the flame. The vegetable world is only vouchsafed movement – compared with a stone again – in growth, and that only when pulled up by the rays of the sun, a fiery source. So trees and plants get their share of the lively element from the outside; in themselves they are cold. But it follows that a gull from the flame is the active capacity. If you want to know if an animal is alive, poke it and see if it moves. If it is fierce use a long stick. So the same phoneme which started out as the sound of the dowsed burning brand is gulled one by one for all the semantic contents in the accompanying psychosemantic tree. The Basque for god is Jinko. He made Life: the Lithic is shai-en-kau, Life-of-Creation, The Creator. Senility is from senile from Latin senere to be old, to show living – as already experienced. Senescence, from the Latin senescere to grow old, is in turn from crescere to grow which in Lithic analysis is kai-rai-sai-ka-re, made-rayed-up-make-verbal marker. In these Lithic analyses the words used to translate the phonemic meanings can only approximate the Lithic thinking which in its own terms was a great deal slicker than the foreign wording suggests whilst at the same time, it has to be admitted, witnesses a fuzz in Stone Age mental processing from which we are still slowly extricating ourselves with unequal success. The Lithic analyses offered in English are hardly neat, but Lithic thinking nevertheless made perfect sense in its day, probably because what made sense in those days did not have to be very clear. Since hominid times we have been precising, but slowly.

Seed (24) is from the Lithic sai-dai, life-bearing (in the sense of birth). The Lithic elements of life, lai-phai, the length of the flesh, refer to its temporal length, while flesh, phai-lai-shai, is the flesh belonging to animal life forms as opposed to animal and vegetable tissue which are both ba. The Latin for seed is semen, sai-mai'n, life-gestating, like Shamash.

Moses and James and Thomas are brothers along with the Egyptian Pharaohs Tutmose and Rameses – there are others – their direct progenitors. The mose and mesi and masi bits are the Lithic elements ma and sai, to earth up or plant (ma) and procreate the seed, or life (sai). The Pharaoh Tutmose is claiming to be begotten by the god Thut, or Tahuti, or Tahu-tai, or Tau-tai, All-knowing and World-bearer. Archbishop Desmond Tutu (who doesn't know this) got his name from Tahuti too. Tahu-tai was an early creator god and supposedly the source of all knowledge, of the intellect and speech, as well as of the world, taun in

Egyptian. Rameses was reckoned to have had Ra, the Sun, plant his seed. James is Ia-mesi, really Iau-mesi, God the Jews call Jaweh or Jehovah planted the seed. In Latin James is Jacobus, Iau kindled the flesh. Thomas was a twin, from tau-mesi, a dual planting of the seed. The late Moshe Dayan, the Israeli general and archaeologist, has dropped the god's name and relies merely on having been pro-created, the seed planted, which must be conceded. He followed Moses in this, who may have been really a James. The hieroglyph for mesi in Egyptian is three fox tails tied together at the top, presumed to be for use as a fly swot in those olden days – no plastics then – with mai-si given the punning semantic content dead-tails and simultaneously suppressor-of life, fly-killing too, in order to make a memorable glyph. A swastika is another piece of linguistic history which goes back to the Sanskrit, when svasti meant well being. The su-a-sai-tai has the same su as in sugar, but here indicating a generally enjoyable condition, and the a-sai-tai is as-actually-becoming (27), well being precisely. That leaves the final ka in swastika. It stands here for the idea of making or kindling. As to the symbol, su is omnidirectional (16) derived from the up direction (10). The -a-sai-tai is then read as that-single-tau. The tau was a T. A single tau had only one side of the cross piece. The swastika is made of half Ts pointing in all four directions. This kind of semantic cats cradling is quite typical of primitive intellectual wrangling. The swastika was a magic symbol promising good fortune and as such it was a popular amulet, at one time to be used to ward off evil influences and promote the friendly forces in the imagined environment. Nazism knew none of this. For Hitler it was just an ancient Aryan sign he promoted as a claim to be standing for everything anciently Aryan. I am not sure even Sanskrit speakers really knew what they had got hold of, in so far as their symbolic significance seems to have been read over an earlier semantic content suggested by the actual shape of the symbol, which in itself offers no support to their phonetic interpretation in Sanskrit. At least there was a double entendre involved. The sign itself indicates an origin in some ways somewhat more mundane but in other ways more intellectual. Spin a swastika, with the clock or against it, and you see a circle, made of infinitesimal rotations of the arms as constituent vectors. This may sound far fetched but then consider the Greek for circle, kuklos: all the corners one after the other smoothed into a loop. Our circle is open to very similar treatment: kai-rai-kai-lai, cornered-rays (which are straight directions)-made-looped.

Salus, Latin for safety, is from the Lithic elements sai-lau, life-smoothed or perhaps at ease-at length, or both. The latter seems to be indicated with creosote a well known timber preservative which is from the Greek. The kreo is flesh (grown literally) and the sote is the past participle of sozein to preserve, to be sau, full of life. Compare Arabic salaam or Hebrew shalom, both greetings, generally trans-lated as Peace! Like Islam they come from the same Arabic verbal form aslama to submit. Or you may prefer direction-smooth – no nasty kinks in it – or spirit-calm, or all three of them together. The sow meanwhile, the mother pig, su in Old English, is full of life and proves her fertility with record litters.

From life it is a short intellectual step to alive life forms (25). We find si- as brer- (a preceding denominator for phenotypes, animal or reptilian) in numerous languages. In English we have snake from si-na-kai, brer-bare-bodied. The Hindi is nag, just the bare body without the brer. The snake is bare of limbs of course as well as without a coat. The colour sepia is the colour of the secretion the fleeing cuttlefish (sepia in Spanish) ejects when pursued by predators. The Spanish fishermen named the cuttlefish Sepia, brer pisser. Cuttle in turn is from Old English codele, akin to Old English cod and Middle Dutch codde for testicle. The Lithic appears to be ka-u-dai, the Ka (or oomph) what does. Hollanders appear to have spotted at an early date removal of the cod led to reduced libido in both animals and men. The cod really referred to the scrotum rather than its contents since cod had the general meaning of a pod or bag, but castration of animals was originally done by the farmer and of men by the victor. In both cases it is to be supposed they cut off the scrotum and contents in one. Indeed you were probably lucky in the case of the male genitalia where the whole tackle makes a handy handful if they did not take your penis at the same time. Certainly, when Egyptian armies won, their cheery soldiers collected phalluses from the wounded and slain on the battlefield as evidence of their win, without which count the Pharaoh might prove disbelieving. Anyway so far as the cuttle fish is concerned his smoke screen tactic appears to have been taken by English speaking sailors as an ejaculation rather than the urination the Spanish favoured. The colour however suggests neither of these but a specialized secretion. Both the languages have been built on the nautical whimsies of the jolly jack tar. In Malaya a snail is siput, brer puti or penis teat, with a glans shaped house on its back. The similarity, it must be said, is only slight, but the usage is confirmed by other Malay examples. Seladang is the wild ox and ladang means clearing or meadow. Siamang is the siamang ape with long arms it uses to swing from branch to branch with an astonishing facility: brer weightless. Si pelandok is brer mouse deer, the brer rabbit of Malay folk law, dainty sly and secretive and no bigger than a prize rabbit but with two needle sharp extended incisors with which he will wickedly slash if trapped. It earns him a whack on the head with a long stick. The pe- is in most cases little more than a substantive preposition in Malay, but here it may refer to his feet. Landok has the semantic content of sly doer, and he treads lightly and leaves few tracks. Siapa, from si-apa, is brer-what? and so who?

The active species above has then been gulled for activity. To slough is the action (25), sai, of letting slide down or lowering (lau), shedding (a skin). The slough of despond is a somewhat similar let down. To slough in Malay is salumba, a sloughing from the flesh. Selulup is a plunge (into water), and berselulup is to be adoing it. Plunge in English is akin to the plumb line with which a weight (plumbum, the heaviest known metal, lead in Latin) is lowered into water to discover its depth. Lead appears to be named after this facility, lai-a-dai, lowering-that-does (because of its weight), and a plumb pa-lau-mai-bai is a piece-lowered-down-going. Hang it over the side and down it goes until it reaches the bottom. Slough is not far from slow: Lithic action-lowered, in place of one of lowering. The Egyptian god Set, enemy of Osiris, is a mistranslation based on the Egyptologists' alphabetic values for Egyptian glyphs – in reality only used latterly for foreign names, etc, which were what enabled the code to be cracked – glyphs intended to be read as syllabic. The letters s-t, transliterated Set, were originally Sai-taun, the action-(of the) world. Hindi has Shaitan, English Satan. It rather looks as if Satan, the root of all evil, is really to be found in the ways of the world, placing it firmly at the door of humanity. Sleep, sa-lai-pai, is a state of lowered livelihood and activity with the eyes lidded. It puts the lid on activity. The Latin is sopire to sleep, liveliness-lowered-verbaliser, whence we get our soporific for which no understanding of how we get it is needed; nevertheless it specifically and quite clearly puts the lid, pai, on activity, sau. But then we are in difficulties because at the very same time sleep is a case of easement too. You can hardly be more at ease than when you are asleep, nightmares excluded. That is the subconscious for you, meanings overlapping. It is not a linear mental capacity, but more a source of arisings from a whole three dimensional texture of memories and promptings, some immediate and strong while others, like a papier-mâché, are leftovers from bits and pieces which have happened to jell because of various quite oblique psychosemantic appeals over millennia, but passed on generation to generation in the linguistic heritage learned by every child. We do not inherit ideas, which are an activity of the brain, any more than we inherit the walks we may take or the races we may run, the activity of our legs, even though the legs, like the brain, are a genetic inheritance. I suspect this is where Noam Chomsky has got it wrong; and certainly the MIT (Massachusetts Institute of Technology) school of cognitive psychology appear to have allowed Darwinian evolutionary theory to take over their minds to the exclusion of common sense.

The sea has nothing to do with the flame, on the contrary in the real world they do not mix. But of all the waters in the world the sea is the one which is always in movement (26). Rivers have white water too, but that is because they are on their way to the sea, sai-a, the active one, or perhaps elided over the millennia from sai-awa, active water, that is to say with waves which come ashore, some modest part of the active spirit of the flame imparted to them. That is Lithic thinking, not mine.

Activeness leads into actuality (27). It is these mini leaps of the human mind, like the jump from the shown, the seen and the active (all gulled from the flame) to the actuality, which spring to mind without recourse to any reasoning, which go to make up not only our common sense but also, almost unbelievably, our finest thinking, our mathematics, philosophy and science. It can be argued that Einstein abandoned reason for a deeper subconscious intuition informed by the prehistoric Tau, a T- shaped reality, just as Karl Marx derived his atavistic dialectical materialism (OK, via Hegel) rather less prettily from the vowel oon of the ancients (a spawns i and then they are followed by the rejoinder u–, counting one, two, both of them, in place of one, two, three) once they had shucked off (risen above) conventional thinking. See chapter 16 on thinking. Many of the initial s- which Eric Partridge has identified as "the general intensive prefix" are just about that, indicating actualities as opposed to abstractions. Latin combuere to burn has past participle combustus from which we get our combustion, which it is tempting to treat as s-tau, become burnt, but in fact it is of course indicative of the past tense merely, actually-become. To sit, Latin sedere, and our seat etc, are to settle oneself comfortably (sai, 19), including to squat around the hearth at ease long before chairs were invented. They are gulled from the easement from the warmth of the hearth which is from the Lithic phonemes hai-are-ta(-he)i, hot or enjoyably-rayed-becoming(aroused). So it turns out a chair, shai-are, which renders you at ease, is just an easement like the hearth. Isis, the Greek for Ai or Au-Siti in the original Egyptian, the world sunset but also Our Lady – the Virgin Mary in Malay – and the setting of the sun or just a seat at the same time. Her hieroglyph is an upright chair or throne. But the original seat was squatting around the hearth. Siti is lady from sai-tai, life form-tapped, that is feminine, with a birth canal, whence life-source. The boys by contrast have bung ends to their urethras, making childbearing out of the question. The Celtic bwoid for the penis, from the Lithic phonemes bau-ai-dai, bunged-that which-of the birth canal, is a bunged urethra, the male's pride and joy spelt out as a blockage preventing the prime propensity of giving birth. That is what a boy is, he is the one with the bung end, a fatal constriction – made just for fun and games, bless him! In prehistory the girls dictated thinking for hundreds of thousands of years before the male riposte developed. Was there a mothers' lib so far back in time it has been forgotten? Progress is a jagged edged process. But perhaps around the hearth there were some scraped hollows to accommodate the rumps of those seeking ease, such as jungle dwellers scrape for their hips to sleep; and even some dried grasses to soften the contours of the earth. Baitna is the Hindi for to sit. Baito is the imperative: sit! It is perfectly polite: please be seated. It has the semantic content let your haunches be parted, or bums apart gentlemen please. Our English bottoms are our two haunches (bau) with the cleavage (tau) between.

In Lithic terms activity and action (34) are virtually the same. Indeed what precisely is the difference in the current English scansions of these two words? Not much. Action concentrates upon the acting, whereas activity in turn concentrates upon the action. Their functional uses are different. You might well call for action, with some particular action in mind. But you would be unlikely to call for activity – in place of torpor? If you did you would likely be asked what activity you had in mind. Anyway it is not hard to pick up some examples of Lithic where the sibilant is used for action. Malay is perhaps the closest to the primal language (Adam speak?). Selah is the bolt of a door, with an uncanny resemblance to slide. Doors bolted against an enemy had massive beams slid in huge brackets. That is no doubt why bolt starts with a bau. It was a substantial burgeon in its own right. In Malaya selah secured light bamboo edifices. The bamboo as a tree boasts many single branches or "bam", like the banana, but they are hollow and lightweight. More general action is found in sound, from sau-un-da, activity-what or whendoes. Sounds generally are the result of movement, perhaps in the surrounding bushes with the stealthy approach of the sabre-toothed tiger on the lookout for a meal. If this seems improbable consider noise, na-ui-sai, show-what is-moving. Slow is lowered action or movement. The German langsam (slow) has the same phonemes reordered. The sepoy or soldier, sipahi in Hindi, is a foot soldier who acts on foot. It is hard to avoid reverting to Malay. Sayat is to cut off bits, sai-a-tai, action-which-cuts or separates, and at the same time what turns one (sa) into two. Which bits is not specified, but it is used of cutting the umbilical cord and also, in a Muslim country, for cutting off the foreskin, circumcision – from cutting around (the glans). The Latin caedere to cut is from the Lithic kai-da-ere, to do the flint knapper's original chopping action from which kai is gulled. In parentheses, ducere to lead, in reverse order is to pull or draw out and so to lead, from Lithic tau-kare, to make with the tau, the feminine pudenda, which in Ancient Egyptian at least was supposed to send out an attractant ray, like the sunbeams which pulled up the crops on raying back on their return journey to the sun. These inferior rays just pulled out and up the boys squatting opposite around the hearth. Al Caeda, the Arabic leadership, has the cutting order but the ducal meaning. We are here right next door to the English ploughshare and the other thirty three words closely akin which Eric Partridge lists with it, all deriving their sense from "the idea to divide or separate by cutting". Their semantic contents come from a former sc- or sk- and it is the ka which provides the cutting. Malays use potong for simple cutting, from pau-tau'n, dual pieces-two'ing. There is no way of telling whether the Malay at one time had this vanishing sk- phoneme too, rather than having to rely upon the -tai at the end to provide the cutting in two on its own. A push is the action of pu, which as a dual can be decomposed as pipi, the penis, which not only protrudes as the penis says, nai, but also pushes. In the same way piesein in Greek is to press down, the action of the schoolboy's pee. The strength,

from strong, (of a push) refers to an action proportionate to the degree it partakes
of the ish or action terau, rayed, to draw it along. A fit in Malay, with alarmingly
vigorous convulsions, sawang, from the Lithic elements sa-au-ang, is action-ex-
treme-one. A sickle for reaping is from sai-kai-lai, action-cut-looping. It is not a
little sick, which is to have one's liveliness subjected to the chop.

Cress is a very lively grower (24) and therefore a fast one (35). But with a ski
the action (26) is one of cutting the planks you ski on, the same as our shingle
which has the little known semantic content, from Middle English skindle, of
wood sawn thin for roofing. All these are akin to Greek schizein to split, as in
schizophrenia.or split brainery, and also our schedule originally a sheet of papyrus
cut to shape, and our garden shed as well, which makes use of cut planks. Greek
phren (heart or brain) is a pointer to the antecedents of our own English brain.
Ph- and b- established a natural linkage in the mind, they were close enough for
that. It was clearly perceived as the recipient of rays from outside just like the
male sexual organ which responded, according to our forebears, to the rays sent
out by the girls. Moods and mentality were originally supposed to be borne in on
rays from without, and were only selected for personalization and taken in piecemeal over many generations. It is still a common retreat into irresponsibility by
the mentally insane Use has a very long derivation from Lithic, now hard to trace.
In Italic languages like Latin it is probably from *utsus, with a revealing ancient
Oscan form uttiuf, accusative plural, with a Lithic expansion u-tai-tai-u-fai, dual-
becomings-dual-pleasurable, comfortable, convenient, convenient in use, useful,
use. The use is a duality of activity, a dual relationship between the user and the
used, like a tool, another dual convenience similarly lai twice over (or more), flat
facile lacquered and gliding in use, easy and so useful.

With that it is time to exit this overgrown chapter – words in s- exceed all
the others by a long chalk – which has grown with the many meanings of the
sibilant, in turn sprung from the strength of the impact on the primitive mind of
the hissing sound of the dowsed brand speaking directly – almost personally – to
our Stone Age forebears when they put it out. Fire was high tech when first it was
tamed, a good deal trickier than the inert stone it displaced, for all the flaws in
flints. Ex for exeat is from ai-kai-sai, as it-makes-ascend, rising above, i.e. beyond
and so outside, out – up and away like batman! Sudden, similarly, is akin to Latin
subitum and the verbal form subire to go under, Partridge suggests the going under is in an underhand way, i.e. to steal upon so as to be suddenly discovered. That
is as may be; but more interesting is sub, under, enjoys the Lithic elements sa-bai
and does not mean go up but on the contrary up-fleshed, fleshed over on top, and
so covered and therefore under what covers it; which is as good an example as you
could wish of the whimsical ability of the human mind to extract even the most
ludicrous and virtual contrary meanings from just a couple of phonemes. The way

the flesh covers the bones, sometimes even recovering them during the course of healing if they have been violently exposed, made the instinct of the flesh so to do clearly apparent to early mankind. Bone itself is what is exposed when the flesh is stripped away. Flesh loomed large in their conscious world, their science, in a way that has dropped out now from ours. There is a final sexual flourish to the chapter taking the time once again from Malay. To show affection is kaseh say-ang, to give or bestow sayang, affection, as Sir Richard Winstedt glosses it "such as from parents or lovers". Are we not back around the hearth in the warm glow of the flame? Sayangkan is to love, experiencing such a warm feeling, surely just as sugar from su-kara makes a sweet taste. Eric Partridge meanwhile presents us with his own "f/e" or "folk etymology" when he hesitantly offers sex as akin to the Latin secus, a cut, from the verb secare to cut, sai-kare, the action of our flint flak-ing forebears once again, making a chopping action, with the cut or slit he has in mind the "female sex", presumably, though he leaves it to the reader to work it out for himself or herself, the vagina which the girls all sport. The Malay recension is surely preferable: sai-kaseh, life-giving. English sex, from sai-kai-sai offers action-making-life and action-making-pleasure, a cozy conjunction from the warmth of the flame around the hearth. Sex has always been a matter of emotion – admit-tedly sometimes coarse (even including rape, from ra-pai, when the rays suppos-edly getting to the male organ supposedly take over) – and never just a matter of intimate geometry, however much that features in the human lexicon.

Notes

1. A gull wing is from the shape of the sea-gull´s wing. A sea-gull is a sea caller, from ga-la, like a gale of wind we call a gale because it is a howler, or a miners´gala which was in origin a harmless sing-song before politics took over, or a nightingale, a night in caller which treats us to a finely modulated sing-song in the night. But the gull wing neither sings nor calls. A charac-ter has simply been picked from the symbolised and named from it. It was the Lithic "Open Sesame!" when language began, and is now known rather inadequately as metaphor, which is why Lithic makes use of the term 'a gull' instead, as here.

2. Were some scientific wiseacre to claim on the contrary shivering comes from some arcane thermally controlled neurochemical reaction, ignorance of which disqualifies the identification, it could be retrieved by personal experience of over enthusiastic dipping in the local cow pond as a boy in inclement weather, when the shivers would sometimes invade the whole body.

3. Of course this can only be a coincidence, but the cat´s cry mimics the intona-tions of the Jewish God, Jaweh or Adonai; and the version with La dividing

the vowels comes quite close to the Arabic God Allah who came later, or maybe earlier if His name derives from El. This in no way impugns either of these Deities – some believe them to be really the same One True God.- since it is merely a matter of linguistic idioms practiced here on earth where the three original vowelisations, eee, aaa and ooo, do seem to have exercised, and even fascinated the hominid mind to an extent it is hard now to understand. It is even possible, as the medium of prelinguistic communication, early folk secretly – even instinctively – treasured their mewing chat long after speech had replaced it, rather as educated Victorians treasured their smattering of Latin and the Classics they once learned, long after they had forgotten it all bar a smidgen. It is also possible to drum up some black humour from the source of the revolutionary Marxian dialectic in the Pliocene Vowel Oon, the first dialectic, both equally absurd when subjected to the cruel light of Lithic derivations. The Vowel Oon is in chapter 15 on the vowels. The Marxian dialectic is finally demolished in chapter 16 on the origins of thinking.

4.   Just keep well away from shrinks who will be keen to pass on to you their favourite fantasies, by means of which they manage themselves to preserve a fragile balance, which at best will therefore fascinate rather than illuminate.

5.   Elsewhere it is noted this extended to copying Sumerian historical myth, including Adam and Eve and their expulsion from the Garden of Eden, which is apparently grounded in reality with the raising of the sea level by three hundred and fifty feet with the melting of the glaciers some thirteen thousand years ago, leaving the padi gardens of Eastern Malaya submerged under the South China Sea, and Malaya – the garden land – only surviving today as the Western hills still above water. There is no difficulty with Malaya, Adam's garden land, surviving twenty thousand years if Lithic can make sense of phonemes lasting six hundred thousand.

6.   Slugs are not formed from the word slow, nor from slip nor slime nor line nor along, but on the contrary all of these words carry some of the same meaningful phonemes and like all verbage acquire their meanings from them. It is necessary to interject these occasional reminders of the proper Lithic hypotheses since critics who are just dippers will otherwise make use of their own misunderstandings to make a mock of them, imagining the words used to indicate Lithic meanings are meant to be copies – often where no copies should be.

7.   The German poet Wolfgang Von Goethe wrote (parodying the Christian teleological philosophy):
      "Glory to God Almighty who designed
      The cork tree for us, having corks in mind".

In my dissolute undergraduate days 60 years ago I was constrained to embelish the master's work as follows:

"And glory too to Man,
Who with God's cork stole His thunder
By capping the Deity's plan
And putting the bottle thereunder".

8. Colman-Gabriel Gostony, ancien professeur au collège Saint-Michel, Saint-Étienne (Loire), et ancien auditeur (1952-1972) à l'École Pratique des Hautes Études, quatrieme section, Sciences philologiques (Sumérien). Paris (Sorbonne). Dictionary of Sumerian Etymology and Comparative Grammar. Published in paperback in Paris in 1975, Éditions E. De Boccard, 11Rue de Médicis, 11. Ouvrage publié avec le concours de la Recherche Scientifique.

9. My uncle, whose wife died quite unfairly long before him, inscribed on her gravestone "Does not the sun rise smiling, at the dawn of another day". After experiencing Japanese prison conditions for nearly four years in Singapore he became seriously religious and reverted to the belief, from the Egyptian Book of the Dead, in the dua taun or second world, along with the second birth into it, on death in the first one we all live in.

10. When trying this tale out on aboriginal boys they would become restless at this stage and if the story were continued would get up and leave, not wishing to be associated in any way with any repetition of the events recounted by this rash foreigner. The Malay for tree is different, pokok in place of kruing. Garden furniture sold in UK today is allegedly made from renewable stocks of timber grown in Borneo, where they do not speak proto Malay, even the Iban and Dayak inhabitants of the deep jungle being later invaders. Yet the timber is declared to be made from renewable "Kruing" timber. Clearly a Senoi guide was asked 'what do you call this one then?' – and replied honestly enough 'We call that a tree'. The Senoi have somewhat more generous categories than the modern entrepreneur in pursuit of timber for his garden furniture. Interrogation is an art form. Compare Budgerigar: 'That is a bright coloured bird" – not a bowl of porridge. What is so delightful is to consider what the folk interrogated must have been thinking at the time about these extraordinary wild interloping white men, with their bits between their teeth, asking the silliest of questions and satisfied with the most commonplace answers any child properly brought up in the jungle could have told them. I remember sometimes seeing a Senoi patriarch fully clad in a G-string – his name was Pa 'Ah: Grandfather 'Ah – looking at me in a slightly patronising manner, no doubt wondering how on earth I was brought up, to pitch in amongst them so singularly ill equipped for life.

11. Sir Wallis Budge. An Egyptian Hieroglyphic Dictionary. Dover Publications Inc. 1978. Vol 2 Page 1086.

12. See Sir Wallis Budge's "Ptah Renpit", where his "renpit" is really "arai en paitaun" and turns out to mean "[who] are in Heaven", a translation of The Lord's Prayer (and Ptah, an ancient god, is an ancestor god, pata ahí, our fathers, or our father).

CHAPTER 15

WA, YA AND THE VOWELS

This is a conjoined chapter for the vowels and the two dipthong consonants Wa and Ya, because their meanings are so closely intertwined it makes no sense to try and treat them separately. Phonetically Wa can have come from the slovening of Ba by way of Va, and similarly it can by misprision sloven back the other way via Va which then gets pronounced as Ba; as also of course Ba can then be spelt Va. There must always be a doubt which was which originally. The phonemes are shown with Ba below rising to Wa in the phonetic tree, because that gradation is already in the phonetics. Ba is at the level of being. Wa is up and away in the empyrian, the insubstantial. Of earth, air, fire and water only earth is fully substantial. Air and water are vowel elements, fluid, shapeless and yielding, without any persistent surface; and fire also is an insubstantial element but arising from the substantial: the flame comes out of the bough where it must therefore have been lurking before. Or so our simple forebears thought. After all if the flame were truly of independent origin it would be found flaming away disembodied on its own without any physical source. Light does this, lightening the sky, but not the flame itself which waits for the light to strike the bough and release the flame within. This kind of thinking may seem far fetched but it is what is required to recapture the Stone Age mind, effectively identical with ours but filled with many different ideas now quite hard to follow.

Vowels only carry tones. It is the consonants which give them substance and split them up, articulating one semantic content from the next. Before speech we hummed and haared, wailed and howled, but we were unable to precise a verbal string of separate phonetic and semantic beads, with each consonant modifying the tone it accompanied. With consonants the supply of meanings could grow to fill the mental spaces, the separate boxes the consonants provided. Indeed with the stringing of the separate beads, not only reflection but an interplay of meanings became available. Twenty beads (phonemes) was probably more than most men could follow through and maintain the thread of meanings from one end to the other. No doubt we started out with just two. The original consonantal phonemes appear to have been no more than a dozen. Moreover there was from an early date the problem we now know as polysemy: the same sounds became over packed with meanings so it was hard, even with the context as guide, to guess the right meaning correctly. Certainly it took time and thought. Pharaoh was still using soothsayers when the lean kine came along. The semantic contents of the twelve chapters in this book with psychosemantic trees for the phonemes involved were an encyclopedia beyond the mind of simple Homo Sapiens (also known as Homo Erectus, who succeeded Habilis) to grasp. We must have started with just the top rows to manipulate at most. The meanings at that stage were so general, fuzzy and ill defined it could be said that the rest of the world lexicon was a virtual prisoner within them waiting to be allowed out through the filter of the bare bottomed naming committees squatting on their hunkers around their Stone Age hearths. Indeed initially each semantic content in turn must have been individually hammered out with many meetings, with trials and errors gradually shaping a common consciousness. There will have been the slow uptake of buffoons, their gray matter in the cortex largely uninscribed. It is still a claustrophobic horror scene to vividly envisage what it must have been like struggling to grasp each symbolism in turn and get young Tarzan hunkered beside you to register his understanding or lack of it. It is a scene anyone interested in etymology should be invited to contemplate at some length. It is necessary to discard all your intellectual clothing and allow yourself a few skins at most, probably not very skillfully scraped or cured. It may even help to imagine the itching and even the slightly rancid smell of the skins as well as their occupants. No doubt there will have been some brilliant boys and girls – at this stage probably for the most part girls – who will have been locked onto the game, texting each other much of the day around the hearth with utterances, just for the fun of the exchanges, much like kids with mobile phones today.

The psychosemantic tree is on page 464. There are three ancient vowels, a (aaa). i (eee), and u (ooo). Aaa was the general vowel, signifying extension because you can keep a vowel going as long as you have breath. It is also unmodulated – which makes it general, as well as an un- when it comes to pairing it off with modulated phonemes. It is also the first vowel because it is the easiest and babies babble first. So, like the letter a, it comes first and can even mean first. I (eee) is the thinned and therefore diminutive reduplicative vowel, diminutive because thinned, and reduplicative because diminutive, and because reduplicative involved in itemisation and numeration, the digital vowel. U (ooo) is the inclusive-completive-substantive vowel because it is uttered from rounded lips and so suggests a circular surrounding pattern which is inclusive, as well as dual, because the other two vowels were only two and so in their case inclusive meant both of them. It is substantive because the inclusive is substantive, a category is implied by inclusion and a category can be substantive: all nouns are categorical. The forty three semantic contents strung together in the psychosemantic tree can be rearranged in several different ways. These trees are supposed to be a guide to the thinking of the subconscious mind which like the dreaming mind is kaleidoscopic, capable of jumping without much consequence from one idea to another with gossamer connections no more substantial than those the psychosemantic trees reveal. Sapiens found himself saying Wa (1) involuntarily when he spent too long in the water, groping for fresh water mussels with his feet, likely sent back in by his elders until he had enough for a meal. For me, dipping in the local mere when still very young, stepping between the cowpats and enduring the nips from duck lice involved, overstaying and emerging with one's mouth ashiver was quite common. We would be toweled and revived by a fond mother with a cat's tongue of plain chocolate now no longer made. The wer-wer-wer of the shivers (7) meant hypothermia and the element that caused it, or else an extremity of funk, and so distress of any kind, building vocabulary from like to like, as heard in the ululation and wailing of the womenfolk in face of death or other disaster. Words like howl and whine and awe and woe are formed indirectly from the sound of shivering. The wind is a whistler, the Lithic wai'n-da, to whistle-does, but unkind with it as the bard had it. Winter is the windy time, Lithic Wai'n-tai-a, whistling-become-one, but a shivering time with it. The chill factor will have been recognized in the Pleistocene. Nothing surprising in that. The Aztec God of creation was 'Wakan Tanka': Fear-making World maker, The Awesome Creator.

How do we know ka means maker? It was the sound of flint on flint, see chapter 5. How do we know Tan meant the world for the Aztecs? Taun was the world for the Egyptians, as in Pai-Taun for Heaven, see chapters 6 and 9. Of course that might not signify if there were no other evidence for contact between Central America and Egypt; or if the same Lithic phonetic meanings were not so widely distributed around the world. But how do you explain the pyramids in Egypt and Central America unless by contact to swap ideas? The flood when the glaciers melted some fifteen thousand years ago – the sea level rose some 350 feet – reinforced the human belief the gods were gods of high places, where natural forces were strongest: particularly the severe discipline of the cold season but also the ethereal shining whiteness of the clean snow, even the lack of mud on the roof of the world. So how to attract the divine spirits to your lowly habitations in the valleys? Well by making them a mountain, if only a relatively small one, to show you knew what they liked and were trying to please them, however punily. Surely they would alight there to inspect your handywork at least. If not, kill for them, to show how much you want to please. In Central America hundreds of thousands of hearts were torn out of living human bodies at the summits of the pyramids and held aloft to show the spirits. Was this not a homicidal mania? Or was it not a mania after all, just because it was accepted by all there at that time as rational

THE PSYCHOSEMANTIC TREE FOR WA, YA AND THE VOWELS

The Phonetic Tree

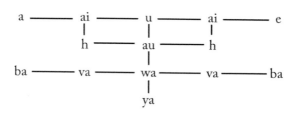

The Semantic Tree

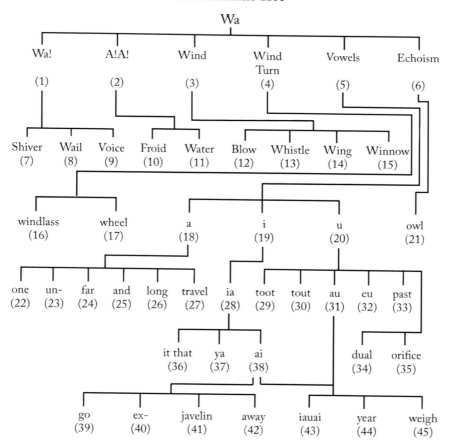

behaviour? Might they all not have been mad together, brain washed into be-lieving the will of the gods was a monstrosity, led by the priests who had in fact invented the whole paraphenalia? All mad? Why not? Meet Sapiens Sapiens! Mutatis mutandis we can see a good deal of the same still today. What must it have been like in those times and places for the maverick spirits who did not swallow hook line and sinker their fellow human beings' inanities and insanities? What indeed!

With this the last chapter dealing with phonetic meanings, with the last psy-chosemantic tree, it is intended to plunge in at the deep end and present the wild-est shores of Lithic hypothesising straight away. The vowels are the oldest parts of speech, as is perhaps recognised when we term the consonants as those elements of speech which have come to be sounded with them. Throughout prehistory it is, I think, clear there were only three vowels. Fine tuning didn`t go any further. Indeed for a long period there may well have been only two. Chimpanzees mostly mew. Is it fanciful to think of them when they are really comfortable and stress free as babbling like babies? Anyway babies babble which is of course why they are called babies, just babblers, starting with the general "ba" which gets uttered when the lightly pursed lips are parted to let out an aaa (26), the unmarked vowel. The prehensile lips of the chimpanzees, which they use for plucking leaves and fruit, come forward quite readily to provide the tubular shape which makes a mew, with something of a whistle in it. The word prehensile throws up a Lithic analysis worth recording. Chambers' brilliant American Dictionary of Etymology defines it as: "adapted for grasping or holding on, from the Latin prehensus, past participle of the Latin verb prehendere to grasp or seize (pre- before, unaccented form of prae + hendere, related to hedera, ivy, in the sense of clinging, and cognate with Greek chandarein to hold; see Get). Related to prey" It is all very well to confidently declare pre- means before (as it does inter alia), but it makes no sense when it is tacked in front of hedere to grasp. What is it about grasping which needs before in front of it? The answer is pre- does not directly mean before. The Lithic makes sense of it when nothing else does. The Lithic for pre- is pai-rai, the surface-seen, which gets to in front, which is of course the surface facing you presenting itself as the front of whatever it is you are looking at. Thence standing before, whence before. Compare panorama, from the Greek, Lithic pan-au-ra-ma, surfaces-that all-see-mass/assembly. The Greek pan for all comes from the same idea, seen in this case as a single surface or picture taking in all of the items making up the panorama. The Greek god Pan, with his pipes or pipi, has a more mischievous derivation. His name is a play on the pa-nai, the orgasmic penis, an eroticism his followers well understood. Priapus had his herms. Ivy clings to the surface, a form of grasping without the limbs. The atmospheric pressure which holds a sucker to a surface was quite unknown to the ancients, and indeed is still little understood by the public. Stiction in olden times was a force from outside, source well known. Hedere is from the Lithic i(h)a-i-terai, it-that-which-attract-ed, pulled (by a ray attracting the ivy to it), causing it to adhere to the surface or pairai. Lips and tails as well as ivy are prehensile, needing some special outside assistance to acquire their extraordinary capacity, unlike the limbs which are made to do their own grasping, but ivy has this attractive gift in excelcis. Holly had a red berry, a colour which came (in a very similar package) from the sun. That is prob-ably why they got in folk songs. Folk relished this esoteric understanding which encapsulated the mysterious element and contradicted the established belief.

For humanity however aaa is the general vowel ab origine, unmarked and rep-resentative of the vowel tones in general. Lips and tongue, the jokers in the pack which mostly generate the stops (the consonants) are out of the way and the doctor can examine your throat. The larynx is open. Aaa is the open sound un-cluttered and continuous for as long as you like to go on with it and have enough breath. All this while the breath is going out. You can in fact gasp an aah! during the breathing in but it does not come naturally at all. A diver surfacing at the last moment may do it. In point of fact a, the extensive vowel was used for 'ever' in Old English with na (ne-a elided) for never. Ah! is an unspecified tone of understand-ing and appreciation, remarkable for the generality of its applicability, so that it can even be used as a refusal to reveal any information at all. The 'ever' version may have come via aw, the oo in this case emphasising the completiveness of the ex-tension, as rather similarly in all, which has a laryat or lanyard looping around the lot – twice! Or else the second l (lai) in all was to indicate this was a spatial (local) extension and not a temporal one? Either way all has its coverage nicely coralled. What aaa actually conveys as a continuous tone is precisely this idea of extension, which can then be applied in a number of ways, not only temporal extension. It can be spatial, proceeding or going; or even quantitive, all or very.

For ooo the lips are pushed forward and rounded. The u vowel is therefore (be-cause a round suggested enclosure) the inclusive, the determinative, the comple-tive and so the substantial; and because it is the second vowel of the two it is also the dual sound, which is the reason why we say two, as also because we counted one, two, both of them instead of one, two, three (as has been reported elsewhere). As an aside at this point, we also admittedly say bilateral as well as bicycle, etc., to indicate the dual, but this is not because b and d are much the same (as con-ventional etymologists are apt to declare), which they are not, but because of the bilateral symmetry of the flesh, which is ba from the lip work; as can be seen in the limbs – the long bits – the breasts – the raised bits of the ladies (siti) – and the bums – just the fleshy bits, like the bottom, the twin fleshy bits with cleavage between. The bubs are twins too, but in Arabic bab is the two lips making a mouth (or gate or entry, as in Babylon, the entry to the Shatt al Arab, the salt lawns leading to the sea, from the Lithic Bab-ai-lau'n. It will be argued there are no really strong reasons on offer why any of these meanings for u should ever have attached to a vowel or to this one in particular. Although there may be some truth in this it is also true that there are no really strong reasons why any of the psychosemantic trees should have arisen and become markers in the mind of man. All are gossamer connections lightly agglutinated in accordance with human whimsy, and stirred in the subconscious pie as attention flits de fleur en fleur from time to time, mostly in the dream time. Psychosemantics are the stuff of dreams but they are by no means nonsensical, just lightly assembled. What is really striking is that so much of what we have in the dark room down below is so similar all around the world, even when the conscious mind has woven so different linguistic patterns out of it on the surface of the conscious mind.

I (eee) is thinned. The tongue is pushed up to narrow the passage for air and diminish the outflow. It is the diminutive, derivative, repetitive, reduplicative, representative vowel. Our forefathers must have paid attention to these common-sense characteristics of the sounds they were uttering, and it will surely have been in the hope of discovering the natural meaning implicit in the exercise in order to make a bridge into the mind of Tarzan hunkered next to them, who might with luck spot the same implications. With the limbs you can gesture when playing dumb crambo, and with the face you can mimic emotional tone, but hardly with the voice unless with echoism, and echoism could stretch quite far with aa-oo for the owl and a wail for 'weeping'(where the echoic vowelisation has been sacrificed to a later grammar). The meanings of vocalisations for the rest were open to speculative notions – the way they were articulated for instance, or some other association which caught the attention as significant.

Together with the three vowels, Lithic postulates the Vowel Oon, the group of three, the first two aaa and eee, packaged within the third, ooo, third because inclusive: aaa the standard, eee the little one, and ooo the container of the other two, making up the oon or inclusive unity. It was a relationship picked partly from the family and sex. Aaa as the general vowel was recognised as the first; or was it the other way around? If aaa and ooo are dad and mum – an O can suggest the feminine sex and the birth canal – aaa is a bit vague to stand for dad's yard just because of its extending propensity. He was however the free ranging hunter, and no doubt often out of breath and breathing hard as he was away loping interminably after game. In any case the three vowels were triune from the start just as the ineffable is today. The first count appears to have gone one, two, both of them, instead of one two three as we do it. It was probably a left over from splitting a flint and then finding the two flakes still fitted together exactly and if put back together carefully you almost had the status quo. It dates the thinking too from the time when the count was only to register a distinction, to distinguish the one from the other, and so the first from the second, positions probably occupied at first by a and u, and then when a second distinction was made in order to accommodate a third item, eee accepted the repetitive role shifting u as the completive to both of them. Eee then, as the repetitive again, became the plural of both of them, and then ooo as the completive could then become all of them. It may seem a long way round to simple iteration and addition but in the early days the birth of mathematics was a long winded business repeatedly pushing the head of the intellect up against its roof. Even the simplest concepts were at one time novel constructs. Figure 1, sketched for chapter 3 is worth a look (page 95). Even a cow can probably tell the difference between one turnip and two, but she is still some way from rationalising the relationship between them or even spotting that such a one exists. She is simply not blessed with the idea of iteration. A bigger pile of veg is just a bigger pile of veg for her. Similarly we had to learn the hard way that a distinction, from dividing or breaking in two, the two distinguished, could be replicated to give rise to iteration and so to numeration. Meanwhile the insidious one, two, both of them of dialectical thinking was taking hold and building into a dialectic which with hindsight can be seen to be the denial of iteration, an anti-math (and also the downfall of the Communist miasma in due course).

Much of this dovetails quite well with some of the exposition in chapter 16, The Origins of Thinking and Figure 3. To distinguish between this and that, it was simple to see this as not that, and so the negative as the opposite of the positive, and then absence of similarity as the opposite of it, absence as opposite, rather like a hole in a molecular metal lattice which can import the equivalent of an opposite electrical charge. Distincta were thus in opposition from day two if not from day one. This is largely derived now from Ancient Egyptian, although long preceding it, but it is not intended to break off to go over all that at this stage. They had the vowels in an oon – as a unit or an inclusive as opposed to an exclusive 'one'. It was not all that far from Thesis, Antithesis and Synthesis, rethought five thousand years later than the Egyptian priests by a German professor, Georg Hegel, who claimed to have invented the liberal dialectic prompted by the Platonic technique of teaching pupils to think by eliciting repetitive responses from them or from a puppet, each response carrying the argument further. Hegel was closely followed by Karl Marx. Boasting he had stood the liberal establishment dialectic on its head, he disfigured political thinking disastrously with his totalitarian determinism for several generations until the whole system imploded from its absurd internal tensions, trying to make everyone fit a bogus psychological configuration. But it is likely to disfigure academic thinking for as long again before the intellectuals can work it out of their teaching systems (or find time to read chapter 16 and pay attention to it). There is black comedy in communism, claiming to be revolutionary, digging up the atavistic thinking from the beginning of the human race and imposing it by force on whole populations with such terrible bloodshed it makes Homo Erectus´ raids and slaughters no more than tea parties on the lawn, with just a bit of ritual killing for entertainment, no more than practice for the mass executions of the last century. Have we become a tad less mad or is it madder?

The Sanskrit for voice is vac, pronounced wac, from the Lithic Wa-ka, fear-make, or sound the alarm, with distinct if tenuous and far flung connection with the Aztec God of Creation, Wakan Tanka mentioned above. The voice was first used to convey emergency information; and speech was to alert the tribe to what was on the cards precisely, rather than just to screech. Speaking is just a refinement of screeching. It came from the need to precise in messaging. More precise thinking came before and forced an outlet in speech. It was certainly a quantum leap in human civilisation compared with which the invention of the wheel is entirely insignificant. It was the beginning of education, where before it was left to everyone individually to make their own way simply by watching how the world went, the snail paced apprentice method. Moreover with speech, understanding became cumulative from one to another and from one generation to the next and as language built so did understanding. Meanings became infectious. Even with everyone joining in the process, progress was slow – to be measured in hundreds of thousands of years, and tens of thousands of generations, a champion football sized crowd or two chain-spread over the millennia, almost too intensive and lengthy a process for the mind to grasp. That was the consonants for you. But this chapter is about the vowels, left overs from pre-speaking times. They were old when the consonants were young, but now they were to be trimmed and sandwiched into compartments. The tones were broken up to be made into chains. We learned to think in bits, which seems to have suited the cellular structure of the brain. Before we finish with the Sanskrit voice we can look at the schoolboy "Cave!" from the Latin imperative of cauere, later cavere, to beware (schoolboys pronounced it KV). "KV!" was the cry on the approach of a beak in the old days when Latin was the schoolboy´s bread and butter. Lithic ca-wa-verbal marker, make-ware!, can also claim cousinship with the Wakan Creator in Central America, as well as with voice. For good measure in Malaya, about equidistant from Panama and Italy, kawal means to keep guard, and berkawal means to be on your guard with an almost identical sense to the schoolboy´s KV. In France cold is froid, pronounced froi, but it apparently comes from the Latin frigere which is to be cold, probably to be frozen stiff or to be rigid in fact, or else the Lithic frei-kare was to cut off the pleasant warmth. Yet the French has swung back towards the pronunciation wa, a metathesis signalled perhaps from the dark room down below.

Water is from the same stable as awan which is water in Ancient Egyptian, with a zigzag glyph, to show a rippling surface, without any rigid structure. Water was an airy element, liquids and air being both fluids without any rigid structure giving them shape: as they label water in India: "pani", from Lithic elements pa-nai, surface none, having no solid surface. Or else it is pa-nai, lip-presented, since drinking water is pinica pani in Hindi. But it is possible to use an adjectival pi-nica, which is 'of the lips' derived from the noun; and then to qualify it further: to drink is to make with the water or with the lips, in fact it brings both derivations together. The Egyptian hieroglyph awan, often taken by academic Egyptologists – who treat the glyphs as alphabetic – as just n, is actually a formalised rippling or shivering surface, a stylised zigzag line awan, a-u-an, go-both-ways, up and down in this case. It is an easily demonstrated fact that an "a! a!" called out stac-cato will gain the attention of an infant, with inhibitory effect. It is a parental alert instinctively understood. There will be some post natal development of the brain needed first, a few months. It appears it was used in the Stone Age when junior approached the water's edge. "Ha! Ha!" probably did for the hearth, with a hand suddenly withdrawn as if just burnt, the adults having learned the hard way that a really good burn elicits an involuntary "Ha!" which means "Ouch, that was Hot!"

The water warning is now spelt aqua or agua and such like, the q or g taking the place of the glotal stop, giving a cross between a! a! and wa! wa! The -ter in water is harder to explain. Terai means drawn along by an Egyptian ray, usually out and up. Might this be spring water which is pure and unadulterated as it is drawn out and up from a source under the ground, so water just means fresh wa-ter as opposed to the saline stuff found in the sea? Or might it just be the ground water for the same reason, since terra in Latin is ground, the land, which in turn is ground (terai in Lithic) and levelled in nature's mill? If so water is ground water. Or is it an agential –tor, doer, the shiver doer, water being always cold in nature? Anyway the range of similar words tends to indicate that. The Greek is hudor, the Russian voda, both look like agentials. Vodka is strong water. Eric Partridge, with no Lithic, treats vodka as "in form a diminutive" like -kin in English, and suggests it is little water because much reduced by distilling. Whiskey appears to be wa-i-ish-kai, water which has been ish-kai, fire kindled, fire water, or anyway a warming tot. During the distillation it has evidently absorbed some of the essence of fire, which is how the Red Indian tribes too read their Lithic. There may be less of it but it is not a waterkins. The Hittite for water was watar and the Sanskrit udan. Ta and da are most often from the Lithic semantic contents becomes or does. There is some further indication in Latin unda, wave, water-of-deed, the water's trick, and the Arabic wadi, a valley, from awa-dai, water-cut or done, with oued, awa-ai-dai, the river water-that which-did it, by flowing down. Winter is the cold wet season, it is a waterer. The Egyptian has hua for water too. In Egypt there were as many ways of referring to anything as the whimsy of generations of priests with a fancy for poesy could devise. Hua however was not one of them. The

Egyptian h was a cockney h, pronounced usually ahi, or achei – whence perhaps our pronunciation aitch – but essentially in use to keep separate two consecutive vowels otherwise liable to be elided or the weaker to be eliminated altogether. With hieroglyphs, a glyph ending in a vowel not appropriate could be modified by a following glyph with a different vowelisation. So there was a requirement for a marker to show this was not the case. Hua will have been actually pronounced ahua, the h replacing the original glotal stop, making it quite likely the model for aqua, agua, etc. The pronunciation of Egyptian has not been attempted in academic circles to date, the glyphs being read as if with consonantal values only, and a minimal vowelisation inserted where essential for pronunciation. Whereas they were originally syllabic. An owl is taken to stand for m for example, when in reality it said aa'maaooo (as owls do). A mouth with parting lips is read as r, when actually it represented arai, arousing, the lips parting. I think it is a mouth anyway. The salacity of these ancient monks should not be under estimated. They may have drawn it sideways on as an in joke. The Egyptian rays were their special preserve, representing what passed for science and theology at the same time, a rosy state of affairs now long past. Hua was not so different from the awan they drew as a zigzag line, or awanu with three zigzag lines for the abyss, u being the inclusive: the infinity of formlessness, all of it, the third line the tertium quid of the dialectic, relating the other two – both of them in fact. Drawing three symbols for the Egyptian priests was ultimate inclusivity[1].

Rain (12) is an intruder in this chapter since it is water which descends in rays with the watery vowelisation over-ruled. Nevertheless the Old English former form regnian shows kinship with Latin rigare to water or irrigate, which in turn, it would appear, took its time from the rain descending in rays as the sunlight was supposed to do, from Ra the sun. If water followed similar pathways it rayed just like the sun. Reigning too, the monarchical function, was a straightening or or-dering role, one which nature already achieved with the rain, perhaps to teach the monarchy its manners. For the Rex to be making rays was euphemistic, but it may have appealed to him as a Roi Soleil. The Old English regnian also illustrates how g could easily slip into the pronunciation y. Rain serves also as an introduction to urine where the opening u stands for water, whatever else the rest is about. The Greek verb ourein meant to urinate, which seems clear. Urine flows out a bit like a (localised) shower of rain. When urinating you are water raying just like the rain which shows off the same trick on an area scale. You are raining water on an in-dividual scale. The Greek can also be compared to the Sanskrit warsam rain, from Sanskrit war for water. Warsam is the active (sai) water which mai or descends to earth (ma). The Sanskrit war (spelt at the time with a v) may well have originally been awar, or awa, starting with the shivers like everyone else. But now we move to Latin urinare which surprisngly means to take a dip, to plunge or dive into the water, apparently from ua-in-are, water-in-to go. By the time the Old English caught up with the Latins there was some confusion in the ranks. Following the Latins we adopted urinate, but while we declared we were having a dip we were actually having a pee, perhaps in anticipation of the trick the Americans dreamed up with their visits to the bathroom later still. We have even confused urine with Latin aureum, gold, from au-rai-u'm, that one-shining-one, which Euphemus himself would have jibbed at. The language Tokharian A, a remote outlier of the Indo European family of tongues (now extinct) amongst the Central Asians, should have the last word. Water for them was wär, the most nearly echoic of a shiver which is werwerwer rather than wawawa (Latin), or wuwuwu (Greek).

Wind (3) probably does a whistle, just as a gale goes la or sings. But why does it whistle? Because it blows. To blow you must either burgeon low, as the petals flatten when a flower opens; or else with a limb (ba) you must swipe with a loop-ing action, thus delivering a physical blow from a looping limb. Boxers, makers with their upper limbs alone, nowadays deliver straight blows, because a looping one signals its approach and loses the weight delivered ultimately from the back leg. But the original blow was an unscientific swipe as the phonemes suggest, and carried the meaning of to wallop, which meant to thrash. Thirdly to blow up a balloon you must make a flow of air, from the Latin flo, I blow. The initial f- is clearly a puff from which the b- comes, a lip or mouth rather than the puff itself. The puff is a powerful phoneme, a gesture of exasperation, expulsion and rejection – which of course is why it fits so neatly into Ancient Egyptian eroticism, which we still follow today. The way lau can be used to indicate fluid flow can be found in chapter 9 for la. It is the instinct of liquids to flow out, down and away if al-lowed free. The au following upon the l is in common guise here: that completed, away, altogether, all. The blow does not tarry any more than the liquid out of an emptied vessel. That is nature´s way. You can not recover a puffed puff any more than you can pick up spilt milk. Had you not wished to lose it you should never have let it out. You should in any case have paid attention to the semantic contents involved, as above.

To wind (4) a handle gives us the vowel sequence uai, o or circular going, and then ´n the Celtic and Germanic verbal ending, and finally a –d from –dai, doing. Prison officers called screws would screw tight the windlass the prisoners were made to turn as punishment so it was stiffer to turn. It was attached to nothing as a pointless insult added to the physical exertion. The winding the windlass (17) provides is a turning la-sai, in a looping or circular action. We are prompted with an initial o (well a w) as with a simple winding, and then with a –lass, a 'looping action' as well. So how does uai suggest a revolution? Partridge refers us to voluble under which he addresses the Latin voluere to roll or cause to roll. A voluble per-son is thus one who has turned over the whole business in his mind and then lets the whole lot out. He is on a roll; but perhaps it would be more accurate to treat the vo- as from uau-, meaning superlative rather than rotational, and the –luble as from lau-balai, a leaking balai or lip-tongue or verbosity. An archipelago, from the Greek is the chief sea (Partridge: as seen from Greece of course) with etymological analysis for pelago, sea in Greek, surface-leaking-location. It refers to the fact water offers no noticeable resistance to penetration: step on deep water and down you go, with the same spirit as a leak. Compare Hindi pani, water, from Lithic pa-nai, surface-nay or none. La we know as circular from the skyline (seen from an atoll island, which ai-s-lan-d, goes-up-[of]ocean-does). An atoll is an island in the Maldive island chain which comes from Malaya Dewi, the Malayan Family or archipelago. The atolls literally are awa-ta-lau, water-born-in a ring, born from the ocean as coral reef islands, and the coral adverts to the very same process from ka-u-ra-a-lai, hard or land-what-rise-from-the briney. Partridge derives coral from the Greek korallion which he proposes to relate to the Hebrew goral, a pebble. The grinding of the goral acquires the grinding or wearing smooth meaning from the grindstones which go round, just as wood grain goes round when a trunk is felled, although it presents itself as longitudinal streaks in a planed plank. Pebbles on the sea shore are ground smooth by the briney, as the wave motion shifts them back and forth across the rocks and sand. The English pebble is pa-i-baba-lai, piece [of rock] which-repeatedly go-in loops and smoothing – acquiring some of water´s instinct to go flat, having it dinned into them, back and forth, back and forth. There is no reason per se why ba should persist as meaning go, just because the sound is made with the lips and the lips are fleshy and the haunch or bum, the fleshy bits, is the source of most of the flesh for the Stone Age butchers and is the muscle the quadrupeds and man use for perambulation, so ba made with the lips thus comes to mean go. That is the way the mind goes and it is no good complaining it is not cricket. It is the essence of human mentality and that is what counts.

We can now return to the uai vowel sequence winding (4) a handle. Since the vowel a is the general unrestricted extensive vowel, ai is extending including that extension of distance which accompanies any departure, and occurs when you go. We know anyway ai can mean going since the Latin ire, to go, with the -re the Latin verbal marker, almost says as much. Uai can therefore always have the idea of oo-going, going in an oo, an o. To roll has the verbal marker up front, and the o line (not the linear line here but the world circling orbital loop one as seen in and from an atoll) follows. Now we can see why we have coined the term wheel (17) for the specialised roller invented recently. It is an uai with a loop in the end, an o goer again in a loop, as may be gathered from uai, the extension in an o already reported. It just keeps rolling along. When the Lithic is spelled out syllable by syllable you have to try to think of the meanings behind the words used, which are those available today, usually unduly precised by now, for the purpose of representing the boorish and unsophisticated approximate fuzzy meanings of early days. So we must allow for a measure of approximation, here clear enough.

To work through the psychosemantic tree on page 464 brings us now to the vowel oon (5). This is a difficult bit. We are trying to penetrate the mind of Homo Erectus. The reader is asked to turn native and shuck off hundreds of thousands of years of conditioning and try only to think in those terms left to him – and this when he will not know what they were. The only evidence we have is what is left to us of his language as preserved like flies in amber in the everyday speech of today – and every stitch of that will be disputed. Life being short no attempt will be made to take academia by storm. Let them sink or let them swim. The world has better things to do. The vowel a bears traces of being the first born. Oon is the inclusive unity but a is the initial one (22) a singularity, a. Sa in Malay is a single upright – Lithic sa is up, as the flame (ish) springs upwards – in full satu is a single cut or scratched stroke used in Malay for the number one. If it was incised or scratched it was probably on stone, an early day procedure since it does not make for speedy recording: we are back in the Stone Age, whether in Eden it was actually cut on bamboo or not. A single line scratched is atomic, with no innards, a blank: you see it in the English an, spelt un-, with the semantic box empty, a negative quality. So if you are under you are (Lithic) an-terai, un-drawn up, or with nether the Lithic elements are ne-terai, negative drawn up. Because of the sexual dichotomy, nai (chapter 11) which comes from orgasm when the breath, held as tension mounts, is let out as it breaks, comes to mean just the erect state, presenting by pushing forward and up; but also simultaneously the open rounded vagina, and so the open category (23) as well. Old Norse blakkr, a white horse, reveals the development of French blanc and English black, both from uncoloured (a-kara and an-kala), in French leaving the colour white and in English without any colour at all, black. With science the English have it, but that is not significant. The bla- is apparently from pla- and means surface (compare Latin pellis, skin, pa surface, la surrounding). A- is un-, and a-ka-ra is un-colour. The colour it was thought was delivered to the eye by the returning ray sent out by the eye, bouncing off the surface seen (an active ray like a radar beam), picking up the colour from the target. With science we now know the eye is passive, picking up the sun's rays reflected from the objects seen. For kara meaning colour in Lithic, compare the Australian aboriginal budgerigar from the original Lithic baji-jeri-gara, where ba-ji is bird (a go-up), jeri is bright (from ish-rai, flame-rayed) and gara is colour. Our own word probably started out (in Latin) from coror, pronunciation eased by changing the r to l, although the etymology is not extant. The Sanskrit for a white horse is karka, the Lithic elements for colour are the same as in the Old Norse, but the whole is here ka-araka, with the first ka- in the sense body and the second uncoloured. But to get back to the vowels, our English away is probably

from au-ai, the completive-going, rather than the derivation generally adopted of
an-weg from on-weg, on the way, since the meaning is far away rather than just
going from the Lithic au-ai. Similarly far is from fa-aa with a cockney (untrilled)
r. The semantics is spelt fa-aa, fare far. Similarly, 'and' (26) spelt semantically is
aa´n-dai, extending-does, not to be confused with ante, from an-tai, un-born and
so unbecome, or anti from an-tai, un-tied or unpaired and so contrary. The words
today are not particularly apposite for the original thinking but we do not have
the original words any longer. The thinking is nevertheless accessible. Long is
from la-au-ng, linear-extensive completive- one in Lithic elements. The purpose
of this book is to provide a lead in to Lithic thinking, which it has taken forty
years to develop. Understanding of where we came from is a great help in cutting
down false assumptions, a hermaneutic Occam's razor.

Travel (28) has an illicit entry here with the vowels because it badly needs
rescuing from Eric Partridge´s confusion of travail, originally meaning hard labour, even the pangs of childbirth, from Latin tripaliare to torture by means of
a three pronged instrument, Lucifer's pitchfork. A palium is of course a pole or
long piece[2] such as was used for palings, a fence made of posts, which were originally substantial standing palings or poles dug into the ground in a line, side by
side, a defensive barrier of tree trunks making a palisade, rather than the largely
ornamental garden palings often painted white today. The Pope wears a pallium,
which is a long flowing piece made into a cloak (which is long shaped) also white.
Beyond the pale or long pieces (but also outside the circle of posts they made)
you were in no man´s land. The Lithic tra-bai-lai, whence travail and travel both
come from the same semantic content: drawing out-of the flesh-lengthy which
is a travail or labour (long muscle action, with some of the length distributed to
the active marker at the end. Well why not?). Drawn out-going-lengthy is travel,
with the flesh precised as the haunch muscles and thus their action of legging it
and going. The drawing out in origin was action at a distance (girls on boys, with
a ray emanating from the birth canal) and came to include a push from the boys
as well as a pull. It was the push which made the travail, the labour when giving
birth. There is nothing to do with the three poles used for torture on other occasions. There, the Tau-rai referred to the rays of the T the symbol for two, which
are at the same time three viewed as rays emanating from their common point
(whence our three from tau-rai, the rays of the tau). Without the key to polysemy
Lithic offers, urinating is confused with skinny dipping, and torturing with travelling, holding their places on the shelves unchallenged by the vulgar consensus of
etymologists.

The middle vowel i (eee) as an item is often translatable as he or it, and the
sequence ia or ai often nowadays dipthongised as e, as 'it that', 'that which', 'the
one that', even he or him (ia in Malay). Typical is Arabic yani, it that presents

itself, Arabic for id est or i.e. Est is from Latin esse to be, which can be analysed as ai-sai, as is living or as is seen, since the sibilant – from the warmth and light of the flame respectively – carries the semantic contents of life and visibility equally. Ya is similarly a vocative in Arabic. Ya sheikh is polite. A sheikh is an elder who has kahi, spirit made or accomplished by a lot of living, shai. Attempts have been made to relate the Arab sheikh to the West Indian chief, a cacique. But Partridge sides with Santamaria: cacique is from Mayan cah-tsik, hand-honoured, with hand the symbol for power, kahi as the actor, since Lithic adds cah (from ka(h)i) as the maker or actor, the tool we all use, which the hand is; so that the cacique is actually a Cahi Tsik, a High Executive, rather than just a symbolic hand. As for the tsik meaning high, Lithic supplies uplifted, as the flame leaps upwards. A spark is iskra (Arabic), a flame maker (or an elevator or a pleasure maker in Lithic) like the English spark which is from ish-para-kai, flame-burning-making. It may seem presumptuous to be thinking in Lithic terms like this, but it is a presumption born of very many years of examination. It is not all plain sailing because the primitive mind did not sail an entirely consistent course. In those days folk were very far from a single theory of everything. There were only small patches of apparent understanding, and they were generally misplaced. Plus ça change!

The Central Senoi aboriginal tribes of the Malayan jungle count in their own way for the first four numerals before adopting the scheme of their Malayan neighbours. One, two, three, four is mi, duak, mpeq, mpon, before following the Malay five, six, seven, eight, lima, enam, tujoh, delapan. The Senoi numbers are a lesson in Stone Age thinking, perhaps they are Adam's numbers copied by the hill tribes who learned the Adamite language of the plains. They are remarkably erudite for a Stone Age mind. But one of the things which obtrudes in the study of primitive thinking is the degree of abstraction which appears to have obtained from day one. These learner speakers were remarkably bright. In chapter 10, mmm, the hum, is identified as a filler, as well as – in the Hamitic languages – a specific filler such that we can read it as 'him', with what follows the description of 'him'. The m' we find in the Senoi numbering system seems to have been a similar initial sound-off as the mind works itself up to the key to its thinking. Mi is from m'i, a single itemisation such as we have seen is the semantic content of the vowel i. Perhaps we could characterise it as "Him single": the singular. Perhaps, to fit better, it came from m'ai slovened to mi. In that case it could be read as him-first-one, the first person singular. A as the first vowel carries a certain priority in its semantic contents which is reinforced today by its position at the head of the alphabet. Alpha and omega are the beginning and the end. Yet it is not clear why a leads the alphabet, since it was not at first the vowel sound it is today, instead being used for a glotal stop. But then no doubt isolated between two general vowels a'a, the principle can transfer from the stop to the adjoined vowel. The Lithic contribution could then be it became the vowel a because of its position at the head of the series. Duak is from Lithic tau-a-kai, dual ways joined, in other words the Tau or T which forms our own two and many other languages' duality. The two strokes of the Tau or T are certainly joined (kai) but kai also had the semantic content of the earth – later spelt Gaia, with the -a ending to make it feminine- because of its hardness, like the struck flint. If you dig a bit you come to bedrock. So it was the hard element, originally from the underlying rocks, which was in turn from the ka-ka sound of flaking flints. The Tau is a prototypical symbolisation and it can be read as the two of the world skeletal structure, the horizontal line the flat earth, and so standing for space, with the vertical line representing time, bearing the world of events upwards and onwards. Perhaps the Tau was the Stone Age Space-Time waiting for Albert Einstein to come along a few hundred thousand years later. What kept him and us so long?

For three, m'peq is from the Lithic m'pai-kai, indicating in this case them-pieces-joined, defining the three arms of the Tau. Alternatively the pai is a dimensioned pai, namely a surface, with the upright of the Tau making three. The top line of the T is expanded to a surface (which it represented ab initio, the flat surface of the earth itself made of two dimensions, which with the vertical stroke makes three. Four from m'pon, in Lithic m'pa-un, him'surface-dual, dual surfaces, which have two dimensions for the horizontal surfaces and two for the vertical surfaces, making four. It is no good suggesting one dimension was common so there were only three. It would take hundreds of thousands of years for this kind of fancy footwork and finesse to come through. If one surface is made of two dimensions, it is not all that unreasonable to argue two will be made of four. Anyway the language says as much, and the Senoi are quite happy with it.

The Malay figures, out of the same stable, show some signs of carrying on the same mystique. In place of mpeq is empat for four, which is surely a redefinition of the same two surfaces, from m'pa-tai, 'them-surfaces-two' again. Lima reverts to body language, lai-m'a, the five linked relatively massive extensions of the torso, the limbs and head. Compare Hindi panch for five, from pa-en-kai, the points of the body. We do not think of the head as in any way equivalent to the limbs so we do not readily lump it in with them, but if you look at the torso without preconception as to the function of any of its members, drawing a stick man for example (as the Chinese did), it is obvious at once there are five ancillary protruding bits, quite regardless of function, which have to be taken into account; unlike a fish which has a single torso, ikan in Malay (and in the Pacific), ika in Borneo and New Guinea, with only some wavey diaphanous extensions by way of fins. This curiosity causes it to be known as piscis in Indo European, using its body as feet in effect, from the Lithic pai-ish-kai-sai, feet-action-body-action, a single torso one or a single torso respectively. Enam is from ai-na'm, which it is not hard to crack as those that-protrude, if still thinking in bodily terms and adding in, slightly mischievously, the boys' little protruder to make up a sixth. This matches our Indo European six and sex, with the original meaning of sex being the (male) genitalia, from sai, activity or acting or action (indicating, slightly mischievously, the pleasure of it also) ka-sai, make life. It has been known for some time, although not for ever, it is the action of the male sexual organ which fertilises the female. It was first supposed it was by physically kindling the life principle aboard the female body, rather as a fire can be kindled by a vigorous and determined twiddling of a stick in a wooden drill hole until the flame bursts forth. Pollenation is a novel conception of which the Bible still knew nothing, supposing the male sperm was seed which of course it is not. The seed is actually concealed within the body of the female and the Patriarchs were wholly unaware of it. For them the seed bearing and fruit bearing plants were boys! Phala meant fruit and phalus. The testicles were regarded as fruiting bodies, somewhere between nuts and plums. Of course nobody expected the animal forms to precisely copy the vegetable avatars. Tujoh is a pass, like seven[3]; but delapan is perhaps from di-la-pan, di-loop-of surfaces, di as in digamma, that is to say the four sides of a surface twice, twice round the edge of a surface like Apollo rounding the sky. It may sound rather advanced. But some seven thousand years ago the Egyptians were drawing a surface (pai) as a square, an abstracted four sided plan view the Egyptologists have identified as the letter p. As every schoolboy knew in my day, the Greeks also called it pi and drew it in elevation, more as a lid or roof (like their 'polis' or 'all the roofs in a loop'making up a city), with two supporters and a lid with a curlicue to make it clear that was the bit which was being represented, and the two supports were just that; though we had not as schoolboys carried out the etymological analysis, still a novelty waiting to be unearthed.

Mixed between ai and au are the analyses of hour and year on offer. Lithic insists they all revolve around Ra, the Egyptian sun, although this is heresy to conventional linguistics which keeps Egyptian, as an unknown, at arms length. Where was the transition, it will be asked. Lithic has no need of transiting since it posits parallel semantic devolution; whilst acknowledging of course that borrowing has often occurred in the course of human intercourse. Horus was the son of Au Sarai (Osiris in conventional speak, but Au Sarai in Egyptian), the World Sunrise, a repetitive come uppance, the resurrection of the world sun. The sibilant phoneme meant the shining light and at the same time the life principle and the up direction, all gulled from the flame, the source of heat, light and a rising flame. The semantics are comparatively simple, but they encapsulate belief in immortality. Does not the sun rise smiling at the dawn of another day? Au, the All, the Totality, refers to both space and time, symbolised by the Tau, the duality. We know it as just a T, but for the Egyptian monks it represented the two world dimensions, space and time. The space was the line across the top and the time dimension was the vertical, that is the rising line. Some time before Einstein the combination of these two elements in human experience had attracted their attention, as at about the same time, or even earlier, it was as the Chinese Tao attracting the attention of the Chinese mandarins as a mental birth or becoming and so a Path or route to understanding. The vertical and horizontal dimensions put together were both eternity and universality, permanence and omniscience. What a prize! What an aspiration! What Simplicity to reflect upon! It was and is a splendid symbol for navel gazing, and the Chinese have done a lot of it. It brings philosophy but not prosperity, as the Chinese are now learning. What prosperity shall we now at last see in China with the lesson now at last learned (unacknowledged) from the West? Was it Marx? No! His philosophy broke the mould; but his philosophy was false. The Chinese illustrate the Golden Rule of life, simply this: third time lucky: Tao, Marx, Capitalism, the philosophy of common sense. Perhaps there is a dialectic there for those who must have it?

Horus comes by a significant aphesis, which just means shortening in a slovening process, from i(h)a-au-rau-sai and the original Lithic was probably he that-one that-was raised-shining. Horus was the personification of the dawn, The Dawn Horus, a son or copy of his father the sun in his permanent avatar, the sun as a rebirth phenomenon, ascending. There is here a nest of prompts for religious sentiments. How, it might be asked, can the single orb be both father and son, the paternal sun giving birth at dawn to himself as if the dawn were a separate entity coming forth from his own being like a son from his father`s paternity? But then how do you manage to count one two both of them? The answer is you have to go back a long way to when the human mind was little troubled by remaining mysteries and just followed through the thought that sprang to mind. Horus was at the same time I-a-u-Ra-u-sai, He-that-unit-Ra-when-shining, a sun unit, and the sun movement was a time unit. It was not exactly Einstein's mc but it did hook space and time up together, one movement coming to represent the other, in the Stone Age a seven day wonder in itself. Ai and Au (in our terms e and o), were approximating a dialectic, nothing to celebrate today: but then e and o don't mean anything for us. None of this is strictly needed to understand the meanings Lithic phonemes acquired, but it is a nice example of the kind of thinking needed to access the Stone Age mind.

Hari in Malay means the day, when the sun is shining, from the Lithic i(h)a-rai, it that-raying. The Greek sun unit horos, i(h)a-u-Ra-u (s), it that-one-Ra-one-substantive marker, was prayed in aid as a year, and hora, it that-one-of Ra, was a season of the year. Greek horos was also used as meaning boundary or limit. I(h)a-u-Rau can be read as it that-where-raised, and so the horizon, which in turn is the boundary between earth and sky. Daytime sun units we know as hours, from

the Latin hora a season, time, hour. The year is another unit of Ra, as is obvious.
It marks the time it takes for the sun to swing between its heliacal rising points
and back again, with the seasonal effects so important to the life of man. It started
out in Old English gear, from Lithic gai-a-rai, the going and return (it is Ra's rays
which give the re- its return again meaning, because they were supposed to go out
and return back pulling up the plants with them on their return trip, just as the
human eye, a feeble sun, reported back with a simulacrum only of what it had met
and felt over), the time it takes for the travel, the journey sideways of the sunrise
from midwinter to midsummer rising and back. It is a refinement on the Greek
which left the unit unspecified. The year is already primed with the ai, with the semantic content of extension or travel, so the g sound could be overlooked as an inessential helper towards the meaning. It can easily change to y, or j, as in German
jahr, or nearer to English the Old Frisian jer and Old Saxon jar. The spelling is
only an approximate guide to the pronunciations which are all much the same,
and none of them paying attention to the original Lithic composition. Latin,
looking as ever to Greek, had hornus meaning of this year. Compare Greek horos,
year. We may conclude the –nus supplied the this, and Lithic confirms nau means
presented, present, as in now. The year and the hour are equally sun units. They are
both cases of the vowel u as a substantive (22), which can be read as one or unit.
The year is its sideways travel while the hour is a portion of its loop or orbit. An
orbit is from au-ra-bai-ti, that one-Ra-goes-ting, a round or circle, and thus the
track of a wheel likewise, not itself a circle, just a rut (from Lithic rau-tai, round-
born or else ray-become. Ra has the potential for round and straight lines equally)
made by a wheel, and also the orbit of the eye, also ra in Egypt because like the
sun it was supposed to emit a ray, in this case an egg shape emitting a ray again.
Roundness was what was supposed to do it. Round orifices as well as orbs were
sources, with some looseness of the criterion when it came to the end of Tarzan's
penis, which was bell shaped or snail shaped rather than ball shaped but nevertheless was taken to perform in accordance with the perceived scheme of things. It is
Apollo, the upper looper, in orbit, who measures the hours and times the crowing
of the cock, and names the pollo dish in Spain and even has a hand in the three
French hens (poules) true love has to give, along with the partridge 'an a perdrix',
or a partridge in French, which the cheery boors (Wayland Smiths) fancy is 'in a
pear tree'; while the poetry is actually hinting at the alternative philosophy with
its esoteric and erotic (Lithic? Yes!) pa-terai, the male erect penis that the witches
were privately thinking of. But the educated male philosophers had forgotten all
about that, ignoring their true linguistic heritage in pursuit of religious ideals they
supposed (only supposed) were incompatible with the old pagan knowledge. It
was a case of emptying the baby out with the dirty bath water.

It must surely be a source of astonishment in the case of a word like horizon and its adjective horizontal that its derivation from the sunrise remains opaque. The Lithic is i(h)a-u-rai-sa-un, a standard expansion to counter slovening and aphesis. A schoolboy, you would have thought, could read that as from it-that-one-rising-of the shine-one (or sun), or else it-that-one-of Ra-the rising. Sai is rising, because the flame leaps upwards. Our own sun is the flame one or shine one, from ish the flame which (inter alia) surely shines. Is not the sun rising a certainty also? And is not 'so', just so, Lithic ish-au, is-that one, as is? The density of meanings that fit is surely in itself an astonishment, as-tau-nai-shai-ment, as-become-evident-showing-ment, with ment also akin to mental. The conventional etymology is from the Latin tonare to thunder and so to stun, but tonare is from the Lithic tau-na, become na, that is to say it momentarily obliterates everything else in the mind, just as an orgasm (from na, the expulsion of breath held as tension breaks) does: a powerful metaphor surely! Maybe you need an overhead lightning strike to bring the meaning home: the clap of thunder heard from immediately beneath can certainly be stunning. Less impressive tones are gulled from this paradigmatic one.

A javelin has a fine gamut of vowels. It is a Celtic weapon, a light spear for throwing at long range, when you need to consider its flight. The geflach, fletched with feathers like an arrow, was a specialisation. The plain javelin was a hurling weapon, gai-, hurl is straight from the Lithic kai- a forceful stroke, originally aimed at a flint rather than a quarry, with the Lithic semantic contents of -u-ai-lai´n what-going-flying added. A javelin was a light throwing spear. Jehovah has even more vowels and they are supposed to be so sacred they can not be pronounced and instead adonai is substituted, really a young man from the Lithic a-tau-nai, that-birth-showing, his birth is near, he is still green behind the ears, but taken to be good looking with it. But Yaweh is taken as an approximately the same vowelisation, and Lithic expands Jaweh's name to I-a-u-a-i. This is neat and poetic and recommends itself on those grounds alone. The question remains what are the sacred semantic contents? The concealment will undoubtedly have been because some secret truth, suitable for revelation only to the initiated, was supposed to lie there. But the mystery will likely lie with the ancients and no harm will be done today by linguistic research. Only the black goddess Kali is wed to darkness and concealment. With i-a-u-a-i we have a pentagrammaton and not a tetragrammaton as is declared. That is not necessarily a disqualifier. Indeed the layers of cover, from the time when it was generally thought that religion should be a recondite affair with truths too traumatic for the common insight, are likely to be diverse. We have the old original vowel oon deployed in particular fashion with a symmetry which calls out for explanation. We are back in the time of the soothsayers who had a much closer acquaintance with the Lithic roots of language than can possibly exist today. Indeed, they could probably have written this chapter in spades.

We have already worked out a good deal of vowelisation in various languages, with the semantic contents the three vowels carried. It-that-one-that-which[is] springs to mind for Iauai. But it offers very little intellectual satisfaction. I-a-u and U-a-i offer more possibilities. Overlapping of phonemes with the meanings read twice is common in Lithic. Two oo's in the middle sound the same as one, just sounded a bit longer. We have an introductory phoneme in both cases (in capitals above), with as followers -au and -ai. We already have read au as the all and the world, the universal term. Egyptian Taun, the world as all that has been birthed and happened, matches Wakan Tanka, the Aztec Creator God, the Awesome World Maker. I-a-u reads as He-that-Universal. U-ai is to follow. U is the completive, absolutely all of it. The ai, the extension, is surely the temporal extension here, and uai means the whole of the universal extension, the eternal, or an aeon. So we have The Universal and Eternal, and we have it entirely in vowelisations which predate the consonants which carry the thousand things of earthly experience. It is a statement of the trans-substantial and a digging deep into the prehistory of the mind. It is a fuller statement of the Tau, which is scratched on rocks as testimony to human or pre-human aspiration from times so distant we do not know what the scratchers even looked like. It splendidly identifies space and time as the two dimensions of human experience and traces them to a source in the Sacred Absolute. Is that not what religion is about? The formulation of the Jewish God is not exactly triune. The principal constituents are an au and an ai, but they are conjoined in the u in the middle, a both of them. It is this conjunction which provides the pabulum for mystical contemplation, the ineffable: the relationship between our experience on earth with its temporalities, and the over-riding timeless eternity (when our earthly experience is dismissed), with a permanent infinite space to go with it. It is simply a Stone Age dialectical triune unity, one two both of them, from before iteration. It is also surely the same perception as the Buddhist Nirvana, a blowing out of all psychic yearning like the flame of a candle – life like a flame – leading to an experience of utter tranquility, without any consonantal perception at all, swimmingly diagnosed as bliss. Anyway it is some way from the seven nubile ladies supposedly awaiting a Wahabi terrorist, arriving hopefully with his ectoplasmic wedding tackle miraculously reassembled intact. Perhaps these are only metaphorical houris, one for each day of a metaphorical week. The life in the spiritual world of the hereafter has no genitalia, so a Wahabi suicidal martyr is certainly heading for the mother of disappointments when he is greeted by the promised virgins. He will have to be making his excuses, for which he has in no way been trained. The goddess Kali will be in ecstacy: her finest hour, with her greatest deception of her own martyrs fulfilled

Young Georg Hegel had no time for the old Jewish God, since He had been adumbrated in a historical process at too early a date for an enlightened age. But he reproduced a secular iauai nevertheless by means of his dialectical hypothesis, which he gradually firmed up as the backbone and explanation of everything. With the dialectical process – and it was effectively a process with a life of its own in antithesis to the natural process – thought and understanding both progressed historically in parallel zigzags, each as in a discussion between two academic disputants each presenting conflicting positions and then reconciling them – in a thoroughly liberal democratic manner. This was his Thesis, Antithesis, Synthesis, a mental spirit world leading the natural one, revealed to him by a study of classical history (comically borrowing from Gibbon's Decline and Fall! The author, we may imagine, would have fallen over laughing). Hegel then added his own German gloss Gibbon would certainly have laughed out of court. His dialectic produced a mental space curiously made up of coat-hangers, two opposite facing arms coming together in a node or synthesis with a hook on it to join on and do duty as the arm of the next coat-hanger and the confrontation it in turn carried, each thesis evoking its contrary doppelganger and rewarded by an automatic resolution in a higher synthesis. The rest was just verbage. Each synthesis in turn acted as the thesis for the next stitch. It was, Hegel supposed, the way the spirit was working out the world through religion. It was packaged as logic, in several volumes. It was German logic, far divorced from the usual meaning of the term. The wide gap made it easier to live in the new territory. Karl Marx was immediately at home in this world of miasmas. It is all drawn out in Figure 2.

German idealism was thereupon headed for a totalitarian world view which would accommodate Oswald Spengler, Joseph Goebels, Nazism, General Petain and Existentialism. A space entirely filled with these coat-hangers suspended from each other to make a loose texture filling the whole universe makes a memorable picture (in Figure 2); and this scheme of arrangement as a historical process has largely satisfied the majority of mankind (particularly those with intellectual pretensions for which they were barely equipped) since it was adopted also by Karl Marx – with only modest adjustments in order to extract it from its lodgement by its author as the prop of conservative society and convert it instead to a revolutionary totalitarianism by (as he himself put it) standing it on its head. Now this determinist and unattractive dialectical materialism was to lead human mentality; instead of Hegel's world of the spirit leading nature. Both schemes were and are equally absurd. Both attracted maniacal leaders to impose its teachings by force, killing even imagined challengers en masse. This is why Kruschev could bang his shoe with such confidence. Nobody could step outside their predetermined natural position presented by their economic and social classification because they were being lived by the materialistic dialectic. Independent thought was impossible. History itself was predetermined (by the coathangers), so that all those riding the wrong coathangers were doomed. Revolution was nevertheless needed to achieve the predetermined outcome and wise men should work for it, by means of every skulduggery they could dream up, although it was inevitable. It probably accounts too for Arthur Scargill's intransigence, almost a match for Kruschev's. The dialectic can get you in a headlock, but once it is seen through it evokes the most extreme disgust. While he lives Mr Scargill will probably be puzzling his brain over history's contradictions. Pooh bear would probably do better. Sapiens Sapiens does not score highly in these encounters. "Could do better". He certainly can, having already mastered iteration, counting from three towards infinity, with scientists even at home with a mathematical infinitessimal calculus Hegel ignored, so busy was he with his world-shaking coathanger technique. Even Klaus Fuchs, an atomic scientist, put the coathangers first, because they were prelinguistic – you simply intuited them directly. Effectively he swopped places with Tarzan; betraying his tennis club, his family, and his country – apparently in that order. The black humour of it all is his only reward, like the other traitorous inadequates with minds capable only of shallow ratiocination along patterned lines picked up from others.

It still has to strike academia that this dialectical process has no warrant in reality whatever. Nothing goes that way. The coathangers are figments. Their only virtue is to provide a route for resuming everything under one simple rubric which is so general and ill-defined that its total irrelevance, and indeed its ludicrous absurdity, is not immediately apparent. In the Marxian redefinition it has proved an excellent selector for an apostolic succession of operators incapable of running a party in a brewery other than by butchering any possible opposition even before it shows its head. The inevitable outcome is the brewers eventually step in and take their premises back again, and it then proves their brains too have no upper storey. The world is set back five hundred years by these sotisseries, emerging at the stage at which it was set back; and can only recover in its own time. Only a genuine historian can rubbish these stupidities which have their origin in German intransigence marrying history with philosophy, and alas genuine historians are now in very short supply thanks to the bad odours of the Hegelian school of history which even reached old Henry Ford's nostrils. He spotted at once Hegelianism was bunk. It is the gulf still keeping the Anglo Saxons out of Hitler's Thousand Year European Reich, with only some young ahistorical characters including a young and wholely naive prime minister with only a legalistic training and some work with a guitar to sustain him, keen to jump through the hoop and dissolve the united kingdom in the European mess of establishment pottage.

A hoop (30), from the Lithic a(h)u-u-pai, is that one-u-surface, a peripheral piece (shaped like the periphery of an O), or the skin of one, the outline; and is indeed a circlet. The Lithic from which the word hoop comes derives periphery from the skin of a circle. Compare with peri in Greek which means around the periphery from the pai-Rai, the skin of the sun seen head on, its perimeter. In chapter 12 it has been used to show the British are Pretani or PeriTauni, periphery of the world ones, living at the periphery of the world in Egyptian times, and validated by the Ancient Egypian language, which is the inspirational origin of Greek and Western civilisation and making the Inuit who eat raw fish the only true Peritauni or Britons today. The West has been reared on an Egyptian amalgam of Semitic and Hamitic (black African) cultures. To be fair the West, once aroused from its dogmatic slumbers by the above injection, has added much of merit its progenitors lacked. The Inuit object to Eskimo, a derogatory term used by their neighbouring tribes for whom firewood was available to cook their meat. Eskimo is from the Lithic Ai-sai-kai-mai-u, as is-alive-body-eating-ones. Sai-kai together is read as alive. The "Ka" was both the structure and the driving force of the body, treated as "soul"; which was dual, for this world and the next. The Sai Ka was the living soul in this the first world, and the kai was of the first and live ka of the body. The Malays call the aboriginal tribes sa-kai, an insulting term much resented: it means single ka folk with a single-cylindered ka with no second cylinder for the next world, animals in short (or is it insects wearing their two bodies together in the first world?) whose prospects can be snuffed out without any harm. In chapter 14 it is demonstrated how the semantic content of the sibilant includes both alive and first. Now a loop begins with an l like Apollo's, the orbiter, and adds an oop like in the hoop. The French tout (31) meaning all is akin to Ancient Egyptian Tau, all the births, becomings, events, the universe. The T is a universe Einstein came to understand, both the elements of becoming – space along the top of the T and time pushing up from below, in a vowel oon or dialectic Einstein spotted, as folk do who shuck off linguistic thinking and conventional linguistics with it. We (31) are the plural of he (35), with he from ahi, or ai, with the original semantic content that which or one it. Ushi in Navaho is our, the plural of shi which means my, which is cognate with sa in Malay which means one, which is also the first person singular. Une is the simple uninclusive unity, but a unit, which unites and forms a unity is the inclusive one (40). Away (39) is the completive of going, from a-u-ai. A way (39) is the substantive of going. To wag (31) is to dual ways go. A waggon is a way go one. But Old Norse Vagga, a cradle, is a wagger which goes to and fro, a rock-a-bye, which goes and goes back (rau-ka, it makes a reversing ray) plus a-bai, that-goes. The solid rock is raised core, per contra. Add it all up and rocking is going both ways, nothing to do with the earth's core brought to the surface the Carthaginians reported in the Canary Islands, in spite of the same phonemes involved, merely due to the polysemy which has arisen as the phonemes and their semantic contents became overloaded. There is nothing wrong with bye from bai standing simultaneously for going and the binary concept bi-, both. The first semantic content is gulled from the action of the human haunch, the second from the two side by side hams, whence our idea of besides: the hams hard by each other in accordance with the binary symmetry of the human body. It was probably wise women with at least some Lithic who composed the nursery rhymes. When you weigh (from Lithic u-ai-gai) with suspended scale pans, the pans are both-ways-going like the wagging Norwegian cradle, but in this case straight up and down to do their job, that is to tell you the weightiest (as long as your point of suspension is slap in the middle), instead of from side to side to kid Norwegian babies they are still in the womb. It is because the scale pans carry the weight that the Latin vehere means to carry, not the other way around. You do not go both ways when you are carrying anything. The wagging pans have clearly been gulled. An anchor is weighed when it is raised. Its weight is carried. It is brought straight up, not up and down like scale pans. A vehicle is thus a little waggon and a little carriage at the same time. A voyage is a way going and a convoy is a kau'n-uai, a joined one-unit travelling, a joint voyage. With Lithic phonemes and their semantic contents you can pick your way through the lexicon with added insight and delight

The Greek for well is eu (32). But it is the neuter case of eus, from ai-u-sai, which meant strong, lively, brave, that which-completive-lively or active – from the flame leaping upwards, indicating activeness as well as liveliness because animals with warm blood are both alive and active, two gulls out of the phoenix's nest. Eric Partridge has more on this. The interrogative que in many language variations is without explanation. Why is judged to be from *kwei. Certainly it is cognate with Y, which actually says u-ai, dual-going or ways, with the ai extensive, a Y junction of possible paths, an interrogative drawn out of it. U is substantive, ai is extensive. What is first firm is then open to decision, it opens indefinitely what was substantiated. Why else is the Y drawn Y? In the lexicon of semantics, as opposed to empty phonetics, Y is critical. It is the question mark verbalised and sketched: what-that-is. It carries the semantics in its configuration. It is thinking drawn out on paper. The T and the Y, the Tau and the Uai, are the twin mnemonics for Lithic, which turns out to be spelt TY for purposes of meditation with an oo added for completeness. Let us call it Tayoo in place of Tao. The semantics are hard pounding, which is why they are shunned. Not only that they are not 'scientifically correct' because they can not be laid out as specimens and measured up to see if the ideas fit the facts. This is not surprising since metaphysics in their entirety are not reducible to mechanics. Linguistics is the metaphysical science. It will not answer to Darwin, and there is a very good reason for this, quite outside any ideological hangups readers may have: it is that thinking is an activity and not an organ. Within the limits of the brain's capacity it is free. Your brain does not decree what Sunday walks you will take, and so neither can your genes. They control physical capacities alone. You have the capacity to take a myriad walks, perhaps an infinity of them to choose from as linguists accept. It leaves the door ajar and the mystery of how the mind relates to the electrical circuitry unsolved, which is a very good thing.

Notes.

1. They were there in fact before they had even invented a coathanger.

2. A pallium can also, of course, instead of a.long piece, mean a (long) surface surrounding, whence a cloak

3. Seven may be from Lithic sai-bai'n, the life giving organs both, or in Latin septem from Lithic sai-pai-tai'm, the life giving-pai-two, that is to say counting the two female points to add to the five points of the body (head, two arms and two legs). It was the eye that was counting.

CHAPTER 16

THE ORIGINS OF THINKING

Writing a book on the origins of speaking, it is inevitable it must lead into the origins of thinking. The development of one has obviously gone hand in hand with the development of the other. Indeed it has sometimes been argued the one has simply become the obverse of the other. Generally it is proposed (wrongly) advances in thinking mirror advances in linguistic achievement: when we find words for new ideas then we start to think in terms of them. In the same way, most people imagine they think in words – probably because when they come to express what they think they find it comes tumbling out in words. But thinking in words is only shallow thinking. Worse, all education is in words (even when accompanied by still pictures or movies – or mathematical symbols); so that education tends willy nilly to reinforce the illusion and keep students thinking at a shallow level, often doing no more than building their vocabulary (more or less esoteric, depending on the quality of the education). Of course it keeps them politically correct as well. The lexicon can indeed function as a very large pair of blinkers, to the conscious mind at least, leaving only the subconscious to its original native untrammelled perceptiveness, its whimsy.

Moreover the recent explosion of information crying out to be mastered, due to explosions in the media, principally the technological and scientific media, has only reinforced this shallowing of thinking. If you have to be well informed, or only apparently coping even, you had better not spend too much time on questioning methodology or exploring epistemological issues. You may not even learn these terms, so busily are you encouraged to attend to informing yourself and memorising data, names, formulae, etc. Students, if their wits are about them, wish for time to digest and mull over, and if they are enthusiastic conspire to give the syllabus another whirl after qualifying. The retake of course has to go by the board later. Some even drop out bemused by the absorption rat-race, judging themselves inadequate or at least in some way not cut out for academic success. They are the sane ones! Academics meanwhile take this as evidence of natural selection and see no need to question academic procedures.

Also there are very few poets left. They are increasingly seen as dropouts or comical rhymesters, and they probably are. In Victorian times they were still re-vered as the deepest thinkers. There are no Lord Tennysons today. With inspira-tion there is still a struggle as we grope for words to formulate and express the idea we perceive, whether dimly (for the most part) or even occasionally with a sudden "Eureka!" feeling, as if a veil were lifted and we suddenly got a flash vision of the reality. But nowadays education is no longer to be treated as a personal struggle for understanding. It is presented as accumulating public knowledge towards cer-titude and certification, with charity where the less well equipped for this hesitate. This is simply wrong and misleading in every particular. It is "Red Brick" learning in the most pejorative sense. We finish up with the reductio ad absurdum of a well stocked memory, the badge of a shallow thinker, treated as a master mind.

Surprisingly, feminism, which might have been expected to provide some check on the male tyranny of the word, has had the reverse effect. Feminists, thinking of themselves as counter attackers, have moved into male territory arguing they can think male thoughts just as well as men. They can of course, perhaps with some upset to their feminine hormone balance; but it is not what is wanted from them. The female mind is the one free from linguistic hang-ups; although there is a view women were originally the instigators of linguistic advance at the origins of speaking, using their articulation to massage the egos of their male partners – in return for meat and sex. They remain natural talkers, still massaging, without falling for linguism themselves, perhaps knowing perfectly well it has been a mild fraud from the beginning. For the males meanwhile speech is ego-massage. Their "objective" subject matters are easily appropriated as extensions of the self. So they get a double ration, their own and their partners' attention. Still, it has to be said, the males are go-getters, and as such they have powered progress ever since our hominid ancestors came down out of the trees, whether the girls care to admit it or not. There is nowadays more in language than merely feminine charms. It is a whole new world of substantive conceptualisation. It is not that the female mind is less capable of contributing to human science; simply that they have not cared to pursue the matter until recently, and the male mind has thought to encourage them in this.

Feminists may wish to interject here that the males have unfairly cut them off from education and stunted their intellectual development over millennia, in extension of their first mischief of similar effect, impregnation. It would be idle to deny these charges; but the male mischiefs were only successful because they were pushing at open doors. For most of the time, the girls were happy to concede! They just wanted babies like their mothers.

Relict of some of the earliest ratiocination is the Dialectic, a term based on the Greek for 'Conversation' or backchat: first interlocutor A has a go and then party B responds. In linguistic terms that is the origin of the dialectic, simply cross-talk.

But it goes back much further and deeper than that. The Dialectic is our Lithic heritage, a nice example of pre-linguistic thinking. It is an irony the Communist Dialectic proves to have been an atavism and not a novelty at all. Jumping many millennia, Klaus Fuchs (the atomic spy) sold out his adoptive country, his family, and even his tennis club cronies because of the Dialectic, which he had to believe was prior to science (a verbalised discipline) because it was pre-linguistic. So he followed Marx's dialectical thinking and gave the science of the West to Russia. This is really quite surprising; Fuchs was certainly no fool in conventional terms. He had scientific 'chutzpah'. He was a practicing atomic physicist. So why did he do it? No doubt his psyche wanted to posture against the everyday. But his mistake is a testimony to the intellectual power of the Dialectic, which has always been perceived – ridiculously – as deep thinking prior to all the methodologies which utilise speaking, and in particular prior to scientific methodologies; something a priori and given, so you can't argue with it.

There is some merit here in being able to trace the Dialectic far back into human history. Ancient Egypt already reveals it as an ancient piece of established mystery; and some notice of the Egyptian mental usage has already been given as "The Vowel Oon", a-i-u (going going gone), as elaborated in Chapter 15 on the vowels. The Dialectic involved fundamental orienting perceptions (as it still does) as to how the world went. These perceptions are not currently reputable any longer; but nevertheless across Europe the dialectical way of thinking is still believed in, at least in decadent academic circles, particularly in France. Even in China the spell also persists, in spite of their very different intellectual idiom. It is to do with moral justification. If benevolence and beneficence still appear to be tied up with dialectical thinking then that is the way academics are inclined to think; historical evidence or even reason notwithstanding.

Plato (550 BC) used dialectical methodology to argue moral cases, basing his approach on Socrates (who proclaimed his debt to Egypt). But the alternate toing and froing of the dialectical process is thousands, or even hundreds of thousands, of years older than both of them. Ancient Egyptian thinking has had to be entirely resurrected along with the Egyptian language, because Wahabi Moslem genocide resulted in the loss of much of the Egyptian cultural heritage as well as their language. It is a permanent cultural disgrace the Muslim community must bear, hardly ameliorated because they kept some of the Egyptian achievements as theirs.

What are the original categories of human thinking? Indeed, prior to that, what is a category – of thinking or anything else? These questions need answering succinctly and with complete clarity if any progress is to be made in clearing up the misconceptions of the last many millennia.

First of all mental perception is fundamentally dictated by our visual sense

– it has been described as the tyranny of the eye, the only non-reflexive sense we possess; all the others (feeling, temperature, pain, taste, hearing even) are personal experiences, but vision is of the world around, and therefore purporting to be objective. The panorama, all that can be seen, is the local phenomenal world, the visible scene. The objective world of objects is given by the eye. Perhaps we trip over it sometimes also, but the pain of stubbing the toe is clearly subjective.

So now we must pause to see what is involved in seeing, and what ideational constructs it entails. Infants open their eyes and learn to focus. What do they see? Focus brings to attention distincta. See figure 3 overleaf. Perhaps the infant is seeing the wallpaper in the nursery. Let us suppose is has a floral pattern, with red flowers on a contrasting ground. With focus, the eye will pick out the contrast at the boundary between a flower and the ground. The mental event is best represented as "Distincta!" or rather let us say "d!", for "See!" in English, and also for "Distinction!": see Sketch 1. The eye will follow this distinction and will trace out a boundary (Sketch 2) and so eventually – in a day or two only – realise there is a bounded area. The bounded area so identified is indeed a category (d'), first the category "Red" (though red may not discriminate colours as yet), later perhaps also or instead the category "flower", but certainly not yet (Sketch 3).

The pivotal point needs to be underlined that the category is derived indirectly from a prior and more elementary identification of a simple distinction or boundary (Sketches 1 & 2), because from the very same distinction (d!) come the pregnant identifications of (d') (Sketch 5), "Red" and "Not-Red" on either side of the boundary line (Sketch 6), and this already has relevance to the Dialectic.

We might tease our understanding of the Dialectic at this stage, debating if this "Not-Red" in Sketch 6 is the opposite of "Red" or if the "Not-Red" is merely the absence of red. We are going to need to be able to recognise the difference between the absence of a property and its opposite if we are to see through dialectical thinking, which confuses them. It is already a challenge to the many potent grave and reverend intellectuals who have not thought in these terms and remain confused by the Dialectic, but then they do not concern themselves with infants whom they probably think of as mewling and puking merely.

The original discrimination (d!) in Sketch 1 – exemplified by distinguishing a change of colour on the nursery wallpaper (but just as well the aureole of an erect nipple for those who fancy a psychologically marked target as trigger (Sketch 4)) – can be represented conceptually as a simple straight line or boundary (Sketch 2). Flower and nipple boundaries are in fact curvilinear of course but the simplest representation of a boundary is an unmarked one, which simply continues, and so a straight line. This is the stage characterised above as d! in Sketch 2. The conceptual odyssey then proceeds as in Sketch 5. As the distinction suggests a distinction-between, no doubt prompted by a flower or nipple pattern which goes

FIGURE 3

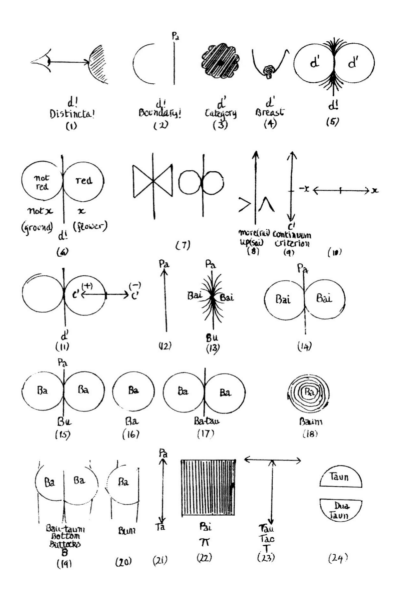

on round to enclose reasonably neat targets, the single boundary line then bends round both ways in the mind as in Sketch 5 to convert the boundary idea to a category, matching more or less the way the eye follows d! around the periphery, until it finds itself isolating not one but two categories (circles, d') separated by d! (Sketch 6). This is probably the source of the butterfly patterns scratched on stone, the acme of Stone Age thinking vouchsafed in triumph to posterity (Sketch 7). Archaeologists have identified it as a butterfly or even a double headed axe, giving a simplistic interpretation to a symbol invented by minds supposedly simplistic. The point is the two categories or butterflies' wings, d', red and not red, are mentally developed from a single discrimination (d!) and they all three appear in the glyph. Purists may wish to challenge the double whammy implicit in my figure of eight or butterfly design (Sketch 5 & 6) showing categorisation from a single boundary identification as sufficient to summon its negative to mind; but I am unmoved by them. We are not talking about a stage which can take in a substantive item on a ground, and the objection is therefore anachronistic. After all if a line merely curls round in the mind will it curl right or left? Obviously it can equally go either way and so it will go at one time one way and at another the other way, so it ends up going both ways; the symmetry of an unmarked mind indeed demands it. So along with our category we get a phantom doppelganger whether we aim for one or not. What are these two? In our example they are "red" (or for the nipple deep browny pink) and "not red" for the ground of the wallpaper (or not-so-browny pink, for the breast): which we can now write in generalised form as "x" and "not x". It would indeed be to rush our fences at this stage to proceed immediately to the more sophisticated double identification of the two as respectively flower and ground (or nipple and breast). Such a double identification only becomes recognisable after the identification of numerous categories in addition to the initial one; so that we meanwhile go on to develop a primitive adjectival mind, noticing and matching qualities all over the place, showing up against their absences – initially it has to be said regardless of perspective and sweet reason as if the whole world were made up simply of bundles of immanent qualities – and then bundles of magic other qualities (the opposites of those observed) and then instincts to go with the properties. We easily might have remarked at this stage the evident identity of the properties of the moon and a Stilton cheese seen end on, had there been in those uncivilised days any Stilton cheeses to be seen. There are still in this primitive mentality no entities as such; only located adjectival universals. If I am right this is an important stage in the development of human rationality. Ability to shuck off the evidence of our senses when false similarities such as the moon and the cheese are presented, so that we are freed from the tyranny of the eye, comes only very many millennia later – if at all.

Meanwhile it has been our misfortune to have another line in our minds, which we have readily confused with the first one, the criterion, the awareness of a differential marker. It is known nowadays as a continuum – shall we call it c!. There is no language which does not recognise the notion of more (Sketch 8), though in earlier language it was sometimes clumsily expressed. Mathematicians, concerned with numbers, mix it up with 'next' these days. It is in fact a difficult concept to get across, as primitive concepts go. Computer buffs as well as symbolic logicians and simple mathematicians too will recognise the "Greater than" sign. Because it is greater, from left to right (the direction of the script) the lines converge reducing the spread, imaginatively to equal a following term of ordinary size. Contrariwise, the "Less than" sign opens out from left to right, so that the initial diminished spread leads to an expansion to catch up with a virtual term on the right of standard size. These terms deserve serious mathematical consideration. The initial term on the left of an equation would have to contract or expand in those ways to equal the term on the right in other words. It is clear "Greater than" and "Less than" are relations developed (logically) from the middle case of equality or "same!" although the original perception probably hardly encompassed this sophistication, coming from a perception somewhat more akin to "What a Brahma!. You don't see many wide mouthed frogs that big these days!" Here we were simply grading things (as to size, or perhaps as to weight – we shall never know). It is hard to get behind these ideas.

The relationship is mathematicised as a gradient and drawn out and formulated in mathematical symbols in numerous ways. But we can surely see today the conceptual schema involved is simply a line or direction with an arrow on it, a vector, for example more is up in Sketch 8. To include less as well as more we need a double arrow, and (pregnantly) an origin or point of reference like ourselves, with a left and right hand, a change-over point from more to less, the equality at source from which more and less are marked deviations, see Sketch 9.

Well-briefed modern boys and girls will recognise this picture at Sketch 9 as the y axis of coordinate geometry used for the analysis of algebraic formulations. As such it has nothing whatever directly to do with the line we also drew vertically in the previous Sketch 6 to distinguish between "red" and "not-red", the first discrimination of the eye, which we mentioned in passing could be generalised as "x" and "not-x" (Sketch 6 again). To point the parallelism which has led to confusion I have drawn the x axis also, simply copying the pattern of Sketch 9 at Sketch 10. These are all simply different schemas, of which there are potentially an infinite number. In both cases (Sketch 6 and 10) the first term now involves x (a coincidence of the symbolism chosen) and the second "not x" and "minus x" respectively. In spite of the fact that linguistically it appears that the absence of x (not x) can without much loss of rigour be represented as a negative, in reality an absence and a negative are clean different things. Quite apart from the math, this becomes clear if we try to think what the negative of "red" might be. Perhaps that colour which when combined with red produces white light, negativing (rubbing out) the red? That suggests complementarity rather than opposition. Moreover, unfortunately there is no such colour, all colour qualities being sui generis and only when all colours (frequencies) are mixed is white light produced. In fact we can not ever see negatives of positives in the real world, only absences, eg of light of one group of frequencies or another. Negatives and positives turn out to be (mathematical) fictions without regard to whether the real world provides any fits for them.

There are for sure presumed polarities, for instance in electronics, basically the potential to attract or repulse, in which respect we find atomic and sub-atomic particles marked. But otherwise negative and positive are cultural constructs much favoured by mathematicians and physicists and of great value in calculations and bank accounts. But they are not presented to the eye, not even by a see-saw, they are abstracts, clearly inferred from experience in the phenomenal world but not part of it. They are to do with shuffling pebbles from one pocket to the other and that sort of thing. They are relative to activities, not to things, coming and going, upwards and downwards, and light and dark for instance. So in the case of electronics, or other subatomic particles schematically opposed, attraction is often regarded as the negative of repulsion, while the absence of attraction is even treated (in semi conductors a hole in place of a particle for instance) as opposite in value and equivalent to a repulsion. Electrons being negative purely by convention, the travel of an electron through the medium is by convention a flow of negative current. So the similar movement of a hole where an electron (or other negatively charged body) might otherwise be is treated as a positive current. But it is the directions which are opposites (strictly reciprocals) not the electron and its absence. A negative is simply a reciprocal vector.

Nothing here so far is new; at most it is perhaps presented differently.

We can now see further however that the category has hybridised. Neither fish nor fowl it has become a red herring. Originally no more than a boundary which closed, it has acquired an outside and an inside, an exclusion zone as well as a centre, simply because it is an extensive presentation in the mind. There is now, if you can anticipate a little, a continuum across the boundary with the point of origin on it (Fig 11). This is something new and even shocking. It is certainly confusing. Hard pounding! It was not in Hegel's or Marx's books.

So now to tie up the relevance to the Dialectic of these two different lines which the mind perceived before speaking – the boundary line or distinction and the sequential line or criterion/continuum – perhaps the essential outlines of the Dialectic should first be spelt out, starting with the Hegelian because it was borrowed with insignificant modifications by Marx and is therefore best known, as well as being still believed in Europe, even unbelievably by some presidents and prime ministers. There are of course published critiques, notably that of the late Isaiah Berlin in Britain; but they are literary, even anecdotal, rather than methodological. The methodology really needs by now to be exposed and demolished once and for all, and it is the analysis in terms of c' and d' which does it.

The Dialectic posits a Thesis (roughly a proposed heading; it is clearly a category): a case in point is Feudalism, (a vague and tentative term to describe Norman society, since much revised but still very much in vogue when Victoria was crowned which was when Marx was formulating his schema for world history). Another more recent application is The Idea of Social and Economic Freedom. Every Thesis is perceived as pregnant with its own opposite, its Antitheses, which arises spontaneously and inevitably from the Thesis, not at all unlike the balloons in Sketch 5. The absence of a category is implied by the existence of one (even just the postulation of one when there is a postulated absence to match); while a continuum is conceived as extending infinitely up and down and so with a positive and a negative. But category and continuum are clean different things – as different as a straight line (the continuum) and a circle (the category). Put them together nevertheless as if they were one and the same and you get this quaint hermaphrodite feature half one and half the other and capable of populating the world and the brain with a comical coat hanger network, a negative implicit in every positive categorisation, with an ability on top to dream up another category embracing the first two. Examples are Capitalism and Totalitarianism, implicit in and therefore inevitably following upon Feudalism and Social and Economic Freedom respectively. There is plenty of room for interpretation here; there will be parties who prefer different examples and may wish to argue vehemently I have got them wrong; and it is true I approach their selection quite casually. Nevertheless the theory is that it is by the development of Thesis, Antithesis and the third term in the Dialectic, Synthesis, the final realisation resulting from the confrontation and then reconciliation of the Thesis and Antithesis, that both the world progresses and at the same time the mind properly comprehends the process by way of these double repetitive elisions, a double whammy neither of which can stand up to examination.

We are now right inside the dialectical thicket. The thesis is the category initially selected (d') and the antithesis is the implied exclusion category (d'), misprised as a negative. This confusion is drawn in Sketch 11. The doppelganger notred arises from the fact every boundary has two sides to it and categorised (Sketch 3) has a within and a without. The negativity of the dialectic however is superimposed on the mere absence of red outside the category simply by confusion with the other (quite different) line, the continuum, which is thus put in Sketch 11 in order to show how these two lines have been confused by Hegel and Marx. It is solely this confusion which enables them to invent the dialectical coat hanger pattern supposedly informing both the world historical process (a miasma) and our mental processes, both at the same time. The synthesis recognises the common origin of the foregoing two and supposes it is the same as a current commonality, which of course it is not. You can always find another category embracing the two preceding ones. In effect you rub out the two lines you have just drawn in and then draw in another one across the differences between the former two, by means of a quick switch from the category arising from a boundary distinction (d') to a criterion/continuum (c') bridging the boundary.

Perhaps it is the most important single aspect of the Dialectic that it is taken to represent both the way we really think and at the same time the way that world events actually unfold. Because clearly if this is the case once you can grasp and accept the Dialectic methodology your thinking ought from then on to be in line with reality, the way the world goes. You are thinking in objective terms, ie the way the objective world proceeds; while the others, poor muts, the subjective thinkers out of kilter with reality, are being suckered. This makes your belief an obstinate one so that you are set to ignore contradictory opinion; and that in turn self selects for a bigoted mind-set as well as the wickedest of tyrannies. Needless to say my own belief is the whole dialectical gamut is all pie in the sky. The pragmatic view is schemes can be invented galore, much like computer software programmes, for one purpose or another, but hardly to provide every kind of analysis by means of a single programme; and so the dialectic has turned out hopelessly impractical, leading to the most painful political and scientific foul-ups and disillusionments.

I have described an early dialectic in Chapter 15 as The Vowel Oon, with the vowels a, i and u in the roles of Thesis, Antithesis and Synthesis. The vowels indeed lend themselves to the representation of pure thought since they flow freely without structure and thus without identification, whereas the role of the consonants is to structure utterances and therefore they are perceived as delineating phenomena, or anyway ideas, discrete chunks of thinking.

The word dialectical itself needs some explanation, being originally from the Greek dia-across and –lectos from legein to read (or choose), that is to say to pick out the meaning of an utterance and so to specify its meaning or import, to read or even to legislate. So the dialect, the way local people talk, is chat but also the logic of speech. I think the speech element is important. It is implicit in dialectic, originally argument and counter argument bandied to and fro as between two folk or perhaps philosophers cross talking in argumentative mood. Then we have to go on to analyse the semantic contents of the term still further: not merely argument and counter argument but prinzip and counter prinzip. Here we access some of the deeper ponderings of the human spirit or psyche. There is first the contrastive consciousness which comes from the very early, even infantile perception of the boundary between red and not red for instance, generally x and not-x as fairly exhaustively discussed already. But then, confusingly, the linear element presents itself alternatively as a continuity at the same time as the discontinuity of the boundary line. The dialectic is caught up in, or perhaps better descends from this confusion of boundary and continuum, a confusion it must be said still able to fuddle the best of brains and lead to the betrayal of patrimony and humanity itself. Witness the brilliant buffoon Doctor Fuchs from chapter 1. The gambit goes precisely like this. First of all conceive of a Thesis and Antithesis on either side of a boundary line; pausing to philosophise as much as you wish upon these contrasted categories whatever they may be, praying in aid, wholly improperly, the positive and negative poles of a continuum with a mid point or point of origin discriminating the two opposite directions. Then comes the Synthesis. Switch about your original point of view entirely now and regard the two elements you have been contrasting as entirely positive and negative aspects of a unifying entity such as a continuum presents. This is your Synthesis. You have as it were stitched up the two elements previously parted, or indeed witnessed their partition and their subsequent over arching unity like a bystander witnessing any other scene change in the everyday world of visual objects. That fixes the whole fandango in the mind. The mind and the world mirror each other in this dance of the coat hangers, the mental gyrations thus guaranteed to reflect precisely the structured processes of reality. This secular neurosis has probably by now killed more than all the world's old religions put together, because it commands the same certainty in assent as the old religions did but with hundreds of times the power for evil at its disposal due to the progress of technology. It is therefore surely bizarre that dialectical thinking is still admired in certain quarters.

It is hard to know whether to dignify Karl Marx with a notice in a chapter on thinking. But he is so much better known and therefore influential than Hegel that his version of the dialectical nonsense deserves proper direct attention. He was a perceptive social critic of his day, which was over a hundred and fifty years ago; but his methodology is hopelessly out of date and was always wrong. His dialectic, which he cobbled together from Hegel by (as he put it) standing Hegel on his head, was the rotten egg in his basket and yet the one beloved by academics for the next century and a half and still admired today even after the communist ideology has failed egregiously everywhere it has been tried. Marx's actual influence has therefore been wholly malign and his intellectual muddles still inform much of the academic establishments around the world. An examination and refutation of the dialectic on scientific and logical grounds is therefore long overdue. Senior wranglers with university tenures have shirked the task or simply failed in it because their thinking never challenged or examined the philosophy involved as too difficult to argue much about. The collapse of Marxism has therefore been merely a matter of practicalities and any hostile critique has been based merely on rival social theory, leaving the aficionados still singing famously to their own scores.

Hegel's dialectic was a contrast and exchange of liberal prinzips which he believed would be fully realised in due course. Marx's was a contrast and exchange of economic factors which he believed would lead to political revolution in due course. In both cases Natural Process was involved, informing both the way the world went and at the same time the process of human thinking. It appears to have struck nobody that these coincidental arrangements were a curiosity, as if it were to be expected from the track record of human thinking to date that we would naturally keep in step with reality. Any set up which positively entailed any such arrangement of affairs, so blatantly contrary to the human record ought surely to have been suspect from first formulation.

There were other curiosities just as bewildering. Economics were naturally determined and their outcomes inevitable and yet they had to be struggled for bloodily. Nobody asked why they could not just sit back and let Nature take its inevitable course. The true answer was because the whole fabricated scheme was bogus; but nobody realised it, whether they looked forward to the denouement with keen anticipation or regarded it as a threat to their livelihoods. The parties were struggling for and against the inevitable, and comically those against won. But it was a black humour killing many millions by the way in the name of the dialectic ands its winning ways.

Marx was a caveman when it came to science. Aristotle must be judged to have known better two thousand years earlier, and he too had one foot in the cave. It was originally Plato's cave in fact. Marx's mind-set was of the 1830s or 1840s at best, twenty years before Darwin when Biology was only present as Linnaean Bottany, a kind of philately merely. Evolution of the rocks was what Charles Lyell had successfully demonstrated in 1830 in his book "The Principles of Geology", in collaboration with my great grandfather, an enthusiastic conchologist (shell collector), and his shell collection which occupied the whole top floor gallery of Merton Hall. I remember it well (the collection). The hard sciences as we now know them, physics, chemistry and of course electronics were simply absent. Straightforward mechanical forces (Newtonian physics), action and reaction, were the scientific paradigms for the historian and philosopher alike, not a lot different from the thinking of our Stone Age hominid forebears as they flaked their flints hundreds of thousands of years before. They just lacked its application to the spheres (courtesy of old Isaac Newton).

The human mind is not primarily oriented towards elucidating the truth. It is much more practical than that; which is how we came down from the trees. The mind merely seeks tools for analysing the world, human destiny, reality, call it what you will.

The dialectic proposed a scheme or process setting out with a Thesis or proposition such as "The moon is made of cheese" or "The world is red"; but which soon got read instead as "Cheese!" for instance, or in the second case "Red!". Whatever else may be said this is clearly categorical thinking. We therefore need to look closely at a category and what may be done with it, as well as what may not. A category is (or comes from) a description, although it can be reduced to just an ostensive description, pointing something out: "That!". So we proceed to examine categories. Thesis, Antithesis and Synthesis, all three of these are categories. We have already been over the way the infant, and quite similarly the infancy of the human race, got its mind around the idea of a category. It can be shown to be an item bounded by a common character, in the case of red for instance a patch of red on a ground which is not red. Humanity is another category just like the red patch although far more complex and controversial to describe. Feudalism and capitalism are categories too. Outside the red patch the ground is not red. Outside humanity are non-human things. Outside feudalism and capitalism there is not any feudalism or capitalism. Inside, the category has determinations but outside they are absent. The category is in no way in opposition to the ground. It is simply in absentia on the ground. The absence of red is not its opposite.

But now a mathematician will tell you the opposite of plus x is minus x. This is where Hegel and Marx messed up. Not x, a ground, is not the same as minus x. X has not been subtracted, it simply is not posited. This is where we need to distinguish a distinction which makes a category from a criterion taken to be a continuum. I don't think the mathematicians had gotten around to this comparison in Hegel's or Marx's day. Frege did not have it. They are two markedly different ideas. We have seen a category already as bounded (by means of a distinction) so that its logical symbol is a boundary, which can of course be represented by a straight line: on one side what the category describes, red for instance, on the other side of the boundary line its absence. It is true a category was first identified as an encirclement but it was derived originally from a barely perceived distinction at a boundary. The thinking can be drawn out as in the Sketches in Figure 3, with the category x shaping up with its doppelganger not x, based on either side of the original distincta.

But there is another kind of criterion altogether which can be represented as a straight line also and so quite easily may be confused with the categorical boundary. One straight line, after all, is exactly the same as the next one. Only in this latter case we are looking straight down it (or up it) instead of across it. This is the line known to mathematicians as a continuum. I believe Berty Russell invented the term. We only met once (at digs in Oxford) and had to beg to differ (on politics only). The best continua are continuous and of infinite extension, by definition unbounded, although that does not of itself distinguish one from a boundary which can also just as well be conceived anyway as infinite. There is after all no chance of red and not red meeting around the corner of the boundary if they press on long enough. Continua do not have to be numerated but they often are, since we often find it handy to make use of graduations when it comes to any extension, gilding the lily for our own convenience. The numbers are a virtual reality to mark out a (supposedly) real space and they can be given a null point or in other words a point of origin and be made as it were into ladders going up and down from there, usually positive numbers going up and negative ones going down. On such a continuum plus x and minus x are indeed opposites; and "not x" is just the zero point. This point can now be made common to these two categories. Distinction and criterion/continuum together can be made to meet at any point of origin, without too much distortion of the mental category if lightly addressed. Otherwise they are clean different ideas, only subject to confusion because of the generality of the straight line which appears to suit them both perfectly well. You can not find an antithesis as Marx did lurking anywhere within a thesis because a category by definition is just a simple category; nor can it therefore combine with the original container to give birth in any way to any kind of summation putting the two together to form a third, the synthesis. That is just free composition outside of any logic, or to be quite blunt with a bogus logic purporting to be prior to thinking, dreamed up by guesswork. A boundary term is made to do double duty as a continuum which has an up and a down. The nearest you can get to that gallimaufry is Stone Age sex, which appears to have been introduced initially in the Lithic scheme of primitive vowelisation. Our first sallies into reasoning came out reeking of the subconscious soup from which they sprung, and it was quite strong stuff. See below. Clear thinking in precise terms rules it out, but daydreaming fishing for original thinking can still conjure it up.

I am obliged to S R Fischer (A History of Language, Page 103) for his notice of Rongo Rongo, the writing of Easter Island. Some 25 mantras in this script survive, most of them appearing superficially to be sketchy mnemonics of various bizarre sexual copulations. But I think they are records of dialectical thinking recorded as fundamentals for meditation. Needless to say I see them as childish and wrong headed also, but not however as evidence of the pornographic mentality of savages that the literal reading of all the copulating would otherwise suggest. Their dialectics were just as dialectical as anything Hegel or Marx turned out, if clothed in language derived from idioms Mrs Grundy would hardly have cared for. Moreover there is added to Hegel the further insight whence originally sprang the dialectic, arising like a miasma from the dream world of the subconscious borne on the confusion of sexual excitement with the purely intellectual stimulus of the Eureka feeling. The Dialectic owes something to a misprision of a plainly sexual pattern. Nikita Kruschev may have been getting more out of banging his shoe on the table than his fellow United Nations delegates could manage. Perhaps at bedrock orgasm is the plain man's Eureka. The latter is said to have sent Archimedes straight from his bath romping through the streets with no clothes on at all. It undoubtedly was for him a great excitement.

But to return to the basics of Rongo Rongo as devised by the Easter Islanders, the inscriptions (all wood carvings) appear to comprise simple telegram style statements in the form A + B = C, glossed as A copulates with B producing C. Whether even math itself arises from the sexual metaphor thrown up by the subconscious is here a red herring, but it could be so. Fischer cites the following example: (Te) Manu mau [phallus =ki 'ai' ki rota ki] ika [ka pute] ra'a". This is translated as "All the birds copulated with the fish: there issued forth the sun". He extracts the elements actually glyphed: Manu (birds) mau (impregnated) ika (fish) ra'a (Ra issued forth). But to look further at what the Easter Islanders were actually thinking we may note that bird is Manu, two phonemes ma- and –nu which can carry the very early semantic contents mass and none. A bird for the Easter Islanders was defined as Brer Weightless. Compare the Australian aboriginal Ba-Ji for bird, which meant Go-Up, those life forms able to overcome their weight, which causes the rest of us to fall to the ground if unsupported. In Malaya there is similarly the Siamang Ape, an acrobatic long armed Gibbon, Si-ama-ang, Brer-mass-less. Mau as well as the earth and so the massive element and so the mass or weight of anything might also be used for earthing up and so the planting of the seed, the impregnation, or even the gestation in the ground or in the womb. In Egypt the god Amun, The Ever Loving One, carried the same semantic content as the Latin amare to love, a-ma-are, as-[when] impregnating-verb ending. In Malay mau is simply to like or want; but in aboriginal Malay it covers lust and sexual possession as well. Words start out with a wide coverage when in short supply and assume specific meanings as they multiply. Ika for fish is the same as ikan in Malay and ika in numerous New Guinea tongues. I-ka-'n is Single-body-one, Brer-limbless. It was the "mana" or mental conceptions of these species, not just their physical conception, which came together in the Easter Islanders' minds when they became conjoined. Copulation was merely their robust and vivid paradigm for any linking together. It meant conjunction. How better to anchor the idea in Sunny Jim's adolescent mind?

So it was simply the elements of weightlessness of the birds and simplicity of structure of the fish, its reduction to basic outline shape, which came together and coming together reached their apogees in the character of the sun; quintessentially weightless and flighty, a super bird, and at the same time the ultimate in minimalist configuration. Thus it was meditation for Rongo Rongo boys and girls. Spot the combinatory characters! It is bogus science of course but you can see it is science of a sort. It is also demonstrably dialectical. A fish is not the antithesis of a bird at first sight, but on reflection the water surface, a major natural interface (d'), divides them just as a distinction (d') divides the categories x and not x: the fish at home swimming below the interface and the bird above it, and both by fin-beat. If the bird is thetic, the fish is antithetic, or else the other way around. One is the reflection of the other with the natural boundary (d') between them. The sun in turn mimics the flying fish, up out of the water with a fine swoop at dawn into the empyrean with the birds, and then disappears down into the deep at dusk back into the fishy element again. These are certainly simple metaphors, but they are not mad or bad. Some fish had an Apollonian temper and would fly short distances while some birds exhibited a remarkable aquarian propensity, diving to join the fish. This put them on the ladder category as well, with a little bit of what they fancied on either side of the source. The abstraction of the abstract adjectivals, the weightless and the simple-shaped adjectival elements, are both characters of our own reductive science, a potent dialectic indeed now with better terms to it, distinguishing (itemising) and then recognising their common elements and bringing them together, nowadays as in chemical formula rather than as man and wife. It is the genesis of the method which is of principal interest when contemplating the origins of thinking. The bird has grown legs for landing gear but the fish remains completely fishy dying when it lands out of water. "Pisces" for fish, from pai-sa-kai, has perhaps the suggestion he carries his legs, pai, in his body, kai, or perhaps better he uses the leg-action-of his body, Brer Motile Body. It is metaphor all along, and so only makes sense in the terms in which it was originally conceived. The fish is born in water and dies out of it but the sun is born out of the water and dies into it, so the sun gets that from the bird, since the bird drowns in water; but how is it born out of it? That is the conundrum for meditation. Is an egg sufficiently watery to keep the metaphorical cats cradle going? The kingfisher was thought to be born from water, at sea, perhaps he was given this role because he clearly had a natural affinity for water and spent so much time diving back into it. We can see the dialectic is silly but the Easter Islanders couldn't. We may be smarter, but not all that much when you look at the twentieth century, ragged out by Hegel and Marx, and the dialectic still a plank in the intellectual firmament even now, after so many millions dead from the hedonistic massage of the psyche by this methodology.

Perhaps the Jewish God was the first, perhaps even the only dialectical God. Jehovah, the Jewish God that Christians witness (with Pagan overtones), was originally "Yahweh" or "I-Au-Ai", the magic combination of vowels 2-1-3-1-2, I-A-U-A-I, which orthodox Jews at one time preferred not to reveal, but held them covered by referring to Him as Adonai instead, the secret virtue being in the vowelisation, A-AU-A-I. With Jaweh there is a symmetry about the central Lithic completive dual vowel u, pronounced oo in English but in Semitic

languages often articulated as a semi consonant Wa. "He-extensive-both-exten-
sive-He" appears to be the semantics concealed in the original appellation. "The
Universal and Eternal": a dialectical God with omnipotent aspects spatial and
temporal brought together in Final Synthesis: Single, plural, both of them, plural, single. We are counting one, two, both of them, from a time before iteration
had been fully worked out. It may be bad math but it is basic for religion, a
dialectical trinity, perhaps even prefiguring Einstein's Space-Time-Both of them:
anyway a thinking man's god, unlike the Christian Trinity which is a comforter
for everybody. All this is some way on from the origins of speaking hundreds of
thousands of years ago. But in all this time Sapiens and then Sapiens Sapiens has
not changed his spots; and only the Lithic hypotheses make sense of any of this
surprising persistence over so long a time.

Hard science (physics) treats its categories as real. An atom is supposed to
be really out there, bolstered by the perfectly valid theory that the world is what
it is and not another thing. The same rule is applied to subatomic particles and
their qualities. But it is all a ghastly mistake. Sure, there are definite things out
there; but they are not the same as we perceive them to be. Of course Emanuel
Kant already knew this. In science this is a truism; a solid table such as Doctor
Johnson kicked, or any other solid body, is in fact a congeries of dancing particles
with electromagnetic fields, and most of the space is just that – space between the
particles – when scientifically described. Our fingers, similarly composed, simply
bounce off the table's fields when they encounter the table's "surface". Moreover
red is not really red; it is a frequency band of that electromagnetic radiation, to
which our optical sensors respond with the mental experience we know as red.
What we experience as red moreover is by no means the same as the electronics
which trigger it. We may be the recipient of rays, but what and where is the screen
on which these phantoms are displayed. We do not now imagine there is a manikin behind the eye reading the pictures from behind as we can sometimes catch
sight of them on the iris from in front. When we sit on a pin and it punctures the
skin we dislike what we fancy we feel. But it is not the same thing as the physical reactions of the nerves involved. The problem is the scientific terms we use to
redefine what we regard as real are also figments as we present them to ourselves.
Science provides us with linguistic refinements for the most part. That is not an
excuse for walking out and going to mystic illuminations, but it is certainly an
opportunity.

Molecular biology copies the hard sciences. But it does not treat of thinking,
only of the brain. We are left with an apparently unbridgeable divide between the
mind and the brain. Science is reasonably content with this, provided the things
which have been scientifically detected out there are given precedence: molecular
biology is prior to psychoanalytic theory for instance. Examining the brain is

scientific. Psychoanalysis (which claims to deal with mental events) is a "cultural construct".

Unfortunately, the distinction between science and cultural constructs is not as helpful as it at first appears, since science too is merely a cultural construct. It is a myth the scientist directly accesses the real world and his determinations are therefore objective. The history of the discipline immediately rubbishes any such idea. This realisation must come as an unwelcome shock to anyone who has walked on the moon – or even sent the walker there. He or she is rightly persuaded the science is objective (gets veridical results) in a way Freud's and other fantasists' waffle is not (does not). Moreover he scores highly for abstraction and precision. Freud too is lavish with his abstractions but he scores less highly for precision. Clearly some cultural constructs are better than others; and what makes them better has to do with the rigour with which fickle fancy is controlled and subjected to severe testing by comparing it with independently deduced "facts" and circumstances. It is the match which validates the science, not the method. Scientists alas are as human as the rest of us or more so and often remain unaware of it. It is hard to know whether it is right to dignify Karl Marx with notice in a chapter on thinking. But his thinking, such as it is, is so much better known and therefore influential than Hegel's that his version of the dialectic deserved attention.

Our consciousness can be (and I think actually should be) analysed in a continuum of developing crispness and informativeness of semantic content. I have labelled the stages in this continuum with Greek letters – chiefly to raise the tone of the piece as mathematicians often do; although the Greek letters do have lip smacking qualities germane to my purpose.

Psi (Ψ), perhaps symbolising a boundary crossing (or perhaps a cactus), designates those sensations which reach our brains and trigger immediate mental events: Ouch!, Hark!, Hot!, Ha!, Wa!, Hard!, Sour!, etc. You hardly need any intelligence for the job. If you are awake and reasonably sober you should get the message. A Chimp would. But I go on from Hot! etc to include in this same sector the other more specific raw emotional and adjectival responses to stimuli: Horror!, Horny!, High!, Hiss!, Hate, Hurtful, Hearty, Hellish, etc. An initial h is not a requirement but it is often a guide because the original element "Ha!" is the sudden compulsive explosion of breath due to shock or exhilaration. Prototype is the Pleistocene foolish boy picking up a white hot stone in mistake for charred wood, to throw it back into the burning hearth, using "Ha!" for hot. The list can be extended to individual taste, and often has been; sometimes with bizarre results when early psychologists have been compiling lists of instincts. There is virtually no limit for a sophisticated mind to the categorisation of primitive traumatic promptings capable of being identified and labelled. But it is probable our first speakers contented themselves with very few; so we shall not bother with all those expansions which are possible. Psi just stands for the crude rude initial primitive psychic output, as input for anything to follow.

Next to Psi is Phi (Φ), originally an Egyptian rude gesture carried over into Greek script (the upright originally penetrating the circle rather than merely crossing it), but here employed for the whole adjacent area of mentality, the identification of phenomena, including the Phi. (Φ) which appears to have started out as Tarzan's penis, here superimposed upon his partner's pudenda. This is the phenomenal level of thinking, simply taking in and mentally digesting crude input, identifying "things" presented to the senses; along with commonsensical ideas of causation, etc. – pre-analytical thinking, in learning terms coming to grips with vocabulary. Phi is adequate for some simple abstractions and analogies arising from them. Given the initial crudity of Psi (Ψ), identification of things is already by comparison an abstract process. Phi identifies both form and function, rescuing us from adjectival guesswork. This is conscious thinking at last, such as we know as commonplace today. A chimp by contrast is mostly stuck in Psi, with only the tip of his accomplishment nosing into Phi, unless dragged forward by human intervention. But the mere identification of phenomena wins no prizes for thinking.

Eventually – after many millennia – we got scientific. I have called reasoned marshalling of phenomena in the mind Pi (Π). It is crisper than Phi and conspicuously requires reasoning. It still allows for a great deal of erroneous ratiocination, but it is where we are at today. Pi is for Pattern, a layout on a surface, conspicuous scheming, everything from the realisation there are regularities in human experience to the modernists' theory of everything. It takes in magic and religion as well as science. It is a broad bailiwick. But it only takes one thin mental slice at a time out of the rich complexity of the reality it seeks to capture, and it is only a representation at one remove from it. Most of humanity's mistakes naturally enough are in this latest sector of intellectual activity, crammed up against the current end of it – including the idea there could or should be a theory of everything!

This leaves Ro (P) for the Reality, confronting the Psi, Phi, Pi series but in no way part of it. Our intellect doodles on the wallpaper while Ro is the real underlying wall our doodling is supposed to represent; which is contrary to the naïve and popular idea that our doodling is progressively getting closer to the real wall and may hope to alight on it given sufficient time and attention. That is a category error. It confuses the wall with the wallpaper. Our ideas must always remain at one remove from reality for as long as we recognise a world outside ourselves, since the wallpaper on which we draw turns out (in reality!) to be papered on the insides of our own heads, a mental construct. Our linguistic and even our mathematical presentations remain just metaphors, in an intellectual medium human enough, but always unreal. There is no Holy Grail in science, there is only representation.

I like this scheme of things because it points up the absurdity of Napoleonic thinking and the other methodologies of the asylum which seek to illuminate Pi by recourse to Psi, as if inspiration were superior to reason, an escape from hard thinking by going back to the primitive end of the spectrum expecting to tunnel from Psi all the way round to come up again at the other end out in front of Pi. That is an illicit move in my gaming. So there you have it. Psi, Phi and Pi is all we know on earth, and in that order; and perhaps even all we need to know – since the rest is developed from the study of Lithic thinking, all unapologetically in the third category, Pi, yet not without benefit of Psi and Phi also.

There is a recent mental module theory which proposes the human mind was divided into separately functioning departments until recently. It is quite unproven. But there is indeed a problem in the archaeological record. How is it that we were fly enough to flake away at hand axes with such precision and yet for a million years or so too thick to get around to decent thinking? The cognitive neurologists have come up with the idea our brains were divided into modules not consciously connected, so that while we could learn the tricks of the trade within any module, we could not apply what now seem to us the lessons of what we had learned to do outside the module concerned. Modules are then up for grabs: sexual (for reproductive skills), social (for clan collaboration), technical (for flaking flints etc), natural (for catching game to eat), and eventually linguistic (for communicating between modules as well as with the neighbours). Sixty years ago when I was at Oxford the students who were studying PPP, the latest syllabus taking in Philosophy, Politics and also Psychology in place of the Economics of PPE, used the old British psychologist MacDougall as exemplar of this temptation to fabricate psychic modules or instincts in excessive profusion, and we coined the coffee drinkers' term "a silly MacDougall". There may still be something of the spirit of this silly MacDougall abroad in the halls of Academe even today.

The inter-modular incapacity really makes better sense if you adopt the position that over this million years or so the hominid brain simply was not thinking consciously at all (or anyway very little) as we understand it, more just apprehending individual skills subconsciously by looking and doing; so that the marvel is better rephrased: how was it that this brainless wonder was making tools without thinking about it at all, simply by following subconscious promptings to copy, without really knowing what he was doing, as we understand it, at all? It goes against the grain of common sense at first; but then parrots can copy human speech, with a noticeably limited range also, and nobody thinks they think through what they are saying or have any knowledge of exactly how they do it. They follow their instinct to squawk the squawks they hear. In the same way perhaps our forebears followed their instincts to copy the flaking they saw, fine tuning the artefact as the parrot fine tunes its articulation. If you think about it, we can ourselves still do as much, for instance when we sing. Perhaps hand axes were effectively sung. Certainly without words to work with hominids could not lay layer upon layer of thinking as we can. They were in exactly the same pickle as trying to do algebra without any notation. It is not theoretically impossible but it is extremely difficult; and without the ability to have a solid (unified categorical) idea and hold it in the mind so as to be able to come back to it with the degree of precision required for further thinking about it, it is indeed impossible.

The question we should be asking ourselves when it comes to getting inside a dumb hominid's mind is what ideas was he having? It is a question which has not been asked because it appears to be unanswerable. We have probably compounded the difficulty by seeking to preserve speaking for a late achievement of Sapiens Sapiens, when in reality our primitive hominid forebears were already articulate yet still pretty beastly with it. Moreover I think you could initially go bashing flints just for the fun of it like a gorilla drumming on his chest, to see and hear them break: "Just look what I can do!"; and then you cut yourself on a sharp edge which results from your flaking. You don't have to go looking for tools. You simply trip over them; they find you. All you need to be able to remember is what hurt last time; and then, and this is what made you human, you have to go back for more of the same, just like the squirrel does with his nuts. If his tail were not so bushy he would be half human at least. He is relatively feeble but quick on the draw and bites. He even has hands, and all that has held him back is the refractoriness of stone – he can not break it. We are not so much featherless bipeds as giant squirrels who shed our pretty tails; and we had the wit or just the good fortune to grow big enough to break stones. You just need hands and a bit of beef behind them for the trick; and memory first of course, but that came in with the herbivores, knowing which bits to bite.

That is a kind of thinking, but it would not win many prizes. It isn't thinking about thinking which is what we really mean when we think about thought; and consciousness is a completely different thing. Every living thing is conscious in the limited sense it is responsive to inputs. A fly contemplates the fly swat and is only defeated when we perforate the weapon so the pressure wave is subtly altered to deceive him, and all this without a single thought in his head that we would recognise as such. None of this fits in too well with the present ideas of the cognitive neurologist, wrapped up in his study of the microphysics of the brain on the grounds you can't ignore science, or even with the cognitive archaeologist looking for inspiration in his catalogue of stone tools. With minds trained to think in terms of their bits and bobs they invent the hominid mind in their image, adding blinkers to taste to account for the deficiencies. That methodology is flawed. They believe our forebears were dumb, but they allow them mental paraphernalia of craftsmen today, only cutting off the bits which elude them in the record.

It is better to start with nothing and think of stone tools as coprolites from the mental digestive system. Nobody nowadays thinks of his stomach as an organ of rational activity but the job it does puts tool making in the shade. I am not forgetting that nowadays we have minds capable of thinking of a complexity almost to match the stomach. But looking around it is clear it is still something of a novelty. Moreover you can easily have a brain without using it, or at least without using it for thinking very much. It wasn't even put there for thinking; it was put there for running the enterprise, as the control centre, a job it continues to do well enough even when we are not thinking but dead drunk or in a coma. The thinking is an accidental and inessential spin off from the nervous system developed for another purpose, namely running the phenotype's engine room. This is in fact the classic evolutionary pattern of adapt and make do, which has engineered novelties galore (conspicuously eyes which focus for instance) as spin-offs from other previous facilities. Although we may value thinking highly, it is not all that important in Darwinian terms. Indeed it is usually regarded – correctly in fact – as outside the rest of evolution. With speech and education, it is argued, survival of the fittest takes a new turn and selection ceases to be natural and becomes cultural instead. Or at least cultural selection is added to the pile. After all we spend a good deal of time these days spoking nature's wheel with medicines and therapies of one kind and another, and even borrowing and diverting her techniques for our own purposes.

We can see now that with a bit more flexibility the bishops might well have won in 1859, and the churches might not now be facing annihilation from scientific progress. They should have dumped the body and argued for the mind as its successor in the struggle for survival, leaving aside where the mind comes from and discussing how we should handle it now we have it as it is. It would be uncharitable to suggest the cognitive gentry are still in something of the same bind as the bishops, but certainly their attempt to treat conscious thinking simply under the biological rubrics of the day – to keep it all scientific – is quite simply misplaced. It is misplaced because with thinking you can produce it cheap and pile it high – according to Chomsky infinitely high – something which does not occur in nature. The mind, and mental activity in Pi (Π), is sui generis. So we can get better results by letting the mind go free, and then of course in tranquillity mulling over what we have, with all the sagacity science can muster. It is a question of de Bono's hats. Academics working on the brain wear one big sombrero with a brim so big it drops to the ground, so that they never take it off (or see out from under it), because doffing it is too much of a discard, unless they are drunk or dreaming. We should not urge them to get drunk but certainly a bit of undisciplined dreaming, allowing their modules to go free and just listening to the music does help. It amounts to a new science of dumping. Einstein would have approved. He surely must have dumped his bits and bobs and launched his mind into empty space with awesome abandon. We know this in fact because he said so. At one time he wrote off language altogether. But he recollected it in tranquillity, as we all must if we wish to avoid the asylum.

To come back to our origins in hominid cognition, they evidently managed without much thinking. Why can we not allow that they simply did not do much conscious thinking at all? Or at least they did not think with the attention to it that we are accustomed to. They worked things out "by guess and by golly" with admirable perspicacity. I am arguing that with hominids it was mostly by golly, the surprise and delight of finding something which worked when you went through the motions; so that it was a spin off from the instinct to show off which under-lay our intellectual development ab origine. For most of the last million years it simply did not occur to do much thinking out loud – the chimp in us got no lessons from futurity in those days. It was just a case of accepting what occurred. For more on the modular mind see Appendix A on the philosophy of language. I have tried to keep the philosophy out of the body of the book as irrelevant to the origins of speaking, but I have included the appendix to try and show I am not altogether lacking in that department.

This chapter so far has – I admit it – skirted and skated round the nub of its proper subject matter, how initially we were habituated to thinking and in what terms we thought. We have come across some pointers merely: the Psi, Phi, Pi, Ro sequential analysis of the mental spectrum; the adjectival mind; the source of categorisation in the recognition of the prior distinction (and so eventually nouns derived from adjectives); together with a good deal of poking fun at those persis-tent aficionados of the atavistic dialectic. This has been a deliberate preliminary in order to clear away some at least of the commonly held misapprehensions which would otherwise immediately confront what follows.

No doubt before speaking the mind dwelt on what was presented to it, just as it still does today. It is most probable we have extracted and distilled our intel-ligence from contemplation of the world around us, as well as within us; if only because it is difficult to see where else we might have got it from. There was, it may be presumed, a grave tendency to snatch at knowledge and jump to all the wrong conclusions, based on perfunctory resemblances (eg the fish, birds and sun in Rongo Rongo) mad metaphors and whimsical prepossessions (eg universal copulations) just as is the case today. Half a million years ago (say) when primi-tive speech was forming, or better when our utterances were being developed to carry an increasing semantic loading, the most difficult bit to accommodate (in our minds these days) about this early stage of prehistory is probably the de-gree of ignorance, and incapacity to cope, which generally obtained. Illiteracy we know, but inarticulacy is largely unexplained, and generally inarticulacy is almost impossible to comprehend. With no speech we must have been nearer monkeys than men so far as our mentality was concerned, regardless of what studies of contemporary physique may reveal. How can we visualise this instinctive brute, with no conscious grasp of reality, beginning to assemble the mental tools for conscious ratiocination, confronting himself and his world? Small wonder there has been a desperate inclination to look to the monkey world for guidance. How does a chimp think? He is pre-articulate. But he is surprisingly teachable, given enough time and effort. What is largely lacking is Simian intention; they are lazy brutes, mentally sluggish, failing if left to themselves to make the most of themselves. Even today we can see the pattern is inter-specific. It is a fair bet our hominid forebears were in the same boat. Their grey matter was there but it lay largely untapped because they did not have the foresight or interest to start using its full potential, to start building its potential. That is one reason why it is most likely it developed in the first place for some other purpose altogether. There can hardly have been any selective advantage in an enlarged organ which lay unused. Perhaps it provided balance for the upright stance, or finger control for all sorts of handy jobs, etc, all without making use of conscious thought. The chimp's own accomplishments solely concern its own betterment, eg signing "Gimme banana". There is no intention there to direct anything else. Yet chimps are far from autistic. They know each other. They can relate to humans. So can a horse, a dog or a cat, of course. A cow or a sheep can accept us but hardly contribute anything intentional. Of course a cow can readily distinguish a daisy from a blade of grass. But she probably does not think about them. That is the point. A monkey and an inarticulate hominid are both in great part cow. But at the same time, the hominid, it turns out, is on a roller coaster to ratiocination – if we speed up the process a bit. This was certainly tied up with a substantial accumulation of grey matter inside his skull, the lid of which rose to accommodate it. Or else the grey matter simply expanded to fill the gap made by the rising lid? That in turn might easily have been from some uninspiring circumstance, like more chewing – or less. Meanwhile hominid instincts will have been purely animal, though his brain provided unprecedented and unlooked for opportunities for building and retaining thought patterns on a vastly extended scale.

I am inclined to think, since there appears as far as one can tell to have been a contemporaneity, that mental usage grew from the taming of fire, on top perhaps of an increased meat diet now that it could be cooked. It literally made us all sit up and think; our culture comes from naked seminars around the hearth, with our warm bellies full of cooked meat, and our warm minds most probably thinking of sex for desert. After all, not only cooked viands but also the warmth around the hearth gazing into the coals must have applied adaptive pressures upon the human frame including the brain. We talk of animals coming into heat. Our hominid forebears were animals every day coming into heat. I believe it was this unnatural heating which led to an enormous increase in the sexual athleticism of the human race. It is not hard to see, when one pictures to oneself any group of hominids, their minds still largely empty, their bellies full, hunkered for the pleasing and relaxing warmth close together around the hearth, perhaps in the mouth of their cave, all of them as bare as the day they were born. The warmth, as well as the proximity and availability of adjacent bodies, will have stimulated the adult parties present sexually. These early folk were inclined, in the absence of ratiocination, to do what came naturally; and what it was can fairly easily be rumbled. You do not need to be a medical practitioner to notice that with heat the vascular system expands increasing the heart rate so that inter alia more blood is pumped to the genitalia, and in turn there is an automatic and involuntary engorgement. Surely our bare bottomed forebears will have noticed this also. Nowadays girls in massage parlours know this and encourage their clients to take hot baths. It makes them smell sweeter and be nicer to know at close quarters as well of course. Even a natural warm climate encourages sex, leaving the British, the Peri-Tauni, around the periphery of the world, notoriously under privileged in that department. That is the real reason, in this air age, for the annual flight of citizens from countries in Northern climes to the sun. With the sun, young folk become ravers and older folk are miraculously enlivened. The Mediterranean littoral has always built a macho male. The steamier African continent is also renowned for its sexual prowess. In India the worship of sex is most highly developed and armed with the Karma Sutra lives are probably shortest because of the overworked heart, added to an ill supplied stomach. Not only is there this connection between climate and sexual activity, surely much increased in a much hotter artificial microclimate around the hearth, but there is also, just as importantly, a change in the ambiance of the sexual relationship. Both sexes are relaxed as well as stimulated by the warmth of the occasion. Orgiastic sex releases more emotion. It could have been this bomb burst of emotion which triggered the birth of the thinking man. If so intellectual activity comes from emotionalism. Long after he was capable of any further orgasm, Tarzan found he still enjoyed thinking about it. He really got thinking. It was perhaps overwhelming sexual emotion which drove him to think, to trawl up out of the subconscious this reflection of what drove him, for further savouring in relative tranquillity. This was mankind hooked on thinking, faut de mieux, his mind in a pink haze as he focused on his earlier pleasuring and planned more for the future.

In short we have swum to civilisation through a sea of sexuality which was the original Open Sesame to fully conscious thinking; and the male genitals have burgeoned beyond all necessity compared with the other apes, simply from countless generations of obsessive and addictive over use, aeons of frenetic sexual activity. It

was around the hearth also, I imagine, that the ladies will have first got out their
needles and tailored stomachers for their menfolk to keep their bellies warm out
hunting and lively on their return, with the innate animal liveliness of the furry
animal life-support systems they were borrowing. Ratiocination is really just refined emotion and without it learning is dreary in the extreme. Thinking is a vehicle just like speaking is, and we have now perhaps identified the original burden
of human thought. We pile Ossa on Pelion when we speak as well.

Mrs Grundy has by now turned her face to the wall, but we should perhaps
meanwhile turn our attention in turn to the Reverend Grundy, not yet comfortable with the idea of orgiastic copulation over aeons, courtesy of the divine flame,
however ancient. Sexual fantasy was indeed the first full dress rehearsal for the
real performance, and (at the risk of being accused of merely punning) this first
full mental address – the word here used in its verbal sense – gave us our first fully
realised mental addresses (nouns) sufficient for all subsequent mental rehearsals,
images imprinted in the cortex as fully conscious images. Moreover the very same
images are, I believe, still there, the lingam still firmly imprinted in the lingo, and
only the concealment of the subconscious mind preserving a fragile decorum.

For the Revd G we can cite the Egyptian head god Amun (Lithic Aa-Mau'n)
"Eternally both inseminator and gestator", "The Ever Loving, both sexes", crude
forerunner indeed of the all encompassing love of the Christian Deity. It should
perhaps be explained (see Chapter 10) Ma comprised a number of derivative semantic contents, including particularly here that of earthing of seed and thus both
insemination and germination; while Latin amare, to love, from the Egyptian via
the Greek, (Lithic A-ma-are), 'As when planting', the male or mali role [mali is
Hindi for gardener], as in Malaya, the Garden of Eden, or at least that peripheral
hilly bit of it left above water when the melting of the glaciers flooded Eden, the
Eastern Lands, under the South China Sea. The resultant diaspora colonised both
Sumer and then Babylon and then Egypt. It was Amun too who first pursued
fully the drive for life after death in its most literal institutional form, again prefiguring Christian belief. This in turn may be why recent biblical scholarship has
located Moses, and the Mosaic religion still professed by the Jews, in Egypt (The
Fatherland in Egyptian) with Moses a priest of the Aton (the Eternal birth canal
in Egyptian) and even possibly a dissident Pharaoh (Devine Penis in Egyptian)
worshiping the Aton as well. If this were the historical pattern the relics of the
Egyptian language to be found in Malay, otherwise hard to explain, would fall
into place.

Recall, after all, is the missing element in subconscious thinking, the mind retains no imprint of its activity, the job is done without a record, certainly without
a record in any detail. I believe that the taming of fire and the consumption of
cooked protein meals around the convivial hearth led to sexual consummations,

no hair pulling needed any more, and sweet dreams thereafter, still remembered on waking. Life became all Rongo Rongo, and this had important consequences quite additional to sexual activity. There was a spin off, as so often with physical evolution. What was sauce for the sexual gander was also sauce for the mother goose (the brain). The same breakthrough into conscious appreciation of hitherto subconscious responses, what was formerly the dream on autopilot could now after the breakthrough lead to conscious appreciation, focused attention, and to quite other diverse matters; prideful consideration for instance of tapping out a hand axe, that is the lesser delights of getting it right at work, of mastering the initially refractory medium which too turned out to yield to slick technique. Wherever there was pleasure in such ego-massage the new found mind would wander. The scrimshaw had begun, leaving Wayland behind doomed, with just the heavy work to do.

It is necessary to point out here, to enable Mrs Grundy to return to the debate, as well as to check any young blades seeking to recapture their authentic roots, that none of this has any current implications for human thinking or conduct, other than the reflection that honesty is often the best policy for understanding. To argue that nothing has changed in a million years, or even just the thick end of it, is blatantly absurd. What has survived as an adaptive response on the part of the human physique as a result of this outburst of frenetic sexual activity long ago, with the fair sex in charge of stoking the fire all day, 24 x 7, is a degree of independence of the menstrual cycle, so that sex is available at all times, a happy circumstance we apparently share only with the Bonobo Pigmy Chimps – and they have evidently achieved it without the benefit of the hearth. We are the only two Hoka Hoka species on earth, the procreational function dumped in pursuit simply of raw stimulation, same sex as well as heterosex. It is a bizarre accident, no part of the original scheme of things (which was for genuine procreation), resulting from suddenly introduced long term overheating in the Pleistocene. Fascinated by the fire, the heat and the flame together, the mind has confronted and out-stared nature. It is the price we have paid for our culture. Now we are stuck with this outmoded fillip we hardly need any more. Now it hinders progress.

I think the original sexual reverie is probably responsible, as much as the present promptings of the gonads, for the sexual content of so much of present day psychologising. Certainly, so far as language is concerned, the sexual prototypes of so much of the lexicon is indicative of our original favourite subject matter. I have even gone one further, suggesting that the subconscious receptacle for these original connections still feeds the conscious minds, indirectly, of each new generation as it apprehends the lexicon both consciously at the superficial (surface) level, and simultaneously at the subconscious level beneath, where the thought patterns flow free and unconstrained by too much language. Down there is the bubble-up element in our mental makeup, humanity's muse, our musings, out of the reach of Mrs Grundy and hard to control.

So far as the subconscious is concerned, it appears to be a halfway house, not wholly unconscious and inaccessible to the conscious mind as the autonomic system appears to be, but not normally recognised by the waking mind. We can remember some of our dreams and can day dream when dozing, but we lose contact with their sourcing when we consciously address them, left only with the shell without the kernel. It is this kernel which I believe Lithic language roots show to be in certain aspects sovereign. Even when awake we can get some shocking promptings from down below, our muse presenting to the waking mind meanings we never intended, triggered by who knows what or how it happens. I have already attempted to sketch spectral lines in the mental curriculum, Psi, Phi, Pi and Ro. Some or all of Psi, the intentional element anyway, originates in the subconscious, outside intentional control. It is a funnel vapouring up strange concatenations from the deeper levels of the mind. Lithic language roots are just one small part of these vapourings. In passing, the fascination of hallucinatory drugs arises in part from the apparent entrée they provide to this area of hyper-vivid primitive and mostly visual perceptions, mixed with a good deal of giddy swirling sometimes appearing yellow and submarine; but in greater part from the relaxation provided by intoxification, surrender to non-thought. Mental poisoning, it turns out, starts out as fun – courtesy of Psi. The audio frequencies of articulation are more effortful and significant than the visual and are blurred out by artificial stimulants; but their sober research is the more rewarding. That leaves tunes, threnodies which flow with rhythm, somewhere in the middle, redolent of the subconscious muse, opening channels to the inarticulate dream-time, dumping the linguistic impedimenta.

We have now introduced the two ideas of the original discriminatory distinction (d), celebrating the boundary between two different textures on the one hand, which went on to generate in the mind the straight line criterion or continuum (c); and on the other hand the unitary bounded area (d') which was then presented by d, as the prying eye of the infant closed the boundary around a nugget. For long this d' must have been a difficult concept for the inarticulate adjectival mind, texturing its universe in an overwhelming and kaleidoscopic avalanche of perceptions, with no mental handrail or any fixed points to guide it. In such a mass or mess it must surely have seemed superogative to go picking out individual nuggets (nouns) as well. Before speech was added the mind undoubtedly roamed somewhat more freely across its experimental inputs. It is useless to pretend there was no mental activity before speech. Squirrel Nutkin disproves it. But the activity was speechless, it could not make use, as we do now, of the conceptual code we find in words. So there were no stepping stones across the mental abyss. In this fix distincta appeared adjectival, popping up all over. Qualities were not entified or separately located. Adjectival terms answer to more or less, their application slipping into the form of a continuum. In this way the continuum virus was fed into the distinction fold; and the category was thus provided with bogus positive and negative poles. The next question we must ask therefore is what senses aided thinking in the absence of language; and the answer must surely be the visual sense. As the eye discerned the world around so the mind discerned the terms in which to think. We have been focusing our thinking ever more closely ever since, with language thinking in nuggets and labelling them, just as the world goes, and then labelling the labels, and so on and so on. It therefore might be possible, it occurred to me, to find traces of the prior thinking patterns when it came to the birth of language. In other words, I accept the view that the development of language followed upon the thinking needed to get it started. Latterly individuals may use vocabulary to stimulate thought but this is a later development. It is hard to believe that language was created from nothing, after all.

Surprisingly, it then turned out, and only after years skirting and skating around the idea, that the very patterns I had chosen in illustration of the eye's analysis of its original journeys of discovery (Figure 3, Sketches 1 to 11) do in fact appear to represent quite well some of the first informing meanings of primitive language roots. I turned my attention to the thought patterns I had drawn and deliberately attempted to label them in Lithic terms. It proved a highly educational exercise. The exercise is here repeated, without a great deal of reconsideration or review, but pretty well as it first occurred to me, with only minor re-ordering for clarity in following through the sequential stages of development of the thinking, my originals having been scribbled across the bottom of a page wherever they would fit in, in some degree of excitement.

We start with the criterion tidied to a simple line as in Sketch 12. I labelled this Pa, because I already had it in mind in company with the burgeoning side developments rounding out (Sketch 13). There is a switch between Sketch 13 and Sketch 14 where the outcome of the thinking in Sketch 14 has led to the "x" and "not x" balloons usurping the labels of the burgeoning process in Figure 13. The finality of the mental process is recognised in Figure 15 where Bai, the burgeoning, has changed to the unmarked Ba, flesh, the pregnant balloons now substantial categories. Here the logic of the pa label is reinforced as the thinned surface tangent of the burgeoned Ba, just as Pa skin is the thinned derivative tangential to ba flesh. A single burgeon may now be abstracted as exemplar of the principal semantic content of the phoneme Ba (Sketch 16). This in turn offers a redefinition of Sketch 15 as two Ba with a cleavage between them. The cleavage – fro n flaking flints, where the effortful strike was taken to sound like "Ka" and the resultant cleavage as the flake was, as it were, spat out, was taken to be like the lesser dental plosive Ta – is added in Sketch 17. At Sketch 18, as an aside, I have shown "Baum" (German for tree) with the completive vowel here indicating all of the tree's growth rings, of which I have only drawn four representing hundreds. At Sketch 19 I have tried to sketch a bottom or buttock, whilst at Sketch 20 I have shown a single bum or haunch. In Sketch 21 we find our original line in Sketch 12 has a double label, both Pa and Ta, the line representing both a dimension and a division. At the bottom of the page Sketches 22, 23 and 24 are from Egyptian. Sketch 22 is the hieroglyph for Pai, being a surface made up of dimensional lines. Sketch 23 is of the Tau or T, a symbol too old to date. It features in the Egyptian ansate cross or ankh. It comprises the dimensions in Sketches 9 and 10. As such it can represent the two dimensions of the surface of a flat world, or even the dimensions of space and time. It also is the symbol Two, and its arms make three rays. Finally there was space for the world in Egyptian, Taun, for which the glyph is a circle divided in two. It provides an opportunity to remark again that Egyptologists have mistaken the glyph for a bun, pronouncing it just t. The under half is Dua Taun, the second world of the dead and the dead sun as it passes under the earth (which was taken to be a disc), gestating in darkness each night before its rebirth on the Eastern horizon each day. Dua Taun is thought to be the Dwat in academic circles.

Bearing in mind the abstraction of a single line from a crooked boundary (Sketch 2) is already a recognition of such as representing a continuum too (because both are just lines), it struck me "Pa" and "Ta" might well be treated as serving as markers for the two directions on this line of double derivation, and so as nodes, apt in turn to be identified as male on top and female thereunder, which is why I have put the labels top and bottom (Sketch 21). These labels are elementary Lithic phonemes, not yet words as we understand them, it must be remembered. There is still a good deal of unstructured swirling in the Lithic mind. We are shaping our thinking and then giving utterance to the labelling. There is a paradox when we subject this to present day customary thinking, because we regard words for things as simples, and abstract shapes and concepts as a posteriori, whereas I am turning it the other way about. The explanation of the paradox is simple: our customary thinking, after aeons of language, tongue wagging in effect, is wrong. We thought in shapes before we thought in words. There is a good deal of evidence, from primitive science, that subjective minds still thought mostly in shapes even after their tongues had been wagging for a comparatively long time. This almost comes to saying before we spoke we mathematicised. Thinking was that difficult, and there was no notation. The math of course stayed simple. Some of the evidence is scratched on rocks as symbols for which anthropologists and archaeologists have been searching for crudities as meanings, without success. Spirals are perhaps the pathetic mementos of the whirligigs of the giddy untutored mind trying to home in on a definition but finding a purchase unobtainable, the whorl its only utterance. Cups are similarly abrasions from dizzy screwing with a hard stone or flint to uncover the essential shape it presented, Adam delving, the product of frustrated mind seeking to relieve its emptiness, to pattern the inane, to escape the nausea. Aesthetes can derive comfortable backing from some of this: here was man the artist while still in his birthday suit expressing himself in primitive art forms before his mind was pinched and trammelled by repressive civilisation. But I see these signs as simply cries of pain, like the mentally disturbed rocking back and forth, or the severely religious similarly in traumatic confrontation with their god. This is Psi, not yet Phi even.

To continue with the line drawings, consider the ongoing development of Pa in Sketch 2 on its own account. It does not curl round. It can only repeat itself (Sketch 22) extending sideways. This after all quite precisely copies the movements of the eye in panning or scanning any scene, particularly a whole panorama, which is simply Greek for the pan or whole coverage of what the eye (Ra from the Egyptian) consumes (Ma from the Lithic) or takes in. I have drawn ten stripes and you can picture them as close together as you like, sweeping out a surface. Moreover Pa has been identified already (Sketch 15) as tangential to Ba, the burgeoning (fleshy) bits. The surface indicated by cross bearings in Sketch 22 is therefore skin; with the phonetics (Pa the thinned diminutive of Ba as skin or surface) making it a triangulation, surely enough to convince an ox – or a hominid – once presented. So surfaces, we now know, comprise extensions in two dimensions, a Tau or T, see Sketch 23. Sketch 23 in fact shows up the shortcomings of my Sketch 22. Clearly Pa is replicable in both directions like Ba, not just in one direction as I showed it. The Tau shows the two dimensions of any surface; and there are two more dimensions, space and time, which it is sometimes taken to represent also; as well as the idea of two in the first place. I rather fancy the semantic root of three in turn is from the Rays of the Tau, there are three: alas, another dialectical intrusion with mystical connotations for musing on. The wise old owl, speaking in Lithic, would howl "terwit terwoo". Howling already had an i, an a and a u (the h was a Cockney h separating two consecutive vowels, one of which is then apt to be dropped in colloquial speech. In the case of the owl's hoot the h was doing double duty, for trauma and for cockney duty together). Ter wit ter wau, is very wise and very doubly wise, for witches who can read it. For long, witchcraft was a poor man's Marxism, stuck with their dialectic, mind and matter in a crazy waltz together. Can we draw the parallel: Marxism as the modern man's witchcraft? The Egyptian owl, by the way, was a more down to earth bird and spoke a different coarser lingo, saying "Aa Mahoo", Always both Ma, viz darkness and death in Egyptian. He was a nocturnal marauder, and the Mau (all the Mas) fixed him later in glyph as the bird for alphabetic M, and he is a lot easier to draw than a vulture. The Egyptian glyph for Taun (Sketch 24) was a circle cut in half, regarded as a bun by Egyptologists. This was because the whole circle, the lip shape for "oo", was an O, as it still is for us. Their idea of the sublunary world was a flat disc like a penny with a dome shaped fly cover over it. The other half of the gismo, the underside of the penny, similarly domed, was the Dua Taun or Second World (misconstrued by the Egyptologists as simply "Duat") ruled over by the dead sun as it travelled across West to East, to be reborn into our Taun and blaze afresh in the sky like Osiris (really Au Sarai in the original Egyptian, Universal Sunrise, promising rebirth after death for all, like the Christians' God later). The sky or Heaven was Pai Taun in Egyptian, Roof of the Universe, (misconstrued by the Egyptologists as "Pet", more like a spit). The original prototypical roof for Semites in the desert was made of goatskins. The divided unity can be drawn both halves together, it can even be unity dividing, and thus a parturition, in which case the O might be taken as the birth canal. The birth canal opens and rounds out to pass the head of the infant in a truly astonishing manner – and they say it hurts – bound to have caught the attention of our simple forebears. The Egyptian Aton, which the Egyptologists think is the disc of the sun, is really the Aa-taun, the Everlasting Birth Canal, the sun which is born from the dark Dua Taun at Dawn and dies diving into the sea at dusk, simultaneously birthing light into the world at sunrise each day and dowsing the light at night. Perhaps there should be a pause here to explain this ancient poetry. The Egyptian mind in ancient times saw the world as a peep show with successive scenes presented, and these re-petitive becomings they articulated as repetitive births, scenic shots. For linguistic purposes, the oo could be the literal round orifice required to make the sound or equally its abstracted signification of totality, in both instances equally using its shape to derive its meanings. The universe was thus the totality of events rather than the totality of locations we think of today.

What I have tried to show with the 24 sketches in Figure 3 is that the mind started out with shapes. I shall be told by academics I have trawled up a whole lot of quite unreliable dream material which can neither be proved nor disproved and it is therefore unscientific, anecdotal (just gossipy) and not worth pursuing. That is why I have included the Egyptian which has linguistic links and the semantics are therefore open to debate, proof or disproof. It may be the material is less un-reliable than unwelcome to academics bent on publishing their own concoctions based on rather different semantic prepossessions. In any case, all the linguistic connections should properly be taken into account before deciding they are in-sufficient to provide a convincing statistical base of correlations. All of science is in reality ultimately statistical. Those who decline to be persuaded of the validity of the linguistic points of contact with the semantic catenas worked out in this study of Lithic should be asked to devise another arbitrary scheme of their own as complex and wide ranging in scope without anything to do with Lithic which can exhibit a similar number of points of contact with language today, in order to show the Lithic correspondences worthless. Or even to just name two they know already.

The central mystery is still how the synapses in the brain come to prompt for the ideas in the mind. It is hard to see how any electronic state of play can at the same time simply be an idea. Recently an indication was vouchsafed me when new digital hearing aids restored sensitivity to a range of higher notes which had been missing for me for very many years, blurring many of the consonants beyond recognition, since I had the misfortune to get blown up while still quite young. The machines immediately reintroduced the missing frequencies but the brain no longer knew how to interpret them. Were they sounds or flavours or visual inputs? It took months (but not many) to recover the full proper audio-responses to the inputs of sounds from the hearing aids, so that the dawn chorus came fully back to life and the consonants lined themselves up once more with the utterances with which speech presented me. The translation of the raw signals and the brain's responses to them to picture, sound, idea, etc is by no means a simple matter, it is a skill which has to be learned. The skill is mysterious and subconscious and perhaps it will always remain so.

Meanwhile it is not irrational to conduct research just as if there actually were a little manikin in there monitoring the brain's performance. The mind has those characteristics in its own performance precisely, learning as it goes along. For all practical purposes there is a virtual ghost in the machine, anyway as long as the machine stays alive, doing its thinking for it. You can not stuff the mind into the brain (as we understand it). It won't go. Maybe it is the brain which needs to go back to the drawing board, and the cognitive linguistics buffs along with it.

CHAPTER 17

CONCLUSIONS

This chapter is included to answer in some measure the question often privately formulated if seldom put: why bother? Authors, especially those aspiring to scientific status to teach the senators wisdom, are inclined to attach too many lessons to their lucubrations. But now that the book is written there is little point in pretending I do not believe in it. It certainly seems to me there is an epochal element in the discovery of Lithic language, not only for semantics but also for the whole field of epistemology and even – at one remove – for mathematics, logic and the philosophy of science itself, which I believe must now recognise even math as derived from the original simple utterances of our hominid forebears. In no way is science thereby impugned, rather it is instated as in most ways the best thinking we have managed so far. But it is still just language. With such expanses of advancement already to our credit by means of the powers of thinking, we must conclude it is premature to draw any conclusions as to what more may or may not be achieved. Certainly in linguistic studies Pandora's box is at least and at last forced ajar. But the work that remains to be done should dwarf progress achieved to date, so that within the present century any contribution my study of Lithic language roots may have made will most probably be ignored and forgotten in the cataract of perceptions to follow, weaving a whole web of interconnected studies and research programmes and leaving my few original semantic catenas looking naked and uninspired. My book, if it is still read at all, will be read just for the patter. In short, the Lithic paradigm is a fertile one.

Fifteen years ago the overall Lithic scheme was presented to Penguin Books and the friendly advice was unequivocal: forget it if you do not wish to be pilloried as a maverick sex maniac. It has to be admitted that the sexual content has if anything increased rather than diminished since then. But this is because the mania is shared with every reader, since if we go back far enough – it is an edifying process in itself – we all have the same forebears and it is their mania. It may be the reader will still wish to slay the messenger; but that would be a pity since some understanding of how we have thought and therefore how we think today is essential for the understanding which everyone seeks. In a permissive age when the internet runs on porn a sober approach to digging up sexual images can surely be expected. At eighty years of age the subject matter is viewed objectively and not as a substitute for indulgence – as some may try to claim. We should not view our Stone Age forebears with over-riding disdain. They had no tele, no universities, no philosophy or politics worth the name, only the experience of daily living with which to occupy their minds. In the same circumstances it seems indisputable modern Sapiens Sapiens would share the same mania today: our principal life work is still to be fruitful and multiply and our principal interest is sexual – now expressed pictorially on television and in the art museums. Internet computing is already closing libraries, and dumbing down culture with soft porn. In fact the internet is said to be largely hard funded by the hard porn photographic filming it offers. That says a lot about Sapiens Sapiens: the sap still runs.

If you have really read this far you will by now likely be getting impatient for the use and purpose of the work if any. This can not of course be made the touch-stone for research, which can therefore prove to be entirely fruitless at the end of the exercise. Otherwise a distortion is introduced from the beginning. However Lithic, as it happens, is invaluable as an educational tool. First of all it puts us all in our place, not entirely estranged from the rest of the animal kingdom, but nevertheless with a uniquely quirky mind often subject to promptings which may not be entirely rational because they arise from our subconscious store of old saws and far from modern instances. Secondly it puts us in serious debt to our hominid forebears, whose burden of often rather silly ideas we still carry within ourselves below the level of conscious knowledge. There is nothing demeaning in that. We have our skill at heart beats etc from much more primitive forebears. We are a patchwork of abilities and functions, a bit like the Sphinx which is a patchwork of different animals with a human head stuck on top. It would be wrong to conclude we have learned nothing important in the last ten thousand years since the Sphinx was carved. We have learned almost everything that makes us what we are. But we need to remember we carry a ball and chain we are not going to escape in another ten thousand years. So much for the theory of everything improbablists are al-ready singing about. They are scientists rhapsodising without the least knowledge of the history and limitations of human thinking, since it can not be empirically addressed, and so they have not addressed it.

Writing on the origins of speaking and basing conclusions on diverse and thinly spread indications in an over rich medium – the world lexicon – is open to challenge as unscientific. There will always be the call for more evidence. It will also keep turning up; both for and against. The truth is science of every kind is in this position; the search for understanding is an amalgam of our own making. It is not the uncovering of a hard reality previously obscured by muddled thinking that most people would accept – the model scientists follow. On the contrary it is simply the invention of the right thinking for doing the job in hand, based on indications, many of them quite slight. Think about the "colours" and "flavours" of sub-atomic "particles" and their constituents; or spend a morning with Einstein and his spatial distortions. It takes quite a bit of habituation before any of this appears "hard"; and it is then the habituation which does it, not the evidence. This is an alarming truth since it implies we are suspended over an abyss supported by nothing more than the accumulated detritus of our own grey matter. But anyone confronting the basic constituents of our linguistic achievements and the thinking that has gone with it, much of it whimsical and some of it preposterous, is bound to come up against these realities. It encourages a proper scepticism and should therefore really be part of the national curriculum in schools, if only to discourage unrealistic meliorism on the one hand and hard posturing leading to terrorism on the other. But teaching the foolishness which has provided the universal pabulum, and received widespread support over aeons is not intellectually correct (IC), since it challenges the intellectual pecking order. An anti-IC stance is even more unpopular than an anti-PC one. Inviting the senators to move over is a recipe for confrontation. The only sane position is to invite the public to the ringside to see the fun; perhaps even to witness an execution, and decide upon the blame.

Next most important, the skids are at last under dialectical thinking, a miasma perhaps even older than speaking. Not even the most intellectual academic, nor the most unintelligent bozo can in future aspire to this kind of short cut to omniscience any more. Chapter 16 on the origins of thinking identifies the errors underlying the dialectic and is an assault upon ideology. In the context of the open society and its enemies, any rebuke to ideological pretentions must surely be benign. Neitzsche freaks and skinheads alike can anyway draw no comfort from their Lithic heritage, simply because of its risible element. The Uber-mensch has feet of clay like the rest of us. Hitler was the classic Superman but really an egomaniac buffoon. Hominid status was not an honourable one; and pride in our origins is raucously amusing. You might almost as well ardently wish to be a monkey. Fascism and terrorism are two sides to the same violent, atavistic and autistic mania, the terrorist worshiping his own club foot in search of the feelgood factor, which must ever escape him unless he capitulates: for he can never overcome his illusions unless he is first of all prepared to lose them, and from this his egotism bars him. He remains thus a spiteful prisoner ranting in the psychic cage he has locked himself in, yowling and catawauling rather than singing, and killing in the meantime in the hope of breaking the bars. His blacks and whites are grays for the rest of us, and we are right and the Usamas are playing the monkey role. The proliferation of terror is a spin off from German Nazism and Mid East copycat Baathism, a privatisation of totalitarianism – as nice an example as anyone could wish of the pervasiveness of mental posturing regardless of overt content or belief.

What is unbelievable to the terrorist Bin Laden and his fellow Wahabi religionists (Moslem heretics) is obvious enough to the observer (as above).

Our present urchin mind-set however can not help him; and Europe as a political organisation remains firmly Fascist even today, the democratic deficit glaring and even brazenly flaunted in Brussels, the new world capital of Fascism with (hopefully) just the genocide left out. Voting "No!" is discreetly described as a failure to communicate with the people, who have in turn failed to understand that they really want the Fascist State. There is even a trace of the Black Goddess Kali whose rules require the abuse and punishment of non believers by deceiving, robbing and if possible by garotting them while sleeping, on the grounds those not with you are against you. Her home base appears to have been in Arabia before Mohammed. It is a desert song. A cold coming they had of it. Her followers in India practicing Thuggee (the garotting, whence the English thug) were expelled in the fifteenth century to become Gypsies, because after being expelled again for anti social behaviour from Egypt in turn they pretended they were Egyptians, gaining bonus marks for deceiving the goy as to their origins. They had picked up some Egyptian folk magic which proved of use to frighten the goy too. The Egyptian Great Gods however do not approve of this deception, effectively taking their names in vain, and a thorough-going curse in Ancient Egyptian in the name of any one of the Egyptian Enead (their nine Great Gods) will send genuine Gypsies scurrying for their lives in hours, where the law takes months or years. You may have doubts about the power of the Egyptian Great Gods in these modern times but Gypsies have none, fearful of their past misdemeanours coming back to haunt them. With all savage beliefs the necessity is to confront them. The only way to break the vicious circle is to educate the Gypsies with their fellow citizens, which is an offence against Kali's rules and finally breaks their bondage when She is seen to be impotent. Until then religious belief in Kali, a mirage arising from the cruel waterless desert, will continue to put them in hostile confrontation with unbelievers as a matter of eventual salvation. The Wahabi tradition has something in common with Kali. It is not a Moslem tradition, but its opposite. It was in fact what the Prophet rebelled against. His jihads (vigorous actions) were against his own tribesmen.

The dialectical idiom is an early and thus a long established one, relatively harmless in moderation but poisonous as an imperative. Dialectic stipulates that whenever you have two related terms in apposition the position is one of opposition. (The detailed analysis, and refutation, is exhaustively covered in chapter 16, on thinking). So ka is antithetic to la, as la is to ma; and ma is to ish and perhaps sa is to ta, with ta antithetic to ka. In semantic terms ka, strike, is antithetic to la, lapse; and la, slight/light, is antithetic to ma, heavy and dark; and ma, dark to sa, bright; and sa, single to ta, split into two, and ta, naturally become to ka, forcefully made. But then we find other pairings: so sa, easy and sweet, is antithetic to la, sly and bitter; and there will be many others but the point is made. These few examples establish the pattern that has heavily influenced human thinking. In chapter 16 it is argued that it was the three vowels which originally triggered the perception. It can also be seen that the vowels are in some sense a legacy from our pre-linguistic past. They are a left over from our tonal howls and cries before we learned to speak by utilising the consonant sounds to break up our cries into the manageable (because precisely reproducible) pieces of speech. What atavistic folk memories they must conjure up in our subconscious minds! Our conscious minds are just the icing on the enormous sponge cake made in the paleolithic kitchens down below. Simple distinction is an early achievement of the human brain. Perhaps it is a pointer to the fact that from the outset prelinguistic thinking was on the road to the dialectic: divide in two, to and fro, there and back, a ping pong in the mind, fallacious ab initio; but nevertheless highly revealing as our road to abstraction. If we go back to the nursery wallpaper in chapter 16 we can see the first perception of the world around us was triggered by the contrast between visual textures. It was a novelty arising from the emergence out of the darkness of the womb into the blazing light of day, and the newly opened eye fastening in the light upon (for example) the contrast of being red and not being red. It was the origin of the tyranny of the eye, pernicious in the absence of further and subsequent ratiocination admitted as evidence. Although prior to language, dialectic does not hold priority over linguistic thinking, and even less over mathematics, a later spin-off from language, now treated as if it provided a direct access to ultimate reality rather than being merely a triumphant composition of the human mind. Klaus Fuchs, a nuclear physicist who spied for Russia, betrayed his tennis club, his family and his country – in that order – because he did not understand this, and could not break free from the Marxist dialectical thinking. Ah well!

More importantly however, the workings of the subconscious mind, indeed its very existence as a calculating entity conscious of semantics on its own, is evidenced by Lithic language survival. Freud had an unconscious he patterned rather unconvincingly with egos, ids, etc., supposed entities he picked from his own dream world. The Lithic subconscious is a bit different, with no real dragons apparent. The Lithic hypothesis is not difficult to understand: the lexicon is made up of sounds with semantic contents and the catena leading to the subconscious, which I do not believe can be broken, goes like this. Lithic language roots are evidenced world wide, originating in the psychosemantic promptings of the aboriginal hominid mind some hundreds of thousands of years ago. They could not be, because of the rate of linguistic change and the noise or blurring this generates, unless there were a means of refreshment in place and continually at work. No such refreshment mechanism can be detected in the conscious mind, which is why academia has denied the possibility of such Lithic survival – and therefore and thenceforth omitted to look for it. But it now follows as day follows night the refreshment does occur, but in another place – in the subconscious.

Jung went on to posit a store for psychological archetypes (of his choice) in a metaphysical World Soul or universal mind from which we mortals' minds were all dependent – shades of Plato's mental archetypes – and to which the privileged at least were able to gain access by insight. He thought this was his unique discovery. Like all discoveries in the mind they often come with a wodge of personal predilections. He effectively located the subconscious he claimed to be able to read, deciphering the archetypes, out there in the other, and not part of the individual mind. It has to be said too he thought the discovery the reward for his intellectual virtue. His was of course a clerical mind. He was also of course of Hitler's generation, though to tell him so would have been to him poison. The Lithic hypothesis in stark contrast keeps everything within the bounds of science, with the subconscious using solely the semantics implicit in the language sent down to it, and the ability to express its self-generated contents available only to its own individual owner, its partner in the same body, knowing only the language it has learned. There is no call for any invention of etherial entities or soul media with broadcasting potential, or for sublimation of location. or action at a distance such as Jung prayed in aid, in order to undercut his publisher.

There is nothing in Lithic which is not in the lexicon if seriously interrogated. Jung´s universal mind is rescued by Lithic from the transcendental limbo in which he left it. The vapourings are traced to their true source, the subconscious mind every individual has. It goes back a long way. At base some say there is even a crocodile mind which some psychopaths discover and summon to the surface – though we were never crocodiles.

The Lithic elements discovered in the foregoing chapters are no more than remnants of the grammar of Ur Speech, which in itself we can never hope to recover, for all those reasons the obscurantists offer for curtailing etymology. Lithic nevertheless is of acute significance. As a first grammar it is a more fundamental guide to the operations of the human mind than the transformational version we apparently contrived, according to Naom Chomsky, aeons later, which is based on speech as we know it, with strings of words looking for ways of conveying meanings more and more precisely, and probably finding them in a slow build up of rules designed to aid understanding. It is understanding which has been the goal from day one, an ambition which is still what makes us believe our world goes round the sun. It is a fact of life you need to understand. It does in fact make the world go round – not love, but the love of comprehension, the eureka feeling, which is much the same as plain love, the recognition of the other and making it your own without any restraint or reservation whatsoever. So force yourself or not, you have to go over the ground in pursuit of understanding, and this includes these days examining instinctive drives, including the most subconscious, as well as their perversions. You must be a rapist, a mutilater of the human form, you must rejoice in the brutal castration by your own hand of your enemies (with an obsidian knife?), and the wholesale slaughter of the innocents. In short you must explore the whole spectrum of humanity and not shrink from it – of course only in the mind – forcing your attention on the most perverse perversities and vilest acts which naturally (if you have been even averagely brought up) you shie away from. Needless to say you may roam the fair uplands of love and affection as well, as antidote to the other, but this you are likely to do of your own volition in any case.

In the foregoing chapters some exercise has been had of the semantic processes whereby meanings have proliferated and diversified, along with the underlying human whimsy which comes largely from our underground store of arcane associations thrusting through to consciousness in largely unrecognisable form; so that, for very many, full awakefulness is never achieved. Potentially we are all zombies, and it is from a very long line of zombies we all proceed, more savage than noble. I have represented the development of speech patterns as spun by Scrimshaw man and Wayland Smith. Scrimshaw precises and constructs, working as if carving a filigree in ivory. You can think of him in caricature as Old Chalky, the Alistair Sims antediluvian schoolmaster. Wayland meanwhile hammers away at his own devices, slovening and slurring for an easy pronunciation, and often spoiling Scrimshaw's finesse.

With bind and bund, pond and pen, open or unpen, even with the Latin ripa for river bank and English trap, to draw shut (the lid)we can, if we try hard, discern an underlying common element which can perhaps be represented by something like the word enclosure. But to understand why words have the meanings they do it is always necessary to expand them back to their full original forms and then examine the underlying elements of meaning they comprise emanating from their constituent phoneme strings. Astoundingly, if this Lithic hypothesis is correct, it is possible to uncover the original symbolisations attributed to the constituent phonemes. Thus what in the above bind-pen group is disclosed is the idea of enclosure, of surrounding even, which survives and resides in the subconscious of mankind, reinstalled for each generation as they learn to speak. Of course this goes against the grain of conventional thinking, because we long ago stopped indulging in this kind of analysis, and it is only in the subconscious that the traces of the methodology still survive. It is the poet's blind bran dip. By definition if it is subconscious it is something we are unaware of, so critics will abound. No hard wiring is required: the Lithic hypotheses supercede the hard wiring of Chomskyan and the Massachusets Institute of Technology's (MIT's) neuro-linguistics.

The p consonant certainly seems to get its enclosure meaning from being the thinned version of the phoneme Ba, which is installed in the subconscious as the sound of flesh on flesh from the lips when saying b. P, the thinned version of b which suggests flesh, is thus identified as the thinned version of flesh and so the skin, leading to surface, lid, roof, cover and then enclosure. Whereupon – and this illustrates the signature tune or modus operandi of the subconscious mind. – the enclosure idea picked up by p feeds back to the prior b. B, as well as flesh, acquires a blocking or bunging function. We may learn from this that in subconscious thinking there are no crisply discriminated categories or pecking orders, as in our waking thinking, but a fuzzier inconsequential relationship of semantic drift. If there is a phonetic contiguity there is a semantic pathway. Meanings flow. The neural networks involved with phonetics and semantics evidently mingle. A wide-awake state is needed to separate them and keep them separated.

The late Jacques Derrida's deconstrucionism has been regarded as iconoclastic and chaotic, but it was intended as the reverse: as an eye-opener to the richness of interconnected meanings accessible in any text. A text is a phonetic string with associated semantic contents. Derrida launched a broadside caveat against simple deductive thinking. He was clearly aware of the subconscious pot pourri over which our waking rational thinking is carried on a gossamer surface. To be sure rational deduction is not to be sneezed at. Scientific conventions are not contra-indicated. But it does seem Derrida, like Eric Partridge, and perhaps the later Wittgenstein, was half way to understanding Lithic. The Lithic hypotheses too amount to a "propositional reconstructionism", and in order to reconstruct thin-king it is necessary to prick the facade of convention. The way we think is simply the way we think. Thinking is not set in Platonic forms. If a new way demonstra-tes its utility by providing the stretch to cover the facts as they become known it will be adopted. Admittedly an Einstein is sometimes needed to break the mould, to make a lateral side-step with a new approach rearranging the scenery. But at other times the side step virtually presents itself. His space-time is metaphor.

The discovery of burnt bones from seventy thousand years ago, and some snail shells in Western Cape Province in South Africa with holes in and signs of wear from threading, has recently led to a reiteration (with a bit of updating) of some of the old and thoroughly suspect dates of crucial cultural landmarks in the his-tory of man. Because writing began in the last ten thousand years it was guessed speaking should be about four times older. The guess is quite groundless; but as nobody knew any better, the views of the academic establishment have been allowed to stand unchallenged. It is in any case no matter of concern. The indi-cations from Lithic of a much longer period of time since our hominid forebears began to speak, say a hundred times longer than the current belief for instance, is similarly a matter of no fundamental concern. We have come the way we have come at the pace at which we have come. Since the time scale is anyway very long, even a factor of a hundred is not a principal matter for contention. It may be we brought with us our barbarous mentality a hundred times longer than is suggested in these chapters. But there seems no reason to assume it, and there is no call for repentance just because I continue to prefer to relate hominid thinking and the origins of speaking to a far remoter period than academia currently allows. Dating is a modern fetish we do not need to share. The timing of prehistoric change is not critical. Nice to think we done it quickly. But there!

Whatever one may think of Chomsky, his transformational grammar is self evidently a late construct, irrelevant to any enquiry as to the origins of speaking. The origins are prior. How any transformational grammar might in turn have originated is a quite separate study. The transformational subconscious is certainly one which could take a Lithic performance in its stride, and perhaps vice versa it could be argued a Lithic subconscious might get up to a bit of transformation later. In any case I suspect our original idioms, still traceable today, will have been involved. They will not be welcome to a wrangler of mathematical bent, heir to a long line of mathematically minded language buffs. But these were his forebears as well as ours, whose thinking I have tried to expose. Words are certainly neither integral nor original and language is learned most readily phoneme by phoneme. Writing is the same, and letter by letter is the way to teach it, making use of an idiom the mind has accommodated for hundreds of millennia and thousands of generations. Teaching words first is mad, even if not certifiable (yet).

Philosophers should take warning from Aristotle. His whole world was one of fantasy. His aether was an insubstantial and so incorruptible element making up all celestial objects, with a natural propensity to move, drawn round the centre of the universe in circles. Air was considered insubstantial. Gases were not yet identified. Wind was evidence of the propensity of the insubstantial to get drawn out just like other things. The ether was ´ai-tahei-arai´, from the Lithic ´that which-vagina-rayed´ – and so drawn out just like the male genitalia whenever they encountered these feminine rays – but being celestial the pull for the ether was of course perfectly circular, an eye watering prospect.

It took two millennia to shake the human mind free from this miasma, in which time, when it proved incorrect, epicycles had been added tier after tier to save the aether from abandon. Aristotle also had the universe composed of four substantial elements, earth, air, fire and water. Earth was massive because it tended to the centre of the earth. Ma, chapter 10, was down, being the opposite of Ish which was up (the flame springs upwards); and so in Lithic phonemes ma was earth (inter alia) which is solid and heavy matter and tends downwards, maintaining the pattern of the Lithic dialectic. The old man had grubbed the science out of his subconscious, just like Hegel and Marx who disinterred the dialectic itself somewhat later. Air belonged above the surface of the earth where it sat passive and immobile. It was not going anywhere until tugged, just like the trouserless boys in the age of the Pleistocene. For Aristotle fire went upwards because its home was at the top of the universe. Like our hominid forebears he had spotted the flame leaps upwards unlike solid objects which possessed ma. His water belonged on the surface of the earth, hugging it as it were, the other boy in the family. Our hominid forebears had liquids instinctively lapsing sideways down sloping surfaces diagonally into the lows, which to my way of thinking was a more accurate characterisation than Aristotle´s when you think how puddles form and rivers flow; but they were quite closely related. That left fire and earth making up the girls team, as life sources but adding matter only! The boys were claiming the spiritual and structural element, almost as if they were the architects with an element of divinity. They knew nothing, or anyway very little about the birds and the bees, but they had probably divined they contributed some kind of permissive input or know-how by vouchsafing conjugation, seen as an opening process – they had evidently explored the hymen with their grubby fingers.

As a last and capstone work, I have kept Aphrodite as a bon bouche for those who have read the rest of the book all through. Apparently she came ashore riding in an outsize conch shell, after generation from the sea foam (apparently thought of as Zeus´s ejaculate) in a particular bay in northern Cyprus, as I have cause to remember, since some considerable time later I found myself rescuing a soldier being inexorably swept out to sea, without any shell to ride on, from the very same bay. Our very different treatments by Father Neptune was, I believe, due solely to the two sides of the bay, the West side the tide sweeps in and the East side it sweeps out, as must have been known in Ancient Greece but had been forgotten since. I was lucky to discover Aphrodite´s secret just in time, and we were washed up on the other side of the bay after an exhausting swim round on the way to Turkey. The boy had cut his foot on a rock and so let his leg hang down as a sail in the current with me thrashing in the opposite direction coastwards. Friends shouted encouragement as we sailed past the Eastern headland on our way out: they would fetch a boat from Larnaca, some fifteen kilometers away. They might as well have asked the Turkish coast guards to keep an eye out for us. As hero of the episode I am proud to say I never thought to drop him off and let him sail away to Turkey on his own; but then the water was warm and welcoming just as it was no doubt for Aphrodite when she sailed in – although she apparently stayed dry and alluring aboard her shell.

Aphrodite was the Greek goddess of carnal love, and Lithic analysis can show it. We do not need to follow the etymologists amongst the ancient Greeks who appear to have got the sea foam rubric from the –phro- bit. From Aa-pahei-rau-dai-tai in Lithic elements we may surely read aa, extensive-pahei rau, all the phaluses in arousal- dai, does, -tai, her vagina; or, more loosely "Without cease her vagina is sending every erect phalus its rousing call". With such a performance it is hardly surprising the Greeks unanimously adopted Her as their goddess, and the very exemplar of erotic love. Eros himself, the mischievous putty of arousal, Lithic a-i-rau (s), he-of-the rays or erection, with his comical minuscule priapism, later airbrushed out altogether so he was given instead a small bow and arrow for the job, was by comparison just hinting. The Lithic Ai-rau(s) for Eros and eroticism at any remove of grammar is easy enough if you understand the sex rays the genitalia were supposed to exchange in olden times, leading to arousal; and are aware the final vowel –u is a completive one: Eros is Ai-rau-s, he of the dual (or reciprocal interacting) rays, with the Greek substantive terminal –s. He was an ever ready (sexual) rayer for all: the sex principle as understood at that time. He was pictured as a cupid, but he was basically a psychosemantic concept arising from the subconscious mind.

Apart from the childishness of the minds which wrapped themselves round these ideas there is some guidance to be gleaned from them on the way we were thinking. First of all, who and where exactly was this potent lady Aphrodite, and how was she able to perform her function in life so omnipresently in everybody´s bed at once, cajoling and inspiring with a single purpose in mind. The answer is of course she was a mental or psychic entity and not a separate personality at all. She was to be found within the subconsciousness of every individual. She was eroticism as it presented itself instinctively to each and every hombre. Where the mind was, there she was, potentially anyway. In other words the erotic instinct was in her recognised as mediated by the conscious mind from promptings from elsewhere. She was a straightforward psychic entity as we would say today. The elsewhere was not understood since the self itself was not yet fully isolated from the environment, and so the subconscious was quite readily treated as a separate party, an outsider – in this case the goddess Aphrodite as with other Greek gods, all representing psychic outputs of one kind or another, mostly mischievous and over sexed. There was a time when this was new: Aphrodite was news. She was discovered. The psyche was still largely being lived by natural influences, internal and external alike, without much conscious attention. But now she was recognised and named doing it, labelled for reference and debate. She was the recognition of subconsciousness in an important area, a half way stage on the way to consciousness of our own independent (conscious) selves. Her role was contemporary and perhaps a trifle illiberal by modern day standards. The Lithic language can be seen to have been first of all absolutely explicit as to its function, pathfinding, stark even; but later probably simply repeated parrot fashion without any conscious understanding of its construction. Aphrodite thus marked our early fixation on sex, like so much else in the primitive lexicon. She was living through us, or better we were being lived by her, all the way from our first hominid compilation of the elements of the lexicon – just as today we are vulnerable to our subconscious promptings which can pull to pieces our consciously constructed personas, leading to "nervous breakdowns" in the modern jargon.

The full and explicit recognition has been sent back down below again, wiped from the slate of conscious attention, as if it were never meant to be brought to the surface in the first place. Freud spotted some of this but unfortunately improvised the semantic contents to suit his personal whimsy. But perhaps that is to press the implications in Aphrodite´s case too far. What is more likely to my mind is that along with the whole of Lithic language its true nature was submerged over the millennia (represssed much as Freud had it) in a revulsion against the dumb crudity, the sheer animality, of our thought and behaviour at the time our hominid ancestors learned to speak. All over the world the species voted for humanity and shucked off their animal origins, and we have been doing it – with notable back slidings on the part of rather too many emotional runts and deviants – ever since. The coarse original semantic contents have thus been tuned out, or at least toned down over the millennia, although vouchsafed astonishing longevity in the subconscious. It is clear the common campus greeting "Hi!" in the States has come a long way from the Ancient Egyptians´ glyph of a rutting drake pronounced ter-hei, or their glyph of a rampant penis, pronounced pa-hei, the whoopee or f...ing piece, and this was only a few thousand years ago. The civilised revolution we are living through is as yet a new born babe.

Our humanity comes nevertheless ultimately from those very animal instincts which humans have aspired to outrun. The word defining the human species, in Lithic form "Hai-u-ma´n", "Enjoying-Both[sexes]-the planting or copulation or begetting", marked the consensual conjugation, warm and cuddly together in the heat close around the hearth, which replaced the solitary chase and subjugation of the female in the rest of the animal kingdom, a flipswitch of emotional confrontations between the sexes we are as a species after a myriad generations still in the process of cementing solid. It was the women who for a few hundred millennia sat and worked around the hearth keeping the fire alight while the menfolk hunted unheated, so perhaps it was to be expected the men thought it was the women who were the nymphs, Lithic nai-em-pahei, the drawers out of their pahei in the warmth when they got back to base. It may indeed require a few more thousand generations before we win through to a uniform genotype enjoining intimate consensual unhurried gentle sexual union enjoyable by both sexes as a matter of course, rather than as an elite achievement. It may not seem much on which to base our humanity at first sight, but on reflection it opens the way of course to a mutual recognition of wants and interests which is the necessary prerequisite for civilised love and affection today. In ending, the derivation of humus makes an apt final run to clear the decks for humanity as above. There have been those who have believed humans identified themselves as the earthlings, the earthy ones. Did this direct Darwin´s attention to earth worms, one wonders? Partridge glosses "human" as "the earthy one, the earth born" (sic!). It was one of his less felicitous guesses: it illustrates the propensity of the human mind to accept any nonsense if there appears to be evidence for it – in the absence of the opportunity to refer to all the evidence which Lithic offers. It may seem some way from the earth to copulation, but the fact is the linguistics relates them: they both share a common functionality, the planting of the seed; and for that reason they share the same lithic phoneme, Ma (see chapter 10). Only a little academic slip is needed to serve up rubbish. Etymology without Lithic offers nothing better than a phonetic scrabble.

It may seem presumptuous to pick a whole string of letters (phonemes) from a single word and then attach meanings to every single one of them, since the human mind surely does not fire with that speed and precision: there is something wrong somewhere. But then it has to be said the letters never sprung onto the page of their own accord either. It was the human mind that put them there. Why? It is surely not such a way out idea there could have been reasons for their selection. Word formation goes back a long way. It may even have been single Sapiens´ signature tune when first arriving on the scene – before Sapiens Sapiens, who conceitedly fancies it was he who learned to speak, his unique achievement marking him out as uniquely intellectual. If it is true – I believe it is – that words formed as a secondary process, from the strings of phonemes put together for the combination of their individual meanings, it will have been at a time when the human mind was indeed thinking in terms of these individual meanings. My guess is we spoke a lot slower in those days as we went through the meaning strings like an old priest fingering his beads. A concomitant of the formalisation of these strings grouped into words was a great saving in ratiocination. When each string had to be analysed to yield its overall meaning, often not immediately obvious for those who had never been sat down to learn their psychosemantic trees, you sometimes even needed a soothsayer for the job, like with "Mene mene tekel upharsin". The Lithic can be read as follows: Mai-nai, mass/amount/weight-protruding/presenting/showing. The repetition indicates plurality, emphasis or both: weigh weigh: you have been weighed in the balance (seven times!). Tekel: compare Hebrew shekel, a weight, from shaqal to weigh from the Lithiic elements sha-i-ka-lai, action-which-make-level, action making level. The weighing pans were hanging from the ends of a stick suspended in the middle. It was the balancing action which was indicated, as if judgmental. Upharsin is from the Lithic A-u-pahei-ra-sai'n, that-un-pleasant-eye-sensed-one, seen to be displeasing, found wanting.

With words, instead of having to recapitulate the meanings of the gamut of phonemes strung along every time, only the meaning which was the end product needed to be learned, in place of each of the constituent phonemic meanings and their combinatory indications. The vocabulary is then of word meanings instead of phonemic meanings. But this surprisingly leads not to less meanings but to more, because the human mind, as it turns out, is quite capable of memorising hundreds of thousands of words and their meanings, not just the few hundred meanings provided by the phonemes with which to compile speech as it was first spoken. Recapitulation is so much easier for us than invention. Mentally we are copy-cats. We copy much better than we compose or analyse. The phonemic meanings which had enabled the human mind to break into symbolisation had become restraints, as generation after generation had each added their mickle to the semantic pile. Verbalisation, the invention of words as simples, was thus a paradigm shift probably greater than any other, perhaps the very marker which in reality distinguishes Sapiens Sapiens from his plain Sapiens predecessor. It is clear the old men will have resisted the switch as they resist every paradigm switch, labelling the Babel which resulted in a judgment of God upon their contemporaries for their insolence in challenging the pre-existing Divine (Lithic) plan. Had God not spoken to their Adam in the old (unsynthetic) phonetics? Would not these new fangled tricks giving every language community a vocabulary of its own, quite outside the dictates of reason, lead to the dissolution of human knowledge and inevitable decline into savagery, with everyone ignorant of what they were really saying? In practice it proved quite otherwise; but one can not help sympathizing with the Babelites. It was pushing off into deep water without any obvious or proven paddle. Semantics became simply a matter of recollected usage, freeing the mind up, and in due course – well eventually – freed of the ties to phonetic structure it became possible to address the phonetics from a straight-forward technical point of view and represent them in symbols for writing. We should not forget the power of untangling what sorts not of itself. It can enable the mind to move forward into areas previously denied to it, as in this case.

Moreover these psychosemantic promptings will today sometimes appear far fetched. Can it really have happened that such trivial indications proved powerful enough pointers to have determined meanings for all time? I believe it can. It seems there were butterflies fluttering over Ecuador long ago in the Stone Age when the human mind was in relative chaos, with little of it operating above the conscious threshold. The original psychosemantic contents I have picked out have survived in the etymological derivations of the languages we use today not because they were ever determined for all time but just because that is what, when it came to it, just happened to match the whimsies of the human race. If we could relive the last few hundreds of thousands of years there is no reason to suppose that the same butterflies would be around in Ecuador, or that the history of human thinking would come out precisely the same again. It is indeed the uniqueness of this human legacy which gives it its principal fascination, a heterogeneous collection of quite disparate original prompts I have named psychosemantic because they were what came naturally from our psychological orientations before conscious consideration had much part to play. The same psychosemantics, which now imprint themselves along with the lexicon on every infant learning to speak, with the Lithic part all below the level of consciousness, can also appear deeply disturbing to those inhabiting a well scrubbed environment, scrupulously sweeping any old dust under their carpets. To learn there are all these Lithic creepy crawlies in residence there is not going to be welcome news for them. They will probably prefer to bumble along in their sanitized emporia with the thirty percent nervous breakdowns at one time or another.

But once you have got used to the idea that there is a subconscious area in the mind which is capable of knowledge of a sort, unsophisticated compared with the hard grafting we have trained ourselves to when we address the world directly and consciously, but nevertheless capable of carrying on a tradition of crude associations sufficient to inform the linguistic record, then you are ipso facto aware that Lithic language is a perpetual accompaniment to rational thinking, just at one remove. In poetic moments I have imagined an unending pie of closely intertwined human bodies stretching back hundreds of thousands of years, miraculously all talking to each other. I have to admit these bodies are naturists, all unclothed and quite unbothered by it, I guess because they symbolise the true nature of their minds, not directly their bodily avatars at all but simply recognising their naked adjacency as the reality of our mental heritage. For the observer there is at first an element of horror in quite so much human flesh so intimately heaped together – a bit like a plague of soldier caterpillars of the Cabbage White butterfly – especially if your imagination starts to play tricks on you and you imagine them squirming together, like at a weekend Californian flower power party. But it fades when it becomes clear they are all alive and well and conversing about anything and everything amongst themselves – as indeed of course they did, though not all at the same time together. As history was really played, Father Time´s spotlight lit up a single belt of humanity at a time. But the chain of discourse, that intimate intercourse of ideas, has never been broken. There is no reason to suppose once language started out it ever had to start again from scratch everywhere on earth. No society was ever rendered dumb, although some have suffered capital punishment unless they changed to the victors´ tongue. The Egyptian language was lost in this way when the Wahabis rampaged across North Africa masquerading as Moslems.

But even Wahabis had Lithic in their subconscious. So Lithic is Perpetual Lithic. It is not all that surprising. We have perpetual legs too, though we use them less and less while talking more and more. It is just the legs are not mediated through the mind. After so many years speech has something of the texture of papier-mache, with a fuzzy semantics where the meanings become tinctures made up of surrounding meanings and fade one into the other. That is why you can often read a group of Lithic phonemes in more ways than one, in much the same way that a deaf person – I am now quite deaf, enough to make normal social inter-course quite difficult – can often make sense of a sentence in more ways than one, sometimes leaving him holding the wrong end of the stick entirely. This can not be used as an argument the Lithic meanings attached to phonemes are so gen-eral as to make so many meanings available that any assemblage is inconclusive. The psychosemantic trees I have tried to present with the chapters dealing with individual phonemes in turn are actually to some extent misleading because there are innumerable pathways in the mind connecting the semantic contents; and the lines of derivation which I have drawn out are simply one strategem for bringing the linkages into consciousness.

My vision of a pie of intertwined bodies stretching across time owes some-thing also to the pie of intertwined meanings in the subconscious minds of those bodies stretching across time. The poet's pie is a congealed congeries of pieces forming a mess or mass, (and the printers' pie is a collection of pieces with letters on them, put in order and the frame then tightened around them to hold them in place for printing). As such it owes nothing to the Lithic etymology of a lid-ded dish as opposed to an open tart and made the printers' pie. The congeries of pieces are what lie under the lidded tart. The pie is a classic case in point for fuzzy semantics since simultaneously pai is both pieces and lid, either or both together, which is probably why it won out as the description for the dish. These ´doubles-entendres´ or double meanings are common with Lithic derivations, as if they settled arguments in the original naming committees: two pointers were better than one. When following through the sequence of constituent atomic meanings, two semantic routes of assemblage were confirmatory and not conflicting.

We can see the same only more so with the Phoenix. The Phoenix palm has a vertical (erect) branchless trunk. Any old trunk, tirau´n-kai is already a drawn out form (kai), and a hard (kai) form with it. Ph- from Pahei meanwhile is a pe-nis, erect, orgasmic, ejaculating (and so presenting), intercourse, a sexual embrace, ecstasy, delight, any of these or all of them together at the same time (see chapter 12 for Pa and chapter 8 for hei). Phoenix, Pahai-oo-i-nai, originally with the phoneme nai suggesting the expulsion of breath at orgasm after holding it as the tension builds, when ejaculating (and so presenting) is later interpreted as merely protruding, exposing, exhibiting and so presenting itself, fundamentally the erec-

tile quality, an erection. Pe-nai(s) is similarly the protruding piece, and so an indicator of what is on the owner´s mind, and so before trousers a witness piece. The
presenting in the case of the phoenix palm tree is clearly the erect trunk, pahai-u-
ai-nai-kai(s), "[like the] penis-one-that is-presenting-shaped", i.e. shaped like an
erect penis. The plain fact is of course the configuration of the one is very little like
the other, but that is not going to interfere with the mischief of human whimsy.
Both articles stick up, and that will do for an audience attuned to think at any
opportunity in sexual metaphor. They thought in terms of sex rather as water ran
down hill. It helps if you have at one time been a schoolboy, however long ago, if
you want to follow the vulgarity of our primitive forebears´ minds. Our earliest
aim was to master expletives rather than to understand, and even today the youth
of the nation take sex to be an opportunity for plaspheming rather than a challenge for their understanding. How does psychology explain this? It surely betrays
a tension brought on by sex. It is surely a consequence of the genitalia sharing
their premises with the urinary tract, an economical design from the structural
point of view which nature invented before the psyche was sufficiently sensitive
to protest. Now the psyche and the physics sometimes grind together like shifting
continental plates. We have invented for ourselves our own conscious natures, at
some points out of kilter with the blind natures we are born with.

The original idiom of the adjectival mind is explained in chapter 16. There was
a sense in which the penis and the palm tree had this commonality of character,
expressed each in its own quite different way each in their animal and vegetable
kingdoms: the shared protocol an adjectival character to be found all over, intelligently picked up in the language. In the case of the palm a bunch of leaves sprouts
out the top, the palm´s vegetative expression of the same ejaculative principle
expressed in sexual conjugation. When the palm leaves die they hang down in
a tinder dry brown mass where the birds nest. Planted close together and fired,
their leaves blaze but the trees survive and foliate and fruit the following year
– like the Phoenix bird. Nowadays they are cut every few years by heros who shin
up the trees with a loop of rope around their bodies and the trunks. The Phoenix
bird could have been modelled on any game bird, a pipi like the quail chick, a
cheeper, and then like the pipi or pan pipe which peeped like the quail chick, and
thereafter the pipi which is a small pipe a bit like a pan pipe although it does not
peep or cheep, the male penis. The penis instead orgasms and in Ancient Egypt
was called pahei (or sometimes bahei) or else more prosaically mai. Mai meant
the earther, the planter, the inseminator, a relatively clinical description. Pahei was
the joy piece or ecstacy shoot. So the Phoenix which started out a bird became
transmogrified into a penis, a rather more subtle string of connections than with
the Phoenix tree which merely shared its erectile character and perhaps its ef-
florescence at the top with the male organ (if you wanted to think that way, as

clearly we did). The fire it dies in and is resurrected is the little death, the orgasm – with a sentient intensity like the flame but of opposite polarity, pleasurable not painful. Just as a tuft of palm leaves could emulate an ejaculation in the minds of our hominid forebears, so the sexual experience could be matched to a fire flaring up, flickering and then bursting into an all consuming blaze. Nobody ever imagined they were actually burning when they copulated. But they thought they were experiencing the same qualititive sequence as the flame, pleasure in a shared protocol with pain, a contrasting pair; and that for them was science, spotting the common patterns in the world and coding them – much like today in fact. No doubt they picked on the motifs they liked to think about, much as (it is popularly argued) scientific research programmes today are environmentally determined, that is to say mediated by the social constraints present in the scientists´ minds as they determine them.

It will be argued the meanings attributed to phonemes are too multifarious, and their combinations offer such polysemy that the semantic strings chosen as evidence carry no conviction. In short, the semantic contents of the phonemes postulated offer such a wide range of meanings that in every case a reading will always be possible, whether it is veridical or not. The argument has force and must be answered. If warranted it opens the way to Lithic being a free composition which can all be dismissed as fiction. But there is only one set of universally consistent meanings available to date, those presented in the present work – or perhaps only two, since alternative derivations occur in interpretations, apparently taken as conclusive when it came to naming things,

Critics will then wish to consider, before accepting Lithic, if the evidences adduced are statistically significant. Statistics are popularly supposed to be the ultimate fabrication, but that is only because statistical theory is so regularly abused. The items adopted for comparison must always be genuine independent variables, so that they must be items with a satisfactory degree of singularity. Establishing the independence of variables is a study in itself, only recently recognised. The whole of philosophy and logic for half a century motored along as if in a trance quite unaware that the idea of independent empirical observations was grossly flawed. It lends tone to the late Arthur Koestler´s characterisation, writing at that very time, of the great scientists as sleep walkers. Once established in the academic world you are probably – all unawares – lost in a thicket, protecting your own achievements, with the truly valid science in second place. In reality observation is subjective at two levels. Nature´s signals which it fires at us may be real and their impact "objective", that is to say reflecting accurately the objects whence they come; but the messages we manage to read into these signals are subjective mental-cum- emotional constructs. So for a paradigm or example, with a pinprick the pain is subjective though the actual puncture is objective (which is not the same as our view of it). The subjectivity of the senses is that simple. In chapter 16 the actual prick is Ro (P) but the pain is Psi (Ψ) see page 44 or 505. But then our psyches go on to inject whimsy, which is Phi (Φ), into every response, often absurdly where ratiocination is involved. Even vision, Psi (Ψ) is a complex mental representation, with its own conventions, of the dance of electromagnetic particles and waves, providing us with a panorama of patterned surfaces for the navigating utility it vouchsafes us. Of course you can introduce further subjective conventions with domains of discourse, symbolic logics and metalanguages, all Pi (Π), to try and insulate the mind from these perceptive misfortunes. But you can not have your cake and eat it: once choiring in these abstract and derivative realms you can not at the same time claim to be directly and objectively observing reality, Ro (P); and you are not! You are subjectively perceiving it.

Statistically it is fair to point out every step in the psychosemantic trees in the chapters on the phonemes, every meaning derived from the original sense has more than one word as exemplar. There are then thousands of complexed meanings and these are for the most part only those prompted by current English usage. World wide there are millions, even an infinity. Each one provides an opportunity of disproof as an independent statistical item. But falsification of the theory does not result from individual cases of misidentification of the evidence but only from wholesale schematic failure, all of the derivations proving false or the majority of them, or there is no subconscious mind, or speech has been intermittent, or a contradictory set of psychosemantic trees is available – not just a rearrangement of the terms but a different set of semantics altogether or none at all. This latter (none at all) is in reality the response already offered by conventional etymologists, but their own word etymologies which disregard the phonemic meanings are far less falsifiable since they are not universally consistent, they only cover single words, or a few words each, and at a phonetic level only – at which level of course under their rubric anything goes. Moreover since they argue for random word roots that is the same as saying there is no evidence for the etymology other than current word use, regardless of meanings, whereas word structure (prefixes, suffixes and infixes) is common ground between Lithic and anti-Lithic. Under the anti-Lithic random rubric the phonemic semantics can not in any case be prayed in aid, although this is unblushingly contradicted when echoism (onomatopaea) is identified. Or, to put it another way, with prefixes etc the build up of words from phonemic components, some at least single phonemes, is admitterd; while from the echoic meanings a direct connection of sound and sense is used.

The fact is the Lithic hypotheses challenge both the current establishment beliefs, wholly untested, that – first – language roots were originally random, and – second – they have anyway changed so much that they contain nothing of any original structure even if it were originally semantically composed in Lithic speak.

Both these established views are false. Roots are not semantically random and the original meanings at the origins of speaking, however long ago it was, can still be traced in the world lexicon today.

The next critique likely to be aimed at Lithic meanings is the opposite of the statistical challenge, on the grounds the meanings are too many to choose from. It is the examples, compared with the number of potential cases, which are not plentiful enough to be significant. With perhaps eight thousand languages to pick from, the majority little known, it must be true the number of examples which can be adduced in a single volume represents only an infinitessimal fraction of all potential examples in the world. However that is not the way statistics work. If a significant number of proven examples exist, the proof may be extended to all or any of the remainder with a clearcut degree of significance. The degree of significance depends upon the number of truly independent confirmatory instances, and only secondarily upon the size of the population from which they are culled. In any case the population can not be expanded to include all the languages, the vast majority, which have not been sampled. The only proviso is the sampling must be of independent variables like the population. This is however a more difficult statistical challenge to rebuff because the statistical computations are too complex to work out. The answer to both challenges therefore is perhaps to issue a challenge on behalf of Lithic in turn. Can the critic put together another scheme as comprehensive which fits in so many cases as well? If he can not put up he should shut up. It does not directly prove Lithic is correct, but it does highlight such a scheme with such consistency as Lithic is not easily compiled; so that such a compilation is at least notable and in need of explanation. That is in fact the way I came, overcoming my own original schematophobia. Volume 2 which will deal with a fair span of languages from Basque to Chinese and from Djeribal (a dead North Queensland aboriginal language) to Ancient Egyptian will very much exacerbate his task.

Earlier (in chapter 1) it was alleged that the whole of the world lexicon, including mankind´s finest thoughts, appear to have been initially hammered out on the anvil of our own genitalia. It was, it seems, genital performance which acted, like a cobbler´s last, as the formative core shaping humanity´s first ratiocination and speech. The source of the metaphors on which Homo Erectus first framed his understanding of the world at large was his own psychological whimsy as he contemplated the fascinations of sex. It was assumed by our semi articulate forebears that the whole of nature followed their own original perceptions; so inevitably they analysed the rest of the world in terms of the ideas they had in their heads, and in a thin crowd there these were obviously those of their home economy, and first of all their own intimate psychosemantic conceptualisations. The Egyptian rays linked sun, eye, brain and sex together in a universal dialectic, action at a distance, there and back linked by their teleological mission. Consequently the animal, vegetable and natural worlds all yielded to their own individual and personal understanding of how things went, a version increasingly absurd but by now so firmly imprinted in the human subconscious that it can influence our conscious thinking still. If you have only a limited stock of perceptions they must necessarily be used to cover the whole of your experience. In the Stone Age the seven day wonder was the miracle of birth and how it was engineered. Vegetation could be propagated just like animal species. The very first geology buffs had even worked out minerals were spawned from volcanos, giant birth canals on the tops of mountains, out of the nether world of fire, a match to some extent of the sun which gave birth to light (fire) on a daily basis from the fiery empyrean believed to be above the heavenly firmament (of stone). Under this rubric volcanos were vulvas, world ones, not human ones or animal ones or vegetable ones; and why not? It was that simple.

It should perhaps be added with some emphasis that our subsequent lucubrations have been devoted to diluting and forgetting, at least to some extent, these original psychosemantic inputs and modifying this original simplistic version of science. It is only our subconscious minds which, trained over the aeons by language to think in our old aboriginal ways, have been prompting us to stay within our old subconscious mental ruts. This is where Wayland Smith has picked up his prompts while Scrimshaw man beavered away to redefine in a much more discriminating mode our perceptions of the real world. This is in fact clearly evidenced by the psychosemantic trees which appear with each of the chapters analysing phonemic meanings. Original motifs, often sexual, have been modified, abstracted and by means of metaphor after metaphor, gulls and buses, removed further and further from our fundamental simplistic orientations. Wayland has just sung the tune got from within, while Scrimshaw has revised and elaborated the lexicon and carried civilisation forward. Of the two it is Wayland who makes the most comfortable bed fellow, because Scrimshaw is often self absorbed and tending to an element of autism. But we can not do without him. It is he that has brought us down from the trees and it is he who will probably introduce a degree of civilisation now we are walking upright on the ground. Give him time!

Appendix A is attached, dealing with the academic philosophy of language in order to keep it out of the main body of the book, where it hardly belongs. Logical disputations have since focused on the philosophy of science, which has nevertheless not advanced much in the past eighty years since Karl Popper first wrote[1]. Most if not all of the "Popperian Knights" who made their way up the civil service ladder on the back of his thinking are already in their graves, but his research programme is still largely intact. The arguments have moved towards relativism – a refuge for scoundrels (who would excuse anything) – as realist theories have crumbled. We have some clever gambits like Tarski´s metalanguages and Kuhn´s paradigm shifts as well as Imre Lakatos´ (mental) research programming. I think almost all of this can be rendered somewhat redundant just by my Psi-Phi-Pi-Ro series and my Wallpaper Theory. We are still gripped by Popper´s ideas on falsification as the best way of assessing theory in chapter 16.

I am indebted to Doctor Chalmers for his book "What is this Thing called Science² which has taught me my Wallpaper Theory is really "Unrepresentative Realism" in wrangler speak; although I still prefer my pictorial version of mental activity, as sketching on the wallpaper how we imagine the real wall behind, to his wranglers´ pie. What is essential for understanding the relationship of all empirical study to the real reality (Kant´s ding fur sich) is to separate the two so that the one is not directly related or in contact with the other. This I do by inserting a cognitive level, the wall paper, (which eventually I locate papered inside our own skulls, having made use of all its virtues papered on the wall). All knowledge is virtual knowledge of virtual reality. In these circumstances haven´t we done well! I also learned from Dr Chalmers that Latokosian research programmes are descriptions of mental approaches and activities and not expeditionary itineraries as I first imagined – a point Dr Chalmers forgets to mention incidentally, so intirely is he taken up within the limitations of his ivory tower and with the wrangling occurring therein. We can all do better, I fancy, just with the expeditionary itineraries. The world is not looking for definitions of truth but for understanding. For that the truth is a handy handrail not to be despised, since it really has no other meaning.

The Oxford University Press report of a symposium on the state of science under the title "Nature's Imagination" edited by John Connell of Jesus College, Cambridge and published in 1995 deserves quotation in full. But here perhaps a short excerpt from the Preface will have to suffice: "Scientific reductionism is a perspective that takes nature and the universe to be deterministic, immutable and non anthropormorphic; a perspective in which all biological and mental events are reducible to properties of matter-energy....[But] Science itself is conditioned by history". This is what historians know as Scientism. It is nowadays the simplistic belief of practical men, who have always taken their ideological environment with a pinch of salt while they got on with their active pursuits; and that includes politicians who these days likely add a whiff at least of dialectical materialism to warrant their otherwise wholly banausic outlook on life. T H Huxley's views were classical Scientism in the nineteenth century, a macho time by any standards. He was in fact a little follower, using Darwin's theories to bludgeon his way to authenticity. It led straight into the massacring civil religions of the twentieth century, the bloodiest on record. The social history merely reinforces the intellectual descent which set the pace. It was a true treason of the clerks. The political puppets just danced to their tune, as ever. Hitler and Stalin are not usually seen as puppets but that is what they were, quick brained but without any understanding of their own. Nazis were actually Socialists, but the socialist intellectuals have dubbed them posthumously reactionaries, and got away with it because German bankers under duress decided to fund them: the treason of German clerks was compounded by the capitulation of German financiers. Both, to be fair, were reeling under the traumas of military defeat, which always brings out the worst in anyone, from whining to cheating. The German slate has still to be wiped clean. Perhaps only the fighting SS can be excused as comrades in arms and even there there was unnecessary brutality. The holocaust SS should all have been put to death and not, as American policy, let off so they would stand up to the Russians, which in the event they never did. Instead they have plotted to reinstate Hitler's plan for a Thousand Year European Reich, officially for European peace, but actually, as followers of the black goddess Kali, in a farcical shot at world domination, an ambition as mad as it is outmoded, kept alive by a political elite which has lost its way.

When Huxley took centre stage in an Oxford debate with the Bishop, Darwin and Lyell were horrified, as indeed was my great grandfather who had more than a smidgeon – perhaps not much more – of responsibility for starting this whole vulgar debate off, since he and Charles Lyell (Darwin's tutor) had worked out the relative ages of the sedimentary rocks from the microscopic shells (species) included within them. My great grandfather was a conchologist who had inherited the nucleus of his collection of shells from his father, an Anglican parson and Prebendary of Winchester Cathedral, with a passion for philately (collecting and ordering things). Some at least of Lyell's book (the epochal and scandalous "Principles of Geology" published in 1830 – it made the case for geological evolution over enormous spans of time contradicting quite precisely the literal version of events in the Christian bible) was worked out in the long gallery which extended the whole length of the top floor of Merton Hall, which was filled with two rows of double fronted glass cabinets holding thousands of shells. I remember them well. They burnt with the Hall round them in 1954. Lyell, a late barrister to earn a living, would weekend at Merton, as his book shows since it notices the Merton Stone, the largest glacial erratic in Great Britain weighing about 25 tons which had been dug up by my farming forebears in the seventeenth century when digging for marl later for the four course Norfolk rotation (which in turn sparked the industrial revolution by presenting so many sturdy beggars for employment in the towns). On the European continent they starved, but in Britain they were put into garden sheds because they smelt too rank (soap came later) to have in the house and were found employment by the division of labour – if all you could do was cut out the sole for a shoe then you passed it to the cobblers indoors when it was done, for the more intellectually demanding stitching operation. Cottage industries became manufactures overnight. Great Britain Ltd gained a half century advantage from this quite modest philanthropy. The late Alan Taylor taught me this – he famously invented the "Cockup" theory of history – when I studied history under him at Oxford nearly sixty years ago.

There is in fact an inclination nowadays amongst philosophers of science to regard Marx and Darwin as fellow workers in the vinyard, confronting religious fuddy duddies with science. This seems to me to be an absurdity. Marx was thinking in the 1830s and found his left over ideas then. He was in fact a left-over from eighteenth century philosophy himself; he said as much himself. He had, he felt, driven a coach and horses through the eighteenth century philosophical tradition. He claimed to have stood Hegel's dialectic on its head, where he made it the foundation of his infamous philosophy of "dialectical materialism". This inversion of Hegel's blunder was to prove sufficient to carry the ancient confusion of thought forward for more than another hundred years, leading in turn to every kind of intellectual corruption amongst academics and politicians alike, and culminating in Stalinism, Nazism, the Cold War and the decay and collapse of Communist regimes around the world. Darwin did not publish until 1859. He was an offshoot of an entirely different and more recent tradition, a science based upon close biological observation of natural species, starting as it happened with the shells included in sedimentary rocks. Philately had come from Linnaeus perhaps: he put the flowers in order. Shells enabled Charles Lyell (born 1800) to disentangle the rock strata of Britain by estimation of their relative ages, judging by the evolution of the forms of the microscopic shells included in them. It was a method no scientist today would countenance because it relied upon the mere assumption that shell forms were getting more convoluted and distorted rather than less, a matter of mere guesswork at the time. However it produced the right results.

What was even more surprising was that Charles Lyell who published his epoch making book "The Principles of Geology" in 1830-1833 did not possess any shell collection to work on himself. He had consulted a number of European conchologists and been engaged as Secretary of the newly formed Geological Society, but he made significant use of the collection of shells housed at Merton. As the shells were species the received wisdom that Darwin was prompted by geological evolution in Lyell's book to think of species evolution for himself is false. In 1859 Darwin fibbed to excuse his old tutor being sent to Coventry by his fellow dons in dog collars. Lyell had taught him species evolution at Cambridge by 1830; and anyway Darwin took Lyell's book with him on his round the world cruise on HMS Beagle. It is all in there and has recently been republished. But Darwin feared if he published species evolution disproving a literal reading of the Book of Genesis in the Hebrew bible it would lead to bloody revolution, and scientists might get their heads cut off. He had therefore cautiously prepared a posthumous volume and was only persuaded to publish when young Alfred Wallace wrote to the President of the Linaean Society in 1859 – it was Charles Lyell – proposing a scheme of species evolution he had worked out for himself, based on his research in South East Asia. Lyell warned Darwin who prepared a paper from his unpublished major work. Darwin's and Wallace's papers were then read to the Linaean Society and Lyell declared Darwin's the winner. All the recognition Wallace got was the Wallace Line dividing Australian species from the South East Asian ones. The media, evidently without reading up the evidence in Lyell's book – they had deadlines to meet even in those sleepy days and had evidently already given up reading books – just copied Darwin's line, so that the fib that he thought of species evolution for himself is in the history books as fact even to this day. None of this has anything to do with linguistics. The Marxist dialectic however has, and it has been demolished already in chapter 16 on thinking. Language understanding should lead to understanding thinking, which is not easy.

Karl von Linné (Linnaeus, 1707-1778), also a parson's son in Sweden, had proposed a scheme of identification of plant species by means of their flower structures which he identified as their male and female sex organs. This relatively blameless philately had so incensed the dominies of the Swedish church that they had no hesitation in declaring von Linné would burn in Hell for his blasphemous mischief. It seems silly now, but poor old Karl was shattered by this prognostication, suffered a nervous breakdown and was confined in an asylum until his death. His system of identification of species however lives on, and young ladies in the nineteenth century collected pressed flowers on the excuse they were displaying speciation, but leaving out the sex. The Prebendary's choice of shells in place of flowers may have suggested itself as a slightly more masculine pursuit, or else was prompted perhaps subconsciously by the reassurance the moluscae's genitalia were all long gone and even the most censorious episcopal overseer could hardly suspect him of any secret salacious interest in his collection. Had he known of the astonishing genital convolutions involved in two moluscs mating, requiring both participants virtually to turn themselves inside out in slow time and intertwine their organs in the open with a good deal of frothing and slime he likely would never have embarked on his hobby. In those days, one has to remind oneself, there was no geology or biology as we understand them. The discovery of giant bones and shells fossilised in quarries and cliffs was a source of puzzlement, and some of these fossils, it had been suggested, must at one time have belonged to species now extinct and their hard parts somehow preserved in the sediment. But there were rival theories such as a provision by the deity to test faith, or else for purposes beyond human comprehension altogether and therefore best left alone.

The Prebendary's views on the matter are not recorded, but he was a genuine believer and he will have been content to leave these mysteries in God's keeping. He is looking down on me as I write, in a portrait painted in the 1820s. His son, however, armed with legal training to test the evidence, was jointly responsible for a mischief which still haunts the church today.

I just ask myself how can it be that I should have uncovered a whole scheme of semantic contents others have overlooked, and so many of them for so long? My wife put an unerring finger on the whole matter on day one when the project was first unfurled: "Why you?" The whole thing narrowly escaped proving a damp squib more than thirty years ago. Doggedness, even bloody mindedness must count for something, but I think the capacity to hold a great many disparate items in the mind on the whole rather aimlessly, doodling perhaps, convinced in my case most human aiming is usually unrewarded, mine anyway, and thus without too much judgmental content is a great help. Add to that a willingness to be entertained by whatever serendipity threw up, the sheer glee at living and thinking and watching the world go by; and underlying it all a great, almost childish, thirst for understanding alongside a refusal to be fooled. There is also the fact my research programme with languages has been pretty useless all along. Perhaps only a bit of a goof would have wished to go on with it. But then you must remember it was for thirty years and more no more than a hobby for me. I never earned my living by it, and certainly never expected to. I have only been writing it consecutively since I was seventy three and able to retire. Until then Lithic just took me away from the hard graft of all the business sums, when I was sleeping quite short hours already. My idea of a break was simply to take off into the Stone Age and have a ball. Just ten minutes a day in the company of Eric Partridge would do, and it was as badly needed as the glass of whisky (or two) which generally went with it. It banished business to its proper place so I slept sound, whether pickling onions were selling well or not.

Finally for the man in the street, and of course equally for his sisters, there is a good deal of fun to be had, once the basic Lithic elements have been learnt, in tracing for himself along with his sisters for themselves the Lithic compositions to be found in words of whatever languages they know, released from the constraints of conventional civilised thinking and back to basics. The audio frequencies are more effortful than the visual but their research is the more rewarding. Even the therapeutic benefits of any such exercise are not to be sneezed at.

This is a short chapter as a settlement. Those hoping to find the pith here, to save reading the rest of it, should go to chapter 18 where the nub of the book has been separated out for them and printed as a synopsis.

Notes

1. Karl Popper. The Logic of Scientific Discovery. Hutchinson. 1968. (As quoted by Chalmers) "What he [a critic] must do is to formulate an assertion which contradicts our own and give us his instructions for testing it. If he fails to do this we can only ask him to take another and perhaps a more careful look at our experiment [or thesis based on it] and think again.

2. A.F.Chalmers. "What is This Thing Called Science", Second Edition, Open University Press. Page 60.

CHAPTER 18

SYNOPSIS

In this chapter a summary is provided in a few pages of the main tenets proposed and evidenced in the whole book, for those in a hurry, reviewers, students, etc, or those otherwise without the patience to give the whole a proper whirl or serious consideration, but who nevertheless still hope to be able to claim to have read the whole of it. It may even be of use as a guide for those ploughing through the book.

1. The origins of speaking go back much further than is conventionally believed at present. Speech was not invented by Homo Sapiens Sapiens but by his hominid forebears who were speaking, after a fashion, for hundreds of thousands of years before he came along. This realisation has a Copernican ring to it, knocking Sapiens Sapiens off yet another perch he has been chirruping from for aeons. It does not in reality diminish him however.

2. The evidence for these origins is historical and circumstantial and not demonstrable like a mathematical theorem. Our earliest history, often described as prehistory, provides few unmistakeable traces because there are no written records. Writing is a very recent achievement. Speaking is a lot older, perhaps a hundred times as old.

3. Language however provides a record of its own early development, but not in the grammar, which like writing is a late addition to the art of speaking. Chomskyan analysis of grammar as a branch of logic, with rules somewhat like mathematical theorems, is of little if any use in unravelling historical language origins. It is a categorical exercise, with intellectual categories superimposed on our original thinking. Unravelling the original syllabic semantics ravelled up over the aeons is mostly simple expansion where the human mouth and mind have conspired together to sloven and slur and then to parrot words instead of understanding their semantic construction. It turns out traces of the original semantic contents attached to elementary phonemes can be found in language spoken today, preserved like flies in amber in the world lexicon. In fact, in the context of discovery, these

semantic traces are first identifiable by back triangulation from modern usages across different language groups. The essential key to uncovering these "Lithic" (Stone Age) language roots is the recognition that phonemes were meaningful when we began to speak. This contradicts current conventional etymology which only allows morphemes, strings of one or more phonemes, often three, to carry any meaning. It was the identification of the meanings of individual phonemes (effectively now the letters of the alphabet) by the bare bottomed hominid naming committees of perhaps some six hundred thousand years ago which enabled them to agree the natural meanings of their utterances based on the consonants.

4.   The evolution of language has been a historical rather than a natural process, and since the term evolution has been taken over by Darwinism the neutral term development is to be preferred for mental activities, regardless of how they may be ultimately based. Universal transformational grammar is a classificatory exercise analysing speech contemporaneously; and as a synchronic research programme it is in any case disqualified for diachronic research.

5.   There was no inevitability in the way hominids attached meanings to the phonemes they found they could utter; only a likelihood, given their common environments both internal and external, that similar sounds uttered would be judged to have similar meanings (semantic contents) the world over. I have called these original semantic contents attributed to the uttered sounds psychosemantic contents – in order to indicate they were dreamed up by the human psyche as the natural meanings of the phonemes they uttered. The naked naming committees hunkered around their hearths jabbering and gesticulating are a vivid mnemonic for primitive language origins. Most of mankind's earliest mental perceptions appear to have been hammered into shape on the anvil of his own genitals, readily available in bare bottomed committee. They did rather well even by modern standards. Indeed in Chapter 16 I suggest it was orgiastic sex heated by the hearth with the taming of fire (sex around the barbie) which jump started recollection, the element missing from the subconscious mind, and triggered conscious thinking (consciousness) – and ultimately civilisation with it. But no doubt unanimity of terminology was in the last resort imposed on individual recalcitrants.

6.   Hominid science was mostly the science of shapes, from the evidences of the eye and the mind was adjectival with properties immanent universals. What else could you think in terms of pictures before speech?

7.   These agreed meanings (psychosemantic contents) were rather general by

our standards, and the phonemes capable of reasonably stable utterance were – and are – rather few, a score or so as in the alphabet, by comparison with a modern lexicon which can comprise a few thousand or hundred thousand words. I have called this Stone Age linguistic substrate Lithic language. It is several orders of magnitude older than the fragmentary proto languages tentatively reconstructed by linguists to date from their presumed, arbitrary and unreasoned roots, which for the most part just muddy the water.

8.   The development of polysemy (see Paragraph 11 below), the meanings which were attached to phonemes before words, proliferating and diversifying as the human mind added tiers to its understanding, probing out into the unknown and unspecified, inevitably led to the doubling up of phonemes, one being used as a qualifier of the other and becoming associated in that role. It didn't require any particular trigger. It was the kind of realisation which would occur even to a chimpanzee. Further doubling and association saw the development of vocabulary until the words resulting finally came to be regarded as nuggets with meanings attached for memorisation as a single unit. Words were not originally atomic, they are molecular, composites ab origine of atomic Lithic elements which by a long way preceded them. This is the core of the Lithic hypotheses, and the central issue for dispute. At the beginning of language it was phonemes which had meanings. Words came later made of sentences of phonemic elements in strings. (The Chinese language shows the most remnants of this original protocol; many of their words are composites to this day).

9.   The evidence words we use today are developed (made up) from the elementary semantic contents of primitive phonemic units turns out to be still around and can be discovered from the structure of words, particularly the traces of common elements (many of them now just letters) in words with allied meanings in different languages. These atavistic semantic contents have been refreshed from generation to generation by every individual learning to speak with their conscious minds, because at the same time all unawares they have been absorbing the background patterns with their subconscious minds; which is how we can still access these patterns of thinking today after aeons of speech. Existing languages have never died, since speaking began, remember. They have been passed down from speaker to speaker, changing all the while but without discontinuity and informed all the while by subconscious Lithic associations. This cancels the claim no phonetic or semantic traces last long because of the slurring and change all languages are subject to, so that the noise rubs them out. The subconscious

mind provides a regular and even constant refresh rate. Each generation has relearned the whole semantic scheme, garnering in the subconscious part of the mind the semantics built up underlying speech.

10. Any single example of these common elements is inconclusive and might arise by accident or happenstance, but the statistical probability of the Lithic language substrate being real, and not merely a miasma multiplies exponentially as cases are added. It is an exercise which has simply been neglected, as hopeless and doomed to failure. Chapters 4 to 16 however, resulting from my thirty year studies of languages ancient and modern, which admittedly are still only partial and introductory, are nevertheless compelling. They are published now as the author, now over 80, veut cultiver son jardin. He read M de Voltaire at secondary school, now impossible.

11. The above Chapters 4 to 16 derive human speaking from the following original semantic contents or meanings attached to uttered phonemes, listed in alphabetical order for the convenience of the alphabetic mind. The lists of derived meanings are skeletal. They are in fact strictly endless, since the work is still in progress. The term semantic contents does not imply utterances are containers, semantic references would do as well. The term phoneme is borrowed from linguistic theory where it is generally contrasted with the further term morpheme, the shortest utterance supposedly capable of carrying meaning. I use the simpler term for these elementary meaningful utterances to distance myself from the theory of morphemic structure which leads to arbitrary random roots, used to mean what they mean for no reason at all. I simply do not go along with this. I believe even hominids reasoned and it still shows. In each chapter a psychosemantic tree traces the derivation of meanings over the millennia as follows:-

Ba   The labial, the sound of lip on lip, mouth, flesh on flesh, flesh, muscle, fleshing out, burgeoning, binary symmetry, the biosphere, being, the haunch (another fleshy bit), to leg it and go, to be fleshed (ie alive), and so to be, and so on.

Ka   The sound of stone on flint, knock, knack, strike, flake, break apart, shape, make, kindle, force, hard, sharp, rock, drive, driving force, life force, male soul, and so on.

Da   An expansion of Ta, birth, become, pass across, do, give effect, reveal, disclose, give, and so on.

Fa   A powerful puff, as for firing a dart from a blow pipe for instance. An approximation of Ba. A dialectical elision of Pa and Ha (one of the naughty bits), the joy piece, the male genitalia, and so on and so on.

Ga   A voiced expansion of Ka (q.v.), impetus, go, and so on.

Ha   A gasp, hot, hideous, harm, harry, horror, haunt, hilarity, hedonism, delight, ecstasy, hooray, joy, rejoicing and so on.

La   With a curling tongue, nasty taste, brackish, the instinct of water to slope down, go flat and become brackish as it goes, slope, slip, slide, lean, ladder, flat, loose, flow, lye, salt water, the ocean, skyline at sea, and so both line and circle, loop, orbit, sun (orbiter), luminescence, light, and so on.

Ma   Stress, hungry, mother, milk, liquid, water, eat, meat, the paired (dialectically opposite) sound with ish: heavy, go down, dead, kill, harm, mass, massive, earth, to earth, plant, impregnate, germinate (seeds), gestate, and so on.

Na   The sound made letting out the breath after holding it – from excitement or anticipation, or both (another naughty bit): orgasm, ejaculate, push, protrude, exhibit, present, the present (now), show, profess, explicate, expositor, prophet; also present, gape, round out, open, empty, null, nil, no, nice, and so on.

Pa   A spit or a puff. The thinned diminutive of Ba, skin, small or thin piece of flesh or foliage, shoot, piece, penis, roof, top surface, visible surface, patch, lid, rim, the ostensive, 'the' in Egyptian, and so on.

Ra   A rapid rattling repetitive sound, the tongue going back and forth almost with the speed of light, repetition, reflex action, light ray (radar style, there and back), ray, rayed, sun, eye, see, seen, colour, straight, elongated, sun rayed, growing, played upon, raise, rise, rouse, engorged, ripe, lots of rises, rough, ruffled, re- and so on.

Ish   The sound of a burning brand extinguished in water. Fire, bright, light (shine), shone on, visible, see, the instinct of the flame for going up, up, vertical, stroke, one, light (weightless), hot, warm, comfortable, pleasant, ease, animal, animal marker, brer, mobile, activity, alive, life, lively, active, and so on.

Ta   The staccato sound or crack of a breaking branch, as opposed to Ka, the clink of flint on flint when knapping stone. To break, to break in two, to cut in two, to divide in two, two, a cut or slit, the vagina, the birth canal, parturition, to give birth, to be born, birth, a coming into being, a becoming, a happening, a natural event as opposed to an agential act, a ray source, a source, and so on.

Wa   Shivering, wet, water, cold, fear, and so on. An easement of a glottal stop.

Vowels – in early speech the vowels were only three: A (aaa), I (eee), and U (ooo), together the a and i made a u or unity:-

* A is the middle general easy vowel and ranks first as the exemplar of continuous unmodulated vowel tones, extension spatial or temporal, ongoing, going, away, un-, ever, omnipresent, eternal, etc; but also as vacuous and empty, air, absence of a quality or structure as with water or air.

* I is the thinned diminutive reduplicative vowel, micro, -ing, -ed, plural, itemisation, it, which, he, I, and so on.

* U is the dual, inclusive, completive, substantive vowel, rounded out, "all done gone finish", "sab khatm ho gaya" in Hindi, dialectically embracing the other two vowels, all of them, both of them, and so on.

12.   The whole human lexicon derives from these simples; though that is not to say that nothing has been added, or that other practices are not in evidence today. I have embarked on the derivation of meanings from each elementary Lithic phoneme in the psychosemantic trees with each chapter on the phonemes, with meanings cascading from each other like the phenotypes in a family tree.

13.   Science before language was (faut de mieux) the science of shapes of things seen as immanent qualities universally apparent; the human eye was king and an absolute monarch – Homo Topologicus – and the eye only began to be superseded as we learned words made up of longish Lithic strings, when the Lithic language roots derived from images were gradually drowned out of the conscious mind, or papered over, by the flood of thinking that speaking unleashed. Now they need to be recovered from the subconscious, the recycle bin, which is only subconscious for the most part due to lack of proper attention. The subconscious still influences conscious thinking, often in astonishing detail.

14.   The subconscious mind is now widely accepted as playing a significant role in everyone's psychology. It informs language, and the primitive meanings locked up in our speech are accessed in the subconscious of every speaker. While we consciously learn to speak our subconscious minds learn the constituent phonemic meanings of the words. That is how these ancient meanings have survived. The waves of language change, mostly driven by fashion in pronunciation and cutting corners, pass over them; but in the subconscious mind they survive. A good deal of idiom in their use survives too, and since this idiom is language specific we learn our mother tongue and it spoils us for after. Specific ideas are not transmitted by the genes and Darwinian evolution is not a direct mechanism for the transmission of the lexicon, and even less the syntax. Brains are organs and can be reconstituted or modified by the genes. Ideas are Activities of the brain and there are no genes to code for what you have thought, any more than there are genes to record what walks you have taken.

15.   The book at no point touches upon myth or religion, it is merely concerned with cognition. It can not be accused of adding to the altercations which have inspired humanity with so much malice and have led to the effusion of so much blood since we learned to express our opinions. The principal interest of this new etymology based on the origins of speaking is not only as a hobby for old linguists but as a pointer to the origins of thinking which I have approached directly in Chapter 16. The central message is one of common heritage – brothers (and sisters) under the skin, in spite of peripheral differences of modern physique and culture. It is inescapable we were and still are a highly sexed species and our intellectual heritage comes with a great deal of sexual metaphor. That all has to be worked over to make sense of the linguistic record. It is not a cause for shame but for understanding.

APPENDIX A

THE PHILOSOPHY OF LANGUAGE

The philosophy of language is annexed as an appendix only, because it is not directly relevant to the main part of the book. There is the consideration if it were left out altogether it would make it easier for hostile academics to rubbish the main body. I suppose philosophy (from the Greek, meaning knowledge-loving approximately, and used historically for top notch wrangling on any subject) covers the theoretical issues arising with any subject matter: the ultimate nature of language in our case, as well as a critique of our knowledge of it, unkindly put the cat's cradles the wit of man has traced around the study of language to date. The only reasonable approach, it seems to me, is to trace historically the positions struck to date, with commentary. It will not be an overly long study since the nature of language per se has not received a great deal of attention, any more than the nature of thinking, since these too often have been regarded as givens and axiomatic, needing no analysis. Nevertheless I have no doubt that in the search for every kind of understanding a true appreciation of the place of language and its implications for the ways in which we think is absolutely fundamental. That anyway is the perception which lies behind my forty years of hobby study of the origins of speaking. It is just unfortunate that my own homework has borne fruit which is very little related to the philosophical contributions to date. All sorts of philosophical schemes have of course held implications for the view you take of language, since philosophy dictates the categories under which thinking proceeds; so in this appendix these implications will be addressed whether they were understood at the time or no.

It was thinking about the philosophy of language – during my philosophical period – currently a gaggle of irrelevancies easily characterized as cat's cradles, which prompted me to come up front with a title for the book to jolt the potent grave and reverend seigneurs of academe into thinking. Then I decided it would put the average reader off, expecting him or her to appreciate Lithic speak from the outset, and so I reduced it to an alternative title. It is the Ishkama bit. It is meant to show we have to get down to actual intellectual analysis of language itself, in stark contrast to the school of neuro-linguistics trying to reconcile our own experience of cognition with their neurological insights. Their neurobiological perceptions do not address our immediate experience on which alone any analysis of the nature of what it is we are doing when we are speaking should be based. Thought is quite different from its neurology, never mind how tightly interlocked at the biological level they may be. It is no more than a recrudescence of the age old division of the historical and scientific traditions. The historian, currently in relative eclipse, says let us see how it happened; and is less good at making up rules on how it will or should happen in future. The scientist just makes up rules that seem good to him, often based on personal whimsy though sometimes on flashes of insight; but he then goes on to test them to destruction winnowing out all but those with some residual utility. Forced to study both disciplines, it seems to me the study of language is primarily a matter of history and does not yield its most revealing insights when investigated with a crudely scientific eye trying out pre-ordained schemes, especially those based on the baggage of biology and math. This straight away divorces me from a century of linguistics. That is not to deny the close relationship between brain function and mentality. It is merely to reject a common research programme, which really implies a congruence of the two and is palpably absurd. In philosophy it is known as a category error. We are far from the science of everything mathematicians hanker after – with no histori-cal sense whatever. That is a Will-o'-the-wisp fashionable in some quarters, a bit like sitting down to design a single computer programme to do everything under a single magic rubric, which is equally absurd. Software buffs will be aware their programmes are highly specific and run on approximations of digital relationships to reality. Science, even with its simplest and most satisfactory and apparently transparent analyses, suffers from the very same limitations in spite of the fact the human mind is much more flexible than any computer programme and actu-ally "understands" what it is doing – it actually has meaning – though not how it does it. Computers by contrast are just dumb Daleks without understanding, just quick. Before we take leave of the neurobiologists however we should recognize there has been some neat thinking on primitive, that is in scientific terms basic, states of mind from them. The recognition of self as a condition of consciousness for instance, includes Julian Keenan's 'mirror test', and some interesting percep-tions from Mithen, Cosmides and Tooby, Gardner, and Fodor on the compart-mentalization of the mind. See the Bibliography at the end of the book.

The study of language theory started out as grammar, "the science of letters", more or less as we understand the study today with a bit of literary expertise thrown in. It was a subjective and systematizing interpretation of language as she is spoke by the grammarian, an intellectual. The first on extant record is Pannini in Sanskrit in 500 BC. To the Greeks belongs the honour of recognizing the phonol-ogy of language, the choice of sounds to symbolize meanings, as originally derived from echoism, or in Greek onomatopoeia which in Lithic is something like "the sounds become the symbols" and in Greek "names making up the words", that is the sounds become the entities, cuckoo for cuckoo and so on. There is no doubt the Egyptians had this beforehand. They were half way to Lithic five thousand years ago. Of course the practice was not so far removed from Lithic in those days. At one time there were probably more educated Greeks in Egypt than in Greece. As a result half the Greek language comes from Egyptian. The Pharaohs were Akkadian adventurers, Semites farming the native Africans. Admittedly they got darker over the millennia from concubinage, but there was no "Black Athena" as Martin Bernal has argued.

The Egyptians believed in natural forces behind every phenomenon. Their hundreds of "gods" were all marked in inscriptions with a pennant blowing in the breeze, a "Natura", which said "Na-", showing, "-tura", the pull or force, they were exemplars of natural forces: Egyptologists nevertheless still think the pennant is a pointed royal axe – what for? – and call it a neter. The Greeks regarded language as "natural", phusike in Greek, where the "phusi-" was from the Lithic "Pa-hei-u-sai", the action[sai] of the phallus [pahei] when roused [hei]; and the "–ke" was from formed, or in form, forming, equivalent to the English –al. The action prayed in aid was of course the biological one to expand and extend, to grow (which the phallus had the trick of doing under your very eyes and in short order). The Greek phusis contrasted to the Greek mind with the nominal or conventional like their laws, nomoi, which I read in Lithic as something like 'presenting the thinking', ie laying down the law which is a nominal deductive business rather than inductive. There was something of the present attempts by scientists to relate linguistics to neurobiology in this. Phusis in Greek was the natural principle of Aristotle's day which informed the animal and vegetable kingdoms, an organic nissus or naturally endowed unentropic drive to develop grow and elaborate. The Egyptians used Ka for a very similar concept, like the Japanese. Probably both got it from the Sumerians, or perhaps the Japanese got it from the Chinese who had it directly from Eden whence the Sumerians emigrated in turn. It was a life force, biological, as in karate, nothing to do with physics in English which concerns the underlying principles which apply to dead nature, the laws of physics and physical chemistry, and only by extension to biology, the organic. It may seem surprising language was not thought of as conventional. But language, it was supposed, had always been there as part of the original divine creation of mankind. To claim mankind had made it up smacked of sacrilege. Would the gods have communicated in manspeak? Adam, after all, spoke with God in the Garden of Eden; and the tale was told in Sumer, and merely borrowed by the Akkadian nomads who conquered Sumer (and were then civilized by the Sumerians for their pains) as part of their creation myth. Adam was not originally a Semite at all, but an Adamite from the

Garden of Eden, the Eastern Garden Land, that is to say the land with riverine irrigated rice paddy now under the South China Sea, flooded when the ice melted leaving only the mountainous hinterland of "Malaya", the "Garden Land" and dispersing the Adamites to Sumer as well as North to China and probably East across the pacific as well. This is how Chinese has some roots and words common to Sumerian as well as Malay so that it has even been suggested that the Sumerians were proto-Chinese! But Malays have no eyefold, and no more did Adam or the Sumerians. For the speakers their language was natural but laws were metalanguage and conventional. That left them with the task of getting the law in line with natural justice of course.

Before Plato and Aristotle, Greek skepticism which was originally from Alexandria in Egypt was universally promulgated by the intellectuals. The Greeks attributed this line of thinking to Pyrrhon who was around in 300 BC, otherwise forgotten. There was also Heracleitus who said you never step twice into the same river: and meant it to apply of course to all our experience of the world, which made apposite judgments hard. Skepticism was the matrix from which Greek philosophy as it is known to us today was born. The skeptics aimed to achieve 'ataraxia', from a-tarai-ka-saia, un-drawn-ka-easy, Greek for a calm resignation in face of the fact the human mind could as happily entertain falsity as truth, there being no way for the mind to distinguish between the two. You only found out when you stepped on the wrong end of the rake. This perception was of course sound, and roughly corresponds with the late Karl Popper's seminal work, "The Logic of Scientific Discovery". He had some equally telling stuff on philosophy, "The Open Society and its Enemies". He was from the Vienna Circle but wrote in English due to Hitler. For Pyrrhon ataraxia was his final position, an early academic bumble. Popper never made it to Pyrrhon's base; his world was nearer to a nightmare.

So far as I can see, the Greek phusis or biological nissus was not necessarily directed and purposive (teleological), but more like a caterpillar waving about on the end of a twig. Today the accepted version of word origins is nominal (from the Greek nomoi) and random, the phonology playing only a misty and minor part in forming meaning, which it takes a poet to spot. In fact the composition of words from random roots is simply assumed, while linguistics buffs have been busy reforming grammar in accordance with mathematical logic, directing attention away from the semantic contents of individual words and eschewing any relationship between sounds and meanings and finding meaning in sentence structure instead, effectively grammatical rules for linking words and phrases into sentences. This is a radical revision: the grammar may have warranted attention, but the discard of everything else was uncalled for. Having thus confused meaning with grammar, the modern grammarians have then had to redefine meaning to get it out from under grammar again. In reality grammar is a structural matter and parts of speech guide sentence structure. Meaning on the other hand is a symbolic matter attaching to words and, in Lithic, to their precursors the semantic contents of phonemes. A prime exemplar of these meanings is the word tiger. The echoic cry "Grrr!", from before speech for when one approached, is transmogrified to Ti-Grrr, Mistress growler, spelt tigre, and anglicized to tiger. That covers hundreds of thousands of years of linguistic development, and thus many thousands of generations of speakers – let us say six hundred thousand years of linguistic development and thus thirty thousand generations of speakers passing the word down each to the next generation: a football crowd playing Chinese whispers! They will however each have had time for a number of goes – in a lifetime perhaps a hundred or more – so I don't find it hard to believe it. We expect changes, but not the total loss of relationships between phonetic signifiers and the signified which is simply assumed by the "noise" theorists in order quite unreasonably to reinforce their case for randomness.

A nice comparison with the tiger's "Grrr" is the word used by speakers of Central Senoi in the jungle of the central spine of Malaya for the bark of a dog "kherrl", which is reported in their creation myth as the cause of the flood when one-tail-of dog-barked-at-a tree, "mi-ikur-chok-kherrl-delong-kruing" in their tongue. (Malay too says one tail [of] dog, but pronounces it sa ekor anjing). It would be wrong to claim Adam spoke Malay. He spoke a language quite close to Lithic and Sumerian which is now lost. This was Adam's flood which drove him from Eastern Malaya or Eden Garden. I never cracked the thinking behind this myth. When I recounted it in Senoi seeking information my audience took off into the jungle for fear it might start up again, so I had to give up. Perhaps the tree stood for the head of the vegetable kingdom and the dog for hunters eating meat. Had the boys been mocking the girls with their digging sticks and their knowledge of agriculture irrigating rice padi, and this climate change was the watery element's revenge, for trying to improve on the nature vouchsafed by the deity, justifying the boys? Adam certainly seems to have had it in for Eve and shopped her to his God. The Malay for tree is pokok or pohon. Kruing however crops up today in advertisements for garden furniture in supermarkets, said to be made from managed forests (in Borneo, where there are no Senoi) from kruing, supposedly the name of a hardwood like teak. It seems clear the entrepreneur enquiring for the name of the timber he was felling (What do you call this one then?) got the answer "It's a tree of course. What do you take me for!" so we are reassured to learn our garden furniture is made of tree. "Kherrl" is quite like Grr! and growl. The r is rasped and the -l is in many words for language too, as if the growl was recognized as doggy language of a sort. Does anyone think Senoi is related to English? Or alternatively is it a psychosemantic echoism? Kruing is easily Lithicised as Kai-rau-'n, a superlatively grown one, the vowel u is the all-done-gone-finished vowel, and pokok is a shoot-what-grown-hard (pa-u-kau-kai), with a trunk in fact. The trunk is recognized in the Malay in its metaphorical meaning of root or origin also (whence all the branches and leaves spring).

The early medieval church, accepting Greek philosophy in much, challenged the idea of simple realism. William of Occam, as well as his razor, introduced a salutary skepticism into the relation of human knowledge to reality. His razor, Res non multiplicanda (things [concepts] should not be multiplied), resulted from his nominalist philosophy. Words as signifiers were only weakly related to the signified, since a word (name) could not cover every aspect of the signified phenomenon, only pick out its most notable aspect. The connection was shrinking, no longer decreed by nature. With this, phonology was randomised. Language was thoroughly disconnected from the external world, the world of nature – which included noises heard but not human language, a human activity in the mind. It should not be thought these fourteenth century churchmen lacked perspicacity. On the contrary they were just as fly as any modern senior wrangler, only they were of course rather less well informed. Grammar was actually regarded as a branch of metaphysics in Occam's day – as of course it is, given a modern interpretation of metaphysics as simply outside physics (and biology). We shall see shortly that Lugwig Wittgenstein's final position was not so far from the medieval stance, which in its philosophy probes the lexicon's connection with the real world; and was also much closer to the Lithic hypotheses than modern neurolinguistics. This is of interest because it suggests it is the neurolinguists rather than the Lithic hypotheses which are the novel oddities with the Darwinian bit between their teeth.

Renaissance scholarship, universally seen as a progressive liberal revolution was actually just as much a rebirth of the old classical philosophy. It was a renaissance because in the dark ages civilization had been set back a thousand years by the savagery of the Germanic races as they overran Roman civilization. Close to my home the fens, drained and cultivated by the Romanised inhabitants, when East Anglia was the bread basket for Europe as the German invaders burned the crops on the continent, after 650 AD with the arrival in England of the Saxons were silted up and provided cover for Hereward the Wake and other local banditi for a thousand years until they were redrained in the seventeenth century by Dutch engineers. On my own home farm, now some three hundred yards East of the Roman farm villa (with pavement discovered in 1870), the forty acre field ("Great Meg") with the villa on it, recently yielded up forty Roman coins dated over three hundred and fifty years, apparently thrown down as libations to the Roman gods to grant a fertile soil and a good crop. I fancy Meg is from the Latin magna, with the translation into the vernacular added. The buildings have just moved three hundred yards in 1700 years – averaging between two and three inches a year. For more than half of this time the farming has been in my family. In yields, financial yields per acre in real terms, since the Romans left we have not seen the same prosperity again. The continental powers, France and Germany, continue to bleed the UK by means of the CAP, and Germany already plans (2001), although France has not noticed yet, the capitalization and modernization of the Eastern European silts to feed the whole of Europe – how else may the Eastern European countries pay their way in the EU? – to the detriment of the French connection which is secured on the 1949 guarante of a CAP guaranteeing European agriculture for France for ever.

Grammar schools taught Latin grammar which was the passport to preferment in the church and university alike. The Romans had taken their philosophy and much else from the Greeks. In the fifteenth and sixteenth centuries the discovery of foreign parts and the exotic languages of the natives, which came with the exploitation of the oceans, did little to displace Latin grammar. Since these barbarian tongues had no written grammar of their own the procrustean categories of Latin grammar were simply superimposed. Indeed the same can be said of the vernaculars of Europe as they came to be written for government purposes. It took a long time for the penny to drop and exotic grammars to be recognized. We were content for twelve hundred years with the grammar laid down by the Latin grammarian Priscian in the sixth century AD – and he had relied largely on the Greek grammarian Dionysus Thrax from seven hundred years earlier still. This is a good chunk of extant history.

The whole of modern linguistics is virtually confined to the last century and a half. Gottlob Frege (1848-1915) was teaching at Jena University in 1872. His first book in 1879, at 31 years of age, explored the logic of mathematics and distinguished meaning as twofold, sense and reference. Sense was roughly the definition, and reference the thing(s) named. He exemplified his perception with the morning star and the evening star as two senses with Venus as the reference of both. Lithic might add "Venus" as another definition or sense (The Visitor), and the actual planet as the reference of all three. His second book in 1884 argued mathematics was founded on logic, which was developed in language which badly needed tidying up. A precise mathematical symbolism was required. We can see linguistics was heading already for an algebra, from which hard thinking was going to be required to shake it loose. But his teaching was ignored until the following century when it was discovered by Bertrand Russell whose Principia Mathematica in collaboration with Alfred Whitehead (copying Isaac Newton), published in 1910-13, fundamentally rehashed grammar as a mathematical exercise by analyzing it in terms of symbolic logic. He called it philosophical logic.

The achievement of symbolic logic is analytical; the sign or symbol is external to the mind, a word for instance which may be written on a page and is what it is and is not another thing. But it invokes in turn in the mind of the observer an idea, subjective and partial. Meanwhile the logician, in this case Gottlob Frege, has been working on the idea thinking in terms of the sign or symbol, and he has cleverly come up with another analysis: the sign or symbol (think of a word) has two aspects, namely first of all a "reference" to the actual real thing to which it refers (think of a stone or a star), and also secondly a "sense" or description or definition. He gives examples: Aristotle as 'the pupil of Plato and teacher of Alexander the Great' or else 'the teacher of Alexander the Great who was born in Stegira' with both of these "senses" having the same "reference", the actual bloke. There may be a spot of categorical parsimony here. With either sense, or indeed with any sense at all, the reference could, as I see it, be to an idea in the head of the thinker rather than immediately to the actual bloke. That idea may then in turn be a sign with sense and reference – with a personal name not much point, but with most nouns (at least with Lithic analysis) a requirement, since the word structures actually started out at least as descriptions. We are certainly close to an infinite regression, or at any rate a lengthy delve into Lithic thinking with meanings analysed through the psychosemantic trees in the chapters on phonemes. These senses or definitions are the entrée for Lithic analysis of meanings. Frege's example of his choice is geometrical: the intersection of lines a and b and the intersection of lines b and c in the case of a triangle where a, b and c are the lines connecting the vertices of the triangle with the mid points of the opposite sides. These two intersections, differently described, define a single point. The lines intersect at the same point! It is another case like the morning star and the evening star above.

Ferdinand de Saussure (1857-1913) was a Swiss academic, whose "Cours de Linguistique Generale" was published posthumously in 1916 in the middle of World War One – the Swiss don't fight. It established structuralism: that is the idea that language is an abstract structure ("langue") as opposed to the actual utterances ("parole"). Instead of the senses of words it was the structure of sentences which needed study, effectively grammar. Structuralism provided much more systematic wrangling opportunity than lexical definitions and it therefore won the day as far as intellectuals were concerned.

Of course Saussure's thinking was around before. There is always a climate of opinion which principal expositors exploit and get the credit for. Wilhelm von Humboldt (1796-1886), a genuine polymath when the scope of human knowledge still allowed such vanities, had hinted at some of it a hundred years before, and Wilhelm Wundt (1838-1920) promulgated structuralism too. It was thought that language shaped thought so that a national language shaped national character. There were those who rejoiced in this in those days. It was a time of chauvinistic politics we are still fighting our way out of. For its recipients language no doubt dictated and dictates their thinking to a remarkable extent. But you have to ask how language got the way it did in the first place. Clearly, before language shaped thought, thought shaped language. It must have done. But once up and running the traffic is both ways. Saussure's structural approach was picked up in the United States where the native Indian languages were proving tough cookies. Their grammar was wildly deviant by European standards. The trouble with Saussure was not that he distinguished between the synchronic (structural) approach and the diachronic (historical and semantic) approach, but that he altogether failed to distinguish them. He thereby introduced two completely different subject matters, somewhat after the shape of Aristotle's distinction between form and matter. Grammar, the form, was simply different in nature from the matter, the study of the semantic contents of words and their developments. Once the philosophers had staked their claims to revising and improving the grammar there was no holding them. The lexicon went out the window. Any linguist worth his salt was bound to a synchronic study of the system of grammar, most recently with expectations of discovering Chomsky's patterns, transformational grammar with a basement floor common to all languages in the subconscious mind where it is supposed to be inborn – carried by the genes (sic), even in the primitive languages being discovered just as they were threatened with extinction around the world. It has been a taxing commitment and by no means a complete success. Linguistics in the USA has moreover for long been hamstrung by the prevalent empiricist hang-ups amongst scientists, refusing to recognize its metaphysical character; and this refusal still determines the tack of the neurologists based at MIT.

What is certain is mathematical thinking has recently demonstrated its ability to reshape language study. That is what modern linguistic philosophy is about. It makes language the tool of theoretical thinking, which you might think would settle the chicken and egg question satisfactorily. The egg preceded the chicken, hatching dinosaurs etc before the chicken was invented. But now it takes a chicken to lay its egg. Now it takes a speaker to contribute a thought.

We have skipped the British colonial judge in India, Sir William Jones, who drew attention to the kinship of Sanskrit and Greek, starting a fashion of comparative linguistics and historical (diachronic, across time) study of language development. Now it is rather dull but it has bred evolutionary rules – although evolution proper does not apply in practice – for phonetic shunts: from bh to b to p, etc, offering a protocol for a blind clockmaker in linguistic change, as if it were a natural process like the evolution of species, which it is not.

Gottlob Frege (1848-1925) was a significant German mathematician as well as a philosopher and therefore not to be lightly challenged. He was prayed in aid by a succession of mathematically minded logicians tackling language, supposedly without prepossession. Before Frege the Classical philosophers had spent their efforts on categorical thinking, largely Aristotle's syllogisms, never probing behind them. The human mind likes a board with small squares on it. As has been seen in chapter 16, entities (categories) are far from being aboriginal concepts and carefree entification (categorization) may be a dangerous snare hindering proper discrimination. The bounded category, based upon the unbounded unlocated distinction separating red from not-red for example an adjectival concept already invented by the adjectival minds of our hominid forebears, as also evidenced today in the mind of the infant exploring his nursery wallpaper (it is in chapter 3 and chapter 16 both) is no good place to start your thinking.

Bertrand Russell's Principia Mathematica provided a symbolic grammar. It was a recognition of the influence of language on philosophy and an attempt to sharpen up the language for the job. The Vienna Circle were somewhat similarly engaged at the same time, and Classical logic was simultaneously up for review. It was a great time for academic intellectuals and a time for painful readjustment for the churches. There is no doubt that the clarity of thinking was much advanced. Natural language however was reinvented in terms of a logical system of grammar, leaving out traditional semantic examination of the lexicon. The rules of grammar usurped all attention. Finally with Chomsky original artificial language was overwritten by a deliberately artificial one and the understanding and classification of languages, especially those facing extinction, was diverted to analysis of their grammar. Philology has yielded place to linguistics at the same time as philosophy has yielded place to logic. Language study has not been served.

The linguistic stretch which Frege and Russell contrived was a revolt against the eighteenth and early nineteenth century idealist systematisers who can I think now be seen as acting out all unawares the last convulsive death throes of the epistemological stance thrown up by the theologians, founded on Plato and Aristotle. The systematisers cover a fair spread, from Kant to Marx and even (let it only be whispered) to Darwin. Structuralism and post modern deconstruction are really only a replay. Chomsky is in Kant's post hole, and the Lithic hypotheses mosey around Frege's sink. The game has gone to second set because of the math that came in with Frege and Russell, which now has to be separated out again. Meaning is semantic, and there is little structural about semantics other than the diachronic trees of etymology. Chomsky's synchronic systematization is an imposition and it harks back to Kant's methodology, adding only some psychological esprit with the subconscious, like Jung's Group Soul carrying ideas from generation to generation for those with the gift to access it. The genes are prayed in aid in replacement of Jung's group soul. Lithic does far better with language as metaphysic in the minds of each generation, with a scientific passage from head to head simply by learning in the here and now in every case, albeit involving the subconscious minds of the participants but via the lexicon and with no magic intergenerational (biological) transference of the metaphysic. Putting ideas into biological inheritance via a language organ is not science but magic. We are born instinctive beings but not wranglers with the ideas in place for play to commence. There is a category mistake here, treating the particular transactional usages of the brain as if they were part of the structure of the organ. Our organs are built by our genes, but not individual ideas, any more than our legs, the pedestrian organs, determine which walks we will take.

What is math? It is a game with simple rules. Reason rules, and consistency counts most. Inconsistency is ruled out, however slightly based merely on linguistic convention. Your sequiturs must resist challenge, but the challenges allowable are only those of logic, a human ability promoted to a superhuman role ruling the universe. Mathematicians equate reason with reality, their minds are apt to become trapped in a single closed system. Math turns out, or rather selects big-brained wranglers – those who make the biggest mistakes. There is a good deal of common sense at the bottom of the bucket like 1+1=2 and 2+2=4 for instance, along with some more difficult equations and transforms, but there is often a good deal of froth at the top where it meets the open air. This appendix is on the philosophy of language. It is beyond its scope to proceed to a philosophy of math.

We need now to undertake a radical analysis of Ludwig Wittgenstein's Tractatus Logico Philosophicus, as a prolegomena to Lithic, in order to clear away many of the obstacles to thinking about thinking that he left us with. He was born in 1883 of plutocratic parentage in Austria Hungary and reckoned he had seen through philosophy, announcing the end of it, its questions and answers being compounded of misunderstandings in language and logic – a splendid research programme but mishandled somewhat in the execution. In aid of all this he produced at length a gnomic document of some 84 pages, Tractatus Logico Philosophicus (A Tract on Logical Philosophy or Philosophical Logic, see Russell above), which he rather engagingly admitted in his preface it was quite possible nobody would be able to follow unless they happened to have already had the same ideas, or something similar, themselves. There is indeed a nugget here: his schema scores more highly for consistency than relevance to the commonplace reality to which the rest of us have access. That is not to say it is a total misfit, but the fact is it allows itself such a spare frame it would fit almost anything. His genius was to cobble together a whimsy quite unlike other contemporary whimsies while all the time engaged in hard pounding in logical terms. In particular he subordinated language to mathematics, which meant treating it as a branch of logic, rather than the other way around, logic as a branch of language. In this he was encouraged by Bertrand Russell, under whom he studied at Cambridge – seeking to teach him at the same time. This curiosity has spawned Noam Chomsky also. In reality language is just language and historically both logic and mathematics have grown out of it. Neither came from dumb hominids after all, they are later developments.

Meditating on Wittgenstein's apothegms, it occurs to me his penultimate view as expressed in his Tractatus was the Stone Age prelinguistic one. He lived, like the Ancient Egyptians also, in a world made up of a succession of pictures or states of play, much like the frames of a cinema film, the same idea we may think which allowed the invention of the cinematograph. These visions he labeled "facts", and collectively "the case". He was a simple realist, originally from the Vienna school of thinking.

There is no doubt, since he says so, he had parlayed this world view to one where his pictures were shaped into (treated as) sets of circumstances, which he then chose to further define as "existing in logical space". By now he was fairly far removed from any picture known to the rest of us, whatever value his construct held for him. It is a quirk of the solipsist mind it can make its own leaps of convenience, fancying them as implicit in the nature of things, quite unaware of the subjectivity involved. I doubt if he had heard of Pyrrhon. It was, so far as one can now see, all in aid of making out that the natural world and logic were in some kind of one to one relationship, so that his magisterial logic handling could be made out to entitle him to dispose of the world on his own terms also.

This is of course an absurdity, or more accurately several absurdities one after another. Anyway by this stage he had also departed rather widely from the Lithic perception, which merely parlayed the pictorial scene by using analogy to abstract semantic patterns from the scenery and apply them across the board. The classic Lithic analogy in building vocabulary was by means of these "gulls". This term is coined for the trick of labelling a character observed in a named phenomenon with the prior name: a gull wing from the shape of the gull's wing, for example, where the gull is named beforehand for it's wailing cry (the same root informing call, gala, gale and gull, all from the two common roots ka/ga and la, which we can label go-la) and the wing picks up its character from that of the gull's wing shape and the gull's name with it, although the wing is silent and neither calls nor sings: the wing is the wing of the singer but it does not itself sing. Interestingly there is an entrée to syntax here: the analogy is of an abstracted aspect from a substantive symbol (noun and adjective in modern terms).

But a gull is far from Wittgenstein's devolution from pictorialisation to propositional representation and then further abstraction to a presentation in logical space. These transmogrifications are, quite frankly, unwarranted. But senior wranglers are apt to wrangle the way they learned. There is an apostolic succession in academic circles which often keeps the same balls in the air for an inordinately (absurdly) long time. One man's philosophy is another man's whimsy, and the passage of history has generally justified the whimsiologists (those exposing the

whimsies) and not those indulging in them. Thus it is that the pressures nowadays on those proposing to follow through any individual schematism are indeed
daunting, and this includes the Lithic hypotheses. That is one reason why the row
to date remains unhoed. The ideology of linguistics has poisoned the wells. Yet the
instinct to shake out evidence into a form enabling a degree of understanding can
not be denied. It must however be done with discretion and a preparedness to tolerate almost any degree of limitation. This is the complete opposite of the wisdom
purveyed at staff colleges, and widely practiced in bureaucratic and technical institutions world wide, where the trick is to achieve as structured a scheme of things
as possible. Edward de Bono has made a killing advocating an alternative strategy
of thinking sideways, as well as deliberately examining circumstances under different heads or "thinking hats". The latter thinking protocol is to review matters
consecutively under radically different aspects, and even other peoples' hats, to
discover how the other coons involved may be seeing things. The hats aren't much
but the lateral thinking is clever. It takes us back to Lithic analogy and the gulls
again, in place of the common modern game plan of logical consequences. De
Bono illustrates the saner side of post modern deconstructionism, much of which
is overly relativistic, denying any one version of events as the reality. The truth of
course is the world is indeed what it is and not another thing, whether we can
spot it or not.

Wittgenstein's personal habits of mind, it can now be seen, were absurd; but
we should admire him nevertheless because he certainly got his mind up and
running – as we all can and should – and was prepared to follow his own nose
all the way. It may not have been an entire success but it has to be said nobody
else's nose will do, so he was not wrong in that. Meanwhile it has also been said
he was in school with Adolf Hitler, intellectually a comparative weakling, and
his toffee-nosed posture may have accounted for Hitler's maniacal anti-Semitism
later. This is interesting since Wittgenstein himself eventually came to adopt a
position not wholly unlike the Nazi philosopher Oswald Spengler, basing understanding on subjective intuition rather than objective science, a position appealing to those who feel themselves geniuses. Wittgenstein's scribblings, when he
finally got around to it, incompletely expressed his thinking, leaving generations
of professional pickers-over to make their sense of them, inadvertently fortifying
his whimsy. The real answer to Wittgenstein is simply to say we do not choose to
think in that way. The emperor has no clothes.

Reading Tractatus Logico-Philosophicus, which is a list of definitions, it soon
becomes apparent many, indeed most of the words he uses are terms of art. They
can not possibly mean for him what they mean for most of us. Here are the first
few noted: Paragraph 2.0121. "If I can imagine objects combined in states of affairs I can not imagine them excluded from the possibility of such combinations".

But surely we can! Even if we might not find such a one we can certainly dream of it. 2.0122. "It is impossible for words to appear in two different roles: by themselves, and in propositions". Has he not come across a dictionary? If he was on to something deeper here he has failed to express it. 3.261."Names cannot be anatomized by means of definitions". Names clearly means something different for him from our general understanding of what names are, which we are quite capable of defining. For instance we give the name carpet to a type of floor covering and we can perfectly easily "anatomize" the name with a definition, for instance a floor covering made of fibres of traditional manufacture with a soft pile. We can go on to describe in complete detail its form of manufacture etc, if we know it. To deny this would be silly. So it is clear "name" (and/or other elements in the proposition) for Wittgenstein means something different. What it means to him, it appears, is an atomic meaning which he imagines is the point or base meaning which is in the nature of a point or base term in logic, atomic and therefore incapable of further anatomisation: just a pun really. A point is the x of mathematics, the exemplar of itemization. It symbolizes one of Wittgenstein's "facts" or prelinguistic 'shots' of the external world, which also is bedrock for Wittgenstein, an axiomatic datum not capable of this anatomisation. I guess his 'shot' is not a gunshot but a camerashot, the panorama at any state of play. Of course such a one would have no further analysis for him by definition, since analysis is logical and the 'shot' is prior to logic. This is a rather important matter since it points the way to a fundamental assumption made by Wittgenstein in his Tractatus, namely that reality (the world we live in) is logico-philosophicus, or even in fact logico-mathematicus. This trick he probably picked up from Bertrand Russell, under whom he studied in Cambridge. In fact it could be said he picked up Russell's ball and ran with it. But the construct resulting actually bore little relation to reality however worthy its credentials as math. Indeed his idea that the 'shots' or frames of external reality are prior to logic sits ill with the conclusion he draws quite soon after that the real world can be defined in logical terms.

Neither Russell nor Wittgenstein had any historical sense, not a scrap between the two of them. They both lived in a glass universe, elegant, see-through and precise, on mental skate-boards since both of them were bright. From these glassy halls they preached their definitive universe made up of neatly interlocking pieces, as if the only world were the world of geometry. Both were somewhat autistic. Autism and egotism, even solipsism, go together. Thus their vulnerability and incompetence in interpersonal relations caused them to construct a carapace for themselves, like the caddis fly worm, but made up of clear-cut intellectual pieces, in which they could choir inviolate and not concern themselves with immeasurable personal exchanges. The result was a determinist ideology like Marxism, which like Marxism their contemporaries could not crack. It was a crystal palace but also a cage with bars made of mathematical tautologies, mental surfaces which bounced you back into the edifice whenever you tried to break out, a hall of mirrors, the biggest mental hephalump trap since the Marxist dialectic, in which the European intelligentsia still wallow and will wallow awhile as yet.

But now we are left astonished Wittgenstein could soliloquize so glibly and self confidently about his flawed presumption, elaborating from one gnomic utterance to the next, pulling in more and more words for his own gloss on them, illustrating in almost every case, like with "name" above, that they were all pieces on his own private chequer board and were being recast to his own Procrustean pattern which he believed was the only true logic. It would still have been a bizarre enterprise had he been right. As it was, his life-and-death struggle with his own sea serpents was left behind for the senators after his death, not wisdom exactly but certainly cats cradles enough to keep them mulling over his rather modest textual contribution in the belief the emperors clothes must be in there somewhere, in pursuit of PhDs and academic tenures. Much of their admiration no doubt was due to the undoubted fact he silenced Bertrand Russell. Anyone who could get the better of Russell, the argument went, must certainly be a senior wrangler.

The reality was he had grasped the wrangler's pressure points (inconsistencies) and worked out the dead ends in wrangling. Russell could not avoid thinking the consequential way he thought. He was a basket case by Edward de Bono's standards. Whatever the weather he sailed a straight course and ran up on the rocks when the terrain confronted him; but he died with his carapace intact on his back. It is the way that mathematicians have. Intellectual integrity is their deity; and the cock crows in vain, they recognize no backsliding. They can even be in a straight jacket and be quite oblivious of it, such is their megalomania. They have their places at the high tables of the world, and that is sufficient for them. At the court of a million years their seats are puny. A smidgeon of the same time scale sees their every idea dismissed as fatuous and forgotten. It is the fatuity which is the point. They are short on understanding, erudite but erroneous, probably from trying too hard when young. A more liberal education is to be found in the crossword puzzle, by comparison of almost infinite variety.

To be half way fair, Wittgenstein discovered the absurdity of many of his own ideas and after eight years in retreat some of it literally in the wilderness, a cottage in North Norway, he returned to Cambridge and lectured for sixteen years several generations of students in his own fashion, without publishing a word. He became finally fascinated by the significance of his own skin, what he owned (within) as contrasted with the alien (without). This was certainly back to basics, what every individual has to work out for himself, even before language. For any individual his skin is his boundary. But in reality it is a boundary with two

sides, each of significance and neither negating the other as Wittgenstein was
inclined to infer. We have sense organs on both sides reporting to control centre,
those looking out sensing the alien while those within sense our own domain.
The two activities, "facts" in Wittgenstein's private terminology, have something
in common. Wittgenstein's idea the internal senses are immediate and given, by
contrast with the external which are derivative and contrived, empirical instead of
known a priori, is simply an unthinking extension of Kantian philosophy which
Wittgenstein imagined he had long ago driven out into the Gadarene Swine (the
philosophers).

His upbringing had been privileged, and liberal where money could buy experience, but astonishingly superficial. He followed his father here, a committed
entrepreneurial achiever. His first adult study was engineering, a relatively banausic discipline, in England; and he had in fact come later to classical philosophy
keen to dismember it. His father was an apostate Jew, a man of the world proud of
his worldly success, said to be the wealthiest man in Austria in his day, the power
of his purse bringing him friendship with the intellectuals as well as the musi-
cians in Vienna. Young Ludwig's philosophy, lately acquired, seems to have stayed
with him in spite of his best efforts to expel it. The total dismantlement of the
elaborate structure of an adult weltanschaung, built up in infancy and adolescence
layer upon layer, later in life is probably a near impossibility. Certainly it involves
a more radical abandonment, even reversal of thinking habits, than Wittgenstein
was readily capable of; whence his spiritual turmoil in his wilderness years. He
had cast off from the shores of conventional wisdom and never again found safe
haven. His posthumous works were posthumous because he never finally adopted
any position in his lifetime. He powerfully challenged the sane world of his day
but he never replaced it. His life left him in a gaping void, a "néant", which the
Lithic hypotheses must now contribute to bridging over. We can see now his reliance on contrasting the immediacy and indubitability of internal sensation – he
sticks to pain as exemplar most of the time – with the empirical uncertainties of
the external senses, seeing and hearing for the most part, but also of course registering hot and cold air and the bruising from heavy whacks, is greatly overdone.
These latter internal sensations are triggered from the outside but sensed internally, and in that not so far from vision of the other, the outside world, which also
– come to think of it – is triggered from the outside but sensed internally.

We can remind ourselves here of the Ancient Egyptians, the earliest thinkers
I know much of, whose gallimaufry of there-and-back rays were called into play
to explain vision (and much else): a ray went out from the eye and contacted,
touched, felt over the panorama, returning with an image of it which it deposited
on the iris of the eye for the homunculus behind to view. The eye's action at a distance was thus tamed, and matched with the hand's sensibility of what it touched

in a manner these old fogies found an acceptable explanation. They actually drew the all-powerful sun's rays with hands on the ends, symbolizing their power to draw the vegetation up with them on their return journey to the sun. Egyptian rays all went there and back like active radar beams, an illusion based on the clear ability of the eye to bring back a picture to the eye, which could actually be seen on the iris: actually a reflection of the light, the eye being a passive sensor and not an emitter at all. Their language may have been crude but they had the business better than Wittgenstein, who was making it up to suit his message to posterity. They kept all their senses internal and reconciled this with messages coming from outside. It would be nice to be able to report they believed in neither the internal nor the external signals they received, but the fact is they appear to have believed in the divine nature of both. Modern science has uncovered bogus sensations, when amputees sense pains or other messages from limbs no longer there, real sensations but uninformative, just as we can mistake what we see. The natures of the respective senses which report internal and external stimuli is not contrapuntal as Wittgenstein wanted them to be to stress the primacy of the emotions like desire and suffering, hope and frustration as the origins of thinking, rather then any calculating (philosophical) thinking. In this of course he was right although he muffed the record. He was grappling with the myriad sottiseries of his day, and he had rumbled many of them.

Wittgenstein's documentation was put into book form posthumously after his death under the direction of Professor von Wright, a Finnish philosopher of Scottish extraction who inherited Wittgenstein's position at Cambridge. In his second avatar Wittgenstein had dumped Descartes' ghost in the machine, a dualistic view not evidenced in reality. He argued for a single integral human personality not fully conscious or "knowing its mind". The Lithic language hypothesis quite nicely matches Wittgenstein's belief in the corruption of thinking from the misapprehension of language. But he insisted internal perceptions (sensed experience), like "I feel a pain", were a priori and not empirical like messages from without. Germans have treated Kant and Hegel like Shakespeare, that is as unchallengeable. Von Wright, who survived into the twenty first century, took Wittgenstein's later sensationalism in his "Philosophical Investigations", published posthumously, one stage further, virtually dumping science for intuition and espousing the radical thinking of Oswald Spengler. Spengler, a runt Nazi philosopher with an outsize grudge for losing the first world war, while employed as a snide secondary school teacher at Blankenberg am Rhein, wrote a world history (Der Untergang den Abendlandes, The Decline of the West) in the 1920s, in which he perceived civilizations as growths like cabbages which burgeoned and decayed. The decay stage was Hitler's decadence. His thinking, like all those who see themselves as geniuses, was a tightly textured mix of brilliance and absurdity.

It was in rejection of this kind of ideology that Burgess and MacLean, as well as the Keeper of the Queen's pictures, embraced instead the other common insanity of the twentieth century, Marxism which had a dialectic supposed to trump science. It cost tens of millions of lives learning it did not. But we have now reviewed the intellectual history of the last century and cleared the decks for the study of thinking, without bothering further with academe.

It is probably best to just announce the true nature of language to be a system of symbols by means of which the utterances of mankind are given specific meanings. This at any rate was the opinion of Ferdinand de Saussure (1851-1913), a Swiss academic and professor at the University of Geneva all his working life. He had already produced an original analysis of the use of Indo European vowels while still a student; and that proved his swan song so far as the historical approach was concerned. He graduated to language as a structural system for study either diachronically (historically) in detail as he had at the outset picking on the vowel changes, or else synchronically – scientifically he would have said or even logically, emphasizing the systemics. He spent the rest of his life lecturing on this latter aspect of linguistics, the systemics turning out to be the grammar.

On the other side of the Atlantic C S Peirce (1839-1914) added his own philosophical analysis of language as the principal sign system of Saussure's "Semiotics", the study of signs and signing. For Peirce a sign was "something which stands to somebody for something". I think we would now prefer to emphasise the relationship is intended to be triadic and say the symbol is a B connecting A to C. Peirce's definition allows B connecting A to A. The Greek "sumbol" means thrown or put together, that is relating things, and the insinuation is the relationship is random, even casual, just falling together, rather than semantic as in the Lithic hypothesis. Peirce's three types of signs were taken as soundly differentiated for a time and provided student material for generations. With the first type, an icon, the relationship between signifier and signified was one of resemblance, principally a configural representation like the Russian religious icon, the most straightforward type; but we might put the cuckoo in front of the icon, as a natural echoism. The second type was an index, or indicator, the relationship being by habitual association, for example smoke indicating fire. We might include the cuckoo here also, the call indicating the bird. The icon could of course qualify as well, the visual representation, perhaps only an outline shape, being just as much an indicator as a bird call. The third type was much in the majority and was arbitrary and had to be learned, such as most words for things, in fact most words. We can however gloss all these types of signs as semantic since they all excite ideas, cuckoos and pictures directly using auditory and visual representations. Indexes like smoke, and cuckoos and outlines if you choose to treat the cuckoo's call as an index of the bird rather than just its auditory representation, and an outline as an indicator of the bloke, all elicit the idea by association with the signifier. Wherever there is smoke there is fire, whenever the cuckoo is heard there is the bird, whenever a good enough icon is presented it is recognized as a representation of the signified. Meanwhile words treated as random signifiers are equally good at evoking the idea, the route is semantic and arises by association just like on hearing the cuckoo. Note that party B is providing the idea. It is not the signified prompting the signifier nor the signified prompting the sign. The two meet, if they do meet, in somebody's mind. We see the smoke and think of fire. We hear the call and think of the cuckoo. We say the word and are thinking of the meaning. But with the words there is more to be said. Uncovering Lithic reveals semantic links overlooked and forgotten over the millennia. Over the millennia psychosemantics have built semantic structures in the subconscious. I think of them as if they were underwater reefs made up of linked meanings, linked by nothing more substantial than the whimsy of the human mind associating analogies, gulls and buses, etc; but for the human mind solid enough material to build a reef. Built into the coral fabric of the reef under the flag of "La" for instance we can find flat and long and line piled on top of slip and slope, lye underlying laut (sea in Malay). These structures are ideational fantasies. They are not inheritable. Each generation rebuilds them over again afresh on the underside of the language they learn, and some no doubt learn them better than others. There was no other route to mutual understanding when first we began to speak. Psychosemantic prompts alone gave any hope of mutual comprehension. The vocabulary must surely have started out extraordinarily small, and grown slowly with it. The reefs were low to start with.

The whole of linguistics has been railroaded since Saussure and Peirce and sidelined into the study of grammar, so that it now takes a massive effort to recover the missing ground and refocus attention on the semantic contents of the whole of speech and not just the logical relationships of the parts of speech the grammarians have been syncopating for a century. Over the past century we have virtually dumped the lexicon for a mess of grammatical pottage. Systematising has known no bounds. Every grammarian since Pannini with any claim to originality has not only recorded language as spoken but has also been unable to resist refashioning it nearer to how he would have wished it to have been. This applies to Professor Chomsky just as much as Pannini all those centuries ago. To some extent the swing to a grammatical focus has been the result of revulsion away from the fanciful etymologies of philologists before the linguistic reformation of the 1900s. Eric Partridge records these as "f/e" or folk etymology. He was guilty of one or two himself.

The logical positivism which originated in the Vienna Circle reckoned sentence meaning was analytical like logic and mathematics, while traditional semantics was synthetic, involving the relationship between human thinking and the phenomenal world. This perception rubbished traditional semantics, down grading it to descriptive names, which were taken to be merely conventional anyway, with etymologies a branch of phonetics. It simultaneously sidelined the historical or diachronic approach replacing it with the new science of linguistic analysis in logical terms. It was a first fine caroling of modernism, but it left out most of language in favour of a linguistic algebra which turned out to be a reformed grammar; and when it had to be found a place was consigned to the subconscious because it was not consciously known to speakers. They inherited it via their genes and used it but did not know it.

I am endebted to John L Casti's elegant synopsis of linguistic theorising over the past fifty years[1]. What has enabled Noam Chomsky to claim we have an organ capable of passing on hereditary ideas as to how we should speak is that it appears that "the poverty of stimulus" when youngsters are learning their language can not explain how they learn it so well. The argument is that some further guidance must be helping them; so it must be neurological. Nevertheless the idea that ideas, rather than just instinctive or emotional dispositions resulting from the organs carrying them, might be heritable seems absurd to many, and certainly to me. Our legs do not carry the walks we will take nor the brain the thoughts we will think. So the question for us is where might this tutorial assistance come from if not from Chomsky's hard wiring of the brain. The answer I believe is twofold, or even threefold. First of all the pattern Chomsky describes is analytical, logical, even mathematical, and quite dubiously relates to the actual development of language. In reality assistance comes from the subconscious processing of the data. Learning is not a simple process. Chomsky himself has described deep structure as not immediately discoverable in the surface structure of language. Lithic language elements similarly are not immediately obvious in the conventional analysis of word structures but nevertheless can be described as a consistent scheme of semantic and phonetic development. It is already suggested in chapter 16 on thinking that the explanation is that processing takes place in the subconscious, which is not immediately apparent when consciously examined. This is very much like Chomsky's transformational grammar, also located in the subconscious. But instead of an unbelievable intellectual cerebral organ, born up-and-running, equipped with thoughts, and quite elaborate thoughts at that, ready to tackle transformational grammar without ever becoming consciously aware of it, the lexicon itself provides the guidance for the subconscious mind with a Lithic scheme of organization, all the way from the dream world, reinforcing the shallow contacts with the conscious rational part of the mind which human experience provides. Language has built this resource piecemeal over the millennia, and passed it on with the language from generation to generation. That already is more believable than grammar booked by the genes. The point is the lexicon as it is learned is both the trigger and the source. Youngsters can avail themselves of this muse more than adults in whom it has been drowned out by very much more conscious verbiage acquired from education education education over many generations. Unlike Kant's high priori or Jung's World Soul or even Freud's overly patterned subconscious, the world lexicon contains all that is required to facilitate learning and it is located in the world we all know and not in any philosophical limbo. It provides a guide to meanings. It comes from the semantics of the Lithic elements, which enlighten the subconscious mind which is speaking Lithic while the conscious mind is acquiring the adaptation thereof, the surface language the child's parents have consciously acquired. We are all simple Neanderthalers under the skin; and it turns out it is this Lithic application of cognitive science which appears to best fit the facts. There really is another way to account for the facts Chomsky uses to validate his transformational grammar. The Lithic language has no need for any transformational grammar, it just enabled us to speak, and the grammarians' gloss on that came long after.

There are other things about Chomsky's approach which jar. His famous non-sense sentence "Colourless green ideas sleep furiously" which he used to display his belief that syntactic rules used to form sentences exist independently of the semantics of the sentence can also be used to indicate almost the reverse: namely his syntactic schemes may be fine but they ignore the actual meanings which comprise the sentence. They have nothing to do with knowledge, they can be used (and are used) to construct nonsense sentences just as well as meaningful ones. This is because the meanings actually reside in the words of which the sentences are made up, and only derivatively in the sentences. Sentences and the grammar that goes with them are copied from word structures tidied up by grammarians in accordance with their various schemes, of which Chomsky's is only the latest. What was really novel about Chomsky's "revolutionary" approach was his understanding the philatelic approach, just collecting languages, was not enough. What was required was new ideas, clear thinking in order to embrace the variety of game plans turning up in exotic tongues. This was fine. It was even true. It involved hard and original thinking. He picked up where symbolic logic left off, that is to say where mathematics led. But mathematical thinking is a minority sport, and always has been. To find mathematical principles hard wired in the brain and inherited for each citizen's self-teach language course was a bridge too far – by far. Primitive language roots demonstrate at least that if Chomsky's grammar is valid it must have come later. It does not fit primitive thinking, of which Chomsky had no direct experience. He is an ivory tower thinker, a true intellectual, politically as well as linguistically. That was the virtue of his approach. He freed linguists from the bind they had gotten into when they rejected the semantic content of language – as if we were all Pavlovian dogs. Chomsky however was carrying baggage too. The ideas he claimed were hard wired were not the ones which informed language from the outset, but another set he had compiled from his contemporary fund of thinking. He was not afraid of metaphysics, but he was not as good a judge of ideas as he imagined. Sentence structure is peripheral to linguistic performance, not central. It is late, not original. It is derivative, not deeper than or prior to semantic structuring which originates with speaking in the very process of word formation, with a grammar of its own.

Chomsky's generative grammar is often designated as "top down" as opposed to the empiricists' school of inductive research which is "bottom up". There is inevitably an element of German high idealism of the materialistic sort in the top down approach, the thinking which has permitted, even encouraged the European totalitarian schools of the past century. So I think the farm boys have it if they can break through the conventional crust and loosen up their thinking. The Sapir-Whorf hypothesis must go too. It comprises two propositions supposedly one implying the other, namely language is prior to thinking, and we think in words; and so, since our words are unique to our language so are our ideas and even our world view. Benjamin Whorf was a fire inspector for an insurance company when he was not writing on language. His thinking was surface thinking, not deep at all. It may even be his own thinking never did get beyond those insights offered by his vocabulary. In reality thought was pretty obviously prior to its expression even if vocabulary trammels our minds, as indeed it does.

Chomskyan linguistics, concentrating on transformational grammar at a deep level which is innate has appealed to the even newer school of cognitive science researching neurolinguistics and claiming computers can think like humans, that thinking is just a dead scheme – almost Skinner's revenge on Chomsky: even mental activity like Chomsky's grammar can be clawed back into the empiricists' fold, disregarding John Searle's demurrer[2]. A spin off is computers can be used as models of brain activity. The theory is bunk and computers can not think in any meaningful sense, for which live brain activity is required. James Joyce described the motive of his "Ulysses", the story in the form of a complete flow of self consciousness over twenty four hours in Dublin, in terms of his perception of the "river of unformed analysis flowing inside our hearts". It makes no sense at all in terms of neuroscience, but it is meaningful all the same.

At the outset of language it was psychosemantics which prompted the meanings attached to the sounds uttered. This was the origin of the symbolization which introduced linguistic skills. If psychic promptings prompted our initial semantic structuring, when did this change over to semantics determined by logical considerations? Like much philosophy, this turns out to be a question posed in terms which are bogus. When the change occurred is a misleading question, since it never did. There is right now on an everyday basis the very same mix of subjective whimsy and odd-ball analogy in play as there was when we first began to put meanings to utterances. There is also today some degree of sweet reason super-added, but this is because with a vast lexicon there is the more scope and requirement for good order and logic in the development of the vocabulary. Yet even the basic mathematico-logical syllogism 1+1=2 is psychologically inspired: we sense items and then we learn that way to enumerate them. Wittgenstein said as much after his conversion[3]. It may be, indeed it is the case that the world performs more or less in accordance with the logical rules we have developed for ourselves over hundreds of thousands of years of trial and error. But the world is not doing the sums. We are. The world's behaviour falls into the patterns we describe (more or less) because it is its nature to do so, regardless of what we think. Science describes nature but nature can not follow the argument. Nature is blind and performance based and outside anything our conscious imagination can tell us, even when it is the nature which is within us promoting our thinking.

When you are picking your way forward trying to frame the terms of procedure in a hypothetical situation such as at the birth of language some six hundred thousand years ago it actually comes easier to coin language appropriate to those circumstances, because clearly current prejudicial baggage does not apply. There is a clean slate of possibilities. Psychosemantics is the term hit upon to describe the combination of the unthinking subjective automatic responses of our primitive forebears confronted with their Paleolithic environment. Stone Age man in a Stone Age environment must have reacted, we must assume, as well as he might. At any rate it appears he was able to reach a number of consensual views sufficient to start language off with enough mutual understanding to keep the process and the progress going. The rest is eventually history after a good deal of prehistory (hundreds of thousands of years) which is missing. Some at least of the missing bits are recoverable as inclusions in the lexicon, like flies in amber, or indeed like the shell inclusions in sedimentary rocks which, with a wild gamble on the evolutionary sequences, enabled my great grandfather (1804-1870) with Sir Charles Lyell (1797-1875) to spell out the evolutionary tale (Lyell's "Principles of Geology" in 1830) for Charles Darwin to copy ("On the Origin of Species" in 1859). Species evolution was used to prove geological evolution and not the other way about as appears in the history books as Darwin pretended, to save his former tutor being sent to Coventry by dons in dog collars. In rather the same way the phonemic semantic contents surviving as inclusions in the lexicon are used 176 years later to establish the semantic evolution of languages all around the world. Mental inclusions guide mental geology. It is a mite more difficult but the story line is the same.

The Encyclopedia Britannica is a reliable middle of the road compilation recording what is academically correct. In it we find "The great majority of word shapes bear no direct relation to their lexical meanings. If they did languages would be more alike". Both statements are false. In order to relate word composition (shape is used to keep it looking as empirical as possible) to meaning all you have to manage is an understanding of the Lithic hypotheses. It still is not easy because of the whimsicality of the human mind often quite hard to follow after a few hundreds of thousands of years. Even geological strata get compressed somewhat in that timescale. Secondly there are always a number of different ways of prompting for meaning, so languages diverge anyway, and we should expect it. The surprise is that most often it turns out more than two people followed a common line of thought. Psychosemantics is a continual surprise today.

Aristotle is quoted also in Britannica: "Speech is the representation of the experiences of the mind". I like this because it recognizes the thinking comes first, because it identifies speech as expressing thought, and above all because it recognizes thought as something which we experience by which I mean as something naturally happening to us without necessarily any particular intention on our part. That is half way as I see it to recognizing the subconscious mind's contribution. Aristotle's apothegm is thus for me of an altogether higher order than the two misleading sentences from the modern hack. It is even curious the encyclopedia makes such a point of countering a position otherwise unmentioned – perhaps fearing poesy? Or else others too have begun to chip away at the randomness of word roots though not as yet in print. Novel ideas are never all that unique, they tend to be in the air; and genetically inherited subconscious grammar has been teasing the linguistic establishment for a number of decades now and must have generated some frictional heat. There is in reality an echoism of one kind or another in every word at coining. But the encyclopedia goes on to suggest the different names for horse in European languages alone proves word formation is arbitrary. It is of course a common presumption, if you can not see a connection, that there is none. The road to perdition may even be paved with such kinds of presumptions.

Horses are unusual in the animal kingdom and have attracted a good deal of human attention and use all round the world. They are renowned for their gameness, spiritedness, strength and speed; and of course they get ridden, when they will even go into battle or confront rioters. Anyone handling a stallion, even a Shetland stallion, learns to show respect. A cow is a coward easily cowed by comparison, although it wears horns and can turn nasty when calving. Now here are the names for horse used by Encyclopedia Britannica to rubbish Lithic, "all unrelated to the animal so named"; "for by far the largest number of words in a language there is no direct association between sound and meaning". There is surely some impatience with what is perceived as time wasting by mavericks showing here. The author is saying there is more important business: anything in the nature of Lithic should be brushed aside as worthless time wasting. So it is necessary to retaliate by deriving all the words for horse supposedly with sound unconnected with any meaning and showing the encyclopedia's conclusions are in each case falsified by the Lithic hypotheses. The show case of the random roots brigade is cracked as follows:-

English Horse. It is from Lithic elements Haurai-sai, hurrah-active or rejoicing in action, the lively spirited animal: down the middle, surely. See chapters 8, 13 and 14 for the phonemic meanings involved. He rejoices in action. What animal? Answer the horse of course. Compare Wahabi, terrorist, Wa-hurrah-living, Terror-rejoicing-habitually.

German Pferd. It is from Lithic Pa-pahei-dai, limbs-rambo-doer. Pa-hei started out as the rampant penis. See chapters 12, 8 and 6.

French Cheval. Compare Spanish Caballo (Caballiero is the horseman riding it, the knight in chess). It is from the Lithic Ka-ba-la-u, Strong-go-leap-one, Strong-galloper, see chapters 5, 4 and 9. Antelopes may be fleeter (size for size) but not stronger.

Latin Equus. It is from the Lithic Ai-Kai-u-s, That which-strong-and headstrong both (-s is the noun ending), literally that which-strengths-both. See chapters 16 on vowels and 5 for the meanings of Ka.

Greek Hippos. It is from Lithic Hei-papau-s, rejoicing-in his four legs-(-s is the noun ending), another gay galloper. See chapters 8 and 12.

We can add immediately for a desert Chinese Ma, the hammer. See chapter 10, and remember the Han horsemen who reached the gates of Vienna.

Albanian Kale (for the chessman too) from the Lithic strong leaper, the galloper again. The knight's move, by the way, is a leaping one too. See chapters 5 and 9. You don't get a cow jumping a five barred gate, it occurs to me.

Malay kuda. It is from the Lithic Kau-da, like Latin Equus, doubly strong-does or doer, ie in strength and aggressive instinct or habit. Then pulling a dictionary from the shelf at random:

Hausa Dauki. It is from the lithic Da-u-kai, Does-double-strong. This looks like a similar double strength to the Latin equus and the Malayan kuda, strong and headstrong, spirited as well as powerful. There is Arab blood in West African horses. The Ka was the physical and spiritual driving force, in this world and the next, and it came South across the Sahara to Nigeria from Egypt.

Egyptian Abara. Budge compares the Hebrew abir. Egyptian aba means to make strong, to endow with soul. The ba was the physical soul inherent in the muscle and flesh which flit with the last breath. Abara is therefore the strong and vehement one. A bull was similarly described, which makes the meaning apparent. It was not to do with the species but the temperament. Also in Egyptian we have Semeseme, Semasema (from the Lithic elements active and heavy), Saisai (Budge compares the Hebrew sus again. The Lithic is active repuplicated), and Khaita (with khaiterai meaning enforcer. Remember the role of the horse pulling fighting chariots in the Egyptian armies. Remember too the root meaning of khai in Lithic, strike from the sound of flint knapping).

The devilling is in the detail, not in the philosophy, mostly ill considered and trifling. Linguistics is first of all etymology. Etymology is as old as philosophy, in fact it must surely be older. It comes from the Greek etymon, coupled with logos. Logos is word and logic, the semantics of words. I believe the Lithic etymon, ai-tau-maun, treated a word as a mental composition or string and that tells us something already: words are complexes and therefore must have constituents, which in my book are the phonemes composing them with the meanings they bring with them. Etymon is a word's first known composition. The Lithic ai-tau-mau-n, as it-born(ie came into being)-minded (or in the mind), the aboriginal or first born meaning. It has to be stressed far too many of these old words with proven ancient histories fit the Lithic categories for doubts to persist for the serious minded. The Lithic language lives, and that is the end on it.

Notes

1. John L Casti. Paradigms Lost. Chapter 4, pages 213-258.

2. Professor JR Searle of the University of California, Berkeley, a philosopher, proposed a procedure where Chinese cards are processed by an uncomprehending operator in accordance with a set or dictionary of syntactic rules without any explanation of their meaning. The dictionary of course was compiled by a Chinese speaker, taking the semantics on the cards into account, so that the question and answer cards made perfect sense where the language was understood although the operator could not crack it and was going by syntactic rules alone. This scenario takes some hard pounding to think through but the effort is well worth while.

3. The best review of modern philosophy of language I have come across is Modern Philosophy of Language edited by Maria Baghramian, (J.M Dent, 1998), starting with Gottlob Frege who published his main work, The Foundations of Arithmetic, in 1890.

APPENDIX B

SKEAT'S ROOTS

The whole of the Reverend William Skeat's Appendix 5 to his Etymological Dictionary of the English Language first published in 1879 to 1882 is republished here by kind permission of the Oxford University Press. He has been described as "the first great English philologist" (Anyway the first great English professor of philology). He was Professor of Anglo Saxon and edited the poetry of Piers Plowman, and in 1899 the Complete Works of Geoffrey Chaucer. In 1901 he wrote Tales from an Eastern Forest (the Malayan jungle), including Salam the Mouse Deer. The mouse deer is known as Kanchil in Malay (Lithic Going-slyly) or Si Pelandok, Brer Dainty Toes. He is the Malayan Brer Rabbit, born and bred in a briar bush. Reducing word origins to core phonetic roots based on an absence of reasoning over the choice of phonology is a false step, but Skeat's research is nevertheless extremely valuable since it collects together examples of words in many languages which the experienced Lithic reader can interpret in meaningful phonemes. For instance, at random, the Sanskrit for owl is uluka (it says he makes an ulu); the Greek is ulau, the Latin ulula, the Anglo-Saxon ule. (The Egyptian is A-maoo, also echoic). The Latin trudere means to push and only thence to intrude and urge. The Lithic speaker will know what intrusion the folk who coined this expression had in mind. Sphuy in Sanskrit means to swell (under SPE-) – the Lithic is easy – and only thence to increase, with Latin spatium for room and space, Latin prosper for prosperous and spes for hope, with Anglo-Saxon spuwan to succeed, and the English speed. Greek tekein is to beget (Lithic from tai-kai-ein, birth-make-verbal) and Sanskrit tan is to stretch, tanu is thin (stretched out) and tantu a thread. William Skeat was no slouch.

V. LIST OF INDOGERMANIC ROOTS

THE following is a brief list of the principal Indogermanic roots that have English derivatives. Those of which examples are either scanty or doubtful are not noticed. Many of the roots here given are of some importance and can be abundantly illustrated. I have added, at the end of the brief account of each root, several miscellaneous examples of derivatives; but these lists are by no means exhaustive, nor are they arranged in any particular order beyond the separation into groups of the words of Greek, Latin, and Teutonic origin.

Many of these roots (but given in forms which are no longer generally accepted) may be found in 'Fick, Vergleichendes Wörterbuch der indogermanischen Sprachen,' in Curtius, 'Greek Etymology, English edition, translated by Wilkins and England,' and in 'Vaniček, Griechisch-Lateinisches Etymologisches Wörterbuch, Leipzig, 1877.' More correct forms are frequently cited by Brugmann and Uhlenbeck, and are here adopted. The chief modern improvements are the substitution of e or o for a in many instances, of ei for i and of eu for u likewise in many instances, and in the treatment of the gutturals.

The account of each root is, in each case, very brief, and mentions only a few characteristic derivatives. Further information may be obtained in the above-mentioned authorities. The English examples are accounted for in the present work. Thus, under the word Agitate, a cross-reference is given to Agent; and under Agent is cited the √AG, to drive; with a reference to Brugmann, i. § 175.

Instead of giving Grimm's Law in the usual form, I omit the Old High German modifications, and use the word 'Teutonic' as inclusive of all other Germanic forms, thus reducing the number of varying bases, as due to 'sound-shifting' of the consonants, from three to two. This being premised, I give a short and easy method for the conversion of 'Indogermanic' roots into the corresponding 'Teutonic' ones; though it must be remembered that each language has ways of its own for representing certain original sounds. Some of these modifications are noticed below.

Let the student learn by heart the following scheme.

Dentals; viz. dh, d, t, th.
Labials; viz. bh, b, p, f.
Gutturals; viz. gh, g, k, h.

This is all that need be remembered; it only remains to explain what the scheme means.

It is to be read in the following manner. When a dental sound occurs (especially at the beginning of a word, for in other positions the rule is liable to exception), an Idg. dh becomes a Teut. d [for dh is followed in the scheme by d]; an Idg. d becomes a Teut. t

[for a like reason]; and an Idg. t becomes a Teut. th (as in English).

In practice, inevitable modifications take place, some of the principal ones being these (I do not give them all).

For dh, as above, Skt. has dh; Gk. has θ; Latin has f (or if the dh be not initial, d or b).

For bh, as above, Skt. has bh; Gk. has φ; and Latin has f (or if the bh be not initial, b).

For gh, as above, Skt. has gh or h; Gk. has χ; and Latin has f or h (or if the gh be not initial, g, gu, u).

Note the threefold value of the Latin f, which may stand, initially, for dh, bh, or gh. Also, that Latin uses c for k, but the c is always hard, having the sound of k before all vowels.

A few selected examples are here noted.

Dentals. Lat. facere, to do, to put, is allied to Gk. τί-θη-μι, I place, and to E. do. From √dhē, to place, put; Sanskrit has dhā, to put. Skt. dva, Gk. δύω, Lat. duo, are cognate with E. two. Gk. τρεῖς, Lat. trēs, are cognate with E. three.

Labials. From the √bher, to bear, we have the Skt. bhar, to bear; Gk. φέρειν, Lat. ferre, to bear; E. bear. Examples of change from the classical p to E. b are very scarce; compare the Lat. labium with the E. lip. Gk. ποús (stem ποδ-); Lat. pēs (stem ped-); E. foot.

Gutturals. From the √ghel, to be yellow, we have the Gk. χολή, gall; Lat. fel, gall, helvus, light yellow; E. gall. The Gk. γένος, Lat. genus, race, is allied to the E. kin; and the Gk. καρδία, Lat. cor, to the E. heart. It is now recognised, however, that there are really three series of gutturals, sometimes named the palatal gutturals, the middle gutturals, and the labialised velar gutturals. Some further information on the more elementary points of comparative philology will be found in my Primer of Classical and English Philology.

I denote the palatal gutturals by GH, G, K; the middle gutturals by G(w)H, G(w), Q; and the labialised velar gutturals by GwH, Gw, and Qw. They cannot always be distinguished, and I am not sure that I have always given them correctly.

The list of Roots given below is arranged in alphabetical order. They may be regarded as elementary bases (usually monosyllabic) which underlie all the various forms that are given by way of example. Each of them may be regarded, to use Brugmann's words, as 'the nucleus (so to speak) of a whole system of word-forms;' and are of much service in grouping words together. But they do not afford any very sure indications of what the primitive Indogermanic was like; 'it must not (says Brugmann) be supposed that the roots, which we in ordinary practice abstract from words, are at all to be relied upon as representing the word-forms of the root-period.'

By way of further illustration, I give a fuller treatment of the first root on the list.

The form **AG** (AK) means that the Indogermanic root **AG** takes the form AK in Teutonic, by the 'sound-shifting' of g to k already noticed above. The sense of the root seems to have been 'to drive, urge, lead, conduct,' and the like. The Skt. form (originally ag) has been palatalised to aj, which is the base of the verb ajami, 'I drive;' the third person singular is ajati, 'he drives;' and the form ajati is taken in Uhlenbeck's Etymological Dictionary of Sanskrit to represent this verb. The Greek infinitive is ἄγειν, and the Latin infinitive is ǎgere. (It is further represented by the Old Irish agaim, 'I drive.') The chief representative of this root in Teutonic occurs in the Icel. aka, to drive (pt. t. ōk); the corresponding AS. form acan (pt t. ōc) took up a new sense, viz. 'to give pain,' as in mine ēagan acaδ, 'my eyes give pain,' or in modern English, ache. I give, as characteristic examples, the words agony and axiom, from Greek; agent, agile, and axis, from Latin; and acre, azorn, and ache, from Anglo-Saxon. How each of these words is connected with the root **AG**, is explained in the Dictionary.

But these are not the only English derivatives from this root. The Latin agere had the pp. actus, whence the E. act, active, actor, actual, actuate, actuary, counteract, enact, exact, transact; while from the base ag- we have also agitate, cogitate, ambiguous, coagulate, cogent, exigent, examine, prodigal. In connexion with the E. agony we may further cite antagonist. And it is very likely that another native English derivative is axle; for the addition of s to the base ag would give a base ags, which would necessarily become aks, accounting for the Gk. ἄξων and the Lat. axis (see **Axis**); and this new base aks would become aks in Teutonic, by the usual 'sound-shifting' from Idg. k to E. h. But the Teutonic hs becomes x in Anglo-Saxon, so that there is no difficulty in connecting the AS. eax, an axle, with the Latin axis; see further under **Axle**.

Similarly, many other roots have often more derivatives than it seemed to me at all necessary to indicate.

AG (AK), to drive, urge, conduct. Skt. aj, to drive; Gk. ἄγ-ειν, L. ag-ere, to drive; Icel. ak-a (pt. t. ōk), to drive. Ex. agony, axiom, synagogue, hegemony; agent, agile, axis; acre, acorn, ache.

AGH (AG), to pull tight(?). Gk. ἄχ-ομαι, I am vexed, ἄχ-ος, anguish; Goth. ag-is, fright, awe. Ex. ail, ⌐we. Cf. ANGH.

AIDH (AID), to kindle. Skt. indh, ɩo kindle; ēdh-as, fuel; Gk. αἰθ-ειν, to burn; αἰθ-ήρ, upper air; L. aed-ēs, orig. a hearth, aestus, heat; AS. ād, a funeral pile, āst, a kiln. Ex. ether; edify, estuary; oast-house.

AK (AH), to be sharp, to pierce. Gk. ἄκ-ρος, pointed; ἀκ-όνη, whetstone; ἀκ-μή, edge; L. ac-us, needle, ac-uere, to sharpen, ac-iēs, edge; AS. ecg, edge. Ex. acacia, acme, aconite, acrobat, acrostic; acid, acumen, acute, acrid, ague, aglet, eager; ear (2), edge, awn, egg (2); ache. Cf. paragon.

AL, to nourish, raise. L. al-ere, to nourish; ad-ol-escere, to grow up; al-tus, raised; Goth. al-an, to nourish; al-ds, an age. Ex. aliment, altitude, adolescent, adult, exalt; old.

AN, to breathe. Skt. an, to breathe; L. an-imus, wind; L. an-imus, spirit; Goth. us-anan, to breathe out, expire. Ex. anemone; animal, animosity, animadvert.

ANGH (ANG), to choke, strangle. Gk. ἄγχ-ειν, to strangle; L. ang-ere, to choke, anx-ius, anxious; Icel. angr, grief. Ex. quinsy (for quin-anc-y); angina, anguish, anxious; anger.

ANQ (ANH, ANG), to bend. Gk. ἀῆκń, to bend, curve; Gk. ἄγκ-υρα, an anchor; Gk. ἀγκ-ών, a bend; L. unc-us, curved, ang-ulus, an angle; AS. ang-el, a hook. Ex. anchor; angle (1); angle (2).

AR, to plough. Gk. ἀρ-όειν, L. ar-āre, AS. er-ian, to plough. Ex. arable; ear (3).

AR, to fit. Skt. ar-as, spoke of a wheel; Gk. ἄρ-μενος, fitted, ἄρ-θρον, joint; ἀρ-μός, joint, shoulder; L. ar-mus, ar-tus, a limb; ar-ma, arms, ar-s, art; Goth. ar-ms, an arm. Ex. harmony; arms, art, article; arm (1).

ARG, to shine. Skt. arj-unas, white (cf. raj-atam, silver); Gk. ἀργ-ός, white, ἄργ-υρος, silver, L. arg-entum, silver, arg-illa, white clay; arg-uere, to make clear. Ex. argent, argillaceous, argument. Also Argonaut.

ARQ, to protect, keep safe. Gk. ἀρκ-εῖν, to keep off; L. arc-ēre, to keep off, arc-a, a box. Ex. arcana, ark.

AUG(w) (AUK), to increase. Apparently allied to **AWEG**(w), **WEG**(w); see **WEG**(w). Skt. ug-ra(s), very strong, ōj-as, strength (cf. vaj, to strengthen); L. aug-ēre, to increase; Goth. auk-an, to increase. Hence **AUG**(w)-**S**, **AUQ-S**, as in Gk. αὐξ-άνειν, to increase,

L. aux-ilium, help. Ex. augment, august, auction, author, also auxiliary; eke (1), eke (2).

AWES, to shine; see **EUS**, **WES**.

BHA [= bhā], to speak, declare. Gk. φη-μί, I say, φή-μη, report, φά-τις, a saying, φων-ή, clear voice; L. fā-ri, to speak, fā-ma, fame, fā-bula, a narrative, fa-teor, I confess. Ex. antiphon, anthem, prophet, euphemism, euphony, phonetic; fate, fable, fairy, fame, affable, confess. See **BHAN** (below).

BHAN (BAN), to speak, declare. Skt. bhan, to speak, declare; AS. ban-nan, to proclaim. Ex. ban, banns.

BHA [= bhā], to shine, to be clear. Skt. bhā, to shine. Hence the extended forms **BHAL**, **BHAN**, **BHAW**.

BHAL, to shine. Skt. bhāl-am, lustre, Lith. bál-ti, to be white, Gk. φαλ-ιός, white. Breton bal, a white streak in an animal's face, AS. bǣl, a blaze. Ex. bald, bald-faced; also bale-fire, beltane.

BHAN, to show, display clearly. Gk. φαίνειν (for *φαν-γειν), to show, φαν-τάζειν, to display, φά-σις, appearance, phase; Irish bān, white. Ex. fancy, hierophant, sycophant, phantom, phenomenon, phase. Also pant.

BHAW, to glow. Gk. φά-ος (for *φαϝ-ος), φῶς, light; φα-έθειν, to shine, glow. Ex. phaeton, phosphorus.

BHEID (BEIT), to cleave, bite. Skt. bhid, to cleave; L. findere (pt. t. fid-i), to cleave; AS. bīt-an, to bite; Icel. beita, to make to bite, to bait. Ex. fissure; bite, bitter, bait, abet, bet. (Cf. bill (1), which Walde refers to an Idg. type *bhid-lom.)

BHEIDH (BEID), to persuade, trust. Gk. πείθ-ω, I persuade; L. fīd-ere, to trust, fīd-es, faith, foed-us, a treaty. Ex. affiance, confide, defy, faith, fealty, fidelity, infidel, perfidious, federal, confederate. Perhaps bid (1). Perhaps bide (disputed).

BHELGH (BELG), to bulge, swell out. Icel. bolg-inn, swollen, from a lost strong verb; Irish bolg-aim, I swell, bolg, a bag, budget, belly, pair of bellows; Goth. balg-s, a bag; AS. belg-an, to swell with anger. Ex. bulge, bilge, budget; bag (?), belly, bellows, billow, bolled. Cf. bulk (1).

BHELS (BELL), to resound. Lith. bals-as, voice, sound; AS. bell-an, to make a loud noise. Cf. Skt. bhāsh (for *bhals), to speak (Uhlenbeck). Ex. bell, bellow, bull (1).

BHENDH (BEND), to bind. Skt. bandh (for *bhendh), to bind; Pers. band, a bond; Gk. πεῖσμα (for *πένθ-σμα), a cable; L. of-fend-ix, a knot, band; Goth. bind-an, to bind. Ex. bind, bend, bond, bundle.

BHER (BER), to bear, carry. Skt. bhr, to support, bhrā-tar-, a brother, friend; Gk. φέρ-ω, L. fer-o, I bear ⌐, for-s, chance (which brings things about); fūr, a thief (cf. Gk. φώρ). Ex. fertile, fortune, fortuitous, furtive; bear (1), burden, bier, barrow, bairn, barm (2), birth, brother; bore (3).

BHER (BER), to cut, bore. Zend bar, to cut, bore; Pers. bur-enda, sharp, cutting; Gk. φαρ-άω (for *φαρ-ρ-άω), I plough, φάρ-αγξ, a ravine, φάρ-υγξ, gullet; L. for-āre, AS. bor-ian, to bore. Ex. pharynx; perforate; bore (1), bore (2).

BHERG, **BHLEG** (BERK, BLEK), to shine, burn. Skt. bhrāj, to shine; Gk. φλέγ-ειν, to burn, L. fulg-ēre, to shine, ful-men (*fulg-men), thunder-bolt, flag-rāre, to burn, flam-ma (*flag-ma), flame; Goth. bairh-ts, bright. Ex. phlox; refulgent, fulminate, flagrant, flame; bright. Also blink, blank.

BHERS (BERS), to be stiff or bristling. Skt. bhrsh-ti-, a point; Icel. brod-dr (*broz-dr), a spike; AS. byrs-t, a bristle, bears, bærs, a perch (fish). Ex. brad, bristle, bass (2).

BHEU (BEU), to dwell, become, be. Skt. bhū, to be; bhav-ana(m), a dwelling, house; Gk. ἔ-φυ, he was; L. fu-ī, I was; AS. bēo-m, to be; bo-ld, a house; Goth. bau-an, to dwell; Lith. bu-ti, to be. Ex. physic, euphuism, imp; future; be, boor, booth, busk (1), bower, byre, by-law, burly, build.

BHEUDH (BEUD), to awake, inform, bid, command. Skt. budh (*bhudh), to awake, understand, bōdh-aya, to inform; Gk. πεύθ-ομαι, I search, ask; AS. bēod-an, to bid. Ex. bid (2), beadle, bode.

BHEUQw, **BHEUGw**, (BEUHw), to bow, bend, turn about. Skt. bhuj, to bend, stoop; Gk. φεύγ-ειν, to flee; L. fug-ere, to flee; AS. būg-an, to bow, bend, bog-a, a bow. Ex. fugitive, fugue, refuge, subterfuge; bow (1), bow (2), bow (3), bight, bout, buxom. See Brugmann, i. § 658; who adds boil (2).

BHLE (= bhlē), Teut. BLE (= blē), to blow. L. flā-re, AS. blā-wan, to blow. Ex. flatulent; blow (1), blaze (2), blast, bladder.

BHLEG, to shine, burn; see **BHERG**.

BHLO (= bhlō), Teut. BLO (= blō), to blow as a flower, to flourish. L. flō-s, a flower, flō-rēre, to flourish; AS. blō-wan, to blow, blō-ma, bloom. Ex. floral, flourish; blow (2), bloom, blossom, blood, bleed, bless.

BHOG, **bhōg** (BAK, bōk), to bake or roast. Gk. φώγ-ειν, to roast, bake; AS. bac-an (pt. t. bōc), to bake. Ex. bake

LIST OF INDOGERMANIC ROOTS

BHREG (BREK), to break (with a cracking noise). L. *frang-ere* (pt. t. *frēg-i*), to break; *frag-ilis*, fragile; Goth. *brik-an*, AS. *brec-an*, to break. Ex. *fragile, fragment, frail; break, brake* (1), *brake* (2). Perhaps *brook* (2).

BHREQ, to crowd close, fence round, shut in. Gk. φράσσειν (*φράκ-γειν*), to shut in, make fast, φράγ-μα, a fence; L. *frequ-ens*, crammed; *farc-ire*, to stuff full. Ex. *diaphragm; frequent, farce, force* (2).

BHREU (BREU), to decoct. L. *dē-fru-tum*, new wine boiled down; Thracian βρῦ-τον, beer; OIrish *bruith*, cooking; AS. *brēo-wan*, to brew. Ex. *brew, broth, brose, bread.* Allied to the above words are, further, Gk. φύρ-ειν, to mix up, mingle together, Skt. *bhuranya*, to be active, L. *fur-ere*, to rage. Ex. *fury*; also *purple.* Also L. *ferv-ēre*, to boil, to be fervent, *fermentum*, leaven; AS. *beorma*, yeast. Ex. *fervent, ferment; barm* (1).

BHREUG (BREUK), to enjoy, use. L. *fru-or* (for *frūg-uor*), pp. *fruc-tus*, I enjoy, *frūg-ēs*, fruit, *frū-mentum* (*frūg-mentum*), corn; AS. *brūc-an*, to use. Ex. *fruit, frugal, furmity, fructify; brook* (1).

BUQ, to bellow, snort, puff; of imitative origin. Skt. *bukk*, to sound; L. *bucc-a*, the puffed cheek. Ex. *disembogue, debouch, embonchure.*

DAK (TAH), to bite, tear, hold fast. Skt. *daç*, to bite; Gk. δάκ-νειν, to bite; Goth. *tah-jan*, to rend; AS. *tang-e*, a pair of tongs. Ex. *tang* (1), *tang* (3), *tongs.*

DAM (TAM), to tame. Skt. *dam*, to tame; Gk. δαμ-άειν, to tame; L. *dom-āre*, to tame; Goth. *ga-tam-jan*, to tame. Ex. *adamant, diamond; daunt; tame.*

DE (=dē), to bind. Gk. δέ-ω, I bind, διά-δη-μα, fillet. Ex. *diadem.*

DEIK (TEIH), to show, point out. Skt. *diç*, to show; Gk. δείκ-νυμι, I show, δίκ-η, justice; L. *in-dic-āre*, to point out, *dīc-ere*, to tell; Goth. *ga-teih-an*, to teach, tell; AS. *tēon* (*tih-an*), to accuse. Ex. *syndic; indicate, dedicate, diction, &c.; dight, index, judge, judicious, &c.; verdict, vindicate; teen, token, teach.*

DEIW (TEIW), to shine. Skt. *div*, to shine; *dēv-a(s)*, God, *div-ya(s)*, brilliant, divine; Gk. Ζεύς (stem Διϝ-), Zeus, δῖ-ος, heavenly, L. *de-us*, God, *dīu-us*, divine, *di-ēs*, day; AS. *Tīg* (gen. *Tīwes*), the god of war. Ex. *Zeus; Jupiter, deity, divine, dial, diary, meridian, jovial; Tuesday.*

DEK, to honour, think fit. Sk. *daç*, to honour, worship; Gk. δοκ-εῖ, it seems fit, δόξ-α, opinion; L. *dec-et*, it is fit, *doc-ēre*, to teach, *discere* (*di-dc-scere*), to learn. Ex. *paradox, dogma, didactic; decent, decorum, docile, disciple.*

DEM (TIM), to build. Gk. δεμ-εῖν, to build, δόμ-ος, a building; L. *dom-us*, a house; Goth. *tim-rjan*, to build. Ex. *dome, major-domo, domestic, domicile* (also *despot*); *timber.* Perhaps L. *dom-inus*, a master, with its derivatives, is from the same root.

DER (TER), to tear, rive. Skt. *dr-nāmi*, I burst open, tear asunder; Gk. δέρ-ειν, to flay, δέρ-μα, skin; Goth. *ga-tairan*, to break, destroy, AS. *ter-an*, to rend. Ex. *epidermis, pachydermatous; tear* (1), *tire* (1), *tire* (4); perhaps *tree, tar, larch.*

DERBH (TERB), to knit together. Skt. *dŗbh*, to bind, *darbh-a(s)*, matted grass; AS. *turf*, turf. Ex. *turf.*

DEU (TEU), to work, prepare. Skt. *dū-ta(s)*, a messenger (?); Goth. *tau-jan*, to do; AS. *taw-ian*, to prepare, to scourge; *tō-l* (*tōu-l*), a tool. Ex. *taw, tew, tow* (2), *tool.* (Hence the final *-t* in *herio-t*.)

DEUK (TEUH), to lead, conduct. L. *dūc-ere*, to lead; Goth. *tiuh-an*, AS. *tēo-n*, to draw, pull. Ex. *duke, ad-duce, &c.; conduit, doge, douche, ducal, redoubt, educate; tow* (1), *tug, tuck* (1), *tuck* (3), *tie, touch, toesin, team.*

DHE (=dhē), weak grade dhe (Teut. *dē, *dō), to put, place, set, do. Skt. *dhā*, to place, put; Gk. τί-θη-μι, I place, set, do, a thing proposed, θέ-σις, a placing, θέ-μις, law, θη-σαυρός, treasure; L. *fa-c-ere*, to do, *fa-c-ilis*, easy to do; AS. *dē-d*, a deed, *dō-m*, judgement, *dē-man*, to judge. Ex. *anathema, hypothec, theme, thesis, epithet, treasure, tick* (2); *fact*, suffix *-fy* in *magni-fy, &c.; -ficent; do* (1), *deed, doom, deem.* Also *creed.* See note to **DO** (above).

DHEGWH (DEG), to burn. Skt. *dah* (for *dhagh*), to burn; L. *fau-illa*, hot ashes; Lith. *deg-ù*, I burn; Goth. *dag-s*, day. Ex. *day.* Cf. *foment*, from L. *fŏu-ēre.*

DHEI (=dhēi), to suck. Skt. *dhē*, to suck; Gk. θη-λή, the breast; L. *fē-lare*, to suck, *fē-mina*, woman, *fi-lius*, son, OIrish *di-nim*, I suck. Ex. *female, feminine, filial.*

DHEIGH (DEIG), to smear, knead, mould, form. Skt. *dih* (*dhigh*), to smear; Gk. τεῖχ-ος, a wall (orig. of earth); L. *fing-ere* (pp. *fic-tus*), to mould, form, feign, *fig-ulus*, a potter; Goth. *deig-an, dig-an*, to knead, *daig-s*, a kneaded lump. Ex. *paradise; fiction, fictile, feign, figure; dough, dairy, lady.*

DHER, to support, hold, keep. Skt. *dhŗ*, to bear, support, maintain, keep, hold, retain; Gk. θρό-νος, a support, seat; θώρ-αξ,

a breast-plate (keeper); L. *frē-tus*, relying on, *fir-mus*, secure. Ex. *throne, thorax; firm, farm.*

DHERS (DERS), to dare. Skt. *dŗṣh*, to dare; Gk. θαρσ-εῖν, to be bold, θρασ-ύς, bold; Goth. *dars*, I dare, *daurs-ta*, I durst. Ex. *thrasonical; dare, durst.*

DHEU (DEU), to run, to flow. Skt. *dhav, dhāv*, to run, to flow; Gk. θέ-ειν, to run (fut. θεύ-σομαι); AS. *dēaw*, dew. Ex. *dew.*

DHEU (DEU), to agitate, fan into flame. Skt. *dhū*, to agitate, fan into flame; *dhū-ma(s)*, smoke; Gk. θύ-ειν, to rush, rage, sacrifice, θύ-ος, incense; θύ-μος, θύ-μον, thyme; L. *fū-mus*, smoke; AS. *dū-st*, dust. Ex. *tunny, thyme; thurible, fume; dust.*

DHEUB (DEUP), to be deep, to be hollow. Lith. *dub-ùs*, deep, *dùb-ti*, to be hollow; Goth. *diup-s*, deep. Ex. *deep, depth, dip.* Variant **DHEUP** (DEUF). Russ. *dup-lo*, hollow, AS. *dȳf-an*, to dive into, AS. *dūfe-doppa*, a diving-bird. Ex. *dive, dove.*

DHEUBH (DEUB), to fill with smoke or mist. Skt. *dhūp-a(s)*, vapour; Gk. τῦφ-ος (*θῦφ-ος), smoke, gloom, stupefaction; τυφ-λός, blinded, dark; Goth. *daub-s*, deaf, (perhaps) *dumb-s*, dumb. Ex. *typhoon, typhus; deaf, dumb?* Allied to **DHEU**, to agitate.

DHREN (DREN), to make a droning noise. Skt. *dhran*, to sound; Gk. θρῆν-ος, lamentation, θρῶν-αξ, a drone-bee; Goth. *drun-jus*, a sound; OSax. *drān*, a drone. Ex. *threnody; drone* (1), *drone* (2).

DHWEL (DWEL), to be confused or troubled. Gk. θολ-ερός, troubled, thick, muddy (as water); θολ-ός, mud; Goth. *dwal-s*, foolish; Icel. *dwel-ja*, to hinder, delay, dwell; AS. *dol*, foolish. Ex. *dull, dwell, dwale.* Perhaps allied to **DHEU**, to agitate.

DHWES (DWES), to breathe, inspire. Gk. θεό-φατος, spoken by God, inspired, θε-ός (*θέσ-ος), God; Lith. *dwes-iù*, I breathe, *dwasê*, breath, spirit, ghost, *dus-ēti*, to breathe hard; Goth. *dius*, a wild animal (cf. L. *animal* from *anima*); AS. *dēor*, a deer. Ex. *theism, theology; deer.*

DO (=dō), to give. Skt. *dā*, to give; Gk. δί-δω-μι, I give, δό-σις, a gift, dose; L. *dō-num*, a gift, *dō-s*, dowry, *da-re*, to give. Ex. *dose; donation, dower, dowry, date* (1), *dado, die* (2), *render, rent* (2), *traitor, treason.* ¶ The verbs *con-dere, crē-dere*, and some others ending in *-dere* are usually referred to the root *dhē.*

DRE (=drē), weak grade dŏr, to sleep. Skt. *drā*, to sleep. Gk. δαρ-θάνειν, L. *dor-mīre*, to sleep. Ex. *dormitory, dormant, dormer-window.*

DREM, to run. Skt. *dram*, to run; Gk. ἔ-δραμ-ον, I ran, δρόμ-ος, a running. Ex. *dromedary.*

ED (ET), to eat. Skt. *ad*, to eat; Gk. ἔδ-ειν, L. *ed-ere*, AS. *et-an*, to eat. Ex. *edible, eat, fret, ort.* Perhaps *tooth, dental.*

EI, to go; whence yē, to go, to pass. Skt. *i*, to go; *yā*, to go; Gk. εἶ-μι, I shall go, L. *i-re*, to go; AS. *ē-ode*, I went. Ex. *proem; ambient, circuit, commence, count* (1), *exit, eyre, initial, issue, itinerant, obit, perish, prætor, preterite, sedition, sudden, &c.* Also *yede.*

EL, to drive. Gk. ἐλ-αύνειν, to drive; L. *al-acer*, brisk. Ex. *elastic; alacrity, allegro.*

ERE, erē (rō), to row. Skt. *ari-tra(s)*, a rudder, AS. *ŗre-rπμός*, an oar; Lith. *ir-ti*, to row; L. *rē-mus*, an oar; AS. *rō-wan*, to row. Ex. *trireme; row* (2), *rudder.*

ES, to dwell, to be. Skt. *as*, to exist, be; Gk. ἐσ-μί, εἰ-μί, I am; L. *es-se*, to be, *s-um*, I am; *abs-ens*, being away; AS. *is*, is, *s-ōð*, true (orig. being). Ex. *suttee; palæontology; absent, present, essence, entity; am, art, is, are, sooth.*

GEN (KEN), to generate, produce. Skt. *jan*, to beget; Gk. γέν-ος, race, γί-γν-ομαι, I am born, L. *gi-gn-ere* (pt. t. *gen-ui*), to beget, *gen-itor*, father, *gn-ascor*, I am born, *gen-us*, kin; Goth. *kun-i*, kin. Ex. *Genesis, endogen, cosmogony; genus, genius, gentile, benign, cognate, indigenous, natal, native, nature; kin, kind* (1), *kind* (2), *kindred, kith.*

GEN (KEN), to know; also gnā, gnō (knā). Skt. *jnā*, to know; Gk. γι-γνώ-σκειν, to know; γνω-τός, known; L. *gnō-scere, nō-scere*, to know, *i-gnō-rāre*, not to know, *gnā-rus*, knowing (whence *narrāre*, to tell); Goth. *kann*, I know; AS. *cnā-wan*, to know. Ex. *gnostic, gnomon; ignorant, narrate, noble; can* (1), *ken, know, cunning, keen, uncouth.*

GER (KER), to grind, to crumble with age. Skt. *jīr-ṇa(s)*, decayed, pp. of *gŗ*, to wear out; *jar-as*, decrepitude; Gk. γέρ-ων, old man; L. *grā-num,* corn; AS. *cor-n*, corn. Ex. *grain; corn, kernel.*

GERPH (KERF), to carve, write. Gk. γράφ-ειν, to incise, write; AS. *ceorf-an*, to carve. Ex. *graphic, autograph, &c.; diagram, &c., grammar, programme; carve.*

GEUS (KEUS), to choose, taste. Skt. *jush*, to like, enjoy; Gk. γεύ-ομαι, I taste, γευσ-τός, to be tasted; L. *gus-tāre*, to taste; Goth. *kius-an*, to choose, *kus-tus*, taste. Ex. *gust* (2), *disgust; choose; choice.*

GLEU (KLEU), to draw together, conglomerate. Skt. *glau,*

LIST OF INDOGERMANIC ROOTS

a lump (Macdonell); L. *glu-ere*, to draw together, *glo-mus*, a clew, *glo-bus*, a ball; AS. *cléo-we*, a clew. Ex. *globe, conglomerate; clew* (*clue*).

GLEUBH (KLEUB), to cleave, to split asunder. Gk. γλύφ-ειν, to hollow out; L. *glūb-ere*, to peel, *glū-ma* (*glūb-ma*), a husk; AS. *cléof-an*, to cleave, split. Ex. *glyptic, hiero-glyphic; glume; cleave* (1), *cleft*.

G(w)EL (KEL), to be cold. L. *gel-u*, frost; *gel-idus*, cold; Goth. *kal-ds*, cold; AS. *cōl*, cool, *ceal-d*, cold. Ex. *gelid, jelly, congeal; cool, cold, keel* (2).

G(w)ER, to assemble. Gk. ἀ-γείρειν (*ἀ-γέρ-γειν*), to assemble, ἀ-γορ-ά, an assembly; L. *grex* (stem *gre-g*), a flock. Ex. *category, paregoric; gregarious, egregious*.

G(w)ER (KER), to cry out (perhaps imitative). Skt. *gir*, voice; Gk. γέρ-ανος, a crane, γῆρ-υς, speech; L. *gr-us*, a crane, *gar-rire*, to talk; Gael. *gair*, a shout, *sluagh-ghairm*, a battle-cry, *slogan*; AS. *cear-u*, care, lament. Ex. *geranium, garrulous; pedigree; slogan; care, crane, jar* (1), *jargon*.

G(w)LEI (KLEI), to stick to. Gk. γλοι-ός, sticky substance, gum; L. *glū-ten*, glue; AS. *clǣ-g*, clay, *cli-fan*, to stick to. Ex. *glue; clay, cleave* (2).

GwEI (QEI), to live; also in the form **GwEIW** (QEIW). Skt. *jiv*, to live, *jiv-a*(s), living, life; Gk. βί-ος, life, also ζά-ω (for *g(w)ȳē-yō), I live, ζώ-ω, I live; L. *uīu-ere*, to live, *ui-ta*, life; Goth. *kwius*, quick, living, active, AS. *cwic*, alive, quick. Ex. *biology, zoology; vivid, vital, victuals; quick*. Also *usquebaugh, azote, zodiac*.

GwEM (QEM), to come, to go, walk. Skt. *gam*, to go; Gk. βαίνειν (*βάν-γειν*), to go, βά-σις, a going; L. *uen-ire*, to come; Goth. *kwim-an*, AS. *cum-an*, to come. Ex. *base* (2), *basis; venture, advent, avenue, convene*, &c.; *come*.

GwER, to devour, swallow greedily. Skt. *aja-gar-a*(s), lit. goat-swallower; Gk. βορ-ά, food, βορ-ός, gluttonous; L. *uor-āre*, to devour. Further allied to Skt. *gal-a*(s), throat; L. *gula*, gullet, throat, *gl-utire*, to gulp down. It seems to be reduplicated in Skt. *gar-gar-a*(s), a whirlpool (which may be partly imitative); Gk. γαρ-γαρ-ίζειν, to gurgle; L. *gur-ges*, a whirlpool. Ex. *voracious;* also *gullet, gully, glut, glutton;* also *gargle, gurgle, gorge, gorget, gorgeous*.

GHA (GA), to gape, yawn. Gk. χά-ος, χά-σμα, abyss, χαίνειν (for *χά-ν-γειν*), to yawn; γ*;ν,a goose; L. *anser*, a goose; G. *gans*, AS. *gōs*, a goose. Ex. *chasm, chaos; goose, gannet, gander*. See **GHEI**.

Base **GHAID** (GAIT), to sport, skip. L. *haed-us*, a kid; Lith. *žaid-žiu*, I play, sport; AS. *gāt*, a goat. Ex. *goat*.

GHEI (GEI), to yawn. L. *hi-āre*, to gape, yawn; AS. *tō-gin-an*, str. vb., to gape open. Ex. *hiatus; yawn*. Perhaps gill (2). See **GHA**.

Base **GHEI-M-** (GEI-M-), cold, winter. Skt. *hi-m-a*(s), cold, *hi-m-a*(m), frost, snow; Gk. χει-μ-ών, winter; L. *hi-em-s*, winter, *hi-bernus*, wintry. Goth. *hibernal, hibernate;* prov. E. *gimmer*, a one-year-old (winter-old) ewe (Icel. *gymbr*).

GHEIS (GEIS), to be hostile (?). Skt. *hēḍ*, to disregard, *hēḍ-a*(s) (for *hēzd-a*(s)), anger, wrath (of the gods); Lith. *žeid-žiu*, I wound; Goth. *us-gais-jan*, to terrify, Icel. *geis-a*, to rage; AS. *gās-t*, a spirit, ghost; *gǣs-tan*, to terrify. Ex. *ghost, aghast*.

GHEL (GEL), to be green or yellow. Skt. *hari-t*, green; Gk. χόλ-ος, χολή-ή, gall, χλω-ρή, verdure, χλω-ρός, greenish, yellowish; L. *hel-uus*, light yellow; AS. *geol-o*, yellow, *gol-d*, gold. Cf. L. *fel*, gall. Ex. *chlorine, choler; yellow, yolk, gold, gall*.

GHEL (GEL), to yell, cry out, cry as a bird. Gk. χελ-ιδών, a swallow; AS. *gell-an*, to yell, sing; *stān-gella*, a staniel; *gal-an*, to sing. Ex. *nightingale, staniel, yell*.

Base **GHEM** (GEM-), from GHZEM-, earth, the ground. Skt. *ksham-ā*, earth, Gk. χαμ-αί, on the ground; Russ. *zem-lia*, earth, land; L. *hum-i*, on the ground, *hum-us*, earth, *hom-o*, man (son of earth), Goth. *gum-a*, man. Ex. *chameleon, chamomile; homage, humble, humane, exhume*. Cf. *bridegroom*.

GHENG(w)H (GENG), to go, stride along. Skt. *jaṅgh-ā*, the leg; Lith. *ženg-iù*, I go, march; Icel. *gang-a*, to go. Ex. *gang*.

GHER (GER), to desire, to yearn. Skt. *har-y*, to desire; Gk. χαίρειν (*χάρ-γειν*), to rejoice, χαρ-ά, joy, χάρ-ις, favour, grace; L. *hor-tārī*, to exhort; AS. *geor-n*, desirous. Ex. *eucharist, chervil; hortatory, exhort; yearn*.

GHER (GER), to seize, grasp, hold, gird. Skt. *hṛ*, to seize, *har-aṇa*(s), the hand; Gk. χείρ (gen. χειρ-ός, χερ-ός), hand; χορ-ός, a dance in a ring or enclosure, χόρ-τος, an enclosure, yard; L. *hor-tus*, yard, garden; AS. *gear-d*, yard. Further allied to χορ-δή, a cord, a string of guts, Lith. *žar-nos*, Icel. *gar-nir*, guts, AS. *gear-n*, yarn. Ex. *cheiromancy, surgeon, chorus, choir; horticulture, cohort,*

court; *yard* (1), *garth, gird* (1), *girth*. Perhaps also *chord, cord;* yarn.

GHERS (GERS), to bristle. Skt. *hṛsh*, to bristle; L. *horr-ēre* (*hors-ēre*), to bristle; cf. *hirs-ūtus*, bristling. Cf. Gk. χήρ, L. *ēr*, a hedgehog; Gk. χαρ-άσσειν, to scratch. Ex. *horrid, hirsute;* perhaps *gorse*. Cf. *urchin, character*.

GHEU (GEU), to pour. Whence also **GHEUD** (GEUT), to pour. Gk. χέ-ειν (fut. χεύ-σω), to pour, χυ-μός, χυ-λός, juice; L. *fū-tis*, a water-vessel, *re-fū-tāre*, to refute (pour back), *fū-tilis*, easily emptied, futile; also *fund-ere* (pt. t. *fūd-i*), to pour; AS. *gēot-an*, to pour; Icel. *gjō-sa, gū-sa*, to gush. Ex. *chyme, chyle* (cf. *alchemy*); *confute, refute, futile, refund, found* (2), *fuse* (1), *confuse, diffuse; ingot, gut; gush, geysir*.

GHREM (GRIM), to make an angry noise. Gk. χρεμ-ίζειν, χρεμ-ετίζειν, to neigh; AS. *grim*, fierce. Ex. *grim, grumble*.

G(w)HAIS, to stick, adhere. L. *haer-ēre* (pt. t. *haes-ī*), to stick; Lith. *gaisz-ti*, to delay, tarry. Ex. *adhere, cohere, hesitate*.

G(w)HEND (GET), to seize, get. Gk. χανδ-άνειν (2 aor. *ἐ-χαδ-ον*); L. *prae-hend-ere*, to grasp, seize, *hed-era*, ivy, *praeda* (for *prae-hed-a*), booty, prey; Goth. *bi-gi:t-an*, to find, AS. *giet-an*, to get. Ex. *prehensile, apprehend, prey, predatory; get, beget, forget*.

G(w)HES (meaning unknown). L. *hos-tis*, orig. a stranger, a guest; also a stranger, an enemy; Goth. *gas-ts*, AS. *gæs-t, gies-t*, a guest. Ex. *host* (1), *host* (2), *ostler, hotel, hospice; guest*.

G(w)HLEU (GLEU), to rejoice (?). Gk. χλεύ-η, sport; Icel. *glau-mr*, glee; AS. *glēo*, glee. Ex. *glee*.

G(w)HRADH (GRAD), to step, walk, go. L. *grad-i*, to step, go; *grad-us*, a step; Goth. *grid-s, grip-s*, a step. Ex. *grade, gradient, gradual, graduate*.

GwHEN, to strike. Skt. *han*, to strike, wound; Gk. θείνειν (*θεν-γειν*), to strike, slay (cf. pt. t. πέ-φα-ται); L. *of-fend-ere*, to strike against; cf. OHG. *gund*, Icel. *gunnr*, AS. *gūð*, war. Ex. *defend, offend, infest, fence, fend*. Also *gonfalon, gonfanon, gun*.

GwHER, to glow. Skt. *ghṛ*, to shine; *ghar-ma*(s), heat, hot season; Gk. θερ-μός, warm, θέρ-ος, summer heat; L. *for-mus*, warm, *for-nax*, furnace. Ex. *thermometer; furnace, fornicate*. Perhaps *warm*.

☞ For forms not found under K, see under Q.

KAM (HAM), to cover over. Gk. *καμ-άρα*, a vaulted place (whence L. *camera*); *κάμ-ινος*, an oven; Goth. *ga-ham-ōn*, to cover with clothes; Icel. *ham-r*, a covering. Ex. *chamber, chimney;* cf. *chemise*.

KAN (HAN), to sing. Gk. *καν-αχή*, a ringing sound; L. *can-ere*, to sing; AS. *han-a*, a cock (singer). Ex. *chant, canto, accent, incentive*, &c.; *hen*.

KEI, to lie down, repose. Skt. *çi*, to recline, rest; Gk. *κεῖ-μαι*, I lie down. Hence also Skt. *çē-va*(s), kind, friendly; L. *cī-uis*, fellow-citizen; OHG. *hī-wo*, husband; AS. *hī-wan*, household servants. Ex. *cemetery; civil, city; hind* (2).

KEL (HEL), to hide. Olrish *cel-im*, I hide; L. *cel-la*, a hut; AS. *hel-an*, to hide, *hel-m*, a covering; *heal-l*, a hall, *hell-e*, hell. L. *oc-cul-ere*, to hide; Gk. *καλ-ιά*, a hut, *καλ-ύπτειν*, to cover; Goth. *hul-jan*, to hide; AS. *hol*, a hole; L. *cēl-āre*, to hide. Ex. *eucalyptus; cell, conceal; helm, hall, hell, hole, hollow*. Or **QEL**, q. v.

KENQ (HENH), to waver, to hang. Skt. *çaṅk*, to hesitate; L. *cunc-tārī* (for *conc-itārī*), to delay; Goth. *hāhan* (*hanhan*), to hang, AS. *hang-ian*, to hang. Ex. *hang, hank, hanker, hinge*.

KER (HER), to project, stand up (?). Skt. *çir-as*, head; Pers. *sar*, head; Gk. *κάρ-α*, head; *κέρ-as*, a horn; L. *cer-ebrum*, brain. Closely allied to Skt. *çṛ-nga*(*m*), a horn (Gk. *κόρ-υμβος*, highest point), L. *cor-nu*, horn, *cer-uus*, stag; AS. *hor-n*, horn, *heor-ut*, hart. Ex. *ginger; sirdar; corymb; cerebral, corner, cornet, cervine, serval; hart, horn, hornet*.

Base **KERD** (HERT), heart. Gk. *καρδ-ία*, *κῆρ*, heart; L. *cor* (gen. *cord-is*), heart; Lith. *szird-is*, Irish *cridhe*, W. *craidd*, Russ. *serdtse*, AS. *heort-e*, heart. Ex. *cardiac; cordial, accord, concord, discord, record, courage, quarry* (2); *heart*.

KERS (HERS), to run. L. *curr-ere* (pp. *curs-us*), to run; OIrish *carr*, a car; AS. *hors*, a horse; Icel. *hross*, a horse. Ex. *current, curricle, course, cursive, concur*, &c.; *car; horse*.

KEU (HEU), to swell out; also, to be hollow. Skt. *çū-na*(s), swollen, *çū-nya*(s), void, hollow; Gk. *κύ-αρ*, a cavity, *κυ-εῖν*, to be pregnant, *κῦ-μα*, a wave (swelling); L. *cau-us*, hollow. Ex. *cave, cavern, cage, gabion; maroon* (2).

KEUDH (HEUD), to hide. Gk. *κεύθ-ειν*, to hide; W. *cuddio*, to hide; AS. *hȳd-an*, to hide. Cf. L. *cus-tōs*, a custodian, Goth. *huz-d*, a hoard. Ex. *custody; hide* (1), *hoard*. Cf. *house, husk*.

KLEI (HLEI), to lean. Gk. *κλī-νειν*, to incline, lean, *κλî-μαξ*, a ladder, *κλî-μα*, situation, climate (slope); L. *in-clī-nāre*, to make to lean; AS. *hli-nian*, to lean, *hlǣ-ne*, frail, lean, *hlā-w*, a hill, declivity. Ex. *climax, climate, clinical*; *incline, decline, acclivity, declivity*; *lean* (1), *lean* (2), *low* (3), *ladder*.

KLEU (HLEU), to hear, listen to. Skt. *çru*, to hear; Gk. κλύ-ειν, L. *clu-ere*, to hear; AS. *klū-d*, loud, *hly-st*, hearing. Ex. *loud, listen.* (The derivation of *client* from L. *cluere* is doubtful.)

KLEU(D), to wash, cleanse. Gk. κλύζειν (*κλύδ-yειν), to cleanse, κλυσ-τήρ, a clyster, syringe; cf. L. *clu-ere*, to cleanse. Ex. *clyster.*

KWEID (HWEIT), to gleam, to be white; allied to **KWEIT**, with the same sense. Skt. *çvind*, to be white; *çvit*, to be white; *çvet-a(s)*, white; Russ. *sviet-ite*, to shine; AS. *hwit*, white, *hwæt-e*, wheat. Ex. *white, wheat.*

KWERP (HWERF), to turn round. Gk. καρπ-ός, the wrist (that turns the hand); Goth. *hwairb-an*, to turn round. Ex. *whirl, wharf, warble.*

KWES (HWES), to pant, sigh, wheeze. Skt. *çvas*, to pant, snort, hiss; L. *quer-or* (pp. *ques-tus*), I complain; AS. *hwēsan* (not *hwǣsan*), to wheeze. Ex. *querulous; wheeze.* (See Brugmann, i. § 355.)

LAB (LAP), to lap with the tongue. L. *lambere*, to lap; AS. *lap-ian*, to lap. (Root *lāb; Brugmann, ii. § 632.) Ex. *lambent, lap* (1).

LAS, to desire. Skt. *lā-las-a(s)*, ardent, desirous, lash, to desire; Gk. λι-λαίομαι (*λι-λάσ-yομαι), I desire; L. *las-c-ivus*, lascivious; AS. *lus-t*, desire. Ex. *lascivious; lust, lusty, list* (4).

LAU (= lāu), to acquire as spoil; see LEU.

LED (= lēd), Teutonic lēt, to let go, leave free. L. *las-sus* (for *lad-tus*), tired, Gk. ληδ-εῖν, to be tired (see Brugmann, i. § 478); Goth. *lēt-an*, to let, let go; AS. *læt*, slow, late. Ex. *lassitude; let* (1), *late, lass.*

LEG, to collect; hence. to put together, to read. Gk. λέγ-ειν, to collect, read; L. *leg-ere*, to read, *de-lec-tus*, choice, *lec-tus*, chosen. Ex. *logic, ecloque, syllogism*, and the suffix *-logy; legend, legion, elect, delight,* &c.

LEGH (LEG), to lie down. Gk. λέχ-os, a bed; L. *lec-tus* (*leg-tus*), a bed; Goth. *lig-an*, to lie down, *lig-rs*, a couch; Icel. *lāg-r*, lying low, *lag*, a stratum, *lög*, a law. Ex. *litter* (1); *lie* (1), *lay* (1), *low* (1), *law, lair, log* (1); *ledger, beleaguer.*

LEI; see REI.

LEIGH (LEIG), to lick. Skt. *lih, rih*, to lick. Gk. λείχ-ειν, to lick; L. *ling-ere*, to lick; Goth. *bi-laig-ōn*, to lick; AS. *licc-ian* (from *ligh-n-*), to lick. Ex. *lichen* (?); *electuary* (?); *lick.*

LEIP (LEIF), to smear, cleave, remain. Skt. *lip*, to smear, anoint; Gk. ἀ-λείφ-ειν, to smear, λίπ-os, fatness; L. *lip-pus*, blear-eyed; Lith. *lip-ti*, to stick, cleave; Goth. *bi-leib-an*, to remain behind, *bi-laib-jan*, to leave behind, *laib-a*, a remnant; Icel. *lif-a*, to remain, to live; AS. *libb-an* (for *lif-jan*), to live. Ex. *synalœpha; life, live, lave.*

LEIQw (LEIHw), to leave, lend. Skt. *rich*, to leave; Gk. λείπ-ειν, to leave; L. *linqu-ere*, to leave, *re-liqu-us*, remaining; Goth. *leihw-an*, AS. *lih-an*, to lend. Ex. *relinquish, relic, relict; lend, loan.*

LEIS, to trace, follow a trace. L. *līr-a* (for *līz-a*), a trace, furrow, *de-līr-āre*, to leave the furrow, become mad; Goth. *lais* (I have followed up the trace), I know, *lais-ts*, a trace, track, AS. *lǣr-an*, to teach, *leor-nian*, to learn, *lār*, lore. Ex. *delirious; last* (2), *last* (3), *lore, learn.*

LENGwH (LENG), to leap over (hence, to go lightly). Skt. *langh*, to leap over, *laghu(s)*, light; Gk. ἐ-λαχ-ύς, light, small; Lith. *lengvu-as*, light; L. *lev-is*, light; Russ. *legk-ii*, light; *legk-oe*, lung; AS. *lung-en*, lung, *lung-re*, quickly. Ex. *levity, alleviate; light* (2), *lights, lungs.*

LEP, to peel. Gk. λέπ-ειν, to peel, λεπ-ίς, a scale, λέπ-ρα, leprosy; L. *lib-er*, bast of a tree (Brugmann, i. § 499), a book. Ex. *lepidoptera, leper; library.*

LEU, to cut off, separate, loosen. Skt. *lū*, to cut off; Gk. λύ-ειν, to loosen; L. *so-lu-ere*, pp. *so-lū-tus*, to loosen, solve; Goth. *laus*, Icel. *lauss*, AS. *lēas*, loose, free from; AS. *los-ian*, to become loose. Ex. *solve, solution, dissolve, resolve; loose, lose, leasing* (falsehood), and suffix *-less.*

LEU, to gain, acquire (as spoil). Prellwitz gives the form of the root as lāw. Gk. λεία, booty, Ion. ληΐη (for *λᾱϝιᾱ); ἀπο-λαύ-ειν, to enjoy; L. *lū-crum*, profit, lucre; Goth. *lau-n*, OHG. *lō-n*, pay, reward. Ex. *lucre; guerdon.*

LEUBH (LEUB), to desire, love. Skt. *lubh*, to covet, desire; L. *lub-et, lib-et*, it pleases, *lub-ido, lib-ido*, lust; Goth. *liub-s*, dear, *ga-laub-jan*, to believe; AS. *lēof*, dear, *luf-u*, love. Ex. *libidinous; lief, love, leave* (2), *furlough, believe, leman.*

LEUQ (LEUH), to shine. Skt. *ruch*, to shine; Gk. λευκ-ός, white; L. *lūc-ēre*, to shine, *lux* (gen. *lūc-is*), light; *lū-men* (for *leuc-men*), light, *lū-na* (for *louc-sna*), moon; Goth. *liuh-ath*, light, AS. *lēoh-t*, light. Ex. *lucid, luminous, lunar, lustre* (1), *illustrate, illustrious; light* (1), *lea.* Also *lucubration.*

LOW (LAW), to wash. Gk. λού-ειν, to wash; L. *ab-lu-ere*, to wash off, *lau-āre*, to wash, *lu-strum*, a lustration; Icel. *lau-g*, a bath; AS. *lēah*, lye, *lēa-ðor*, lather. Ex. *ablution, alluvial, deluge, dilute, laundress, lave, lotion, lustre* (2), *lustration, lute* (2); *lye, lather.*

MAGH (= māgh), Teut. (MAG), to be strong; also in the form **MAG** (MAK). **1.** Skt. *mah-ant-*, great, large; Gk. μῆχ-os, means, expedient, μηχ-ανή, a machine; Goth. *mag*, I may, *mah-ts*, might, AS. *mag-en*, might, main. **2.** Skt. *majman*, strength; Gk. μέγ-as, L. *mag-nus*, great; AS. *mic-el*, great. Ex. *Magi, magic; machine; maxim, May, major, mayor, main* (2), *master; may* (1), *maid, main* (1), *might, mickle, much.*

ME (= mē), to measure; also **MED** (MET). Skt. *mā*, to measure, Gk. μῆ-τις, counsel; L. *mē-tior*, I measure. Also L. *med-itāri*, to consider about, *mod-us*, a measure; AS. *met-an*, to mete. Ex. *metre; meditate, moderate, modern, modest, measure, mensuration; mete, meal* (2), *moon, month;* also *firman.*

MEI, to diminish; also to hurt, diminish. Skt. *mi*, to hurt, diminish; Gk. μι-νύειν, to diminish, μεί-aw, less; L. *mi-nuere*, to diminish; *mi-n-or*, less; Goth. *mi-n-s*, less. Ex. *minor, minute, minim, diminish, minister, minnow, mis-* (2), prefix. See below.

MEI, to change, exchange; also as **MEI-T** (MEITH), to exchange, to change for the worse, deprave. L. *com-mū-nis* (Old L. *com-moi-nis*), common, mutual, AS. *mā-n*, wickedness; Lith. *mai-nas*, barter; MHG. *mei-n*, false. Hence Gk. μοῖγ-os, thanks (good return), L. *mūt-āre* (Old L. *moit-āre*), to exchange; Goth. *maid-jan*, to alter, deprave, *ge-maith-s*, maimed; AS. *ge-mǣd*, troubled in mind, mad. Also Skt. *mith-as*, mutually, *mith-yā*, falsely (hardly L. *mit-tere*, to send away, OHG. *mid-an*, to avoid); Goth. *missa-* (prefix), *mis-*, wrongly. Ex. *common, mutable, mutual, community, moult; mean* (2), *mis-* (1), *miss* (1), *mad.* See above.

MEIGH (MEIG), to wet. Skt. *mih*, to sprinkle, *mēh-a(s)*, urine; Gk. ὀ-μιχ-έω, L. *ming-o*, AS. *mig-a*, I make water; Goth. *maih-stus*, dung, AS. *meox*, dung. Ex. *mistle-toe, missel-thrush, mixen.*

MEIK (MEIH), also **MEIG**, to mix. Skt. *miç-ra(s)*, mixed, *mik-sh*, to mix; Gk. μίγ-νυμι, I mix, μίσγ-ειν (*μίγ-σκ-ειν), to mix; L. *misc-ēre* (*meik-sc-*), to mix; AS. *mi-sc-an*, to mix. Ex. *miscellaneous, mix, mixture; mash.*

MEIT; see **MEI** (2) above. **MEIT** (Teutonic); see *mite* (1).

MEL (MEL), to stain. Gk. *mal-a-*, dirty; Gk. μολ-ύνειν, to sully, μέλ-as, black; L. *mul-lus*, red mullet. Ex. *melancholy; mullet.* (But not *mole* (1).)

MEL, to grind; whence **MEL-D** (MEL-T). Skt. *mlā*, to be worn down, *mṛd-u(s)*, soft; Gk. μαλ-ακός, soft, μαλ-άχη, mallow; Gk. ἀ-μαλ-ός, soft, ἀ-μαλδ-ύνειν, to soften; L. *mol-ere*, to grind, *moll-is* (for *mold-uis*), soft; OIrish *mel-im*, I grind; AS. *mel-u*, meal, *melt-an*, to melt. Also **MEL-DH** (MEL-D). Gk. μαλθ-ακός, soft, tender, mild; AS. *mild-e*, mild; Goth. *muld-a*, mould (1), *mould-e*, mould. Ex. *malachite; molar, mill, mollify, mauve; meal* (1), *mellow; mallow; melt, malt; mild, mould* (1). Cf. *mole* (3), *s-melt* (1).

MELG (MELK), to milk. Skt. *mṛj*, to rub, wipe, stroke; Gk. ἀ-μέλγ-ειν, to milk; L. *mulg-ēre*, to milk, AS. *melc-an*, to milk. Der. *milk;* cf. *milt* (2).

MEN, to remember, to think. Skt. *man*, to think, mind, understand, *man-as*, mind, *mnā*, to remember; Gk. μέν-os, spirit, courage, μέ-μον-a, I wish, μαν-ία, madness, μέ-μνη-μαι, I remember, μνή-μων, mindful; L. *me-min-i*, I remember, *men-s*, mind, *mon-ēre*, to remind; Goth. *mun-an*, to think, AS. *ge-myn-d*, memory. Ex. *automaton, amnesty, mania, mnemonic, mental, monition, monster, monument, comment, reminiscence; man, mind;* cf. *mean* (1).

MEN, to remain. Gk. μέν-ειν, to remain; L. *man-ēre*, to remain. Ex. *mansion, manor, manse, menial, menagerie, messuage, permanent, remain, remnant.*

MEN, to project. L. *ē-min-ēre*, to jut out, L. *men-tum*, the chin, *mon-s*, mountain, *min-æ*, things ready to fall, threats; (perhaps) Goth. *mun-th-s*, AS. *mūð*, mouth. Ex. *eminent, prominent, mountain, mount* (1), *mount* (2), *amount, promontory, menace, commination, amenable, demeanour, mound.* Perhaps *mouth.*

MER, to die. Skt. *mṛ-ta(s)*, dead; Gk. ἀμ-βρο-τos (for ἀ-μρο-τos), immortal; L. *mor-s*, death, *mor-i*, to die, *mor-bus*, disease; AS. *mor-ð*, death, *morð-or*, murder. Ex. *amaranth, ambrosia, mortal, morbid; murder.*

MER, to remember; see **SMER**.

MEUK, to wipe away. Skt. *much*, to loosen, free, shed; Gk. ἀπο-μύσσειν (*-μυκyειν), to wipe away, μυκ-τήρ, nose, snout, μύξα (*μυκ-σα), nozzle of a lamp; L. *mūc-us*, mucus, *ē-mung-ere*, to wipe away. Ex. *match* (2); *mucus.*

MU, to make a suppressed noise (imitative). Skt. *mū-kas*, dumb; Gk. μύ, μῦ, a sound of muttering, μύ-ειν, to close lips or eyes; L. *mu-ttum, mū-tum*, a slight sound, *mu-ttire, mū-tire*, to mutter, *mū-tus*, dumb; E. *moo*, to low; cf. *mum*, a slight sound. Similarly, Gk. μύ-σ-της, one who is initiated, μυ-σ-τήριον, a mystery, secret (thing muttered). Cf. L. *mur-mur-āre*, to murmur. Ex. *myth, mystic, mystery; mute, mutter, motto.* Cf. *mumble, murmur.*

MUS, or **mŪS**, to steal. Skt. *mush*, to steal; *mūsh-as*, a stealer, rat, mouse; Gk. μῦς, a mouse, L. and AS. *mūs*. Ex. *mouse, muscle, niche.* And see *musk*.

NE, to bind together, to spin; see **SNE**.

(E)NEBH (eNEB), to swell out, to burst (?) Skt. *nabh*, to burst, taken as the root of *nābh-i-*, the hub, nave of a wheel, *nābh-il-a(m)*, navel; Gk. ὀμφ-αλός, navel, boss of a shield; L. *umb-o*, boss of a shield, *umb-il-icus*, navel; AS. *naf-u, nab-u*, nave, *naf-el-a, nab-ul-a*, navel. Ex. *umbilical; nave* (1), *navel; auger* (for *nauger*).

(E)NEBH, to burst forth (?), to spread (?). Perhaps the same as the above. Skt. *nabh-as*, cloud, mist, vapour; Gk. νέφ-ος, cloud; L. *neb-ula*, cloud; G. *neb-el*, cloud. Ex. *nebula, nimbus.*

NEDH, to bind, tie. Skt. *nah* (for **nadh*), to bind, pp. *naddha-s*, bound, tied; L. *nōd-us*, a knot. Ex. *node, nodule.*

NEK, to perish, die. Skt. *naç*, to perish; Gk. νέκ-υς, a corpse, νεκ-ρός, dead; L. *nec-āre*, to kill, *noc-ēre*, to hurt. Ex. *necromancy; internecine, pernicious, noxious, nuisance.*

(E)NEK, (E)NENK, to attain to. Gk. ἐ-νεγκ-εῖν, to bear, put up with; L. *nanc-isci* (pp. *nac-tus*), to acquire; Goth. *ga-nah*, it suffices, *ga-nōh-s*, enough. Ex. *enough*.

NEM, to allot, share, take. Gk. νέμ-ειν, to portion out, νέμ-ος, pasture, νόμ-ος, custom, law; L. *nem-us*, grove, *num-erus*, number; Goth. *nim-an*, to take. And perhaps L. *em-ere*, to buy (orig. to take). Ex. *Nemesis, nomad, numismatic; number; nimble numb.* Perhaps *exempt, example, redeem, assume, &c.*

NEU, to nod. Gk. νεύ-ειν, to nod; L. *nu-ere*, to nod, *nū-tāre*, to nod. Ex. *nutation.*

NEUD (NEUT), to enjoy, profit by, use. Lith. *naud-à*, use; AS. *nēot-an*, to enjoy, use, employ, *nēat*, domestic cattle. Ex. *neat* (1).

oNOG(w)H (NAG); base of the sb. 'nail.' Skt. *nakl.-a-*, nail, claw (an abnormal form); Gk. ὄνυξ (stem ὀνυχ-), nail, claw; L. *ung-uis*, nail; Lith. *nag-as*, nail; AS. *nægel*, nail. Ex. *onyx; nail.*

NOGw (NAKW); base of the adj. 'naked.' Skt. *nag-na(s)*, naked; L. *nū-dus* (**nog(w)edos*), nude; Russ. *nag-oi*, naked; Goth. *nakw-alks*, AS. *nac-od*, naked. Ex. *nude; naked.*

OD (ŏd, od), to smell. Gk. ὄζειν (for **ὄδ-yειν*), to smell, pt. t. ὄδ-ωδ-a; L. *od-or*, smell, *ol-ere* (**od-ere*), to smell. Ex. *ozone; odour, olfactory, redolent.*

OID (AIT), to swell. Gk. οἰδ-άνειν, to swell; AS. *āt-an*, pl. oats. Ex. *oats.*

OQw (AH), to see. Gk. ὄσ-σε (for ὄκ-yε), the two eyes; ὄψομαι (**ὄπ-σομαι*), fut. tense, I shall see, ὄπ-ωπ-a, pt. t., I have seen; ὀφ-θαλμός, eye; Russ. *ok-o*, eye. Perhaps ὀφ-θαλμός, eye (it is suggested that the diphthong is due to association with Goth. *aus-ō*, AS. *ēar-e*, ear). See Brugmann, i. § 681 (c). Ex. *optics, ophthalmist, canopy; ocular, oculist, antler;* perhaps *eye*.

PA (pā), Teut. FA (fō), to feed, nourish. Gk. πα-τέομαι, I feed upon; L. *pā-scere* (pt. t. *pā-ui*), to feed, *pā-nis*, bread; Goth. *fō-d-jan*, to feed, AS. *fō-da*, food, *fō-dor*, fodder. Ex. *pastor, pastern, pester, pannier, pantry, pabulum, company; food, fodder, feed, foster.* Perhaps *father.*

PAK, PAG (= pāk, pāg) (FAH), to fasten, fix, hold, secure. Skt. *paç*, to bind; Gk. πάσσαλος (**πάκ-yαλος*), a peg; L. *pac-isci*, to stipulate, agree, *pax* (**pac-s*), peace; Goth. *fag-rs*, AS. *fæg-er*, fair. Also Gk. πήγ-νυμι, I secure, fasten, L. *pang-ere*, pp. *pac-tus*, to fasten, *pāg-ina*, a page (perhaps *pro-pāg-āre*, to peg down, propagate by layers); Gk. πηγ-ός, firm, strong (and perhaps L. *pāg-us*, a village). Ex. *pact, propagate* (?), *page* (2), *compact, pale* (1), *impinge, peace, pay* (1), &c.; *fair, fain, fang.*

PAU (FAU), to cease, leave off. Gk. παύ-ομαι, I cease, παύ-ειν, to make to cease, παῦ-σις, a pause, παῦ-ρος, small, L. *pau-cus*, small, *pau-per* (providing little), poor; Goth. *faw-ai*, pl., few. Ex. *pause, pose* (with *re-pose, com-pose*, &c.); *pauper, poor; few.*

PED (FET), to go, fetch. Skt. *pad*, to fall, go to, obtain, *pad-a(m`*, a step, trace, place, abode; *pād-a(s)*, a foot; Gk. πέδ-ον, ground, πέδ-η, a fetter, ποús (gen. ποδ-ός), a foot; L. *pēs* (gen. *ped-is*), foot, *ped-ica*, a fetter; AS. *fōt*, foot, *fet-ian*, to fetch, *fet-or*, fetter. Ex. *tripod, parallelopiped; pedal, pedestal, pedestrian, pawn* (2), *pioneer, oppidan, impede, expedient; foot, fetter, fetch, fetlock.*

PEI (FEI), to hate. Skt. *piy*, to revile, scoff; Goth. *fi-jands*, hating, *fai-an*, to blame. Ex. *fiend, foe, feud* (1).

PEI (FEI), to swell, to be fat. Skt. *pi-van*, swelling, full, fat; Gk. πί-ων, fat; Icel. *fei-tr*, fat, AS. *fǣ-tt*, fat. Ex. *fat.*

PEIK, PEIG, to scratch, cut, adorn, paint. Skt. *piç, piṃç*, to cut, prepare, adorn; Gk. ποικ-ίλος, variegated, parti-coloured. Also L. *ping-ere* (pp. *pic-tus*), to paint. Ex. *picture, pigment, paint, orpiment, orpine; depict, pimento, pint.*

PEIS, to pound, stamp. Skt. *pish*, to pound, bruise; Gk. πίσ-ος, a pea (cf. πτίσ-μα, peeled grain); L. *pins-ere*, to pound, grind (pp. *pis-tus*), *pi-lum* (for **pins-lum*), a pestle; *pis-tillum*, a small pestle. Ex. *pea, pestle, piston, pistil.*

PEK (FEH), to comb. Gk. πέκ-ειν, to card wool; πόκ-ος, wool; L. *pec-tere*, to comb; OHG. *fah-s* (AS. *fex, feax*), hair. Ex. *pectinal;* and cf. *pax-wax.*

PEL (FEL), to flay, skin (?). Gk. -πελας, skin, in ἐρυσί-πελ-ας, inflammation of the skin; L. *pel-lis*, AS. *fel-l*, skin. Ex. *erysipelas; pell, pellicle, pelisse, pilch, surplice, peel* (1); *pillion; fell* (2), *film.*

PEL, to fill; see **PLE**.

PELT (FELTH), to fold. Gk. πλάσ-σειν (for **πλάτ-yειν*), to form, mould, shape; δι-πλάσ-ιος, two-fold; Goth. *falth-an*, AS. *feald-an*, to fold. Ex. *plastic, cataplasm; fold.*

PEQw, to cook, to ripen. Skt. *pach*, to cook; Gk. πέσσειν, to cook, πέπ-των, cooked, πέπ-ων, ripe; L. *coqu-ere* (for **pequere*), to cook; Russ. *pech(e)*, to bake. Ex. *pepsine, dyspeptic, pip* (2), *pippin, pumpkin; cook, kitchen, precocious, apricot.*

PER (FER), to go through, experience, fare, travel. Skt. *pṛ*, to bring across, causal *pār-aya*, to conduct across; *par-as*, beyond, further, *par-ā*, away; Gk. περ-άω, I press through, pass through, πόρ-ος, a way, πορ-θμός, ferry, πορ-εύω, I convey, πορ-εύομαι, I travel, πεῖρα (**πέρ-ya*), an attempt; also πρό, before, πρῶ-τος, first, πέρ-υσι, beyond, παρ-ά, beside, πέρ-ι, around, over; L. *per-itus*, experienced, *ex-per-irī*, to try, *per-i-culum*, danger; *por-ta*, gate, *por-tus*, harbour; also *prō*, before, *per*, through; AS. *far-an*, to go, fare, *fǣr*, panic, fear; also *for*, for, fore, before, *fyr-st*, first. Ex. *pirate, pore* (1); *peril, experience, port* (1), *port* (2), *port* (3), *port* (4); *fare, far, fear, ford, frith* (2). Also *peri-*, prefix, *para-*, prefix; *pro-*, prefix, *præ-*, prefix, *prime; for, fore, first, for-* (1), *for-* (2), *from.*

PER, to produce, afford, allot. Gk. ἔ-πορ-ον, I brought, gave; L. *par-ere*, to produce, bring forth, *re-per-ire*, to find; (probably) *par-s*, a part, *por-tio*, a portion. Ex. *parent, parturient, repertory, part, portion.*

PET (FETH), to fall, to fly, to hasten towards, seek, find. Skt. *pat*, to fly, fall upon, *pat-ra(m)*, a wing, feather, leaf; Gk. πέτ-ομαι, I fly, πί-πτ-ειν, to fall; πτ-έρυξ, a wing; L. *pet-ere*, to seek, *im-pet-us*, attack (falling upon, flying at), *penna* (**pet-sna*), a wing; AS. *feð-er*, a feather. Ex. *peri; asymptote, symptom, diptera, coleoptera, lepidoptera; compete, impetus, perpetual, appetite, petition, propitious, pen* (2); *feather.*

PET (FETH), to spread out, lie flat. Gk. πετ-άννυμι, I spread out, πέτ-αλον, flat plate, leaf, πατ-άνη, flat dish; L. *pat-ēre*, to lie open, *pat-ulus*, spreading, *pat-ina*, dish; AS. *fæð-m*, fathom. Ex. *petal, paten; patent.* Prob. also *expand, pass, pace*, &c., from L. *pand-ere*, to spread, which seems to be allied to *patēre.*

PEU, to beget. Skt. *pu-tra(s)*, son; Gk. παῖς (**παϝ-ίς*), son; L. *pu-er*, boy. Ex. *pedagogue; puerile.* (Perhaps L. *pū-pus*, boy, belongs here; cf. *pupa, pupil, puppet.*)

PEU (FEU), to cleanse, purify. Skt. *pū*, to cleanse, purify, *pū-ta(s)*, pure, *pāv-aka(s)*, purifying, (also) fire; Gk. πῦ-ρ, fire; L. *pū-rus*, pure, *pu-tus*, cleansed, *pu-tāre*, to prune, clear up, reckon; AS. *fȳ-r*, fire. Ex. *pyre, pyrites; pure, purge, compute*, &c.; *fire.*

PI, pī (fī), imitative; to chirp, pipe. Gk. πι-πί-ζειν, to chirp, L. *pi-p-ire, pi-p-āre*. Ex. *pipe, pibroch, pigeon.* Cf. *fife.*

PLĀQ, PLĀG(w) (FLŌH, FLŌK), to strike, strike down, strike flat. Lith. *plak-ù*, I strike; Gk. πλάξ (gen. πλακ-ός), a flat surface, πλακ-οῦς, a flat cake; also πληγ-ή, a stroke, πλήσσειν (πλήκ-yειν), to strike; L. *plac-enta*, a flat cake, *planc-a*, a plank (cf. Gk. πλάκ-ιν-ος, made of boards); also *plāg-a*, a stroke, *plang-ere*, to strike, to lament; Goth. *flōk-an*, to lament; Gk. φlach, flat; AS. *flōc*, a fluke, flat fish. Ex. *placenta, plank; plague, plaint; fluke* (1), *fluke* (2). Cf. *flay.*

PLAT (=plăt), to spread out. Skt. *prath*, to spread out; *pṛthu-*, broad; Gk. πλατ-ύς, broad, flat, πλάτ-ος, breadth, πλάτ-η, blade of an oar, plate, πλάτ-ανος, a plane-tree; L. *plat-essa*, a plaice, *plant-a*, sole of the foot, spreading shoot, plant. Ex. *plate, place; plaice, plant, plantain, plane* (3). Cf. *field.* Allied to *flat.*

PLE (=plē), lengthened form of **PEL** (FEL), to fill. Skt. *pṛ*, to fill, *pūrṇa(s)*, filled, *pur-u-*, much; Gk. πίμ-πλη-μι, I fill, πλή-ρης, full, πλή-θω, I am full, πολ-ύς, much; L. *plē-re*, to fill, *plē-nus*, full, *plē-bes*, throng, people, *plū-s*, more, *po-pul-us*, people, *mani-pul-us*, a handful; AS. *ful-l*, full, *fyl-lan*, to fill. Ex. *plethora, polygon; plenary, plebeian, plural, popular, maniple, implement, complete, replete; full, fill, fulfil.*

PLEK (FLEH), to plait, weave, fold together. Gk. πλέκ-ειν, to plait, πλοκ-ή, a plait; L. *plec-tere*, to plait, *plic-āre*, to fold; Goth. *flah-ta*, a plaiting of hair; OHG. *flah-s*, AS. *fleax*, flax. Ex. *plait, pleach, plash, ply* (1), with compounds, *complex, simple, duplex, triplicate, explicate, supplicate, suppliant, supple; flax.*

PLEU (FLEU), to swim, float, flow. Skt. *plu*, to swim, fly, jump, *flāv-aya*, to inundate; Gk. πλέ-ειν (fut. πλεύ-σομαι), to sail, float, πλύ-νειν, to wash; L. *plu-it*, it rains, *plu-uia*, rain; AS. *flô-wan*, to flow, *flô-d*, a flood. Also AS. *flêo-t-an*, to float, *flêo-t*, a fleet, *flo-t-ian*, to float. Ex. *pluvial, plover; flow, float, fleet* (in all senses), *flit, flutter, flotsam.*

PNEU (FNEU-S), to blow, breathe. Gk. πνεῦ-μα, breath; AS. *fnéos-an*, to breathe hard, *fnor-a*, a sneezing. Ex. *pneumatic, neeze, s-neeze;* cf. *s-nore.*

PREI (FREI), to love. Skt. *pri-ya(s)*, dear, beloved; Russ. *priiatele*, a friend; Goth. *fri-jôn*, AS. *frê-on*, to love, whence the pres. part. *fri-jônds, frê-ond*, loving, a friend; AS. *frêo*, free, *fri-ð*, security; *Fri-g*, the wife of Woden. Ex. *friend, free, frith* (1), *Friday.*

PREK (FREH), to pray, ask, demand. Skt. *prachh*, to ask; L. *prec-āri*, to pray, *proc-us*, a wooer; *poscere* (*porc-scere), to demand, *postulāre* (from *poscere*), to demand; Goth. *fraih-nan*, to ask. Ex. *pray, precarious, imprecate, postulate.*

PREUS (FREUS), to burn; also, to freeze. Skt. *prush*, to burn; L. *pruina* (for *pruzwina*), hoar-frost, *prūr-ire* (*prūsire > *prūzire*), to itch; AS. *frêos-an*, to freeze. Ex. *prurient; freeze, frost.*

PU, pū (FU, fū), to be foul or putrid. Skt. *pū-ti-ka-*, foul, *pūy*, to stink, *fūy-as*, pus; Gk. πῦ-ον, pus; L. *pū-s*, matter, *pū-rulentus*, purulent, *pū-tidus*, stinking, *pu-tridus*, putrid; AS. *fū-l*, foul. Ex. *pus, purulent, putrid; foul, file* (3), *filth.*

QAL (HAL), to cry out. Skt. *kal-a-s*, low sounding; Gk. καλ-έω, I summon; L. *cal-āre*, to proclaim, *clā-māre*, to cry out; OHG. *hal-ôn*, to call, G. *hell*, clear-sounding; AS. *klô-wan*, to low. Ex. *calends, clamour, claim, clear, council; haul, hale* (2), *low* (2).

QAP (HAF), to seize, hold. Gk. κώπ-η, a handle; L. *cap-ere*, to seize; Goth. *hafjan*, AS. *hebban*, to lift, heave; AS. *haf-oc*, hawk, lit. 'seizer' (cf. Late L. *cap-us*, a hawk). Ex. *capacious, capable*, &c.; *heave, hawk, haft;* perhaps *behoof.* Also *captive, capsule, ease* (2), *cater;* and numerous derivatives of L. *capere.* (For the initial q in *qap*, see Brugmann, i. § 635.)

QAR, to sing, cry aloud. Skt. *kār-u-*, a singer; Gk. καρ-καίρειν, to resound, κῆρ-υξ, a herald; L. *car-men*, a song. Ex. *charm.*

QAR (HAR), to love. Irish *car-aim*, I love; L. *câr-us*, dear; Goth. *hôr-s*, an adulterer. The initial q is suggested by Lettish *kârs*, desirous; Brugmann, i. § 637.

QAS, to cough. Skt. *kâs*, to cough; Lith. *kos-ti*, to cough; AS. *hwôs-ta*, a cough; Irish *cas-achdas*, a cough; W. *pâs*, a cough (whence AS. *ge-pos*, a pose, a cough). Ex. *pose* (3).

QEI, to be lucky (?). W. *coel*, an omen; Hesychius quotes Gk. κοῖλυ· τὸ καλόν; L. *cêl*, an omen; Goth. *hail-s*, AS. *hâl*, whole. Ex. *whole, hale, holy, heal, health.* (For initial q see Brugmann, i. § 639.)

QEL (HEL), to raise up. Lith. *kél-ti*, to lift; Gk. κολ-ωνός, κολ-ώνη, a hill; L. *ex-cel-lere*, to surpass, *cel-sus*, high, *cul-men*, a summit, *col-lis*, a hill; AS. *hyl-l*, a hill, *hol-m*, billow. Ex. *colophon; culminate, column, excel; hill, holm.* (For initial q see Brugmann, i. § 633.)

QEL (HEL), to drive on. Skt. *kal-aya*, to drive, *kâl-aya*, to drive on; Gk. κέλ-λειν, to drive, κέλ-ης, a runner; βου-κόλ-ος, a herdsman (ox-driver); L. *cel-er*, swift. Ex. *bucolic; celerity.*

QEL (qêl), to shelter. Teut. HEL, to hide. Gk. καλ-ύ, a shelter, hut, κάλ-υξ, calyx; L. *oc-cul-ere*, *cêl-āre*, to hide, *cal-ix*, a cup, *cel-la*, a cell, *cl-am*, secretly; AS. *hel-an*, to cover, hide. Ex. *calyx; conceal, occult, cell, clandestine;* (perhaps *supercilious*); *hell, hole, hull* (1), *hall, helmet, holster.* (On the initial q see Brugmann, i. § 641.)

QEND, to shine; L. *cand-êre;* see **SQEND.**

QER, to make. Skt. *kr*, to make; *kar-man*, work, deed; Gk. κρέ-ων, ruler; L. *cre-āre*, to make, create, *cre-sc-ere*, to grow, OLat. *cer-us*, creator, *Cer-es*, goddess of the growth of corn. Ex. *create, cereal, crescent, increase, concrete, accretion, accrue, crew*, &c.

QERH (HERF), to cut. (Probably for SQERP; see SQER, to shear.) Skt. *kr-pāṇa(s)*, sword; Lith. *kerp-ù*, I cut, shear; Gk. καρπ-ός, fruit, κρώπ-ιον, sickle; L. *carp-ere*, to pluck fruit; AS. *hærf-est*, harvest. Ex. *harvest.* Cf. *carp* (2).

QERT, to bind together. Skt. *kat-a(s)*, for (*kar-tas), a mat; *chrt*, to bind together; Gk. κύρτ-αλος, (a woven) basket; L. *crât-ês*, a hurdle; AS. *hyrd-el*, a hurdle. Cf. Skt. *krt*, to spin. Ex. *hurdle.* (For the initial q see Brugmann, i. § 633.)

QEUQ (HEUH), to bow out, to hunch up. Skt. *kuch-as*, the female breast; Lith. *kauk-arà*, a hill; Goth. *hauh-s*, high; Icel. *haug-r*, a hill. Ex. *high, how* (2). Cf. *huge.*

QOU (HAU), to strike, to hew. L. *cū-dere*, to strike, *in-cū-s*, an anvil; Russ. *kou-ate*, to hammer; G. *hau-en*, AS. *héa-wan*, to hew. Ex. *hew, hoe, hay.*

QREU (HREU), to wound. Skt. *krav-i-*, raw flesh, *krū-ra(s)*, wounded, raw; Gk. κρέας (*κρέϝ-ας), raw flesh; L. *cru-dus*, raw, *cru-or*, blood; Lith. *krau-jas*, blood; AS. *hrêa-w*, raw. Ex. *crude, cruel; raw.* Perhaps *rue* (1).

QwEI (HWEI), to rest. Skt. *chi-ra(s)*, long-lasting, long; OChurch Slav. *po-či-ti*, to rest; L. *qui-ês*, rest, *tran-quillus*, tranquil; AS. *hwî-l*, a while (quiet time), Goth. *hwei-la*, rest. Ex. *quiet, tranquil, coy, quit; while, whilom, whilst.*

QwEI, to expiate, pay for. Skt. *apa-chi-ti-*, expiation; Gk. ἀπό-τι-σις; also ποι-νή (L. *poe-na*), a penalty, τί-νω, I pay a penalty. Ex. *penalty, pain, pine* (2), *penance.* (See Brugmann, i. § 652.)

QwEL (HWEL), to move, go round, turn, drive. Skt. *char, chal*, to move; Gk. πέλ-ειν, to be in motion, πόλ-ος, pole, axis of revolution; L. *col-us*, a distaff, *col-ere*, to till, *in-col-a*, inhabitant, dweller in; OSlav. *kol-o*, a wheel; AS. *hwêol*, a wheel (which see). Ex. *pole* (2); *colony; calash; wheel.* Cf. L. *collum* (for *col-sum*), neck (from its turning); whence E. *collar.*

QwEP (= q(w)êp), to breathe, to reek. Lith. *kwêp-ti*, to breathe, *kwâp-as*, breath, vapour; L. *uap-or*, vapour; Gk. καπ-νός, smoke. Ex. *vapid, vapour.* (See Brugmann, i. § 193.)

RAD (RAT), to gnaw. Skt. *rad*, to scratch, gnaw; L. *râd-ere*, to scrape; *rôd-ere*, to gnaw; AS. *ræt*, a rat. Ex. *rase, rash* (2), *rasorial, razor, abrade, erase, rodent; rat.*

RE (= rê), to think upon; whence **REDH** (rêdh), Teut. RED (= rêd), to provide, accomplish. L. *rê-ri*, to consider (pp. *ra-tus*); Skt. *râdh*, to achieve, accomplish, prepare; Goth. *ga-rêd-an*, to provide; AS. *rêd-an*, to counsel, interpret, read. Ex. *rate* (1), *ratify, ratio, ration, reason, arraign; read, riddle* (1).

REBH (REB), to cover. Gk. ἐ-ρέφ-ειν, to cover, ὄ-ροφ-ος, a roof; OHG. *râf-o, râv-o*, a beam, Icel. *râf*, a roof, *rap-tr* (= *raf-t-r*), a rafter. Ex. *raft, rafter.* (Not *roof.*)

REG (REK), to stretch, stretch out, reach, straighten, rule. Skt. *rj*, to stretch; Gk. ὀ-ρέγ-ειν, to stretch; L. *reg-ere*, to rule, *ê-rig-ere*, to erect, set upright, *rectus* (*reg-tus*), right, *rêx* (gen. *rêg-is*), king, ruler; Goth. *uf-rak-jan*, to stretch out, *raih-ts*, right, AS. *rih-t*, right. Ex. *rajah; regent, regal, regulate, reign, rule*, &c.; *right, rack* (1), *ratch, rake* (3). Also *rich.* Perhaps *rogation.*

REI, to distil, flow. Skt. *ri*, to distil, drop; L. *ri-uus*, a stream, *rî-tus*, a custom, rite (cf. Skt. *rîti-*, a going, way, usage). (Some connect Goth. *rinnan*, to run.) Ex. *rivulet, rival, rite.* Perhaps *run.* A parallel form is LEI, to melt, to besmear. Skt. *lî*, to melt, dissolve; L. *li-nere*, to besmear, *lî-mus*, mud; AS. *lî-m*, lime, *lâ-m*, loam. Ex. *lime* (1), *loam.*

REIDH (REID), to ride, be conveyed. OIrish *riad-aim*, I drive, ride; AS. *rîd-an*, to ride. Ex. *ride, road, raid, ready.*

REIP (REIB), to tear down, tear. Gk. ἐ-ρείπ-εσθαι, to be torn down, to fall in ruins; L. *rîp-a*, bank (with steep edge); Icel. *rîf-a*, to rive, to tear. Ex. *river; rive, rift, riven.*

RET, to run along, rotate. OIrish *reth-im*, I run; Lith. *rit-ù*, I roll; Skt. *rath-a(s)*, a chariot, car; L. *rot-a*, a wheel. Ex. *rotate, rotary, round, roll, rouleau, rotund*, &c. Also *barouche, roué.*

REU, to hum, bray, roar; imitative. Skt. *ru*, to hum, bray, roar; Gk. ὠ-ρύ-ομαι, I howl; L. *rū-mor*, a noise, report; cf. also *ru-gire*, to bellow, *rū-men*, the throat. Ex. *rumour, ruminate; rumble.* Cf. *raucous.*

REUD (REUT), to weep, bewail, wet with tears. Skt. *rud*, to weep, bewail, *rôd-ana(m)*, weeping, tears; L. *rud-ere*, to cry out; AS. *rêot-an*, to weep, Icel. *rjôt-a*, to wet, only in the pp. *rotinn*, rotten, orig. 'soaked.' Ex. *rot, rotten, ret.* Extended from REU.

REUDH (REUD), to be red. Skt. *rudh-ira(s)*, red, *rudh-ina(m)*, blood; Gk. ἐ-ρευθ-ειν, to redden, ἐ-ρυθ-ρός, blood, L. *rub-er*, red; AS. *rêad*, red. Ex. *erysipelas; rubric, rubescent, rubicand, rissole, rouge, russet; red, ruddy, rust.*

REUP (REUF), to break, seize, pluck, rob. Skt. *rup*, to feel spasms, *lup*, to break, injure, spoil, seize, rob; *lôp-tra(m)*, booty, loot; L. *rump-ere* (pp. *rup-tus*), to break; Goth. *bi-raub-ôn*, to rob, AS. *rêof-an*, to break; *rêaf*, spoil. Ex. *loot; rupture, eruption*, &c.; *route, rout* (1), *rut* (1), *rob, robe; reave, bereave.*

SA (= sâ), to satiate. Gk. ἄ-μεναι (*σᾱ-μεναι), to satisfy; ἄ-δ-ην, enough; L. *sa-t*, *sa-t-is*, enough, *sa-t-ur*, full; Lith. *sa-t-ùs*, sated, full; Goth. *sa-th-s*, full; AS. *sæ-d*, sated. Ex. *sated, satiate, satisfy, satire, assets; sad.*

SAG (= sâg), Teut. SÔK, to perceive. Gk. ἡγ-έομαι, I guide, I suppose; L. *sâg-ire*, to perceive by the senses; Goth. *sôk-jan*, AS. *sêc-an*, to seek. Ex. *sagacious, sagacity; seek.* Probably allied to *sake* and *soke.*

SAL, to leap. Gk. ἅλ-λομαι (*σάλ-γομαι), I leap, spring; L. *sal-io*, I leap, *sal-to*, I dance. Ex. *salient, salmon, assail, saltation, desultory, exult, insult, result, resilient, sally, saltire.*

SAUS, to become dry, to wither. Skt. *çush* (for *sush), to become dry; Gk. αὔ-ειν (*σαυσ-ειν), to become dry, wither; αὖσ-τηρός, harsh; AS. *sêar*, sere, withered. Ex. *austere; sear, sere.*

SE (=**sē**), to cast abroad, sow, scatter. Gk. ἵ-η-μι (for *σί-ση-μι), I cast, send forth; L. se-rere (pt. t. sē-ui), to sow, sē-men, seed; Goth. sai-an, AS. sā-wan, to sow, sǣ-d, seed. Ex. season, secular, Saturnine, seminal; sow (1), seed.

SED (SET), to sit. Skt. sad, to sit; Gk. ἕζομαι (for *σέδ-yομαι), I sit; L. sed-ēre, to sit; AS. sit-tan, to sit, pt. t. sæt; Russ. sied-lo, Polish siod-lo, a saddle. Ex. cathedral, chair, chaise, polyhedron; sedentary, see (2), sell (2), size (1), size (2), also assiduous, assess, &c.; sit, set, seat, settle (1), settle (2). Also nest, saddle, soot.

SEGH (SEG), to bear, endure, hold in. Skt. sah, to bear, endure, overcome, restrain; sah-as, power, victory; Gk. ἔχ-ειν (*σέχ-ειν), to hold, have (fut. σχ-ήσω), σχ-ῆμα, form, σχ-ολή, stoppage, leisure; Goth. sig-is, victory. Ex. epoch, hectic, scheme, school; perhaps sail.

SELQ (SELH), to draw along. Gk. ἕλκ-ειν (*σέλκ-ειν), to draw, ὁλκ-άς, a heavy ship, hulk, ὁλκ-ός, a furrow; L. sulc-us, furrow; AS. sulh, plough. Ex. hulk; sulcated.

SEQ (SEG), to cut, cleave. L. sec-āre, to cut; Russ. siek-ira, an ax; OHG. seg-ense (G. sense), a scythe; AS. sag-a, a saw, sig-ðe, sí-ðe, a scythe; seeg, sedge. Ex. section, segment, secant, saxifrage, sickle; saw (1), scythe, sedge.

SEQw, to follow, accompany. Skt. sach, to follow; Gk. ἕπ-ομαι, I follow; L. sequ-i, to follow, sec-undus, following, soc-ius, a companion. Ex. sequence, &c.; sect, second, sue, suit, suite, social, associate.

SER, to string, put in a row. Gk. εἴρ-ειν (for *σέρ-yειν) to string (as beads); L. ser-ere, to join together (pp. ser-tus); Icel. sör-vi, a necklace. Ex. series, assert, concert, desert (1), dissertation, exert, insert.

SERP, to slip along, glide, creep. Skt. srp, to creep, sarp-a(s), a snake; Gk. ἕρπ-ειν (*σέρπ-ειν), to creep; L. serp-ere, to creep. But hardly rēp-ere (*srēp-ere ?), to creep. Ex. serpent. Probably not reptile.

SEU, to beget, produce. Skt. sū, to generate, sū-nu(s), a son, sū-kara(s), a hog; Gk. σῦ-s, ὕ-s, a sow, υ-ιός, a son; L. sū-s, pig, su-īnus, belonging to pigs; AS. su-gu, sow, su-īn, swine, su-nu, a son; cf. OIrish su-th, birth, fruit. Ex. sow (2), swine, son.

SEUG, SEUQ, to suck. (Both forms occur; the former answers to Teut. SEUK.) 1. L. sūg-ere, to suck; OIrish sūg-im, I suck; AS. sūc-an, to suck. 2. L. sūc-us, juice; AS. sūg-an, to suck. Ex. suction; suck, soak; also sowans. Also succulent.

SIEU, to stitch together. Skt. siv, to sew, syū-ti-, sewing; Gk. κασ-σύ-ειν, to stitch together, ὑ-μήν, hymen; L. su-ere, to sew; Goth. siu-jan, AS. sēow-an, sīw-ian, to sew. Ex. hymen; suture; sew, seam. Perhaps hymn.

SKAG (SKAK), to shake. Skt. khaj (for *skaj, *skag); to move to and fro; AS. scac-an, sceac-an, to shake. Ex. shake, shock (1), shog; perhaps jog.

SKEI, to shine. Skt. chhā-yā, shade, image, reflected light, splendour; Gk. σκι-ά, shade; Goth. skei-nan, AS. sci-nan, to shine. Ex. shine, shimmer, sheer (1).

SKEUBH (SKEUB), to agitate, shake. Skt. kshubh, to be agitated; kshōbh-aya, to shake; Goth. af-skiub-an, to push away; AS. scūf-an, to shove, push. Ex. shove, sheaf.

SKEUD (SKEUT), to shoot. Lith. szaud-yti, to shoot; AS. scēot-an, to shoot. Ex. shoot, sheet, shot, shut, shuttle; scot-free, skittish, skittles.

SKHED (SKET), to cleave, to scatter. Skt. skhad, to cut, kshad, to carve; Gk. σκεδ-άννυμι, I scatter, disperse, σχέδ-η, a tablet (slice); L. scand-ula, a shingle. Ex. scat-erian, to scatter, shatter. Ex. schedule; shingle (1); scatter, shatter.

SKHEI, whence **SKHEID, SKHEIT**, to cleave, part, shed. 1. Skt. chhid, to cut, divide; Gk. σχίζειν (*σχίδ-yειν), to split; L. scind-ere, to cleave. 2. Goth. skaid-an, AS. scād-an, to shed, separate, part, scid, a thin slip of wood. Ex. schism, schist, zest; shed (1), shide, skid; shingle.

SKLAUD (sklāud), to shut. L. claud-ere, to shut; OFries. slūt-a, slūt-a, to shut; G. schliess-en, to shut. Du. sluit-en. We also find SKLEU; as in Gk. κλείς, Doric κλᾱ-ίς, a key; L. clāu-is, a key; L. clāu-us, a nail. Ex. close (1), close (2), enclose, clause, include, &c.; slot. Also clavicle, clove (1), cloy.

SLEB (=slēb), Teut. SLEP (=slēp), to be relaxed; hence, to sleep. L. lāb-i, to glide, lāp-sāre, to slip, lapse, lab-āre, to totter; Russ. slab-uii, slack, weak; AS. slēp-an, to sleep, LowG. slapp, lax, relaxed. Ex. lapse, elapse, collapse, illapse, relapse; sleep.

SLEG (=slēg), to be slack. Gk. λήγ-ειν, to leave off, λαγ-αρός, slack; L. laxus (*lag-sus), lax, lang-uēre, to be weak; AS. slac, slack, loose. Ex. lax, relax, leash, lease (1), lessee, relay (1), release, relish; slack. And see lag, languish.

SMEI, to smile, laugh. Skt. smi, to smile, smē-ra(s), smiling; Gk. μει-δάω, I smile; L. mi-rus, wonderful, mi-rārī, to wonder at; Swed. smi-la, to smile. Ex. admire, marvel, miracle, mirage, mirror; smile.

SMELD (SMELT), to melt. Gk. μέλδ-ειν, to melt; Swed. smält-a, to smelt. Ex. smelt, smalt. See **MEL**.

SMER, to remember. Skt. smr, to remember, record, declare; Gk. μέρ-ιμνα, sorrow, regret; μάρ-τυς, a witness; L. me-mor-ia, memory, remembrance, me-mor, mindful; AS. mur-nan, to mourn. Ex. martyr; memory, remembrance, commemorate, memoir; mourn. Cf. demur.

SMER, to rub over, smear. Gk. σμύρ-ις, emery for polishing, μύρ-ον, ointment; Icel. smjör, grease, butter; AS. smer-u, fat, grease, smir-ian, to smear. Ex. smear, besmear, smirch.

SMERD (SMERT), to pain, cause to smart. Skt. mrd, to rub, grind, crush; Gk. σμερδ-αλέος, terrible; L. mord-ēre, to bite; AS. smeort-an, to smart. Ex. mordacity, morsel, remorse; smart. Cf. muzzle.

SNA (=**snā**, **snāu**), to bathe, swim. Skt. snā, to bathe; Gk. νή-χειν, to swim, να-ρός, liquid, νη-ρός, wet, νά-ειν, ναύ-ειν, to flow, να-ïs, να-ιάς a naiad, ναῦ-s, a ship; L. nā-re, to swim, nau-ta, sailor, nāu-igāre, to navigate, sail, nāu-is, a ship. Ex. aneroid, naiad; nave (2), naval, navigate, navy, nausea, nautical, nautilus, navvy, natation.

SNE (=snē), to bind together, fasten (with thread). Skt. snā-yu-, tendon, muscle, str.ng, snā-va-, sinew, tendon; Gk. νέ-ω, I spin, νῆ-μα, thread; L. nē-re, to spin; OIrish snā-th, thread, snā-that, a needle; Goth. nē-thla, a needle; AS. snō-d, a fillet. Cf. also Gk. νεῦ-ρον (from *snēu), nerve, sinew, cord. Also, from a base SNER, Gk. νάρ-κη, cramp, numbness; L. ner-uus, nerve, sinew; perhaps AS. near-u, narrow (closely drawn), snear-e, a noose, snare. Ex. neuralgia, narcotic, narcissus; nerve; snare, snood, narrow. And see sinew.

SNEIGwH (SNEIW), to snow. Gk. νείφ-ει, it snows, νίφ-α, accus., snow; L. ningu-it, it snows, niu-em, accus, snow; Irish sneach-d, snow; Goth. snaiw-s, AS. snāw, snow. Ex. snow.

SNER, SNEU (snēu ; see under SNE.

SPE (= spē), to increase, have room, prosper. Skt. sphāy, to swell, increase, sphā-ti-, increase; L. spa-tium, room, space, pro-sper, prosperous, spē-s, hope; AS. spā-wan, to succeed. Ex. space, prosperous, despair, desperate; speed.

SPEK (SPEH), to spy, observe, see. Skt. spaç-a(s), a spy; Gk. σκέπ-τομαι (for *σπέκ-τομαι), I see, σκοπ-ός, a spy, an aim; L. spec-ere, to see, spec-iēs, appearance, spec-tum, to behold; OHG. speh-ōn, to watch. Ex. scope, sceptic, bishop; species, special, spectre, speculate, spectator, suspicion, esfry, sfy, &c.

SPER, SPHER, to struggle, kick, jerk. Skt. sphur, to throb, struggle; Gk. σπαίρ-ειν, ἀ-σπαίρ-ειν, ἀ-σπαρ-ίζειν, to struggle convulsively, σφαῖρ-α, a ball (to be tossed); L. sper-nere, to spurn, despise; AS. spor-nan, to spurn, kick against; perhaps G. sich sper-ren, to struggle, fight. Ex. sphere; spurn, spur, spoor; perhaps spar (3). Cf. sparrow.

SPER, to scatter, sow. Gk. σπείρειν (*σπέρ-yειν), to scatter, sow. Ex. sperm, sporadic. See below.

SPHERG, Teut. SPERK, SPREK, to burst noisily, crackle, scatter abroad. Skt. sphūrj, to crash, burst forth, be displayed; Gk. ἀσφάραγ-ος, a cracking, crackling, ἀ-σπάραγ-ος, asparagus, shoot of a plant; (perhaps) L. sparg-ere, to scatter; AS. spearc-a, a spark of fire, Icel. sprak-a, to crackle (cf. AS. sprec-an, to speak), AS. spræc, a shoot, a spray. Ex. asparagus; speak, spark (1), sparkle, spark (2), spray (2). Perhaps sparse (and derivatives). Cf. spray (1). See above.

SPIW, SPIEU, to spit out, vomit. Skt. shthīv, to spit; Gk. πτύ-ειν (from *σπyυ-yειν), to spit; L. spu-ere, to spit; AS. spīw-an, Goth. speiw-an. Ex. spue, spew. (Of imi'ative origin; so that the form of the root is indeterminate.)

SQAP (SKAF), to dig, scrape, shave ; **SQAB** (SKAP), to cut, scrape, shape. 1. Skt. skāp-yειν, to dig, σκαπ-āη, a spade; Goth. skab-an, AS. scaf-an, to shave. 2. L. scab-ere, to scrape ; Lith. skab-ūs, cutting, sharp; Goth. ga-skap-jan to shape. Ex. shave, scab, scabious, scabby, shabby, shaft. Also shape, capon.

SQEL, to cleave, split, divide. Gk. σκάλ-λειν, to hoe; Lith. skel-iù, I split; ONorse skil-ja, to sever, separate; Goth. skal-ja, a tile; AS. scell, shell. Ex. scale (1), scale (2), scall, scald (2), skill, shell. See shelf, shield.

SQEND, to spring up, climb. Skt. skand, to jump up, ascend; Gk. σκάνδ-αλον, the spring of a trap; L. scand-ere, to climb, scā-la (for *scand-la), a ladder. Ex. scandal, slander; scan, ascend, descend, scale (3), escalade.

SQEND, to shine, glow. Skt. chand, çchand, to shine, chand-ra(s), moon, chand-ana(s), sandal-wood tree; L. cand-ēre, to shine, cand-idus, white. Ex. candle, candid, incense, candour, chandelier, chandler, incendiary, &c. Also sandal-wood.

SQER (SKER), to shear, cut, cleave. Gk. κείρειν (κέρ-yειν), to shear, cut; Lith. ker-wis, an ax; AS. scer-an (pt. t. scær, pp. scor-en), to shear. Ex. *shear, share, sheer* (2), *shard, scar* (2), *scare, shore.* Cf. *scorpion, sharp, scarp, scrape.* And see **QERP, SEQ.**

SQEU (SKEU), to perceive, observe, beware of. Skt. *kav-i-,* wise, a seer, prophet, poet; Gk. κοέω, I mark, θυο-σκό-ος, an inspector of an offering; L. *cau-ēre,* to beware, *cau-tio,* caution; AS. *scēa-wian,* to look, behold. Ex. *caution, caveat; shew, show, scavenger, sheen.*

SQEU (SKEU), to cover, shelter. Skt. *sku,* to cover; Gk. σκῦ-τος, κύ-τος, skin; L. *cu-tis,* skin, *scū-tum,* a shield, *ob-scū-rus,* covered over, dark; OHG. *skiu-ra,* a shed, stable; Icel. *skjō-l,* a shelter, cover; AS. *hȳ-d,* hide, skin; Icel. *skȳ,* a cloud. Ex. *cuticle, obscure, escutcheon, esquire, squire, equerry; hide* (2), *scum, skim, sky, sheal, shieling, scowl.*

SREBH, to sup up, absorb. Gk. ῥοφ-έειν, to sup up; L. *sorb-ēre,* to sup up; Lith. *srēb-ti,* to sup up. Ex. *absorb.*

SREU (STREU), to flow. (Observe the insertion of T in Teutonic.) Skt. *sru,* to flow, *srō-ta(s),* a stream; Gk. ῥέειν (fut. ῥεύ-σομαι), to flow, ῥεῦ-μα, flood, ῥυ-θμός, rhythm (musical flow); Irish *sruaim,* stream; AS. *strēa-m,* stream. Ex. *rheum, rhythm, catarrh, diarrhœa, emerods; stream, streamer.*

STA (= stā); see **STHA.**

STAQ (STAH), to be firm. Skt. *stak,* to resist, Zend. *staχ-ra-,* strong, firm; OPruss. *panu-stac-la-,* steel for kindling fire; OHG. *stah-al,* OMerc. *stēl-i,* steel. Ex. *steel.*

STEBH; see **STEMBH.**

STEG(w), also **TEG(w)** (TEK), to cover, thatch. Skt. *sthag,* to cover; Gk. ἁ-στέγ-ειν, to cover, στέγ-ος, τέγ-ος, roof; L. *teg-ere,* to cover, *teg-ula,* tile, *tog-a,* garment; Irish *tigh,* a house; AS. *þæc,* thatch; Du. *dak,* thatch, *dek-ken,* to cover. Ex. *protect, tegument, toga, tile; thatch, deck;* also *shanty* (old house).

STEIG(w) (STEIK), to prick, pierce, stick, sting. Skt. *tij,* to be sharp, Zend. *tigh-ra-,* sharp, *tigh-ri-,* an arrow; Gk. στίζειν (*στίγ-γειν), to prick, στίγ-μα, a prick; L. *in-stig-āre,* to instigate; Goth. *stik-s,* a point; AS. *stic-e,* stitch (in the side). Ex. *stigma; instigate;* allied to *instinct, distinguish, stimulate, style* (1); cf. *tiger, stick* (1), *stitch, sting.*

STEIG-(w)H (STEIG), to stride, to climb. Skt. *stigh,* to ascend; Gk. στείχ-ειν, to go, march, στίχ-ος, a row, στοίχ-ος, a row; Lith. *staig-ùs,* hasty; AS. *stīg-an,* to climb. Ex. *acrostic, distich, hemistich; sty* (1), *sty* (2), *stile* (1), *stair, stirrup.*

STEMBH, STEBH (STEMB, STEB), to make firm, set fast; **STEMB** (STEMP), to stamp, step firmly. Skt. *stambh,* to make firm or hard, stop, block up; *stambh-a(s),* a post, pillar, stem, *stabh,* to fix, prop; Gk. ἁ-στεμφ-ής, fixed, fast, στέμβ-ειν, to stamp; AS. *staf,* a staff, prop, *staf-n, stem-n,* a stem of a tree; AS. *stemp-an,* to stamp, *stap-ul,* a post, pillar, *step-pan,* to step. Ex. *staff, stave, stem* (1), *stem* (2); also *stamp, step, staple* (1), *staple* (2); perhaps *stump.*

STEN, TEN (THEN), to groan, to stun, to thunder. Skt. *stan,* to sound, sigh, thunder; Gk. στέν-ειν, to groan; Στέν-τωρ, Stentor (loud-voiced); Lith. *sten-éti,* to groan, AS. *stun-ian,* to make a din. Also Skt. *tan,* to sound; L. *ton-āre,* to thunder; AS. *þun-or,* thunder. Ex. *detonate; stun, thunder; astonish, astound.*

STER, whence **STREU,** to strew, scatter, lay down. Skt. *star-a-,* a layer, bed; *stṛ,* to scatter, spread; *tār-as,* pl. stars; Gk. στόρ-νυμι, I spread out; L. *ster-nere,* to scatter, spread out (pp. *strā-tus*), *stru-ere,* to lay in order, heap up, build; Goth. *strau-jan,* to strew; AS. *strēow-ian,* to strew, scatter, *strēaw,* straw. Ex. *asterisk, asteroid; street, structure, instrument, consternation, stellar; stratum; strew, straw, star.*

STER, to be firm or rigid. Skt. *sthira(s),* firm, fixed; Gk. στερ-εός, solid, stiff, στεῖρα (*στερ-ya), a barren cow; Goth. *stair-ō,* a barren woman; L. *ster-ilis,* sterile, barren. Ex. *stereoscope, stereotype, sterile;* and cf. *stark, starch.*

STEU, probably for **STHEU,** to fix firmly. Skt. *sthav-ira(s),* fixed, firm; Gk. στῦ-λος, a pillar, στο-ά, a porch, σταυ-ρός, an upright pole or stake; L. *in-stau-r-āre,* to construct, build, restore; Goth. *stiu-r-jan,* to establish, OHG. *stiu-r-a,* a prop, staff, paddle, rudder; AS. *stēo-r,* a paddle or rudder. Ex. *stoic; star-board, steer* (2); *store, restore.* Cf. *steer* (1). Allied to **STHA.**

STEUD (STEUT), to strike. Skt. *tud,* to push; L. *tund-ere* (pt. t. *tu-tud-i*), to strike, beat; Goth. *staut-an,* to strike. Ex. *contuse, obtuse; stutter;* perhaps *tot, stoat.* And see *toil* (1).

STHA, STA (= sthā, stā), to stand, stand fast. Skt. *sthā,* to stand; Gk. ἴ-στη-ν, I stood, ἵ-στη-μι, I set, place; L. *stā-re,* to stand, *si-st-ere,* to set; G. *sthen,* to stand. Further allied to Goth. *standan,* AS. *stondan* (pt. t. *stō-d*), to stand, AS. *sted-e,* a place, stead; from a Teut. base STA-D. Also to AS. *stō-w,* a place. Ex. *statics, apostasy,* &c.; *stage, stamen, stamina, station, statute,* &c.; *stand, stead, stow, stall.* And cf. *stammer, stem* (3), *stool, stud* (1), *stud* (2).

SWAD (SWAT), to please the taste. Skt. *svad,* to taste well, to season; *svād-u-,* savoury, sweet; Gk. ἥδ-ύς, sweet; L. *suā-uis* (for *suad-uis*), sweet; O.Sax. *swōt-i,* sweet; AS. *swēt-e,* sweet. Ex. *suave, suasion, persuade, assuage; sweet.*

SWEID (SWEIT), to sweat. Skt. *svēd,* to sweat; *svēd-a(s),* sweat; Gk. ἶδ-ρώς, sweat; L. *sūd-āre,* to sweat, *sūd-or,* sweat; AS. *swāt,* sweat. Ex. *sudorific; sweat.*

SWEN, to resound, sound. Skt. *svan,* to sound; *svan-a(s),* sound; L. *son-āre,* to sound, *son-us,* sound; AS. *swin-sian,* to resound. Ex. *sound* (3), *sonata, sonnet, person, parson, sonorous, unison,* &c. Cf. *swan.*

SWEP (SWEF), to sleep. Skt. *svap,* to sleep; Gk. ὕπ-νος, sleep; L. *sop-or,* sleep, *somnus* (for *swep-nos*), sleep; AS. *swef-n,* a dream. Ex. *hypnotise; soporific, somnolence.*

SWER, to murmur, hum, speak. Skt. *svr,* to sound, *svar-a(s),* sound, voice, tone; L. *su-sur-rus,* murmur, whisper; AS. *swer-ian,* pt. t. *swōr,* to affirm, swear; *swear-m,* a swarm of bees. Ex. *swear, answer, swarm.*

TAK, to be silent. L. *tac-ēre,* Goth. *thah-an,* to be silent. Ex. *tacit; taciturn, reticent.*

TAU (= tāu), Teut. (thāw), to melt, thaw. Skt. *tō-ya-,* water; Gk. τή-κειν, to melt; L. *tā-bēs,* decay; AS. *þā-wian,* to thaw. Ex. *tabid, thaw.*

TEG(w), to cover; see **STEG(w).**

TEK (THEH), to beget. Gk. τεκ-εῖν, 2 aor. inf. of τίκτειν, to beget; AS. *þeg-en,* a thane; orig. boy, servant. Ex. *thane.*

TEKTH (tekþ), to fit, prepare, hew out, weave. Skt. *taksh,* to form, prepare, cut, hew; Gk. τέχ-νη, art, τέκτ-ων, carpenter; L. *tex-ere,* to weave; OChurch Slav. *tes-ati,* to hew. Ex. *technical, architect; text, subtle, toil* (2). (For the form of the root, see Uhlenbeck, Skt. Dict.)

TEL (THEL), to bear, tolerate, lift. Skt. *tul,* to lift, *tul-ā,* a balance, weight; Gk. τελ-αμών, belt for shield or sword, τάλ-αντον, balance, talent, τλῆ-ναι, to endure; L. *tol-lere,* to bear, *lā-tus* (for (tlātus = τλη-τός), borne; *tol-erāre,* to endure; AS. *þol-ian,* to endure. Ex. *talent, atlas, tantalise; extol, tolerate, trot, elate, prelate, relate, oblate, prolate, dilate, delay, collation, legislator, translate; thole* (2).

TEM, to be dark. Skt. *tam-as,* gloom; L. *tem-ere,* in the dark, blindly, rashly; *ten-ebræ,* darkness. Ex. *tenebrious, temerity.*

TEM, to cut. Gk. τέμ-νειν, to cut, τομ-ή, a cutting, τόμ-ος, part of a book (section), τέμ-ενος, sacred enclosure, τέν-δ-ειν, to gnaw; L. *tem-plum,* sacred enclosure, *ton-d-ēre,* to shear. Ex. *anatomy, tome; tonsure, temple.*

TEN (THEN), to stretch. Skt. *tan,* to stretch, *tan-u-,* thin (stretched out), *tan-tu-,* a thread; Gk. τείνειν (*τέν-γειν), to stretch, τόν-ος, tension, tone; L. *ten-d-ere,* to stretch, *ten-ēre,* to hold tight, *ten-uis,* thin; Goth. *than-jan,* to stretch out; AS. *þyn-ne,* thin. Ex. *hypotenuse, tone; tenacious, tender, tenuity, tend, tense* (2), *tent* (1), *tendon, tendril, tenor, tempt, tentative, toise,* &c.; *thin; dance.*

TENG, to dip, steep. Gk. τέγγ-ειν, L. *ting-ere,* to dip; OHG. *thunch-ōn,* G. *tunk-en,* to dip. Ex. *tinge, tincture, tint, stain.*

TENG (THENK), to consider, ponder on. L. *tong-ēre,* to think; Goth. *thagkjan* (= *thank-jan*), to think. Ex. *think, methinks, thanks, thought.*

TENQ (THENH), to be strong, grow thickly. Skt. *tañch,* to contract; Pers. *taug,* tight; Lith. *tenk-ù,* I have sufficient, *tank-us,* close, tight; Goth. *theih-an,* AS. *ge-þēon* (pp. *ge-þung-en*), to thrive; ONorse *þēt-tr,* tight. Ex. *thee* (2), *tight.*

TEP, to be hot. Skt. *tap,* to be warm; Russ. *top-ite,* to heat; L. *tep-ēre,* to be warm. Ex. *tepid.*

TER (THER), to pass through, reach; go through, rub, turn. (Two roots of the form TER, 'to go through,' and 'to rub, turn,' have probably coalesced.) 1. Skt. *tar-a(s),* a passage, ferry, *tār-a(s),* penetrating; *tār-aya,* to take across, *tir-as,* prep., across, through, over; Gk. τέρ-μα, goal, end; *in-trā-re,* to pass into, *trā-ns,* going through, across; Goth. *thair-h,* through; AS. *þȳr-el,* a hole. Ex. *avatar; enter, term, transom, trestle, through, thrill, thirl, thrum.* 2. Gk. τρῆ-σις, a boring through, τέρ-ετρον, a borer; L. *ter-ere,* to bore, rub; *tor-nāre,* to turn. Ex. *turn; trite, tribulation, detriment.*

TERQ (THERH), to twist, turn round. Skt. *tark-u-,* a spindle; Gk. ἄ-τρακ-τος, a spindle; L. *torqu-ēre,* to twist. Compare also (from Teut. THWERH) AS. *þweorh,* perverse, transverse, tord. *þverr,* perverse. Ex. *torment, tortu·e, torch, nasturtium, torsion, tort, tortoise.* Cf. *thwart, athwart, queer.*

TERS (THERS), to be dry, to thirst. Skt. *tṛsh,* to thirst; Gk. τέρσ-ομαι, τέρσ-ειν (for *ters-ēre*), to parch, pp. *tos-tus, terr-a* (for *ters-a*), dry ground; Goth. *thaurs-jan,* to thirst, *thaurs-tei,* thirst. Ex. *torrid, torrent, terrace, tureen, toast, terrier, inter, fumitory; thirst.* Perhaps *test.*

TEU (THEU), to be thick or fat. Skt. *tu,* to increase, be powerful, *tav-a(s),* strong; Gk. τύ-λος, τύ-λη, a hard swelling;

L. *tu-m-ēre*, to swell up, *tŭ-ber*, a round root, *tum-ulus*, a mound, *tum-ultus*, uproar ; Lith. *tau-kas*, fat of animals, *tù-k-ti*, to be fat ; AS. *þéo-h*, thigh, *þū-ma*, thumb, *þéa-w*, muscle. Ex. *tumid, tumult, tumulus, protuberance ; thigh, thumb, thews.*

TEUD (THEUT), to strike ; see **STEUD**.

TRE = **trē** (THRE, thrē), to twist ; from **TER**, to turn. AS. *þrā-wan*, to twist, throw ; *þrǣ-d*, thread. Ex. *throw, thread.*

TREM, also **TRES**, to tremble. Skt. *tras*, to tremble ; Gk. τρέ-ειν, (for *τρέσ-ειν), to tremble ; L. *terr-ēre* (for *ters-ēre*), to scare, cause to tremble. Also Gk. τρέμ-ειν, L. *trem-ere*, Lith. *trim-ti*, to tremble. Ex. *terror ; also tremble, tremulous, tremendous.*

TREUD (THREUT), to push, crowd, urge. L. *trūd-ere*, to push, urge ; Goth. *us-thriut-an*, to vex greatly, G. *ver-driess-en* ; AS. *þréot-an*, to afflict, vex, urge. Ex. *abstruse, extrude, intrude, obtrude, protrude ; threat, threaten.* Cf. *thrust.*

UL, to howl (imitative). Skt. *ul-ūka-*, an owl ; Gk. ὑλ-άω, I howl, ὀλ-ολ-ύζω, I shriek ; L. *ul-ul-a*, an owl ; AS. *ūl-e*, an owl. Ex. *owl, howl.*

WADH (WAD), to walk slowly, to wade. L. *uād-ere*, to go ; *uad-um*, a ford ; AS. *wad-an*, to wade. Ex. *evade ; wade.*

WAQ (WAH), to swerve, go crookedly, totter ; also **WAG** (WAK), to bend, totter. Skt. *vak-ra(s)*, crooked, bent, *vañch*, to go crookedly, totter, waver ; L. *uac-illāre*, to waver, reel ; AS. *wōh*, crooked, bent. Also L. *uag-us*, wandering, going aside ; Lith. *wing-is*, a bend of a river, *weng-ti*, to flinch, to shirk work, OHG. *wink-an*, to move aside, to waver ; AS. *wanc-ol*, wavering, weak. Ex. *vacillate, vague ; wench, woo.* Cf. *wink, winch.*

WAN (= **wā-n**), to fail, lack, be wanting ; from the root **WA** (wā), with the same sense. Skt. *ū-n-a(s)*, inferior, wanting ; Gk. εὐ-ν-ις, bereft ; L. *uā-n-us*, vain ; Goth. *wa-n-s*, deficient. Ex. *vain ; wane, wanion, want, wanton.* Cf. *vacant.*

WE (= **wē**), to blow. Skt. *vā*, to blow ; Gk. ἄ-η-μι (ἄ-ϝη-μι), I blow ; L. *ue-ntus*, wind ; Goth. *wai-an*, to blow, *wi-nds*, wind ; Lith. *vė-jas*, wind ; Russ. *vie-iat(e)*, to blow, *vie-ter'*, wind ; AS. *wi-nd*, wind, *we-der*, weather. Ex. *ventilate, fan ; wind* (1), *weather.*

WEBH (WEB), to weave. Skt. *ūrṇa-vābh-i-*, a spider, lit. ' wool-weaver ' ; Gk. ὑφ-αίνειν, to weave ; G. *web-en*, AS. *wef-an*, to weave. Ex. *weave, web, weft, woof, weevil.* Cf. *wafer, wasp.*

WED (WET), to wet, moisten. Skt. *ud-an-*, water, *und*, to moisten ; Gk. ὕδ-ωρ, water ; L. *und-a*, wave ; Russ. *vod-a*, water ; Goth. *wat-ō*, water, AS. *wæt-er*, water, *wēt*, wet. Ex. *Hydrogen ; hydra ; undulate, abound, redundant, surround ; wet, water, otter ; vodka.*

WEDH (WED), to redeem a pledge, to pledge. L. *uas* (gen. *uad-is*), a pledge ; Goth. *wad-i*, AS. *wed-d*, a pledge ; Lith. *wad-oti*, to redeem a pledge. Ex. *wed ; wage, wager, gage* (1), *engage.*

WEG (WEK), to be vigorous or watchful, to wake ; hence the extended form **WEKS** (WEHS), to increase ; hardly allied to **AUG(w)**. Skt. *vaj-ra(s)*, thunder-bolt (from its strength) ; *vāj-a(s)*, vigour ; L. *ueg-ēre*, to excite, arouse, *uig-ēre*, to be vigorous, *uig-il*, watchful ; AS. *wac-an*, to come to life, *wac-ian*, to watch. Also Skt. *vaksh*, to grow, Goth. *wahs-jan*, to wax, AS. *weax-an*, to wax. Ex. *vegetable, vigour, vigilant ; wake* (1), *wake* (2), *wax* (1).

WĒG(w) (WEK), to be moist or wet. Gk. ὑγ-ρός, moist ; (perhaps) L. *ū-dus*, moist, *ū-mor*, moisture ; Icel. *vōk-r*, moist. Ex. *hygrometer ; wake* (1). Perhaps *humid, humour* ; and see *ox*.

WEGH (WEG), to carry, convey, remove. Skt. *vah* (for *vagh*), to carry, *vāh-a(s)*, a vehicle ; Gk. ὄχ-ος (*ϝόχ-ος), a chariot ; L. *ueh-ere*, to carry, convey ; *uē-na*, a vein (duct) ; AS. *weg-an*, pt. t. *wæg*, to bear, carry, *weg*, a way, *weeg*, a wedge (mover), *wæg-n*, a wain. Ex. *vehicle, vein ; weigh, way, wain, waggon, wey, wag.* Perhaps *vehement.*

WEI, to bind, wind, plait. Skt. *vī*, *vay-a*, to weave, *vi-ta(s)*, wound, *vī-tasa(s)*, a kind of reed ; Gk. *ī-téa*, a willow ; L. *uī-tis*, a vine, *uī-men*, a twig, *ui-ēre*, to bind ; AS. *wī-r*, a wire, *wī-ðig*, a willow, withy. Ex. *vine, ferrule, vice* (2) ; *wire, withe, withy, wine.* And see *wind* (2).

WEID (WEIT), to know, to wit ; orig. to see. Skt. *vid*, to know, *vēd-a(s)*, knowledge ; Gk. εἶδ-ον (for *ϝεῖδ-ον), I saw, οἶδ-a (for *ϝοῖδ-α), I know ; L. *uid-ēre*, to see, *uī-sere*, to go to see, visit ; Goth. *wit-an*, to know, *wait*, I know. Ex. *Veda ; history, idol, idea ; vision, visit, &c. ; wit* (1), *wit* (2), *witness, wiseacre ; ywis, wise.* Also *advice, &c.*

WEID, to sing. Gk. ἀ-είδ-ειν (for ἀ-ϝείδ-ειν), to sing ; ἀοιδ-ή, ᾠδ-ή, a song ; cf. OIrish *faed*, W. *gwaedd*, an outcry, shout. Ex. *ode, epode, palinode.*

WEIG (WEIK), and **WEIQ** (WEIK), to give way. (1) Skt. *vij*, to fear, *veg-a-s*, speed, haste ; Goth. *wik-ō*, succession ; AS. *wic-an*, to give way, *wāc*, weak, *wōc-an*, to weaken ; *wic-u*, a week (change of phase of the moon) ; *wic-e*, a wich-elm. (2) Gk. εἴκ-ειν (for *ϝείκ-ειν), to give way ; L. *uic-is* (gen. case), change ; OHG. *weh-sal*, G. *wech-sel*, change. Ex. *weak, week, wich-elm ; vicissitude, vicar.*

WEIK (WEIH), to come to, to enter. Skt. *viç*, to enter, *vēç-a(s)*, a settler, a neighbour, *vēç-man*, a house ; Gk. οἶκ-ος (for *ϝοῖκ-ος), a house ; L. *uīc-us*, a village, *uīc-īnus*, neighbouring ; Goth. *weih-s*, a village. Ex. *economy, diocese ; vicinage, wick* (2), *bailiwick.*

WEIP (WEIF), to tremble, shake, vibrate. Skt. *vēp*, to tremble ; cf. L. *uib-rāre*, to tremble ; ONorse *veif-a*, to vibrate, flap, flutter. Ex. *waif, waive ; cf. vibrate.*

WEIQ (WEIH), to fight, conquer. L. *uinc-ere*, pt. t. *uīc-i*, to conquer ; Goth. *weih-an*, to contend ; AS. *wīg*, war. Ex. *vanquish, victory, convict, evince, convince, &c.*

WEIQ (WEIH), to give way ; see **WEIG**.

WEL, to will, to choose, like. Skt. *vṛ*, to choose, select, prefer, *var-a(s)*, a wish ; L. *uel-le*, to wish ; Goth. *wil-jan*, to will, *wil-ja*, will, *wal-jan*, to choose, *wail-a*, well. Ex. *voluntary, voluptuous ; will* (1), *will* (2), *well* (1), *weal, wealth, welcome, welfare.*

WEL, to wind, turn, roll ; well up (as a spring). Skt. *val*, to turn here and there, turn round, *val-ana(m)*, a turning, agitation ; Gk. ἑλ-ιξ, a spiral, ἐλ-ίσσειν, to turn round ; OHG. *wel-la*, a billow, AS. *wel-la*, a well or spring. Also in the form WEL-W ; cf. Gk. εἰλύ-ειν, to enfold, L. *uolu-ere*, to roll, Goth. *af-walw-jan*, to roll away. Ex. *helix ; voluble, volute, revolve, &c. ; valve ; well* (2), *wallow, waltz, welter.* Also *wale ; cf. walk.*

WEM, to vomit. Skt. *vam*, Gk. ἐμ-εῖν, L. *vom-ere*, to vomit. Ex. *emetic ; vomit.*

WEN, to honour, love, strive for, seek to get. Skt. *van*, to serve, honour, ask, beg ; L. *uen-us*, love, *uen-erāri*, to honour, *uen-ia*, favour ; AS. *win-nan* (pt. t. *wann*), to fight for, labour, endure (whence *I. win*). Hence also AS. *wūñchh*, to wish, AS. *wūsc*, a wish. Ex. *venerable, venereal, venial ; win*, also *winsome, wish.* Allied to *wean, ween, wont* ; and to *won* (to dwell).

WEQw, to cry out, to speak. Skt. *vach*, to speak, *vach-as*, speech ; Gk. ἔπ-ος, a saying, a word ; L. *uox* (gen. *uōc-is*), voice, *uoc-āre*, to call. Ex. *epic ; voice, vocal, avouch, advocate, invoke, &c.*

WER, to cover, surround, defend. Skt. *vṛ*, to screen, cover, surround, *vṛ-ti-*, an enclosure, *vār-aya*, to keep off ; Gk. ἔρ-υσθαι, to protect ; Goth. *war-jan*, AS. *wer-ian*, to protect. Ex. *warren, warison, garret ; weir.* Cf. *aperient, cover.*

WER, to be wary, observe, see. Gk. ὁρ-άω (*ϝορ-άω), I observe, see ; L. *uer-ēri*, to guard against, to fear ; AS. *wær*, wary. Ex. *revere, reverend ; beware, wary.* Also *ward, guard.* Perhaps also *ware* (1), *worth* (1).

WER, to speak. Gk. εἴρ-ειν (for *ϝέρ-γειν), to say ; ῥή-τωρ (*ϝρή-τωρ), a speaker, orator. Hence **WERDH**, to say. O. Irish *ford-at*, they say (Stokes-Fick, p. 274) ; L. *uerb-um*, a word ; AS. *word*, a word. Ex. *verb, word* ; also *rhetoric.*

WERG (WERK), to work. Skt. *vṛj-apas* ; Gk. ἔργ-ον (*ϝέργ-ον), work ; ὄργ-ανον, an instrument ; Goth. *waurk-jan*, to work ; AS. *weorc*, work. Ex. *organ, orgy, chirurgeon, surgeon ; work, wrought, wright, work.*

WERGH (WERG), to strangle, choke. Lith. *wersz-ti*, to strangle ; MHG. *ir-werg-an*, to strangle ; AS. *wyrg-an*, to strangle, worry. Ex. *worry.*

WERT (WERTH), to turn, become. Skt. *vṛt*, to turn, turn oneself, exist, be ; L. *uert-ere*, to turn ; Goth. *wairth-an* (pt. t. *warth*), to become ; AS. *weorð-an*, to become. Ex. *verse, vertex, vortex, prose, avert, averse, convert, &c. ; worth* (2), *weird, -ward* (suffix). Also *verst.*

WES, to clothe, put on clothes. Skt. *vas*, to put on clothes ; Gk. ἕσ-θος (*ϝέσ-θος), clothing, ἕννυμι (*ϝέσ-νυμι), I clothe ; L. *ues-tis*, clothing, garment ; Goth. *was-jan*, to clothe ; AS. *wer-ian*, to wear clothes. Ex. *vest, invest, divest, vestment ; wear* (1) ; *gaiter.*

WES, to dwell, live, be. Skt. *vas*, to dwell, to pass the night, to live, *vās-tu*, a house, *vas-ati-*, a dwelling-place ; Gk. ἑσ-τία, a hearth, ἀσ-τύ, a city ; L. *Ves-ta*, goddess of the household, *uer-na*, a home-born slave ; Goth. *wis-an*, AS. *wes-an*, to be. Ex. *vernacular, Vesta, vestal ; was, wast, were, wert.* Cf. *wassail.*

WES, to shine ; also as **AWES, AUS (āwes, āus)**, to shine. Skt. *vas*, *uchchh*, to shine ; *ush*, to burn ; *vas-antas*, spring ; Gk. ἤ-ως, ἠ-ώς, Æolic αὔ-ως, dawn, ἔ-αρ (for *ϝέσ-αρ), spring ; L. *aur-ōr-a* (for *aus-ōs-a*), dawn, *uēr* (for *ues-r*), spring, *aus-ter*, south wind ; AS. *éas-t*, adv., in the east. Ex. *vernal ; east, Easter.*

WIDH, to lack. Skt. *vidh*, *vindh*, to lack, be in want of (Macdonell) ; Gk. ἠ-ίθ-εος, unmarried ; Skt. *vidh-avā*, bereft of a widow ; L. *uid-ua*, a widow ; AS. *wid-uwe*, a widow. Cf. L. *di-uid-ere*, to divide (pp. *di-uī-sus*). Ex. *widow* ; also *divide, division.*

YAG (yāg, yag), to worship, reverence. Skt. *yaj*, to sacrifice, worship, *yaj-yu(s)*, worshipping, pious ; Gk. ἅγ-ιος, holy. Ex. *hagiographa.*

YES, to ferment. Skt. *yas*, to exert oneself, *yēsh*, to bubble, seethe ; Gk. ζέ-ειν (perf. mid. ἔ-ζεσ-μαι), to seethe, ζέσ-μα, a decoc-

ON THE ORIGINS OF SPEAKING

tion, ζεσ-τός, sodden; ἐκ-ζε-μα, a pustule; AS. *gis-t*, yeast. Ex. *eczema*; *yeast*.

YEU, to drive away, preserve from. Skt. *yu*, to drive away, preserve from, keep aloof, *yāv-aya*, to drive away; L. *iu-uāre* (pp. *iū-tus*), to assist. Ex. *adjutant, aid, coadjutor*.

YEU, to bind, to mix. Skt. *yu*, to bind, to fasten, join, mix; *yū-sha-*, pease soup; L. *iū-s*, broth; Gk. ζύ-μη, leaven. Ex. *zymotic*; *juice*. See **YEUG, YOS**.

YEUG, to join, to yoke together. Skt. *yuj*, to join, connect *yug-a(m)*, a yoke; Gk. ζεύγ-νυμι, I yoke, ζυγ-όν, yoke; L. *iung-ere*, to join, *iug-um*, a yoke, *con-iux*, a spouse, *iux-tā*, near; AS. *geoc*, yoke. Ex. *syzygy*; *jugular, conjugal, join, junction, joust, jostle*; *yoke*. See **YEU**.

YOS (= **yōs**), to gird. Zend *yās-ta-*, girt; Gk. ζώννυμι (for *ζώσ-νυμι), I gird, ζώ-νη, a girdle, ζωσ-τήρ, a girdle; Lith. *jos-ta*, a girdle. Ex. *zone*. See **YEU** (2).

APPENDIX C

SUMERIAN OR WHAT PROFESSOR IFRAH KNOWS

Babel I believe is correctly identified in the Bible. It was the Akkadian (Semitic) take over from the Sumerians which marked the demise, in that part of the world at least, of the age old consciousness of the Lithic language idiom, which could (in theory) be deciphered by anyone at all who was fully acquainted with the principles of speech developed over hundreds of thousands of years up to that time. It is hard to imagine these days Semitic culture as a hill-billy outfit, but I believe that is what it was, they were fighters and doers rather than thinkers. "Shem" came from the setting sun, the Semites were Western barbarians to the Sumerians who were immigrants from an eastern Eden. The first migrations out of Africa settled where East was. It was in the direction of the sunrise. "Shem" is from the Lithic elements Shai-mai, Sun-set ones, Westerners. As outsiders, so far as the Sumerians, Those-who-went-West were concerned, the Shem were able to bestow upon humanity a freedom from the dead hand of the old convention which had trammeled and confined the mind for countless hundreds of generations. It was a far greater emancipation than any encountered since. These Semitic wild men simply tore up the bedrock of literate civilization and cheerily carried on without it, paying homage to the empty forms of Sumerian language and math to start with but never adopting Sumerian thinking, just some of their myth as factual.

These conclusions I have firmed up from my study of Professor Georges Ifrah´s epoch making book, six hundred double pages long, "The Universal History of Numbers from Prehistory to the Invention of the Computer", and in particular his chapters on Sumerian and Akkadian, which I have approached in almost pi-ratical fashion and ransacked for cases illustrating the Lithic hypotheses. The fact is I have not had access myself to the work on the Sumerian language of the last few decades, before which what was known was rudimentary, so that I wrote it off and gave it up. I should make it absolutely clear that Professor Ifrah is in no way responsible for any of the speculations I have hung on his language data or the use I have made of his original work – without, I have to say, first seeking his permission. So I advertise his genius but do not quote him.

Numbers were recorded before writing proper was current. So the oldest records so far deciphered are of numbers and through them of course we have access to the primitive thinking which lay behind them. In so far as the language is deciphered, the numbers can be quarried for Lithic language roots. In Sumerian, number symbols were based on the clay pellets previously used to record quantity, which came to be enclosed in clay bullae or hollow balls sealed with cylinder seals to authenticate the record. Units were short cones or elongated roly-polys of clay. In so far as the cones were pointed it seems to me they give some indication that they were already designated shi, because shi had the meaning upright direction and the cones were pointing upwards, while the alternative roly-polys professor Ifrah points out may well have been modelled on sticks used earlier as tallies. Tens were pellets of clay, spherical roly-polys. Sixties were larger cones, larger copies of the vertical pointers. 600s were similar large cones but with a rounded impression on one side, the mark for ten, making sixties ten, or a sixty worth of tens, in place of a sixty worth of ones which the large pointed cone on its own conveyed. 3600, the next unit up (60 X 60) was a larger ball, a jumbo ten.

When these calculi, literally stones (from the original pebbles, Greek khalix, kha-lai-kai's, solid-ocean-shaped, used for counting as simple tallies before numbers), came to be written down on the outsides of bullae a large and a small round nosed reed were used, or one with a large and a small end. The Cone and long roly-poly became a snub nosed notch made by impressing the reed obliquely to give length to the impression it made, while the round roly-poly became a circular impression with the stylus applied vertically. This latter technique of course was already in use to mark ten on the solid 600s counter.

Now the Lithic contributions to these schemes I will briefly attempt to disclose in what follows. It suggests to me incidentally the Sumerians were perhaps still conscious of Lithic semantic roots and passed them on in some measure to the Western languages as well as the Semitic ones. I have in mind here Stephen Oppenheimer's book "Eden in the East", which purports to demonstrate the Garden of Eden is now under the South China Sea due to the great glacier melt as the Ice Ages started to recede, only the highlands of Malaya remaining above water. "Eden" is the Orient, Ai-tai'n, as it [the sun] is born in Lithic phonemes. Orient from Latin oriens is a very similar concept, au-rai-en(s), that one/where-rising, where the sun rises, the orient. Malaya means garden land, but you have to know what the ancients described as a garden. It was not a matter of parterres or rose beds. That was all a long way in the future. What made a garden was irrigation, in Lithic Ma-lai, Ma earth, lai flooding. Lai in Lithic was the instinct of water to run down into the lows. The ancient riverine civilisations were founded on digging channels (canals) leading the water from the river to run down into the paddi fields. Malaya is not noted for its irrigation, being far too hilly for this kind of technique in ancient days. But the lowlands to the east of Malaya have great river beds still traceable beneath the shallow seas, the birthplace of the technique, from which the Sumerians were expelled by the rising tides. Their expulsion brought the technique first to Iraq; and then to Egypt when the Semites had learnt from the Sumerians. The harsh Semitic Cains of those days learned the skills of the alien Sumerian Abels, the irrigators.

So the Sumerians came by sea from Eden as their lands shrank, bringing their civilisation, such as it was, with them. The Semites, descendants of Shem in the Bible, were the Westerners so far as the Sumerians were concerned, Shem or (Lithic) Shai-mai, Sun goes-down ones, or the light extinguished ones, or life murdered ones: Western barbarians. They were the Akkadians who attacked out of the Western deserts. We should remind ourselves here of all the other associations of shai and sai in the Lithic subconscious mind, as the subconscious mind became the receptacle for the Lithic perceptions rejected by the barbarians. Ish, fire, from the sound made by the dunked burning brand, shai and sai flamed, warmed around the hearth, cosy, comfortable, even randy (from the relaxing warmth around the hearth), su altogether warmed, enjoyment, pleasure, leisure, delighting, delightful, delight. Compare Sanskrit Su-kara, pleasure-maker for sugar, a nice taste, Sanskrit Turkish delight, delight maker in Lithic. The Semites learned from the Sumerians after defeating them, Cain versus Abel. They were never in Eden, for them it was a Shangri-La denied by the rising tide to mankind for ever because (Shem supposed) of the hubris of the Sumerians who had it too good and knew too much, as well as being a great deal better dressed after their seminal experience in this department. The Sumerians were banished for ever and the Semites borrowed their predicament. I think God must have chosen them later, perhaps after an early Pharaoh (Pa-hei-Ra-au-hei, Ra's Penis, may He ever be praised) thought to cut back his foreskin so his glans, the rounded out knob on the end, always stuck out ever ready to ray and initiate a sexual encounter, as befitted the Divine Organ with its erogenous rays; where before He had had to wait for the equivalent feminine ray to be fired first to withdraw His muzzle cover, so he could respond in proper fashion; and Abraham ("Aba-Ra-Ha-mai"), Father-God's-Great Joy-Engendered, God's Favourite Son, then proseletised the trick, in order to similarly promote all of the male sex over their sisters; and no doubt at the same time to advance the male dialectical God over the Cow Goddess, the wet nurse of the human race, sometimes known as Isis, or in the original Egyptian Au-Siti, Universal Lady – Sai Ti, vertically tapped, the Sumerian symbol was the pubic triangle with its vertical slit, offering warmth and pleasure. Mrs Grundy might not care for these rather earthy early derivations but, in Sumer and before, any consideration of her would have been an anachronism.

The Sumerian for the number one was ges, gesh. The Lithic derivation of the phonemes kai and Shai, slovened over the millennia to Gesh here, are as follows. Kai is from the clack of flint on knapped flint, conjuring up simultaneously the conceptions of striking and hardness, whence flake, chip and then inscribe as developments of the striking. In Gesh the kai element should I think be read as inscribed, or perhaps struck out or struck in. Shai comes originally from the dunked brand which said ishsh, whence fire, whence inter alia that principal sun or fire source, a volcano in the sky, spitting out fire as light. Then also as the flame leaps upwards that upward nissus precisely, and so high up as in sierra in Spanish and shan in Chinese for high mountains, and a whole lot of other meanings developed in chapter 14 which are not strictly germane in this context.

Shang in Chinese is up, and dji in many aborigine languages across Australia means up also. Here the upward direction is the relevant semantic content; and in particular and quite precisely Kai-Shai, whence Gesh, means a carved or inscribed upright. All around the world stone age folk have kept tally of quantity by scoring ||||| and so on, sometimes improving the count by scoring the fifth line across the first four, to make a handful or five barred gate which publicans with slates and other primitives are said to employ still to this day. Gesh also meant wood in Sumerian, and this has to be explained. Perhaps it was the earlier meaning and as some tallies were sticks, bamboo counters perhaps, Professor Ifrah speculates numbers may have been referred to as woods or sticks. But Lithic semantic contents can handle the nomenclature without any of these assumptions. Kai, as well as the striking and carving could also refer to the medium, rock and rock hard, and shai was flame and burning before ever it was up. Wood was thus the hard flammable element in the stone age vocabulary, by contrast with rocks which were Gaia (the Greek for the solid earth), Gai-aaa, Hard for Ever. The Egyptian was Geb, from Kai Bai, Hard [in its very] Being. You can get from Bai to being in chapter 4. In those days before blast furnaces the minerals were adamantine, unchangeable, while wood had this extra utility as fuel. It is no surprise to find these contrasting properties reflected in the language. Stone admittedly is ultimately from Ish-tau-'n, fire born'n, stun, stan, stone; whereas stand from sto stare in Latin is to become upright (from ish-ta), and then to stay that way. Standing stones are monuments to Lithic language roots, whatever else those who erected them had in mind. For the Sumerians it would appear an upwards stroke was the definition of singularity. There is more on this concept in chapter 16 on thinking. It was a criterion rather than a category, as worked over in that chapter, a simple upright I, not a T of dual dimensions from whence the categorical loop of collation, paradigmatically the circle, was derived. Shu, all the uprights (digits), is hand in Chinese to this day. They were counting on their fingers. Sa is one in Malay, sometimes elaborated to the fuller form of which it is supposed to be the abbreviation, Satu, the upright dimension of the Tau cross, or else the –tau being the cut made. In English it is just the seeds which do the shooting up, and not the fingers.

Professor Ifrah has a lot more on Gesh in Sumerian. As well as unit, one, from the semantic derivation of the inscribed upright stroke, it carried other more interesting meanings: the erect phallus, male and man. The male Lithic mind never strayed far from its own genitalia, a trait we have I believe in some measure inherited. The Lithic elements Kai and Shai evidently suggested sexual pointers as well as numerical indicators. Since Kai could mean kindle as well as knap and strike – struck flints sometimes emit sparks – "Kindled-go-up" will have appeared to our hominid forebears as neat thinking for an erection, the girls with their sexual rays up to their mischief again hunkered around the hearth in their birthday suits winking at the boys they fancied. Once you have established that etymology, to be male was to respond thus. Adam was a gardener watering the earth. He was the mali which is from the Sanskrit root for gardener. He was the mali or male fecundating the female also and making her fertile. To be male was to be a man, homo, the one that also does all the planting of the seed. Here is the explanation of the curious similarity of the roots for humanity and the soil which has caused some simpletons to speculate our forebears regarded their species as earth bound in some way, where they should have been directing their attention to etymology. We shall see shortly that mai the downward directed nissus was used to indicate the secondary sex the female, the gardener's or planter's pleasure[1], the fertile soil planted by Adam the gardener, gravid not spry like man the hunter, an earth grubber, adept with their grubbing sticks, but not a runner. Male chauvinism is certainly recorded in the oldest language roots, and may even in part have been inspired by them. On reflection the two processes are essentially the same, since the original linguistic roots are psychosemantic, that is they arise from human thinking in response to the surrounding environmental prompts, internal as well as external.

The Sumerians appear not to have highly regarded the Tau as a numeral symbol. Their Tau or Tao followed a different dialectic, from birth to becoming and so to a route or path, a way for going. It is in chapter 6. For the number 2 the Sumerians used Min, and the Lithic semantic contents of this phoneme "ma", whence mai and mi, can I think show why. Of the consonants only the sibilants (hisses) sh and s and the hums m and n can be uttered continuously for as long as you have breath. As such they were in a way honorary vowels. Not only that but with the sibilants the breath is obviously being expelled from the mouth, while with the hums it clearly is not because the mouth remains shut and indeed you can still hum, if not quite so comfortably, while holding your nose as well. All the other consonants are strictly and solely breaks between vowels or point initials, and it is only the vowels with them that can be continued indefinitely, particularly aaa, as medical wisdom has spotted. So the sibilants and hums were supposed in Lithic times and terms to be out on their own, a pair of non vowels but not merely consonants either, breaks between vowels but not solely confined to that role, making them rather special twins. Cutting cackle, ma was identified as the opposite pole to Sa of the same criterion, they were polar opposites, a complementary pair. That implied ma meant down because sa meant up. Most of the meanings of the ma phoneme follow from that one very early, and one is inclined to say original psychosemantic content, although there was confirmatory evidence for our hominid forebears they were on the right track in so far as men said "Hrmph!"or some such, in clearcut cases just "Mmmm!"as they heaved away at a heavy rock. The reason is that maa is the expression of a stressed stomach, the muscles under stress or from the stress of hunger itself. Weight expressed the go-down instinct which could crush your foot just as the flame expressed the go-up instinct which could burn your hand. In both cases the trick was to keep out of the line of fire of these natural drives, just as we duck today when bullets are flying about. So the second Sumerian incised vertical stroke, if it was to be distinguished in its nature from the first and named must be described as a down stroke if the first already had the up tag for its name: QED. They were thinkers, after their kind. These immanent instincts of phenomena were anthropomorphic and simplistic for today, but they passed muster as wisdom for hundreds of millennia and nobody spotted anything wrong; so we should perhaps exercise some caution before placing our full dependence upon the workings of the human mind today.

It is perhaps moderately relevant to interject here that since sa and ma were identified as opposing poles of the same directional criterion, that is having an astonishing commonality not immediately apparent, sama, the two ends of the criterion, came to stand for their commonality and meant same across a wide spectrum of languages, and not confined to any one of the single families identified today. Partridge has a fine collation over four columns on pages 584 and 585, but without offering any reasoning towards explaining the meanings. The term criterion itself is indeed an elaborated blood relative of Gesh, since karai is engraved and terai is a drawn out or stretched out and thus a straight line, originally thought of as a division between two categories rather than as I use it as a polar discriminator. The Greek krisis from which criterion is derived, curiously meant sifting. Kara-sisi(si) is to make, or better break down, into all the verticals, ie individual items, in this case grains or particles rather than sticks or strokes. Etymology is full of these whimsical twists you need a nimble mind to pick up.

They did not crop up in a twinkle, they were brewed over the millennia. A criterion separates out not a pile of grain but a particular item.

Three in Sumerian was es, esh. Since a is the unmarked general continuative (vowel) and esh is from the Lithic ai-shai – whence since i is the diminutive reduplicative, we would be justified in thinking this stood for continuous duplication of upright strokes, with the meaning many, as perhaps it originally did. But if so it appears the Sumerian psyche redefined it as 'an other upright' or 'a go-on-one' – leaving you to divine it was meant to be added to the previous two, a thoroughly clumsy representation of three, suggestive of the mental confusion which undoubtedly existed over this third digit because of the dialectical Tau (the triune twins, a and i, with u, both of them) getting in the way. Does it perhaps mark the derivation of numeration from the original simple distinction between one thing and another. Es or Esh was another single upright to add to gesh and min: one up, two down, three up again.

Four was limmu which appears to have been contrived from the Lithic elements Lai-en-mu, a loop or link or assemblage (category)-of-two mins, a looping or pooling of two mins, putting two mins together, (mu dual is two mi), two twos making four. If min was two, mu was already four since u was the dual completive substantive vowel. Don't bother about the presence or absence of terminal –n. It is only a terminal when it is terminal.

Five was ia, certainly succinct Lithic. The phoneme i, the diminutive reduplicative is used in that sense precisely: items, you might say; followed by the first vowel, general and therefore inclusive, all as well as first, one, unity, unit. The first item-unit or lot of items, originally a hand of digits, is five. We are in he right area because the Sumerian for hand was shu – all the fingers upright which was evidently the fingers being counted by being raised one by one.

Six, 'as' or 'ash' is then just aa + shi: aa is extend or go on + shi, one upright: add one (making six).

Seven, imin, we may then similarly conclude is elided from ia-min, five and two which is seven. Perhaps in turn elided from ia-aa-min, five-add-two.

Eight is Ussu and is probably from the Lithic elements u-su-su, u the dual, su doubled, su doubled again, 2 X 2 X 2, which makes eight. At one time this will have ranked as a clever piece of figuring, the average intelligence liable to get lost somewhere between the first and the second su. Once you could get this methodology into your head you were half way to becoming a Sumerian accountant. But why should shu mean doubled when it also meant a hand of five fingers raised in the digit before eight? Refer to chapter 14. The sibilant, from flame gulled warm, to warm blooded, to live, to active, to action. In Sumer the sibilant meant all those, that is any of them: dual action was Sumerian for times two.

Nine is ilimmu, elided from ia-lai-en-mu, one a-pooled-dual two, 5 and a bunch of two twos (mu is the dual of mi) which makes nine. The elision involved in ilimmu is routine. Math was an esoteric art in those days and we are beginning to see why.

Ten was u, written o, and is the inclusive "one" or unity or unit. Originally the vowels were treated as markers sometimes but at other times as standing on their own. So a was a but i could appear as ai and vice versa; and u could be au and vice versa. These became the dipthongs e and o. In other words it was moot whether i and u were merely glosses on the general vowel a or independent vocables making up a trinity with a. The issue is still unresolved. We still have a Holy Trinity, a whole which is a trinity, a single but at the same time Triune God, a synthetic dialectic with three elements, Tria Juncta in Uno, Iauai the dialectical deity, and now Marx's gloss on it all, reinventing the wheel in the form of dialectical materialism. From a rational point of view the Vowel Oon is an atavistic thinking habit, but that in no way impugns any Deity caught up in its web. This dialectical thinking was never any part of a Divine scheme, simply the result of Lithic language roots which did not know how to count beyond two (which was treated as a division into two, a parturition – a birth originally) and when challenged to go beyond that step the primitive mind misconstrued the idea of a third step forward as some kind of consummation of the first parturition, namely its reconciliation making the two whole again, pulling back from any further brain damage, a repair job rather than another item. Consequently we lisped one, two, both of them; originally our whole numeration, strictly limited and ill informed, actually handling only the first two items, a division and not an iteration at all. It went one, ie the split, making two and then what you had got, a pair, both of them, and after that just a mass more of them (many). That is why a number of languages still have a dual case as well as a proper plural, as also why u can stand for dual and then all of them in both senses, a dual or a totality for the Lithic mind. As Professor Ifrah remarks the classical Chinese for forest was three trees, the third sign indicated the completive, the totality as well as a third item, or perhaps even before a third item, instead just a plurality: one, another, lots of others. Similarly the sign for man three times meant a crowd, the whole gamut of them; and in Egypt three glyphs were repeated for the plural or three lines after the glyph would do, and the pronunciation indicated by the three lines, though Professor Ifrah does not mention it – or perhaps know it, since I believe it to be my own discovery – was u. This pattern was strictly unanswerable to reason and was therefore bumblingly imagined as indicative of Ultimate Reality beyond comprehension, by early religionists as well as by Marxists rather more recently. In both cases delving in the subconscious for mystical inspiration led to what ultimately turns out to be a comicality. Klaus Fuchs was a notable example of a proto-Sumerian mind set, with nuclear physics superimposed. These dredged up illuminations can be identified because they present themselves as prior to logic from persistence in the mental matrix from the beginning of time, or at any rate of human thinking. On reflection it ought to appear that such reliance upon our Lithic psychosemantic perceptions is never warranted. Caveat Emptor! Those who buy into these kinds of thinking patterns are setting themselves up for some nasty surprises: eventually a self revelation as patsies bent on stealing the Emperor's clothes. Nevertheless these are not all joke figures in the West, mere Scargills of academia. They include senatorial figures gracing university high tables, cabinet offices and scientific institutions handling nuclear physics. Meanwhile in Sumeria ten was just circular and symbolised the first bundling into a unit other than the singular. These numbers have been very parsimonious with the verbage, so we are inclined to wonder, in an age notorious for its verbosity, if so much meaning can be derived from so little. Be reassured. In chapter one the tale of Yosemite in California is told. Officially translated as the Navaho word for a bear, it is actually the sentence in Navaho "That is our tribal mother!", (Ia-ushi-ma-i-tai). We moderns are the mavericks using word strings long enough to make a whole sentence. We waffle. The Navaho uses seven phonemes where we use twenty one letters – and then go on to identify their sentence as a single word.

Professor Ifrah leaves out the teens and goes next to twenty, so we proceed to twenty too, recorded as nis or nish, which is from the Lithic nai-shi, another one (to be added to the first ten unit). It got to mean another one in a fairly roundabout way from new, as also now. Its original psychosemantic content was to orgasm, as the sexual excitement mounted and held breath was suddenly let go with a hominid gasp identified as Naaa. It acquired the extension to copulate, and this in turn involved an erect, protruded, presented penis, possibly as a dumb crambo invitation, whence the idea to present, presented, and then simply present, the present, nau or now in English, and so new. The Gallic gesture, for some reason, appears to have been a hand held one, maintenant. Presenting was an introduction, showing for the first time was new, and at the very time it was now, the present. Similarly "No" was apparently from the same nau, declining further concourse: "I regret Madam I have already performed, I can perform no more, my tank is empty – try further down the row". A Malay medic presenting an aboriginal patient with two pills to be swallowed with a glass of water explained "Na! Do biji ubat", Here you are, two individual little bits of medicine.

Thirty was usu, Lithic u-shu, unit (ten)-[and] dual strokes – one up and one down remember – two more [tens], making three of them which is thirty. We would be inclined to read ushu as ten + five (a fist of fingers), making fifteen. But we would have been put to the bottom of the class, as if there was something seriously wrong with our thinking.

Forty was nismin, literally twenties two. It got shortened to nimin and even nin. This slovening is par for the course throughout linguistic development.

Fifty was ninnu, from the shortened form of forty nin, plus u, another ten (u or oo). There is also in my view also en, concertina'd to the second n here, meaning, as in Ancient Egyptian of (from ai'n, that which): forty of ten. It is of interest because the sense of our 'of' is generic for a number of other more specific prepositional relations, and this is a case in point. The nn in ninnu is two twenties and the twenties were composed of two tens so the nin in fifty is really four tens. So the nin en is four tens of (postposition) ten. The 'of' is taken to mean another one of the same ten. It is quirky thinking but it is thinking.

Sixty was ges, gesh again, just like one, and its figure was simply a larger vertical stroke, the Big One. This suggests that although one for the Sumerians had started out as a simple singularity, it had by the time they could count to sixty become an inclusive one also, thus suitable to lend itself to an inclusive unit such as sixty. In cases of doubt it could be distinguished uniquely by adding –ta, making geshta. The Tau or Ta (T) stood for the two dimensions (of a surface) in Lithic, and therefore paradigmatically for dual or the two of them, in this case a second Gesh unit.

Six hundred, the next unit in the whimsical Sumerian numeration in alternate ten and sixty units – Professor Ifrah reckons to have cracked their thinking accommodating the twelve finger joints of the sophisticated elite (the Sumerians) at the same time as the earlier five upright fingers used by the peasants (the pre Sumerian savages) – was simply geshu, sixty times ten (u, pronounced oo and written o).

3600, the next unit in the alternate decimal and sexagesimal system, sixty times sixty, Gesh times Gesh, took off. It was pronounced Sarai or some such, a round direction, sun shaped indeed, a categorical shape because it enclosed its own area included by its periphery. In Ancient Egyptian Ra was the sun, the eye of the day, and sent out its rays, straight rays of light, a surprising performance for an entity so evidently sold on its round shape. In parentheses here however there was precedent for this kind of conjunction in the Lithic mind, since la and lai, for reasons disclosed in chapter 9, already defined the straight line presented by the skyline at sea, as well as a loop or circle when viewed from a small enough island or out of sight of land in a boat; and hence by analogy an orbit, the sun's loop (Apollo). It lent itself to some intricate juggling with these contradictory concepts to distinguish them in use. The Egyptian sun rays meanwhile raised green plants, in Lithic elements raisai geraien plants, and caused them to rise and grow, raisai and gerau again in their original Lithic elements. The Egyptians drew sunbeams with hands on the ends to emphasise their propensity to pull back up the plants when the rays returned to the sun. The Egyptian rays were identified as reciprocal because of this function, as also with the human eye, also ra, which sent out its ray from the central pupil and received a picture back on the iris (irais) where you could see a little reflection when the light was right and the manikin inside your head was able to view it from behind giving him a sight of what was in front of him. The eye grabbed only a surface presentation, it lacked the power to actually pull the panorama up. Sex rays were of intermediate power. They could pull out and up, or round out their targets, but only the specific targets for which they were designed. They could not fashion a ramrod or a pot, which required handiwork besides. Since you can sometimes see the motes in a sunbeam, the tiny dust or smoke particles from which the light is reflected making the beam, suggested a string or stream of infinitesimally small baby suns to which the sun was giving birth. This perception, a wholly erroneous notion, was pregnant nevertheless with later abstractions which would prove useful to science. Anyway Gesh times Gesh, pronounced Shara or Sharai, was a big circular impression in the clay fit for 3600 tiny items, a sunbeam quantity of particles, a very long string of pellets. There can be no doubt that at the birth of language and probably indefinitely thereafter patterns were adjectival patterns and the adjectival mind expected to find them obtaining equally everywhere.

When I had worked out the Lithic underpinning of the Sumerian number nomenclature – hard pounding for me and no doubt still harder for the gentle reader – I found in the following chapters Professor Ifrah had himself worked out most of it without the benefit of any Lithic language elements that I had prayed in aid. This was a proper correction to any satisfaction I felt, but at the same time a kind of confirmation the Lithic elements which fitted were relevant and right. They made sense of what was written quite a number of millennia ago, late for Lithic but still well soused in Lithic thinking.

The Akkadians, probably named by the Sumerians, originally Agade, the non cultivators, literally "not ground cutters", were pastoral nomads from the light soils of Arabia, beduin, Bai-tau-in, bumming-born-ones, born on the hoof; to the Sumerians uncivilised. Their most famous king, somewhat loosely named Nebuchadnezar (604-562 BCE) in the Bible (in Aramaic, some time later) when properly read was actually called "Naibu Agadenai Shar", Of all the Naibs [governors, but literally explicator-bums] of the Akkadians Shar [that is Sunray or Source of Light]. He was as Professor Ifrah puts it Babylon's last glory. It was conquered by Cyrus of Persia in 539 BCE, twenty three years after his death. The Akkadians were Semites, children of Shem in the Bible, which simply meant Westerners in Sumerian, natives of the lands of light soil to the West of where the Sumerians had invaded and settled, which we can derive from the original Lithic phonemes: shai, which as we know the Sumerians used in other contexts for meanings concomitant with the flame which hisses when dunked so that the sibilant became its signature sound, and sheds light as it leaps upwards; and then the hum mai which meant the contrary downward instinct for concealment. The sinking of the light meant the west where it takes place. In France the sun still sinks in the sea, mer; while in India it glows red, merah, over the Western Ghats. The Akkadians themselves preferred to call themselves Hebrews, Eber originally, Eberu the plural, the Travellers, from the Lithic elements Ai-bai-are, bummers, nomads, non diggers again, pastoralists, from the Middle West now renamed the Middle East to suit the Europeans who see themselves as The Westerners. Their unfulfilled longing to finally locate could lead to heightened spirituality but also to suicide and even homicide when continually frustrated. Just like the terrorist, they were locked in a psychic bind they could not escape without shedding their earliest and most fundamental beliefs.

The other tribes of Ham and Japheth labelled in the Bible were victims of rather sharper treatment when it came to picking their totems (totems are ancestors from Au-tau-tau-ma in the original Hawaiian, All-the generations-dead. You can see them one below the other on their Totem poles) in the Bible, named in turn by the children of Shem. There is always a subtle advantage in taking the minutes, it becomes possible on many occasions to subtly ensure the Whig dogs do not get the better of it.

The African tribes were the children of Ham, and the goys were descended from Japheth. The African tribes started for the Shem when they got to Egypt and then to the Sudanese border, much as the Wogs started at Calais for the British Empire. The African tribe there, the Dinka (The Indigenous) and other similar tribes were all conspicuously long bodied which by a curiously roundabout way of thinking gave their womenfolk a fixation on pulling their babies' penises in infancy in order to elongate them to match. It is apparent the technique can be surprisingly, even startlingly effective, since the tissue has nothing much in the way of sinew in it and remains extraordinarily plastic being so designed by nature to provide a neat fit later to save on pollen. Unsurprisingly under this treatment Sudanese boys grew up somewhat over valuing their virility which they displayed, generally going trouserless under a tropic sun. Hai-mai, the Lithic elements for Ham meant rejoicers in the maying, the planting of the seed, in this case not in the soil but insemination. They were the original Morris dancers, but in their case without the costumes and with no need for any of the other accoutrements. They were thus identified as sex addicts by the more properly brought up Shem, addicted in their case to shortening their genitalia to improve their own performance that way – the clippers labelling the gentler pullers obscene. The slander has stuck and been hung quite unfairly on all the Negroid races of Africa ever since, Africa itself descends from Aa-pherai-ka, the country of continuous fornicators. However there is another interpretation of Africa which Mrs Grundy would much prefer which points up the slander: Continuous Fine Sunshine Country, a fairyland of fine weather and fine views –Ra is Sun and Eye equally, The land of sunshine which charms the eye. There are plenty of cases where Lithic analysis throws up a fundamental substrate straight from the Pleistocene of extreme coarseness, but open to redefinition with the original blunt elements shaved away to offer a slightly more civilised recension. This faithfully reflects the actual process of development of the human mind. What is equally of interest is how the phonemic meanings provide such scope for phoneme sentences of lengthy strings. It was the only speech in the Pleistocene.

Japheth and his lot came in for criticism of their sexual mores too, so far as the Shem were concerned. If the Hamites were too forward the Japheths were too backward at coming forward. I-a-pahei-ta(h)I, They-un-penises-cut. They kept their muzzle covers on and ran about in the woods, turning into the European goys, although one must suspect it was a jibe at the expense of the Sumerian sober-sides originally. The Japheths were the uncircumcised worshipers of unclean cow goddesses, the wet nurses of the human race, who could only get it up courtesy of their partners when the feminine rays triggered them and withdrew their muzzle covers for them, allowing their own plumped up emitters in turn to come into play and engage: they were mollies led by the nose by their womenfolk, settled, domesticated, hardly real men at all. They had no racing camels for fighting, only draft animals; and one suspects as a final clincher (although there is no direct evidence for it, but the surviving garden dwellers in Malaya are by comparison hairless wonders)their beards were not as bushy or as black. Later when in Egypt the Shems confided in the Hams the pickle the Japheths were in, the Hams not only enthusiastically adopted circumcision but made a rite of passage out of it; and they even confiscated the girls little pistolets as well and stitched up their emitters for good measure in order to ensure full male sexual control. The lunacy beats on us still, just as before. The Stone Age still rules, lurking below the conscious threshold and mocking our conscious minds; its stronghold below is millions of years older than yesterday's conscious thinking. We think we are rational beings but at the core we are not, only at the edges; and the edges may be more fun but the core is more serious.

The Akkadian records are more profuse than the Sumerian, and there is the advantage when trying to translate them that the Shem have prospered and still speak versions of the language of their forefathers. At the Palace of Nuzi near Kirkuk scores of Abnati have been recovered. The word heads the lists of animals and their numbers written on the outsides of the clay bullae (hollow balls) which contain counters inside. A duplicate system of abnu was in use, translated as stones (since that is what they often were), calculi used for calculating – adding and subtracting to and from the collection. For abnu the Lithic appears to be

A-bai-nau, un-flesh-indicators, imperishable or permanent indicators; while for the Abnati we have the imperishably (a-ba) recorded (na-tai) – parts of speech were largely optional in those days. The abnu were originally just pebbles, until they thought of the wheeze of using shaped clay counters to stand for different livestock, so they could put the whole farm in a single bulla. It would be nice to report the refinement was a single day's work but in fact it took generations, to judge by the large number of little collections of stones found. Professor Ifrah's translation of Permanent Record as things and permanent indicators as stones hardly does justice to his Akkadian forebears, or their Sumerian maths teachers; although since the permanent counters were pebbles for a long while pebbles may well have come to be known as counters; but the name was framed for pebbles in use. Four thousand years ago folk were primitive but not all that simple. They even recognised some grammar, and when the Cains had conquered the Abels in Sumer they were of course able to imbibe wisdom from the Sumerian spring, reaching them all the way from the Garden of Eden East of Malaya, whence the Sumerians had come.

Now Professor Ifrah's discoveries from the Sumerian-Akkadian texts on cuneiform tablets of the second millennium BCE are prayed in aid, and added to from records in the Baghdad Museum as well as Yale University Library and from S J Lieberman's research papers in the American Journal of Archaeology No 84 and Hebrew Union College Annual No 58 of 1987, as well as B Landsberger's contributions in Materialen zum Sumerischen Lexicon, Rome, 1937 which he consulted.

Abnu equates with Sumerian Imna, Imnana and Naim, which in Lithic phonemes offer I-mai-nai, with insignificant variations. The repetition of the –na- merely reinforces the plurality provided by the initial i. The reading is individual(i)-mud/clay (mai)-representations (nai): the clay calculi the Sumerians were using to enclose in their bullae as permanent records, which could not be altered without breaking the bullae stamped with a seal, when the game would be up.

Next we have Sumerian Nig-sid, translated as accounting with the Akkadian nik-kas-si to match the Sumerian. This follows from Sumerian Sid to count, with Akkadian Manu ditto. In Sumerian Si is the vertical (from the flame which springs upwards, see chapter 14) and thence the tally stick marks for numbers and the vertical marks written for numbers, and so the numeral one – in Malaya, the Garden Land of Eden, one is still Sa. For Sid, the Lithic elements Sai-da mean to do or distinguish or think the verticals or numbers, viz to count them. But in the Akkadian manu, equivalent to Sumerian Sid, ma is the multiplicitous earth which comes in individual grains of soil, as well as the instinct to go down and so weight and weighing, the measuring of quantity; while nu is our old friend presented or presentation: the presentation and measurement of quantity. So now we can go to the Sumerian Nig-sid, the Nig from the Lithic elements nai-ka, apparent or explicit (Nai) make (ka): so the whole is to make explicit the thinking of the verticals or digits – precisely the accountants role still today. Their weakness of course is also unchanged: they think in bare units instead of in fully fleshed real terms. The Akkadians to match that put down their Nik-kas-si, Nik- the Sumerian Nig- spelt in Akkadian letters + kas, ku, inscribed marks + si, vertical units, or better together kasi, just numbers. The nik provided all the explication, not mentioning the thinking about it all which was Sumerian.

There are more Sumerian-Akkadian doublets in Professor Ifrah's book. Sumerian Lu-na-na he translates man of the stones where we prefer man of the counters. There is no doubt that for the Sumerians man was Lu, all done gone finish (u) long (Lai), the long one or the tall one, because he walked upright, extended, just as the Papuan cannibals defined human meat as long pork, I will guess from the taste, a whitish meat like pig because of our similar dietary habits; more or less omnivorous. It is the leaf eaters who have red meat: veal and sucking pig are white. The "na-na" Professor Ifrah translates as stones and we have already corrected this to indicators, originally from pushing forward or presenting (a sexual invitation) amongst our simian forebears, originally the erect penis or banana. The grizzly details are all spelled out in chapter 11 for the phoneme Na. The man of the stones or counters was a metrologist or accountant. The Akkadian equivalent was Sa abne-e. Sa for man because he walked upright, perhaps directly translating the Sumerian perception or else one like the royal 'one'. Similarly abne-e is probably only the Sumerian abnu in drag, abai-nai in lithic terms, imperishable indicators again, with –e conjoined from the Lithic plural –ai, they or that which, here a redundant plural marker. The man with the small clay objects [calculi] is Professor Ifrah's preferred translation.

Then we have counting stick, Sumerian Ges-sid-ma, strictly wood-count-quantity. The ma could be mud/clay, which suggests clay roly polys rather than sticks although it is undeniable ges can also mean wood, as already disclosed above. Of course it could be read wood count mud but the two do not go well together. Ma had weight and measurement and quantity or amount among its derivatives – largely from its opposition to sha which could shine forth – and so, as a hidden invisible element, the workings of the mind. In Akkadian we have is-si-mi-nu-ti and is-si-nik-kas-si. We are asked to make is- into the equivalent of gesh if we are to go along with wooden sticks. It could of course mean flammable and that standing alone could define wood for the simpler Akkadians. However the Akkadians may have been more inclined to use rushes from the marshes than trees which in the Middle West whence they came were and are in notably short supply. In which case they might refer to them as just ish rather than gesh. As against that, in fact they usually wrote reeds as ge or gi, scribers, a description from use not connected with any natural flammable qualities at all. It is moot because the mi-nu-ti could be mud presenting things or amount presenting things, clay counters or measuring counters. To make, in the English language, I am reminded here originally meant to mould and so to make – perhaps a pot or dough, with the real element conveying the making residing in the ka and not the ma which was just the medium, or pig in the middle. However mai-nu is not so far from manu, which we have already accepted as presenting the quantity or value, from the multiplicity of the soil, and the mass for measuring, so mi-nu could also carry that signification. Indeed ma, mai and mi were, I suspect, virtually interchangeable. I do not really care about the outcome, which is right, once the Lithic elements have been given free expression and the Lithic methodology an airing.

Sangu, according to Professor Ifrah, meant both priest and the manager of the temple wealth. It is tempting to see kinship with san in Sanskrit as well as in San Francisco and perhaps even savant; and a guru is a teacher. The flame, ish, has an ethereal quality which could be the Lithic origin of the san (from Latin sancta) as well as savant; and the r in guru could be merely an intrusive interpolation simply to give the articulation a bit more body. Gu must be from the Lithic element Kau, perhaps meaning fully fashioned, and so adept, earlier just fashioned or made and originally chipped out of a flint, echoic of the clack of stone on flint striking an artefact out. The sham in Sanskrit is moot. It can be written Shamshkrit, which makes me toy with Shamash-skrit, viz Holy or religious writing like hieroglyph, with hiero meaning holy from the Egyptian habit of Hei Ra, worshiping the sun god, Ra. Here the sun was shamash, Up Down Up, Light Dark Light, helios, (ahi-lai-u([s]), the cycler. Just to attach Him to your script appears in the case of those speaking Sanscrit sufficient on its own to make the script holy, ie perfect enough to be appropriate for religious purposes, no doubt old fashioned and overly con-servative to the point of losing touch with the speakers of the vernacular, Prakrit. Prakrit was parole as we would say, while the Sanskrit was langue with all its grammatical nuances dreamed up by an elite with insufficient of a practical nature to occupy their time and attention. Pannini has a lot to answer for. Both sweetness and light are priestly qualities, nominally at least, and both come from Shamash, the sun, sweetness etymologically, light physically.

The word sangu, number adept, is written in cuneiform the same way as the verb manu which means to count, in Lithic terms multiplicity (ma) presented/demonstrated (nu). Sangu, Numbers Adept, is written perhaps with a vertical upstroke while manu, numbers demonstrator may be written with a very similar down stroke. Both are accountants. We can perhaps derive the rather later Latin Manus hand from manu the counter using the fingers of one hand pointed to by a finger of the other. Earlier I toyed with the Ancient Egyptian Mai (planter, inseminator, penis)+ nu presenter: back to those hearthside sexual orgies in the

Pleistocene which are recounted in chapter 16, with young Tarzan reduced to using his hand to get started and make an offer. It is not beyond the wit of man to
accommodate both meanings, even by way of a jape as also as some confirmation
the meanings are natural and therefore confirmed as on the right lines, matches
in more ways than one, their meanings essentially the same all over. One meaning
was evidently meant for Mrs Grundy while the other simultaneously accommodated boys' humour.

Elam was an Asianic tribe, neither Sumerian nor Semite. Susa, the capital was
about two hundred miles South East of Babylon. Their language is for the most
part unreadable, as yet undeciphered. Their land was less fertile than Sumer's. It
may well be they were the remnants of the previous inhabitants of Sumer, pushed
aside when the Eastern Eden, the Garden of Malaya, was inundated by the rising
seas and the inhabitants became Sumerians (immigrants to the West) seeking
refuge in the land of Elam. They will, one may surmise, have known where they
were heading and probably had had long term mercantile relations with the folk
whom they found it a necessity of state to dispossess. They will have been aware of
the suitability of the land between the two rivers for irrigated padi, and may even
have already taught the Elamites how to go about it in the Persian Gulf before
it was inundated. In any case the Elamites actually called themselves Haltami.
Elam was merely the masticated version the Sumerians got their mouths round.
If we wish to discover the meaning the Elamites gave to their own nomenclature
then we should analyse Haltami. H was often a cockney H to separate two vowels
merely: it was pronounced Ahi and said the same as Ai. At other times it was a
strong H or Ha! and conveyed some sharp sensational or emotional response. I
think the original one was "Hot!" as young Tarzan, way back in the Pleistocene,
burnt his fingers, perhaps picking up a hot stone imagining it was a burnt stick to
throw back into the fire. It is all in chapter 8. With Haltami it does not fit the case
to start with what was almost an expletive, so we can safely plump for the cockney
H. So the Lithic elements are Ai-lai-ta-mai, or perhaps as a second try Ai-al-lai-
tamai, those that-at-the rivers-twin. Thamuz or Damuzi was originally an Asiatic
figure, sprung from Shamash, and that is how he devolved into Thomas the twin.
Now we can see why it may well have been the Elamites the Sumerians displaced.
It may not have been a brutal and sudden eviction, but a gradual usurpation of
space by the newcomers, not unlike the absorption of the Danish invaders in the
Danelaw of East Anglia under population pressure from the Huns behind them
in the ninth century of the Common Era, CE. You can now find villages in two
parts, one originally Saxon, the other Danish. In this case the Danes were the less
civilised pagans and were absorbed by the Saxons, though it appears they smelled
sweeter or had another edge on the Saxons who were probably less handsome,
since over the centuries the girls voted with their feet and as a result the churches

now tend to be marooned at the Saxon end while the life, the shop and the public house, as well as the great majority of the population, are now to be found at the newcomers' end. With the Sumerians the boot appears to have been on the other foot. The population spoke Sumerian and would still today, had they not fallen victim to Semitic imperialism and been dispossessed and eliminated. Elam is supposed to mean the Land of God, but this is clearly a Semitic invention, since El- is Lord and God in the Semitic tongues. The Elamites are rather unlikely to have called themselves by a name in a foreign tongue. Not only that but Land of God would in all probability have been the other way about: Mahel for example; and in any case there is no reason to believe ma meant land in Elamite. If Haltami was pronounced Yalatami, then slovening to yelaami would be written in consonants, just LM, and misconstrued as Elami in the natural course. It seems this is precisely what happened. Ya-la-ta-em-i can come from the Lithic it that-rivers-two-of-ones, the original dispossessed Mesopotamians.

In the middle of the third millennium BCE, 4500 years ago, the ruler of Elam was of the dynasty Shamash, the sun (Up-down-up as before). His name was Untash-Gal. Gal we know was big (tall, long framed) in Sumerian from ka-lai, body-long; and Lugal meant king (Big Man). Lu was man. Un-Ta-Shai is uncommonly like Ta-Un-Shar, World-of-light, the Light of the World, probably a religious Big Man as well as wielder of the secular power. Compare Su-tan in Ancient Egyptian, Light of the World, or indeed Highest in the World, the Pharoah's favourite title, with his wife the Queen Bee (Bee-ti). The hieroglyph was a queen bee, or possibly a queen white ant. They are (aerial) travellers (bai) just like the bee, and their queens a tad more fertile. Su-tan in Egyptian glyphs contemporaneously with Elam, were first a shoot of barley (Se in Sumerian) the tall crop – or big (barra)-lay (grass) in English – and the second, which the Egyptologists fancy for some reason to be a bun called Ti, was in fact taun, the top half of the disc universe, on which mankind lived and moved and had his being, cooped up under the sky like a cheese mite under a cheese cover, pronounced Ta-un, the Universe as we know it, the Universal, the All, strictly Ta-u, all the birthings or becomings, the sum total of events, a rather different definition of the universe than our purely locative version. Toying with all these calculi enclosed in bullae, we were perhaps, for the accountants poking all those counters into the bullae, inhabiting a world not unlike a bulla: the lid of the world as well as the floor was believed to be equally solid. Was it the real world, as they saw it, which gave them the idea in the first place of making a copy of it, the bulla – the stick men reaching for reality?

The Sumerian for the early abacus, a board with columns ruled on it, so that addition and subtraction, and even multiplication and division with more difficulty, could be carried out physically using counters, pebbles or fancy carved pieces, which were moved from column to column in exact imitation of the mental carrying between columns when doing mental arithmetic with a column of figures these days, was Ges-su-me-ge. Ges is our old friend wooden board or else the incised upright number one and thus a number. Su meant hand, as it still does in China (a very conservative country still uniquely saddled with much of the original Lithic idioms of speech), but it really meant all the uprights (su), fingers used raised upright one by one to count. The fingers were used to count on, so it appears you put them up as you counted, probably pushing them with the index finger of the other hand to give emphasis to the exercise. All the fingers made a hand of fingers just like a hand of bananas. Of course unlike a hand of bananas a hand of fingers can be used as a counting unit because of its inestimable virtue of always having the same number of fingers on it, and quite a handy number at that, neither many too many nor too few, as well as being conveniently carried by the accountant with him wherever he went, all respects in which any hand of bananas would have been totally wanting. As each finger stood for a number the hand, a bunch of them, stood for the total of them, in the first instance five, the first numerical base – soon discarded for both hands and the base ten. It helps to know the vowel u (oo) from the birth of speaking was the inclusive vowel, with the lips rounded to an O. Su had the sense of Siu, si-all of them. Si was a singular number, in Sumerian the number one, a single raised finger. Su was thus readily usable as a total of (five) single numbers, and then with only a little further generalisation as just a total, five or other. As Professor Ifrah remarks, without benefit of any Lithic semantic contents, "The word su literally means hand. In certain contexts however it also means total, totality, alluding to the hand which assembles and totalises". I think his functional assembly route is just fiction. In reality it is the hand which is the assembly, not the assembler, and we can deduce this from the u vowel which is what is carrying the totalisation all along, not the hand as a functional item at all. What it is totalling is the si, the up raised fingers, five or ten, hand or hands, or else the dual si, two fingers.

Gesh Su thus resolves itself into Wood Totalisation or totalisator board. For -me-ge Professor Ifrah opts for –me- as "rite" or "prescription", and the whole as freely translated: "the determination of that which must be done [that is the ge?] according to the rules [that is the me]"; or "an action which is performed according to precise order as well as a prescribed order". Apparently he is quoting A Deimel from "Sumerischen Lexicon, Scripta Pontificii Institutu Biblici, Rome, 1947. It is quite a lot to get out of Gessumege: fifteen words in English from five phonemes in Sumerian. For the –me-ge we can propose the following. Me is from the Lithic elements ma-i, probably meaning many, like the grains of the earth (ma) from which certainly can be extracted the idea of a great quantity, (just as in the Latin Mille, like mud); and then further off just the generalised idea of quantity, and even measuring the quantity from ma the instinct to go down which earth has in fair measure, and which can be ascertained by weighing the downward force (ma) contained in a quantity. Ge, used right at the beginning of the same word in Sumerian, is hard and also incised and so inscribed, all good Lithic semantic contents from kai. So may we not invoke another semantic content, that of the spark from the flint, kindling, creating (kids as well as figuring), certainly inseminating in Ancient Egyptian; but here in the case of figures just multiplying. My own translation of Gessumege is Board Totalisator Adding and Multiplying. The ritual invoked above can be left over to another place, as can the rules: Professor Ifrah is welcome to dip into chapter 10 for the phoneme Ma if he is still around.

Luges-su-mun-ge Professor Ifrah has as "literally a man (Lu) who manipulates the rules (mun) with a reed (ge)on the wood (Ges), of the tablet understood". This is all very well but is it all there or even the gist of it? My recension is man (lu) board (ges) total (su) of quantities (mun)making (ge). You can put in minimal grammatical guides such as we use today to make the translation smoother: The man with the board for making the quantity totals, or slightly more freely, the man with the board for totalling quantities.

Meanwhile Professor Ifrah is away on the next definition of an abacist: Lu-su-mun-gi, which he defines as a "symbolic variant" of the first which I take to mean the symbols are different as indeed they are. Before it was gesh-su-ma-ge. Gesh is out and –ge has changed to –gi – perhaps a scribal quirk or just a spelling error, never a strong point in the accountants' armoury. That leaves us with the man making the totals of quantities without the board – though he must have surely had one, as how else in those far off days could he achieve the necessary simple addition and subtraction of large numbers. Mental arithmetic had not yet been invented, and even the grey beards still needed their ruled lines and counters. Professor Ifrah's recension is a man (lu) who finds the total(su) with a reed (ge)according to the rules (mun). Professor Ifrah, I think, had not entirely freed himself from thinking in modern language terms with all the grammatical niceties and particularisations, none of which were yet extant 5000 years ago. They still used stilted Lithic idioms as if to the manner born, as indeed they were. This finally leaves us with the Babylonian for abacist which is read as Sa-da-ab di-mi and Sa-su-ma-ki-i, in Lithic terms the man (sa) distinguish imperishable (da-ab, ie the tablet for writing on) distinguish quantity (da-mi); and the man (sa) total (su) of the amount (ma) creator (ki-i). In Akkadian the number 60, the Sumerian base for numbers but not the Akkadians' who used ten like most everybody else, is shu-shi, two hands of singles, a total numerical, a sum used as a base.

This has been only a glance at a few Sumerian words. It has provided an opportunity for flexing the muscle of Lithic analysis. There is much more to be done.

Notes.

1. Female has the Lithic elements Fai-malai, fully expanded Pa-hei-ma-lai. Pa-hei in Ancient Egyptian had an unmistakeable glyph, the penis, (also pronounced mai, the mayer, in Lithic the earther or planter of the seed, the inseminator), where hei had the semantic content rejoicing, joy while the pa- as the thinned diminutive of Ba which initially meant flesh (from the fleshy lips which said it) suggested either the skin or surface, etc, or a small shoot or fleshy piece. So Pahei, later fei or fai and then fa and even just the letter f conveyed to the Egyptian mind something like the Joy Shoot, not unlike the joystick the young pilots of the first world war found sticking up between their legs which they manipulated to direct the plane. The female was the mali or gardener propagating the seed. The family on the other hand is linked (lai) by the pha-mai, the insemination.

SELECT BIBLIOGRAPHY

Legend. OUP = Oxford University Press. CUP = Cambridge University Press. Books are listed under author(s) where given, with title, publisher, edition (where relevant) and date. The subject matter is not always immediately apparent from the title. But space does not allow further guidance here.

Ablay M. Spoken Here. Arrow Books. 2005.

Adorno T & Horkheimer M. Dialectic of Enlightenment. Herder & herder. Verso. Allen Lane. 1973.

Allegro JM. The Sacred Mushroom & the Cross. Hodder & Stoughton. 1970.

Aitchison J. Language Change. Progress or Decay? Fontana Paperbacks. 1981.

Aitchison J. The Seeds of Speech. Language Origin & Evolution. CUP. 1996.

Aitchison J. The Language Web. CUP. 1997.

Albanian English Dictionary. OUP. 1998.

Alderson AD & Iz F. Oxford English Turkish Dictionary. OUP. 2nd Edn. 1978.

Anderson SR & Lightfoot DW. The Language Organ. Linguistics as Cognitive Physiology. CUP. 2002.

Appleyard David. Colloquial Amharic. Routledge. 1995.

Armenian-English English-Armenian Dictionary. Hippocrene Books. 1995.

Arnold D, Atkinson A, etc. Essays on Grammatical Theory & Universal Grammar. OUP. 1989.

Assagioli R. Psychosynthesis. Turnstone Books. 1965.

Aulestia Gorka and White Linda. Basque-English English-Basque Dictionary. University of Nevada Press. 1992.

Austin JL. How to do Things with Words. 1962. CUP. 1980.

Ayto J. Dictionary of Word Origins. Bloomsbury Publishing Ltd. 1990.

Baghramian M. Modern Philosophy of Language. JM Dent. 1998.

Baigent M. Ancient Traces. Viking. Penguin Group. 1998.

Baker Mark C. The Atoms of Language. OUP. 2002.

Barkow JH, Cosmides L, Tooby J. The Adapted Mind. OUP. 1992.

Barnhart R. Chambers Dictionary of Etymology. Chambers. 1988.

Barsky RF. Noam Chomsky, a Life of Dissent. ECW Press Council. 1997.

Barthes R. The semiotic Challenge. Basil Blackwell. 1988.

Bayram A, Serdar Turet S & Jones G. Hugo Turkish Dictionary. Hugo's Language Books.

Basque-Spanish Spanish-Basque Dictionary. Academia Montiano, Bilbao.

Baugh AC & Cable T. A History of the English Language. 1951. 3rd Edn. Routledge & Kegan Paul. 1978.

Becker E. The Birth and Death of Meaning. Penguin. 1972.

Beckford S & A. Philipino Dictionary. Hippocrene Books. 1988.

Ben Yehuda. English-Hebrew Hebrew-English Dictionary. Simon & Schuster. 1961.

Bendix EH. The Uses of Linguistics. New York Academy of Sciences Vol 583. 1990.

Berlin I. Against the Current. Essays on the History of Ideas. Random House. 1955.

Berlin I. Karl Marx. Fontana. Harper Collins. 1995.

Berlitz Swahili for Travellers. 1974. 13th Printing. 1991.

Berlitz Norwegian Dictionary. 3rd Printing. 1996.

Berlitz C. Native Tongues. Grenada Publishing Ltd. 1983.

Bermant C & Weitzman M. Ebla. Weidenfeld & Nicolson, Book Club Associates. 1978.

Bermudez JL. Thinking without Words. OUP. 2002.

Bernal Martin. Black Athena. Vol 1. Vintage. 1987.

Bernal Martin. Black Athena. Vol 2. Free Association Books. 1991

Betro MC. Hieroglyphics. Abbeville Press Publishers. 1996.

Bickerton D. Language and Species. University of Chicago Press. 1990.

Bierce A. The Devil's Dictionary. 1911. Folio Society. 2004.

Blackmore S. The Meme Machine. OUP. 1999.

Brandreth G. Pears Book of Words. CUP. 1997.

Breal M. The Beginnings of Semantics. Stanford University Press. 1991.

Brothers L. Friday's Footprint. How Society Shapes the Human Mind. OUP. 1997.

Brown A. The Darwin Wars. Simon & Schuster. 1999.

Brown I. Book of Words. Jonathon Cape. 1934.

Brown CM & Hagoort P. The Neurocognition of Language. OUP. 1999. Paperback. 2000.

Bryson B. Mother Tongue. Penguin. 1990.

Budge EAW. The Egyptian Book of the Dead. 1895. Routledge & Kegan Paul. 1967.

Budge EAW. Egyptian Language. Routledge & Kegan Paul. 16th Impression. 1978.

Budge EAW. An Egyptian Hieroglyphic Dictionary. 1920. 2 Volumes. Dover Publications. 1978.

Burchfield R. Unlocking the English Language. Faber & Faber. 1989.

Burgess A. Language made Plain. 1964. Flamingo. Fontana Paperbacks. 1975.

Burgess A. A Mouthful of Air. 1998. Hutchinson. Random House UK Ltd 1992.

Burling R. The Talking Ape. How Language Evolved. OUP. 2005.

Byrne R. The Thinking Ape. OUP. 1995.

Cahen L. Serbian Pocket Dictionary. Kegan Paul Trench Trubner. 1920.

Calvin WH. How Brains Think. Weidenfeld & Nicholson. 1997.

Campbell J. Grammatical Man. Allan Lane. 1982.

Cassells German Dictionary. 1978. 3rd Edn. McMillan. 1980.

Cassells. New Latin Dictionary. Original 1854. 5th Edn, 3rd Impression. 1971.

Casti JL. Paradigms Lost. 1991. Abacus. 2000.

Cavalli-Sforza LL. Genes, People & Languages. Allen Lane. Penguin Press. 2000.

Chafe Wallace. L. Meaning and the Structure of Language. University of Chicago Press. 1970.

Chantrell G. Oxford Dictionary of Word Origins. OUP. 2002.

Cheturvedi M & Tiwari B N. A Practical Hindi English Dictionary. National Publishing House. 4th Edn. 1978.

Chetwin B. The Songlines. Picador, Pan Books, Jonathan Cape. 1988.

Chetwynd T. A Dictionary of Symbols. Granada Publishing. 1982.

Chinese Dictionary. Harper Collins. 2005.

Claxton G. Noises from the Dark Room. Harper Collins. 1994.

Chomsky N. Reflections on Language. Random House 1976.

Chomsky N. Language & Responsibility. Harvester Press, Sussex. 1979.

Chomsky N. The Chomsky Reader. Random House. 1988.

Chomsky N. On Nature & Language. CUP. 2002.

Christiansen MH & Kirby S. Language Evolution. OUP. 2003.

Cirlot JE. A Dictionary of Symbols. Routledge & Kegan Paul. 1962.

Cohane JP. The Key. Fontana/Collins. 1973.

Collins. Chinese Dictionary. Harper Collins. 2005.

Collins. English Dictionary. BCA. Harper Collins. 1999.

Collins. English Japanese Dictionary. Harper Collins. 1993.

Collins. Pocket Irish Dictionary. Harper Collins. 1997.

Collins. New Italian Dictionary Harper Collins. 1st Edn 1995.

Collins. Spanish Dictionary. 1971. 4th Printing 1985.

Collins D. The Human revolution, from Ape to Artist. 1976. Phaedon Press. BCA. 1976.

Colman AM. Oxford Dictionary of Psychology. OUP. 2001.

Concise Routledge Encyclopedia of Philosophy. Routledge. BCA. 2000.

Corballis MC. The Lopsided Ape. OUP. 1993.

Corbridge-Patkaniowska M. Polish. English Universities Press. 1973.

Corominas J. Breve Diccionario Etimologico de la Lingua Castellana. Editional Gredas SA. 3rd Edition. 1973.

Coulson M, Gombrich R, Benson J. Sanskrit. Hodder & Stoughton. 2nd Edn. 1992.

Cowan JG. Myths of the Dreaming. Prism Press, Dorset. 1994.

Crossthwaite H. Ka. Metropolitan Publications, Princeton. 1992.

Crum WE. A Coptic Dictionary. 1939. OUP. 1979.

Crystal D. Linguistics. Pelican. 1971.

Crystal D. Cambridge Encyclopedia of the English Language. CUP. 1995.

Cummings J. Thai Phrasebook. Lonely Planet Publications, Australia. 4th Edn 1999.

Dalby A. Dictionary of Languages. Bloomsbury Publishing plc. 1998.

Darwin C. On The Origin of Species. 1859. JM Dent. 1973.

Davies JP & Hersh R. Descartes' Dream. Penguin. 1986.

Dawkins R. Climbing Mount Improbable. Viking. 1996.

Dawkins R. The Ancestor's Tale. Weidenfeld & Nicolson. 2004.

Deacon T. The Symbolic Species. The Co-evolution of Language & the Human Brain. Penguin. 1997.

De Grazia A. Homo Schizo. Metron Publications, Princeton. 1983.

Dehaene S. The Number Sense. Penguin. 1997.

Dennett D. Consciousness Explained. Penguin Group. 1993.

Dennett D. Kinds of Minds. Weidenfeld & Nicolson. 1996.

Dennett D. Darwin's Dangerous Idea.

Dent GR &Nyembezi CLS. Scholar's Zulu Dictionary, Shuter & Shooter 8th Impression. 1982.

De Santillana G & von Dechend H. Hamlet's Mill. David R Godine. 1977.

Deutcsher G. The Unfolding of Language. William Heineman. 2005.

Dhont H, etc. South Pacific Phrase Book. Fijian, Hawaiian, Kanak, Maori, Niuean, Rapanui, Raratongan, Samoan, Tahitian, Tongan. Lonely Planet, Australia. 1999.

Dieckhoff HC. Pronouncing Dictionary of Scottish Gaelic. Gairm Publications. 1998.

Dillon M & O'Croinin D. Irish. 1961. Hodder & Stoughton. 12th Impression. 1979.

Dixon RMW. A Grammar of Yidin. CUP. 1977.

Dixon RMW & Ackenwald AY. The Amazonian Languages. CUP. 1999.

Dixon RMW & Blake BL. Handbook of Australian Languages Vol 5. OUP. 2000.

Doblhofer E. Voices in Stone. Paledin. Granada Publishing. 1973.

Doke CM, Malcolm DM, Schakana JMA & Vilakazi BW. Zulu Dictionary. Witwatersrand University Press. 1990.

Donnald M. A Mind so Rare. WW Norton & Co. 2001.

Doyle T& Meara P. Lingo. How to Learn a Language. BBC Books. 1991.

Dunbar R. Grooming, Gossip and the Origin of Language. Faber & Faber. 1996.

Echols J & Shadily H. Indonesian-English Dictionary. Cornell University Press. 1961.

Eco U. The Search for the Perfect Language. Fontana Press. 1995.

Eco U. Serendipities. Language & Lunacy. Weidenfeld & Nicolson. 1999.

Eco U. Kant & the Platypus. Vintage, Random House. 2000.

Ellwell-Sutton LP. Colloquial Persian. Routledge & Kegan Paul. 1971.

Encarta World English Dictionary. Bloomsbury Publishing plc. (2172pp). 1999.

Evans HM & Thomas WO. Complete Welsh-English & English-Welsh Dictionary. Christopher Davies. 1975.

Finnish Dictionary. Holt, Rinehart and Winston Ltd. 1978.

Finnish Dictionary. William Collins & Sons. 2nd Edn 1987.

Fischer SR. A History of Language. Reaktion Books, London. 1999.

Flavell L and R. Dictionary of Word Origins. Kyle Cathie Ltd. 1995.

Fodor JA. Concepts. Where Cognitive Science went Wrong. OUP. 1998.

Foley WA. The Papuan Languages of New Guinea. CUP. 1986.

Fontana D. The Secret Language of Symbols. Pavilion Books Ltd, London. 1993.

Fontana Dictionary of Modern Thought. Fontana Collins. 1977.

Foucault M. The Archaeology of Knowledge. Tavistock Publications. 1972.

Frazer JG. The Golden Bough. A Study in Magic & Religion. 1922. MacMillan. 1976.

French Dictionary. Harrap. 1982.

Gaelic-English English-Gaelic Dictionary. MacAlpine & MacKenzie.1979.

Gardner A. Egyptian Grammar. 1927. Griffith Institute, Oxford. 3rd Edn. 1982.

Goossen IW. Navajo Made Easier. Northland Press. 1967.

Gostony C-G. Dictionnaire d'Etymologie Sumerienne et Grammaire Comparee. Editions de Boccaro. Paris. 1975.

Gratzer W. The Undergrowth of Science. OUP. 2000.

Green J. The Slang Thesaurus. Elm Tree Books. 1986.

Greene J. Psycholinguistics. Chomsky and Psychology. Penguin. 1972.

Greenfield S. The Human Brain. Weidenfeld & Nicolson. 1997.

Gregory R L. The Oxford Companion to the Mind. OUP. 1987.

Hagger N. The Fire & the Stone. A Grand Unified Theory of World History and Religion. Element Books Ltd, Dorset. 1991.

Halliwell JO. Dictionary of Archaic Words. 1850. Bestseller Publications Ltd, London. 1989.

Hamilton AW. Easy Malay Vocabulary. 5th Edn. Australian Publishing Co Pty 1944.

Hart CWM & Pilling AC. The Tiwi of North Australia. Holt Rinehart & Winston. 1978.

Hawker CL. Simple Colloquial Persian. Longmans Green & Co. 1942.

Heller I, Humez A & Dror M. The Private Lives of English Words. Routledge & Kegan Paul 1983.

Hendrichson R. QPB Encyclopedia of Word & Phrase Origins. Facts on File Inc. 1997.

Hillian D. Word Lore. W & R Chambers Ltd, Edinburgh. 1984.

Hofstadter DR. Godel, Euler, Bach. An Eternal Golden Braid. Penguin. 1979.

Hofstadter DR. Le Ton Beau de Marot. Harper Collins. 1997.

Honderich E. The Oxford Companion to Philosophy. OUP. 1995.

Horgan J. The Undiscovered Mind. Weidenfeld & Nicolson. 1999.

Hoshima T & Marcus R. Lao for Beginners. Tuttle Language Library, Tokyo. 1981.

Humphrey N. A History of the Mind. Chatto & Windus. 1992.

Hunter J. Papua New Guinea Pidgin Phrase Book. Lonely Planet Australia. 1986.

Ifrah G. The Universal History of Numbers from Prehistory to the Invention of the Computer. 1994. Harvill Press. 1998.

Jackendoff R. Foundations of Language. OUP. 2002.

Jakobson R & Waugh L. The Sound Shape of Language. Harvester Press. 1979.

Janov A. The Primal Revolution. Abacus. 1978.

Janson T. Speak. A Short history of Languages. OUP. 2002.

Japanese English Dictionary. OUP. 1986.

Jaynes J. The Origin of Consciousness in the Breakdown of the Bicameral Mind. Penguin. 1976.

Jenner T. Tsze Teen Piao Muh (Guide to the Chinese Dictionary). Luzac & Co, London 1907.

Johnson AT & Smith HA. Plant Names Simplified. 1931. Landsmans Bookshop. 1986.

Johnson F. Standard Swahili Dictionary. 1937. OUP. 1964.

Johnson Samuel. Dictionary of the English Language. Times Books. 1983.

Jones S. The Language of the genes. Harper Collins. 1993.

Jones S. In the Blood. God, Genes and Destiny. Harper Collins. 1993.

Jung C. Man & his Symbols. 1964. Picador. Pan Books Ltd. MacMillan. 1978.

Kallir A. Sign and Design. Vernon, Richmond, Surrey. 1961.

Katan NJ. Hieroglyphs. British Museum Publications. 1980.

Katzner K. The Languages of the World. Routledge & Kegan Paul. 1975.

Kenny A. Wittgenstein. Pelican. 1975.

Kenny A. Frege. Penguin Books. OUP. 1995.

Kerr J. A Most Dangerous Method. Sinclair Stevenson. 1994.

Kohn M. A Reason for Everything. Faber & Faber. 2004.

Kovekses Z. Metaphor. OUP. 2002.

Kraft C H & Kirk-Green A H M. Hausa. Hodder & Stoughton. 9th impression. 1985.

Kriel TJ, Prinsloo DJ & Sathekge BP. Popular Northern Sotho Dictionary. Pharos, Capetown. 4th Edn. 1997.

Kroeber AL. Handbook of the Indians of California. Publications Inc. 1976.

Langenscheidt. Portuguese Dictionary. 1984.

Langer SK. An Introduction to Symbolic Logic. Dover Publications. 3rd Edn. 1967.

Leakey R and Lewin R. Origins. MacDonald & Jane Publishers. BCA. 1977.

Leech G. Semantics. Pelican. 1974. Penguin. 1983.

Levy GR The Gate of Horn. Faber & Faber. 1948.

Levy-Bruhl L. How Natives Think. 1926. Princeton University Press. 1985.

Levy-Strauss C. Structural Anthropology. 1963. Penguin Books. 1977.

Lewin R. The Orign of Modern Humans. Scientific American Library. HPHLP NY. 1993.

Lewis CS. Studies in Words. CUP. 2nd Edn. Canto. 1990.

Lewis N. The Book of Babel. Penguin Boks. 1994.

Liddell and Scott. Greek English Lexicon. OUP. 1889. 1980 Impression.

Lieberman P. On the Origins of Language. MacMillan. 1975.

Lieberman P. Eve Spoke. Picador. MacMillan Publishers. 1998.

Lockwood WB. A Panorama of Indo European Languages. Hutchinson. 1972.

Loritz D. How the Brain Evolved Language. OUP. 1999.

Lyell C. Principles of Geology. 1830. University of Chicagp Press. 1990.

Lyons J. New Horizons in Linguistics. Pelican. 1970.

Lyons J. Chomsky. Fontana. William Collins. 1978.

Lyons J. Language Meaning & Context. Fontana. 1981.

Macdonnell AA. A Practical Sanskrit Dictionary. 1924. OUP. 1976.

Mace J. Modern Persian. Hodder & Stoughton. 11th Impression. 1983.

MacWhorter J. The Power of Babel. William Heineman. 2001.

Manser MH. Bloomsbury Good Word Guide. 1988. Bloomsbury Publications. 1990.

Martsinkyavilshute V. Lithuanian Dictionary. Hippocrene Books. 1993.

Matthews PH. Concise Dictionary of Linguistics. OUP. 1997.

Mazar A & Trone A. Voices from the Past. Harvey House Inc. New York. 1967.

Mazonowicz D. Voices from the Stone Age. Allen & Unwin. 1975.

McAlpine. Gaelic Dictionary.

McFarland GB. Thai English Dictionary. Stanford University Press. 1944.

Marsack CC. Samoan. 1962. English Universities Press. 1975.

Mengham R. The Descent of Language. Bloomsbury Publishing Ltd. 1993.

Miller G. Language & Speech. W H Freeman. 1981.

Miller G. The Science of Words. Scientific American Library. 1991.

Mithen S. The Prehistory of the Mind. Thames & Hudson. 1996.

Mol F. Maa Dictionary. Marketing & Publishing Ltd, Nairobi. 1978.

Moore J & Rodchue S. Colloquial Thai. Routledge. 1994.

Moore T & Carling C. Understanding Language: towards a Post Chomskian Linguistics. MacMillan Press Ltd. 1982.

Moore T & Carling C. The Limitations of Language. McMillan Press. 1988.

Nichols J. Linguistic Diversity in Space & Time. University of Chicago. 1992.

Nichols J. Sounds Like Life. The Pasteza Quechoah Language of Ecuador. OUP.

Norrman R. & Haarberg J. Nature and Language. Routledge & Kegan Paul. 1980.

Nuckolls JB. Sounds Like Life. OUP. 1996.

O'Connor JD. Phonetics. 1973. Penguin Books. 1978.

Onions CT. Oxford Dictionary of English Etymology. 1996. OUP 1970.

Oppenheimer S. Eden in the East. Weidenfeld & Nicolson. 1998.

Oxford English Dictionary on CD.

Papermac. 1811 Dictionary of the Vulgar Tongue. Digest Bookstore. 1982.

Payne J. Colloquial Hungarian. Routledge. 1987.

Partridge E. Origins. A Short Etymological Dictionary of Modern English. 1958. Routledge & Kegan Paul. 1978.

Partridge E. A Dictionary of Slang. 1937. Routledge. 8th Edn. 2000.

Partridge E. From Sanskrit to Brazil. Hamish Hamilton. 1951.

Payne J. Colloquial Hungarian. Routledge. 1987.

Perrott DV. Concise Swahili English Dictionary. Hodder & Stoughton. 1978.

Piggott S. The Dawn of Civilisation. Thames & Hudson. 1961.

Pinker S. The Language Instinct. Allen Lane, Penguin Press. 1994.

Pinker S. How the Mind Works. Allen Lane, Penguin Press. 1997.

Pinker S. Words & Rules. Weidenfeld & Nicolson. 1999.

Pinker S. The Blank State. Allen Lane. 2002.

Pinnock PS. Xhosa. A Cultural Grammar for Beginners. African Sign Press. 1994.

Pinnock PS. Xhosa Dictionary. Via Afrika. 1997.

Popper KR. The Logic of Scientific Discovery. Hutchinson & Co. 9th Impression. 1977.

Pribram KH. Brain & Perception. Lawrence Erlbaum Associates. 1991.

Radin P. Primitive Man as Philosopher. 1927. Dover Publications. 1957.

Ravin Y. Lexical Semantics without Thematic Roles. OUP. 1990.

Recoeur P. The Rule of Metaphor. Routledge & Kegan Paul. 1978.

Reed AW. Concise Maori Dictionary. AH & AW Reed Ltd, Wellington. 1981.

Rees N. Dictionary of Word & Phrase Origins. Cassell. 1996.

Renfrew C. Before Civilisation. Jonathan Cape. 1973.

Renfrew C. Archaeology and Language. Pimlico. Random House. 1987

Ridley M. The Origins of Virtue. Softback Preview. 1997.

Room A. Dictionary of True Etymologies. 1986. Routledge & Kegan Paul. 1987.

Room A. The Cassell Dictionary of Word origins. Cassell. 1999.

Rowlands EC. Yoruba. Hodder & Stoughton. 1969.

Rudelson JJ, Central Asia Phrasebook. Uyghur, Uzbek, Kyrgyz, Kazakh, Pashtu, Tajik, Tashkorghani, Turkmen, Burushashki, Khowar, Kohistani, Mandarin, Mongolian, Russian, Shina, Wakhi, Lonely Planet Publications. 1961.

Safire W. William Safire on Language. 1980. Avon Books. Hearst Coorporation. 1981.

Samuels ML. Linguistic Evolution. CUP. 1972.

Savage-Rumbaugh S, Shankar SG, Taylor TJ. Apes, Language & the Human Mind. OUP. 1998.

Schapiro W. Collins Russian Dictionary. William Collins Sons & Co. 1985.

Scientific American. Human Communication Language & its Psychological Bases. 1981

Searle J. Mind Language & Society. Weidenfeld & Nicolson. 1999.

Shipley JT. Dictionary of Word Origins. Philosophical Library Inc. 1945.

Shlain L. The Alphabet versus the Goddess. Allen Lane. Penguin Press. 1999.

Skeat WW. An Etymological Dictionary of the English Language. 1879-82. OUP. 1983.

Slobin D I. Psycholinguistics. Scott Foresman & Co. 1974.

Smith N & Wilson D. Modern Linguistics. The results of Chomsky's Revolution. Pelican. 1979.

Speake J. Dictionary of Foreign Words and Phrases. OUP. 1997.

Spender D. Man Made Language. Routledge & Kegan Paul. 1980.

Springer SP & Deutsch G. Left Brain Right Brain. WH Freeman & Co, San Francisco. 1947.

Stanislawski J. Polish Dictionary. Minerva Publishing Co. 1941.

Steffanllari I. Albanian-English, English-Albanian Dictionary. Hippocrene Books Inc. 7th Edn 2003.

Sternberg RJ & Ben-Zeev T. Complex Cognition. The Psychology of Human Thought. OUP. 2001.

Stevens A. Ariadne's Clue, A Guide to the Symbols of Humankind. Allen Lane. Penguin Press. 1998.

Sturrock J. Structuralism. Paladin Grafton Books. 1986.

Talk Now CD. Funda isi Xosa.

Taylor I. Words and Places, 1911. J M Dent. EP Publishing Ltd. 1978.

Taylor JR. Linguistic Categorisation. OUP. 1989.

Todd L. Pidgins and Creoles. Rutledge & Kegan Paul. 1974.

Tolstoy I. The Knowledge & the Power. Reflections on the History of Science. Cannongate Publishing. 1990.

Trask R L. Key Concepts in Language & Linguistics. Routledge. 1999.

Urdan L. Dictionary of Differences. Bloomsbury Publishing. 1988.

Uys I. The English Afrikaans, Xhosa, Zulu Word Lists. Queillerie Publishers, Capetown. 1996.

Vietnamese Dictionary. Nka Sach Khai-Tri, Saigon.

Walker E. Explorations in the Biology of Language. Harvester Press. 1978.

Walsingham Lord Fauna Hawaiiensis Vol 1 Pt 5. Microlepidoptera. CUP 1907.

Watterson B. Introducing Egyptian Hieroglyphs. Scottish Academic Press. 1981.

Weiner J. Frege. OUP. 1999.

Whitney WD. The Life and Growth of Language. Dover Publications. 1979.

Wylie.Frank. Chinese English Dictionary.

Williams HR. Chinese. Hodder & Stoughton. 1947. 8th Impression. 1980.

Williams HW. Dictionary of the Maori Language. 1844. AR Shearer. 7th Edn. 1975.

Williams R. Ket Words. 1976. Flamingo. Fontana paperbacks. 1983.

Wills C. Exons, Introns and Talking Genes. OUP. 1992.

Wills C. The Runaway Brain. The Evolution of Human Uniqueness. Harper Collins. 1993.

Wilson H. Understanding Hieroglyphs. Michael O'Mara Books Ltd. 1993.

Winstedt R. Dictionary of Colloquial Malay. Kelly & Walsh. 1949.

Winstedt R. Malay English Dictionary. Marican & Sons. 4th Edition. 1962.

Winstedt R English Malay Dictionary. Marican & Sons. 2nd Edition. 1960.

Wittgenstein L. Tractatus Logico Philosophicus. Routledge & Kegan Paul. 1974.

Wittgenstein L. Philosophical Investigations. Blackwell Publishing. 1953. 3rd Edn 2001.

Wood WM. South East Asian Phrasebook. Burmese, Chinese, Filipino, Indonesian, Laotian, Malaysian, Thai, Vietnamese. Thomas Cook Publishing. 2000.

Woodhouse S C. English-Greek Dictionary. Routledge & Kegan Paul. 1910. 2nd Impression reprint 1979.

Wray A. The Transition to Language. OUP. 2002.

Wuolle A. Standard Finnish-English English-Finnish Dictionary. Holt Rinehart & Wilson. 1986.

Yule H & Burnell AC. Hobson-Jobson. 1886. 2nd Edn 1903. 3rd Edn 1985. Routledge & Kegan Paul. 1986.

Zimmer C. Evolution. The Triumph of an Idea. William Heineman. 2002.

ISBN 141207697-8